THE INFLUENCE OF THE LAW ON THE ASSESSMENT PROCESS

Special education laws have significantly shaped assessment practices. As discussed in Chapter 2, the first special education law was passed by Congress in 1975. In 1990, the law was revised as the Individuals with Disabilities Education Act (IDEA). The most recent revision of the law is the 1997 Amendments to the Individuals with Disabilities Education Act (IDEA), Public Law 105–17. IDEA 1997 is having extensive effects on the assessment and teaching of exceptional students. Additional information about IDEA 1997 is at **http://www.ed.gov/offices/OSERS/IDEA/the_law.html.**

IDEA 1997 makes major changes in the law (Senate Report on the IDEA Amendments, 1997; Yell & Schriner, 1997) which

- strengthen the role of parents
- ensure access to the general education curriculum and reforms
- focus on teaching and learning while reducing unnecessary paperwork requirements
- assist education agencies in addressing the costs of improving special education and related services for children with disabilities
- give increased attention to racial, ethnic, and linguistic diversity to prevent inappropriate identification and mislabeling
- require that transition planning begins when a child is 14 years old
- ensure that schools are safe and conducive to learning
- encourage parents and educators to work out their differences using nonadversarial means

Two segments of IDEA 1997 that directly shape assessment procedures are (1) the provisions related to the individualized education program (IEP) and (2) the procedural safeguards and parents' rights.

The Regulations for IDEA 1997

As noted, many of the new features of the 1997 Individuals with Disabilities Education Act affect the assessment of students with learning disabilities. The Regulations for IDEA 1997—issued by the Department of Education on March 12, 1999—clarify the IEP procedures and provide guidelines for schools and teachers. The major issues of the regulations are described in Appendix F of this book. Of particular note in regard to the IEP are the regulations affecting the IEP and the general curriculum, and the Regular Education Involvement in the IEP. Further information on the regulations is available at **http://www.ideapractices.org.**

Learning Disabilities explores the latest special education laws and how they influence assessment practices, including the Department of Education's 1999 Rules and Regulations for Implementing the 1997 Individuals with Disabilities Education Act (IDEA).

Learning Disabilities

Learning Disabilities

Theories, Diagnosis, and Teaching Strategies

EIGHTH EDITION

Janet W. Lerner

NORTHEASTERN ILLINOIS UNIVERSITY

Houghton Mifflin Company BOSTON   NEW YORK

To Eugene

Senior Sponsoring Editor: Loretta Wolozin
Associate Editor: Lisa A. Mafrici
Editorial Assistant: Carrie Wagner
Project Editor: Rebecca Bennett
Senior Production/Design Coordinator: Carol Merrigan
Senior Manufacturing Coordinator: Priscilla Bailey

Cover Design: Catherine Hawkes, Cat & Mouse
Cover Image: Joe Tilson, *The Homeric Hymn to Hermes II,* 1992, oil on canvas on wood relief. Photo courtesy of the artist and Theo Waddington Fine Art Ltd., London, England.

Chapter opening photographs: Chapter 1: © Bob Daemmrich/Stock Boston; Chapter 2: © Jean-Claude Lejeune; Chapter 3: © Bob Daemmrich/The Image Works; Chapter 4: © Jean-Claude Lejeune; Chapter 5: © Jean-Claude Lejeune; Chapter 6: © Jean-Claude Lejeune; Chapter 7: © Spencer Grant/Stock Boston; Chapter 8: © James Carroll; Chapter 9: © Bob Daemmrich/The Image Works; Chapter 10: © Elizabeth Crews; Chapter 11: © Index Stock Photography, Inc.; Chapter 12: © Elizabeth Crews; Chapter 13: © Don B. Stevenson/The Picture Cube; Chapter 14: © Annie Dowie/The Picture Cube.

Printed in the U.S.A.

Library of Congress Catalog Card Number: 99-71944

ISBN: 0-395-96114-9

123456789-QF-03 02 01 00 99

Brief Contents

Contents

Preface

The condition of learning disabilities is widely recognized as a problem leading to serious difficulties in school learning and often in adult life. The field of learning disabilities continues to be dynamic, influential, and responsive to advances in research, policy, and major changes in society. The eighth edition of *Learning Disabilities: Theories, Diagnosis, and Teaching Strategies* reflects these rapid advances and changes.

Individuals with learning disabilities encounter unexpected difficulties in some types of learning. Learning disabilities can impede learning to talk, listen, read, write, spell, reason, recall, organize information, or perform in mathematics. Described as a weakness among a sea of strengths, the condition of learning disabilities is especially perplexing because each individual has a unique combination of talents and characteristics, of strengths and weaknesses. Children and youth with learning disabilities are found in every classroom, but because learning disabilities cannot be seen, the condition is too often neglected. Unless these students are recognized and treated, they are destined to become educational discards. Identifying and helping students with learning disabilities are the primary concerns of this book.

AUDIENCE AND PURPOSE

Learning Disabilities: Theories, Diagnosis, and Teaching Strategies, Eighth Edition, is an introductory text written for both undergraduate and graduate students who are taking a first or second course in learning disabilities. It is designed to provide a comprehensive view of the field and offer teaching strategies to general education classroom teachers, special education teachers, school psychologists, administrators, language pathologists, counselors, and related professionals. This book will be particularly useful for preservice teachers and inservice classroom teachers who are increasingly responsible for teaching students with learning disabilities in inclusion classes. The text also brings parents the necessary background information to better understand their child and the problems he or she faces.

The approach of the book is varied so that readers may gain a comprehensive overview of this complex subject. Teachers need to understand the diverse theoretical approaches within the field; know procedures for assessing and evaluating students; possess skills in the art of clinical teaching; be familiar with teaching methods, strategies, and materials; and know the requirements of special education laws. This book deals with each of these essential topics.

REVISIONS IN THIS EDITION

- *The 1997 Individuals with Disabilities Education Act.* This edition explains the features of the new laws for special education (IDEA 1997) and the Department of Education's 1999 regulations for implementing IDEA 1997.

- *Useful Web addresses.* This edition includes web addresses for resources that the reader can find on the Internet.

- *Inclusion.* Most students with learning disabilities are now in inclusive general education classrooms for services. Chapters 3, 4, and 5 contain expanded and up-to-date information about responsible inclusion practices and describes how special and general education teachers can work together to make inclusion work.

- *Linguistically and culturally diverse children.* Chapters 4 and 6 discuss the changing demographics of the children in our schools, and addresses the growing number of linguistically and culturally diverse students who also have learning disabilities. This revision also explores methods for assessing and teaching these students.

- *New findings about the teaching of reading.* Chapter 11 describes new evidence about the need for explicit and structured instruction for teaching decoding skills and phonics to students with learning disabilities. The text also incorporates the value of literacy-based instruction in the teaching of reading.

- *Attention Deficit Disorder.* Chapters 2, 7, and 13 expand the coverage of ADD/ADHD to meet the needs of an increasing number of students who are being diagnosed with ADD/ADHD.

- *Early precursors of learning disabilities.* Chapters 2, 7, and 13 also examine the early signs of learning disabilities exhibited by young children, including problems with phonological awareness and rapid naming. Chapter 8 provides many intervention strategies for young children.

- *Recent brain research.* Chapter 7 contains exciting new findings about the brain and learning. This revision reports the neuroscience information on the brain and the implication of this research for individuals with learning disabilities.

- *Adolescents and adults with learning disabilities.* Chapter 9 provides current information on the discussion of the problems of adolescents and adults with learning disabilities and offers strategies to help them.

- *Using computer technology.* Chapters 2, 8, 11, 12, and 13 discuss the rapid advances in computer technology and how the computer can be used for students with learning disabilities.

■ *New approaches for assessing learning disabilities.* Chapter 3 explores new assessment approaches, discusses recent information about the use of intelligence tests in the identification process, and provides alternatives to using eligibility criteria formulas for identification.

■ *The role of parents.* Chapter 5 covers current perspectives on the essential role of parents, the problems that parents face, and the importance of establishing healthy home-school partnerships.

■ *Nonverbal learning disabilities.* Aside from academic problems, some students with learning disabilities have nonverbal learning disabilities and social skills problems. Chapter 14 contains a discussion of nonverbal learning disabilities.

This text strives to provide a fair and clear explanation of new and controversial issues in the field while still presenting the basic foundations, concepts, and strategies that have helped teachers, parents, and students over the years. There are many short case examples and case studies to illustrate major points, as well as two longer case studies that offer practical applications of the theories and procedures.

COVERAGE AND FEATURES

This book is organized into four major sections. Part I is an overview of learning disabilities which includes important features of the 1997 Individuals with Disabilities Education Act. Chapter 1 presents learning disabilities as a field in transition, and Chapter 2 looks at the field's historical perspectives and emerging directions.

Part II deals with the assessment-teaching process. Assessment and clinical teaching are viewed as interrelated parts of a continuous process that involves trying to understand students and help them learn. Assessment is discussed in Chapter 3, with special emphasis on how the 1997 Individuals with Disabilities Education Act affects the Individualized education program (IEP). Chapter 4 examines clinical teaching, the elements that make teaching successful, and the relationship between teaching and assessment. Chapter 5 provides coverage of the growing inclusion movement, the various placement options, and methods for general education and special education teachers to work together.

Part III deals with theoretical issues and expanding directions. Chapter 6 examines basic psychological theories of learning disabilities, including the contributions of developmental, behavioral, and cognitive psychology. Chapter 7 discusses medical aspects of research, assessment, and treatment. In Chapter 8, the focus is on early childhood with an examination of the precursors of learning disabilities in young children. This chapter also includes a discussion of perceptual and motor problems. Chapter 9 focuses on adolescents and adults with learning disabilities and includes a discussion of transition.

Part IV bridges the gap from theories to teaching strategies, dealing with the heart of the challenges that accompany teaching children and youth with learning disabilities. The chapters are organized by academic areas.

Every chapter has two sections, Theories and Teaching Strategies. Each Theories section examines the theoretical framework for teaching that particular content area; each Teaching Strategies section offers teachers practical suggestions and methods for teaching that academic subject. Chapters 10, 11, and 12 discuss language in its various forms. Chapter 10 looks at oral language, specifically listening and speaking; Chapter 11 investigates reading—both reading skills and reading comprehension; and Chapter 12 addresses written language, including written expression, spelling, and handwriting. Chapter 13 analyzes disorders in mathematics concepts, skills, and problem solving. Chapter 14 discusses nonverbal, social, behavioral, and emotional implications of learning disabilities.

To make this text easy to study and more appealing to use, the following features have been included.

Chapter outlines for each chapter present the major headings as an advance organizer and handy checklist for students to use in learning chapter material.

Summaries conclude each chapter and highlight—in a clear point-by-point format—the major ideas presented in the chapter.

Questions for Discussion and Reflection are provided after each chapter to offer an opportunity to pull together and elaborate on the major ideas of the chapter.

Key Terms follow each chapter, list important terminology, and provide an opportunity for students to review their knowledge of key concepts.

Case Examples are interspersed throughout most chapters. These short illustrative vignettes and discussions demonstrate real-life situations.

Case Studies are longer and more comprehensive than Case Examples, and are designed to show practical applications.

Print and Multimedia Resources appear at the end of the book and offer the reader print references, suggested videotapes, and relevant Internet resources.

The Appendixes contain useful information for teachers. Appendix A is an extended Case Study. Appendix B consists of a phonics quiz and a brief review of important phonics generalizations. Appendix C is a listing and brief description of commonly used tests. Appendix D lists contact information for publishers and organizations. Appendix E is a glossary of important terms, and Appendix F presents major issues from the Department of Education's 1999 Regulations for Implementing IDEA 1997.

ACCOMPANYING LEARNING AND TEACHING RESOURCES

The eighth edition of *Learning Disabilities* is accompanied by an extensive package of student and instructor resources.

Study Guide with Cases

The *Study Guide with Cases* that accompanies this text is a supplementary resource designed to help students learn the content and concepts presented in this textbook. It provides practice in using the field's important specialized vocabulary and in understanding key concepts and systems. It also provides applications of ideas, brief quizzes for review and illustrative case studies.

Each chapter is divided into seven parts: *Objectives,* or major goals of the chapter; *Terms You Should Know,* a series of important vocabulary terms and definitions for students to match; *Key Points,* questions about the key ideas of the chapter; *Seeing the System,* questions related to tables and drawings presented in the text; *Application and Synthesis,* open-ended activities, discussions, and debate questions; *Rapid Review Questions,* a multiple-choice quiz on the chapter; and *Case Study,* a brief case and accompanying questions that illustrate a topic in the chapter.

The final section of the *Study Guide with Cases* contains answers to the questions for each section.

Instructor's Resource Manual with Test Items

The *Instructor's Resource Manual with Test Items* contains a vast array of instructional support material, including *Sample Syllabi, Chapter Instructional Guides,* and *Assessment Materials.* Learning objectives, lecture-discussion outlines, key terms and definitions, suggested activities, and transparency masters in each chapter's *Instructional Guide* provide visual reinforcement instruction. *Assessment Materials* for each chapter contain multiple-choice, short-answer, and essay questions, as well as additional ideas for performance assessment.

Computerized Test Bank

The test items contained in the printed *Instructor's Resource Manual* are also available in an electronic form for use with PC and Macintosh computers.

The Houghton Mifflin Company Teacher Education Station web site.

This site provides resources for beginning and experienced education professionals. It includes information about new books, key learning themes, and links to other Houghton Mifflin Teacher Education web sites developed especially to support new and practicing teachers.

ACKNOWLEDGMENTS   *Learning Disabilities: Theories, Diagnosis, and Teaching Strategies* grew out of my experiences working in public schools with students who had reading and learning disabilities and from teaching courses in learning disabilities in colleges and universities. The work was considerably influenced by feedback from students enrolled in my courses. Students; colleagues; and organizations such as the Learning Disabilities Association of America, the Division of Learning Disabilities of the Council for Exceptional Children, International Dyslexia Association, and the National Center for Learning Disabilities also alerted me to new concepts, programs, assessment instruments, and intervention strategies. I am indebted to many authors of books and articles, to speakers at conferences, and to educators in school districts and universities with whom I have worked. In addition, I have learned by listening to and meeting with professionals and parents at conferences held in various communities throughout the country.

I wish to thank the following reviewers, who read the manuscript at various stages and provided helpful suggestions and criticisms:

Dr. Victor S. Lombardo, Professor, Marshall University Graduate College, Special Education

Dr. Laurie U. deBettencourt, University of Virginia

Dr. Cleborne Maddux, Professor, Department of Counseling and Educational Psychology, University of Nevada, Reno

Dr. Jeanne C. Faieta, Edinboro University

I also wish to acknowledge the editors at Houghton Mifflin who skillfully guided me through the processes of writing this book: Loretta Wolozin and Carrie Wagner.

As my first college instructor in special education and as a stimulating and provocative scholar and writer, the late Dr. Samuel A. Kirk played a significant role in the inception of this book. I also wish to acknowledge my family—Susan, Laura, Dean, James, Aaron, Lee, Sue, Anne, and Sarah. Finally, I wish to acknowledge my husband, Eugene, who continues to provide the encouragement and support every author needs.

Janet W. Lerner

Learning Disabilities

Overview of Learning Disabilities

Learning Disabilities: A Field in Transition

CHAPTER OUTLINE

This is a book about learning disabilities, a problem that impedes learning for many children, adolescents, and adults, affecting their schooling and adjustment to society. Part I provides an overview of the field of learning disabilities, with some basic concepts (Chapter 1) and a historical perspective and discussion of current and emerging directions (Chapter 2).

This introductory chapter gives the reader the broad scope of the field: the problem of defining learning disabilities, the diverse characteristics of learning disabilities, manifestations at different ages and stages of life, the prevalence of learning disabilities in our schools, and the multidisciplinary nature of the field.

THE ENIGMA OF LEARNING DISABILITIES

The power of awareness is an important factor in alerting parents, educators, health professionals, and the general public to the condition of learning disabilities. The **Coordinated Campaign for Learning Disabilities (CCLD)** was established in 1998 to increase public awareness of learning disabilities. To make more people aware of practical information and resources about learning disabilities, the CCLD banded together with six other major learning disabilities organizations, and they are now all working with the Advertising Council to increase public awareness. The web site for CCLD is **http://www.ldonline.org** (Coordinated Campaign for Learning Disabilities, 1998).

The term **learning disabilities** refers to a neurobiological disorder related to differences in how one's brain works or is structured. This brain variance affects a person's ability to speak, listen, read, write, spell, reason, organize information, or do mathematics. If provided with the right support and intervention, children with learning disabilities can succeed in school and have successful, often distinguished careers later in life. Parents can help their learning-disabled child achieve success by fostering the child's strengths, knowing the child's weaknesses, and understanding the educational system as they work with professionals and learn about strategies for dealing with specific difficulties (Coordinated Campaign for Learning Disabilities, 1998).

The enigma of the youngster who encounters extraordinary difficulty in learning, of course, is not new. Throughout the years, children from all walks of life have experienced difficulties in learning. In fact, some of the world's most distinguished people had unusual difficulty in certain aspects of learning. Moreover, the condition we call *learning disabilities* occurs in all cultures, nations, and language groups. The case of Tony in the case example shows the effects of learning disabilities and the problems that parents encounter in identifying the problem.

CASE EXAMPLE

TONY—THE PUZZLE OF LEARNING DISABILITIES

The case of Tony illustrates the enigma of learning disabilities and the difficulty parents encounter. Tony's parents have long been aware that their son has severe problems in learning. As an infant, Tony was colicky and had difficulty in learning to suck. His early speech was so garbled that no one could understand him, and frequently his inability to communicate led to sudden temper tantrums. The kindergarten teacher reported that Tony was "immature"; his first-grade teacher said he "did not pay attention"; and succeeding teachers labeled him "lazy" and then "emotionally disturbed." Tony's distraught parents attempted to find the source of his learning problems to alleviate his misery and theirs. They desperately followed suggestions from many sources, which led to a succession of specialists and clinics dedicated to treating such difficulties.

One clinic detected a visual problem, and as a result Tony received visual training exercises for several years. An opinion of emotional disturbance at another agency led to years of psychotherapy for both Tony and his parents. Another expert placed Tony on a special diet for a period of time. The family pediatrician said that the boy was merely going through a stage and would grow out of it. Yet despite this wealth of diagnosis and treatment, Tony still cannot learn. He is unhappily failing in school, and, understandably, he has lost faith in himself.

The problems encountered by Tony and his parents are typical. Each profession viewed Tony's problem from its own perspective and saw only part of the picture. What is needed instead is a unified, interdisciplinary approach to the problem of Tony's learning disabilities—a coordinated effort by members of the various participating professions.

Some Eminent People with Learning Disabilities

Nelson Rockefeller, who served as vice president of the United States and governor of the state of New York, suffered from severe dyslexia, a form of learning disability in which the individual encounters extreme difficulty in learning to read. His poor reading ability kept him from achieving good grades in school, and the affliction forced him to memorize his speeches during his political career.

In describing his feelings about growing up with a learning disability, Rockefeller (1976) recalled,

> I was dyslexic . . . and I still have a hard time reading today. I remember vividly the pain and mortification I felt as a boy of eight when I was assigned to read a short passage of scripture at a community vesper service and did a thoroughly miserable job of it. I know what a dyslexic child goes through . . . the frustration of not being able to do what other children do easily, the humiliation of being thought not too bright when such is not the case at all. But after coping with this problem for more than 60 years, I have a message of hope and encouragement for children with learning disabilities and their parents. (pp. 12–14)

As a child, Thomas Edison, the ingenious American inventor, was called abnormal, addled, and mentally defective. Writing in his diary that he was never able to get along at school, he recalled that he was always at the foot of his class. His father thought of him as stupid, and Edison described himself as a dunce. Auguste Rodin, the great French sculptor, was called the worst pupil in his school. Because his teachers diagnosed Rodin as uneducable, they advised his parents to put him out to work, although they doubted that he could ever make a living. Woodrow Wilson, the scholarly twenty-eighth president of the United States, did not learn his letters until he was 9 years old and did not learn to read until age 11. Relatives expressed sorrow for his parents because Woodrow was so dull and backward (Thompson, 1971).

Albert Einstein, the mathematical genius, did not speak until age 3. His search for words was described as laborious and, until he was 7, he formulated each sentence, no matter how commonplace, silently with his lips before speaking the words aloud. Schoolwork did not go well for young Albert. He showed little facility with arithmetic, no special ability in any other academic subject, and great difficulty with foreign languages. One teacher predicted that "nothing good" would come of him. Einstein's language disabilities persisted throughout his adult life. When he read, he heard words. Writing was difficult for him, and he communicated badly through writing. In describing his thinking process, he explained that he rarely thought in words; it was only after a thought came that he tried to express it in words at a later time (Patten, 1973).

These persons of eminence fortunately were somehow able to find appropriate ways of learning, and they successfully overcame their initial failures. Many youngsters with learning disabilities are not so fortunate.

The Cross-Cultural Nature of Learning Disabilities

The condition of learning disabilities is a universal problem that occurs in all languages, cultures, and nations in the world. The problem is neither confined to the United States nor to English-speaking countries. Accumulating research shows that in all cultures there are children who seem to have normal intelligence but have severe difficulty in learning oral language, acquiring reading or writing skills, or doing mathematics. The International Academy for Research in Learning Disabilities (IARLD), an organization dedicated to fostering international research on learning disabilities, publishes a journal called *Thalamas,* and has a web site at **http://come.to/iarld/.**

Clinical reports of the personal travails of children from all corners of the world are remarkably similar. In the following excerpt, for example, a Chinese adult remembers his first baffling failure in a Chinese school; the story parallels the bewildering episodes that children with learning disabilities face in our own schools (Lerner & Chen, 1992).

> The condition of learning disabilities is a universal problem that occurs in all languages, cultures, and nations.
> *(Elizabeth Crews)*

My first recollection of learning problems occurred at age 7, when I entered the first grade in school in Taiwan. My teacher wrote [characters] on the blackboard and the pupils were to copy this board work into their notebooks. I vividly remember that I was simply unable to perform this task. Observing how easily my classmates accomplished the assignment, I was perplexed and [troubled] by my inability to copy the letters and words from the board.

Research reports about learning disabilities come from many parts of the world—Denmark, the United Kingdom, The Netherlands (Gersons-Wolfenberger & Ruijssenaars, 1997), New Zealand (Chapman, 1992), Australia, Germany (Opp, 1992), Italy (Fabbro & Masutto, 1994), Mexico (Fletcher & DeLopez, 1995), Portugal (da Fonseca, 1996), Chile, Canada (Wiener & Siegel, 1992), Russia (Korkunov, Nigayev, Reynolds, & Lerner, 1998), and Israel (Shalev, Manor, Auerbach, & Grodd-Tour, 1998). The problem appears in children learning an alphabet-based system of written language (such as English) or with children learning a logographic (pictorial) system of written language such as Chinese (Hsu, 1988) or Japanese (Yamada & Banks, 1994). It occurs in children learning written languages that follow regular phonetic rules (such as Spanish) and in written languages with irregular spelling (such as English).

In our schools today, children from many different backgrounds, cultures, environments, and languages receive instruction through learning disabilities programs. Understandably, difficulty in school learning may occur when the language, values, or customs of the child's culture differ substantially from those of the school. However, the problem is compounded when the child also has learning disabilities. For students with culturally diverse backgrounds, the problems arising from the cultural differences and those from learning disabilities are difficult to untangle (Markowitz, Garcia, & Eichelberger, 1997). Some parents reflect cultural attitudes that a child with a disability is a personal failure. These parents may not wish to admit that their child has a disability, may refuse to attend individualized education program (IEP) meetings, or may even keep a child with a disability at home as a face-saving gesture. (Children with learning disabilities who are culturally and linguistically diverse are further discussed in Chapter 10.)

DEFINITIONS OF LEARNING DISABILITIES

The term learning disabilities was first introduced in 1963. A small group of concerned parents and educators met in Chicago to consider linking the isolated parent groups active in a few communities into a single organization. Each of these parent groups identified the children of concern under a different name, including perceptually handicapped, brain-injured, and neurologically impaired. If these groups were to unite, they needed to agree on a single term to identify the children. When the term learning disabilities was suggested at this meeting (Kirk, 1963), it met with immediate approval. The organization today known as the Learning Disabilities Association (LDA) was born at this historic meeting. The LDA web site can be found at **http://www.ldanatl.org.**

Although the term *learning disabilities* had immediate appeal and acceptance, the task of developing a definition of learning disabilities proved to be a formidable challenge. Indeed, defining this population is considered such an overwhelming task that some have likened learning disabilities to Justice Potter Stewart's comment on pornography: impossible to define, "but I know it when I see it."

Formulating a definition of learning disabilities that is acceptable to all has been difficult. A number of definitions have been generated over the years, but each has been judged by some to have certain shortcomings. This chapter discusses three of the influential definitions: (1) the definition in the federal law (IDEA, 1997), (2) the Interagency Committee on Learning Disabilities definition, and (3) the National Joint Committee on Learning Disabilities definition.

The Federal Definition: Individuals with Disabilities Education Act (IDEA)

The most widely used definition first appeared in 1975 in **Public Law 94–142,** the **Education for All Handicapped Children Act.** It was also incorporated in **Public Law 101–476,** the **1990 Individuals with Disabilities Education Act (IDEA),** and is in the **1997 Amendments to IDEA (PL 105–17).** The definition of learning disabilities in the federal law is the basis of most state definitions and is used by many schools (Mercer, Jordan, Alsop, & Mercer, 1996).

There are actually two parts to the federal definition. The first part was adopted from a 1968 report to Congress of the National Advisory Committee on the Handicapped. It is the definition of learning disabilities in the 1997 Individuals with Disabilities Education Act:

The term "specific learning disability" means those children who have a disorder in one or more of the basic psychological processes involved in understanding or in using language, spoken or written, which disorder may manifest itself in imperfect ability to listen, think, speak, read, write, spell, or to do mathematical calculations. The term includes such conditions as perceptual handicaps, brain injury, minimal brain dysfunction, dyslexia, and developmental aphasia. The term does not include a learning problem which is primarily the result of visual, hearing, or motor handicaps, of mental retardation, of emotional disturbance, or of environmental, cultural, or economic disadvantage.

The second part of the federal definition is considered operational; it first appeared in a separate set of regulations for children with learning disabilities (U.S. Office of Education, December 29, 1977). The regulation states that a student has a specific learning disability if (1) the student does not achieve at the proper age and ability levels in one or more specific areas when provided with appropriate learning experiences and (2) the student has a severe discrepancy between achievement and intellectual ability in one or more of these seven areas: (a) oral expression, (b) listening comprehension, (c) written expression, (d) basic reading skills, (e) reading comprehension, (f) mathematics calculation, and (g) mathematics reasoning.

To summarize, the federal definition of learning disabilities as contained in IDEA 1997 includes the following major concepts:

1. The individual has a *disorder in one or more of the basic psychological processes*. (These processes refer to mental abilities, such as memory, auditory perception, visual perception, oral language, and thinking.)

2. The individual has *difficulty in learning,* specifically, in speaking, listening, writing, reading (word-recognition skills and comprehension), and mathematics (calculation and reasoning).

3. The problem is *not primarily due to other causes,* such as visual or hearing impairments; motor handicaps; mental retardation; emotional disturbance; or economic, environmental, or cultural disadvantage.

4. A severe discrepancy exists between the student's apparent **potential for learning** and his or her low level of achievement. In other words, there is evidence of underachievement.

Other Significant Definitions

Other definitions of learning disabilities have been recommended. The two most significant definitions are those by the National Joint Committee on Learning Disabilities (NJCLD) and the Interagency Committee on Learning

Disabilities (ICLD). (See "The NJCLD Definition of Learning Disabilities" and "The ICLD Definition of Learning Disabilities.")

The Need for Several Definitions

What conclusions can be drawn from this review of the definitions of learning disabilities?

1. *Learning disabilities has become an established discipline.* The condition of having a learning disability has wide recognition and general acceptance. Children and adults, experts and novices, all have an implicit notion of what constitutes a learning disability. Many disciplines, professionals, organizations, and nations are now identifying individuals with learning disabilities.

2. *Learning disabilities is not a single condition.* The goal of finding a single definition acceptable to all may be unfeasible. The problems of learning disabilities are highly individual, and the solutions applied to those problems must be adaptive and flexible. Learning disabilities are not a single condition but rather a class of related and partially overlapping conditions (Keogh, 1994).

3. *Several definitions of learning disabilities are needed.* Different definitions are required for various professionals, populations, age levels, and degrees of severity. Different definitions also serve different purposes, including identification, assessment, instruction, advocacy, and research. Rather than trying to force the various attributes of learning disabilities into a single, all-encompassing definition, we must acknowledge that these characteristics reflect different types of learning disabilities (Keogh, 1994).

COMMON ELEMENTS IN THE DEFINITIONS

The various definitions of learning disabilities have several elements in common: (1) central nervous system dysfunction, (2) uneven growth pattern and psychological processing deficits, (3) difficulty in academic and learning tasks, (4) discrepancy between achievement and potential, and (5) exclusion of other causes. The nature of each of these elements and the problems that surround them are examined in the following sections.

Central Nervous System Dysfunction

Although not always stated directly, implied in many of the definitions is the view that learning disabilities are related to neurological factors. All learning originates within the brain and, consequently, a disorder in learning can be caused by a dysfunction in the central nervous system. Educational and

THE NJCLD DEFINITION OF LEARNING DISABILITIES

The **National Joint Committee on Learning Disabilities (NJCLD)** is an organization of representatives from several professional organizations and disciplines involved with learning disabilities. The NJCLD definition is as follows:

> *Learning disabilities* is a general term that refers to a **heterogeneous** group of disorders manifested by significant difficulties in the acquisition and use of listening, speaking, reading, writing, reasoning, or mathematical abilities.
>
> These disorders are intrinsic to the individual, are presumed to be due to central nervous system dysfunction, and may occur across the life span. Problems in self-regulatory behaviors, social perception, and social interaction may exist with learning disabilities but do not by themselves constitute a learning disability.
>
> Although a learning disability may occur concomitantly with other disabilities (for example, sensory impairment, mental retardation, or serious emotional disturbance) or with extrinsic influences (such as cultural differences or insufficient/inappropriate instruction), it would not be a result of those conditions or influences. (National Joint Committee on Learning Disabilities, 1997, p. 29).

Here are the main points of the NJCLD definition:

1. *Learning disabilities are a heterogeneous group of disorders.* Individuals with learning disabilities exhibit many kinds of behaviors and characteristics.

2. *Learning disabilities result in significant difficulties in the acquisition and use of listening, speaking, reading, writing, reasoning, and/ or mathematical skills.*

3. *The problem is intrinsic to the individual.* Learning disabilities are due to factors within the person rather than to external factors, such as the environment or the educational system.

4. *The problem is presumed to be related to a central nervous system dysfunction.* There is a biological basis to the problem.

5. *Learning disabilities may occur along with other disabilities or conditions.* Individuals can have several problems at the same time, such as learning disabilities and emotional disorders.

Source: Used by permission of the National Joint Committee on Learning Disabilities.

THE ICLD DEFINITION OF LEARNING DISABILITIES

The **Interagency Committee on Learning Disabilities (ICLD)** is a government committee that was commissioned by the U.S. Congress to develop a definition of learning disabilities. It included representatives of twelve agencies within the Department of Health and Human Services and the Department of Education. A key addition by the committee was the inclusion of social skills deficits as a characteristic of learning disabilities (1987), an addition that has drawn some criticism (Silver, 1988). The major points of the committee's definition are as follows:

1. *The child can have difficulties in listening, speaking, reading, writing, reasoning, mathematics, or social skills.* Unlike the federal definition, the ICLD includes social disabilities.
2. *Learning disabilities can occur concomitantly with other conditions.* This definition specifically mentions socioenvironmental influences and attention-deficit disorders.
3. *Learning disabilities are intrinsic to the individual and are presumed to be caused by central nervous system dysfunction.* The disorder in learning is presumed to be caused by an impairment in brain function.

environmental events can, of course, modify the process of learning and influence brain function, making it worse or better. In many cases, the neurological condition is difficult if not impossible to ascertain by medical examination or external medical tests. Dysfunction of the central nervous system is therefore often presumed and determined through observation of behavior. Neuroscience and medical research (Chapter 7) shows growing evidence that learning disabilities has a neurological basis. Although teachers are chiefly concerned with behavioral and educational aspects, the medical contributions remain important. Historically, medical scientists played a key role in the creation of the field (see Chapter 2), and the medical profession currently takes an active part in research, diagnosis, and treatment (see Chapter 7).

Uneven Growth Pattern and Psychological Processing Deficits

This element of the definition refers to an irregular or uneven development of the various components of mental ability. Mental ability, or intellect, is not a single capacity; rather, it is composed of many underlying mental abilities. For the individual with learning disabilities, these component abilities or subabilities do not develop in an even or normal fashion. That is, while some of the components are maturing in an anticipated sequence or rate, others are lagging in their development, thereby appearing as symptoms of the learning problem. This uneven growth pattern results in *intra-individual differences,* or strengths and weaknesses in different mental processes (Kirk & Chalfant, 1984). (See Chapter 6). A key phrase within the federal definition—*a disorder in one or more of the basic psychological processes* (italics added)—refers to this component of the definition.

The concepts of an uneven growth pattern, intra-individual differences, and psychological processing disorders have become the basis of much of the assessment and instruction in learning disabilities. About 88 percent of the states include a process/language component in their state definition (Mercer et al., 1996; Frankenberger & Fronzaglio, 1991).

language component

Difficulty in Academic and Learning Tasks

Individuals with learning disabilities encounter different types of problems in learning. One child's obstacle may be in the acquisition of speech and oral language; another's may be in reading, arithmetic, handwriting, motor skills, written expression, thinking, or nonverbal learning. (See Part IV for discussions of each specific area of learning.) As noted earlier, the federal definition lists seven specific academic areas in which learning disabilities can be detected. Lyon (1997) views learning disabilities as failure to learn a specific skill or set of skills after validated teaching of that skill. All fifty states include difficulty in academic learning as a component of their definition of learning disabilities (Mercer et al., 1996).

Discrepancy Between Potential and Achievement

Another element common to many definitions of learning disabilities is the identification of a gap between what the student is potentially capable of learning and what the student has in fact learned or achieved. The operational portion of the federal definition states that the child with learning disabilities has a **severe discrepancy** between achievement and intellectual ability in one or more of seven areas. Most state definitions of learning disabilities (about 98 percent) include the concept of a discrepancy between achievement and potential (Mercer et al., 1996).

To determine if a discrepancy exists between potential and achievement, one must ask three essential questions (each of which raises serious problems):

1. *What is the individual's potential for learning?* Judgments about a child's potential, ability level, or capacity are usually based on such

measurements as intelligence tests, tests of cognitive abilities, clinical judgments, or other means. Often an intelligence, or IQ, test is used. IQ tests are criticized as being inaccurate measures of intelligence, as being racially and culturally biased, and as measuring achievement rather than intelligence. There is much current discussion about using measures other than IQ to determine a child's potential (Fletcher, 1998; Lyon, 1994, 1995a; Stanovich, 1993). (This topic is discussed further in Chapter 3.)

2. *What is the individual's current achievement level?* The **current achievement level** refers to a student's current performance. Tests that are used to measure the individual's performance have imperfections. Many academic tests have poor validity, reliability, and standardization (Farr & Carey, 1986; Salvia & Ysseldyke, 1998), and the score may not reflect the child's achievement level.

3. *What degree of discrepancy between potential and achievement is "severe"?* The important word here is *severe*. A one-year discrepancy at the second-grade level is more severe than a one-year discrepancy at the eleventh-grade level. Further, should a severe discrepancy be measured by a fixed amount of time (such as one year or three years), or should a ratio or some statistical measure or formula be used?

Each state, school district, or evaluation team must establish its own method of defining a "severe" discrepancy. Many of the states (about 66 percent) quantify the learning disability, using one of several forms of "discrepancy formulas" to determine if a child is eligible for learning disabilities services (Mercer et al., 1996; Frankenberger & Fronzaglio, 1991; National Center for Learning Disabilities, 1994).

Discrepancy formulas, with their uses and shortcomings, are discussed in Chapter 3. A number of scholars question the validity of identifying students with learning disabilities through a discrepancy formula (Lyon, 1995a, 1997; Fletcher & Foorman, 1994; Stanovich, 1993). The policy of using a discrepancy between IQ and achievement to identify a student with learning disabilities is criticized for several reasons (Mather, 1998; Fletcher, 1998; Lyon, 1995a, 1997; Stanovich, 1994):

- The criterion of IQ-achievement discrepancy is predicated on failure. This procedure (coined the "wait-and-fail" model) requires that a child fall behind a predicted level of performance to be eligible for services. This practice often results in services being delayed until third grade and beyond. Unfortunately, while the child waits to cross a threshold of failure to be eligible for services, he or she can develop many negative conditions resulting from school failure, such as low self-esteem and loss of interest and motivation.

- This discrepancy component of the definition stresses the criterion of underachievement and thus minimizes other aspects of the definition, especially the concept of disorders in basic psychological processes and phonological problems. Since there are many reasons besides learning disabilities for an individual to be underachieving—such as poor teaching, lack of motivation or interest, or psychological or emotional factors—the criterion of underachievement alone is insufficient.

Exclusion of Other Causes

This component of the definition reflects the notion that learning disabilities are not primarily the result of other conditions, such as mental retardation, emotional disturbance, visual or hearing impairments, or cultural, social, or economic environments. About 98 percent of U.S. states have incorporated the exclusion component in their state definition (Mercer et al., 1996; Frankenberger & Fronzaglio, 1991).

In practice, the exclusion component of the definition of learning disabilities becomes difficult to implement because children often exhibit co-existing problems. Teachers who work with children with other disabilities often observe that many students appear to have two problems—their primary impairment plus their learning disabilities. It is hard to determine which problem is primary and which is secondary. There is growing acceptance of the idea that other conditions often co-occur with learning disabilities, as indicated in the NJCLD and ICLD definitions.

CHARACTERISTICS OF LEARNING DISABILITIES

Individuals with learning disabilities are a heterogeneous population. Many different characteristics are associated with learning disabilities, but each individual is unique and will present only some of these characteristics.

Diverse Characteristics

Students with learning disabilities exhibit a variety of learning and behavioral traits, and no individual will display all of them. Some students have disabilities in mathematics, whereas others excel in mathematics. Attention disorders and **nonverbal learning disabilities** are symptomatic problems for many students with learning disabilities but not for all. Further, certain kinds of characteristics are more likely to be exhibited at certain age levels. Young children are more likely to be hyperactive than adolescents. In addition, deficits are manifested in different ways at different age levels. For example, an underlying language disorder may appear as a delayed speech problem in the preschooler, as a reading disorder in the elementary student, and as a writing disorder in the secondary student. During the evaluation process, an assessment team will determine which characteristics an individual presents and how these traits impede that student's learning.

The implications of each of these learning and behavior characteristics are complex, and they are discussed in detail throughout this book. With these cautions in mind, we can now briefly note the common characteristics of learning disabilities.

Disorders of attention.   Students with attention problems may not focus when a lesson is being presented, have a short attention span, be easily distracted, and have poor concentration ability. They also may be hyperactive or impulsive. Students with learning disabilities with these characteristics may have coexisting attention-deficit disorders (ADD) (Children with ADD are discussed in Chapters 7 and 14).

Poor motor abilities.   Some children with learning disabilities have difficulty with gross motor abilities and fine motor coordination, and they exhibit general awkwardness and clumsiness and have spatial problems (see Chapter 8).

Psychological process deficits and information-processing problems. Children with learning disabilities often have problems in processing auditory or visual information. For example, many are poor in recognizing the sounds of language (phonological awareness), in quickly recognizing letters or words (visual perception), or in short-term memory tasks (see Chapter 8).

Failure to develop and mobilize cognitive strategies for learning.   Many students with learning disabilities do not know how to go about learning and studying. They lack organization skills, have not developed an active learning style, and do not direct their own learning (metacognitive functions) (see Chapters 6, 9, and 11).

Oral language difficulties.   Many individuals with learning disabilities have basic underlying language disorders. This characteristic appears with problems in listening, language development, speaking, vocabulary development, and linguistic competencies (see Chapter 10).

Reading difficulties.   About 80 percent of the students with learning disabilities have disabilities in reading. They have problems with learning to decode words, with basic word-recognition skills, or with reading comprehension (see Chapter 11).

Written language difficulties.   Writing is a very challenging task for many students with learning disabilities, and they do poorly in situations that require written work (see Chapter 12).

Mathematics difficulties.   The major problem for some students with learning disabilities involves difficulties in quantitative thinking, arithmetic, time, space, and calculation facts (see Chapter 13).

Nonverbal learning disabilities: problems with social skills.   The major problem for some individuals with learning disabilities involves social skills. These individuals have not learned how to act and talk in social situations, and their social skills deficits make it hard to establish satisfying social relationships and make and keep friends (see Chapter 14).

Gender Differences

Clinics and schools identify four times as many boys than girls who have learning disabilities. However, gender research shows that actually there are as many girls with learning disabilities as boys, but they are not being identified. Boys tend to exhibit more physical aggression and loss of control, visual-motor abilities, spelling ability, and written language mechanical aptitude. Girls with learning disabilities tend to have more cognitive, language, and social problems and to have severe academic achievement deficits in reading and math (Lyon, 1995a, 1997; Shaywitz, Fletcher, & Shaywitz, 1995; Shaywitz, Shaywitz, Fletcher, et al., 1990; Shaywitz & Shaywitz, 1988; Vogel, 1990b). Girls with learning disabilities who are not identified are an underserved group that is at significant risk for long-term academic, social, and emotional difficulties.

Explanations of why more boys than girls are identified with learning disabilities include *biological causes* (males may be more vulnerable to learning disabilities), *cultural factors* (more males may be identified because boys tend to exhibit more disruptive behaviors that are troublesome to adults), and *expectation pressures* (the expectations for success in school may be greater for boys than for girls).

Multiple Intelligences and Learning Disabilities

Many teachers and parents have observed that their students with learning disabilities have incredible talents that are generally undervalued or not well represented in our school curricula. According to Howard Gardner (1983, 1993), people possess **multiple intelligences,** at least eight different types of intelligence (Figure 1.1).

1. *Verbal/linguistic intelligence* is related to words and language, spoken and written, and to sensitivity to different functions of language—qualities of writers and poets.
2. *Logical/mathematical intelligence* refers to abilities with quantitative thinking, numbers, and logical patterns—qualities of mathematicians and scientists.
3. *Visual/spatial intelligence* includes the ability to visualize objects and the ability to create internal mental images and pictures—qualities of artists, architects, and engineers.
4. *Musical/rhythmic intelligence* includes sensitivities to tonal patterns, rhythms, and musical expressiveness—qualities of musicians.

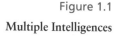

Figure 1.1

Multiple Intelligences

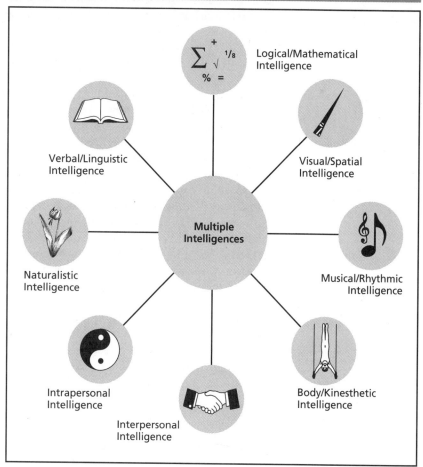

Source: Adapted from *Frames of Mind: The Theory of Multiple Intelligence,* by Howard Gardner, 1983, New York: Basic Books.

5. *Body/kinesthetic intelligence*   is related to abilities to control one's physical movement—qualities of athletes and dancers.

6. *Interpersonal intelligence*   includes skills in dealing with other people—qualities of salespeople and politicians.

7. *Intrapersonal intelligence*   refers to inner states of being, self-reflection, and knowledge of one's self—qualities of persons with accurate self-knowledge.

8. *Naturalistic intelligence*   refers to individuals who are attuned to nature, animals, and plant life—qualities of farmers, forest rangers, and gardeners.

The degree to which each type of intelligence develops depends on many variables. Much of school learning calls upon linguistic intelligence, the very area of difficulty for many individuals with learning disabilities. Some students with learning disabilities encounter great difficulty learning to read but possess superior abilities in other areas, such as mathematics, music, athletics, or art. These individuals may have a deep reservoir of creativity and intellectual power and unusual strengths in originality, insight, knowledge, humor, and emotions (Hearne & Stone, 1995; Coben & Vaughn, 1994; Waldron & Saphire, 1990; Vail, 1990).

Sometimes their talents are so unusual that they are recognized as gifted or talented children. Characteristics of **giftedness** include spontaneity, inquisitiveness, imagination, boundless enthusiasm, and emotionality; and these same traits are often observed in children with learning disabilities. Often children with learning disabilities, like gifted children, seem to require a great deal of activity. They may find regular classroom environments uninviting or have difficulty attending to the classroom instruction. If their learning needs are not being met, they may respond by becoming fidgety, inattentive, and even disruptive (Lerner, Lowenthal, & Lerner, 1995).

It is especially important that school failure for these children does not lead to the withholding of opportunities to learn and to frustration, failure, or depression. Teachers can meet the unique needs of students whose strengths and talents lie outside the narrow view of knowledge as being purely linguistic by

- Helping students bypass their deficits as they access their areas of strengths.
- Modifying assignments and curricula for these students so their true abilities may be demonstrated.
- Creating an environment that nurtures personal creativity and intellectual characteristics.

WIDENING AGE SPAN OF THE LEARNING DISABILITIES POPULATION

When the initial small group of concerned parents and professionals first sought to obtain help for their children and to promote the field of learning disabilities, their efforts focused on the pressing needs of the elementary-level child. Today, we recognize that learning disabilities become evident at many stages of life and that the problem appears in a different form at each stage.

Figure 1.2 illustrates the number of children identified with specific learning disabilities at different age levels, ranging from age 6 through age 21 (U.S. Department of Education, 1998). The number of students gradually increases from age 6 to 9, a majority of students are in the 10 to 13 age range, and the number decreases sharply from ages 16 to 21. This pattern suggests that substantial numbers of children with learning disabilities are identified in the age range of 9 through 14. Most children are not identified

Figure 1.2

Age Distribution of Students with Learning Disabilities

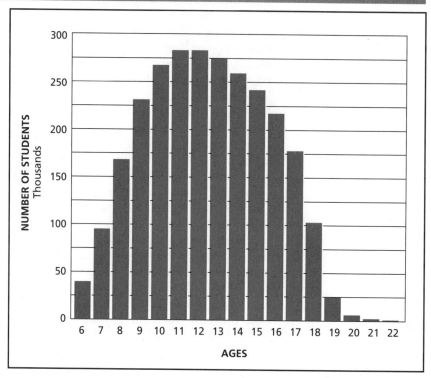

Source: To Assure the Free Appropriate Public Education of All Children with Disabilities. Twentieth Annual Report to Congress on the Implementation of the Individuals with Disabilities Education Act, by the U.S. Department of Education, 1998. Washington, DC: U.S. Government Printing Office, Table AA6, p. A–14.

until age 9, and the decrease during the teen years may relate to the large dropout rate of adolescents with learning disabilities.

Each age group (preschoolers, elementary children, adolescents, and adults) needs different kinds of skills. Therefore, certain characteristics of learning disabilities assume greater prominence at certain age levels.

The Preschool Level

Because growth rates are so unpredictable at young ages, educators are generally reluctant to identify preschoolers under a categorical label, such as learning disabilities. As discussed in Chapter 8, very young children (under age 6) who appear to have learning disabilities are often identified under a noncategorical label, such as *developmental delay*. However, experience and research show that intervention for young children is very effective and that educational efforts have a high payoff (Lerner, Lowenthal, & Egan, 1998).

Among the characteristics displayed by preschool children with learning disabilities are inadequate motor development, language delays, speech disorders, and poor cognitive and concept development. Common examples of problems at the preschool level are the 3-year-old who cannot catch a ball, hop, jump, or play with manipulative toys (poor motor development); the 4-year-old who does not use language to communicate, has a limited vocabulary, and cannot be understood (language and speech disorders); and the 5-year-old who cannot count to 10, name colors, or work puzzles (poor cognitive development). In addition, preschoolers often exhibit behaviors of hyperactivity and poor attention. The problems and treatment of the preschool child are so unique that a special chapter of this text (Chapter 8) is devoted to young children with learning disabilities. Data for 3–5-year-old children are not counted by category of disabilities (e.g., learning disabilities), but 4.6 percent of all children receiving special education services are in the 3–5 age group (U.S. Department of Education, 1998).

The Elementary Level

For many children, learning disabilities first become apparent when they enter school and fail to acquire academic skills. The failure often occurs in reading, but it also happens in mathematics, writing, or other school subjects. Among the behaviors frequently seen in the early elementary years are inability to attend and concentrate; poor motor skills, as evidenced in the awkward handling of a pencil and in poor writing; and difficulty in learning to read. The case study describes Fred's difficulties in school.

In the later elementary years, as the curriculum becomes more difficult, problems may emerge in other areas, such as social studies or science. Emotional problems also become more of an impediment after several years of repeated failure, and students become more conscious of their poor achievement in comparison with that of their peers. For some students, social problems and the inability to make and keep friends increase in importance at this age level. About 41 percent of all children with learning disabilities are in the 6–11 age group (U.S. Department of Education, 1998).

The Secondary Level

A radical change in schooling occurs at the secondary level, and adolescents find that learning disabilities begin to take a greater toll. The tougher demands of the middle school and high school curricula and teachers, the

CASE STUDY

LEARNING DISABILITIES AT THE ELEMENTARY LEVEL

That day stands out starkly in my memory. I was at the blackboard, carefully printing the words that my first-grade teacher had asked me to write. As I stepped back from my work, the laughter of my classmates told me I'd done something terribly wrong. What was so funny? I was confused by the laughter. "Fred," the teacher admonished, "you wrote all of your *e*'s backward."

During second grade, things became worse. No matter how hard I tried, I couldn't grasp simple math—even adding 2 and 2 was difficult. I kept wondering, *What's wrong with me?*

By the third grade, my parents became increasingly concerned. I remember my mother plaintively asking, "What'll become of Fred?"

Note: This child became one of the world's leading brain surgeons and pioneered many surgical techniques.

Source: Based on "What'll Become of Fred?" by F. Epstein, 1994, *Reader's Digest,* February, pp. 46–50.

turmoil of adolescence, and the continued academic failure combine to intensify the learning disability. Adolescents are also concerned about life after completing school. They may need counseling and guidance for college, career, and vocational decisions. To worsen the situation, a few adolescents find themselves drawn into acts of juvenile delinquency (Learning Disabilities Association of America, 1995).

Because adolescents tend to be overly sensitive, some emotional, social, and self-concept problems often accompany a learning disability at this age. Most secondary schools now have programs for adolescents with learning disabilities. Although this age group is considered throughout this text, some of its unique features and some special programs for adolescents are discussed in Chapter 9. About 59 percent of all children with learning disabilities are in the 12–21 age group (U.S. Department of Education, 1998).

The Adult Years

By the time they finish schooling, some adults overcome their learning disabilities, are able to reduce them, or have learned how to compensate or circumvent their problems. For many adults, however, the learning problems continue, and vestiges of their disorder continue to hamper them as they grow older. Both reading difficulties and nonverbal social disabilities may limit their career development and may also hinder them in making and keeping friends. Many adults are voluntarily seeking help in later life to cope with their learning disabilities as illustrated in the case example. Problems of adults are discussed further in Chapter 9.

CASE EXAMPLE

AN ADULT WITH LEARNING DISABILITIES

When I left school at the age of 15, the only qualifications I possessed besides years of failing was the reading ability of a 6-year-old. I could not even spell my own name. It was like living in a dark shadow, and at times it was like hell. If I didn't know or understand what was being said, I would never ask for clarification. I was too scared and nervous.

I was frustrated and tired of people humiliating me. I tried to hide my illiteracy by doing things like carrying a card in my wallet with the different amounts of money spelt on it so I could slip it out and withdraw some money from the four banks in town.

I couldn't trust my own reading ability when reading instructions on medicine bottles. I had checks returned to me many times because the words and figures didn't match. I couldn't read the instructions on how to use the public telephone in an emergency. I applied for a horticultural apprenticeship but was turned down five times in five years.

I decided to enroll in the Adult Learning Assistance Program. My dream was to learn to read and write. I had three wonderful tutors who gradually helped me learn to read and write. Gradually I became more confident and convinced that I could learn to read successfully.

Source: Based on "Overcoming Illiteracy: The Toughest Marathon," by Michael Marquet, 1994, *Reading Today, 12*(2), p. 17.

PREVALENCE OF LEARNING DISABILITIES

What percentage of the children in our schools have learning disabilities? Estimates of the prevalence of learning disabilities vary widely—ranging from 1 percent to 30 percent of the school population, with about 5 percent receiving services in the schools. The number of children and youth identified as having learning disabilities depends largely on the criteria used to determine eligibility for services. The more stringent the identification criteria, the lower the prevalence rate. If only severe cases of learning disabilities are admitted to the program, a low percentage of pupils in the school will be identified. Conversely, the more lenient the criteria, the higher the prevalence rate. If mild as well as severe learning disabilities are admitted for service, the prevalence rate will rise.

Increase in Children Identified as Having Learning Disabilities

Before the passage of Public Law 94–142 in 1975, there were only estimates of the number of children with disabilities who were being served in our schools. With this law, a nationwide count was accomplished through the written **individualized education program (IEP),** which was written for each student in special education. This child-count information indicates that the number of students identified as having learning disabilities has increased steadily. The first year the law was implemented (1977–1978), fewer than 800,000 children (or 1.8 percent of the enrolled school population) had received services under the category of learning disabilities in 1977. The percentage had increased to 5.5 percent, or over 2.6 million, by the school year 1996–1997 (U.S. Department of Education, 1998). Figure 1.3 shows the steady increase in the percentage of students identified with learning disabilities over the years.

Why has the category of learning disabilities experienced such a rapid increase? Several explanations are suggested.

1. *More awareness of learning disabilities.*   Public awareness of the condition of learning disabilities has increased. As a consequence, parents, educators, and students are exerting additional pressure on the schools to provide adequate services for students with learning disabilities.

2. ***Improvement in procedures for identifying and assessing learning disabilities.***   Improved evaluation and assessment techniques have identified many children who previously would have gone unidentified.

Figure 1.3

Percentage of Students with Learning Disabilities in Enrolled School Population

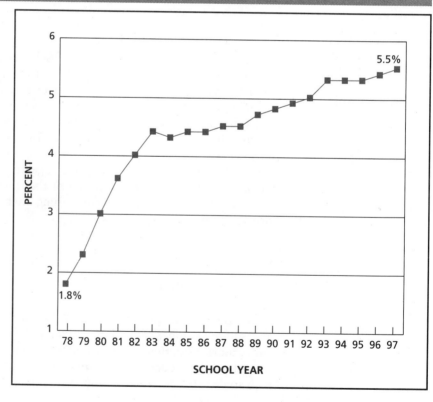

3. *Social acceptance and preference for the learning disabilities classification.*   Many parents and administrators prefer the classification of learning disabilities because it does not carry the stigma of other areas of disability. Some students who once would have been classified as having mental retardation or behavior disorders are increasingly being classified under the rubric of learning disabilities. For example, as noted in point 5, the number of children classified under **mental retardation** has decreased significantly.

4. *Cutbacks in other programs and lack of general education alternatives for children who experience problems in the regular class.*   Over this period, there has been a decrease in the funding of many programs (such as Title I programs, which are federally funded remedial programs in regular education) and a lack of adequate remedial programs, such as remedial reading.

5. *Court orders.*   A number of court decisions found that the classification of minority children as mentally retarded was discriminatory. Some of these children may be identified under the classification of learning disabilities (U.S. Department of Education, 1991a). In contrast with the increases in learning disabilities, there has been a long-term decrease in the number and relative proportion of children and youth identified with mental retardation.

Comparison of Learning Disabilities and Other Disabilities

Comparisons of learning disabilities with other categories of disabilities are revealing. In Table 1.1, the first column lists each type of disability, and the second column shows the percentage of each disability in terms of school enrollment. The third column shows the portion of each disability as a percentage of all children identified under special education; Figure 1.4 displays this information as a pie chart. Learning disabilities is the largest category, accounting for over half of the children receiving special education services.

SHIFTS IN THE SETTINGS FOR DELIVERING SERVICES

Most students with learning disabilities (about 80 percent) receive services in regular classrooms and/or resource rooms. Approximately 42 percent are served only in regular classrooms, and 39 percent are served through resource rooms for a portion of the day and in regular classrooms for the balance of the day. About 17 percent of the students with learning disabilities are served in separate classes. Other placements make up one percent and include separate schools, residential facilities, and homebound or hospital settings (U.S. Department of Education, 1998). The percentages of students

Table 1.1

Percentage of Children
with Disabilities, Ages
6–17, School Year
1995–1996

Category of Disability	Percent of Estimated Enrollment	Percent of All Disabilities
Learning disabilities	5.53	51.1
Speech/language impairments	2.28	20.1
Mental retardation	1.16	11.4
Emotional disturbance	0.92	8.6
Multiple disabilities	0.19	1.7
Hearing impairments	0.14	1.3
Orthopedic impairments	0.14	1.3
Other health impairments	0.34	3.1
Visual impairments	0.05	0.5
Autism	0.07	0.6
Deaf-blindness	less than 0.01	less than 0.1
Traumatic brain injury	0.02	0.2
All disabilities	10.83	100.0

Source: From *To Assure the Free Appropriate Public Education of All Children with Disabilities.* Twentieth Annual Report to Congress on the Implementation of the Individuals with Disabilities Education Act, by the U.S. Department of Education, 1998, Washington, DC: U.S. Government Printing Office.

with learning disabilities age 6 to 21 who are served through different educational environments are displayed in a pie chart in Chapter 5 (Figure 5.2).

The percentage of students with learning disabilities served in the general classroom is increasing as a result of an inclusion policy in many schools. **Inclusion** refers to the practice of placing students with disabilities in the general education classroom for instruction. The inclusion movement is growing rapidly. As more and more children with disabilities are placed in the general classroom in neighborhood schools, the placement of these students has changed dramatically. The U.S. Department of Education reports that about 18 percent of students with learning disabilities had been placed in general education classrooms for instruction in 1988, but the number increased to 42 percent in 1996. In 1988, 59 percent of students with learning disabilities had been placed in resource rooms, but this placement decreased to 39 percent in 1996. These data are summarized as follows:

Changes in Placements of Students with Learning Disabilities

	1988	1996
General Class (inclusion)	27.6 percent	42.3 percent
Resource Room	59.2 percent	39.3 percent

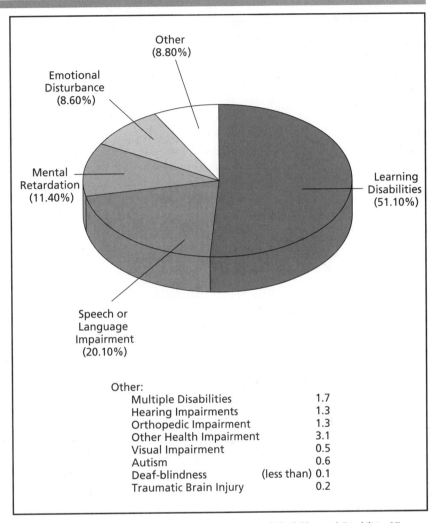

Figure 1.4

Composition of Students with Disabilities

Other (8.80%)

Emotional Disturbance (8.60%)

Mental Retardation (11.40%)

Learning Disabilities (51.10%)

Speech or Language Impairment (20.10%)

Other:
Multiple Disabilities	1.7
Hearing Impairments	1.3
Orthopedic Impairment	1.3
Other Health Impairment	3.1
Visual Impairment	0.5
Autism	0.6
Deaf-blindness (less than)	0.1
Traumatic Brain Injury	0.2

Source: From *To Assure the Free Appropriate Public Education of All Children with Disabilities.* Nineteenth Annual Report to Congress on the Implementation of the Individuals with Disabilities Education Act, by the U.S. Department of Education, 1997. Washington, DC: U.S. Government Printing Office.

Earlier placement practices that were designed to integrate special education students into general education classes were known by various terms, including *mainstreaming, regular education initiative,* and *integration* (Kauffman & Hallahan, 1995; Fuchs & Fuchs, 1995; Stainback & Stainback, 1992).

More information about the changes in placements of students with learning disabilities is provided in Chapter 5 (see Table 5.2).

COLLABORATION: THE NEW ROLE FOR LEARNING DISABILITIES TEACHERS

With the inclusion movement and the placement of more students with learning disabilities in the general education classroom, the specialist in learning disabilities must become more adept at collaboration. This role includes coordinating the efforts of other professionals, building a cooperative interdisciplinary team that works together, providing support to classroom teachers, and becoming actively involved in teaching children in many settings, including general education. The learning disabilities specialist should be equipped to serve as a highly skilled coworker and collaborator (see Chapter 5).

Without a coordinated effort, each professional may see the student with learning disabilities in terms of her or his own perspective, much as the fabled sightless scholars of India are said to have "seen" the elephant. In the proverbial tale, one scholar felt the elephant's trunk and concluded the elephant was like a snake; another, feeling the leg, said it resembled a tree trunk; the third, feeling the tail, believed the elephant was like a rope; the fourth touched the ear and thought the elephant was a fan; the fifth felt the tusk and likened the elephant to a spear; and the last man, feeling the side, said the elephant was like a wall. Similarly, since each professional sees but one part of the student with a learning disability, there is a risk that each may blindly misinterpret who the student actually is. An important task of the learning disabilities specialist is to integrate the various professional services to effect an understanding of the whole person.

DISCIPLINES CONTRIBUTING TO THE STUDY OF LEARNING DISABILITIES

Learning disabilities is a multidisciplinary field to which several disciplines (primarily education, psychology, language, and medicine) make major contributions. In addition, other professions in the helping and research fields participate in and advance the work done for people with learning disabilities. The mingling of disciplines has resulted in a multidisciplinary breadth to the body of thought in this dynamic and changing field.

Education

The contributions of the field of education have a practical framework, for educators must deal with the reality of teaching students. Special educators, classroom teachers, reading specialists, physical educators, and secondary teachers focus on the learning behavior of the student. The educators' expertise includes knowledge about subject-area sequences, understanding of the relationships among curricular areas, acquaintance with a variety of school organizational patterns, and knowledge of materials and methods. The very term *learning disabilities,* with its emphasis on the learning situation instead of the causes of the disorder, demonstrates the impact of educators on the field.

Psychology

Psychologists—particularly specialists in child development, learning theory, cognitive psychology, and school psychology—have had a significant influence in shaping the field. The psychological perspective has also led to a keener awareness of the psychodynamic and affective consequences of learning disabilities.

School psychologists have had an especially direct influence because they have observed, tested, evaluated, and characterized the outward behavior of children. The work of child development specialists, which focuses on the developmental processes of the normal child, has become the basis for many concepts of the atypical child. Learning theorists have enriched the field with their behavioral analyses of subject content areas, which identify tasks to be taught and behaviors to be expected. Behavioral theory and cognitive psychology are among the contributions of learning theorists to learning disabilities research and training (See Chapter 6).

Language Disciplines

Professionals in the fields of speech and language pathology, language development, linguistics, and psycholinguistics recognize that many of their concerns overlap with those of their counterparts in the field of learning disabilities. Speech and language pathologists have studied ways to assess language disorders and ways to teach those who have them. The work being done in linguistics (the study of the nature and structure of human language) and in psycholinguistics (the study of the relationship of language development to the thinking and learning processes) has also added to the learning disabilities knowledge base. A renewed interest in the puzzle of language acquisition, kindled by the concepts in psycholinguistics and developmental language, has increased our understanding of the child with learning disabilities. Knowledge of how the typical child learns language is invaluable in developing the ability to diagnose and treat children with language difficulties. Conversely, the study of the language disorders of exceptional children can clarify our understanding of how all children acquire language. (See Chapter 10.)

Medicine

The medical specialties (represented by both practitioners and researchers) contributing to the field include pediatrics, neurology, ophthalmology, otology, psychiatry, pharmacology, endocrinology, and nursing, particularly school nursing. By education and practice, medical specialists are cause-oriented—always searching for the etiology, or source, of a health problem. They view learning disabilities as pathological conditions, and their major contributions therefore have been in identifying the causes of learning disorders. Physicians are the key specialists for the medical diagnosis. Neuroscientists have made remarkable discoveries about the brain and learning (see Chapter 7).

Other Professions

Many other professionals also play important roles in the research and literature on learning disabilities. Optometrists have made key advancements concerning the visual function. Audiologists have contributed important concepts relating to hearing and auditory perception and training. Social workers, occupational therapists, and guidance counselors have also been instrumental in the growth of the field. In addition, research findings from fields such as genetics and biochemistry have provided important information.

One must also consider parents as vital contributing members of the multidisciplinary team. Parents have known their child for the longest period of time and have the most at stake. The parents' input and help can be both extremely supportive of and enriching to the understanding of students with learning disabilities.

Finally, individuals with learning disabilities can be advocates for themselves. Some individuals are very resourceful in understanding themselves and the nature of their learning problems. They successfully take the needed steps to help themselves learn and work within the environment to reach their goals.

Chapter Summary

1. This chapter introduced the field of learning disabilities by presenting accounts of the lives of accomplished people who experienced severe learning problems as children and discussing the cross-cultural nature of the problem; discussing and evaluating several definitions of learning disabilities; analyzing five elements common to most definitions; describing the characteristics of people with learning abilities; looking at the expanding age range of the learning disabilities population; analyzing the prevalence of learning disabilities; examining the new settings for serving children with learning disabilities and the new role of the learning disabilities teacher; and describing the contributions of the various disciplines involved in the learning disabilities field.

2. Learning disabilities have affected the lives of many eminent people as children, including Nelson Rockefeller, Thomas Edison, Auguste Rodin, and Albert Einstein.

3. Learning disabilities occur in all cultures. The condition affects individuals of all nations, cultures, and languages.

4. Defining *learning disabilities* has proved to be a formidable task. The definition that appears in federal legislation has become the basis for state and local district definitions and many learning disabilities programs. The operational part of the federal definition states that a student can be identified as having a learning disability if an evaluation team finds a severe discrepancy between the student's achievement and intellectual ability in one or more of several areas: oral expression, listening comprehension, written expression, basic reading skill, reading comprehension, mathematics calculation, and mathematics reasoning. In addition to the federal definition, others have been proposed, including those by the National Joint Committee on Learning Disabilities (NJCLD) and the Interagency Committee on Learning Disabilities (ICLD).

5. There are five elements common to most definitions of *learning disabilities*: neurological dysfunction, uneven growth pattern, difficulty in academic and learning tasks, discrepancy between achievement and potential, and exclusion of other causes. Each adds to our understanding of learning disabilities, but each also raises certain issues in the field.

6. Students with learning disabilities display many different and diverse characteristics; no individual will exhibit all characteristics. In addition, certain difficulties are more prevalent than others at particular ages. The possible characteristics include problems in attention, motor abilities, perception, cognitive strategies, oral language, reading, written language, mathematics, and nonverbal social skills. More boys than girls are identified with learning disabilities. However, research shows that there are as many girls with learning disabilities as there are boys with them. The notion of multiple intelligences suggests that students with learning disabilities have other kinds of intelligences not recognized by the school.

7. There is recognition that learning disabilities affect people differently in various stages of life. Preschoolers, elementary-age students, adolescents, and adults manifest different problems and characteristics. The age range has expanded over the years, and each age group requires different intervention and teaching strategies.

8. The percentage of children with learning disabilities in school is now 5.5 percent for ages 6 through 21. More students are classified as having learning disabilities for several reasons: more awareness of the problem, improved procedures for identifying learning disabilities, social acceptance and preference for the learning disabilities classification, a decrease in other types of remedial services, and court orders concerning other disabilities.

9. Inclusion, a growing trend, is a policy by which students with learning disabilities are placed in the general education classroom. The number of students in general education classes is increasing while the number in resource rooms is decreasing.

10. A growing responsibility for the learning disabilities teacher is collaboration with classroom teachers and other school personnel.

11. Several disciplines participate in the study of learning disabilities, making it a multidisciplinary field. These disciplines are education, psychology, language, medicine, and other helping and research professions. Each specialization has important contributions to make to the field.

Questions for Discussion and Reflection

1. What are the various definitions of learning disabilities that have been proposed, and how do they differ? Do you think it is important to formulate a single definition of learning disabilities? Why or why not?

2. What are the five dimensions or components common to most of the definitions of learning disabilities? Discuss the nature of each component and the controversies surrounding each one.

3. The age range of individuals with learning disabilities has expanded over the years. Describe the characteristics of each of the four general age levels.

4. The number of students classified as having learning disabilities has increased substantially since the 1975 special education law (Public Law 94–142). Discuss the reasons for this increase.

5. How has the role of the learning disabilities teacher changed? Discuss the new responsibilities.

6. The field of learning disabilities is interdisciplinary. What are the various professions that contribute to the field, and what is the nature of their contributions?

Key Terms

central nervous system dysfunction *(p. 12)*

Coordinated Campaign for Learning Disabilities (CCLD) *(p. 4)*

giftedness *(p. 19)*

heterogeneous *(p. 10)*

inclusion *(p. 26)*

individualized education program (IEP) *(p. 23)*

Interagency Committee on Learning Disabilities (ICLD) *(p. 11)*

learning disabilities *(p. 4)*

mental retardation *(p. 25)*

multiple intelligences *(p. 17)*

National Joint Committee on
Learning Disabilities (NJCLD)
(p. 10)

nonverbal learning disabilities
(p. 15)

potential for learning *(p. 11)*

Public Law 94–142, 1975
Education for All Handicapped
Children Act *(p. 9)*

Public Law 101–476, 1990 Individuals with Disabilities Education Act (IDEA) *(p. 9)*

Public Law 105–17, 1997 Amendments to the Individuals with Disabilities Education Act (IDEA 1997) *(p. 9)*

severe discrepancy *(p. 14)*

2

Historical Perspectives and Current Directions

CHAPTER OUTLINE

This chapter traces the roots of the field of learning disabilities and looks at the current directions. Theories, concepts, and research findings that advanced the thinking within the field were generated by many individuals and stem from several related disciplines. Each contribution added to and redirected earlier theories and, in turn, inspired further research and investigation. It is convenient to divide the history of learning disabilities into four distinct periods (see Figure 2.1):

1. *Foundation phase* (about 1800–1930).   Marked by basic scientific investigations of brain function and dysfunction.

2. *Transition phase* (about 1930–1960).   Research findings about brain dysfunction were applied to the clinical study of children with problems in learning, and professionals began to develop assessment and treatment methods for those children.

3. *Integration phase* (about 1960–1980).   Characterized by the rapid growth of school programs for students with learning disabilities; the eclectic use of a variety of theories, assessment techniques, and teaching strategies; and the enactment of legislation designed to protect the rights of children and youth with disabilities.

4. *Current phase* (1980–present).   New directions have expanded the scope of the field. Among the highlights of the current period are special education law, the inclusion movement, culturally and linguistically diverse students with learning disabilities, attention deficit disorder, nonverbal learning disorders, education reform policies, and the increasing use of computer technology.

THE FOUNDATION PHASE: EARLY BRAIN RESEARCH

The foundation phase, 1800–1930, was a period of basic scientific research on the functions and disorders of the brain. Many of the early brain researchers were physicians involved in investigating the brain damage of

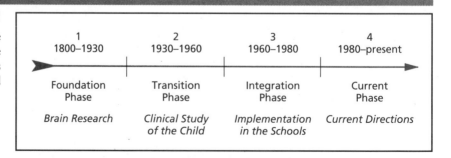

Figure 2.1

Time Line: Phases in the Development of the Learning Disabilities Field

1 1800–1930	2 1930–1960	3 1960–1980	4 1980–present
Foundation Phase	Transition Phase	Integration Phase	Current Phase
Brain Research	*Clinical Study of the Child*	*Implementation in the Schools*	*Current Directions*

adult patients who had suffered stroke, accidents, or disease. These scientists gathered information by first studying the behavior of patients who had lost some function, such as the ability to speak or read. In the autopsies of many of these patients, they were able to link the loss of function to specific damaged areas of the brain. Some of the highlights of this foundation period are reviewed in this section.

A widely held notion in the nineteenth century was the belief in *phrenology*, which held that abnormal behavior and brain function could be predicted by examining the shape of the skull. Bumps on the head were thought to reveal information about the brain. In the 1860s, Paul Broca refuted the phrenology notion with his discovery during autopsies of adult patients who had lost the ability to speak and had subsequently died; he found that certain areas of the brain (in the left frontal lobe) were damaged (Broca, 1879). The importance of his discovery is widely recognized, and the loss of the ability to speak is often called *Broca's aphasia*. John Hughlings Jackson (1874) added to this knowledge by showing that the areas of the human brain are intimately linked, so that damage to one part will reduce overall general functioning. Carl Wernicke (1908) described another portion of the brain (the temporal lobe) as the location for the function of language understanding.

Sir Henry Head (1926) produced major contributions about aphasia, or the loss of speech, by developing a system for data collection and a test for diagnosing **aphasia**. Head showed that patients with aphasia did not suffer from generalized impairment of intellectual ability even though they had sustained brain damage and had lost language skills. James Hinshelwood (1917), an ophthalmologist, studied the condition of *word blindness*, which he defined as the inability to interpret written or printed language despite normal vision. Reporting on the case of an intelligent boy who was unable to learn to read, Hinshelwood speculated that the problem was due to a defect in the angular gyrus, a specific area of the brain.

Kurt Goldstein (1939), a physician who treated brain-injured soldiers during World War I, showed that brain damage affects an individual's behavior. Among the characteristics he noted in the brain-injured soldiers were *perceptual impairment* characterized by foreground-background (or figure-ground) difficulties, *distractibility* to external stimuli, and *perseveration* (the behavior of being locked into continually repeating an action). Heinz Werner and Alfred Strauss (1940) continued Goldstein's work, expanding the study from brain-injured soldiers to brain-injured children.

In the 1930s the field of learning disabilities proceeded from the foundation phase—with its focus on the study of the brain—to the transition phase—the clinical study of learning problems in children. However, brain research did not end. In fact, interest in this area is today greater than ever. Advancements in scientific technology allow much more sophisticated ways to study the brain. Some of the more recent discoveries about the brain that have implications for learning disabilities are discussed in Chapter 7.

THE TRANSITION PHASE: CLINICAL STUDY OF CHILDREN

During the transition phase (about 1930–1960), scientific studies of the brain were applied to the clinical study of children and translated into ways of teaching. Psychologists and educators developed instruments for assessment and teaching. During this period investigators also analyzed specific types of learning disorders.

A number of scientists played important roles in developing this phase of the field. Foremost among them was Samuel T. Orton (1937), a neurologist, whose theory of the lack of cerebral dominance as a cause of children's language disorders led to the development of a teaching method known as the Orton-Gillingham method (see Chapters 7 and 11). The International Dyslexia Association (formerly The Orton Dyslexia Society) was created to honor Orton and to continue his work. It is an active force in the field of learning disabilities today. An educator in the 1940s, Grace Fernald (1988), also contributed to this period by establishing a remedial clinic at the University of California at Los Angeles, where she developed a remedial approach to teaching reading and spelling (see Chapters 11 and 12). Maria Montessori (1964), a physician who worked with at-risk young children in Italy, demonstrated the value of using carefully planned materials and a structured environment to encourage children to learn and to develop cognitively.

Among the other pioneers who helped develop the field of learning disabilities during this period are William Cruickshank, Ray Barsch, Marianne Frostig, Newell Kephart, Samuel Kirk, and Helmer Myklebust; their contributions are discussed in pertinent chapters of this book. During the transition phase, terminology changed many times, and various phrases were used to describe the problem—*brain-injured children*, *Strauss syndrome*, *minimal brain dysfunction*, and finally *learning disabilities*. The progression of terms reflects the historical progress of the field. Each term filled a need in its time, but each had inherent shortcomings.

The Brain-Injured Child

Pioneering work conducted by Alfred Strauss and Laura Lehtinen (1947) was reported in their book *Psychopathology and Education of the Brain-Injured Child*. They identified a new category of exceptional youngsters, classifying them as **brain-injured children**. Many of these youngsters had previously been classified as mentally retarded, emotionally disturbed, autistic, aphasic, or behaviorally maladjusted. Most of them exhibited such severe behavior characteristics that they were excluded from the public schools. (It is important to remember that at that time public schools had the right to exclude children with disabilities.) Further, the medical histories of these children indicated that they had suffered a brain injury at some time during their prenatal or postnatal lives.

Seeking a medical explanation for the behavioral characteristics, Strauss hypothesized that the behaviors and learning patterns of these children were manifestations of brain injury. This diagnosis was unique at the time because other professionals had explained the behavioral abnormalities of many such children as stemming from emotional origins. Strauss believed that other children who exhibited characteristics similar to the subjects in his studies had also suffered an injury to the brain.

Strauss believed that the injury to the brain occurred during any of three periods in the child's life: *before* birth, the prenatal stage; *during* the birth process; or at some point *after* birth. An example of an injury occurring before birth is an infection such as German measles (rubella) contracted by the mother early in pregnancy and affecting the fetus. An example of an injury during birth could be any condition that would seriously reduce the infant's supply of oxygen during the birth process (anoxia). After birth, the brain could be injured by a fall on the head or an excessively high fever in infancy or early childhood. Although such events could produce other disabilities (such as mental retardation or physical impairments), Strauss believed that they could also precipitate behavior and learning problems.

Strauss identified the following behavioral and biological characteristics of brain-injured children.

Behavioral Characteristics   It is of historical interest to note that Strauss stressed behavioral characteristics more than learning characteristics. As leaders in learning disabilities sought supportive legislation from Congress in the 1960s and 1970s, they shifted the emphasis to disorders in learning. Currently, many of the behavioral characteristics first identified by Strauss are recognized as key characteristics of children with attention deficit disorder.

Perceptual Disorders   The child with a **perceptual disorder** may either experience a figure-ground distortion that causes confusion between the background and foreground, or may see parts instead of wholes.

Figure-ground distortion is an inability to focus on an object without having its background or setting interfere with the perception. One teacher noted that when she wore a particular dress with polka dots, the children with perceptual disorders seemed compelled to touch it to verify what they thought they perceived. The ambiguity in perception that the normal observer senses in Figures 2.2 and 2.3 can help one understand the unstable world of the child with a perceptual disorder. In Figure 2.2, one is to determine whether the picture is the face of an old woman or a young woman. In Figure 2.3, one is asked to look at the drawing and then to sketch it from memory. (Even copying this figure while viewing it may prove to be difficult.) These illustrations contain reversible figure-ground patterns that produce confusion, or a shifting of background and foreground, much like that constantly experienced by a child with perceptual disorders.

Figure 2.2

Do you see a young woman or an old woman in this picture?

Figure 2.3

Examine this drawing and then try to sketch it from memory.

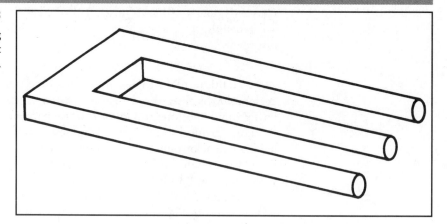

Seeing parts instead of wholes can be illustrated with the capital letter *A*. A child with a perceptual disorder might perceive three unrelated lines rather than a meaningful whole. Or instead of the whole figure of a square, the child might perceive four unrelated lines. A child might also focus on an irrelevant detail in a picture and thereby lose the meaning of the entire picture.

Perseveration   A child with perseverative behavior/**perseveration** continues an activity once it has started and has difficulty changing to another. For example, after writing the letter *a* the three times required in a writing lesson, the perseverative child may not be able to stop but instead will continue this activity until the entire page is filled with *a*'s. One such child continued this activity onto the desk and up the wall. Another example of perseveration is the child who persists in singing a song from a television commercial over and over.

Conceptual Disorders   A child with **conceptual disorders** is unable to organize materials and thoughts in a normal manner. This is a disturbance in the cognitive abilities that affects comprehension skills in reading and listening. One 10-year-old girl was unable to differentiate the concepts of *sugar* and *salt;* since the two substances have a similar appearance, she confused the words symbolizing those concepts. Today there is renewed interest in the thinking problems of individuals with learning disabilities and in instruction in cognitive strategies (see Chapters 6 and 9).

Behavioral Disorders   Strauss noted that brain-injured children were hyperactive, explosive, erratic, or otherwise uninhibited in behavior. They were continually in motion, blew up easily, and were easily distracted from the task at hand.

Distractibility   The behavior of **distractibility** refers to the inability to concentrate or inattentiveness. Today, children with these characteristics are seen as having hyperactive and impulsive behavior and are identified as children with attention deficit disorder.

Biological Characteristics   In Strauss's thinking, children could be diagnosed as brain injured without positive evidence of any of the following three biological signs.

Soft Neurological Signs   This term refers to subtle rather than obvious or severe evidence of neurological abnormalities. An awkwardness in gait, for example, is considered a **soft neurological sign**. Another soft sign is difficulty in performing fine motor skills, such as buttoning or cutting with a scissors.

A History of Neurological Impairment   This characteristic refers to evidence in the medical history of brain injury that occurred before, during, or after birth.

No History of Mental Retardation in the Family   Strauss felt that it was important to rule out familial or inherited types of mental retardation. Since his interest was in the effect of brain damage on a child with a potentially normal brain, he excluded from his investigation those children who had mental retardation resulting from inherited factors.

Strauss's initial work alerted physicians to events that might be related to brain injury. An alarmingly large number of possibilities are identified as potential causes of such injury. In the *prenatal stage*, injury could result from such conditions in the mother as the RH factor or from diseases during pregnancy such as rubella. It could also be caused by the mother's smoking or use of alcohol, prescribed medication, or illicit drugs during pregnancy. During the *birth process*, insufficient oxygen; prematurity; a long, hard labor; a difficult delivery; or a purposely delayed birth could injure the baby's brain. *After birth*, childhood diseases (such as encephalitis and meningitis), the dehydration and extremely high fevers that accompany illnesses, some head injuries sustained in accidents, and baby shaking have also been linked to brain injury. (It must be remembered, however, that these events are merely *possible* causes of brain injury. Many children with case histories of such events apparently escape harm, whereas other children with clear symptoms of brain injury have no such events in their case histories.)

Teaching the Brain-Injured Child   Besides developing a theory of the brain-injured child, Strauss and Lehtinen (1947) presented a plan for teaching such children. Their suggested methods, materials, and settings differed dramatically from those of a regular classroom. For example, they designed a learning environment that reduced distraction and hyperactivity. All stimulating visual materials such as bulletin boards or pictures were removed, and the windowpanes were painted to conceal overstimulating outside views. Further, they recommended that the teacher avoid wearing jewelry and dress in a manner that would reduce distractions. The students' desks were placed against a wall, behind a screen, or in a partitioned cubicle. Special materials were constructed to aid students in the perception of visual forms and in the organization of space and form. The initial classes for brain-injured children were in a private school setting.

Strauss's work and theory were welcomed because they offered an alternative diagnosis for children who previously had been given many other labels, such as badly behaved, emotionally disturbed, lazy, careless, or stupid. This fresh view was most welcome to parents who had been blamed for creating psychological distress that caused disorders in their children, had been told that their children did not fit into a public school setting, or had vainly sought a sensible diagnosis. This new approach offered such parents a meaningful, logical, and hopeful analysis of their child.

Strauss and his coworkers laid the foundation for the field of learning disabilities by (1) perceiving similar characteristics in a diverse group of children who had been misdiagnosed by specialists, misunderstood by parents, and often discarded by society; (2) planning and implementing educational settings and procedures for teaching these children successfully; and (3) alerting many professions to the existence of a new category of disabilities.

The Search for Other Terminology

Doubts about the usefulness of the term *brain-injured* arose soon after the publication of Strauss and Lehtinen's book in 1947. Critics pointed out that the term was confusing. Also, it was difficult to use the medical term *brain-injured* in communicating with parents, and the term was frightening to children. Other terms were soon suggested to identify these children.

The term *Strauss syndrome* was recommended by Stevens and Birch (1957) to pay tribute to Strauss's pioneering work. This term focused on the behavioral characteristics, not the learning characteristics. The "Strauss syndrome" child exhibited the following behaviors:

1. Erratic and inappropriate behavior on mild provocation
2. Increased motor activity disproportionate to the stimulus
3. Poor organization of behavior
4. Distractibility of more than the ordinary degree under ordinary conditions
5. Persistent faulty perceptions
6. Persistent hyperactivity
7. Awkwardness and consistently poor motor performance

Minimal brain dysfunction (MBD), a term recommended by Clements (1966), classified children with various brain impairments along a scale ranging from mild to severe. At the severe end of the scale are children with obvious brain damage, such as cerebral palsy or epilepsy. At the opposite end are children with minimal impairments that affect behavior and learning in more subtle ways. Clements recommended the term *minimal brain dysfunction* to describe the child with near-average intelligence and with certain learning and behavioral disorders associated with deviations or dysfunctions of the central nervous system. Thus, MBD differentiated the minimally involved child from the child with major brain disorders. Many medical professionals employed the term *MBD* when diagnosing children.

Clements classified the many terms (over thirty-eight) being used to refer to these children by sorting them into two groups: (1) terms that identified the *biological causes* of the condition (for example, neurological dysfunction or brain injury), and (2) terms that identified the *behavioral consequences* (such as hyperactivity or distractibility).

Acceptance of the Term "Learning Disabilities"

None of the many recommended terms for describing these children received general acceptance. It was clear that another term was needed that would more meaningfully describe these children's conditions. In 1963 Samuel Kirk first proposed the term *learning disabilities* at a meeting of concerned parents and professionals (Kirk, 1963). Accepted immediately, *learning disabilities* continues to be used and appears to be a satisfactory term which gained rapid acceptance. It is an umbrella concept, encompassing many diverse types of learning problems without identifying the specific area of the student's deficiencies. Its advantages are that it focuses on the educational problems, avoids the medical implications, and seems to be acceptable to parents, teachers, and students. The term *learning disabilities* has now been written into law in the United States and other countries throughout the world. It successfully serves as a recognized way to refer to individuals with the problems that are the concern of this book.

THE INTEGRATION PHASE: RAPID EXPANSION OF SCHOOL PROGRAMS

During the integration phase (about 1960–1980), learning disabilities became an established discipline in the schools throughout the United States. The field grew rapidly as learning disabilities programs were established, teachers were trained, and children began to receive services. (Some events that occurred in a later phase are discussed in this section because they are a logical extension of and closely related to major events of the integration phase.)

Rapid Growth of Public School Learning Disabilities Programs

One of the first attempts to establish a public school learning disabilities program occurred in Syracuse, New York (Cruickshank, Bentzen, Ratzeburgh, & Tannhauser, 1961). This demonstration-pilot project adapted and refined the educational methods proposed by Strauss and Lehtinen (1947) for brain-injured students in the public schools. The early plans for teaching these students called for the following conditions in the teaching environment (Cruickshank et al., 1961):

1. Reducing unessential visual and auditory environmental stimuli
2. Reducing the space in which the student works
3. Providing a highly structured schedule
4. Increasing the stimulus value of the teaching materials

By the 1960s and 1970s, public school learning disabilities programs were rapidly being established throughout the nation. Several forces promoted this needed development: parental pressures, the increase in professional information, the availability of teacher training programs, and the first state laws requiring services for students with learning disabilities. Most of the early programs were for students at the elementary level. Children were placed in special classes, following the traditional delivery system in special education at that time. Later in this period, resource room programs were introduced, and the secondary schools also began to serve adolescent students with learning disabilities. Many new tests and teaching materials were developed during this period to serve the growing number of students identified under the category of *learning disabilities* in the schools.

Increased Legislative Support for Teacher Training

A major advancement in the field occurred in 1969, when Congress passed the **Children with Specific Learning Disabilities Act (PL 91–230)**. For the first time, the field of learning disabilities was acknowledged in federal law, with funding provided for teacher training. This law set the stage for including learning disabilities in subsequent federal and state laws.

In the 1970s, federal funding supported the development of learning disabilities model programs throughout the country. Called **Child Service Demonstration Centers (CSDCs)**, these were model projects that provided opportunities for innovation and experimentation, and stimulated the development of learning disabilities practices throughout the nation (Mann et al., 1984).

THE CURRENT PHASE: EMERGING DIRECTIONS

A number of key issues affect students with learning disabilities at the present time. In a relatively new field, one expects many changes in direction and the development of new concepts and ideas. Some occur as natural extensions of ongoing programs, others result from shortcomings experienced in earlier programs, and still others result from outside pressures. In this section, we look at several major contemporary trends—special education laws, the inclusion movement, serving culturally and linguistically diverse students, attention deficit disorder, nonverbal learning disabilities, the educational reform movement, and the impact of computer technology.

Special Education Laws

As noted in Chapter 1, the legislation that had the greatest influence on the establishment of learning disabilities services in our public schools was the 1975 federal special education law known as **Public Law 94–142 (or the Education for All Handicapped Children Act)**. In 1990, this law was updated as the **Individuals with Disabilities Education Act (IDEA) (PL 101–476)**. In 1997, IDEA was updated as the **Individuals with Disabilities Education Act of 1997 (PL 105–17)**. Under this series of laws, summarized in Table 2.1, all children and youth ages 3 through 21 with disabilities have the right to a free and appropriate public education. Further, each state must have a plan that is in compliance with the federal law.

Individuals with Disabilities Education Act (IDEA)　The 1990 Individuals with Disabilities Education Act (IDEA 1990) continued the mandates of the

Table 2.1

Series of Special
Education Laws

Public Law Number	Name of Law	Date Passed
PL 94–142	The Education for All Handicapped Children Act	1975
PL 101–476	Individuals with Disabilities Education Act (IDEA) of 1990	1990
PL 105–17	Individuals with Disabilities Education Act (IDEA) of 1997	1997

earlier 1975 law PL 94–142 but added several important features. The term *disabilities* was used instead of *handicaps,* which is now considered a pejorative term. The word *individuals* replaced the word *children.* IDEA 1990 also recognized two new categories of disabilities, *autism* and *traumatic brain injury,* and it required transition plans for adolescents with disabilities.

The 1997 Individuals with Disabilities Education Act Amendments (PL 105–17) sharpen IDEA by (Yell & Schriner, 1997):

- strengthening the role of parents (see Chapter 5)
- extending the full rights and protections to preschool children with disabilities (see Chapter 8)
- ensuring access to the general education curriculum and reforms (see Chapter 5)
- focusing on teaching and learning while reducing necessary paperwork requirements (see Chapter 5)
- assisting education agencies in addressing the costs of improving special education and related services to children with disabilities
- giving increasing attention to racial, ethnic, and linguistic diversity to prevent inappropriate identification and mislabeling (see Chapter 10)
- ensuring that schools are safe and conducive to learning (see Chapter 14)
- encouraging parents and educators to work out their differences using nonadversarial means (see Chapter 5)

The Rules and Regulations for IDEA 1997   In 1999, the Department of Education wrote the Rules and Regulations to implement the 1997 Individuals with Disabilities Act. These Rules and Regulations provide guidelines for schools and parents as they implement the law. They are discussed further in Chapters 3 and 5 and in Appendix F.

Basic Concepts of the Individuals with Disabilities Education Act (IDEA)
The Individuals with Disabilities Education Act (IDEA) is considered civil rights legislation that guarantees education to individuals with disabilities.

The law alters former educational practices that led to exclusion, neglect, and substandard treatment of persons with disabilities. The critical features of IDEA that have implications for identifying, assessing, and serving students with learning disabilities are discussed in relevant sections of this book. Among them are the *individualized education program* or IEP (Chapter 3), *procedural safeguards* (Chapter 3), *least restrictive environment* (Chapter 5) and *continuum of alternative placements* (Chapter 5), and *parent involvement* (Chapters 3 and 5).

IDEA recognizes that individuals with disabilities need special education or related services. Federal categories of disabilities under IDEA include learning disabilities; mental retardation; hearing disabilities; speech and language disabilities; visual disabilities; emotional disturbance; orthopedic disabilities; other health-impaired, deaf-blind, multiple disabilities; autism; and traumatic brain injury.

Other Special Education Laws: Section 504 and the Americans with Disabilities Act (ADA)   Two additional laws affect students with disabilities in the schools. Section 504 of the Rehabilitation Act requires that accommodations be made for individuals with disabilities in institutions that receive federal funds. The Americans with Disabilities Act (ADA) protects people with disabilities from discrimination in the workplace. Both laws are discussed further in Chapter 5.

The Inclusion Movement

As discussed in Chapter 1, the placement practice known as inclusion is growing rapidly in our schools. Inclusion is the policy of placing children with disabilities in general education classrooms for instruction. Support for placing children with disabilities in general education classrooms is a component of the law called the **least restrictive environment (LRE)**, which indicates that children with disabilities should, to the greatest extent appropriate, be instructed with children who do not have disabilities. Inclusion and the role of general education are also bolstered by several new features of the 1997 IDEA. The effects of the expanding inclusion policy are evident in Table 2.2, which shows that the placement of children with learning disabilities in regular classrooms increased from 15 percent in 1985–1986 to 42 percent in 1995–1996.

The topic of inclusion continues to be controversial among parents, educators, administrators, and legislators. Advocates of inclusion believe that placing students with disabilities in general education classrooms will provide those students with greater access to their general education peers, raise expectations for student performance, help general education students be more accepting of diverse students, and improve coordination between regular and special educators (U.S. Department of Education, 1997; Stainback & Stainback, 1992). Other educators are more cautious about the value of inclusion. They worry that children with learning disabilities will not receive

Table 2.2

Percentage of Students
with Learning
Disabilities Placed in the
Regular Classroom

Year	Percentage
1985–1986	15
1989–1990	21
1995–1996	42

Source: To Assure the Free Appropriate Public Education of All Children with Disabilities. Twentieth Annual Report to Congress on the Implementation of the Individuals with Disabilities Education Act, by the U.S. Department of Education, 1998. Washington, DC: U.S. Government Printing Office, p. A–52.

the intensive, direct, and individualized teaching they need in the general education classroom. These educators emphasize that special education requires discovering what is unique about each child with learning disabilities and finding individually designed instruction to meet the particular needs of that child. They worry that much research shows that students with learning disabilities are poorly served in general education classrooms (Zigmond et al., 1995; Zigmond, 1997; Kauffman & Hallahan, 1997). (The subject of inclusion is discussed further in Chapter 5.)

Collaboration   For effective integration of students with learning disabilities into general classrooms, inclusion practices must be carried out in a responsible way with sufficient support in those classrooms (Vaughn & Schumm, 1995). A key element of this support is **collaboration** between special education and general education teachers. Engaging in the process of collaboration has become a growing responsibility for learning disabilities teachers.

There are several different models of collaboration. In some the special educator works only with the classroom teacher and provides no direct services to the children. In others the special educator both collaborates with the classroom teacher and provides direct services (Friend & Cook, 1996). (The topic of collaboration is discussed further in Chapter 5.)

Cultural and Linguistic Diversity

Cultural and linguistic diversity aptly describes the rapidly changing school population in the United States and in Canada. By the year 2000, over 36 percent of the school population in the United Sates will consist of African-American, Hispanic, and Asian-American students (Ortiz, 1997). Many of these culturally and linguistically diverse (**CLD**) students also have learning disabilities (Ortiz, 1997; Artiles & Trent, 1997; U.S. Department of Education, 1997; Artiles, Trent & Kuan, 1997). Table 2.3 shows the percentage of students with learning disabilities by racial/ethnic groups from data collected by the Office of Civil Rights.

Table 2.3

Percentages of Students with Learning Disabilities by Race/Ethnicity

Race/Ethnic Group	Percentage with Learning Disabilities
White, non-Hispanic	5.7
Asian/Pacific Islander	2.0
Hispanic	5.7
Black, non-Hispanic	5.7
American Indian	7.3

Source: U.S. Department of Education. (1998). *To Assure the Free Appropriate Public Education of All Children with Disabilities.* Twentieth Annual Report to Congress on the Implementation of the Individuals with Disabilities Education Act. Washington, DC: U.S. Government Printing Office, p. II–22.

In urban schools and certain geographic locations, the percentage of linguistically and culturally diverse students with learning disabilities is even higher. Although Spanish speakers represent 76 percent of the language minority population, more than 100 distinct language groups are served across the United States, including Spanish, Korean, Polish, Arabic, and Vietnamese (Ortiz, 1997).

Cultural and linguistic diversity aptly describes the rapidly changing school population. (© Elizabeth Crews)

One of the greatest challenges our schools face is educating students from all cultures, whatever their geographic origin, socioeconomic status, or language. Cultural pluralism recognizes the rich contributions of the participating cultures in our nation and promotes the conviction that each culture can make a worthy contribution to the overall American society. The differences that exist among the various cultural populations in our schools can be a positive force in society. Children benefit by maintaining their cultural identities, and society is enriched by the mosaic created by this diversity.

Learning disabilities occur in all cultures and ethnic groups. The population of students with learning disabilities reflects the cultural diversity of our nation. Teachers must appreciate their cultural contributions; assessment procedures must be fair and must consider each child's culture, language, and background; and appropriate services must be offered to all children (Artiles & Trent, 1997).

Learning English is particularly challenging for children with learning disabilities whose native language is not English. These children have two basic problems: limited English proficiency and learning disabilities. Many do not have a good grasp of their native language, yet they are expected to learn and function in English. For these children, teachers must draw upon instructional methods from both bilingual education and special education (Gersten, Brengelman, & Jiminez, 1994; Ortiz, 1997). (Recommendations for helping children with limited English proficiency and learning disabilities are presented in Chapter 10.)

Attention Deficit Disorder

Attention deficit disorder constitutes a chronic neurological condition characterized by developmentally inappropriate attention skills, impulsivity, and, in some cases, hyperactivity. Two different terms are used to refer to this condition: (1) **attention deficit disorder (ADD)**, which is used by the U.S. Department of Education as well as by the schools; and (2) **attention deficit hyperactivity disorder (ADHD)**, which is taken from the diagnostic criteria in *Diagnostic and Statistical Manual of Mental Disorders*, 4th edition (DSM-IV) (American Psychiatric Association, 1994), and is used by physicians and psychologists.

ADD is a complex and puzzling condition for many children in our schools, including many who also have learning disabilities. Research indicates that 30 to 62 percent of the children with ADD have co-occurring learning disabilities (Flynn, 1998). With increasing frequency, physicians and psychologists are diagnosing children with ADD or ADHD. These children have difficulty staying on task, focusing attention, and completing their work. They are easily distracted, racing from one idea or interest to another, and they may produce work that is sloppy and carelessly performed. They impart the impression that they are not listening or have not heard what they have been told. Children with attention deficit disorder have attentional problems and/or problems with hyperactivity, displaying symptoms of age-inappropriate hyperactive behavior (Lerner & Lowenthal, 1999; Lerner, Lowenthal, & Lerner, 1995; Goldman, Genel, Beznan, & Sianetz, 1996).

The condition of attention deficit disorder is not listed as a separate category of disability in the special education law of IDEA. However, the regulations for IDEA 1997 (1999) and a policy memorandum by the U.S. Department of Education (September 16, 1991b) clarify that children with this disorder are eligible for special education services and can be identified under one of three existing special education categories: *other health impaired*, *learning disabilities*, or *emotional disturbance*.

The number of children identified under the category *other health impaired (OHI)* increased substantially because many children with ADD are served under OHI. In fact, the number of children identified as OHI increased from 56,165 in the Department of Education 1992 report to 160,663 in the 1998 report, an increase of over 200 percent. (See Figure 2.4.) Some children with attention deficit disorder may not be identified under IDEA, but under the law known as Section 504 of the Rehabilitation Act, they are eligible for accommodation in the regular classroom. The category of eligibility and the type of educational services available depend on the nature of the child's disability.

Figure 2.4

Increase in the Number of Children Identified as "Other Health Impaired" (OHI)

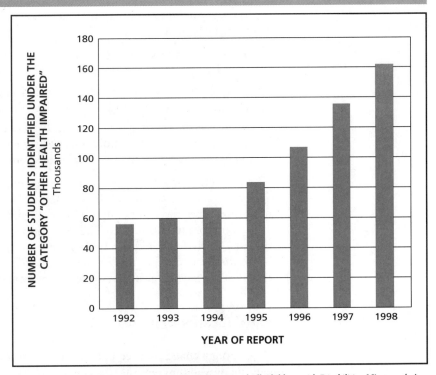

Source: To Assure the Free Appropriate Public Education of All Children with Disabilities. Nineteenth Annual Report to Congress on the Implementation of the Individuals with Disabilities Education Act. Washington, DC: Government Printing Office, 1991–1997.

Three types of attention deficit hyperactivity disorder (ADHD) are defined in the fourth edition of the *Diagnostic and Statistical Manual of Mental Disorders* (American Psychiatric Association, 1994). They are (a) primarily inattentive, (b) primarily hyperactive-impulsive, and (c) a combination of *a* and *b*. Additional information about attention deficit disorder is presented in greater detail in Chapters 7 and 14.

A useful web site for ADD is located at **http://www.CHADD.org**.

Nonverbal Learning Disabilities

Nonverbal learning disabilities (NLD) affect some children and adults who manifest serious social problems. NLD is described as a neurological syndrome consisting of specific assets and deficits (Semrud-Clikeman & Hynd, 1990; NLD web site; Rourke & Conway, 1997; Thompson, 1997; Teeter & Semrud-Clikeman, 1997). Asperger's Syndrome is a severe nonverbal learning disorder.

Individuals with nonverbal learning disabilities (NLD) have specific strengths which include early speech and vocabulary development, remarkable rote memory skills, attention to detail, early reading development, and excellent spelling skills. These individuals have the verbal ability to express themselves eloquently. Persons with NLD also have strong auditory retention.

However, individuals with NLD have specific deficits and areas of dysfunction. They include

- *Motor clumsiness* (Lack of coordination, severe balance problems, and difficulties with graphomotor skills, specifically in writing)
- *Visual-spatial-organizational deficits* (Lack of image, poor visual recall, faulty spatial perceptions, and difficulties with spatial relations)
- *Social relationships* (Lack of ability to comprehend nonverbal communication, difficulties adjusting to transitions and novel situations, and deficits in social judgment and social interaction)

Individuals with nonverbal learning disabilities are thought to have a right-hemisphere dysfunction. In addition to having trouble with social relationships, they have difficulties with mathematics, visual-spatial relationships, and organization (Rourke & Conway, 1997). Since the major difficulty for individuals with NLD appears in the social sphere, this condition is discussed further in Chapter 14. A web site for nonverbal learning disabilities is located at **http://www.nldline.com**.

The Educational Reform Movement

Major policy changes in regular education profoundly affect students with learning disabilities. Several recent national study commissions on the poor quality of U.S. schools have culminated in an **educational reform movement**.

Increasing Curriculum Demands   The pursuit of excellence in our schools translates into increasing curriculum requirements and raising the standards of academic competence. In all these recommendations for curriculum changes, little consideration is given to what will happen to special education students. Many special educators fear that as these policies are implemented, special education students—including those with learning disabilities—will be the losers. Being unable to meet the educational standards set by the pursuit-of-excellence movement, some students with learning disabilities will be denied a high school diploma and thus denied the opportunity to complete their schooling. Further, if general education teachers are held accountable for the academic excellence of their students, they will be reluctant to accept the responsibility for hard-to-teach students. Some special educators predict that the push for excellence may widen the schism between regular and special education (Salvia & Ysseldyke, 1998). (The implications of the excellence-in-education movement for adolescents with learning disabilities is further discussed in Chapter 9.)

More Testing of Students with Learning Disabilities   Another implication of the educational reform movement that affects the entire educational system is the call for more accountability through the measurement of student performance. Vanderwood, McGrew, and Ysseldyke (1998) report that fewer than half of the states have required that students with disabilities participate in the statewide testing programs. One of the reasons that these students are excluded is that they are expected to perform poorly on the tests and therefore lower the scores of the school when they are compared with those of other schools.

However, IDEA 1997 outlines several new requirements concerning the participation of students with disabilities in statewide or districtwide assessments. The individualized education program (IEP) must document which portions of the curriculum and which goals and standards are relevant for each student in special education and what accommodations in assessment are appropriate for each individual student (Yell & Schriner, 1997).

Computer Technology

The pace of change occurring with computer technology is so rapid that even computer experts find it hard to keep up. New technologies virtually enter the marketplace on a daily basis. No sooner do we familiarize ourselves with one technology than better and more advanced technologies emerge. The most cutting-edge technologies become old in just a matter of a few months. Computers continue to increase in power and decrease in cost, and more and more people heve access to them. Many of these new technologies are geared toward improving the quality of life of individuals with learning disabilities (Raskin & Higgins, 1998; Male, 1997).

Many students with learning disabilities have a special facility with computers. *(© Jean-Claude Lejeune)*

With computer technology bursting into the classrooms at all levels, computers have also become tools for instruction of students with learning disabilities. Moreover, research shows that computer use is effective with these students. Although they may experience many academic problems in school, many seem to have a special facility with computers (Raskin, 1998; Raskin & Higgins, 1998). Several descriptions of current and emerging computer uses that have important implications for students with learning disabilities follow.

1. *The World Wide Web and Email*

    Among the most exciting computer applications for both teachers and students are the Internet, the **World Wide Web** (**WWW**), and **email**. With a computer, a modem, a telephone line, and a subscription to an online service, students can get into cyberspace and onto the "information highway." With email students can send and receive mail, make friends, and communicate with other students throughout the world. Unlike "snail mail" (regular mail), email allows people to send and receive messages at any time of the day or night. It encourages students to engage in meaningful peer-to-peer writing, join interest bulletin boards, and get involved in "chat groups."

    The World Wide Web provides a way to display information on the Internet. The Web is made up of interconnected pages or "sites," each containing textual and graphic information on specific topics. Users can link up to pages that interest them. For example, students can go to the

"White House" and visit its occupants at **http://www.whitehouse.gov**. We are only at the beginning stages of what is called *cyberspace* and can expect many more applications in the near future for students with learning disabilities (World Wide Web and Special Education, 1998; Boone & Higgins, 1998; Male, 1998). You can "surf" the Web at **http://www.cec. sped.org/bk/tec-jour.htm** to find more information about using the World Wide Web with students with learning disabilities.

2. *Assistive Technology and the Technology Act*

   Assistive technology refers to technological devices that enable users with disabilities to move, play, communicate, write, speak, and participate in many activities that would be unavailable to them without the computer (Lerner, Lowenthal, & Egan, 1998; Messerer, 1997). Lewis (1998) offers ways that students with learning disabilities can use assistive technology to overcome barriers in print, in communication, and in learning.

   Overcoming Print Barriers   There are assistive devices to help students with learning disabilities who have problems with reading and writing. Alternative options include taped books, devices that read print books aloud, and "talking" computer programs.

   Overcoming Communication Barriers   Assistive devices to help students who experience difficulty with written communication include word processing programs, spelling and grammar aids for editing assistance, programs to help writers organize their thoughts during the planning stage of the writing process, and voice input devices to dictate the written message.

   Overcoming Learning Barriers   Technology offers alternatives to traditional learning approaches, such as audiotapes, CD-ROM instruction, videodisk instruction, and the Internet.

   The **Technology Act** was first passed by Congress in 1988 and was reauthorized in 1994 (PL 103–218, 1994). This law recognizes the need for persons with disabilities to access and use assistive technology devices and provides funding to support assistive technology (Bryant & Seay, 1998; Lewis, 1998).

3. *CD-ROM Technology*

   CD-ROM drives and compact discs make multimedia-based applications possible through their large storage and retrieval capability. With CD-ROM software, programs can use text, speech, graphics, pictures, audio, and video, and students can interact with the computer program as they solve problems and make choices. With electronic reference materials, such as encyclopedias on CD-ROM, students can explore and obtain information by browsing through topics or searching for specific information. Electronic storybooks on CD-ROM offer high-interest stories, and words can be highlighted or read aloud by the computer.

4. *Videodisk Technology*

   This cutting-edge technology uses a videodisk, which looks like a large compact disc—a shiny, metallic silver disc about the size of a long-playing (LP) record. The videodisk stores large amounts of information that can be accessed nonlinearly by the computer. It is possible to store and randomly access up to 30 minutes of full-motion video or 54,000 frames (still images like slides) on each side of a videodisk. This technology is promising for students with learning disabilities because it provides concrete visual representations of concepts in an appealing format (Hofmeister, Engelmann, & Carnine, 1989).

5. *Tutorial Software*

   These software programs are designed to teach new materials and provide direct instruction. Good tutorial programs require a response that resembles the skill being taught, limits the amount of new information presented at one time, provides corrective feedback, and provides a management system (Hasselbring & Goin, 1993). Students with learning disabilities can have the concept taught many times. Tutorial programs that take advantage of the advances in technology are even more effective.

6. *Drill-and-Practice Software*

   Drill-and-practice programs are designed to give students practice with previously learned skills and concepts. Students with learning disabilities need many repetitions and a large amount of practice; they need to overlearn to be able to do something automatically. Good drill-and-practice software provides practice of acquired skills, offers many opportunities for practicing in an interesting way, emphasizes speed of responding, and monitors and evaluates student progress (Hasselbring & Goin, 1993). With the new computer capability, such as multimedia, color, sound, animation, and interaction, these programs are becoming more appealing to students.

7. *Word Processing*

   Word processing is a boon for students with learning disabilities who have difficulty in handwriting, spelling, and written composition. One student with learning disabilities wrote:

   > I didn't learn how to write until I learned how to use a computer. This sounds ironic, but in my past writing was spelling, and since I could not spell, I could not write. When I discovered a word processing system with a spell check, I finally understood that writing involved putting thoughts and ideas into some kind of written form. Knowing that the computer would catch my spelling errors, I began to ignore my spelling. Then I began to look at writing as content. (Lee & Jackson, 1992, p. 23)

Computers can help students with learning disabilities by providing a one-on-one interactive environment in which students can practice recently acquired reading skills as often as they wish, and spend more time in learning tasks.

Specific applications of computer technology appear throughout this text: with young children (Chapter 8), in teaching reading (Chapter 11), in word processing and written language (Chapter 12), and in mathematics (Chapter 13).

Learning Disabilities Organizations

Early in the history of learning disabilities, parents and professionals organized to further the cause of learning disabilities and to strengthen efforts to help students. A critically important event was the establishment in 1963 of an organization for parents and professionals that today is called the Learning Disabilities Association (LDA). Over the years, the LDA has been extremely effective in bringing the cause of learning disabilities to the attention of legislative bodies and teachers and other school personnel, and in helping parents when they discover that their child has learning disabilities. For example, when the "Dear Abby" newspaper column briefly mentioned the LDA in response to a letter about learning disabilities, the organization's national headquarters in Pittsburgh received thirty thousand inquiries from readers.

The Council for Exceptional Children (CEC) established a separate division for special educators interested in learning disabilities in 1968. This division is now called the Division for Learning Disabilities (DLD) and has over eleven thousand members.

Other organizations for professionals working with learning disabilities are the Council for Learning Disabilities (CLD) and the International Dyslexia Association. In addition, many professional organizations in fields such as reading, speech and language, and pediatrics have subgroups or special-interest committees concerned with learning disabilities.

Brief descriptions and addresses of organizations that support or are involved with learning disabilities follow.

CHADD (Children and Adults with Attention Deficit Disorder)   A national alliance of parent organizations to provide information to parents of children with attention deficit disorder. CHADD, Suite 185, 1859 North Pine Island Road, Plantation, FL 33322. CHADD can also be reached at **http://www.CHADD.org**.

Council for Exceptional Children   An organization for professionals in Special Education. CEC, 1920 Reston Drive, Reston, VA 22091. CEC's web site is at **http://www.cec.sped.org**.

Division for Learning Disabilities   A unit for professionals within the Council for Exceptional Children (CEC). DLD, Council for Exceptional Children, 1920 Association Drive, Reston, VA 22091.

International Dyslexia Association   This organization honors Samuel T. Orton, a physician who studied children with language disorders. It combines the interests of both medical and educational professionals interested in dyslexia and language-learning disorders. It has state and local units as well as the international organization. International Dyslexia Association, Inc., Chester Building, Suite 382, 8600 La Salle Road, Baltimore, MD 21286–2044. It can also be reached at **http://www.interdys.org**.

Learning Disabilities Association   A parent organization with active professional participation as well. It is a national organization with state and local chapters. LDA, 4156 Library Road, Pittsburgh, PA 15234. LDA can be reached at **http://www.ldanatl.org**.

National Center for Learning Disabilities   Provides financial support for research on learning disabilities. National Center for Learning Disabilities, 38 Park Avenue, Suite 1420, New York, NY 10016. It can be reached at **http://www.ncld.org**.

International Reading Association   An organization for persons interested in all aspects of reading. International Reading Association, 800 Barksdale Road, Newark, DE 19711.

AHEAD (Association on Higher Education and Disability)   An international organization of professionals committed to full participation in higher education for persons with disabilities. P.O. Box 21192, Columbus, OH 43221. Phone (614) 488-4972. It can also be reached at **http://www.ahead.org**.

Journals and Periodicals

Some journals and periodicals that feature articles, research, program descriptions, tests, materials, and organizational activities follow.

Annals of Dyslexia   International Dyslexia Association, Chester Building, Suite 382, 8600 La Salle Road, Baltimore, MD 21286–2044.

ASHA   American Speech and Hearing Association, 9030 Old Georgetown Road, Washington, DC 20014.

Exceptional Children   Council for Exceptional Children, 1920 Association Drive, Reston, VA 22091.

Exceptional Education Quarterly   PRO-ED, 5341 Industrial Oaks Boulevard, Austin, TX 78735.

Exceptional Parent   P.O. Box 102, Boston, MA 02117.

Focus on Exceptional Children   Love Publications, 6635 E. Villanova Place, Denver, CO 80222.

Intervention   PRO-ED, 5341 Industrial Oaks Boulevard, Austin, TX 78735.

Journal of Applied Behavior Analysis   Department of Human Development, University of Kansas, Lawrence, KS 66045.

Journal of Learning Disabilities   PRO-ED, 5341 Industrial Oaks Boulevard, Austin, TX 78735.

Journal of Reading   International Reading Association, 800 Barksdale Road, Newark, DE 19711.

Journal of Special Education   PRO-ED, 5341 Industrial Oaks Boulevard, Austin, TX 78735.

Learning Disabilities: A Multidisciplinary Journal   Learning Disabilities Association, 1415 Library Rd., Pittsburgh, PA 15234.

Learning Disabilities Quarterly   Council for Learning Disabilities, P.O. Box 40303, Overland Park, KS 66204.

Learning Disabilities Research and Practice   CEC, Division for Learning Disabilities, 1920 Association Drive, Reston, VA 22091.

Reading Research Quarterly   International Reading Association, 800 Barksdale Road, Newark, DE 19711.

The Reading Teacher   International Reading Association, 800 Barksdale Road, Newark, DE 19711.

Remedial and Special Education   PRO-ED, 5341 Industrial Oaks Boulevard, Austin, TX 78735.

Teaching Exceptional Children   Council for Exceptional Children, 1920 Association Drive, Reston, VA 22091.

Chapter Summary

1. The history of the field of learning disabilities can be divided into four phases: (1) foundation, (2) transition, (3) integration, and (4) current.

2. The foundation phase covers the period from 1800 to 1930. It was an era of basic scientific research on the brain and its disorders.

3. The transition phase covers the period from 1930 to 1960. During this time, researchers conducted clinical studies of children who were having difficulty learning, and psychologists and educators developed instruments for assessment and remediation. The progress of the field was marked by a series of terms that were used to describe the child who was not learning. The term *brain-injured child* was introduced by Alfred Strauss. Other suggested names included *Strauss syndrome* and *minimal brain dysfunction* (MBD). The term *learning disabilities* was first proposed in 1963.

4. The integration phase occurred between 1960 and 1980. During this period there was widespread and rapid implementation of learning disabilities programs in schools across the nation.

5. The current phase covers 1980 to the present. This period represents emerging developments, such as the special education law, inclusion, collaboration, cultural and linguistic diversity, attention deficit disorder and nonverbal learning disorders, and computer technology.

Questions for
Discussion and
Reflection

1. Describe the four distinct historical phases in the development of the field of learning disabilities. Discuss how each phase contributed to the discipline of learning disabilities.

2. Discuss some of the terms that have been used over the years to describe individuals with learning disabilities. Why have many of these descriptive terms not received general acceptance?

3. What is the series of three federal special education laws that regulate special education programs in the schools? Discuss the differences among IDEA 1997, IDEA 1990, and PL94–142. How does the federal definition compare to other definitions?

4. Discuss some of the current directions in the field of learning disabilities and how these directions will affect learning disabilities programs in our schools.

5. What is meant by *inclusion*? Why is it a controversial subject?

6. Describe some of the ways that computers can be used with students with learning disabilities.

Key Terms

aphasia *(p. 37)*

assistive technology *(p. 55)*

attention deficit disorder (ADD) *(p. 50)*

attention deficit hyperactivity disorder (ADHD) *(p. 50)*

brain-injured child *(p. 38)*

Child Service Demonstrations Centers (CSDCs) *(p. 45)*

Children with Specific Learning Disabilities Act (PL 91–230) *(p. 45)*

collaboration *(p. 48)*

conceptual disorders *(p. 41)*

cultural and linguistic diversity (CLD) *(p. 48)*

distractibility *(p. xx)*

educational reform movement *(p. 52)*

email *(p. 54)*

The Education of All Children with Disabilities Act of 1975 (PL 94–142) *(p. 45)*

Individuals with Disabilities Education Act of 1990 (IDEA) (PL 101–476) *(p. 45)*

Individuals with Disabilities Education Act of 1997 (IDEA) (PL 105–17) *(p. 45)*

least restrictive environment (LRE) *(p. 47)*

minimal brain dysfunction (MBD) *(p. 43)*

nonverbal learning disabilities (NLD) *(p. 52)*

perceptual disorder *(p. 39)*

perseveration *(p. 41)*

soft neurological signs *(p. 41)*

Technology Act *(p. 55)*

World Wide Web (WWW) *(p. 54)*

The Assessment-Teaching Process

3

Assessment

CHAPTER OUTLINE

The three chapters of Part II highlight the interrelated elements of the assessment-teaching process. They are *assessment* (Chapter 3), *clinical teaching* (Chapter 4), and *systems for delivering educational services* (Chapter 5).

Assessment must be linked with teaching if one is to truly understand and help a troubled student. Attention to only one of these components splinters the effort and shortchanges the student. For example, routinely teaching skills or using methods or materials without considering a student's unique problems may be ineffective because such teaching does not meet the student's needs. Similarly, if assessment only results in selecting a diagnostic label, the procedure does not provide guidelines for the student's learning.

This chapter focuses on assessment. It examines the uses and models of assessment, investigates the effects of the law on the assessment process, and analyzes the assessment decisions and different kinds of assessment information. It considers current views on using discrepancy formulas for eligibility for services, and the new focus on standards and accountability. In this chapter, we also begin a case study (which continues in Chapters 4 and 5) to illustrate assessment-teaching procedures and to demonstrate the relationships between assessment, teaching, and service delivery.

USES OF ASSESSMENT INFORMATION

Assessment is the process of collecting information about a student that will be used in forming judgments and making decisions concerning that student. There are two major reasons for conducting an assessment in special education. The first is *classification*. The law requires that a student must be classified as having learning disabilities or another category of disability (see Chapter 4) to become eligible for special education services. The more important reason for assessment, however, is *planning instruction*. The critical assessment information can be used to help the student learn.

The closer the connection between educational assessment and instruction, the more effective the assessment-teaching process will be. Assessment that focuses on curriculum and teaching is needed for guiding instruction. Although the initial assessment occurs before instruction begins, the astute clinical teacher continues to probe and evaluate during the teaching process. Even after the initial assessment, the teacher should remain alert to the student's responses and changing needs. During the teaching process, the evaluation should continue through discerning observation and questioning.

The assessment process serves several purposes:

1. *Screening.* Detecting pupils who may need a more comprehensive examination. In the screening process, a cursory evaluation is given to ascertain which students need a more intensive evaluation.

2. *Referral.* Seeking additional assistance from other school personnel. On the basis of observation and classroom performance, the teacher (or others) requests an evaluation of a student.

3. *Classification.* Determining a student's eligibility for services. Students are assessed for purposes of judging the need for services and classifying the category of disability.

4. *Instructional planning.* Assisting in planning an educational program for an individual student. The assessment information is used to formulate instructional goals and objectives, to decide on placement, and to make specific plans for teaching.

5. *Monitoring pupil progress.* Reviewing a student's achievement and progress. Many approaches can be used, including traditional formal tests and alternative or informal measurements.

MODELS OF ASSESSMENT

Students are referred for an evaluation because they are experiencing academic problems. Through the evaluation process, school personnel attempt to answer questions such as these: Why is this student having difficulty in learning? What specific characteristics impede learning for this student? and How can this student be helped to learn? The evaluation process helps to identify the nature of the problem and the student's strengths and weaknesses.

Two general approaches for assessing learning disabilities can be used: (1) traditional assessment and (2) alternative assessment. Schools generally use both methods to obtain a comprehensive picture of the student (Poteet, Choate, & Stewart, 1993).

Traditional Assessment

Traditional assessment procedures that rely on standardized tests are frequently used. The scores from these tests allow the examiner to compare the student's performance with the performance of a group of students who are comparable in terms of age or with a norm-referenced group on whose performance the test was standardized.

Standardized tests are statistically designed so that one-half of the students are below the mean (average) and one-half are above. Of course, communities want all of their children to score above average. The humorist Garrison Keillor lampoons this notion in his tales of the mythical town of Lake Wobegon, where "all the children are above average."

Many of the commonly used standardized tests are judged by psychologists and educators to be statistically adequate in terms of their reliability, validity, and standardization. The use of traditional standardized tests is discussed in more detail later in this chapter under the topic of formal standardized tests.

Standardized testing is criticized for a number of reasons: (1) many educators are finding that standardized tests do not provide enough information about the student; (2) the tests may not assess what the student is learning in class; (3) standardized tests may be biased against culturally diverse populations; (4) the pressure for high test scores may sway teachers to use class time to prepare students to take the tests; and (5) the tests focus instruction on segmented skills instead of higher-order thinking and creativity (Poteet, Choate, & Stewart, 1993).

Alternative Assessment

Disenchantment with traditional testing led educators to turn to alternative assessment procedures. Interest in **alternative assessment** is growing because it assesses the child in the natural setting, uses the school curriculum, and capitalizes on what the student actually does in the classroom. Alternative assessment approaches encourage students to produce, construct, demonstrate, or perform a response. Several types of alternative assessments are presented in this section; others are described in the section on informal assessment (see p. 85).

Authentic and Performance Assessment   **Authentic assessment** makes realistic demands and is set in real-life contexts, such as at school or at home. (In contrast, a formal test often is not related to the child's curriculum.) Examples of authentic assessment situations include actually reading a passage (reading), giving a persuasive speech (oral expression), writing a letter to the editor (written expression), or using mathematics to solve a real-life problem (mathematics)(Elliot, 1988).

Performance assessment is closely related to authentic assessment in that performance tests are designed to assess what the student actually does in the curriculum. This assessment requires that the students actively perform some classroom task (produce, demonstrate, perform, create, construct, apply, build, solve, plan, show, illustrate, or explain). Although teachers have used performance assessment as part of the day-to-day classroom activities for many years, the new focus is on systematizing this process (Elliot, 1988; Poteet, Choate, & Stewart, 1993).

Portfolio Assessment   In **portfolio assessment**, multiple samples of a student's actual class work over an extended period of time are collected. This portfolio is used to evaluate the student's current achievement level and progress over time. Portfolio assessment is often used to measure reading and writing progress. Samples of student work can be used to determine achievement and progress in all academic areas.

A portfolio might contain the following kinds of materials: selected samples of daily work done in the classroom, academic classroom tests (for example, in spelling or mathematics), checklists of behavior, sample stories, writing drafts at various stages of development, science projects, art samples, a teacher's observational notes, or the results of group projects.

Assessment is authentic when it requires realistic demands and is set in real-life contexts, such as at home or at school.
(© Elizabeth Crews/ Stock Boston)

In deciding what samples to collect, the teacher must first consider the goals of the instructional program, and the samples should then reflect these goals. For example, the portfolio might include samples of the objectives in the individual education program (IEP). Students can be responsible for organizing their own portfolios. Since portfolios serve as mirrors of the process of learning in the classroom, they should be available for student-teacher conferences or for parent conferences (Salend, 1998).

Dynamic Assessment   In **dynamic assessment,** the teacher tries to evaluate the student's ability to learn in a teaching situation rather than attempt to determine what the student has already learned. The procedure is first to engage in instruction that is active and flexible and then to observe how well the student can learn under favorable conditions.

A key element in dynamic assessment is the social environment in which the learning occurs. When a healthy reciprocal relationship exists among teacher and students, the students' ability to learn will grow and flourish. The teacher can evaluate how well a student performs in an interactive teaching environment and can make a subjective judgment rather than rely on test scores (Palinscar, Brown, & Campione, 1991; Feuerstein, 1979). **Reciprocal teaching** offers the teaching side of dynamic assessment (see Chapter 4) (Palinscar & Brown, 1984).

THE INFLUENCE OF THE LAW ON THE ASSESSMENT PROCESS

Special education laws have significantly shaped assessment practices. As discussed in Chapter 2, the first special education law was passed by Congress in 1975. In 1990, the law was revised as the Individuals with Disabilities Education Act (IDEA). The most recent revision of the law is the 1997 Amendments to the Individuals with Disabilities Education Act (IDEA), Public Law 105–17. IDEA 1997 is having extensive effects on the assessment and teaching of exceptional students. Additional information about IDEA 1997 is at **http://www.ed.gov/offices/OSERS/IDEA/the_law.html.**

IDEA 1997 makes major changes in the law (Senate Report on the IDEA Amendments, 1997; Yell & Schriner, 1997) which

- strengthen the role of parents
- ensure access to the general education curriculum and reforms
- focus on teaching and learning while reducing unnecessary paperwork requirements
- assist education agencies in addressing the costs of improving special education and related services for children with disabilities
- give increased attention to racial, ethnic, and linguistic diversity to prevent inappropriate identification and mislabeling
- require that transition planning begins when a child is 14 years old
- ensure that schools are safe and conducive to learning
- encourage parents and educators to work out their differences using nonadversarial means

Two segments of IDEA 1997 that directly shape assessment procedures are (1) the provisions related to the individualized education program (IEP) and (2) the procedural safeguards and parents' rights.

The Individualized Education Program (IEP) as an Assessment-Teaching Process

A major provision of the law is the requirement that an **individualized education program (IEP)** be formulated for each student identified as having a disability. In IDEA 1997, the IEP remains the cornerstone of services for all children and youth with disabilities.

The IEP serves two purposes:

1. *It is a written plan for a particular student.* The IEP is a written statement developed by the IEP or case conference team that prescribes specific educational objectives and placement for an individual student.

2. *It is a management tool for the entire assessment-teaching process.* In this sense, the IEP also serves a much broader purpose. As the core of the entire assessment-teaching process, the IEP involves all assessment evaluations as well as all teaching procedures. It becomes the critical link between the student with learning disabilities and the special teaching that the student requires.

Thus, the IEP is intended to be a management tool for ensuring that the education designed for an individual student is appropriate for that student's special learning needs and that the special education services are actually delivered and monitored. The IEP represents an entire accountability system in miniature—an outline of learner expectations, assessment strategies, and performance standards (Erickson et al., 1998). Figure 3.1 illustrates the stages of the IEP assessment-teaching process.

Procedural Safeguards and Parents' Rights

Procedural safeguards have been designed to protect the rights of parents and students. In IDEA 1997, **parents' rights** have been considerably expanded and are summarized in the Parents' Rights and Procedural Safeguards box on p. 71.

The Regulations for IDEA 1997

As noted, many of the new features of the 1997 Individuals with Disabilities Education Act affect the assessment of students with learning disabilities. The Regulations for IDEA 1997—issued by the Department of Education on March 12, 1999—clarify the IEP procedures and provide guidelines for schools and teachers. The major issues of the regulations are described in Appendix F of this book. Of particular note in regard to the IEP are the regulations affecting the IEP and the general curriculum, and the Regular Education Involvement in the IEP. Further information on the regulations is available at **http://www.ideapractices.org**.

STAGES OF THE ASSESSMENT- TEACHING PROCESS

The assessment-teaching process follows a sequence of stages. As indicated in Figure 3.1, there are three broad stages: referral, assessment, and instruction. Each of these stages is subdivided, making six stages in all. These six stages meet the legislative mandates of the IEP. The case study described at the end of this chapter and continued in Chapters 4 and 5 illustrates the assessment-teaching process.

Figure 3.1

Stages of the IEP Process

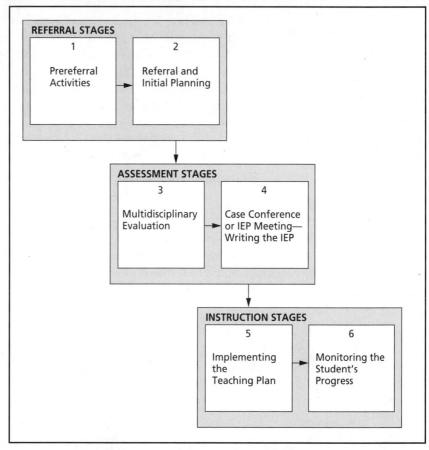

Source: From *Cases in Learning and Behavior Problems: A Guide to Individualized Education Programs*, by J. Lerner, D. Dawson, and L. Horvath, 1980, Salem, WI: Sheffield Publishing Co., p. 3.

Referral Stages

The **referral stages** begin the process and involve prereferral and referral activities.

Stage 1: Prereferral Activities   **Prereferral activities** are preventive intervention measures taken by general education classroom teachers to meet the needs of students who are having difficulties in their classrooms. Teachers take these measures before referring students for a special education case study. If the measures are successful, the prereferral interventions make the referral unnecessary. Many school districts and some states now require evidence that prereferral activities have occurred before a referral is initiated.

Prereferral intervention is a less cumbersome means of gathering data about a student's performance than the formal multidisciplinary evaluation. A peer group of colleagues helps the classroom teacher analyze the student's

Table 3.1

Parents' Rights and Procedural Safeguards

1. Parents must *consent in writing* to several phases of the IEP process: (1) to having their child evaluated; (2) to the IEP, including plans and placement as set forth in the written IEP; and (3) to the three-year reevaluation plan. (Parental consent is needed if the IEP team uses existing information and assessments to develop the three-year evaluation. The parents can also request that new assessment information be obtained for the three-year evaluation.)

2. The assessment must be conducted in the student's *native language* or mode of communication, and the findings must be reported in the parents' native language.

3. The school or local education agency (LEA) must ensure that tests are *not racially or culturally discriminatory*.

4. Parents have the *right to see all information* that is collected and used in making decisions. Parents can request an explanation of all evaluation procedures, tests, records, and reports.

5. Parents have the *right to mediation* at no cost. **Mediation** is voluntary and involves attempts to solve disputes between the school district and the parents of a child with a disability.

6. Parents and students have the *right to an impartial due process hearing* if they disagree with the IEP decision or if the voluntary mediation is unsatisfactory. There are certain provisions to have the school pay attorneys' fees if the parents prevail in a lawsuit.

7. The *confidentiality* of the student's reports and records is protected under the law.

academic and/or behavior problems and recommends interventions and accommodations for the classroom. The classroom teacher then tries the suggested methods to help the student. The prereferral stage is important because the decision to refer a student for a multidisciplinary evaluation has serious consequences. Once a student is referred, the probability is high that the student will be declared eligible for services (Salvia & Ysseldyke, 1998).

Three prereferral intervention models are the consultation, the teacher assistance team, and peer collaboration.

■   In the *consultation model*, a consultant in a school building takes on the responsibility of responding to the teacher's prereferral requests. The steps of the consultation model are as follows:

1. The referring teacher requests a consultation about a student.

2. The consulting teacher explores possible interventions with the referring teacher.

3. The suggested interventions are implemented in the classroom and then evaluated.

4. If further decisions are needed, the consulting teacher observes the student in the classroom and then holds a conference with the referring teacher.

5. If the student's problem persists, a formal referral for a special education evaluation is made.

■   In the *teacher assistance team* prereferral *model*, three general education teachers in the school, plus the referring teacher, meet to brainstorm to find ways to help the referring teacher develop a plan to improve the student's performance in the classroom (Salvia & Ysseldyke, 1998; Chalfant & Pysh, 1989, 1993). Teacher assistance teams substantially reduce the number of learning disabilities referrals (Chalfant & Pysh, 1989).

■ The *peer collaboration model* requires that several general education classroom teachers work together to develop effective instructions and behavioral interventions for their students. Teachers work together as partners in restructuring a problem and seeking solutions. The peer team collaborates in four areas (Pugach & Johnson, 1988):

1. Describing the problem
2. Summarizing the problem
3. Developing at least three potential interventions
4. Finding a practical way to evaluate the intervention strategy

Stage 2: Referral and Initial Planning   The initial **referral** of a student for evaluation can come through several sources: the parent, the teacher, other professionals who have contact with the student, or a self-referral by the student. After a referral is made, school personnel must follow it up. Parents must be notified of the school's concern and must give written permission for an evaluation. In addition, decisions must be made about the general kinds of assessment data needed and the people who will be responsible for gathering this information.

Assessment Stages

The **assessment stages** are the core of the process and involve the tasks of developing and writing the IEP.

Stage 3: Multidisciplinary Evaluation   At this stage, specialists representing various disciplines obtain pertinent information by assessing academic performance and behavior in areas related to the suspected disability. (For example, specialists for the multidisciplinary evaluation might be a school psychologist, school worker, school nurse, speech and language pathologist, learning disabilities specialist, or reading specialist.) The law (IDEA) refers to a **multidisciplinary evaluation** and outlines the procedures for gathering the assessment information.

Several features of the law regulate the multidisciplinary evaluation. Testing must be administered by trained personnel. The tests must be appropriate, validated for the purpose used, and as free as possible from cultural or racial bias. Evaluation materials must be administered in the student's native language. The evaluation team must represent several disciplines and include at least one teacher or other specialist in the area of the suspected disability. This means that if the condition of learning disabilities is suspected, at least one person knowledgeable about learning disabilities will be involved in the multidisciplinary evaluation. Although the multidisciplinary specialists responsible for collecting the assessment data may meet as a team, the multidisciplinary team should not be confused with the case conference (or IEP) team. In the multidisciplinary team, specialists administer tests, obtain other evaluation data, and determine the student's eligibility for learning disabilities programs. In the case conference (or IEP) team, participants meet to make decisions and write the IEP.

Special regulations in the law state that in evaluating learning disabilities, the multidisciplinary team must prepare a written report of the evaluation. The report must include the following information:

1. Whether the student has a specific learning disability
2. The basis for making the determination
3. The relevant behavior noted during the observation of the student
4. The relationship of that behavior to the student's academic functioning
5. The educationally relevant medical findings, if any
6. Whether there is a severe discrepancy between achievement and ability that is not correctable without special education and related services
7. The determination of the team concerning the effects of environmental, cultural, or economic disadvantages

Stage 4: The Case Conference (or IEP) Meeting—Writing the IEP After the multidisciplinary information is gathered, the parents are contacted to arrange the **case conference meeting.** It is at this meeting that the IEP is written.

Participants at the IEP meeting must include the following (IDEA, 1997):

1. The parent(s) or legal guardian
2. At least one regular education teacher if the child is in regular education or being considered for regular education
3. A special education teacher
4. An LEA (local education agency) representative knowledgeable about general curriculum and resources available within the school district
5. A person who can interpret the instructional implications of evaluation results (may be one of the previously mentioned members)
6. The child, if the situation is appropriate
7. Any other person invited by the parent or the school who has knowledge or special expertise regarding the child, including, when appropriate, related services personnel

The contents of the IEP must include these components (IDEA, 1997):

1. Present levels of the student's performance (How does the disability affect his or her involvement and progress in the general education curriculum?)
2. Measurable annual goals, including **benchmarks** or **short-term objectives,** related to

    a. meeting the child's needs to enable him or her to be involved in the general curriculum

    b. meeting other needs resulting from the disability

3. Special education and other services necessary for the student to meet annual goals, such as supplementary aids, any program modifications, or support for school personnel

4. An explanation of the extent to which the child will not participate in general education

5. Individual modifications in the administration of achievement tests (or an explanation of why such modifications are not appropriate) and how child will be assessed

6. A projected date for beginning services and anticipated service frequency, location, and duration

7. Measures of progress toward annual goals and an explanation of how parents will be kept informed of their child's progress

Other Considerations. The IEP team should also consider (Yell & Schriner, 1997):

1. The child's strengths, most recent evaluation, and parental concerns

2. The language needs of an LEP (limited English proficient) child

3. The child's communication needs

4. The use of assistive technology, if needed

    Before a student is placed into a special education program and services begin, the parents must agree to the IEP plan in writing.

Instruction Stages

The **instruction stages** occur after the written document has been completed and involve the teaching and the monitoring of the student's progress.

Stage 5: Implementation of the Teaching Plan   This is the teaching portion of the assessment-teaching process. It occurs after the IEP document has been written. In this stage, the student is placed in the agreed-upon setting and receives instruction designed to help him or her reach the goals and objectives or benchmarks set forth in the IEP. This stage involves implementing the plan through teaching (see Chapters 4 and 5).

Stage 6: Monitoring the Student's Progress   This stage calls for the review (at least annually) and reevaluation of the plan in terms of the student's progress. The IEP must include plans to show how this evaluation will be accomplished, who will conduct it, and what assessment instruments and criteria will be used. IDEA 1997 requires that the child's parents be informed of his or her progress toward reaching annual goals (via benchmarks) as often as parents of nondisabled children are informed. The parents can receive IEP report cards.

ASSESSMENT DECISIONS

The purpose of the assessment is to collect and analyze information that will help in planning an educational program that will improve a student's learning. The following issues are considered in formulating the assessment and writing the multidisciplinary evaluation report.

Determining Present Levels of Performance

The procedures for determining the student's **present levels of developmental and educational performance** generally include the following steps:

1. Review the information gathered by the multidisciplinary team.
2. Determine subject and skill areas for which an IEP should be developed.
3. Determine if sufficient evaluation data are available and, if necessary, gather additional evaluation information through standardized tests, alternative assessment measures, or observations.
4. Designate the student's current performance levels in the subject and skill areas to be developed. The performance level can be stated in terms of traditional norm-referenced measurements (such as test scores that indicate grade level or a percentile) or from alternative assessment measures (such as a performance assessment of the class mathematics assignment).
5. Consider the general education curriculum requirements.

Gathering Additional Information

Additional information must be obtained to provide a comprehensive picture of the student. *Classroom observation* is required to provide information about the student's behavior in school and how that behavior affects the academic problem. For example, what does the student do during the independent reading activity period? The **case history** information also gives useful information about past health, absences from school, family moves, changes in schools, teacher's comments, and grades over time—all of which can be valuable in understanding the student's problem. It is also important to determine whether the student has the *prerequisites* or readiness skills for the targeted academic learning.

To gain insight into the interrelatedness of the student's difficulties, it is necessary to look for clusters of characteristics. For example, a student with a severe handwriting problem may also have a motor difficulty in fine motor skills. Or a student with a reading problem may have an underlying oral language disorder. A student who does poorly in oral expression may have a history of delayed speech, speech motor difficulties that affect articulation, and difficulty in remembering words.

Considering the Discrepancy Between Performance and Potential Ability

The operational portion of the definition of learning disabilities has been a discrepancy-based procedure. That is, the child with learning disabilities has a severe discrepancy between achievement (what a student has actually learned) and intellectual ability (what the student is potentially capable of learning). Achievement refers to the student's present performance level or academic skills (i.e., in reading, mathematics, etc.). Intellectual ability refers to the student's potential for learning and is usually measured with an intelligence or IQ test. The discrepancy is the difference between the achievement and the potential for learning.

A discrepancy provides one way to judge if a child has learning disabilities and is eligible for services in the schools. Schools often calculate the **discrepancy score** by using a mathematical formula that quantitatively establishes the amount of discrepancy between achievement and potential. Most schools (about 98 percent) use a notion of discrepancy to identify students with learning disabilities. (Mercer, Jordan, Allsop, & Mercer, 1996; Frankenberger & Fongalgio, 1991). Several discrepancy formulas are described later in this chapter in the box entitled "Methods for Determining the Discrepancy Score Deviation from Grade Level" on page 102.

Problems with Using the IQ-Achievement Discrepancy Formula   At the present time, the practice of using a discrepancy formula to identify students with learning disabilities is questioned by some researchers and practitioners (Mather, 1998; Fletcher, 1998; Fetcher, Francis, Shaywitz, Lyon, Foorman, Stubbing & Shaywitz, 1998; Tomlan & Mather, 1996; Lyon, 1995a; Stanovich, 1993; Mather & Roberts, 1994; Shaw, Cullen, McGuire, & Brinckerhoff, 1995). The following issues prompt this questioning:

- *How useful is the IQ score in establishing a child's potential?*   Researchers are asking serious questions about the IQ test itself. Is it a type of achievement test rather than a measure of intellectual potential? The child with learning disabilities may have a depressed score on the IQ tests because of the very characteristics of his or her disabilities. For example, a deficit in language may lower the IQ score, lessen the discrepancy, and therefore make the child ineligible for learning disabilities services. In addition, IQ test scores can be adversely affected by the child's culture and personal experiences (Mather & Healey, 1990; Swanson, 1993).

- *Discrepancy formulas vary from state to state.*   Different states (as well as different school districts) use different discrepancy formulas to identify learning disabilities, and they also use different tests in their evaluations. Consequently, a child may be identified as having learning disabilities in one state or school district but not be eligible for services in another. As Shaw et al. (1995) note, learning disabilities do not disappear when the child crosses the state boundary.

■ *A discrepancy formula does not identify learning disabilities in young children.*   The aptitude-achievement discrepancy is based on school failure in academic skills. Since young children have not as yet been exposed to academic skills, the discrepancy formula is not useful for identifying young children with learning disabilities. The discrepancy formula is coined "the wait-and-fail" approach because the child must wait several years and fail academically or perform below a predicted performance level to be eligible for services. Yet we know that early intervention and preventive instruction in kindergarten or first grade is the most effective instruction (Foorman, Francis, Fletcher, Schatsneider, & Mehta, 1998).

■ *Do schools use discrepancy formulas to identify students with learning disabilities?*   In actual practice, IEP teams do not consistently use discrepancy formulas to determine whether a student is eligible for learning disabilities services. MacMillan, Gresham, and Bocian (1998) found that school teams that did not use discrepancy scores identified more children with learning disabilities than did researchers who used the discrepancy approach.

Alternatives to the IQ-Achievement Discrepancy   Several different alternatives to the IQ-achievement discrepancy model have been suggested to identify learning disabilities (Mather 1998; Fletcher 1998; Lyon, 1995a; Shaw et al., 1995; Fletcher et al., 1994; Bateman, 1994). The following are some suggestions:

1. *Assess discrepancies among academic skills.*   For example, the child who excels in mathematics but does poorly in reading displays an intra-individual academic skills discrepancy. Stanovich (1993) suggests using "listening comprehension" as a measure of potential.

2. *Assess discrepancies among cognitive skills.*   Children with learning disabilities may exhibit discrepancies among the various cognitive skills. Shaywitz, Fletcher, and Shaywitz (1995) suggest looking for an "unexpected" academic problem, such as reading due to phonologically based problems, in a child who has a learning disability but many cognitive strengths in areas such as concept formation, reasoning, and critical thinking.

3. *Assess the phonological-core variable.*   Many children with learning disabilities display phonological processing problems and also slowness in naming. Children with these specific deficits could be identified and could receive instruction in these specific skills (Mather, 1998; Stanovich & Siegel, 1994).

4. *Use more clinical judgment.*   When quantitative measures are ineffective, the clinical skills of the assessment team could identify the students in need of learning disabilities services. The evaluation teams should take into account other information that is less quantitative, such as

observational reports, information provided by teachers and parents, and other information revealed through test performance. For example, how does the student's performance in language tasks compare with his or her performance in nonverbal, manual tasks? Do attentional problems interfere with the student's performance on tests? (Mather, 1998).

5. *Separate eligibility and services.* Under current practice, when a student is classified as having learning disabilities, the student becomes eligible for special education services. The paradox is that if the student's academic skills improve sufficiently due to good instruction, the student may no longer be eligible for services because the discrepancy is no longer enough and consequently he or she will be dropped from learning disabilities services. If the student needs learning disabilities services again a few years later, the student will no longer be classified as having learning disabilities and will have to go through the entire referral, assessment, classification, and eligibility process again. The Learning Disabilities Association (LDA) therefore recommends that a student's eligibility be separated from prescribed educational services (LDA Position Paper, 1990).

Setting Annual Goals—Benchmarks or Short-Term Objectives

What **annual goals,** (benchmarks or short-term objectives) should be set for the student? (In the 1997 IDEA, the former category *short-term objectives* has been replaced by benchmarks or short-term objectives. Both terms have the same general meaning.)

Annual goals are general estimates of what the student will achieve in one year. They should represent the student's most essential needs, and priorities for each subject area. For example, an annual goal in mathematics could be that the student learns to multiply and divide.

Benchmarks or short-term objectives are designed to move the student from his or her present performance level to the annual goal. There are usually several benchmarks or short-term objectives which are sequential, specific in terms of behavior and criteria, and manageable for both student and teacher. For the annual goal, the benchmarks or short-term objectives could be the following:

1. The student will add numbers involving carrying in two digits (for example: 578 + 389).

2. The student will subtract numbers involving regrouping in two digits (for example: 311 − 289).

3. The student will multiply and divide through products of 81.

4. The student will multiply two-digit numbers by one-digit numbers (for example: 25 × 9).

5. The student will divide numbers by two-digit divisors (for example: (237 ÷ 25).

Deciding on Services

What specific special education and related services are to be provided? To what extent will the student be in regular education classes? These decisions are related to where the student will be placed for the delivery of services. (The various options for placement are discussed in Chapter 5.) In addition, decisions must be made about the extent to which the student will be placed in the least restrictive environment (that is, with students who do not have disabilities). In IDEA 1997, the general curriculum is presented to be the appropriate beginning point for planning an IEP for a student. The general education curriculum is the preferred course of study for all students (IDEA, 1997). (The terms *general education* and *regular education* are both commonly used and are interchangeable.)

Monitoring Progress

How will the student's progress be monitored and measured? It is necessary to determine whether annual goals (and benchmarks or short-term instructional objectives) are being met. What measurement instruments will be used? Who will be responsible? A sample format for evaluating annual goals (and benchmarks or short-term objectives) appears in Table 3.2.

Developing a Teaching Plan

What teaching plan is appropriate for this student? Although not required in the IEP, a plan must be developed for teaching. The plan should take into account all the information about the student: strengths and weaknesses, developmental levels, skills learned as well as those not yet assimilated, age, interests, and attitudes. Planning strategies require that teachers have a broad knowledge of methods, materials, approaches, curriculum areas, child development, and, most important, the students themselves.

Finally, the assessment process involves continuous reappraisal; it must be revised and modified as more knowledge of the students is acquired through teaching and as the students themselves change as they learn.

OBTAINING ASSESSMENT INFORMATION

To answer many of the questions described earlier, information can be obtained from five major sources: (1) the case history or interview; (2) observation; (3) rating scales; (4) informal measures; and (5) traditional standardized tests. Often several kinds of information are gathered at one time, or one assessment procedure may lead to another. For example, the observation of a student may suggest that a specific test should be used. Or speech misarticulation, along with frequent misunderstandings of the examiner's conversation, could suggest an auditory difficulty and lead to a decision to administer formal tests of auditory acuity and discrimination.

Table 3.2

Sample Format for IEP Annual Goal in Mathematics

Instructional Area: Mathematics
Annual Goal: Student will learn multiplication and division computation skills

Short-term objectives (Benchmarks)	Evaluation of benchmarks or short-term objectives				Results of evaluation skills		
	Tests, materials, and evaluation procedures to be used	Criteria of successful performance	Evaluation schedule	Date objective mastered	Not existing	Emerging	Aquired
1. Student will add numbers involving two renamings	Will compute 20 addition problems requiring two renamings	85% accuracy	End of first grading period	10/10			x
2. Student will subtract numbers involving two renamings	Will compute 20 subtraction problems requiring two renamings	85% accuracy	End of second grading period	11/14			x
3. Student will multiply and divide through products of 81	Will complete a fact sheet containing 20 multiplication and division facts and products through 81 within a specified time	65% accuracy	End of third grading period	1/15		x	
4. Student will multiply two-digit numbers by one-digit numbers	Appropriate mastery test included in mathematics text	75% accuracy	End of fourth grading period			x	
5. Student will divide numbers by two-digit divisors	Appropriate mastery test included in mathematics text	75% accuracy	End of fifth grading period		x		

Source: Adapted by permission from *Illinois Primer on Individualized Education Programs*, Springfield, IL.: State Board of Education, 1979, p. 36.

Case History

The information obtained through a case history contributes insights and clues about the student's background and development. During an interview, parents share information about the child's prenatal history, birth conditions, and neonatal development, the age of developmental milestones (sitting, walking, toilet training, and talking), the child's health history (including illnesses and accidents), and learning problems of other members of the family. The student's school history can be obtained from parents, school records, and school personnel (such as teachers, nurses, and guidance counselors).

The interviewer must try to establish a feeling of mutual trust, taking care not to ask questions that might alarm parents or make them defensive by indicating disapproval of their actions. The interviewer should convey a spirit of cooperation, acceptance, and empathy while maintaining a degree of professional objectivity to guard against excessive emotional involvement and consequent ineffectiveness.

Skillful interviewers are able to obtain much useful information during the case history interview. They gather information in a smooth, conversational manner and go beyond routine questions, garnering more information and impressions than the questions themselves ask. Case history information and impressions are integrated with knowledge obtained through clinical observation, traditional tests, and alternative assessment measures. Table 3.3 illustrates the kind of information obtained through the case history interview.

Case History Interview Forms   Many case history interview forms are available. Some are quite lengthy and complete, procuring information in many domains. **Adaptive behavior scales** that question the extent to which individuals adapt themselves to the expectations of nature and society are often used. An informant (usually the mother) provides the information during an interview. Commonly used adaptive behavior scales are listed below. Appendix C contains additional information about these instruments.

- *The Vineland Adaptive Behavior Scales.*   There are three different versions of these scales: *Interview Edition, Survey Form*; *Interview Edition, Expanded Form*; and *Classroom Edition.* They all assess the domains of communication, daily living skills, socialization, and motor functions. Ages birth to age 19.

- *Adaptive Behavior Inventory.*   This inventory interviews an informant and yields information about self-help skills, communication skills, social skills, academic skills, and occupation skills. Ages 6 to 9.

- *Conners Teacher Rating Scales; Conners Parent Rating Scales.*   There are several versions of this test. They yield information about conduct disorders, anxiety, restlessness, obsessive/compulsive behaviors, and antisocial, hyperactive, and immature behaviors. Ages 3 to 19. (An early version of the Conners inventory appears in the *Student Guide* that accompanies this text.)

Table 3.3

Case History Information

Identifying information

Student: name, address, telephone, date of birth, school, grade
Parents: father's name and occupation, mother's name and occupation
Family: siblings' names and ages, others in the home
Clinic: date of interview, referral agency, name of examiner

Birth history

Pregnancy: length, condition of mother, unusual factors
Birth conditions: mature or premature, duration of labor, weight, unusual circumstances
Conditions following birth: normal, needing special care

Physical and developmental data

Health history: accidents, high fevers, other illnesses
Present health: habits of eating and sleeping, energy and activity level
Developmental history: age of sitting, walking, first words, first sentences, language difficulties, motor difficulties

Social and personal factors

Friends
Sibling relationships
Hobbies, interests, recreational activities
Home and parent attitudes
Acceptance of responsibilities
Attitude toward learning problem

Educational factors

School experiences: skipped or repeated grades, moving, change of teachers
Preschool education: kindergarten, nursery school
Special help previously received
Teachers' reports
Student's attitude toward school

Observation

According to Yogi Berra, "Sometimes you can observe a lot just by watching." **Observation** of the student is a required part of the assessment of learning disabilities, and the information it produces can make a valuable contribution. Whereas many attributes of the student are inadequately identified through testing or case study interviews, the skillful observer can often detect important characteristics and behaviors of the child in the classroom setting.

Observation of student behavior often corroborates findings of other assessment measures. For example, a skillful observer can note whether the child is attending to the lesson or is engaged in other activities. One astute observer overheard Washington, who was being evaluated because of poor reading, warning another child that for his bad behavior he would no doubt get "H-A-L-L." The observer perceptively inferred that Washington's incorrect spelling might be related to problems in phoneme awareness and auditory processing. Later testing confirmed that hypothesis.

Observation is also useful for shedding light on a student's general *personal adjustment*. How does the student react to situations and people? What is the student's attitude toward the learning problem? Has the school problem affected the student's social and home life? Has it drained the student's energy? Is the student's attitude one of interest or seeming indifference? During one testing situation the teacher observed three children in the class—Ricky, Pat, and Duster. When the work became difficult, Ricky gave up completely and simply filled in the blank spaces with any answer. Pat tensed up and refused to continue his work. Duster refused to guess and was afraid to make a mistake, so she struggled with a single item on the test for as long as she was permitted. These observations gave the teacher valuable information about each student.

Motor coordination and development can be appraised by observing the student's movements and gait. Can the child hop, skip, or throw and catch a ball? How does the student attack a writing task? Is there a contortion of the body while writing? What is the general appearance of the student's handwriting? How does the student hold a pencil? Must the student expend an inordinate effort in trying to make the handwriting presentable?

The child's *use of language* is readily assessed through observation. Is there evidence of articulation problems or infantile speech patterns? Does the student have difficulty finding words? Does the student possess an adequate vocabulary? Does the student speak easily, haltingly, or perhaps excessively? Does the student use complete sentences or single words and short, partial phrases? Is the sequence of sounds correct in words (for example, *aminal* or *psghetti*)? The student's native language is an important consideration in today's culturally diverse school population. What is the student's primary language and facility with English?

Games and toys offer activities for making observations of the child and also serve as a way to build rapport. For example, one can observe the student's ability to zip a zipper, tie a shoelace, button clothing, or lock a padlock for clues about *fine motor coordination* and *eye-hand relationships*. Games such as phonic rummy or phonic bingo give clues to the student's *phonics abilities* and *auditory skills*.

Observations of everyday classroom behavior provide much authentic information. For example, while reading, how does the student react to an unknown word? Does he or she stop and look to the teacher for help, look at the initial consonant and then take a wild guess, attempt to break the word into syllables, or try to infer the word from context?

Rating Scales

Behavior **rating scales** require teachers or parents to record their observations and impressions of students in a measurable fashion. Figure 3.2 shows a 24-point rating scale designed to help teachers identify pupils with learning disabilities in their class. Teachers rate the 24 behaviors on a 5-point scale (with 1 indicating poor behavior, 5 good behavior, and 3 average behavior). The highest possible score is 120 (5 × 24). In one study, the mean score of the children classified as normal was 81, and the score of the children identified as having learning disabilities was 61 (Myklebust & Boshes, 1969).

Figure 3.2

Rating Scale of Student Behavior

	POOR				GOOD	
	1	2	3	4	5	
AUDITORY COMPREHENSION						
1. Ability to follow oral directions						1
2. Comprehension of class discussion						2
3. Ability to retain auditory information						3
4. Comprehension of word meaning						4
SPOKEN LANGUAGE						
5. Complete and accurate expression						5
6. Vocabulary ability						6
7. Ability to recall words						7
8. Ability to relate experience						8
9. Ability to formulate ideas						9
ORIENTATION						
10. Promptness						10
11. Spatial orientation						11
12. Judgment of relationships						12
13. Learning directions						13
BEHAVIOR						
14. Cooperation						14
15. Attention						15
16. Ability to organize						16
17. Ability to cope with new situations						17
18. Social acceptance						18
19. Acceptance of responsibility						19
20. Completion of assignments						20
21. Tactfulness						21
MOTOR						
22. General coordination						22
23. Balance						23
24. Ability to manipulate						24

Teachers' judgments of students' behavioral characteristics are useful for identifying students with learning disabilities, and rating scales help in this process. Two scales, the *Pupil Rating Scale (Revised): Screening for Learning Disabilities* and the *Devereaux Elementary School Behavior Rating Scale*, are described in Appendix C.

Rating scales are frequently completed by teachers and parents in assessing ADHD (attention deficit hyperactivity disorder). Table 3.4 shows some of the commonly used rating scales used for assessing ADHD.

Informal Measures

Informal assessment measures are useful and practical alternative assessment procedures that test students on the ordinary materials and activities they are currently working with in the classroom. A major advantage of using classroom materials for informal tests is that the assessment is as close as possible to the expected behaviors. Informal tests also give teachers freedom in administration and interpretation. For example, a teacher can encourage the student during the assessment or give the student more time to complete the test. Such adjustments put students at ease and help ensure that they will give their best effort. Informal measures can also be given more frequently than formal tests and can be administered over a period of time rather than in a single session. In addition, they can use a variety of materials and procedures, can be given during regular instruction periods, and are less expensive than formal tests.

In this section we present several informal measures for teachers to use. Some informal tests are also provided in other pertinent chapters: informal reading tests (Chapter 11), informal motor tests (Chapter 7), and tests of phonological awareness (Chapter 10).

Table 3.4

Rating Scales for ADD/ADHD

Name	Publisher	Comments
Conners Teacher and Parent Rating Scales	Multihealth Systems	Parent scales and teacher scales. Several versions of each.
Child Behavior Checklist (Achenbach & Edelbrock)	University of Vermont, Department of Psychiatry	Teacher scales and parent scales.
Attention Deficit Disorder Evaluation Scale	Hawthorne Educational Services	Home version and school version.
Attention Disorder with or without Hyperactivity (ACTeRS)	Metritech, Inc.	Parent form and teacher form. Spanish version.

Informal Graded Word-Recognition Test   This type of test can be used as a quick method to determine the student's approximate reading level. It is also useful in detecting the student's errors in word analysis. An informal graded word-recognition test can be constructed by selecting words at random from graded basal reader glossaries. Table 3.4 illustrates such a list; the words were selected from several basal reader series and from graded reading vocabulary lists. The informal graded word list can be given as follows: (1) type the list of words selected for each grade on separate cards; (2) duplicate the entire test on a single sheet; (3) have the pupil read the words from the cards while the examiner marks the errors on the sheet, noting the pupil's method of analyzing and pronouncing difficult words; and (4) have the pupil read from increasingly difficult lists until three words are missed. The level at which the student misses only two words suggests the instructional level at which the pupil is able to read with help. The level at which one word is missed suggests the pupil's independent reading level, or the level at which the pupil can read alone. The level at which three words are missed suggests a frustration level, and the material is probably too difficult.

Informal Arithmetic Test   An informal arithmetic test can be easily devised to point out weaknesses in students' basic computational skills (Underhill, Uprichard, & Heddens, 1980). The informal survey test illustrated in Figure 3.3 can be used for sixth grade (Otto, McMenemy, & Smith, 1973). The difficulty level of the test could be increased or decreased, depending on the grade level being tested.

The informal arithmetic test should include several items of each kind so that a simple error will not be mistaken for a more fundamental difficulty.

Curriculum-Based Assessment   **Curriculum-based assessment (CBA)** is a type of performance assessment that is widely used in special education. CBA strengthens the connection between assessment and instruction by

Figure 3.3

Informal Survey Test: Sixth-Grade Level

ADDITION	300	37			
	60	24		234	123
	407	6	271	574	324
	2	19	389	261	451
SUBTRACTION	765	751	7054	8004	90327
	−342	−608	−3595	−5637	−42827
MULTIPLICATION	36	44	721	483	802
	×10	×83	×346	×208	×357
DIVISION	2/36	12/36	6/966	16/1061	13/8726

Source: W. Otto, R. McMenemy and R. Smith, *Corrective and Remedial Teaching,* Copyright © 1973 by Houghton Mifflin Company. Used by permission.

Table 3.5

Informal Graded Word-
Recognition Test

Preprimer	Primer	Grade 1	Grade 2
see	day	about	hungry
run	from	sang	loud
me	all	guess	stones
dog	under	catch	trick
at	little	across	chair
come	house	live	hopped
down	ready	boats	himself
you	came	hard	color
said	your	longer	straight
boy	blue	hold	leading

Grade 3	Grade 4	Grade 5	Grade 6
arrow	brilliant	career	buoyant
wrist	credit	cultivate	determination
bottom	examine	essential	gauntlet
castle	grammar	grieve	incubator
learned	jingle	jostle	ludicrous
washed	ruby	obscure	offensive
safety	terrify	procession	prophesy
yesterday	wrench	sociable	sanctuary
delight	mayor	triangular	tapestry
happiness	agent	volcano	vague

evaluating the student in terms of the curricular requirements of the student's own school or classroom. For example, if the student is expected to spell certain words in the classroom, the assessment measures the student's performance on those words (Tindal & Nolet, 1995; Fuchs & Deno, 1994).

The teacher first determines the area of the curriculum or the individualized education program (IEP) goal that the student is expected to learn. The student is then assessed through frequent, systematic, and repeated measures of that learning task. Performance results are graphed or charted so that the student's progress is clearly observable to both the teacher and the student.

CBA offers a useful and accountable assessment procedure for students with learning disabilities. Using direct and repeated measures, CBA displays the student's performance changes over successive time periods (such as days or weeks).

Deno (1985) used CBA to monitor growth in reading through frequent measurements of the number of words the student read aloud during 1-minute reading samples. The example of a curriculum-based assessment chart shown in Figure 3.4 shows the improvement in oral reading performance over a fourteen-week period. The chart shows the number of words read correctly in 1-minute reading samples. Period A is a base line, measured over three successive days; Period B shows progress after a target instructional program has been used and measurements have been taken weekly (on Mondays) for fourteen weeks. The dashed line shows the IEP objective, which is reading seventy words per minute within fourteen weeks.

Criterion-Referenced Tests **Criterion-referenced tests** measure a student's mastery of specific skills. For example, does the pupil recognize *-ing* endings? Does the student know the meaning of the prefix *dis-*? Can the student subtract single-digit numbers through 10? The teacher can set an acceptable criterion for mastery, such as 90 percent. When that performance level is reached, the student is taught the next skill in the sequence.

Criterion-referenced tests *describe* rather than *compare* performance, measuring mastery levels rather than grade levels. In contrast, ***norm-referenced tests*** (or traditional standardized tests) compare the pupil's performance to that of other children of the same age. This difference can be illustrated in a nonacademic area of learning such as swimming. In criterion-referenced terms, a child would be judged as being able to perform certain tasks, such as putting his or her face in the water, floating, or doing the crawl stroke. In contrast, in norm-referenced terms, the child would be tested and judged to swim as well as an average 9-year-old.

Figure 3.4

A Curriculum-Based Assessment Chart Monitoring an Individual Student's Progress

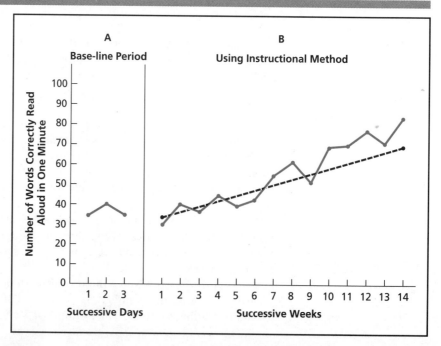

Criterion-referenced tests are useful because they provide a means of accountability. Although it is often difficult to show that a student has improved in terms of percentiles, stanines, or even grade-level scores, the teacher can show that the student has learned certain specific skills in terms of mastery of criterion-referenced measures.

Some commercial criterion-referenced tests used in special education are the *Brigance Diagnostic Inventories, Key Math—Revised, Standard Reading Inventory,* and *Prescriptive Reading Inventory* (see Appendix C).

Diagnostic Teaching   **Diagnostic teaching** is an extension of the assessment process whereby a perceptive teacher continues to collect assessment information while teaching the student. Typically, after giving tests, the teacher still has much to learn about the student and can do so by developing lessons that teach and test simultaneously and by noting the student's reactions to these lessons. Diagnostic teaching is also referred to as "trial lessons" or "teaching probes."

Assessment information about the student's learning styles can be obtained through short lessons. For example, the following procedure can indicate whether the student learns well through a sight-word method. First, teach some words visually by putting a few words on cards. Say the word while the student is looking at the word. A short time later, test the student to see if she or he remembers a certain word. Students who have fairly good visual memories will have little difficulty remembering the word after a few repetitions. A similar procedure can be used in a diagnostic teaching session to assess a student's auditory and phonics learning abilities.

A commercial instrument that incorporates the diagnostic teaching concept is *DARTTS (Diagnostic Assessments of Reading with Trial Teaching Strategies* (Roswell & Chall, 1994). Another commercial test that uses a probing technique to get at the student's learning style is the *Learning Styles Inventory* (The Price Systems).

Formal Standardized Tests

Traditional assessment uses **formal standardized tests,** commercially prepared instruments that have been normed or standardized on large groups of students. Formal tests require strict procedures in administration, scoring, and interpretation. These tests are also called *norm-referenced* because their scores are derived from their administration to a large group of children. A formal test has the following characteristics:

- The test is usually available in more than one form so that a student can be examined more than once without obtaining a high score due to practice.
- The test is accompanied by a manual giving directions for administration, scoring, and interpretation.
- The manual contains grade norms, age norms, and possibly percentile ranks or some form of scaled scores.

- The manual has information on validity (the degree to which the test measures what it is supposed to measure). The manual also shows reliability (consistency or similarity of performance). A reliability coefficient of 0.90 indicates that if the test were given to the student again, it is 90 percent likely that the student would obtain a score in the same range.

The examiner should know the techniques of using and interpreting tests and be thoroughly familiar with the specific test being used. Frequently, the value of a test may be not so much in the final test score as in the measurement of a particular subtest performance, the profile of all the subtest scores, or the clinical observations of the student during the test. The evaluator who has had extensive experience with a test may find that some parts used alone yield the necessary information.

Adequacy of Formal Tests Used in Learning Disabilities   In interpreting test scores, it is important to follow certain precautions. The score indicates only a small sample of behavior at one moment in time. By their very nature, all tests give only a limited measure of a person's abilities.

The integrity of formal tests is judged on (1) *standardization*—On what group was the test standardized? (2) *reliability*—Are the test results consistent? and (3) *validity*—Does the test measure what it claims to measure?

Informal assessment procedures measure student progress using classroom materials and activities. *(Jean Claude Lejeune)*

Many of the tests used to assess learning disabilities are inadequate by these criteria (Salvia & Ysseldyke, 1998). Yet these tests can be useful in the assessment process. It is important to know the limitations of the test and to use the information in proper perspective. A single score gives only a small part of the information, and teachers should not overgeneralize the implications of a specific test. If multiple sources of data are used in the assessment, test scores can provide a rich harvest of leads for assessment and teaching.

Formal tests can be viewed as a means of providing two levels of information about the student. General tests sample general, or global, areas of functioning and determine whether a student is performing at, above, or below age level in a given area. **Diagnostic tests** give a microscopic view of the components of some area of performance, enabling the teacher to analyze the student's functioning in specific subskills and to supply direction for remediation.

Some commonly used formal tests of both types are identified in this chapter and in each of the chapters in Part IV. A listing of tests and their publishers is presented in Appendix C.

Tests of Mental Abilities and Mental Processes   The purpose of general intelligence tests is to assess the global aspects of intellectual ability. These tests provide information about the student's aptitude for learning and specific cognitive attributes. Certain intelligence tests are usually administered by psychologists; others may be given by teachers with appropriate training.

Commonly used individual intelligence tests that are typically administered by psychologists are the *WISC-III (Wechsler Intelligence Scale for Children—Third Edition)*, the *Stanford-Binet Intelligence Scale—Fourth Edition*, and the *Kaufman Assessment Battery for Children (K-ABC)*. The *WISC-III* provides three IQ scores: verbal, performance, and full-scale IQ scores. The mean of each IQ score is 100, and the standard deviation is 15. (The WISC-III is described in greater detail later in this chapter.) The Stanford-Binet has fifteen subtests grouped into four areas: verbal reasoning, quantitative reasoning, abstract/visual reasoning, and short-term memory. A score is obtained for each area as well as an overall intelligence score. The mean overall IQ score is 100, and the standard deviation is 16. The Kaufman Assessment Battery for Children (K-ABC) classifies mental abilities as sequential processing or simultaneous processing.

Some tests of cognitive ability that can be given by teachers with training are listed in Figure 3.5. (See Appendix C for more description of these tests.) Two widely used tests of mental abilities are described next.

Wechsler Intelligence Scale for Children—Third Edition (WISC-III)   This test comprises thirteen subtests organized into two groups—verbal and performance. The verbal and performance subtests are administered in alternating order to maintain the child's interest during testing. These subtests are described in Figure 3.6.

Figure 3.5

Tests of Cognitive
Ability that Can be
Given by Teachers with
Training

Tests of Cognitive Ability of the *Woodcock-Johnson Psychoeducational Battery—Revised* (This test is described in greater detail later in the text.)

The *Kaufman Brief Intelligence Test* (K-Bit) is a short test that measures two distinct cognitive functions through two subtests: Vocabulary Subtest (verbal: uses expressive vocabulary and definitions); and Matrices Subtest (nonverbal: uses pictures and abstract designs).

The *Slosson Intelligence Test—Revised* is a relatively short screening test.

The *Detroit Tests of Learning Aptitude—3* are intended for use with children ages 6 through 18.

The *Detroit Tests of Learning Aptitude—Primary—2* are intended for younger children, ages 3 through 12.

The *McCarthy Scales of Children's Abilities* are designed to assess young children, ages 2½ to 8½.

The *Illinois Test of Psycholinguistic Abilities* (ITPA) was one of the first tests of mental processes designed expressly to analyze subskills of mental function.

The *Goodenough-Harris Drawing Test* estimates intellectual maturity through an analysis of a child's drawing of a person.

Verbal Tests	*Performance Tests*
Information	Picture Completion
Similarities	Coding
Arithmetic	Picture Arrangement
Vocabulary	Block Design
Comprehension	Object Assembly
*Digit Span	**Symbol Search
	*Mazes

*Supplementary subtest.

**Supplementary subtest that can substitute only for Coding.

The WISC-III is designed so that a scaled, or standard, score of 10 indicates average ability for age in the particular subtest. The test yields a Full-scale IQ score, a Verbal IQ score, and a Performance IQ score. Information about a student's strengths and weaknesses in language and performance areas can be interpreted by comparing the Verbal score to the Performance score. In addition, examiners frequently garner additional clinical information by going beyond the global scores and analyzing the student's performance on specific subtests and through clusters of subtests (Salvia & Ysseldyke, 1998).

Woodcock-Johnson Psychoeducational Battery—Revised (WJ-R)   This is an individually administered, multiple-skill test battery. It can be used on subjects from 3 to 80 years of age and has two parts: (1) tests of cognitive

Figure 3.6

Subtests of the Wechsler
Intelligence Scale for
Children—Third
Edition (WISC-III)

WISC-III Verbal Tests   These tests use oral language for administration and student responses. Their descriptions follow.

Information: In this test, the examiner orally presents a series of questions about common events, objects, places, and people. The child's answers indicate knowledge about this common information.

Similarities: In this test, the examiner orally presents a series of pairs of words. The child explains the similarity of the common objects or concepts the words represent.

Arithmetic: This test is a series of orally presented arithmetic problems. The child mentally solves the problems and responds orally.

Vocabulary: This test is a series of orally presented words. The child orally defines the words.

Comprehension: This is a series of orally presented questions. Formulating the answer requires the child to solve everyday problems or to understand social rules and concepts.

Digit Span: This test is a series of orally presented number sequences. The child must repeat verbatim the number sequences for digits forward and in reverse order for digits backwards.

WISC-III Performance Tests   These tests are presented visually, and the subjects respond by performing some task. Their descriptions follow.

Picture Completion: This test consists of a set of colorful pictures of common objects and scenes, each of which is missing an important part. The child identifies the missing part.

Coding: This test consists of a series of simple shapes (Coding A) or numbers (Coding B), each paired with a simple symbol. The child is required to draw the symbol in its corresponding shape (Coding A) or under its corresponding number (Coding B) according to a key.

Picture Arrangement: This is a set of colorful pictures presented in a mixed-up order. The child rearranges the pictures into a logical story sequence.

Block Design: This test consists of a set of modeled or printed two-dimensional geometric patterns. The child replicates the patterns using two-color cubes.

Object Assembly: This is a set of puzzles of common objects, each presented in a standardized configuration. The child assembles the puzzle parts to form a meaningful whole.

Symbol Search: This is a series of paired groups of symbols, each pair consisting of a target group and a search group. The child scans the two groups and indicates whether a target symbol appears in the search group.

Mazes: This test, printed in a response booklet, is a set of increasingly difficult mazes. The child solves the maze using a pencil.

ability and (2) tests of achievement. It can be administered by teachers and is designed so that a discrepancy analysis can be developed by comparing aptitude and achievement scores. The test uses clusters of scores for interpretation, and a computer program is available to assist the user in calculating and interpreting the student's performance. The Cognitive Ability

". . . I can't go bowling tonight, Freddie, I'm cram-
ming for an IQ test tomorrow. . ."

subtests of the Woodcock-Johnson Psychoeducational Battery are described in Figure 3.7

Analysis of the Subtest Scores of Intelligence Tests   The current view of intelligence is that it is not a single general factor but rather many separate abilities (Sternberg, 1985). The WISC-III provides three IQ scores: a Verbal IQ, a Performance IQ, and a Full-Scale IQ. Another intelligence test, the K-ABC (Kaufman Assessment Battery for Children), divides intelligence into sequential thinking (thinking in logical order) and simultaneous thinking (an immediate grasp of an idea). The multiple-intelligence theory of Gardner (Gardner & Hatch, 1989) conceives of eight separate intelligences—linguistic, logical-mathematical, spatial, musical, bodily-kinesthetic, intrapersonal, interpersonal, and naturalistic.

   Many of the intelligence tests provide scores for each of their subtests in addition to the overall IQ score. Clinicians find it useful to analyze the subtest scores to obtain clinical information about a student's component cognitive abilities. In some cases the analysis of subtest scores might show wide

Figure 3.7

**Cognitive Ability
Subtests of the
Woodcock-Johnson
Psychoeducational
Battery—Revised (WJ-R)**

WJ-R Tests of Cognitive Ability

The Standard Battery of cognitive subtests consists of the following seven tests.

Memory for Name: Consists of auditory-visual tasks in which the individual learns the names of nine pictures of space creatures.

Memory for Sentences: Tests the ability to repeat orally presented sentences.

Visual Matching: Consists of a timed assessment of skill in identifying two identical numbers in a row of six numbers.

Incomplete Words: Consists of words with one or more missing phonemes that the individual is to identify.

Visual Closure: The individual must identify visual stimuli. The pictures are distorted, incomplete, or have patterns superimposed on them.

Picture Vocabulary: Tests the ability to identify pictured objects or actions.

Analysis-Synthesis: Tests the ability to analyze the parts of an equivalency statement and then put them back together to solve a novel equivalency statement.

The Supplementary Battery of cognitive subtests consists of the following fourteen tests.

Visual Auditory Learning: A miniature learning-to-read task in which a person is required to associate unfamiliar visual stimuli (rebuses) with familiar oral words and to translate sequences of rebuses into sentences.

Memory for Words: Requires the individual to repeat lists of unrelated words; the lists range in length from one to eight words.

Cross-out: Timed, match-to-sample tasks in which the individual must locate five drawings in a set of twenty that match the stimulus.

Sound Blending: The subject must merge sounds into words.

Picture Recognition: Requires the individual to recognize a subset of pictures that have been presented with distracting pictures.

Oral Vocabulary: Requires the individual to give synonyms or antonyms in response to stimulus words read by the examiner.

Concept Formation: Tests the ability to identify the rule for a concept, given instances and noninstances of the concept.

Delayed Recall—Memory for Names: Requires the subject to recall, after one to eight days, the names of the space creatures learned in the first test.

Delayed Recall—Visual-Auditory Learning: Requires the subject to recall, after one to eight days, the symbols learned in the eighth test.

Numbers Reversed: Tests the ability to repeat in reverse order a series of orally presented digits.

Sound Pattern: Requires the subject to listen to two complex sound patterns and tell if they are the same or different.

Spatial Relations: Requires the subject to match shapes.

Listening Comprehension: An oral cloze task in which the subject listens to a passage and supplies the word.

Verbal Analogies: Requires the subject to draw comparisons about word meanings.

variability (or "scatter") in different components of mental functioning. In other cases clusters of scores might indicate a student's strengths and weaknesses in specific areas of learning.

For example, in the WISC-III test, four factor-based index scores can be calculated: verbal comprehension, perceptual organization, freedom from distractibility, and processing speed. These factor-based scales, like the IQ scales, have a mean of 100 and a standard deviation of 15 (WISC-III Manual, 1991, p. 7). The four factors are made up of four subtests.

1. *Verbal comprehension.* Information, Similarities, Vocabulary, and Comprehension
2. *Perceptual organization.* Picture Completion, Picture Arrangement, Block Design, Object Assembly
3. *Freedom from distractibility.* Arithmetic, Digit Span
4. *Processing Speed.* Coding, Symbol Search

Measurement experts are cautious about overinterpreting the clinical importance given to individual subtest scores, cluster scores, and recategorized groups of subtest scores (Kavale & Forness, 1987a, 1987b; Taylor, Partenio, & Ziegler, 1983). The reliability of a test's total score is much stronger than the reliability of a single subtest score.

Bias in Intelligence Testing   The use of IQ tests continues to be controversial. School policies about the use of intelligence tests have been influenced by class-action lawsuits that found bias in intelligence testing. In an early lawsuit, *Larry P.* v. *Riles* (1979), the court ruled that IQ testing was racially and culturally discriminatory when used as the sole criterion for placing children in classes for the mentally retarded. As a result of this case, the state of California stopped using standardized intelligence tests to identify educable mentally retarded black children. However, in a later class-action case, *Pase* v. *Hannon* (1980), the judge examined the items on the intelligence tests and ruled that he could find little evidence of bias (Salvia & Ysseldyke, 1998; Galagan, 1985). The issue of bias in assessment through the use of intelligence tests continues to be debated in both the courtroom and academic research.

Reading Tests: Survey Tests and Diagnostic Tests   General survey-type tests of reading yield a general score of silent reading and give an indication of the level at which a child reads. Table 3.6 lists some of the widely used general survey reading tests, and they are described in Appendix C.

Diagnostic reading tests differ from general reading tests in that they analyze the processes by which the child attempts to read, providing information on *how* the child reads rather than indicating only the reading level. By analyzing specific errors, the examiner can determine whether the problem is poor word-attack skills, a lack of familiarity with certain phonic elements (such as vowels, consonant blends, and diphthongs), inadequate sight vocabulary, or a slow reading rate. A few of the useful diagnostic

Table 3.6

**Commonly Used
Academic Tests**

General reading tests
California Achievement Tests: Reading
Gates-MacGinitie Reading Tests
Metropolitan Achievement Tests: Reading
SRA Achievement Series: Reading
Stanford Achievement Test: Reading

Diagnostic reading tests
Analytic Reading Inventory
DARTTS (Diagnostic Assessment of Reading with Trial Lessons)
Diagnostic Reading Inventory
Gates-McKillop-Horowitz Reading Diagnostic Tests
Stanford Diagnostic Reading Test
Test of Reading Comprehension (TORC)
Woodcock Reading Mastery Tests—Revised

Comprehensive batteries of academic tests
California Achievement Tests
Iowa Tests of Basic Skills
Metropolitan Achievement Tests
SRA Achievement Series
Stanford Achievement Test
Wide-Range Achievement Test—III (WRAT-III)

Diagnostic academic tests and test batteries
Brigance Diagnostic Comprehensive Inventory of Basic Skills
Kaufman Test of Educational Achievement (K-TEA)
Key Math—Revised
Peabody Individual Achievement Test—Revised (PIAT-R)
Stanford Diagnostic Mathematics Test
Test of Written Spelling—2
Woodcock-Johnson Psychoeducational Battery—Revised: Achievement Tests

Motor tests
Bruininks-Oseretsky Test of Motor Proficiency
Peabody Development Motor Scales
Southern California Perceptual-Motor Tests

Language tests
Ammons Full-Range Picture Vocabulary Test
Carrow Elicited Language Inventory
Clinical Evaluation of Language Fundamentals—Revised (CELF-R)
Goldman-Fristoe Test of Articulation
Houston Test for Language Development
Peabody Picture Vocabulary Test—Revised
Templin-Darley Tests of Articulation
Test of Adolescent Language—2 (TOAL-2)
Test of Language Development—2 (TOLD-2)
Test of Language Development—2—Primary
Test of Written Language—2 (TOWL-2)
Test for Auditory Comprehension of Language—Revised

reading tests are listed in Table 3.6 and are also discussed in Chapter 11 and described in Appendix C.

Comprehensive Batteries of Academic Tests General test batteries measure performance in academic skills in reading, arithmetic, spelling, and grammar. These comprehensive batteries are also listed in Table 3.6 and described in Appendix C.

Diagnostic Academic Tests and Test Batteries Diagnostic tests for academic areas are designed to provide more in-depth information than the general tests. They can be given to one child, not a group, and they provide information on several academic areas. Commonly used tests are listed in Table 3.5 and described in Appendix C.

One widely used individual diagnostic battery of achievement is the *Woodcock-Johnson—Revised, Tests of Achievement*. This battery contains fourteen achievement subtests. Four academic areas are measured through nine tests in the standard achievement battery: (1) reading (tests of letter-word identification and passage comprehension); (2) mathematics (tests of calculation and applied problems); (3) written language (tests of dictation and writing samples); and (4) knowledge (tests of science, social studies, and humanities). The supplementary battery of academic achievement consists of five subtests designed to provide additional information: word attack, reading vocabulary, quantitative concepts, proofing, and writing fluency. The subtest scores of the Woodcock-Johnson test can be combined into seven cognitive factor clusters, four scholastic-aptitude clusters, two oral language clusters, and three total scores.

Motor Tests Examples of diagnostic tests that evaluate motor performance are listed in Table 3.6 and discussed in Chapter 8 and Appendix C.

Language Tests Speech-screening tests of articulation include tests of articulation, tests of the ability to understand words, tests of syntax, tests of language comprehension, and tests of written language. These tests are listed in Table 3.6 and discussed further in Chapter 10 and Appendix C.

Screening Tests for Visual and Auditory Acuity Students with learning disabilities should be checked for sensory deficits. Vision- and hearing-screening tests may be given by learning disabilities teachers who are trained in the administration of these tests, or by the school nurse or some other school staff member. Students who fail the screening tests are referred to an eye or ear specialist for a professional examination.

Vision-screening instruments are the *Keystone Visual Survey Service for Schools* and the *Ortho-rater*. These instruments use stereoscopic slides to screen for near-vision and far-vision acuity, eye-muscle balance, and fusion. (See Chapter 7 and Appendix C.)

The *audiometer* is an auditory screening instrument used to screen for hearing problems. Students who fail the screening should be referred for a professional hearing examination. (See Chapter 7.)

USING A DISCREPANCY FORMULA TO DETERMINE ELIGIBILITY FOR LEARNING DISABILITIES SERVICES

The most critical decision of the assessment process is whether the student under consideration has learning disabilities and will be eligible for learning disabilities services. Making decisions about classification and eligibility is the responsibility of the IEP team, which should take both qualitative and quantitative factors into account. One method of establishing eligibility for the learning disabilities category is to use a *discrepancy score*, a mathematical calculation for quantifying the discrepancy between achievement and potential. As noted earlier in this chapter, some researchers and practitioners question the validity of IQ-achievement discrepancy procedures and call for other methods to identify learning disabilities. Still, it is important to be familiar with discrepancy procedures because most states and districts rely on IQ-achievement discrepancy scores to establish **eligibility criteria** for learning disabilities (Mercer et al., 1996; Frankenberger & Harper, 1987).

"I'm not an underachiever. You're an overexpecter."

Methods for Determining the Discrepancy Score

The discrepancy score refers to the quantitative difference or gap between a student's potential for learning and current achievement. Several quantitative methods for determining a discrepancy score are used in schools or are suggested by measurement specialists (Reynolds, 1985; Forness, Sinclair, & Guthrie, 1983; Cone & Wilson, 1981): (a) deviation from grade level, (b) potential-achievement discrepancy based on grade scores or age scores, (c) potential-achievement discrepancy based on standard score comparisons, and (d) potential achievement discrepancy based on regression analysis. Each method has certain advantages as well as certain limitations. These and other methods for identifying learning disabilities are described in the box entitled "Methods for Determining the Discrepancy Score Deviation from Grade Level."

Combining Qualitative and Quantitative Data

Many parents and teachers are concerned about the use of formulas for making decisions about their children, maintaining that there is no substitute for clinical judgment and experience (Mastropieri, 1987; Chalfant, 1989). Indeed, decisions about eligibility for learning disabilities services should not be made solely on the basis of a discrepancy formula. Discrepancy scores focus exclusively on the relationship between potential and achievement measures and ignore other learning characteristics unique to individuals with learning disabilities. Many human and clinical factors cannot be put into any formula, and other imperative information must also be considered. Observations, informal measurements, and the experience of teachers and parents are important considerations in the eligibility decision.

STANDARDS AND ACCOUNTABILITY

As a nation, we are taking education very seriously. Almost all of the states have set specific standards for expected performance and have established an accountability system to measure student performance. Accountability in education denotes a system for informing those inside and outside the education arena of the direction in which schools are moving. The states are setting high standards and most of them now administer statewide assessments to measure the progress of students meeting these standards. (Erickson, Ysseldyke, Thurlow, & Elliot, 1998; Elliot, 1998)

Including Students with Learning Disabilities in Statewide Assessments

In the recent past, students with disabilities, including learning disabilities, were excluded from statewide tests. The reasons for this exclusion were concerns about the test scores of students with disabilities lowering the overall scores of a school and concerns about the effect of assessments on the self-esteem or emotional health of students with disabilities (U.S. Department of Education, 1997; Yell & Schriner, 1997). However, states have now begun to hold schools accountable for the educational results of all students, including students with disabilities (Erickson et al., 1998; U.S. Department of Education, 1997).

The 1997 Amendments to IDEA outline several new requirements concerning the participation of students with disabilities in statewide assessments. The states want assessment information so that they might know how students with disabilities are progressing toward the general education curriculum goal. The 1997 Amendments to IDEA require that students with learning disabilities participate in statewide assessments. A plan for how the student with learning disabilities will be assessed must be part of the IEP and must include a statement of whatever modifications may be needed for her or his participation in the assessments.

Accommodations for Assessment

Alternate assessment refers to ways to make accommodations in assessment for students with disabilities. Alternative assessment procedures must be written into the IEP. Figure 3.8 provides examples of common assessment accommodations for students with learning disabilities.

Figure 3.8

Examples of Common Assessment Accommodations for Students with Learning Disabilities

TIMING	**SETTING**
• Extend the time allotted to complete the test.	• Give to small groups.
• Alter time of day that test is administered.	• Give in hospital setting.
• Administer test in several sessions over thecourse of the day.	• Use study carrel.
• Administer test in several sessions over several days.	• Use separate room.
• Allow frequent breaks during testing.	
PRESENTATION	**RESPONSE**
• Use audiocassettes.	• Dictate to scribe.
• Read test aloud.	• Record answers.
• Use large-print versions.	• Use word processor.
• Give repeated directions.	• Transfer answers from booklet to answer sheet.
• Use magnification devices.	

Source: Adapted from Inclusive Assessment and Accountability Systems, by Erickson, Ysseldyke, Thurlow, & Elliot, 1998, *Teaching Exceptional Children, 31* (2), p. 8. Copyright © 1998 by The Council for Exceptional Children. Reprinted by permission.

METHODS FOR DETERMINING THE DISCREPANCY SCORE DEVIATION FROM GRADE LEVEL

This chart describes several methods for quantifying a discrepancy score to determine a child's eligibility for learning disabilities services.

Deviation From Grade Level

This method identifies students with learning disabilities by identifying students with achievement scores that are significantly below their current grade placement. Schools set guidelines to determine the amount of deviation from grade level needed for learning disabilities eligibility. The following guidelines illustrate the deviation from grade level method (Richek, Caldwell, Jennings, & Lerner, 1996).

Deviation from Grade Level Eligibility Criteria

Primary grades—more than 1.0 year below current grade level
Intermediate grades—more than 1.5 years below current grade level
Junior high school—more than 2.0 years below current grade level
Senior high school—more than 2.5 years below current grade level

The deviation from grade level method is easy to administer, but it has statistical shortcomings. The method discriminates against students with higher IQ scores who should be performing above grade level; since they actually are at grade level, they will not receive services. The method also tends to identify low achievers rather than students with learning disabilities (Cone & Wilson, 1981).

Potential-Achievement Discrepancy Based on Age or Grade Scores

These methods of obtaining the discrepancy score are frequently used and are based on the discrepancy between potential and achievement when both are converted to either age-level scores or grade-level scores. A statistical shortcoming is that these scores do not take into account the tests' error of measurement, nor do they have a comparability of norms across tests: that is, the grade-level or age-level scores on one test are not comparable to those on another test (Cone & Wilson, 1981).

Three different methods are described here: (a) the mental grade method, (b) the years-in-school method, and (c) the learning quotient method.

Mental Grade Method   This is the simplest method. It uses the student's mental age to assess reading expectancy (Harris, 1964). To determine the reading expectancy grade (RE), the examiner subtracts five years from the student's mental age (MA):

$$RE = MA - 5$$

Thus, a child with an MA of 13 would be expected to read as well as the average 13-year-old or average eighth-grade student. An MA of 7 suggests a reading expectancy of the average 7-year-old, or second-grade student.

The expected reading level and the student's present reading level are compared to determine whether a discrepancy exists. For example, Tony, who is 10 years, zero months, old, has an IQ score of 120. Using the mental grade method, his reading expectancy grade is 7.0. If he reads at the 4.0 grade level, he has a three-year discrepancy in reading:

$$7.0 \text{ (RE)} = 12 \text{ (MA)} - 5$$

Years-in-School Method   This method (Bond, Tinker, Wasson, & Wasson, 1984) suggests that the mental grade method does not take into account the years of school exposure and therefore gives an inaccurate expectancy in some cases, especially when the IQ score is particularly high or particularly low. In the first case, it would overestimate expectancy, and in the second it would underestimate it. These authors calculate the expectancy grade with the following formula:

$$RE = \frac{\text{years in school} \times \text{IQ score}}{100} + 1.0$$

Ten-year-old Tony is in the middle of the fifth grade and therefore has been in school for 4.5 years. Using this formula with his IQ score of 120, his reading expectancy grade is 6.4:

$$RE = \frac{4.5 \times 120}{100} + 1.0 = 6.4$$

If Tony reads at the 4.0 grade level, the discrepancy between his expectancy and achievement levels is 2.4 years.

Learning Quotient Method   Another method to measure the discrepancy between achievement and IQ is the learning quotient method. This method takes three factors into consideration: mental age (MA), chronological age (CA), and grade age (GA) (Myklebust, 1968). Since each factor contains certain errors, an average of the three—called expectancy age (EA)—tends to minimize error.

$$EA \text{ (expectancy age)} = \frac{MA + CA + GA}{3}$$

The child's learning quotient (LQ) indicates the percentage of what the student is capable of learning. The learning quotient (LQ) is the ratio between the present achievement (AA) and the expectancy age (EA).

$$LQ \text{ (learning quotient)} = \frac{AA \text{ (achievement age)}}{EA \text{ (expectancy age)}}$$

The school can designate a target LQ (learning quotient) score for eligibility for learning disabilities service—for example, an LQ score of 89 or less. This means that the child is learning less than 90 percent of what he or she is capable of learning.

Potential-Achievement Discrepancy Based on Standard Score Comparisons

The method of standard score comparisons avoids some of the statistical problems inherent in comparing age and grade scores. All scores are converted to standard scores that are based on the same mean and standard deviation. The standard score on a mental ability (IQ) test can then be readily compared with the standard score on an achievement test. In judging discrepancy, if the difference between the obtained standard scores is greater than one or two standard errors of difference, then the student is viewed as eligible for learning disabilities services.

Although the standard score comparison method meets many of the statistical requirements, it does not take into account certain statistical properties known as regression toward the mean (Reynolds, 1985; Cone & Wilson, 1981).

Potential-Achievement Discrepancy Based on Regression Analysis

Regression analysis is a statistical procedure to measure discrepancy that is favored by many measurement experts. The regression equation provides a statistically determined expected achievement range for a specific IQ score. It indicates whether a student's achievement scores are in the range of what would reasonably be considered normal limits for the student's IQ score. This method adjusts for the phenomenon of regression toward the mean, a statistical tendency for scores that are especially high or low to move toward the mean when measured a second time (Reynolds, 1985; Cone & Wilson, 1981).

However, the regression analysis method is also criticized. Many of the tests used in learning disabilities assessment fail to meet acceptable psychometric standards (Salvia & Ysseldyke, 1998). Regression analysis is a precise, sophisticated technique that is being used on tests that are rather gross measures of behavior (Willson, 1987). (One software package that makes discrepancy calculations for determining eligibility for learning disabilities is the Discrepancy Determinator [DD1], from TRAIN, Inc.; the address is given in Appendix D.)

Instruction in test-taking strategies can offer students a fair chance and put them on an equal footing with other test takers (Hughes, Schumaker, Deshler, & Mercer, 1988). A quality called *test-wiseness* is the ability of the student to use the characteristics and formats of the test and/or the test-taking situation to receive a high score (Hughes, Salvia, & Bott, 1991). Good test takers possess the quality of test-wiseness. Students who enroll in commercial test-taking courses to prepare themselves for specific examinations do better on the exams. If children and schools are to be judged on the basis of test scores, should they be helped in playing the game of test taking?

Students with learning disabilities desperately need test-taking skills. At the present time, they can receive modifications in taking certain tests, such as the ACT and SAT (such as extended time limits), and high school juniors can take the PSAT for the purpose of practicing for the SAT. Since the students' performance on these competitive tests play such a key role in the decisions affecting their lives, students with learning disabilities need all the help they can get. The web site for the ACT is **http://www.act.org** and the web site for the SAT is **http://www.ets.org**.

INTRODUCTION TO THE CASE STUDY

This chapter presents the first part of an extended case study. The direction of every case is influenced by the theoretical orientation of the case investigators, which affects many factors: (1) how the student's learning problems are analyzed; (2) the kinds of assessment questions asked; (3) the selection of evaluation measures and tests; (4) the interpretation of case data; (5) the recommended placements for services; and (6) the proposed instructional strategies. Because solving the puzzle of a learning disabilities case is an art as well as a science, professionals may differ about many aspects of a case. (Another extended case study is presented in Appendix A.)

The following case study, that of Rita G., illustrates the stages of the assessment-teaching process (shown earlier in Figure 3.1). The information presented in this case study is based on an actual case. Identifying information has been altered to maintain confidentiality. This case study is broken into three segments, which are presented in the three chapters of Part II. With reference to the stages of the IEP, the case study is presented as follows:

PART I of Case Study	Stage 1: Prereferral information and activities	Chapter 3
	Stage 2: Referral and initial planning	
PART II of Case Study	Stage 3: Multidisciplinary evaluation	Chapter 4
PART III of Case Study	Stage 4: Case conference (or IEP) meeting: Writing the IEP	Chapter 5
	Stage 5: Implementing the Teaching Plan	
	Stage 6: Monitoring the student's progress (and reevaluation)	

Rita G.

Identifying Information
Name of Student: Rita G.
Age: 9.0 (Nine years, zero months)
Current placement: Grade 3.6. General education
third-grade class.

STAGE 1: PREREFERRAL INFORMATION AND ACTIVITIES

Rita G's third-grade teacher, Steve Martinez, requested a prereferral staffing for her. In his request, Mr. Martinez reported that Rita cannot work independently; she seems unable to organize and plan when faced with a problem task, such as thinking through an arithmetic word problem or solving problems in other curriculum areas. When doing a class assignment, she answers one or two items and then becomes distracted by other activities going on in the classroom and does not complete her work. Although Rita recognizes words in reading, her reading comprehension is inconsistent, and her work is usually not completed. On the day Mr. Martinez made the prereferral request, Rita's total morning's work consisted of writing four spelling words five times each. Mr. Martinez also reported that Rita never engaged in conversations with him and rarely asked questions either in class or of him personally. He did note that in her school records her first-grade teacher had described Rita as inquisitive, but she showed no evidence of that quality in his class.

The prereferral team meeting was held soon afterward. The team consisted of Mr. Martinez, the building principal, and the fourth-grade teacher. After discussing Rita's performance in class, the team concluded that the assigned work in the class may be too difficult for Rita. The team made several suggestions: Provide Rita with texts and workbooks at the second-grade level and give her individual assignments in these materials. Change Rita's seating to the front of the class so that Mr. Martinez would have closer contact with her. Talk to the second-grade teacher about Rita's work last year. Obtain some high interest–low-reading-level books from the library for Rita to use. Check to see that she has her assignment book before she goes home.

Mr. Martinez followed up on these suggestions for several weeks. Unfortunately, Rita objected to being given different assignments from those of her classmates. She complained that she was being given "baby" work. She did not read the library books. She also began to hide her papers at home and lost her assignment notebook. Her mother reported that Rita purposely broke pencils when doing homework. Also, Mr. Martinez could not contact Rita's second-grade teacher because she had moved out of town. Rita's academic functioning at school grew worse; she was failing in several subjects. Mr. Martinez decided to call in Rita's mother to discuss recommending an educational evaluation.

STAGE 2: REFERRAL AND INITIAL PLANNING

Mr. Martinez met with Rita's mother to discuss her daughter's problems in school. Mrs. G. said that she was worried because the problem was becoming critical. Rita kept saying she was dumb and hated school, and it was becoming increasingly difficult to get her to go to school. She frequently complained of stomachaches in the morning. Mr. Martinez and Mrs. G. agreed to refer Rita for an educational evaluation in the hope that it would provide information to help plan an appropriate educational program for her. Mrs. G. signed the informed consent form so that the evaluation could proceed.

Mr. Martinez submitted a referral and discussed Rita's problem with the special education coordinator in the school. The initial planning for Rita's evaluation included the following kinds of assessment information: classroom observation, auditory and visual acuity; a relevant developmental and educational history; measures of intellectual aptitude; measures of present levels of academic functioning; a measure of adaptive behavior, learning strengths and weaknesses; and an interest inventory.

Note: The information gained from this evaluation is presented in the continuation of the case of Rita G. in Chapter 4.

Chapter Summary

1. This chapter examines the initial portion of the assessment-teaching process: the assessment of learning disabilities. Assessment is the process of gathering pertinent information about the student to make the critical decisions about teaching. The uses of assessment include screening, referral, classification, instructional planning, and monitoring student progress.

2. There are two models of assessment used with students with learning disabilities: traditional assessment and alternative assessment. Alternative assessment includes performance assessment, portfolio assessment, and dynamic assessment.

3. Federal and state laws have greatly influenced the assessment process. The new federal legislation known as IDEA 1997 and state versions of this law have had the greatest impact.

4. The IEP (individualized education program) has two functions: It is a written plan for a particular student, and it also regulates the entire assessment-teaching process.

5. Parents' rights or procedural safeguards must be considered during the assessment process. They include obtaining parental consent, giving tests in the student's native language, using tests that are free of racial and cultural bias, giving parents the right to see all information, informing parents about mediation, respecting the right to a due process hearing, and ensuring confidentiality.

6. The assessment-teaching process has six stages: (1) prereferral activities; (2) referral and initial planning; (3) multidisciplinary evaluation; (4) the case conference (or IEP) meeting; (5) implementation of the teaching plan; and (6) review and monitoring of student progress.

7. Prereferral activities include those activities that the teacher tries in the classroom before making the referral. Three procedures are consultation, use of the teacher assistance team, and peer collaboration.

8. Referral and initial planning consists of the formal procedure of initiating the special education study for the student.

9. Multidisciplinary evaluation is the process of obtaining assessment information through testing and other means. This information is obtained by various specialists in the school.

10. The case conference (or IEP) meeting is the meeting with the parents and other school personnel at which the IEP is written.

11. Implementation of the teaching plan refers to both placement and teaching to reach the prescribed long-term goals and short-term objectives or benchmarks.

12. Review and monitoring of the student's progress must take place and the IEP must be reevaluated, at least annually.

13. Several decisions must be made during the assessment process. Many of these decisions are based on requirements in the law concerning the IEP.

14. Assessment information can be obtained in several ways: from the case history or interview, from observations and rating scales, through informal measures, and through formal standardized testing.

15. Eligibility criteria help to determine if the student has learning disabilities and is eligible for learning disabilities services. The multidisciplinary team takes into account both qualitative and quantitative information and may consider discrepancy scores, which measure the discrepancy between the student's achievement and potential. The four discrepancy measures are deviation from grade level, discrepancy based on grade- and age-level scores, discrepancy based on standard-score comparisons, and discrepancy based on regression analysis measures.

16. The demand for accountability and the school reform movement are increasing. In IDEA 1997, students with learning disabilities must be included in statewide testing.

Questions for Discussion and Reflection

1. Compare and contrast two models of assessment: traditional assessment and alternative assessment.

2. Describe the six stages of the individualized education program (IEP) process. What is the purpose of each stage?

3. The 1997 Individuals with Disabilities Education Act (IDEA) provides important procedural safeguards for students with learning disabilities. Discuss four of the parents' rights or procedural safeguards described in this chapter.

4. IDEA 1997 specifies the participants for the IEP meeting. Describe each of the participants.

5. What are the five ways of obtaining data for an evaluation of a student with learning disabilities? Give examples of information that might be obtained in each way.

6. Discuss the meaning of the phrase "discrepancy between potential and achievement" in relation to assessment of students with learning disabilities. What are the implications of this concept for assessment of

students with learning disabilities? What are some of the reasons behind criticism of discrepancy formulas?

7. Describe several accommodations that can be made for testing students with learning disabilities.

Key Terms

adaptive behavior scales *(p. 81)*

annual goals *(p. 78)*

alternative assessment *(p. 66)*

assessment stages *(p. 72)*

authentic assessment *(p. 66)*

benchmarks *(p. 73)*

case conference meeting *(p. 73)*

case history *(p. 75)*

criterion-referenced tests *(p. 88)*

curriculum-based assessment (CBA) *(p. 86)*

diagnostic teaching *(p. 89)*

diagnostic tests *(p. 91)*

discrepancy score *(p. 76)*

dynamic assessment *(p. 66)*

eligibility criteria *(p. 99)*

formal standardized tests *(p. 89)*

individualized education program (IEP) *(p. 68)*

informal assessment measures *(p. 85)*

instruction stages *(p. 74)*

mediation *(p. 71)*

multidisciplinary evaluation *(p. 72)*

norm-referenced tests *(p. 88)*

observation *(p. 82)*

parents' rights *(p. 69)*

performance assessment *(p. 66)*

portfolio assessment *(p. 66)*

prereferral activities *(p. 70)*

present levels of developmental and educational performance *(p. 75)*

procedural safeguards *(p. 69)*

rating scales *(p. 84)*

reciprocal teaching *(p. 68)*

referral *(p. 72)*

referral stages *(p. 69)*

short-term objectives *(p. 73)*

traditional assessment *(p. 65)*

4 Clinical Teaching

CHAPTER OUTLINE

This chapter reviews the teaching portions of the assessment-teaching process. Assessment is only a starting point; the process continues with teaching—a special kind of teaching required to help students with learning disabilities. We call it **clinical teaching**.

The goal of clinical teaching is to tailor learning experiences to the unique needs of a particular student. Using all the information gathered in the assessment, including an analysis of the student's specific learning characteristics, the clinical teacher designs a special teaching program. Assessment does not stop when teaching begins. In fact, the essence of clinical teaching is that assessment and instruction are continuous and interlinked. The clinical teacher modifies the teaching as new needs become apparent.

Many different intervention strategies can be used in clinical teaching. A clinical teacher is a "child watcher." Instead of concentrating solely on what the student *cannot* do, the teacher observes in detail what the student *does* do. For example, by observing the kinds of errors a students makes, the clinical teacher can obtain much information about the student, such as the student's current level of development, way of thinking, or underlying language system. A student's oral reading errors can furnish insight into the student's way of thinking.

Clinical teaching can also be seen as an alternating test-teach-test process, with the teacher alternating roles as tester and teacher. First the student is tested; a unit of work based on the resulting information is then taught. After teaching, the student is again tested to determine what has been learned. If the student performs well on the test, the clinical teacher knows that the teaching has been successful and plans for the next step of learning. If the student performs poorly on the test, the teacher must reassess the teaching plan, analyze the errors to try to determine the cause of the failure to learn, and develop a new course of action for teaching.

Clinical teaching, then, implies a concept of and an attitude about teaching. It does not require any one particular instructional system, educational setting, or style of teaching. It can be used by special teachers, by classroom teachers, or in team collaboration. Clinical teaching can also be applied in many settings: a general education classroom, a resource room, a special class, or a one-to-one setting. It can be used with many different intervention strategies or teaching methods. A variety of terms are used to describe this instruction, such as *remediation, intervention, educational therapy, instructional strategies*, or simply *good teaching*; and these terms are often used interchangeably.

CLINICAL TEACHING CYCLE

The clinical teaching process can be viewed as a cycle, with each stage of the process as a point along a circle, as diagrammed in Figure 4.1. The phases of the clinical teaching process are (1) assessment, (2) planning,

CASE EXAMPLE

THE CLINICAL TEACHING APPROACH

- Ann, a third grader, read, "I saw a large white house" as, "I saw a large white horse." A teacher might respond by concluding that Ann is wrong and that her error must be corrected. The clinical teacher, however, would respond by thinking, "That's an interesting error. I wonder what caused that response? What is involved in Ann's approach to learning or her processing of information that caused her to do that?" The teaching that followed would depend on the analysis of this error—whether it is related to a deficiency in visual perception, an inadequate sight vocabulary, poor visual memory, lack of word-attack skills, or too difficult a text. Subsequent teaching and testing would evaluate the analysis.

- John read, "Now he had been caught" as, "Now he had been catched." Again, teaching will depend on whether the clinical teacher analyzes this error as a lack of phonics skills, insufficient attention to word endings, or an underlying difference between the reader and the language used in the text.

- In another area of academic performance, Debby failed the arithmetic story problem in the testing situation. Observation revealed that although Debby could read the words of the story and perform the arithmetic calculations required, she could not visualize the story's setting. She could not picture in her mind's eye the items to be calculated in the arithmetic story problem. The clinical teacher speculated that Debby's arithmetic failures were related to her identified difficulty in spatial orientation and visualization. This hypothesis was supported by the observation that Debby could not remember how to get to school, to the store, or to a friend's house from her home and that she constantly lost her way in the outside hall. In this case, the teaching was directed toward strengthening Debby's visualization skills and her ability to visualize the situation in arithmetic story problems.

- Saul, a high school student, was failing in most of his subjects. He appeared to be uninterested and uninvolved in his school courses. Although his reading word-recognition skills were good, his reading comprehension was very poor. When questioned in class, Saul usually quickly blurted out the first answer he thought of, which was also usually wrong. His impulsive behavior was the same in written work. After carefully observing Saul's behavior and responses, his teacher inferred that Saul did not have a dependable system for learning. He did not know how to become actively involved in the learning task. He responded impulsively because he had not learned how to stop, think, and monitor his responses before answering questions. In short, he lacked learning strategies. The instruction that ensued focused on teaching Saul strategies for learning.

(3) implementation, and (4) evaluation, leading to (5) a modification of the assessment and then to new planning, new forms of implementation, and a continuing cycle of clinical teaching.

Clinical teaching is unique in several ways. First, *it requires flexibility and continual decision making.* Too often curriculum procedures are determined not by the teacher but by the materials being used. The search for

Figure 4.1

The Five Phases of the
Clinical Teaching Cycle

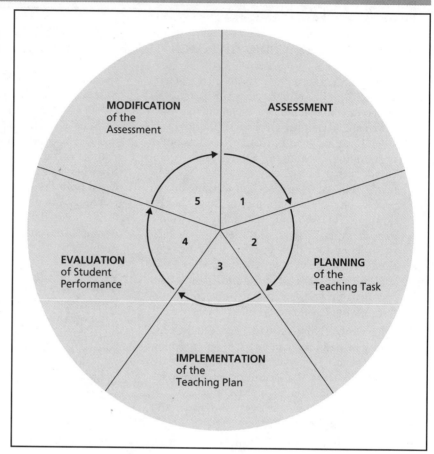

the "perfect" package or materials to teach academic skills can be viewed as an attempt to minimize the teacher's need to make decisions. In most elementary and secondary classes, textbooks dominate instruction, becoming the de facto curriculum (Kameenui, 1991). For example, the basal reader is the predominant instructional tool for teaching reading in 90 to 95 percent of the classrooms across the country; once the reading textbook series has been selected, many of the teaching decisions can be found largely in the reader itself. The textbook has many built-in instructional decisions, with step-by-step and day-by-day directions, a teacher's manual, and workbooks. Thus, in many classes, the textbook structures the curriculum, replacing the teacher as the decision maker. The clinical teacher, however, cannot rely on a textbook.

A second feature of clinical teaching is that *it is planned for a unique student* rather than for an entire class. Curriculum lessons in the regular class are designed for the "average" student. But the *best* method for teaching a class may not be the best method for teaching an individual student with unique behaviors and needs.

A third feature of clinical teaching is that *it can be accomplished in a variety of placements*. The student may be taught within a group or an inclusion setting and by either the general education classroom or the special education teacher. Clinical teaching reflects an attitude on the part of the teacher. What is important is the teacher's ability to interpret feedback information and to be ready to make decisions. Teachers should be sensitive to the individual student's learning style, interests, shortcomings, strengths, levels of development and feelings, and adjustment to the world.

Many critical decisions must be made about what and how to teach. In many respects teaching remains an art. One can never tell where a teacher's influence stops. (Zigmond, 1997; Bateman, 1992).

ECOLOGICAL CONSIDERATIONS

The **ecological system** refers to the various environments within which a person lives and grows. The environments of the home, the school, the social group, and the culture influence a student's desire and ability to learn. Learning competencies depend on positive interactions with the various environments. Recognizing the effects of the ecological system, realizing that learning, attitudes, and progress depend on positive interactions with the various environments, is an important feature of clinical teaching.

Home Environment

The home is the child's first environment. The child's home experiences during the first five or six years influence cognitive development and lay the foundation for later school performance. As the child's first teachers, parents can provide intellectual stimulation and emotional well-being. The development of self-concept, self-esteem, interest in literacy, and a curiosity about learning all depend on the support and encouragement parents provide within the home. Parents become role models for their child, and when their child experiences school difficulties, a supportive family relationship becomes especially important. A dysfunctional home environment contributes to school problems. The child's learning disabilities also have an impact on members of the family (Turnbull & Turnbull, 1996).

School Environment

A substantial portion of a student's day is spent in school, and school experiences exert dramatic effects. An integral part of the school experience is the student's relationships with peers and with school personnel (including teachers, aides, administrators, office personnel, and maintenance staff). The school environment encompasses more than teaching and learning academic subject matter. In addition to the academic curriculum, students must cope with a "hidden curriculum" of expected values and behaviors. They must learn complex rules for participating in a classroom, such as learning how to be recognized and how to demonstrate what they know.

Many students with learning disabilities not only encounter academic difficulty but often have problems acquiring appropriate school behaviors. They often have unsatisfactory relationships with teachers and classmates in the school environment, receive much less praise and acknowledgment for their efforts, and are more likely to be criticized, shown disapproval, and even ignored (Brooks, 1997; Haager & Vaughn, 1995; Vaughn, Zaragoza, Hogan, & Walker, 1993). Teachers who are sensitive to how such negative factors can discourage learning can take measures to provide a nurturing school atmosphere. (See Chapter 14.)

Social Environment

A student's social environment also has significant consequences. Everyone needs mutually satisfying relationships with friends. Friendships serve as the basis for further social growth and provide opportunities to build confidence in the social realm. Children who develop normally in the social sphere learn social skills in a casual and informal manner, assimilating through incidental experiences appropriate ways of acting with people.

For many students with learning disabilities, however, the social environment becomes another sphere of dismal failure. Often they are not socially perceptive or adept at discerning the nuances of everyday living. They are unaware of how their actions affect others and how their behavior is interpreted. Their unsatisfying social experiences, in turn, can adversely affect school learning. Many of the characteristics that underlie academic learning disabilities also create the disability in the social sphere (Schumaker & Deshler, 1995; Condermon, 1995; Bryan, Sullivan-Burnstein, & Mathur, 1998; Brooks, 1997; Haager & Vaughn, 1995). Strategies for helping students with learning disabilities to cope with social problems and nonverbal learning disabilities are further discussed in Chapter 14. See also the case example entitled "Learning Disabilities in the Social Environment."

Cultural and Linguistic Environment

In today's pluralistic society, the student's cultural and language environment is an extremely critical consideration. Our nation's school population consists of students from many different ethnic, language, and cultural populations. One of our nation's greatest challenges is to educate all students regardless of culture, geographic origin, socioeconomic status, or native language. In some cases, students discern a conflict between the traditional values of the school they attend and the values of their culture. For students

Mutually satisfying friend-ships serve as the basis for further social growth and provide opportunities to build confidence in the so-cial realm *(© James Carrol)*

with learning disabilities, problems stemming from disabilities are com-pounded by dimensions of the student's cultural system (Ortiz, 1997; Bos & Fletcher, 1997).

Understanding the student's culture and language background is essen-tial for effective teaching, and teachers should appreciate the unique contri-butions of each culture. By the time children enter school, they have already absorbed many of the values and behaviors of the culture in which they were raised, which have major ramifications for school success. The child's language is one obvious consideration. If the school expects all children to be fluent in English, students from families that speak another language will be at a disadvantage. Another consideration is that many schools ex-pect students to work independently and to compete for grades and recog-nition. This expectation will be in conflict with the attitudes of cultures in which cooperation and peer orientation are valued more than the qualities of independence and competitiveness. A similar assumption—that students should do their own work and that helping others is cheating—may also produce conflicts if the culture of the students makes them less willing to compete and more interested in cooperating with their peers (Ortiz, 1997; Artiles & Trent, 1997; Cummins, 1996; Moll & Gonzalez, 1994).

CASE EXAMPLE

LEARNING DISABILITIES IN THE SOCIAL ENVIRONMENT

Betsy is a first grader who encountered difficulty in the social environment (Osman, 1979). Betsy had trouble both understanding verbal communication and talking to her classmates. She hugged and touched every prospective friend until the classmate backed away. She made connections with people by feeling and touching—a behavior characteristic of much younger children. When Betsy liked someone, she wanted to show it and did so by hugging, kissing, and grabbing. The other first graders were able to play together and convey thoughts to each other by talking. They did not need to touch to feel liked, and they thought Betsy was strange. When Betsy sensed the other children's rejection, she became even more possessive. The more she was rebuffed, the more she tried to make a friend—the wrong way. By age seven, Betsy expected to be rebuffed by her classmates and unconsciously provoked them. She would ask, "Do you like me?" at inappropriate times, inviting a negative response. Because of her complaints of mistreatment at the school bus stop, Betsy's mother drove her to school. This provoked taunts from the other children, which she hated. Eventually, her claim that "nobody likes me" was based more on reality than on Betsy's imagination.

Teachers can create an atmosphere that builds on cultural and linguistic diversity in the following ways:

- Select activities that help students become aware of the contributions specific cultural and linguistic groups have made to North America, the United States, and to the world
- Encourage students to demonstrate culture-specific knowledge and skills
- Help students develop a sense of identity and pride by acquainting them with accomplishments of eminent and successful people who share their cultural or linguistic background
- Use cooperative teaching methods for a portion of the day to encourage peer cooperative learning
- Use activities that explore cultural differences in perceptions, beliefs, and values

A CLASSIFICATION OF TEACHING METHODS

Remember that old high school cheer?

"Slant to the left. Slant to the right. Stand up, sit down, fight, fight, fight." This cheer applies to the pendulum effect we witness in teaching methods. One method is popular for the moment, only to be replaced by a new method that comes into vogue.

In this section we try to sort out the confusing array of recommended instructional methods by suggesting a classification model of teaching methods. Figure 4.2 classifies the many teaching methods within three types: analysis of (1) the student, (2) the curriculum (or content) to be learned,

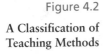

Figure 4.2

A Classification of
Teaching Methods

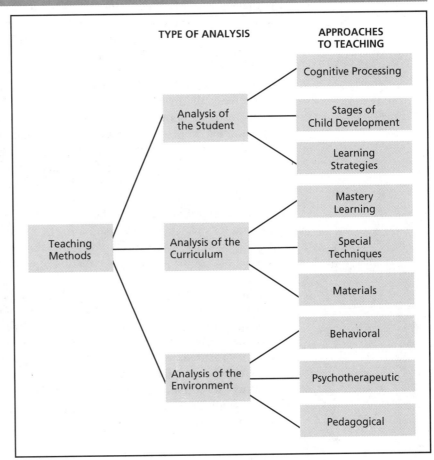

and (3) the environment in which the learning occurs. Each type of analysis is further subdivided into three specific methods of teaching, making a total of nine methods. Each method has merit as well as certain limitations and shortcomings. In the following discussion, each method is briefly examined, along with some criticisms of it. (These methods and the theories underlying them are also discussed in Chapter 6 and in the curriculum areas throughout Part IV.)

Analysis of the Student

The first three methods of teaching concentrate on an analysis of the student and how the student functions as a learner.

Cognitive Processing Approaches   **Cognitive processing** refers to the mental processes involved with learning and thinking. The underlying premise is that deficits in certain mental operations are related to difficulties in learning. Furthermore, in planning for instruction, it is useful to consider the student's cognitive processing abilities and disabilities. In the field of learning disabilities, views about cognitive processing have expanded over the years, going from the early approach of psychological processing disorders to the contemporary views stemming from cognitive psychology.

As with all the methods of teaching, cognitive processing methods should be used along with other approaches to teaching. Teachers must understand the scope and sequence of curriculum and be familiar with developmental and behavioral models of instruction. For example, Jeff's teacher may use direct instruction to teach phonics to Jeff. But because his teacher is well aware of Jeff's difficulty with auditory processing and perception, she will be attuned to the difficulty Jeff has in perceiving certain sounds and will make accommodations in her teaching. In general, the closer the teaching is to the academic work, the more effective it is likely to be. For example, the teaching of visual discrimination of letters is more closely related to reading than is the visual discrimination of geometric shapes.

Psychological Processing Disorders   Early in the development of the field of learning disabilities, the emphasis was on children's **psychological processing disorders**—on the mental processes of perception and perceptual disorders (visual, auditory, tactile, and kinesthetic perception). Teaching methods focused on (1) *strengthening the cognitive deficits* (for example, students who had deficits in auditory perception would receive training in auditory perception), (2) *teaching through the student's processing strengths* (for example, if students had strengths in visual processing, a method of teaching that capitalized on those strengths would be selected), or (3) *doing both* (the teacher would build the deficit area while also teaching through the strengths) (see Chapter 6).

The concepts embodied in the notion of psychological processing disorders became an integral part of the field of learning disabilities. In fact, the current definition of learning disabilities in federal law (IDEA 1997) contains the phrase *psychological processing disorders*. The concepts underlying psychological processing continue to be useful, and the idea remains a cornerstone of the field of learning disabilities.

Cognitive Psychology   **Cognitive psychology** provides a more comprehensive and elaborate notion of the relationship between cognitive processing and learning disabilities.

It is defined as a scientific endeavor to "understand the nature of human intelligence and how people think" (Anderson, 1990, p. 1). In applying the theories of cognitive psychology to learning disabilities, cognitive psychology looks at higher-level mental processes such as attention, language, problem solving, memory, information processing, and higher-order thinking (Torgesen, 1993; Stanovich, 1993). In terms of teaching, the procedures focus on (1) determining the mental processes needed for learning, (2) identifying the specific mental processes needed for school learning, and (3) providing the link between these mental processes and teaching methods. (Deshler, Ellis, & Lenz, 1996). Teaching methods involve strengthening memory and attention, strengthening phonological awareness, developing thinking skills, and linking new information to what the student already knows.

An understanding of the concept of cognitive processing and of the child's strengths and weaknesses in various mental operations is useful in evaluating the student's learning problems and in planning for teaching. Theories of cognitive processing are discussed further in Chapter 6.

Stages of Child Development Approach   In the **stages of child development** approach to teaching, the teacher analyzes the student in terms of a specific sequence of stages of normal development, such as Piaget's developmental stages (see Chapter 6). In this approach, the teaching begins at the lowest unaccomplished stage in the sequence. Once skills at this stage are learned, the instruction moves on to the next sequential stage.

This approach implies that schools should not create learning problems by pushing children to learn tasks for which they are not ready. It is important to know the stages of human development and the stage at which an individual child is functioning. Sensitive teaching helps the child move from one stage to the next. (See Chapters 6 and 8.)

An interactive developmental model is proposed by Levine et al. (1993). This model emphasizes the multidimensional mechanism underlying learning disabilities; that is, one must consider many interacting developmental elements when assessing a child's learning disabilities.

The stages of child development approach has been criticized by those who point out that with students with learning disabilities, we must do more than simply wait until children mature. Intervention and direct instruction may be necessary to help the child's abilities develop and emerge.

Learning Strategies Approach   **Learning strategies** offer another **approach** to teaching by analyzing how students with learning disabilities go about learning, remembering, solving problems, and understanding. Students with learning disabilities tend to be inefficient learners because they lack systematic ways of learning, remembering, or directing their learning. These students do not know the secrets of being a successful student: how to study, how to integrate new material with what they already know, how to monitor their learning and problem solving, how to remember, or how to predict what is going to happen. (U.S. Department of Education, 1997).

A *learning strategy* is defined as an individual's approach to a task when it includes how a person thinks and acts when planning, executing, and evaluating performance on a task and its outcomes. The learning strategies approach to teaching students with learning disabilities includes both cognitive (relating to thinking processes) and behavioral (relating to overt actions) elements that guide student planning, performance, and evaluation of strategy engagement (Lenz, Ellis, & Scanlon, 1996; Deshler, Ellis, & Lenz, 1996).

Students with learning disabilities need instruction in learning strategies. They need to learn to direct and control their own learning and to generalize those strategies to areas of the curriculum, such as reading, spelling, and mathematics (Rosenshine, 1997; Harris & Pressly, 1991; Deshler, Ellis, & Lenz, 1996).

The goal of learning strategy instruction is to teach strategies in a manner that is effective (i.e., the strategy is learned and generalized by the student) and efficient (i.e., the strategy is learned to an optimal level with a minimum amount of effort by both the teacher and the student) (Lenz et al., 1996). Learning strategies instruction is also discussed in Chapters 6, 8, and 11.

Analysis of the Curriculum

The next three methods for teaching analyze the content to be learned, rather than the student who is learning.

Mastery Learning Approach   A useful teaching method that analyzes the content to be learned is the **mastery learning approach**. This perspective presumes that the student must learn each of a sequence of skills in order to learn a task. Learning each skill of a task is likened to climbing the rungs on a ladder. Each rung must be touched in climbing to the top; the learner who misses some rungs may fall off.

The steps of the mastery learning approach are as follows. First, a sequence of skills in a subject area (reading, arithmetic, spelling, and so forth) is established. The teacher attempts to determine how far the student has gone along that sequence, what the student does not know within the sequence, and where in the sequence teaching should begin. The skill of reading, for example, is analyzed as consisting of many skills and subskills; by mastering the component subskills, the student should master the skill of reading. Teachers using this approach must have a thorough understanding of the **skills sequence** in each subject area.

Critics of the mastery learning approach question the premise that a student must acquire each specific subskill to learn a task or subject. They suggest that learning occurs in a more holistic fashion and that it is counterproductive to insist that a child learn each subskill. For example, proponents of "whole-language" reading instruction argue that learning occurs in a holistic rather than in a step-by-step fashion (Goodman, 1992; Richek, Caldwell, Jennings, & Lerner, 1996).

Special Techniques Approach   Unlike the usual developmental methods used in the regular classroom, the special techniques approach offers a highly differentiated way of teaching. A special teaching technique is sometimes named after the originator or the popularizer of the approach (for example, the *Orton-Gillingham method* or the *Fernald method*). The special technique sometimes has an esoteric or vaguely medical name (such as the *neurological impress method*). Special techniques usually use explicit direct instruction. These special methods are often used as remedial methods for one-to-one use.

Since most research compares the effects of methods on large groups, it is difficult to know if any one method has been the best for an individual student. Some of the special techniques are described in the discussion of reading in Chapter 11.

Materials Approach   Publishers' materials become the basis of yet another approach to teaching in that the materials guide and direct the teaching. The basic decision facing teachers using this approach is the choice of materials. Once that choice is made, the materials themselves, not the teachers, become the decision makers. The materials give step-by-step procedures, select the skills to be taught, provide practice activities, and give the questions to be asked. **Basal readers** are often used (or misused) in this way.

Such reliance on materials lessens the teacher's role. As noted earlier in this chapter, clinical teaching requires constant and active decision making. The danger for teachers who follow the materials approach is that they may become educational clerks, allowing materials to dictate what is to be taught and how.

Nevertheless, if they are not misused, publishers' materials can prove to be a valuable tool for instruction. Certainly, teachers should be familiar with a wide variety of materials.

Analysis of the Environment

The next three methods of instruction are based on the analysis of the environmental conditions in which the learning occurs.

Behavioral Approach   The **behavioral approach** to teaching concentrates on the environmental conditions surrounding the learning. Using principles of reinforcement theory and operant conditioning, behavioral management methods are intended to eliminate undesired behaviors and to establish specific desired behaviors. As discussed in Chapters 6 and 14, a premise of behavioral theory is that if a response is rewarded (reinforced) when it occurs, it will tend to be repeated. Behavioral management focuses on three components known as *ABC*: the *antecedent event* (stimulus), the ***target behavior*** (the behavior to be changed), and the *consequent event* (response or reinforcement). (These are illustrated in Figure 6.1.) The antecent or stimulus and the consequent event (or reinforcement) are environmental events that can be modified to bring about the desired target behavior. Little effort is spent trying to analyze underlying causes of the student's learning disability or the student's cognitive processes. Instead, the emphasis is on finding ways to change learning behavior by modifying the environment.

The behavioral approach to teaching students with learning disabilities uses reinforcements to improve the student's performance. The success of the behavioral method is demonstrated through continuous measurement, or graphing, or by giving points or reinforcements to show the measurable changes in the learning behavior. (See Figure 14.2.)

The field of learning disabilities benefited tremendously from the contributions of behavioral methods to teaching. Certainly, skill in behavior management should be among the competencies of all learning disabilities specialists (Alberto & Troutman, 1998).

The behavioral approach is criticized for its excessive focus on specific skills and its failure to consider more holistic styles of learning. Some teachers find fault with the practical applications of behavioral management, complaining that time does not permit the careful recording and monitoring that the method requires (Kohn, 1993).

Psychotherapeutic Approach   The **psychotherapeutic approach** to teaching concentrates on the student's feelings (or **affect**) and relationship with the teacher. The psychodynamics of learning are too often lost in the labyrinth of materials, techniques, methods, cognitive processing, and baseline measurement. Failing students are unhappy in the learning situation. Their frustrations, poor ego development, and feelings of inadequacy all lead to continued failure in learning. What is needed, this approach suggests, is a reversal of this downward cycle of failure by building feelings of success and establishing a healthy psychodynamic relationship between teacher and student.

Research demonstrates that when students with learning disabilities develop a positive affect, they improve academically (Yasutake & Bryan, 1995). Even if a child is well adjusted when entering school, continued failure in school learning is likely to have unfavorable effects. As the pupil grows older, these feelings of failure, frustration, and oversensitivity tend to increase. By the time the student reaches adolescence, emotional problems are almost always in evidence.

The goal of this approach is to rebuild self-concept, foster hope and assurance, and let students know that the teacher understands the problem and has confidence in their ability to learn and succeed. The emphasis is on providing appropriate environmental conditions to improve the students' self-confidence and establish a healthy relationship with the teacher.

There are many reported cases of dramatic improvement in academic learning after a student has worked with a tutor who was untrained in the sophisticated skills and knowledge of the learning disabilities profession yet was able to establish a point of meaningful contact with the student. Specific techniques for building self-esteem and self-confidence are presented later in this chapter and in Chapter 14.

Like the other approaches considered here, the psychotherapeutic approach to teaching has its critics. Despite the obvious need for considering psychodynamic factors, critics charge that *exclusive* use of this approach may result in the creation of "happy failures," students who have learned to be content with their academic failure.

Pedagogical Approach   The last method of teaching uses the old-fashioned term **pedagogy**, which means simply the art of teaching. One specialist observed that the major cause of reading failure is *dyspedagogia*, a term coined to indicate a lack of good teaching (Cohen, 1971). If poor teaching causes failure, it follows that good instruction promotes successful learning. In fact, research consistently shows that the teacher is the most important variable in a pupil's learning. The most significant factor is not the materials or the methods but the teacher. Despite this consistent finding that the teacher is the key ingredient for successful learning, we are not certain what qualities a successful teacher possesses. Is the most important quality empathy, kindness, ability to structure the class, enthusiasm, creativity, flexibility, ability to individualize instruction, consistency, knowledge of the field, love of children, assessment skills, familiarity with materials, competency in specific skills, or clinical intuition? Or is good teaching possibly a judicious combination of all these qualities?

Research findings on effective teachers are inconclusive. Without a precise understanding of the qualities that make up the good teacher, the plea for "good teaching," although obviously important, does not offer *the* answer.

Implications of the Classification System

The classification system just presented consists of three types of analysis and nine methods of teaching. In practice, these methods are not mutually exclusive, and effective teachers use several concurrently. Each method of teaching has strong support and contributes to the total teaching system. Each method is also vulnerable to criticism. Teachers must have some knowledge, skill, and expertise in each method but must also recognize the shortcomings and limitations of each.

Teachers should not be overdependent on a single approach to teaching. Such a flaw is exemplified in the box entitled "A Fable for Teachers." The point of the fable is that each student is different and that no one method can be relied on as the "best" way for teaching in every case. Learning disabilities cannot be corrected or "cured" by a specific teaching method or training technique. There is no magic formula for teaching children with these problems. Teachers should have a wide range of instructional materials and techniques at their disposal and be imaginative and flexible enough to adapt them to the particular needs of each student.

CONTROLLING THE INSTRUCTIONAL VARIABLES

The teacher and the school can do relatively little about many factors related to learning disabilities. The home environment or the genetic or biological makeup of the student may be key elements contributing to the learning problem, but usually such variables cannot be modified by the teacher. Other factors that can be changed by teachers should receive careful consideration. Variables in learning that can be readjusted by teachers include the difficulty level, space, time, language, and interpersonal relationship between pupil and teacher.

A FABLE FOR TEACHERS

Once upon a time the animals decided they must do something educational to help their young meet the problems of the world. A school was organized where they adopted a curriculum consisting of running, climbing, and swimming. To make it easier to administer, all of the animals took all the subjects. Of course, the duck was excellent in swimming—in fact, he was better than the instructor; running, however, was a weak area for him. Therefore, he had to stay after school and drop swimming in order to practice running. Now, this was kept up until his webbed feet were badly worn, and soon he became only average in swimming. However, average was an acceptable criterion in this school, so no one was concerned about it—except, of course, the duck. While the rabbit was good in running, he was not up to par in swimming and suffered a nervous breakdown because of the makeup work required to improve his swimming. By the end of the year, an abnormal eel that could swim exceedingly well and also run and climb had the overall highest average and was consequently named valedictorian of the class.

Source: From "A Fable for Teachers," 1974, *Reading Today International, 3*(2), p. 1.

Difficulty Level

The *difficulty level* of material can be modified to meet a student's present performance and tolerance levels. The concept of **readiness** applies here, as well as Vygotsky's notion of the **zone of proximal development (ZPD)** (Vygotsky, 1962). (See Chapter 6.) Many students are failing tasks simply because the tasks are too difficult and the required level of performance is far beyond their present ability. Expecting a student to perform a task far beyond tolerance level can result in a complete breakdown in learning.

Another factor to be considered is the *sequential skills* of the subject area. Certain tasks normally precede others. Students who have not acquired oral language will probably do poorly in the written tasks of reading and writing. Students who have not learned addition cannot be expected to succeed in multiplication.

Many skills or responses must be overlearned so that they become automatic. If skills are to be used in or transferred to new situations, they must be internalized. This internalization permits a shift from the conscious, cognitive level to the automatic response (or habitual) level. For example, in reading, the student initially may use phonic skills in a conscious, deliberate way to decode words; later, the process should become automatic for effective reading.

Space

Space refers to the physical setting, which should be conducive to learning. Among the ways to modify space are using partitions, cubicles, screens, special rooms, and quiet corners and removing distracting stimuli. Space also involves the student's work area, such as the size of the paper and the desk surface. The school environment should not be a distraction from learning.

The goal of space control is to slowly increase the amount of space with which the student must contend. Gradually, students must internalize their own controls so that they can get along in an unmodified space environment.

Time

There are a number of ways to control *time* in the teaching setting. Lessons for students with a very short attention span can be limited so that they can be completed in less time. For example, one row of mathematics problems can be assigned instead of an entire page. The work page can be cut into squares or strips to shorten the time required to complete one section. Fewer spelling words can be given to learn. In timed exercises, the allotted time can be increased. Time can be broken into shorter units by varying the types of activity so that quiet activities are followed by livelier ones. Planned activity changes, such as having the student come to the teacher's desk or walk to a shelf to get supplies, can be useful breaks during long lessons. Homework assignments can be shortened. The goal is to gradually increase the time that the student works on a task.

Language

Language can also be modified to enhance student learning. To ensure that language clarifies rather than confuses, teachers should examine the wording of their directions. The language should match the student's level of understanding. For students with severe disabilities, the language quantity must be reduced to the simplest statements. Techniques to simplify language include reducing directions to "telegraphic speech," or using only essential words; maintaining visual contact with the learner; avoiding ambiguous words and emphasizing meaning with gesture; speaking in a slow tempo; touching the student before talking; and avoiding complex sentence structure, particularly negative constructions.

The Interpersonal Relationship

The *interpersonal relationship factor*, or the **rapport** between the pupil and teacher, is of paramount importance. Without it, learning is not likely to take place; with it, learning frequently occurs in spite of inappropriate techniques and materials or other shortcomings. The importance of the pupil-teacher relationship is discussed in the next section in the context of building self-esteem and motivation.

BUILDING SELF-ESTEEM AND MOTIVATION

Clinical teaching requires an affirming teacher-pupil relationship. Although effective teaching requires objectivity and a thorough knowledge of curriculum, skills, and methods, it also requires a subjective understanding of the pupil as a whole individual with feelings, emotions, and attitudes (Brooks, 1991, 1997). Students with learning disabilities often feel lost and frightened because they have suffered years of despair, discouragement, and frustration. Feelings of rejection, failure, and hopelessness about the future are always present, affecting every subject in school and every aspect of the student's life:

> For twelve long years of school and after, he contends with a situation for which he can find no satisfactory solution. When schoolwork becomes insurmountable, the child has few alternative resources. An adult dissatisfied with his job may seek a position elsewhere or find solace outside of his work; he may even endure these difficulties because of a high salary or other compensations. For a child who fails, however, there is no escape. He is subjected to anything from degradation to long-suffering tolerance. Optimum conditions may lessen the child's misery, but proof of his inadequacies appears daily in the classroom. In the end, he is held in low esteem, not only by his classmates, but also by his family. (Roswell & Natchez, 1977, p. 2)

Teachers should realize that learning disabilities may influence every aspect of the student's world. It is important to recognize the emotional impact of failure on the student. Not only are parents and teachers displeased with the child, but the parent's anxiety often becomes uncontrollable. The parents wonder whether their child is retarded or just plain lazy. If they are assured that his or her intelligence is normal, even the most loving parents can become so alarmed at their child's inability to learn that they tend to punish, scold and threaten, or even reward with the hope of producing desired results. Teachers also feel frustrated by their inability to reach the child.

The child tries his or her best to function under these adverse conditions. Then, when failure continues, the child can become overwhelmed and devastated. These feelings linger after school and on weekends. The notion that he or she does not measure up hangs over him relentlessly.

An important responsibility for the clinical teacher, therefore, is to motivate students who have been failing, to build their self-concept and **self-esteem**, and to interest them in learning. Success in learning has a beneficial effect on personality, enhances feelings of self-worth, and rekindles an interest in learning. Such teaching can be considered therapeutic (Brooks, 1991, 1997). The following principles offer guidelines for therapeutic teaching.

Rapport

A good relationship between the teacher and student is an essential first step in clinical teaching. Much of the success in clinical teaching depends on the establishment of such rapport. The teacher must accept the pupil as a human being worthy of respect in spite of a failure to learn. A healthy relationship implies compassion without overinvolvement, understanding without indulgence, and a genuine concern for the student's development. Because the student lives in a continuing atmosphere of rejection and failure, the relationship with the clinical teacher should provide a new atmosphere of confidence and acceptance. It is extremely difficult for a parent to retain an accepting yet objective attitude, and the student becomes very sensitive to the parent's disappointment. Parents are often unaware of their child's reaction to their efforts. For example, one well-intentioned father, observed in a public library helping his son pick out a book and listening to him read, was overheard saying, "I'll tell you that word one more time, and then I don't want you to forget it for the rest of your life." This is not an attitude that is conducive to learning.

Shared Responsibility

Involvement of both the student and the teacher is another factor in clinical teaching. Students should participate in both the analysis of their problems and the evaluation of their performance. In the same collaborative spirit, the student should take an active role in designing lessons and choosing materials.

Structure

Providing structure and establishing routines are important factors for introducing order into the chaotic lives of students with learning disabilities. Many students need and welcome such order. Structure and routine can be provided in many aspects of teaching—in the physical environment, in the sequence of activities, and in the manner in which lessons are taught.

Sincerity

Students are skillful in detecting insincerity, and they will soon detect dishonesty if a teacher tells them they are doing well when they know otherwise. Instead, the teacher might try to minimize anxiety about errors by saying that many students have similar difficulties and by conveying confidence that together they will find ways to overcome them.

Success

"Life is not so much a matter of holding good cards, but sometimes of playing a poor hand well." This pithy observation was made by Robert Lewis Stevenson (cited in Katz, 1997), and it aptly applies to individuals with learning disabilities. Many students and adults with learning disabilities achieve success by understanding the nature of their learning problems and learning to use their strengths.

Achieving goals in learning and acquiring a feeling of success are of paramount importance. Lessons must be designed and materials selected to permit students to experience success. For example, the teacher can obtain books at the reading level that meets the student's areas of interest. In addition to selecting the appropriate level of difficulty of teaching materials, the teacher can make students conscious of their success and progress by praising good work, by using extrinsic rewards as reinforcement, and by developing visual records of progress through charts and graphs.

Interest

The chance of successful achievement increases when a teacher provides materials based on the student's special interests. Student interests can be determined through conversations with the pupil or by administering interest inventories. Using materials in the student's area of interest gives the student a strong motivation to learn.

Students have diverse reading interests that include sports, adventure and action, history, science, stories about people, mysteries, and humor. Teachers can develop valuable reading lessons from materials that students have an interest in—*TV Guide*, newspapers, baseball and football programs, record jackets, popular magazines, and even computer manuals. The first real interest in reading shown by some high school students is stimulated by the necessity of passing a written test in order to get a driver's license. Engaging this interest, some teachers have successfully used the driver's manual to teach reading. A favorite author or series books have been the impetus for other youngsters to become readers.

Once a real interest has been tapped, students often make great strides. Antonio, an eighth-grade boy with learning disabilities, found the first book he ever read from cover to cover, *The Incredible Journey,* so fascinating that he was completely oblivious to class changes, ringing bells, and classroom incidents from the time he started the book until he completed it. Maria developed an interest in successful women, who had in her words "made it." Her teacher helped her find many books and articles that related stories of successful women in many fields. Her reading improved dramatically after she read these materials. Dave had a keen interest in the Chicago Bulls basketball team. His teacher helped him find newspaper stories about the games and biographies of the players. His interest led him to read more, and his reading improved. Sometimes a television show or a movie based on a

Acceptance and self-respect are important to any student's self-esteem and motivation. *(© Jeffrey W. Myers/FPG International)*

book can spark an interest. After seeing a television show about *Robinson Crusoe*, Juan, who had severe reading problems, was introduced to a simplified version of this book. His teacher reported that he became so immersed in the story that he would grab the book as soon as he entered the room for their daily session. Fairy tales have great appeal for many children, and primary teachers are aware of the sheer delight and excitement of children when they read a simple version of the classic themes in their reading books.

Once in a while, dramatic changes occur in a student's attitude and outlook because of clinical teaching. When such a change occurs because of a book the child has read, it is sometimes called **bibliotherapy**. Learning about the experiences of others can foster release and insight as well as hope and encouragement. Students with personal problems (for example, children who are short, overweight, or unpopular, or who have physical or academic disabilities) identify with book characters who suffer similar problems. Such students can be helped by the characters' resolution of their problems.

Peter, a seventh-grade student with learning disabilities, identified with Houdini, the great escape artist. He read all the books he could find on

Houdini in the school library and in the public library. During this period, Peter's teachers observed personality and attitude changes as well as tremendous improvement in his reading.

The right book can be a powerful tool to build interest, provide motivation, and improve academic learning.

CURRENT TRENDS FOR INSTRUCTION

In this section, we will examine some of the emerging trends in instruction for students with learning disabilities. The intervention topics include accommodating students with learning disabilities in general education classrooms, effective teaching practices, promoting active learning, reciprocal teaching, learning strategies instruction, and collaborative practices.

Accommodations for Students with Learning Disabilities in the Regular Education Classroom

Most students with learning disabilities (81 percent) spend at least a portion of their school day in general education classrooms. About 42 percent of these students have full placement in the general education class, while 39 percent are in resource rooms for a portion of the day and in the general education class for the rest of the day. (U.S. Department of Education, 1998).

In addition, accommodations in general education classrooms must be made for students identified under Section 504 of the Rehabilitation Act. These students have disabilities that "limit one or more of life's major activities," but they are not eligible for special education under the school's criteria for eligibility. Many of the Section 504 students have attention deficit disorders. For students identified under Section 504, "**reasonable accommodations**" must be made in general education classrooms.

Most of the states now have accommodation guidelines. The most frequently used accommodations for assessment are classified as the following (U.S. Department of Education, 1997):

- *Modifying the setting* (taking a test in a separate room, a carrel, or small group)
- *Modifying the scheduling* (extended time, breaks during testing, or testing on certain days)
- *Modifying the presentation* (using large print, giving verbal instead of written directions, or tape-recording directions)
- *Modifying responses* (students responding via computer-generated or scribe-recorded answers, pointing to answers or marking in booklets instead of on answer sheets)

The general education teacher has much of the responsibility for teaching the increasing number of students with learning disabilities and Section 504 students in her or his classroom. An essential support to meet this responsibility is *collaboration*, a well-planned and coordinated effort between regular and special education teachers (Fuchs & Fuchs, 1998; Idal, 1997; Monda-Amaya, Dieker, & Reed, 1998; Friend & Cook, 1996). (The topic of collaboration between general and special educators is discussed in Chapter 5.)

Ways that classroom teachers can modify the classroom and their instruction include (Lerner, Lowenthal, & Lerner, 1995):

Improving Organizational Skills   Difficulty in organizing their lives is characteristic of children with learning disabilities. The lack of organization results in incomplete assignments. These students need to learn how to plan ahead, how to gather appropriate materials for school tasks, how to prioritize the steps to complete an assignment, and how to keep track of their work. The following are some steps to help students organize.

- Provide clear routines for placing objects—especially regularly used objects such as books, assignments, and outdoor clothes—in designated places so they can be found easily.
- Provide the students with a list of materials needed for a task. Limit the list to only those materials necessary to complete the task.
- Provide a schedule so that the student knows exactly what to do for each class period.
- Make sure the students have all homework assignments before leaving school. Write each assignment on the board and have the students copy it. Or write the assignment for a student in a pocket notebook.
- Provide students with pocket folders to organize materials. For example, place new work on one side and completed work in chronological order on the other.
- Use a different color folder for each subject.

Increasing Attention   A short attention span is another characteristic of students with learning disabilities. These students may initially be attentive, but their attention soon wanders. The following activities will help students attend and prolong their concentration (Lerner et al., 1995).

- Shorten the task by breaking a long task into smaller parts. Assign fewer problems—for example, fewer spelling words or mathematics problems.
- Shorten homework assignments by giving fewer problems.
- Use distributed practice. Instead of a few long and concentrated practice sessions, set up more short, spaced, and frequent practice sessions.
- Make tasks more interesting to keep the student's interest. Encourage children to work with partners, in small groups, or in interest centers.
- Alternate highly interesting and less interesting tasks.
- Increase the novelty of the task. Tasks that are new or unique are more appealing and will increase attention.

Improving the Ability to Listen We erroneously assume that students know how to listen. Students with learning disabilities frequently miss important instructions and information because they are not actively listening. They may even be unaware that a message is being given. Teachers expect students not just to hear or recognize the words that are spoken, but also to comprehend the message. The following strategies can help students acquire better listening skills.

- Make instruction simple by using short, direct sentences. Give one instruction at a time. Repeat it as often as necessary. Make sure the student knows all the vocabulary being used.

- Prompt the student to repeat instructions after listening to them. Later, have the students repeat to themselves information they have just heard to build listening and memory skills.

- Alert the student by using key phrases—for example, "This is important," "Listen carefully," or "This will be on the exam." Some teachers use prearranged signals, such as hand signals or switching the lights on or off before giving directions.

- Use visual aids (such as charts, pictures, graphics, key points on a chalkboard, or overhead transparencies) to illustrate and support verbal information.

Adapting the Curriculum Often the teacher can change, modify, or adapt the curriculum without sacrificing its basic integrity. Even a small change can be beneficial for the student.

- Select high-interest materials to reinforce the basic curriculum. Use manipulatives, or hands-on materials, whenever possible. Create activities that require active participation, such as talking through problems and acting out steps. Many students learn better when they actually do something in addition to just listening and observing.

- Use visual aids to supplement oral and written information. Use learning aids such as computers, calculators, and tape recordings to increase motivation.

- Modify tests, allowing the student to take tests orally instead of writing the answers. Teach students how to cross out incorrect answers on multiple-choice tests.

Helping Students Manage Time Managing time is a common problem area for many students with learning disabilities. They get pulled away from the task at hand and become involved with new challenges. They become procrastinators, a trait they retain into their adult lives. The following activities are designed to help students with time management.

- The How I Spend My Time chart (Figure 4.3) can be kept by the student to develop a sense of time and what must be accomplished in a

Figure 4.3

How I Spend My Time

NAME					DATE		
ACTIVITY	Monday	Tuesday	Wednesday	Thursday	Friday	Sat	Sun
Classes							
Studying							
Social							
Television							
Exercising							
Working							
Reading							
Sleeping							

given time span. The student can make a spreadsheet, bar chart, or pie chart with a computer to illustrate time use.

■ Set up a specific routine and adhere to it. When disruptions occur, explain the situation to the students as well as appropriate ways to respond.

■ During the school day, alternate activities that are done sitting and those that involve standing and moving about.

■ Make lists that will help students organize their tasks. Have them check off tasks as they complete them.

■ Use behavior contracts that specify the amount of time allotted for specific activities.

Effective Teaching Practices

The *effective teaching studies* are a collection of research investigations about the qualities and characteristics of schools, classrooms, and teachers that produce high-achieving students.

The studies found that effective teachers are academically focused and capable of teaching explicit skills using the following procedures (Rosenshine, 1997; Brophy & Good, 1986; Rosenshine & Stevens, 1986):

■ Begin each lesson with a short review of previous learning.

■ Begin each lesson with a short statement of goals.

■ Present new material in small steps, and provide students with time to practice after each step.

■ Give clear explanations and detailed instructions.

■ Provide a high level of active practice for all students.

■ Ask a large number of questions, check for student understanding, and obtain responses from all students.

- Guide students during the initial practice.
- Provide systematic feedback and corrections.
- Provide explicit instruction and practice for seatwork, exercises, and when necessary, monitor students during seatwork.

In addition, effective teachers for students with learning disabilities use the following procedures: give explicit instruction, give praise, use good management, offer a good attention and emotional climate, provide opportunities for responding time, and use active learning strategies (Morsink et al., 1986).

Explicit Instruction   Many students with learning disabilities need explicit, direct instruction. **Explicit instruction** means teachers clearly state what is to be taught and explain what needs to be done. Students are not left to make inferences from experiences that are unmediated by such help. In explicit instruction, students are provided with models of appropriate methods for solving problems or explaining relationships. They are amply supported during the stages of the learning process, and they are provided with adequate practice (U.S. Department of Education, 1997; Cazden, 1992). Table 4.1 provides some principles of explicit instruction (U.S. Department of Education, 1997; Carnine, Jones, & Dixon, 1995).

Praise and Management   Teachers should provide contingent praise for appropriate learning and social behavior. Students with learning disabilities need many opportunities for success. The teacher's attention to misbehavior often increases the frequency of that misbehavior. (See Chapter 14.)

Attention and Emotional Climate   Students with learning disabilities need attention and sufficient helping behavior from teachers. Studies show they are more likely to receive such attention and help from a special teacher in a special class than from a regular teacher in a general education classroom (Bateman, 1992; Baker & Zigmond, 1990).

Opportunities for Responding Time   Students with learning disabilities need sufficient time to think and to respond. They also need many opportunities to respond, answer questions, or give an opinion. Studies show that general education classroom teachers spend more instructional time with high achievers than with low achievers, giving low achievers less opportunity for responding. Further, the time spent with low achievers is often spent in disciplinary or corrective activities than in academic learning (Bateman, 1992; Kauffman, Gerber, & Semmel, 1988; McKinney & Hocutt, 1988).

Promoting Active Learning

The importance of instruction that promotes **active learning** is advanced by research in contemporary cognitive psychology. Active learners (1) attend to instruction, (2) attribute results to their own efforts, (3) relate tasks and ma-

Table 4.1

Principles of Explicit Instruction

- Provide students with an adequate range of examples to exemplify a concept or problem-solving strategy.
- Provide models of proficient performance, including step-by-step strategies (at times) or broad generic questions and guidelines that focus attention and prompt deep processing.
- Provide experiences where students explain how and why they make decisions.
- Provide frequent feedback on quality of performance and support so that students persist in performing activities.
- Provide adequate practice and activities that are interesting and engaging.

Table 1, p. 164, Principles of Explicit Instruction in R. Gersten, (1998), "Recent advances in instructional research for students with learning disabilities: An overview." *Learning Disabilities Research & Practice*, 13(13), p. 162–170.

terials to their knowledge and experience, and (4) actively construct meaning during learning. Instruction for active learning capitalizes on the child's interests, stresses the importance of building background knowledge prior to teaching, and encourages the active involvement of students. The theory emphasizes the concept that learning and behavior emerge from the interaction of three components: the learning environment, the learner, and the teaching material (Wittrock, 1988; Resnick, 1987). Table 4.2 provides guidelines for fostering active learning.

Scaffolded Instruction

Scaffolding refers to teacher supports at the initial stage of a student's learning of a task. An analogy is made to the scaffold used by builders. A scaffold is a temporary structure used to support a building in the early stages of construction and then removed when it is no longer needed. In teaching the student, the metaphor of a scaffold is used to describe supports that the teacher provides for the student in the early stages of learning a task that is beyond student's level of competency. These supports are removed when they are no longer necessary. (Stone, 1998; Rosenshine, 1997).

The concept of **scaffolded instruction** is often linked to Vygotsky's (1962) notion of the zone of proximal development (ZPD). The term ZPD refers to the difficulty level for effective learning; it is neither too easy nor too difficult for the child (see Chapter 6). Also, Vygotsky notes that learning depends upon the social interaction of an experienced adult (teacher) and the learner (student). The teacher provides the support or scaffolding that the student needs during the initial stage of learning the task (Stone, 1998; Rosenshine, 1997).

For scaffolding to be successful, a child must enter an exchange with some prior understanding of what is to be accomplished. The scaffolding procedure uses an ongoing interaction in which the teacher provides carefully

Table 4.2

Guidelines for Promoting Active Learning

Encourage interactive learning	Learning emerges from the interaction of three components: the environment, the learner, and the teaching material. Teachers should interrelate these three components.
Recognize the importance of prior experience	Integrate the children's background knowledge and experience into the learning activities. Learning is dependent on what children already know.
Prepare children for the lesson	Preparation for learning leads to improved understanding, motivation, and storage of information. Expose children to key concepts before they are presented in the lesson.
Encourage active involvement	When children are actively involved in their learning, they are more successful learners than when they take a passive role in the learning process.
Structure lessons for success	There is a positive correlation between learning, self-concept, and positive attitudes. Teachers should structure lessons to provide opportunities for children to experience success.
Teach "learning to learn" strategies	Teachers can help children become aware of their learning processes. For example, asking children how they found a solution to a problem will assist them in understanding the strategies they use to learn.

calibrated assistance at the child's leading edge of competence (Stone, 1998). Examples of scaffolds include simplified problems, modeling of the procedures by the teacher, thinking aloud by the teacher, and teacher mediation to guide the student to think through the problem. Reciprocal teaching, described next, is an example of scaffolded instruction.

Reciprocal Teaching

In Chapter 3 on assessment, we discussed the model of dynamic assessment. **Reciprocal teaching** is the instructional link of dynamic assessment. In teaching reading comprehension, reciprocal teaching assumes the form of a dialogue in which teachers and students take turns leading discussions about a shared reading text (Palinscar, Brown, & Campione, 1991). The initial study on reciprocal teaching was conducted by Palinscar and Brown (1984). The researchers used reciprocal teaching to train a group of seventh-grade poor readers, whose scores were about 2.6 years below grade level, in reading comprehension. The students were trained in four learning strategies: *summarizing* the content of a passage, *asking questions* about a central point, *clarifying* the difficult parts of the material, and *predicting* what would happen next.

The reciprocal teaching procedures follow four steps: (1) the teacher and students read the material silently; (2) the teacher explains and then models the strategies of summarizing, questioning, clarifying, and predicting by saying out loud the thoughts that she or he used in those learning strategies; (3) everyone reads another passage, and the students are given the responsibility of demonstrating out loud for the other students in the group. At first, many of the students may be hesitant and their demonstrations imperfect. The teacher provides guidance, encouragement, and support (scaffolding) to help the students perfect their demonstrations. Finally, (4) each student demonstrates abilities in the strategies of summarizing, questioning, clarifying, and predicting.

The reciprocal teaching procedure has been investigated in a number of studies, and it has been shown to be an effective approach to instruction. Students improved in their ability to summarize, question, clarify, and predict using reading passages. Students also showed improvement in their scores in reading comprehension (Palinscar, Brown, & Campione, 1991).

The key principles of reciprocal teaching instruction are (Palinscar et al., 1991):

- Learning is considered a social activity, initially shared among people but gradually internalized to reappear again as individual achievement.

- The dialogue or conversations between teachers and students guide the student's learning.

- The teacher plays a mediating role, shaping learning opportunities and bringing them to the attention of the learner.

- Assessment is a continuing, ongoing process that occurs during the reciprocal teaching.

Instruction in Learning Strategies

Instruction in learning strategies plays an increasing role as an instructional method for students with learning disabilities. Learning strategies are discussed in several sections of this book—particularly in Chapter 6 (the theory underlying these methods), Chapter 8 (in relation to adolescents with learning disabilities), and Chapter 11 (in the context of reading). Instruction in learning strategies helps students with learning disabilities take charge of their own learning, become active learners, acquire a repertoire of learning strategies, be able to select the appropriate strategy for the learning situation, and be able to generalize the strategy to other situations (Deshler et al., 1996).

The model for teaching learning strategies to students with learning disabilities, which was developed at the University of Kansas Institute for Research on Learning Disabilities, has eight steps: (1) pretesting, (2) describing the strategy, (3) teaching modeling, (4) verbal practice, (5) controlled practice, (6) advanced practice, (7) posttesting, and (8) generalization (Deshler et al., 1996; Lenz et al., 1996). (See Chapter 9.)

TASK ANALYSIS   **Task analysis** is a useful procedure for teaching students with learning disabilities. The purpose of task analysis is to plan the sequential steps for learning a specified skill. Task analysis breaks down the complexity of an activity into easier steps; these steps are organized as a sequence, and students are taught each step of the sequence. The goal is to move the student to the desired level of skill achievement. The skill of buttoning, for example, entails a sequence of component subskills: grasping the button, aligning the button with the buttonhole, and so forth. The teacher must consider the following: (1) What are the important, specific educational tasks that the student must learn? (2) What are the sequential steps in learning this task? (3) What specific behaviors does the student need to perform this task? The steps in this process are shown in the box entitled·"Steps of Task Analysis" (on p. 144).

The following are examples of the task analysis of instruction sequences to reach a curriculum goal:

- *Task of analysis of long division* includes the steps (or subskills) of estimating, dividing, multiplying, subtracting, checking, bringing down the next digit, and then repeating the process. Each step must be planned for, taught, and assessed.

- *Task analysis of writing a report* by using the school library includes the skills of knowing alphabetical order, using the card catalogue (or a computer terminal), finding books on a subject, using a book index to find information on a topic, getting a main idea from reading, and knowing language usage skills (Slavin, 1991).

- *Task analysis of recognizing a word* might include the skills of recognizing initial consonants, recognizing short vowels, and blending.

In addition to analyzing the task, it is useful to analyze the learner in terms of the task. (1) What abilities does the student need to understand and perform the task? For example, does the task require language, memory, problem-solving, auditory, or visual abilities? (2) Does the task require one ability or several, and must the student shift from one to another? (3) Is the task primarily *verbal* or *nonverbal*? (4) Does the task require *social* or *nonsocial* judgments? (5) What *skills* and *levels* of involvement are needed? Is failure due to the manner of presentation or to the mode of response expected? (Johnson, 1967).

An example of task analysis of the learner might involve spelling. Two spelling tasks might differ significantly in presentation and mode of response: one spelling test might require the pupil to underline the correct spelling from among four choices; another might require the pupil to spell orally a spoken word. The visual-memory, language, and motor requirements of these two spelling tasks are quite different.

The case study that follows is a continuation of the case of Rita G., which was begun in Chapter 3. Part II of the case study covers Stage 3 of the IEP process, the Multidisciplinary Evaluation.

RITA G.

STAGE 3: MULTIDISCIPLINARY EVALUATION

The multidisciplinary team for Rita's case consisted of the school psychologist, school nurse, social worker, and learning disabilities teacher. Each member of the team was responsible for administering certain tests and gathering specified evaluation information. A summary of the multidisciplinary evaluation appears next.

Classroom Observation

The learning disabilities teacher and the social worker observed Rita in her third-grade class. The learning disabilities teacher's observation took place during an arithmetic lesson. Mr. Martinez was giving the class practice in solving word problems in two-digit addition and subtraction, using place value. He read a problem to the class; students were expected to visualize the situation and then perform the calculations on paper to find the answer. The lesson was followed with practice on similar written word-story problems in a workbook, and students were asked to complete five problems. Rita did not volunteer the answer to any of the oral problems, and she did not write the calculations to find the answer to the problems during the lesson. In the seatwork portion of the lesson, Rita attempted the first problem but had difficulty staying on task. She did not even attempt the other four problems. Inspection of her work showed she could not line up the numbers in the addition problem and, consequently, made mistakes in addition. She had many erasures and crossouts.

The social worker observed Rita during a fifteen-minute "free" period. During this time, none of her classmates interacted with Rita, and she just stared out of the window for the entire period.

Auditory and Visual Acuity

The school nurse tested Rita for hearing and visual impairments.

Hearing   The school nurse administered an *audiometer* hearing screening test. Rita's hearing tested within the normal range.

Vision   The school nurse used the *Keystone Visual-Screening Service* for School visual screening test to screen Rita's vision. No visual difficulties were noted.

Developmental and Educational History

The social worker interviewed Mrs. G. to obtain the case history information. Rita is the older of two daughters in an English-speaking household. Her father is a salesman; her mother a homemaker. Rita's birth and prenatal history were reported as normal. Her birth weight was 7 pounds, 10 ounces. Rita had a high fever at six months of age and was hospitalized for two days. She had chicken pox at age five. Otherwise, her medical history appears to be normal.

Mrs. G. said that Rita's motor development seemed to be normal. Rita crawled at six months and walked at one year, but she seemed to fall and bump into things frequently. She had much difficulty learning to feed herself and learning to dress herself. She still has trouble with certain tasks, such as tying shoelaces. She did not like to play with "educational" types of toys that had to be put together. Mrs. G. described Rita as "clutzy." Language development seemed to be normal; Rita had babbled at six months, said her first word at about one year, and used two-word sentences at eighteen months.

Rita attended a nursery school at age 4 but, according to Mrs. G., was not enthusiastic about going to preschool. Rita began to experience problems in kindergarten. The kindergarten teacher told Mrs. G. that Rita showed difficulty in fine motor coordination and seemed "immature" for a 5-year-old. The first-grade teacher said she did not always pay attention and did not complete her work. The second-grade teacher said she did not try hard enough and her work was very "sloppy." Rita does not have any close friends and usually plays with younger children.

Mrs. G. felt the major problem now was that Rita was failing third grade and that she did not want to go to school.

Measures of Intellectual Aptitude

The school psychologist administered the *Wechsler Intelligence Scale for Children—Third Edition* (WISC-III). Rita's overall performance was within the average range with a Full-Scale IQ score of 109. Her Verbal IQ score was 128 and her Performance IQ score was 87. These WISC-III scores suggest a discrepancy between Rita's verbal and performance abilities. Her aptitude strengths were in areas that use language; her weaknesses were in tests in which she had to visualize objects in space, or plan and manipulate objects, and in arithmetic. (The mean for the IQ scores on the WISC-III is 100; the mean for the subtest scores on the WISC-III is 10. The school psychologist noted that Rita seemed to give up as soon as items became difficult and did not seem to have any system for attacking challenging problems. When items became hard for her, Rita seemed helpless and simply said, "I can't do that. It's too hard for me." Her WISC-III scores were as follows:

WISC-III Full Scale IQ: 109
Verbal IQ: 128
Performance IQ: 87

Verbal subtest scaled scores

Information	13
Similarities	14
Arithmetic	8
Vocabulary	14
Comprehension	11
Digit Span	13

Performance subtest scaled scores

Picture Arrangement	7
Coding	6
Picture Completion	8
Block Design	8
Object Assembly	7
Symbol Search	7
Mazes	5

Present Levels of Academic Functioning

Rita's current academic skill levels were determined by assessment in the areas of mathematics, reading, handwriting, spelling, adaptive behavior, learning strengths and weaknesses, and interest. In addition, her classroom work was observed and analyzed. Curriculum-based assessment was given in reading and mathematics. Assessment results are summarized next.

Mathematics Mathematics testing included the mathematics tests of the *Peabody Individual Achievement Test—Revised* (PIAT-R), the *Key Math—Revised, and the Brigance Inventory of Basic Skills.* Rita scored substantially below grade level in all these mathematics tests. Her grade placement at the time of the test was 3.8, and her mathematics scores ranged between grade 1.8 and 2.5, making her between one and one-half years to two years below her present grade in mathematics. Her most serious mathematics difficulties were in the areas of numerical reasoning and word problems. She also did poorly in addition, subtraction, and multiplication. Her scores were low in fractions and division, but she has not had instruction in these areas in the classroom.

Reading Rita was given the reading tests of the *Brigance Inventory of Basic Skills,* the PIAT-R, the *Woodcock Reading Mastery Tests—Revised,* and the *Gray Oral Reading Tests, Third Edition* to test reading achievement. In general, Rita scored satisfactorily in tests of word recognition, but her performance dropped considerably when reading comprehension was required. When she was observed during the reading, she seemed to lose her place and had difficulty concentrating on the material. Her word identification, phonics skills, and reading vocabulary are adequate. Difficulties in reading appear when she is required to use higher conceptual skills in reading comprehension. Her reading comprehension is at the independent reading level of second grade. Her word-recognition skills are at the fourth-grade level.

Handwriting Rita's handwriting skills were assessed with the *Brigance Inventory of Basic Skills* and through observation. Handwriting poses a major problem for her. The third-grade handwriting curriculum calls for shifting from manuscript to cursive writing. However, Rita has resisted making the change and asked Mr. Martinez if she could continue using manuscript writing. She is left-handed and has always had much difficulty performing this visual-motor task. Her written papers are a painstaking task for her to complete and require much effort and time. Even then, the final product is usually illegible and has a very sloppy appearance. She begins many letters from the bottom, moving to the top of a line. Tall letters are the same size as small letters. Her pencil grasp is unusual, and she keeps her nonwriting right hand in a folded, tense position. Written expression could not be tested because of her extremely poor handwriting skills.

Spelling Rita's spelling was tested with the spelling tests of the PIAT-R, the *Brigance Inventory of Basic Skills,* the *Woodcock-Johnson Psychoeducational Battery—Revised Tests of Achievement,* and the *Wide-Range Achievement Test—III.* She scored at the second-grade level. Analysis of her spelling errors showed that she usually spelled words according to phonics rules, for example, *frend* for *friend, laf* for *laugh,* and *tok* for *talk.* She showed poor visual memory for irregularly spelled words.

Adaptive Behavior

Information on Rita's adaptive behavior was obtained by the social worker, who used the *Vineland Adaptive Behavior Scales* in interviewing Rita's mother. Rita's lowest scores were in the areas of daily living skills and socialization. These scores supported her mother's comments that Rita relies on other people to tell her what to do and that she has made no friends and plays mostly with her younger sister. They also support Mr. Martinez's observation that Rita lacks the motivation to organize herself to complete school work and will often "just sit there."

Learning Strengths and Weaknesses

Rita was given the *Developmental Test of Visual-Motor Integration* by the learning disabilities teacher. Rita's score was equivalent to that of a 6-year-old, or three full years below her chronological age. Although she could copy simple designs, such as the circle and plus sign, she had difficulty with the triangle, diamond, and other more complicated shapes. She appears to have a weakness in visual perception abilities.

Rita's auditory discrimination was tested with the *Goldman-Fristoe-Woodcock Test of Auditory Discrimination.* Her scores were adequate on this test, suggesting a strength in auditory discrimination.

Other learning strengths included good phonics skills, an adequate sight vocabulary, and good verbal skills. All the specialists on the multidisciplinary team noted Rita's weaknesses in attention and concentration. They also noted that she lacked cognitive strategies to approach learning situations. Rita had become a passive learner and did not actively seek out ways to enhance her learning.

Interest Inventory

The learning disabilities teacher gave Rita an informal interest inventory. Rita indicated that she likes to watch television and eat. She said that her playmates include her younger sister and her sister's friend. Rita does not receive an allowance, but she earns money by taking out the garbage. She spends the money she earns on candy. In response to the question, "Do you like school?" she said, "Sometimes and sometimes not." After some prompting, she admitted that a good school day meant that the teacher had not yelled at her. Rita's favorite subject is music; she dislikes gym and arithmetic.

Note: The case study of Rita G. is continued in Chapter 5.

STEPS OF TASK ANALYSIS

Step 1. Clearly state the learning task (the behavioral objective).

Step 2. Break the learning task into the steps necessary to learn the target skill and place these steps into a logical teaching sequence.

Step 3. Test informally to determine the steps that the student can already perform.

Step 4. Begin teaching, in sequential order, each step of the task analysis sequence.

Chapter Summary

1. Clinical teaching is an integral part of the assessment-teaching process.

2. The concept of tailoring learning experiences to the unique needs of a particular student is the essence of clinical teaching.

3. The clinical teaching process can be viewed as a five-stage cycle of decision making that consists of assessment, planning, implementation, evaluation, and modification of the assessment.

4. The student's ecological environment includes the home environment, the school environment, the social environment, and the cultural environment. Each has an impact on the student's learning.

5. A classification system of intervention classifies approaches according to the type of analysis performed: analysis of the student, analysis of curriculum, and analysis of the environment.

6. One of the critical options available to teachers is to change certain variables in the school setting: difficulty level, space, time, language, and the interpersonal relationship between teacher and student. By modifying these elements, the teacher controls certain variables that affect learning.

7. Clinical teaching requires not only a sound foundation in methods and practices but also the ability to establish an understanding and empathic relationship with the pupil. Six therapeutic principles—rapport, shared responsibility, structure, sincerity, success, and interest—can help in creating such a relationship.

8. Emerging instructional trends include instructing students with learning disabilities in general education classrooms, using effective teaching practices, promoting active learning, scaffolded instruction, reciprocal teaching, and instruction for learning strategies.

9. Task analysis involves analyzing the small sequential steps of a specific skill.

Questions for Discussion and Reflection

1. Teachers should consider the student's ecological system. Discuss the various environments in which students live that can affect their learning. What changes are occurring in today's society in terms of the ecological system of children?

2. Discuss three different approaches to teaching students with learning disabilities based on the Classification Model of Teaching Methods.

3. Teachers can do little about many of the factors related to learning disabilities. Some variables, however, can be controlled or adjusted by the teacher. Describe and give an example of three instructional variables that teachers can control.

4. Why is it important to consider ways to accommodate students with learning disabilities in the regular classroom? Name three ways that general education classroom teachers can make modifications for students with learning disabilities.

5. Other students in the classroom may complain that it is not "fair" to make modifications and accommodations for students with disabilities because the students are not all being treated in the same way. How would you respond to these comments?

6. Compare and contrast the *explicit instruction* approach and the *active learning* approach. What are the advantages of each of these approaches for students with learning disabilities?

7. Describe task analysis. Give an example of an instructional sequence (or the steps to learning a specific skill).

Key Terms

active learning *(p. 136)*

affect *(p. 124)*

basal readers *(p. 123)*

behavioral approach *(p. 123)*

bibliotherapy *(p. 131)*

clinical teaching *(p. 112)*

cognitive processing *(p. 119)*

cognitive psychology *(p. 120)*

ecological system *(p. 115)*

explicit instruction *(p. 136)*

learning strategies approach *(p. 121)*

mastery learning approach *(p. 122)*

pedagogy *(p. 124)*

psychological processing disorders *(p. 120)*

psychotherapeutic approach *(p. 124)*

rapport *(p. 127)*

readiness *(p. 126)*

reasonable accommodations *(p. 132)*

reciprocal teaching *(p. 138)*

scaffolded instruction *(p. 137)*

self-esteem *(p. 128)*

skills sequence *(p. 122)*

stages of child development *(p. 121)*

target behavior *(p. 123)*

task analysis *(p. 140)*

zone of proximal development (ZPD) *(p. 126)*

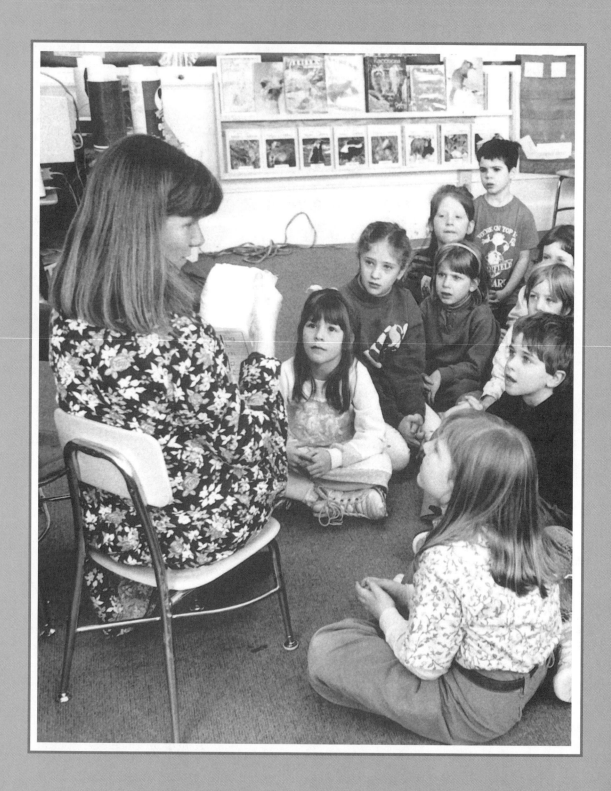

5

Systems for Delivering Educational Services

CHAPTER OUTLINE

T his chapter examines educational placement, the third element of the assessment-teaching process. To discuss placement for students with learning disabilities, we focus on the following issues: important concepts about placement; placement options for students with learning disabilities; methods for promoting partnerships between general education and special education teachers; competencies for learning disabilities teachers and general education teachers; and parents and families. This chapter also concludes the case study of Rita G.

IMPORTANT CONCEPTS ABOUT PLACEMENT

In what *place* a student with learning disabilities will receive instruction is an important component of the assessment-teaching process and a key decision that is made by the IEP (individualized education program) team. The topics of **placement** and inclusion are probably the most hotly debated issues in the field of learning disabilities, as well as other categories of disabilities. **Inclusion** refers to the placement of children with disabilities into regular or general education classes for instruction, with appropriate supports. The inclusion movement is a growing practice in our schools. (Both the terms *regular education* and *general education* are commonly used and are interchangeable.)

The inclusion movement has engendered impassioned responses from teachers, parents of students with and without disabilities, administrators, researchers, and policy makers. The debate essentially reflects two perspectives:

(1) the view that children with disabilities, including learning disabilities, have a right to participate in environments as close to normal as possible and to benefit socially and academically from being in the mainstream of society and school. This view also contends that other settings for instruction are harmful and stigmatizing (Stainback & Stainback, 1992, 1996; McLeskey & Waldron, 1995).

(2) the view that the nature of the problems encountered by students with learning disabilities require individual, intensive, explicit instruction that cannot easily be provided in the regular class (Zigmond, 1995, 1997; Kauffman & Hallahan, 1997; Fuchs & Fuchs, 1995). This view maintains that students with learning disabilities need instruction beyond that which can be provided in the general education classroom.

The effectiveness of inclusion for students with learning disabilities remains controversial. Both groups cite research and a sense of "what is right" to support their views. Nevertheless, the inclusion movement is escalating within our schools. The steady increase of the placement of students with learning disabilities in regular classes for instruction is striking. In the past seven years, the percentage of students with learning disabilities who had only regular class placement increased from 18 to 42 percent. During that same eight-year period, the percentage of students with learning disabilities in resource rooms decreased from 59 to 39 percent (U.S. Department of Education, 1990, 1998). (Figure 5.3 on p. 158 in this chapter depicts these changes.)

To appreciate the full implications of the inclusion movement, it is necessary to know certain basic concepts about placements for instruction in special education. The child's placement is determined when the case study team holds the IEP (individualized education program) meeting. The type of educational placement, or the place where the student will receive services, is written into the IEP.

The federal special education law (the 1997 Individuals with Disabilities Education Act) contains two significant provisions related to placement for services: (1) the **continuum of alternative placements** and (2) the **least restrictive environment**.

Continuum of Alternative Placements

The continuum of alternative placements provision specifies that schools make available an array of educational placements to meet the varied needs of students with disabilities for special education and related services. The placement options include general (or regular) education classes, resource room classes, separate classes, separate schools, and other types of placements as needed.

Table 5.1 contains a brief list, with explanations, of alternative placements for students with all categories of disabilities. The placement options are ordered from the least restrictive to the most restrictive environment. As used in this context, the term *restrictive* refers to the placement of students with disabilities with nondisabled students. The placement of students with disabilities with regular students in general education classes is therefore considered the least restrictive option. Placement in a separate class or separate school in which only students with disabilities are served is a more restrictive environment. It is important that teachers not lose sight of the continuum of services (Langone, 1998).

Least Restrictive Environment

The second important provision in special education law in regard to placement is the least restrictive environment (LRE), which has been the cornerstone of the inclusion movement. Successful adults with disabilities have learned to function comfortably in society and the community—an unrestricted environment composed of all people. To promote normalization and experiences in the greater society, the LRE provision aims to ensure that, to the extent appropriate, students with disabilities have experiences in school with regular (or non–special education) students. Translated into practice,

Table 5.1

Continuum of
Alternative Placements

General education class	Includes students who receive most of their education program in a general education classroom and receive special education and related services outside this classroom for less than 21 percent of the school day. It includes children placed in a general education class and receiving special education within this class, as well as children placed in a general education class and receiving special education outside this class.
Resource room	Includes students who receive special education and related services outside the general education classroom for at least 21 percent but not more than 60 percent of the school day. This may include students placed in resource rooms with part-time instruction in a general education class.
Separate class	Includes students who receive special education and related services outside the general education classroom for more than 60 percent of the school day. Students may be placed in a separate class with part-time instruction in another placement or placed in separate classes full-time on a regular school campus.
Separate school	Includes students who receive special education and related services in separate day schools for more than 50 percent of the school day.
Residential facility	Includes students who receive education in a public or private residential facility, at public expense, for more than 50 percent of the school day.
Homebound/hospital environment	Includes students placed in and receiving special education in hospital or homebound programs.

this means that when the IEP team makes decisions about placement, the team must attempt to choose the least restrictive environment for each student. Placements that include students who do not have disabilities are less restrictive.

Figure 5.1 illustrates the placements described in Table 5.1 but in reverse direction. The base is less restrictive and the top is more restrictive in terms of contact with non-disabled students. It is a version of the classic cascade model of the continuum of alternative placements first suggested by Deno (1970). This model implies that students with mild learning disabilities would be more likely to receive services in level I (the regular education class) or level II (the resource room). Students with severe learning disabilities would be more likely to receive services in level III (the separate class). In many cases, the team recommends services from several placement options—for example, the separate class and the resource room concurrently. As a particular student progresses in learning, changes in the educational placements may be needed to keep pace with the student's new educational needs.

Figure 5.1

A Model of the Continuum of Alternative Placements

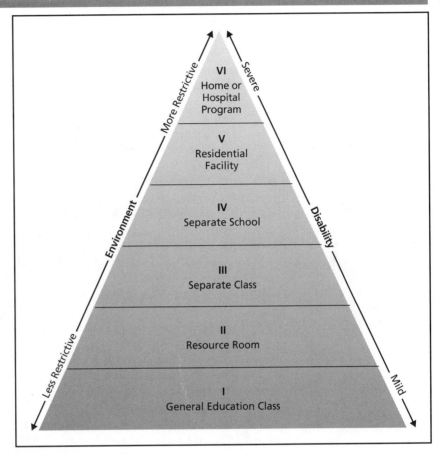

This classic cascade of services model for special education is criticized by inclusion proponents as obsolete because it leads to the labeling and separation of children. Instead, they recommend that placement should be with the child's peers and should be based on chronological age (Langone, 1998).

Integrating General and Special Education

A progression of practices over the years were designed to integrate general and special education. In the early days of special education, there were special classes or schools for each category of disability. Special classes were established for students with mental retardation, for children who were blind or deaf, and for children with learning disabilities. An influential article by Lloyd Dunn (1968) is credited with initiating the idea of integrating special education students into less restrictive settings. Dunn suggested that some students with mental retardation who had been placed in special classes could benefit from other placements (MacMillan, Semmel, & Gerber, 1995).

In the years since Dunn's article, we have seen many changes in the placement system and a call for progressively more integration. We look at three placement models that promote integration for students with learning disabilities: mainstreaming, the regular education initiative, and inclusion. None of these terms is mentioned in special education law, and each is progressively more encompassing.

Mainstreaming   **Mainstreaming** refers to the practice of gradually placing selective students with learning disabilities in the regular education classroom for instruction, when teachers believe the child will benefit from an integrated placement. Within the philosophy of mainstreaming, students with learning disabilities are carefully integrated in regular education classrooms, perhaps for a single subject or for a portion of the day. The goal is to slowly increase the amount of time the student spends in this class. The mainstreaming plan is carefully worked out and monitored for an individual student by special and general educators.

The Regular Education Initiative   The **regular education initiative (REI)** is a concept that was first proposed by the Office of Special Education and Rehabilitation Services within the U.S. Department of Education (Will, 1986). REI goes further than mainstreaming and recommends fundamental, major revisions in where and how students with learning disabilities receive services. The premise of REI is that students with learning disabilities, as well as other children with learning and behavior problems, can be served more effectively through the general education classroom than through the special education system (Reynolds, Wang, & Walberg, 1987; Lilly, 1986; Wang, Reynolds, & Walberg, 1986).

The rationale for the regular education initiative is described by Will (1986). Many youngsters with various learning problems in our schools currently are not eligible for special education services. In addition, children with disabilities are stigmatized when they are placed in special education programs that separate them from their peers. Further, there is little emphasis placed on early prevention; special education students are usually identified after serious learning deficiencies have been discovered. The intent of the REI was to serve children with many types of mild problems including children with disabilities, children considered at-risk, children with limited English proficiency, children in poverty, and others, in the regular education classroom.

Inclusion   As noted, inclusion refers to the instruction of students with disabilities in the regular classroom education, with appropriate supports to meet their individual needs. One interpretation of inclusion is known as **full inclusion,** which has the goal of placing *all* children from *all* categories of disabilities and *all* degrees of severity into their neighborhood schools in regular education classes. An underlying aim of full inclusion is to restructure the schools to eliminate special education, which is viewed as an unnecessary "second system" (The Association for Persons with Severe Handicaps, TASH, 1993; Thousand & Villa, 1991; Villa & Thousand, 1990; Villa, Thousand, Meyers, & Nevin, 1996).

The philosophical ideologies of inclusion are the normalization of children through integrated regular classes and the elimination of labels for children with disabilities. An added argument for inclusion is the notion that society artificially constructs the disability labels of children, and the belief that a large part of this problem would disappear by doing away with labels.

Many parents and professionals have reservations about inclusion for all students with learning disabilities. A provocative question is whether the stigma comes from the label or from the child's failure to learn. Kauffman & Hallahan (1997) point out that learning disabilities would not exist in a society that did not value literacy. The reality is, however, that we live in a society that does value literacy, and a person who does not know how to read suffers in this society. Many special educators and parents worry that the inclusion placement will not meet the individual needs of many students with learning disabilities. The heart of IDEA (the Individuals with Disabilities Education Act) is the *individualized* education program (IEP). Many students with learning disabilities need individualized clinical teaching and explicit instruction, which is extremely complex and difficult to provide in a regular classroom, so students with learning disabilities who are placed there are often neglected (Zigmond, 1995, 1997; Stone, 1998).

Individualized placement decisions can be made only if there is a continuum or variety of placements from which to choose (Bateman, 1995). When full inclusion is the only option, schools no longer offer a continuum of alternative placements (or choices), such as resource rooms and special classes. For many students with learning disabilities a regular class setting may be appropriate; for others, however, the inclusion classroom may become a complex failure-producing situation. They need more intensive instruction than can be provided in a general classroom. One size does not fit all, and lumping all students with learning disabilities into the general classroom ignores the notion of individual planning (Hallahan & Kauffman, 1997; Roberts & Mather, 1995).

It is also important to recognize that the placement or setting is not a treatment; what goes on *in* that setting is the treatment (Kauffman & Hallahan, 1997; Zigmond, 1995, 1997). Roberts and Mather (1995) suggest that research does not support the effectiveness of inclusion for students with learning disabilities. The intervention needs of students with learning disabilities are often neglected, and their educational outcomes are disappointing (Zigmond, 1995, 1997). In addition, classroom teachers are not receiving supports for special needs children in their classes (Yasutake & Lerner, 1996; Zigmond, 1995, 1997). Many learning disabilities organizations have published position papers stating that the inclusion model may not meet the needs of students with learning disabilities (Hallahan & Kauffman, 1995). For example, the Council for Exceptional Children policy states that "a continuum of services must be available for all children, youth, and young adults" (Council for Exceptional Children, 1995).

Responsible Placement Practices

To make integrative and inclusion placements more effective, it is essential to provide sufficient support through multidisciplinary teams of professionals who mutually adjust their collective skills and knowledge to create unique, personal programs for each student. Ideally, all staff members are involved in making decisions, teaching, and evaluating the students' needs and progress.

Vaughn and Schumm (1995) suggest the following guidelines for responsible placement: (a) the student and family are considered first, (b) teachers choose to participate in inclusion classrooms, (c) adequate resources and supports are provided, (d) models are developed and implemented at the school level, (e) a continuum of services is maintained and evaluated continuously, and (f) ongoing professional development is provided. More detailed guidelines, gathered through experience and research, follow (Zigmond, 1995; Vaughn, Schumm, & Arguelles, 1997; Langone, 1998; Vaughn & Schumm, 1995).

1. *Help teachers through a team approach.* Regular classroom teachers are sometimes hesitant and even fearful about providing for the needs of special students in their classrooms. To succeed, such placements require a team approach and should be a shared responsibility of all of the educators in the school.

2. *Provide supportive services.* When students with learning disabilities are served in general education classrooms, they often need some supportive services. Providing such services is the responsibility of the special education teacher.

3. *Plan for social acceptance.* Many students with learning disabilities experience difficulty in being accepted socially by their peers in the general education classroom. By itself, placement in a general classroom may not lead to greater social interaction or increased social acceptance.

4. *Teach students appropriate classroom behaviors.* Acceptable classroom behaviors are even more important than academic competencies as predictors of success in the general education classroom. Important behaviors for classroom success include interacting positively with other students, obeying class rules, and displaying proper work habits. Special education teachers should prepare students for integration by teaching these essential classroom behavior skills. For example, if the regular class requires the student to work independently on an assign-

ment for thirty minutes, the special education teacher should prepare the student for that situation by making the same work demands in the special education setting.

Regulations for IDEA 1997

The regulations to clarify the 1997 Individuals with Disabilities Act (IDEA 1997) were issued by the Department of Education on March 12, 1999. Several of the regulations affect the placement of students with learning disabilities, especially regulations regarding the involvement in the general curriculum of students with learning disabilities. See Appendix F for a further discussion of major issues in the regulations. Additional information about the regulations is available at **http://www.ideapractices.org.**

PLACEMENT OPTIONS In selecting an educational placement for a particular student, the case conference IEP team should consider the severity of the disability, the student's need for related services, the student's ability to fit into the routine of the selected setting, the student's social and academic skills, and the student's level of schooling (primary, intermediate, or secondary). Teams often recommend a delivery system that combines elements of several types of placements.

Parents must agree to the placement in writing. If parents and school personnel disagree, parents can ask for mediation at no cost to the parents, or either party can request a hearing. In the two cases described in the Case Example: "Selecting a Placement," different educational placements are recommended.

In what type of placements are students with learning disabilities currently receiving their instruction? Figure 5.2 displays the percentage of students with learning disabilities (ages 6 through 21) in the various educational placements. The great majority (over 81 percent) spend much, most, or all of their time in general education classes. This group includes students whose educational placement is the regular classroom only (42 percent) and those who are placed in both a resource room and a regular classroom (39 percent). About 18 percent of students with learning disabilities are placed in separate classes. A small percentage (1.0 percent) are in other settings, including separate schools (0.7 percent), residential facilities (0.1 percent), and homebound and hospital settings (0.2 percent) (U.S. Department of Education, 1998). The various placement options are described in this section. As already noted, most students with learning disabilities receive services through the regular education classroom, resource room and regular class, or special class.

When no one placement option seems ideal, a combination placement may be a viable alternative. For example, a student could be in a special class for a portion of the day or week and in a general education classroom for the remainder of the time.

Figure 5.2

Placements of
Students with
Learning Disabilities

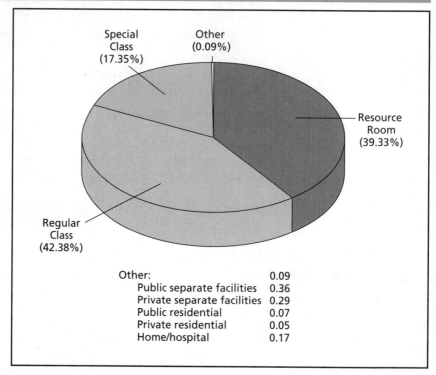

Other: 0.09
    Public separate facilities   0.36
    Private separate facilities 0.29
    Public residential   0.07
    Private residential   0.05
    Home/hospital   0.17

Source: Data taken from U.S. Department of Education (1998). To Assure the Free Appropriate Public Education for All Children with Disabilities. Twentieth Annual Report to Congress on the Implementation of the All Children with Disabilities Education Act. Washington DC. Government Printing Press. Appendix A, Table 52.

Significant changes have occurred in the placement of students with learning disabilities because of the inclusion movement. As shown in Figure 5.3, over an eight-year period, the percentage of students with learning disabilities who were placed in the regular education classroom increased from 17.6 percent to 42.4 percent. During this time frame, the percentage of students with learning disabilities in resource rooms decreased from 59.2 to 39.3. The percentage of children in separate classes decreased from 21.7 to 17.4. There was a decrease in other placements from 1.5 percent to less than 1 percent.

Regular Education Class

The **regular or general education classroom** placement is the least restrictive option for students with learning disabilities. Successful integration of students with learning disabilities in the general education classroom requires careful planning, teacher preparation, team effort, and a complete

CASE EXAMPLE

SELECTING A PLACEMENT

- José, age 12, was judged to have mild learning disabilities and has been receiving resource help for the past year. His word-recognition reading skills are now at grade level, but his reading comprehension and arithmetic, although very much improved, still require special education instruction. José has improved in his attention skills. He now knows how to study and can attend to an assignment for a period of 30 minutes. José still has a speech articulation disorder that requires the services of the speech and language teacher. His IEP recommendation for placement is that he be placed in the regular education classroom and that the teacher receives support from the learning disabilities teacher. In addition, José will receive related services in speech.

- Lucinda, also age 12, was judged to have severe learning disabilities. Last year she was enrolled in a special school; now she is returning to the regular school. Lucinda's reading skills are at the primary level, and she has extremely poor skills in arithmetic, spelling, and language. In addition, she has a severe social disability and does not easily relate to adults or peers. Lucinda is returning to the regular school with great fear and reluctance. She needs a very supportive placement, one offering a predictable routine and surroundings as well as an opportunity to develop strong social relationships with a few people. Because Lucinda has displayed a remarkable talent for creative art and enjoys working with a variety of art media, the IEP recommendation for her placement is that she receives services in a separate class but that she also is placed in the regular art class.

support system. Mere physical placement in a general education classroom is not enough to ensure academic achievement or social acceptance. As already noted, students with learning disabilities have specific needs that require targeted instruction and attention. Such students in regular education classes receive special education and related services outside this classroom for less than 21 percent of the day (U.S. Department of Education, 1995).

Two ways to deliver education services to these students in a regular education class are through direct services and indirect services. In **direct services,** the learning disabilities teacher works directly with the *child* in the general education class. In **indirect services,** the learning disabilities teacher works with the general education *teacher,* who then instructs the student. Often students with learning disabilities in a regular education class placement receive a combination of direct and indirect services (Zigmond, 1995).

Ideally, general and special educators share responsibility for teaching. The special educator may consult with the classroom teacher, provide materials for the student, or actually teach the student within the general education classroom. The classroom teacher must also have the skills, knowledge, and willingness to work with the students with learning disabilities placed in their classrooms. In-service and continuing education of

Figure 5.3

Changes in Placements
for Students with
Learning Disabilities

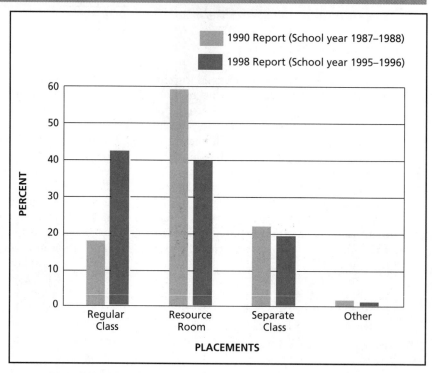

Source: U.S. Department of Education, (1990, 1998). To Assure the Free Appropriate Public Education for All Children with Disabilities. Twelfth and Twentieth Annual Reports on the Implementation of the All Children with Disabilities Education Act. Washington, D.C.: Government Printing Office.

classroom teachers are critically important, as is the coordinated effort of all school personnel—regular teachers, special teachers, related personnel, and administrators.

In addition, there are some students with learning disabilities in the regular classroom who do not meet the school's criteria for learning disabilities but who are eligible to receive services under the regulations of **Section 504 of the Rehabilitation Act.** The students must be given a Section 504 Learning Plan, which is less stringent that an IEP. A sample Section 504 Learning Plan is shown in Figure 5.4.

Resource Room

A **resource room** is an educational setting that provides assessment services and remedial instruction to students with disabilities on a regularly scheduled basis for a portion of the school day. Students spend most of the school day in the regular education classroom. (According to the U.S. Department of Education [1995], students in resource rooms spend 21 to 60

Figure 5.4

Learning Plan for a Student in a General Education Classroom under Section 504 of the Rehabilitation Act

Student: _____ School: _____ Grade: _____

Date of
Implementation: _____ Termination: _____ Review: _____

Statement of Student's Performance as it Relates to this "Plan": _____

_____

INTERVENTION/ STRATEGY	IMPLEMENTOR(S)	MONITORING DATE	COMMENTS

percent of their time outside the regular classroom.) The resource room offers flexibility in terms of the curriculum offered, the time students spend in the program, the number of students served, and the teacher's time. The resource room is a supporting element for regular education instruction. However, as noted in Figure 5.3, the number of students receiving resource room instruction is decreasing.

Care must be taken in scheduling students for resource programs. For example, if the pupil enjoys physical education, the teacher should avoid preempting this period for the resource room session. In addition, the classroom teacher must be consulted about the optimum time for the student to leave the classroom. Resource rooms should be pleasant and have an abundant supply of materials. Because students with learning disabilities often have short attention spans, it is wise to provide a change of pace by planning several activities during a teaching session.

Resource rooms have the following characteristics:

- The resource room teacher is located in the same building with classroom teachers, administrators, and students, and therefore may be readily accepted by them. The resource room teacher's schedule is flexible so that he or she can collaborate with the classroom teacher.

- Resource rooms enable students with learning disabilities to benefit from specific instruction while remaining integrated with their friends and peers in school.

- Resource programs are flexible enough to fit the level of the schooling. Primary school resource programs can be very different from those serving secondary school students.

- The resource room teacher should be a highly competent and personable individual who is able to coordinate efforts with classroom teachers, make educational and behavioral assessments, design and implement individualized instruction, and work effectively with parents and families.

- The resource room should be attractive and well organized. Since the student is in the general education classroom for a large part of the day, assessment and instruction must be related to the regular class, and instruction in the two settings should be coordinated.

Separate Class

The **separate class** within the school was one of the first placements used in the public schools to provide education to students with learning disabilities. Early classes had specially equipped rooms designed to reduce environmental distractions, and teaching techniques were highly structured and exacting (Cruickshank, Bentzen, Ratzeburgh, & Tannhauser, 1961). Although some features have changed, many of the elements of these early classes are still evident today. Separate classes are typically small, containing about six to fifteen students at a time. A wide variety of materials is available to the teacher. The separate class offers the opportunity for highly individualized and closely supervised intensive instruction. It serves students for more than 60 percent of the day (U.S. Department of Education, 1995). Even with the extensive inclusion movement, the percentage of students with learning disabilities in special classes remained at about 20 percent.

Some separate classes are *categorical* (consisting only of students with learning disabilities); others are *cross-categorical* (consisting of students with various disabilities, usually learning disabilities, emotional disturbance, or mental retardation).

The separate class benefits certain students with learning disabilities. They appear to have a better self-concept than similar students in regular classrooms, possibly because regular class competition sets achievement criteria that these students cannot meet. In separate classes certain students with learning disabilities make greater strides in both academic and social areas. With its lower teacher-pupil ratio, this setting offers more intensive individualized instruction in which students spend more time learning. The separate classroom may provide the most appropriate setting for the kind of intensive and comprehensive intervention needed by students with the most serious and severe learning disabilities (C. Smith, 1991).

A goal of separate class placement is to help students organize themselves for increased independent learning so that eventually they will be able to take part in a less restrictive environment. Sometimes the first step in the transition involves having the student receive some instruction in the resource room. Students may continue the transition by participating in a limited way in a regular education class for a selected subject, and their participation is then gradually increased. If the transition is to be effective, a good working relationship must be maintained between the teacher of the separate class and the teacher of the regular education class.

Separate School

Separate schools are special educational facilities established specifically for students with learning disabilities. These schools are often private, but they may be publicly supported. Students may spend more than 50 percent of the day in a separate school (U.S. Department of Education, 1995). Some students attend the separate school full time. Others attend only half a day and may spend the balance of the school day in the public school.

The disadvantages of separate schools include the high expense to parents, the traveling distance, and the lack of opportunity to be with other students for some portion of the school day. Separate schools also have some advantages, however. They often serve students with learning disabilities well, and they sometimes provide the only feasible option for certain students. The pilot programs they develop are often adopted later by separate class or resource room teachers.

Residential Facility

Residential facilities usually provide full-time placement for students away from their homes. The students receive education in a public or private residential facility, at public expense, for more than 50 percent of the school day (U.S. Department of Education, 1995). Relatively few students have disabilities severe enough to warrant such placement. However, in some cases—if the community lacks adequate alternative facilities, if the behavioral manifestations are extremely severe, and if the emotional reaction among other members of the family is debilitating—residential placement on a 24-hour basis may be the best solution for both the student and the family.

Although residential schools are the oldest provision for dealing with children and youth with disabilities, they have many disadvantages. They remove the student from home and neighborhood, emphasize the student's disability, and provide fewer opportunities for social experiences in the larger community. As public and private schools and other community agencies develop more services, the need for residential placements decreases. Nonetheless, as noted earlier, for certain youngsters residential placements remain the most appropriate choice, and they have successfully helped students learn, adjust to the world, and achieve very successful careers and lives for themselves.

Homebound or Hospital Environment

Children in homebound or hospital settings usually have a medical condition requiring these placements. The school sends teachers to these settings to provide instruction.

One-to-One Instruction

One-to-one instruction occurs when one adult works with one child. It is one of the most effective types of teaching, and the research shows that it leads to substantial improvement in student achievement (Slavin, 1991). It works because the teaching is highly individualized, and the child receives intensive instruction over a period of time by a skilled teacher who can tailor the instruction to the specific child's needs. Sometimes students with learning disabilities need one-to-one instruction, and they tend to do well with this individualized instruction (Slavin, Karweit, & Wasik, 1994; Pressley & Rankin, 1994; Wasik & Slavin, 1993; Kirk, 1986; Bloom, 1984).

In the real world, of course, the cost of schools providing a teacher for each child is impractical, and so parents must often turn to private specialists or clinics to receive this highly individualized form of instruction. Therefore, it is important for schools to seek ways to get as close as possible to one-to-one instruction. Methods for doing this include using computer instruction and using other aides and volunteers as tutors in the classroom (Slavin, 1991).

Computers also offer a way to individualize teaching. A good computer software program is like a tutor because it presents the information, gives students abundant practice, assesses their level of understanding, and provides additional information if it is needed. Computer programs can be quite effective in presenting ideas and in using pictures or graphics to reinforce concepts. Since most students are motivated by the computer, they will work longer and harder than they will with paper-and-pencil tasks.

Using aides and volunteers offers another way to approximate one-to-one instruction. The volunteer movement is alive and growing. Some 60 reading and literacy groups support one-to-one programs, using volunteer adult tutors. Moreover, research demonstrates that tutoring works, increasing a child's reading achievement, confidence, and motivation, in addition to providing a sense of control of his or her reading ability (America Reads Challenge, 1998). Even when children receive the very best in-class instruction, some still need extra time and assistance to meet the high levels of reading skills needed in school, in the workplace, and throughout life. Tutors can provide the explicit instruction that produces positive results (America Reads Challenge, 1998; Snow, Burns, & Griffin, 1998; CIERA, 1998). Tutoring is especially critical during the long school breaks, such as summer vacation. Research shows that during these vacation periods, children lose many skills they had learned (Wasik, 1998).

PROMOTING PARTNERSHIPS BETWEEN GENERAL AND SPECIAL EDUCATION TEACHERS

Procedures that promote partnerships between general and special educators become especially important as more and more students with learning disabilities are placed in the regular class for instruction. Finding ways to facilitate this regular education/special education team effort is important for successful inclusion of students with learning disabilities. Regular and special educators must work together as equal partners (Langone, 1998). Instructional models that facilitate this partnership, including coteaching, peer tutoring, collaboration, and cooperative learning, are described in this section.

Coteaching

Coteaching represents another partnership between general and special education teachers. Coteaching occurs when two or more teachers deliver instruction to a diverse group of students in a regular classroom (Vaughn, Schumm, & Arguelles, 1997; Friend & Bursuck, 1996). Both the general classroom teacher and the learning disabilities teacher actively share in the teaching. Coteaching can be mutually satisfying, but both partners must be willing to share and accept responsibility. In fact, coteaching has been likened to marriage. In order for coteaching to be effective, both partners have to feel that they are making 100% effort and want things to work out. Five different types of coteaching are described in Figure 5.5 (Vaughn, Schumm, & Arguelles, 1997).

Peer Tutoring

Peer tutoring is a strategy in which two children work on a learning task together. One child is the *tutor* and serves as a teacher; the other child is the *tutee* and is the learner. The children work in pairs, so peer tutoring supports one-to-one teaching in the regular classroom. The peer tutor helps the student tutee learn, practice or review an academic skill that the classroom teacher has planned. Examples of peer tutoring tasks are saying aloud or writing spelling words, reading sentences, or solving a mathematics problem. Types of peer tutoring include *same-age peer tutoring* (in which one student in the classroom tutors a classmate) and *cross-age peer tutoring* (where the tutor is several years older than tutee) (Utley, Mortweet, & Greenwood, 1997; Greenwood, 1996; Slavin, 1991).

Both the tutor and the tutee benefit from the peer-tutoring experience. For the tutee, there are gains in academic achievement. The child is able to learn more effectively from a fellow student who is closer to the thinking process of the child than that of an adult. For the tutor, there are also academic benefits because the best way to really learn something is to teach it to someone else. It also offers the tutor a sense of accomplishment. There are other advantages of peer tutoring: the tutor serves as a model of appropriate academic and nonacademic behavior, and the relationship

Figure 5.5

Types of Coteaching

TYPE	DESCRIPTION
A. One Group: One Lead Teacher, One Supportive Teacher	One teacher teaches the entire group; the other teacher provides "supportive learning activities." Either teacher can serve in both roles.
B. Two Groups: Two Teachers Teach Same Content	The class is divided into two heterogenous groups. Each teacher works with one of the groups to provide students with more opportunities to interact and respond. This may be followed by a wrap-up session with the whole class.
C. Two Groups: One Teacher Re-teaches, One Teacher Teaches Alternative Information	Students are assigned to one of two groups, based on their levels of knowledge and skills for an assigned topic. These groups are temporary and apply only to the assigned topic.
D. Multiple Groups: Two Teachers Monitor and Teach. Content May Vary.	Activities are arranged in designated areas throughout the classroom. Students can either be assigned or select a particular activity area. Teachers provide mini-lessons for the activity group and monitor the progress of students in the activity group.
E. One Group: Two Teachers Teach Same Content	Two teachers direct a whole class of students. Both teachers work cooperatively, teaching the same lesson at the same time. (For example, a science teacher presents a lesson on electricity; and the learning disabilities teacher supports the lesson by giving examples, highlighting key ideas, and assisting students with strategies for remembering and organizing the content of the lesson.)

Source: The ABCDEs of Co-Teaching by J. S. Vaughn, J. Schumm, and M. Arguelles. *Teaching Exceptional Children, 30* (2), 1997 26–29. Copyright © 1997 by The Council for Exceptional Children. Reprinted by permission.

between the two children offers opportunities for establishing additional social relationships within the classroom.

Research continues to show that peer tutoring is a successful and validated strategy (Fuchs & Fuchs, 1998; Fisher, Schumaker, & Deshler, 1995; Utley, Mortweet, and Greenwood, 1997; Greenwood, 1996). Peer tutoring is relatively easy for teachers to implement. It is a practical way to provide supports for children with learning disabilities in inclusion classes, and most important, children like peer tutoring.

Classwide peer tutoring is a more organized version of peer tutoring that involves the entire class. Tutor-tutee pairs work together on a classwide basis. At the beginning of each week, all students are paired for tutoring, and these

In peer tutoring, two children work on a learning task together; with one child serving as the teacher (tutor) and the other child as the learner (tutee). *(Anne Dowle/ The Picture Cube)*

pairs are then assigned to one of two competing teams. Tutees earn points for their team by responding to the tasks presented to them by their tutors. The winning team is determined daily and weekly on the basis of the highest teams' point total (Utley, Mortweet, & Greenwood, 1997; Greenwood, 1996).

Collaboration

The process of **collaboration** involves people with diverse areas of expertise (such as classroom teachers and learning disabilities teachers) as they interact to find creative solutions to mutually defined problems (such as teaching students with learning disabilities in general classes) (Langone, 1998; Friend & Cook, 1996; Sugai & Tindal, 1993). As noted earlier, collaboration activities are essential to meet the needs of students with learning disabilities in general education classrooms.

Friend and Cook (1996) see collaboration as a style of interaction, that is, a way that individuals or groups work together. Successful collaborations involve (1) mutual goals, (2) voluntary participation, (3) parity among participants, (4) shared responsibility for participation and decision making, (5) shared responsibility for outcomes, and (6) shared resources. Figure 5.6 presents a summary of principles of effective collaboration, showing activities that work and those that do not work.

Activities to Promote Collaboration   The following activities are intended to promote a spirit of cooperation within a school (Voltz, Elliot, & Harris, 1995; Friend & Cook, 1996; Sugai & Tindal, 1993). After reviewing them, you may find that high-level cooperation already exists at your school.

Figure 5.6

Principles of Effective
Collaboration

Principles	Activities That Work	Activities That Do Not Work
Establish common goals: Successful partners share mutual goals and a common philosophy.	▪ Developing a relationship ▪ Engaging in small-scale efforts initially ▪ Sharing the same philosophy	▪ Engaging in a long-term commitment without having established a relationship
Participation should be voluntary: Collaboration cannot be forced by directives from superiors. Individuals must take mutual responsibility for a problem and freely seek solutions.	▪ Involving key stakeholders ▪ Inviting participation	▪ Working with only one or two individuals on something that will impact many
Recognize equality among participants: Each person's contribution to an endeavor is equally valued and each person has equal power in decision making. A team of individuals shares equal responsibility for moving toward a common goal.	▪ Using names, not titles, when interacting ▪ Rotating and sharing team roles (e.g., facilitator, timekeeper, recorder) ▪ Structuring ways to facilitate participation	▪ Calling John Jacob "Professor Jacob" instead of "John" ▪ Reserving the role of facilitator for a select few
Share responsibility for participation and decision making: Individuals involved in a collaborative effort are expected to share the responsibility for both participation and decision making.	▪ Sharing perspectives about decisions ▪ Brainstorming before decision making ▪ Balancing between coordination of tasks and division of labor ▪ Clear delineation of agreed-upon actions as follow-up	▪ Assuming that tasks must be divided equally and that each party must participate fully in each activity ▪ Placing decision-making responsibility with one individual or party
Share accountability for outcomes: Everyone shares in the outcomes, whether they are successful or not. When successful, all share in the celebration. When unsuccessful, all share responsibility for failures.	▪ Acknowledging risks and potential failure ▪ Celebrating successes together ▪ Embracing failures together, adopting a "learning from failures" mindset	▪ Trying to determine *who* is to blame ▪ Giving awards to individuals for team efforts
Share resources: Each individual has some resources to contribute to the shared goals.	▪ Identifying respective resources ▪ Having mutual goals ▪ Highlighting the benefits of sharing ▪ Joint decision making about resource allocation	▪ Protecting, not revealing, resources ▪ Having no mutual goals and disparate benefits ▪ Using own resources after depleting others' resources

Source: Adapted from "True or False? Truly Collaborative Relationships Can Exist Between University and Public School Personnel," by T. Vandercook, J. York, and B. Sullivan, 1993, *OSERS News In Print, 5* (8), p. 3. Copyright 1993 by the U.S. Department of Education.

Making Time for Collaborative Activities   Productive work requires space, time, and the assurance of uninterrupted sessions. If planning, communicating, and evaluating are not specifically scheduled, there will be insufficient time in the crowded school day for these purposes.

Coaching   Coaching is a way to help teachers learn and put into practice useful techniques for working with students with learning disabilities. The learning disabilities teacher takes on the role of a coach, giving instruction and demonstrating a specific teaching skill, and the classroom teacher becomes the partner and learns the skill. The coach and partner jointly decide on the skill they wish to practice. Essential elements of the coaching method include demonstrations by the coach, practice by the partner, and transfer of the skill into the classroom.

In-service Education   It is essential to provide in-service training for all persons involved with students with learning disabilities. Classroom teachers, as well as administrators, paraprofessionals, and other specialists, should be urged to participate in the in-service sessions.

Demonstration of Methods and Materials   Materials, methods, techniques, and tests can be demonstrated or used in trial periods with students in the classroom. Publishers' materials—videos, tapes, and so on—can also be used for this purpose. Teachers are usually interested in learning about useful new items.

Case Study Discussions   An in-depth discussion of a particular case can be a useful way of presenting certain concepts and principles. Emphasis may be on assessment, intervention, or some other aspect of the case. Involving participants in the case under discussion can be an effective way to make a point or to teach a concept. *Cases in Learning and Behavior Problems: A Guide to Individualized Education Programs* (Lerner, Dawson, & Horvath, 1980) is designed for group participation in case studies.

Guest Speakers and Conferences   New ideas, new approaches, and fresh perspectives can be gained from guest speakers invited to address the group. Attendance at local, state, and national meetings also renews energy, interest, and ideas.

Newsletters   A written communication which may be issued biweekly, monthly, or quarterly can be developed by the learning disabilities teacher to update classroom teachers and others about ideas, materials, and happenings in the field.

Communication   Communication is key to collaboration. If problems are allowed to continue without an opportunity for face-to-face communication, dissatisfaction increases and misunderstandings develop. To avert such situations, oral and written communication must be clear. Effective collaborators are active listeners, are sensitive to the contributions and ideas of others, and recognize nonverbal messages. They give and ask for continuous feedback and are willing to say, "I don't know" and to give credit to others.

Problem Solving   Successful problem solving requires shared perceptions among all participating team members. Procedures for problem solving include the generation of alternative solutions through brainstorming, the anticipation of possible consequences of actions, and an open, positive, problem-solving attitude. Effective collaborators are available for troubleshooting and follow-up and remain objective throughout the problem-solving process. When problems arise, they must be resolved. Problems should not be ignored, and resolutions should not be forced by the use of power. Successful collaborators develop problem-solving strategies. They also place all information out in the open so that the problem can be considered by all participants.

Cooperative Learning

Cooperative learning is a method of promoting learning among students through cooperation rather than through competition. Instead of competing against each other, students work together to seek solutions to problems (Johnson & Johnson, 1986). Advocates of cooperative learning believe it can foster positive relationships among students with disabilities and other students in the regular education classroom.

COMPETENCIES FOR LEARNING DISABILITIES TEACHERS

The responsibilities of teachers of students with learning disabilities are difficult to define because they are changing so rapidly. Learning disabilities teachers are expected to (1) set up programs for identifying, assessing, and instructing students; (2) participate in the screening, assessment, and evaluation of students; (3) collaborate with classroom teachers to design and implement instruction for students; (4) use both traditional and authentic assessment methods; (5) participate in the formulation of individualized education programs; (6) implement the IEP through direct intervention, coteaching, and collaboration; (7) interview and hold conferences with parents; and (8) perhaps most important, help students develop self-understanding and gain the hope and confidence necessary to cope with and overcome their learning disabilities.

To accomplish these goals, effective learning disabilities teachers need two kinds of competencies: (1) competencies in professional knowledge and skills (having the information and proficiencies for testing and teaching), and (2) competencies in human relationships (the art of working with people).

Professional Knowledge and Skills

Competencies in knowledge and skills encompass the professional knowledge base that learning disabilities teachers need. This technical role requires competencies in assessment and diagnosis, curriculum, instructional practices, managing student behaviors, planning and managing the teaching and learning environment, and monitoring and evaluation. Learning disabilities teachers must also know theories of learning and must possess strategies for teaching oral language, reading, written language, mathematics, behavior management, social and emotional skills, and pre-vocational and vocational skills.

Human Relations Abilities

The art of working with people comprises the second and growing responsibility for learning disabilities teachers. As services for students with learning disabilities move from special classes and resource rooms to general education classes, the focus of the teacher's role is shifting from provider of direct instruction to that of coteacher, consultant, and collaborator (Langone, 1998). Thus, the effective learning disabilities teacher will be proficient not only in professional knowledge and skills but also in the ability to deal with people.

Collaboration requires teachers to be caring, respectful, empathic, and open. They must be able to establish good rapport with others, remembering to display appropriate responses to another's stage of professional development. A positive and enthusiastic attitude, combined with a willingness to learn from others, is essential. As they work with others, learning disabilities teachers must be able to manage personal stress, remain calm in time of crisis, and respect divergent points of view.

In a collaborative partnership, both general and special educators come to the classroom with identifiable strengths and weaknesses. Both teachers can provide each other with useful strategies for instruction learners (Langone, 1998).

PARENTS AND THE FAMILY The child with learning disabilities exacts a tremendous emotional toll on parents. Parents of these children face many of the same problems as teachers do but in greatly magnified intensity. The child is in school for a few hours a day in a limited and controlled situation, but for the parent, it is 24 hours a day, seven days a week, with no vacations, in all kinds of situations and with all types of demands.

It is important for school personnel to consider the strengths of the family. Involvement of parents and families through family-school collaboration is encouraged through informal communication (such as written notes between school and home, parent involvement in the classroom and in extracurricular activities, face-to-face conferences, telephone contact, and technology options, such as email and the Internet) (U.S. Department of Education, 1997; Turnbull & Turnbull, 1996).

Parents can play a crucial role in helping their child. They must (1) be informed consumers, continually working to learn more about the baffling problem of learning disabilities; (2) be assertive advocates, seeking the right programs for their child at home, in school, and in the community; (3) work to make sure that their child's legal rights are being recognized; and (4) be firm in managing their child's behavior while remaining empathetic to their child's feelings, failures, fears, and tribulations. Parents must also give time and attention to other members of the family and try to make a life for themselves. There are no easy answers or simple solutions for parents of children with learning disabilities (Turnbull & Turnbull, 1996). For an account of a parent's role in helping a child with learning disabilities, see the box entitled, "A Mother's Thoughts."

Parenting a child with learning disabilities is challenging, but it can also be rewarding. Parents need support from the school, the extended family, and other professionals. With this support, encouragement, and the sharing of expertise, the child can emerge from the school years academically, emotionally, and socially intact, and prepared for the challenges ahead.

Parents' Rights

The 1997 IDEA (Public Law 105–17) strengthens the rights of parents and families in the educational process of their children. A fundamental provision of the law is the right of parents to participate in the educational decision-making process. Parents have the right to (ERIC, 1998):

- a free appropriate public education for their child
- request an evaluation of their child
- notification whenever the school wants to evaluate their child or change the child's educational placement
- informed consent (parents understand and agree in writing to teaching plans and may withdraw their consent at any time)
- obtain an independent evaluation of their child
- request a reevaluation of their child
- have their child tested in the language that the child knows best
- review all of their child's school records
- be informed of **parents' rights**
- participate in their child's IEP (individualized education program) or IFSP (Individual Family Service Plan) for young children

A MOTHER'S THOUGHTS

My son has a learning disability. He went to elementary school at a time before students with learning disabilities were identified. I remember his coming home from first grade and crying over his reader. He could not decode! The only way he managed to get through first grade was to memorize the readers he brought home. He accomplished this by going over and over them with me. I don't think his teacher was ever aware that he memorized.

The tests in second grade were longer; we had to labor over the stories together many times each night. In the spring of his second year our family was transferred for a short period to New York. My son was accepted at his father's old private school, where he finally learned to read. He read slowly, but he was reading.

Spelling was another matter. Try though he might, he simply could not hear the vowel sounds. They all sounded alike to him. His visual memory was also unreliable. I kept one of the science papers he wrote in second grade. It was all about how "gravy helps people on earth."

Teacher comments were predictable. "He is immature." "He could do it if he would just try." "He's just sloppy because he rushes through his work." "He's just lazy." If they had only been with him night after night as he cried over his homework.

My son was lucky. I continued to work with him. As he grew older, he learned to compensate somewhat. He typically avoided classes that required much writing. I typed and edited most of his papers for him. By his sheer determination he made it through school, college, and eventually law school.

Source: From A Mother's Thoughts on Inclusion by Carr, M. N. (1993) *Journal of Learning Disabilities, 26*(9), 590–592. Copyright © 1993 by PRO-ED, Inc. Reprinted by permission.

- be informed of their child's progress at least as often as parents of children who do not have disabilities are informed
- have their child educated in the least restrictive environment possible
- voluntary mediation or a due process hearing to resolve differences with the school

The Family System

A family of five is like five people lying on a waterbed. Whenever one person moves, everyone feels the ripple. (Lavoie, 1995)

It is useful to view the family as a system. The fundamental idea of the family systems theory is that whatever happens to one part of a family or system affects all the other parts. In the family system, all members of the extended family are interdependent, and each member has interactive effects on all other members. The family system involves the child, parents, siblings, grandparents, other people living in the home, or those who are part of the child's family.

The entire family system is affected by a child with learning disabilities. Day-to-day living can be stressful from the start. As infants, these children may be irritable, demanding, and difficult to soothe, making parents feel incompetent, confused, and helpless. As the child enters school and begins to face learning failure, the parents may have feelings of guilt, shame, and embarrassment. As they become frustrated, they may blame each other for their youngster's problems. One parent may accuse the other of being too strict or too lenient in raising their child, putting extra strain on the marital relationship. Siblings and other family members are also affected when a brother or sister has learning disabilities. The siblings may be embarrassed or feel angry or jealous if their parents pay more attention to the sibling with learning disabilities.

For these reasons, in some cases it is necessary to include the entire family in the treatment process, with counseling for the family system an important part.

Stages of Acceptance

When parents are faced with the quandary of a child with learning disabilities, they are likely to pass through a series of predictable **stages of acceptance** (Kubler-Ross, 1969). These stages are universal and apply to anyone who experiences a loss. In this case, the parents have lost their hope for a normal child.

The parents go through a mourning process when first told that their child has learning disabilities. The stages in the process are shock, disbelief, denial, anger, bargaining, depression, and acceptance. There is no factor that predicts the order in which the parent experiences these stages, the number of stages that the parent goes through, or the length of time that is spent in each stage. Nor is the process linear; the parent often returns to an earlier stage.

Shock is the numb, distancing feeling that engulfs the parents when the bad news is being delivered.

Disbelief is the stage in which parents do not believe the diagnosis.

Denial is a stage in which parents refuse to even consider that the child has a learning disability, and they may seek an alternative diagnosis.

REACTIONS OF PARENTS OF CHILDREN WITH LEARNING DISABILITIES

Denial

There is really nothing wrong!
That's the way I was as a child—not to worry!
He'll grow out of it.

Blame

You baby him!
You expect too much of him.
It's not from my side of the family.

Fear

Maybe they're not telling me the real problem.
Is it worse than they say?
Will he ever marry?
Go to college?
Graduate?

Mourning

He could have been such a success, if not for the learning disability.

Bargaining

Wait until next year.
Maybe the problem will improve if we move.
I'll send her to camp.

Anger

The teachers don't know anything.
I hate the neighborhood, this school, this teacher, etc.

Guilt

My mother was right. I should have used cloth diapers when he was a
    baby.
I shouldn't have worked during her first year.
I am being punished for something, and my child is suffering as a result.

Source: Adapted from R. Lavoie, "Life on the Waterbed: Mainstreaming on the Homefront," *Attention!* 2 (1), 1995, p. 27. Used by permission.

Anger occurs as the denial breaks down and the child's condition becomes more real and apparent. Angry feelings are exhibited when parents say, "Why did this happen to me?" or "It isn't fair."

Bargaining is evident when the parent decides that dedication will somehow alleviate their child's condition.

Depression is evident when the parent makes statements like: What's the use? Why even bother? Nothing is going to change. What will happen to my child? The parent may despair of ever finding a solution and feel sad and helpless.

Acceptance is the stage at which the parents can look past the disability and accept the child as he or she is. A stage beyond acceptance is to *cherish* the child for those differences and for how that child has made the parents' lives better.

For some statements parents typically make when expressing these and other emotions, see the box entitled "Reactions of Parents of Children with Learning Disabilities." This "roller coaster" of emotions has a profound impact upon the parent and upon interactions with the child. Since the two parents will probably not go through these stages at the same time, each must learn to respect the other's right to travel through the stages at a different rate.

The goal is to reach acceptance so that the parent is able to make placement decisions that are unclouded by undue emotionality. When parents accept their child along with his or her disabilities, they are then able to provide for the child's special needs while continuing to live a normal life and tending to family, home, civic, and social obligations (Gallagher, 1995; Lavoie, 1995).

Parent Support Groups and Family Counseling

Establishing healthy parental attitudes and ensuring parent-teacher cooperation are, of course, desirable goals. Two procedures—parent support groups and family counseling—can help in meeting these goals.

Parent support groups offer parents a way to meet regularly in small groups to discuss common problems. They can be organized by the school, family service organizations, professional counselors, or parent organizations (such as the Learning Disabilities Association, or LDA). The opportunity to meet with other parents whose children are encountering similar problems tends to reduce the parents' sense of isolation. Furthermore, such parent support groups have been useful in alerting the community, school personnel, other professionals, and legislative bodies to the plight of their children.

Family counseling offers parents help in accepting the problem, in developing empathy for the child, and in providing a beneficial home environment. Guidance counselors and social workers often play important roles in providing such help. Often the first step in parent or family counseling is helping the parents get over their initial feelings. In addition to the feelings already mentioned, the initial period of reaction may include feelings of mourning, misunderstanding, guilt, deprecation of self, or even shame. Parents may respond to these feelings by turning away in confusion, or they may overreact, become aggressive, and try to break down doors to get things done. These aggressive parents are much needed in our profession, for they are the ones who keep the educators moving. Educators should empathize with parents to help them get through the initial period of reaction.

Parent support groups and family counseling offer the following benefits:

1. Helping parents understand and accept their child's problem.

2. Reducing anxieties stemming from apprehension about the psychological and educational development of their children. Parents can discover that they are not alone; other parents have similar problems and have found solutions.

3. Realizing that they are an integral part of their child's learning, development, and behavior. They can learn to perceive their children differently and to deal with their problems more effectively.

4. Learning about discipline, communication skills, behavioral management, parent advocacy, special education legislation, social skills development, helping one's child make friends, home management, and college and vocational opportunities.

Parent-Teacher Conferences

Parent-teacher conferences are a bridge between the home and school. Both parents and teachers tend to shy away from these private conferences, parents fearing what they will hear and teachers fearing that parents will react negatively. Yet these conferences, at which the student's progress and problems are discussed, should be viewed as an opportunity to help the student. Parents and teachers can work together to enhance progress.

In setting up a conference, teachers should try to reassure parents that they are going to communicate with another human being. Teachers must impart a sense of confidence without being arrogant, and should convey a sincere interest in the student and respect for the parents. They should discuss problems in a calm manner, avoiding technical jargon. Parents want to understand the nature of their child's problems, and diagnostic data and current teaching approaches should therefore be interpreted and explained. The parents must also be helped to become sensitive to the nature of their children's learning problems and to those tasks that are difficult for them. Parents also want to know what they can do at home.

SUGGESTIONS FOR PARENTS

1. *Be alert to any hint that your child is good at something.* By discovering an area of interest or a talent, you can give your child a new chance for success. Even small tasks, such as folding napkins or helping with specific kitchen chores, can give a sense of achievement.

2. *Do not push your child into activities for which the child is not ready.* The child may react by trying half-heartedly to please you; rebelling, either actively or passively; or just quitting or withdrawing into a world of daydreams. When a child is forced to meet arbitrary and inappropriate standards imposed by the adult world, learning becomes painful rather than pleasurable.

3. *Simplify family routine.* For some children, mealtime can be an extremely complex and stimulating situation. Your child may be unable to cope with the many sounds, sights, smells, and so on. It may be necessary at first to have the child eat earlier and then gradually join the family meal—perhaps starting with dessert. Search for other such examples in your routines.

4. *Try to match tasks to the child's level of functioning.* Think about the child's problem and figure out some way to help. For example, easy-to-wipe surfaces and break-proof containers can reduce mess and breakage when the child uses these materials. Drawing an outline of the child's shoes on the closet floor can indicate left and right.

5. *Be direct and positive in talking to your child.* Try to avoid criticizing; instead, be supportive and provide guidance. For example, if your child has trouble following directions, ask him or her to look at you while you speak and then to repeat what you have said.

6. *Keep the child's room simple and in a quiet part of the house.* As far as possible, make the room a place to relax and retreat.

7. *Help your child learn how to live in a world with others.* When a child does not play well with other children, parents may have to go out of their way to plan and guide social experiences. This may mean inviting a single child to play for a short period of time, arranging with parents of other children for joint social activities, or volunteering to be a den mother or Brownie leader.

8. *Children need to learn that they are significant.* They must be treated with respect and allowed to do their own work. They should learn that being a responsible and contributing member of the family is important—probably more important than learning the academic skills demanded by the school.

9. *Keep your outside interests.* Try to relinquish your child's care to a competent baby sitter periodically. Parents need time off for independence and morale boosting.

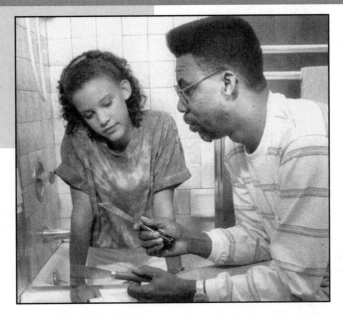

A child's self-esteem benefits from a parent's support
of a child's interests, talents,
and related activities.
*(© Laima Druskis/
Stock Boston)*

Suggestions for Parents

Some useful things parents *can* do are presented in the box entitled "Suggestions for Parents." Teachers may also wish to recommend reading materials to parents to help them become better acquainted with the problem of learning disabilities and with ways of helping their children. A selection of appropriate books for parents is given in the box on page 178.

The case study starting on page 177 completes the story of Rita G., which was begun in Chapter 3 and continued in Chapter 4.

CASE STUDY, PART III

RITA G.

STAGE 4: THE CASE CONFERENCE

The case conference team that met to discuss Rita included the school psychologist, the learning disabilities teacher, Mr. Martinez (her third-grade teacher), and Rita's parents, Mr. and Mrs. G.

The case conference team agreed that Rita has a number of strengths. They include facility with oral language; intelligence within the overall normal range, with high abilities in verbal areas; an understanding and supportive family and a playful relationship with her sister; good word-recognition skills in reading; a grasp of phonics skills; and an above-average listening-speaking vocabulary.

Her weaknesses include poor problem-solving skills in arithmetic computation and mathematics word problems; slow, laborious, and illegible handwriting, related to general visual-motor and spatial problems; and difficulty in reading comprehension. Rita has developed a passive attitude toward learning, and she cannot attend to a task without becoming distracted. She lacks organizational skills and does not use efficient learning strategies. In addition, Rita has poor social skills.

The case conference team concluded that Rita has learning disabilities. She has a severe discrepancy between her potential and her achievement in academic areas. Her learning problems are not primarily the result of other known disabilities such as mental retardation or due to economic or cultural disadvantages. Rita has difficulties with visual-motor perception, social interactions, attention, and learning strategies.

The annual goals developed for Rita focused on improving skills for written communication, improving mathematics skills—calculation and arithmetic word-story problems, improving reading comprehension, developing cognitive learning strategies, and developing better social skills. Benchmarks (or short-term objectives) were written for each of these five goals.

The case conference team recommended that Rita be placed in the regular third-grade class. The regular third-grade teacher and the special education teacher would coordinate their efforts through coteaching and other classroom supports. Rita's father said that he thought this would be a good arrangement because Rita would receive the special teaching she needed and still be part of the third-grade class.

The information and decisions were written into Rita's individualized education program. The IEP was signed by all of the case conference team members, including Rita's mother and father. The annual goal concerning improvement in the skills of writing for cursive is shown below. A few selected benchmarks (or short-term objectives) for this goal are also presented.

Annual Goal Writes legibly, using cursive writing, one paragraph consisting of ten sentences.

Benchmarks (or short-term objectives)
Cursive writing
1. Traces two cursive letters using a stencil
2. Copies ten letters using cursive writing in upper and lower case on a chalkboard.
3. Writes legibly all letters using cursive writing in upper and lower case on paper.
4. Writes name in cursive writing.
5. Writes legibly five short words in cursive writing from a model.
6. Writes legibly a sentence from a model.
7. Writes legibly a paragraph with five sentences.
8. Writes legibly a paragraph with ten sentences.

STAGE 5: IMPLEMENTING THE TEACHING PLAN

The learning disabilities teacher and Mr. Martinez, Rita's third-grade teacher, developed more specific plans to meet the objectives stated in the individualized education program. A summary of these plans is discussed briefly in this section.

Rita would be placed in Mr. Martinez's third-grade classroom. Through a team partnership between the learning disabilities teacher and Mr. Martinez, the two could share the activities for Rita's instruction. Coteaching would allow Rita's learning disabilities teacher and regular education teacher to work with her in different kinds of groups. The use of peer tutoring would provide Rita with more individual practice and instruction. In addition, Rita would receive some resource room help if it were needed.

The instruction in mathematics and reading would be linked to the curriculum-based assessment data. Rita's deficits in visual-motor skills were taken into account in planning a skills approach to arithmetic. The learning disabilities teacher and Mr. Martinez decided to use concrete materials to establish basic number concepts for addition, subtraction, and multiplication. Opportunity for drill and practice was planned by using a number of different manipulative materials and some computer mathematics drill-and-practice software.

A computer typing software program would also be used to teach Rita typing skills. The plan was that after she learned to type, she would be taught word processing and then would move into lessons in written expression. It was felt that it would be worthwhile to try to teach Rita cursive writing, since many occasions in daily life require handwriting. However, since her writing problem is so severe, Rita's progress should be monitored very carefully and her progress reevaluated continually. Another specific plan was to help Rita develop more efficient learning strategies. She would be taught to self-monitor her attention to keep herself on task and self-rehearsal strategies to improve her approach to learning.

The plan also included the provision of more opportunities for social interaction in the classroom through assigning Rita to committees and through peer work. (These are only a few of the implementation activities.)

STAGE 6: MONITORING PROGRESS AND REVIEW

The learning disabilities teacher and Mr. Martinez will review Rita's progress informally on a monthly basis. An annual review is planned for the middle of the following year, when Rita will be in fourth grade. She will be tested in mathematics computation, mathematics reasoning, written expression, and reading comprehension. Also, the information gathered through instruction linked to curriculum-based assessment will serve to monitor progress continuously.

Chapter Summary

1. Important concepts for planning the placement for students with learning disabilities are the continuum of alternative placements and the least restrictive environment.

2. The term *continuum of alternative placements* refers to the array of educational placements in the schools to meet the varied needs of exceptional students.

3. The 1997 Individuals with Disabilities Education Act (IDEA) (PL 105–17) requires that students be placed in the *least restrictive environment*. This means that, to the greatest extent appropriate, they should be with students who do not have disabilities.

4. Several approaches for integrating general and special education include mainstreaming, the regular education initiative, and inclusion.

5. Special and general education students must be integrated into general education classrooms in a responsible way.

6. The continuum of alternative placements available to meet the needs of students with learning disabilities includes the general education classroom, the resource room, the separate class, the separate school, the residential facility, and the home or hospital environment. Each of the placements is successively more restrictive in terms of the student's opportunity to interact with students without disabilities. One-to-one instruction between teacher and student is very effective but also very costly.

BOOKS FOR PARENTS

Barkley, R. (1995). *Taking charge of ADHD: The complete authoritative guide for parents.* New York: Guilford Press.

Cordoni, B. (1992). *Living with a learning disability.* Carbondale, IL: Southern Illinois University Press.

Goldstein, S., & Mather, N. (1998). *Overcoming underachievement: An action guide to helping your child succeed in school.* New York: John Wiley.

Hall, S., & Moats, L. (1999). *Straight talk about reading: How parents can make a difference during the early years.* Chicago: Contemporary Press.

Lerner, J., Lowenthal, B., & Lerner, S. (1995). *Attention deficit disorders: Assessment and teaching.* Pacific Grove, CA: Brooks/Cole.

Osman, B. (1997). *Learning disability and ADHD: A family guide to learning and learning together.* New York: John Wiley.

Silver, L. (1998). *The misunderstood child: A guide for parents of children with learning disabilities.* New York: Times Books.

Smith, S. (1991). *Succeeding against the odds: Strategies and insights from the learning-disabled.* Los Angeles: Jeremy P. Tarcher.

---

7. Methods for promoting the partnership between general and special education include peer tutoring, collaboration, coteaching, and cooperative learning.

8. Peer tutoring is a system of having one student teach another student.

9. Collaboration is the coordinated effort of the learning disabilities teacher and the general classroom teacher to provide services for students with learning disabilities in the regular classroom. Collaboration is a growing responsibility for learning disabilities teachers. Various activities for promoting collaboration are suggested.

10. In coteaching, two instructors, a regular classroom teacher and a special education teacher, teach a diverse group of students in the regular education classroom.

11. There are two types of competencies for learning disabilities teachers. The professional knowledge and skills competencies involve the technical knowledge about the field and skills in testing and teaching. The human relations responsibilities require sensitivity and skill in dealing with people. As learning disabilities teachers interact more with other school staff, the human relations aspect of the job grows in importance.

12. Families and parents are vital components of the student's education. In the family system, all members of the extended family are interde-

pendent, and each member has interactive effects on all other members of the family system. Parents go through stages of mourning before they reach the stages of acceptance. Parent support groups and family counseling are effective in helping parents understand their children and their problems and in finding ways to help their children within the home.

13. Parents' rights have been strengthened through the 1997 IDEA federal law.

14. Parent-teacher conferences can become a bridge between home and school and can involve parents in the educational process.

Questions for Discussion and Reflection

1. Discuss two key concepts about placement that are features of the special education law. Do you think these two features are compatible or in conflict? Explain your position.

2. Discuss some of the recent trends in placement for students with learning disabilities. How do you think these trends will affect students with learning disabilities?

3. Inclusion is one of the recommended placement plans for students with learning disabilities. Describe the advantages and shortcomings of the inclusion placement model. What do you think the future holds for inclusion?

4. What are the three most common school placements for students with learning disabilities? Compare and contrast these placements.

5. Discuss activities for coteaching between the learning disabilities teacher and the general education teacher.

6. What are the various responsibilities of the learning disabilities teacher? How are they changing?

7. How has the 1997 IDEA federal law approached parents' rights? Which rights were strengthened?

Key Terms

collaboration *(p. 165)*

continuum of alternative placements *(p. 149)*

coteaching *(p. 163)*

direct services *(p. 157)*

family counseling *(p. 174)*

full inclusion *(p. 152)*

inclusion *(p. 148)*

indirect services *(p. 157)*

least restrictive environment *(p. 149)*

mainstreaming *(p. 152)*

one-to-one instruction *(p. 162)*

parent support groups *(p. 174)*

parents' rights *(p. 170)*

peer tutoring *(p. 163)*

placement *(p. 148)*

regular education initiative
(REI) *(p. 152)*

regular or general education
classroom *(p. 156)*

residential facilities *(p. 161)*

resource room *(p. 158)*

Section 504 of the Rehabilitation
Act, Americans with Disabilities
Act *(p. 158)*

separate class *(p. 160)*

separate schools *(p. 161)*

stages of acceptance *(p. 172)*

Theoretical Perspectives and Expanding Directions

6 Theories of Learning: Implications for Learning Disabilities

art III examines underlying theories and expanding directions in the field of learning disabilities. It covers the relevant theories of learning (Chapter 6) and pertinent information in several areas—medicine (Chapter 7), early childhood (Chapter 8), and adolescence and adulthood (Chapter 9).

This chapter explores the contributions of theories from the various branches of psychology to the field of learning disabilities. Fundamental concepts from developmental psychology, behavioral psychology, and cognitive psychology have advanced our understanding of learning disabilities, with implications for assessment, instruction, and research.

THE ROLE OF THEORY

"If you don't know where you are going, any road will take you there." This advice is as applicable to learning disabilities as it is to other facets of life. Theories help us to understand the foundations of learning disabilities. By shedding light on the nature of the learning problems encountered by the student, theories suggest a basis for instructional methods. Those who teach without theories may follow the road that leads nowhere.

The Need for Theory

In a visit to a hypothetical classroom, we might see all the children in the room using the latest in instructional materials—"Mother Hubbard's Cure-All"—enticingly packaged material composed of colorful boxes, machines, and supplementary items. This program, which the publisher assures the user is based on extensive research and the most recent scientific evidence, is purported to cure students with learning disabilities and to improve students without learning disabilities. The program contains all forms of teaching media: videotapes, transparencies, worksheets for duplication, computer software, Internet sites, workbooks, CD-ROMs, games, and even books. It also contains a teacher's manual that explains the foolproof, step-by-step directions on *how* to use the items in the package. Everything is carefully described, except *why* a particular activity is to be used. The theoretical basis for the method has been eclipsed by the latest educational package.

The point of this somewhat cynical view of pupils engulfed in orderly instruction without a theoretical basis is that such activity may be wasteful. In their enthusiasm to "do something," prospective teachers want "practical" methods and techniques, and they question the need to study theory. Understandably, knowledge of methods and techniques is indispensable, but in too many classrooms across the country, teachers are busily engaged in neat, orderly techniques, completing page after page or step after step in sequential fashion without knowing why. As a result, much of the work is probably wasteful of all resources—time, effort, money—and, most important, of children.

The Purpose of Theory

The purpose of theory is to bring form, coherence, and meaning to what we observe in the real world. Underlying any assessment or instructional procedure should be a theory of teaching or learning. Theory is helpful in sorting and evaluating the bewildering deluge of new materials, techniques, machines, gadgets, methods, and media confronting the educator.

Theories in this context are meant to be working statements. Theories are not meant to be ideas "frozen into absolute standards masquerading as eternal truths" or "programs rigidly adhered to" (Dewey, 1946, p. 202). Theories are meant to serve as guides in systematizing knowledge and as working concepts to be modified in the light of new knowledge. John Dewey considered theory the most practical of all things because it provides a guide for action, clarifies and structures thought, and creates a catalyst for further research.

Theory building is a process. Every discipline is built on the concepts and ideas contributed by earlier theorists. Theories are challenged, modified, and strengthened as researchers and practitioners test the theory's relevance and usefulness. The modified theory in turn leads to changes in assessment and instructional practices.

The investigations of the complex problems of learning disabilities during the past thirty or so years led to substantial reforms in theories and instructional practices. Moreover, the theories generated in the field of learning disabilities also have significant applications in other areas of special education and in general education.

We now turn our attention to three major theories in psychology and their implications for learning disabilities: developmental psychology, behavioral psychology, and cognitive psychology.

DEVELOPMENTAL PSYCHOLOGY

Developmental psychology offers an important theory for understanding learning disabilities. A key notion in developmental psychology is that the maturation of cognitive skills, or thinking, follows a sequential progression. An individual child's ability to learn depends on his or her current maturational status. Further, this theory implies that attempts to speed up or bypass the developmental process may actually create problems. Jean Piaget, the celebrated developmental psychologist, remarked, "Every time I describe a maturational sequence in the United States, an American asks: 'How can you speed it up?'"

Developmental Delays

Developmental delays (or maturation lag) mean a slowness in specific aspects of development. According to this point of view, each individual has a preset rate of growth for various human functions, including cognitive abilities (Bender, 1957). Discrepancies among the various abilities indicate that the abilities are maturing at different rates, with some abilities lagging in their development. Developmental delays are sometimes temporary. Thus many children with learning disabilities are not so different from children without them; rather, it is more a matter of *timing*.

The developmental perspective suggests that society actually creates many learning disabilities. The school curriculum may have set expectations in terms of age of learning. Learning problems occur when children are pushed into performing academic tasks before they are ready to do so. The demands of schooling thus cause failure by requiring students to perform beyond their readiness or ability at a given stage of maturation. Vygotsky (1978), the Russian psychologist reasoned that children learn when the instruction is directed to their *zone of proximal development* (ZPD). If the child's abilities do not mesh with the instructional level, learning cannot occur.

The following studies show that many young children manifest developmental delays or maturational lags that lead to academic problems as they get older.

- Koppitz (1973) studied students with learning disabilities over several years and concluded that these children were immature and needed more time to learn and to grow up. When given the needed extra time, along with the help necessary to compensate for their slowness in maturation, many did well academically. Koppitz observed that these children may require one or two more years than other pupils do to complete their schooling.

- Silver and Hagin (1966, 1990) found evidence of maturational lags in young children, including delays in spatial orientation of symbols, auditory discrimination, and left-right discrimination. When these subjects were reevaluated as young adults aged 16 to 24, many no longer had maturational lags. A great number of the problems had disappeared.

- de Hirsch, Jansky, and Langford (1966) conducted an extensive study aimed at finding factors that predicted reading failure in kindergarten children. They found that the tests that were most sensitive to differences in maturation were the ones that best predicted reading and spelling achievement in second grade. They concluded that maturational status is the crucial factor in predicting reading achievement.

- Levine (1987) and Levine & Swartz (1995) describe how neurodevelopmental variations in students with learning disabilities and learning disorders lead to academic failure. Levine and his colleagues also emphasize the importance of recognizing developmental variations in children and providing instruction to ameliorate them.

- The collection of studies from the National Institute of Child Health and Human Development (NICHD) (Torgesen, 1998; Lyon, Alexander, & Yaffee, 1997; Lyon, 1996) show that children who are likely to have difficulty in learning to read exhibit developmental delays in several areas of maturational development, including phonological awareness. The NICHD studies showed that explicit instruction during the preschool and early primary years helps these children overcome these developmental delays and achieve academically.

Make copy 3
Flow

Piaget's Maturational Stages of Development

Jean Piaget, who is recognized as a pioneer in developmental psychology, spent his life studying the intellectual development of children. Piaget's observations of the maturational stages of thinking in children showed that cognitive growth occurs in a series of invariant and interdependent stages. At each stage, the child is capable of learning only certain cognitive tasks. As the child goes through a series of maturational or developmental stages, the child's ability to think and learn changes with age. The quantity, quality, depth, and breadth of learning that occur depend upon the stage during which the learning takes place (Piaget, 1970). Piaget provided a schematic description of the typical child's stages of development:

1. Sensorimotor stage: Birth to age 2.   The first two years of life are called the **sensorimotor period.** During this time, children learn through their senses and movements and by interacting with the physical environment. By moving, touching, hitting, biting, and so on and by physically manipulating objects, children learn about the properties of space, time, location, permanence, and causality. Some children with learning disabilities need more opportunities for motor exploration. (Motor learning is discussed in Chapter 8.)

2. Preoperational stage: Ages 2–7.   Piaget called the next five years of life, ages 2 to 7, the **preoperational stage.** During this stage children make intuitive judgments about relationships and also begin to think with symbols. Language now becomes increasingly important, and children learn to use symbols to represent the concrete world. They begin to learn about the properties and attributes of the world about them. Their thinking is dominated largely by the world of perception. (The subject of perception is one of the concerns of Chapter 8.)

One characteristic of the preoperational stage is that young children can attach only one attribute or function to an object. For example, three-year-old Josephine was confused when her mother was the emergency substitute teacher in her nursery school class. Josephine was visibly baffled and upset as she exploded, "You can't be a teacher; you're a mother!"

3. Concrete operations stage: Ages 7–11.   The period between ages 7 and 11 is called the **concrete operations stage.** Children are now able to think through relationships, to perceive consequences of acts, and to group entities in a logical fashion. They are better able to systematize and organize their thoughts. However, their thoughts are shaped in large measure by previous experiences and are linked to the concrete objects that they have manipulated or understood through the senses. For example, at this stage a child can recognize a set of four objects without physically touching and counting them.

4. Formal operations stage: Age 11.   The fourth stage, that of **formal operations,** commences at about age 11 and reflects a major transition in the thinking process. At this stage, instead of observations directing thought,

thought now directs observations. Children now have the capacity to work with abstractions, theories, and logical relationships without having to refer to the concrete. The formal operations period provides a generalized orientation toward problem-solving activity.

The transition from one level to the next depends on maturation, and the stages are sequential and hierarchical. An implication for teaching is that students need ample opportunities and experiences to stabilize behavior and thought at each stage of development. Yet the school curriculum frequently requires students to develop abstract and logical conceptualizations in a given area without providing sufficient opportunity for them to go through preliminary levels of understanding. Attempts to teach abstract, logical concepts divorced from any real experiential understanding on the part of the student may lead to inadequate and insecure learning. The teacher may think students are learning the concepts, but they may be giving only surface verbal responses. Some examples of surface learning without understanding are given in the Case Example entitled "Developmental Theory and Maturation."

Piaget used the following experiments to illustrate that children's concepts about *conservation* develop according to their maturational stage of thinking. In one of Piaget's conservation experiments, two balls of clay of equal size were placed on a scale to demonstrate to the child that they were equal. When one ball of clay was then flattened, 8-year-olds were likely to predict that they were still the same weight. Four-year-olds, however, said that the flattened ball weighed more. In another experiment, an equal amount of liquid was poured in each of two identical glasses. When the liquid from one glass was then emptied into a tall, thin container, 5-year-olds were convinced that the tall, thin glass contained more liquid, but 7-year-olds knew there was no difference in volume. From experiments such as these, Piaget concluded that the child's ability to understand the principles of conservation develops naturally through the maturational process.

Implications of Developmental Theory for Learning Disabilities

The following are some implications of maturational theory for students with learning disabilities:

- A major cause of school difficulty is immaturity. All individuals have a natural development and time for the maturation of various skills. What is sometimes thought to be a learning problem may be merely a lag in a student's maturation of certain processes.

  Research shows that younger children in the early grades tend to have more learning problems than older children in that grade, a phenomenon called the "birth date effect." When the month of birth was

CASE EXAMPLE

DEVELOPMENT THEORY AND MATURATION

- Illustrations of young children who have surface verbal skills without an in-depth understanding of concepts are frequently amusing. One kindergarten child explained with seemingly verbal proficiency the scientific technicalities of a spaceship being shot into orbit. His apparently precocious explanation ended with "and now for the blastoff . . . 10-3-8-5-6-1!"

- The maturation of the cognitive ability to categorize objects was apparent when each of three children, ages 7, 9, and 11, was asked to pack clothes for a trip in two suitcases. Sue, the 11-year-old, was adultlike in her thinking, packing day clothes in one case and night clothes in another. Dean, the 7-year-old, had no organizational arrangement and randomly proceeded to stuff one suitcase with as much as it would hold and then to stuff the second with the remainder. Laura, the 9-year-old, made an organizational plan that called for clothes above the waist to go in one suitcase and clothes be-

low the waist to go in the second. The top parts of pajamas and a two-piece bathing suit were placed in one suitcase and the bottoms in the other. Each child had categorized in a manner appropriate to the individual's maturational stage.

- Schools sometimes neglect the need for prelogical experiences and learning in their attempts to meet the current trend to teach abstract concepts and logical thinking in the primary grades. In instituting a modern mathematics program in one district's kindergarten, the teachers were advised that an understanding of the one-to-one correspondence was a higher and more important cognitive level than other kinds of number learning. Therefore, games like "Ten Little Turtles" and other enjoyable counting experiences were unfortunately dropped from the kindergarten curriculum because these activities did not develop "logical thinking."

compared with the percentage of children referred for learning disabilities services, the younger children (those born near the cutoff date for school entrance) were much more likely to be referred for learning disabilities services (Diamond, 1983; Di Pasquale, Moule, & Flewelling, 1980).

- The educational environment may actually hinder rather than assist the child's learning by making intellectual demands that require cognitive abilities that a child may not have yet developed. Cognitive abilities are qualitatively different in children from those of adults. Cognitive abilities develop sequentially; as children mature, their ways of thinking continually change. Schools must design learning experiences to enhance children's natural developmental growth.

- The concept of **readiness** refers to the state of maturational development and prior experiences that are needed before a target skill can be learned. For example, readiness for walking requires a certain level of development of the neurological system, adequate muscle strength, and

In the preoperational stage (ages 2–7), children make intuitive judgements about relationships and language becomes increasingly important. *(© Elizabeth Crews)*

the development of certain prerequisite motor functions. Until a toddler has these abilities, attempts to teach the skill of walking are futile. To illustrate readiness in a very different area of learning, a student must have acquired certain mathematics skills and knowledge to profit from a course in calculus.

Readiness skills are picked up in an incidental fashion by some learners. For students with learning disabilities, special instruction is needed to help them strengthen the precursor or readiness abilities they need for their next step of learning. Sensitive teachers can help children acquire these abilities by being aware of the child's stage of maturation and of any developmental delays that they have.

Ironically, with all our attempts to be "scientific" about decisions made in education, one of the most important decisions—when to teach a child to read—is based on *astrology*. The star under which the child is born, the birth date, is the key determining factor of this crucial decision because it determines when the child enters school and begins formal school learning.

BEHAVIORAL PSYCHOLOGY

Behavioral psychology helps us understand how learning behavior is shaped, and this branch of psychology significantly influences the way we teach. For over fifty years, since the seminal work of B. F. Skinner (who is considered the father of behavioral psychology), the concepts of behavioral psychology have flourished, producing major and productive applications for promoting learning. In the field of learning disabilities, behavioral theories provide a systematic foundation for research, assessment, and instruction (Haring & Kennedy, 1992).

In this section, we discuss the application of behavioral psychology for explicit teaching and direct instruction. The applications of behavioral theories to other areas of learning disabilities are discussed in other relevant chapters of the book: assessment (Chapter 3), effective teaching (Chapter 4), motivation (Chapter 14), and behavior management (Chapter 14).

The Behavioral Unit

A core of behavioral psychology is the **behavioral unit,** which has three key components—A, B, and C. As illustrated in Figure 6.1, "A" is the **antecedent event** (or stimulus); "B" is the **target behavior** (or child's response); and "C" is the **consequent event** (or reinforcement).

The target behavior "B" is the child's response. It is helpful to think of the target behavior as an event sandwiched between two sets of environmental influences—those that precede the behavior (antecedent event or stimulus) and those that follow the behavior (consequent event or reinforcement). Changing a student's behavior requires an analysis of these three components.

To illustrate the relationship among the three behavioral events, the teacher's goal, in this example, is to have Bonnie lengthen the time she engages in silent reading. The *antecedent event* (or stimulus) is the teacher's action: assigning a silent reading period. The *target behavior* (or response) occurs when Bonnie reads for 2 minutes. The *consequent event* (or reinforcement) occurs when the teacher reinforces Bonnie's reading behavior by praising her or giving her a reward.

It should be noted that critics of reinforcement theory have suggested that it is too controlling. A recent outspoken challenger of the theory that incentives lead to improved quality and increased output in the workplace and in schools is Alfie Kohn in his popular book *Punished by Rewards: The Trouble with Gold Stars, Incentive Plans, A's, Praise, and other Bribes*

Figure 6.1

Components of the Behavioral Unit

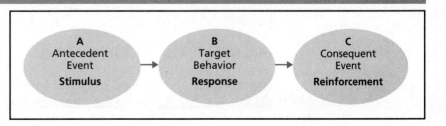

(Kohn, 1995). Kohn derides rewards as bribes which do not lead to long-term changes in behavior.

Explicit Teaching and Direct Instruction

direct instruction

Behavioral theories of instruction focus on the curriculum and on the tasks to be learned. Instructional practices stemming from behavioral theory are called *explicit teaching* or *direct instruction*. Other terms used for this kind of teaching include *mastery learning* and *sequential skills teaching*.

Explicit teaching means that teachers are clear about the specific skills to be taught and explicitly teach each step or skill rather than leave it up to the learner to make inferences from his or her own experiences in order to learn (Gersten, 1998). As noted in Chapter 4, in explicit teaching students are provided with (1) models for solving problems or explaining relationships, (2) ample support during the stages of the learning process, and (3) ample practice. Table 4.1 provides the key principles of explicit instruction (Gersten, 1998; U.S. Department of Education, 1997).

models support practice

Direct instruction is very similar to explicit teaching. The term *direct instruction* has been used for a longer period of time than *explicit teaching* and is based on behavioral orientation. However, it also focuses on academic skills that students need to learn and on the structuring of the environment to ensure that students learn these skills (Tarver, 1992; Lovitt, 1991; Algozzine, 1991). Direct instruction (Rosenshine, 1986; Rosenshine & Stevens, 1986):

- is academically focused, teaching academic skills directly
- is teacher directed and controlled
- uses carefully sequenced and structured materials
- gives students mastery of basic skills
- sets goals that are clear to students
- allocates sufficient time for instruction
- uses continuous monitoring of student performance
- provides immediate feedback to students
- teaches a skill until mastery of the skill is achieved

Behavior Analysis

Behavior analysis is the application of behavioral psychology to teaching. It requires that teachers analyze a specific task that students are to learn and determine the skills needed to learn that task. These skills are then placed in an ordered and logical sequence. Such teaching involves helping students accomplish a task by learning each skill they have not yet mastered. Even complex behaviors can be analyzed to determine their component parts or subskills. Students are taught each of the subskills they do not know. By learning all of the subskills, the students accomplish the desired complex behavior.

The steps involved in teaching a child to swim illustrate the behavioral analysis approach. First, analyze the steps involved in swimming—for example, floating, treading water, holding one's breath under water, and kicking. Next, teach the child each skill in its sequence, help the child combine the skills, and finally, observe the child swimming across the pool. Although this example does not demonstrate an academic task, the same procedures would apply to teaching, reading, mathematics, or writing.

These steps are involved in behavior analysis:

1. State the objective to be achieved or the task to be learned in terms of student performance.

2. Analyze the skills needed to perform that task.

3. List the skills to be learned in their sequential order.

4. Determine which of these skills the student does not know.

5. Teach one skill at a time. When one skill has been learned, teach the next skill.

6. Evaluate the effectiveness of the instruction in terms of whether the student has achieved the objective or learned the task.

For a summary of the guidelines for instruction based on behavior analysis, see Table 6.1.

Stages of Learning

All individuals need a period of time "to know" a concept that is being taught. Few people fully grasp a concept the first time they are exposed to it. This phenomenon is even more apparent in students with learning disabilities. In planning instruction, therefore, it is important to consider the student's **stage of learning**. Among the stages involved in learning knowledge, concepts, and skills are acquisition, proficiency, maintenance, and generalization:

1. *Acquisition.*   At this stage, the student is exposed to the new knowledge but has not fully grasped it. The student needs extensive teacher support and direction in using the knowledge. (For example, José is shown the 5's tables in multiplication, the concept is explained to him, and he is just beginning to understand it.)

2. *Proficiency*.   At this stage, the student begins to grasp the knowledge but still needs practice with it. (José now is given practice with the 5's

Table 6.1

Guidelines for
Instruction Based on
Behavior Analysis

Guidelines	How to do it?
Set goals and objectives.	■ Structure learning tasks as clear academic goals ■ Use task analysis to break goals into manageable steps.
Provide rapidly paced lessons and carefully sequenced materials.	■ Sequence and structure materials and lessons to help students master one step at a time. ■ Use a fast pace so that learning becomes automatic through over-learning.
Offer a detailed explanation with many examples.	■ Make sure that students understand the task. ■ Provide detailed and redundant instructions and explanations. ■ Use many examples.
Provide many opportunities to practice the new skill.	■ Ask many questions. ■ Offer many active practice opportunities. ■ Help students develop automaticity so they can do do the activity with ease.
Give students feedback and correction.	■ Help students learn new material through teacher feedback. ■ Give immediate, academically focused feedback and correction.
Assess student progress.	■ Actively monitor student progress to check on learning. ■ Make adjustments in teaching as necessary.

tables with flash cards, computer games, oral and written drill work, and various kinds of reinforcements.)

3. *Maintenance.*   The student now can maintain a high level of performance after direct instruction and reinforcement have been withdrawn. (José can now do the 5's tables by himself rapidly without reinforcement and teacher direction.)

4. *Generalization.*   At this point the student "owns" the knowledge and has so internalized it that he or she can apply it to other situations. (In our example, José can now apply his knowledge of the 5's tables to mathematics problem-solving activities.)

Expectations and instructional plans are necessarily different for each stage of learning. Teachers who are aware of the student's stage can provide appropriate instruction to help the student move from one level to the next. Students with learning disabilities will need a great deal of support at each stage, may move through the stages at a slower rate than that of other children, and may need specific help to transfer to the next stage, particularly the generalization stage.

DIRECT INSTRUCTION

A description of a parent instructing a son at a Little League game is a slightly exaggerated example of direct instruction, which was provided by humorist Dave Barry (1990, p. 18).

To participate in this highly popular sport, all you need to do is get a small child who would be infinitely happier just staying home and playing in the dirt, and you put a uniform on this child and make him stand for hours out on a field with other reluctant children who are no more capable of hitting or catching or accurately throwing a baseball than they are of performing neurosurgery. Then you and the other grownups stand around the perimeter and leap up and down and shriek at these children as though the fate of the human race depended on their actions.

The object of the game is to activate your child if the ball goes near him, similar to the way you use levers to activate the little men in table-hockey games. Your child will be standing out in right field, picking his nose, staring into space, totally oblivious to the game and the ball will come rolling his way, and your job is to leap violently up and down and shriek "GET THE BALL! GET THE BALL!!" repeatedly for several minutes until your child finally is aroused from his reverie long enough to glance down and discover, to his amazement, the ball. The ball! Of all things! Right there in the middle of a Little League game! While your child is staring at the ball curiously, as if examining a large and unusual tropical insect, you switch to yelling: "THROW THE BALL! THROW THE BALL THROW THE BALL THROW THE BALL! THROW THE BALL, DAMMITT!!" After several minutes of this an idea will start to form somewhere deep inside your child's brain: Perhaps he should throw the ball. Yes! It's crazy, but it just might work! And so, seconds before you go into cardiac arrest on the sideline, your child will pick up the ball and hurl it, Little-League style in a totally random direction, then resume picking his nose and staring off into space. As you collapse, exhausted, the ball will roll in the general direction of some other child, whose poor unfortunate parent must then try to activate HIM. Meanwhile the other teams' parents will be shrieking at THEIR children to run around the base in the correct direction. It is not uncommon for 150 runs to score on one Little League play. A single game can go on for weeks.

Source: *Aging Bull* by Dave Barry, printed in the Chicago Tribune Magazine, June 10, 1990, pp. 14–20. © 1998. All rights reserved. Tribune Media Services. Reprinted with permission.

Implications of Behavioral Theory for Learning Disabilities

Behavioral theories have important implications for teaching students with learning disabilities:

1. *Explicit teaching and direct instruction are effective.*   It is important for students with learning disabilities to receive direct instruction in academic tasks. Teachers should understand how to analyze the components of a curriculum and how to structure sequential behaviors.

2. *Explicit teaching and direct instruction can be combined with many other approaches to teaching.*   When the teacher is sensitive to a student's unique style of learning and particular learning difficulties,

direct instruction can be even more effective. For the child who lacks phonological awareness, for example, the sensitive teacher can anticipate difficulties in learning phonics during a direct instruction lesson. To learn the skill, this child will need more time, practice, review, and alternative presentations of the concepts. The sensitive clinical teacher will use knowledge of both the curriculum and the individual child in planning instruction.

3. *The student's stage of learning should be considered.* In planning instruction, teachers must consider the student's stage of learning for a particular concept. We cannot expect students to learn a new area completely the first time they are exposed to it. Students with no learning problems make many attempts to learn something so well that they can generalize it to other situations. For students with learning disabilities, going through the stages of "knowing" will take even longer, and they will need explicit or direct instruction to make the application at each stage.

COGNITIVE PSYCHOLOGY

Cognitive psychology focuses on the human processes of learning, thinking, and knowing. **Cognitive abilities** are clusters of mental skills that are essential to human functions. They enable one to know, be aware, think, conceptualize, use abstractions, reason, criticize, and be creative. Theories about the nature of cognitive and mental processes lead to a better understanding of how human beings learn and how the cognitive characteristics of learning disabilities affect learning. Cognitive theory also suggests a guide for teaching students with learning disabilities.

Concepts in cognitive psychology have been broadly elaborated over the years, and changes in the field of learning disabilities reflect these elaborations. A progression of ideas from cognitive psychology has influenced the field of learning disabilities: (1) the term *disorders of psychological processing* refers to the idea that launched the field of learning disabilities and continues to be an influential concept; (2) the *information-processing model* is a model of learning that emphasizes the flow of information within a person's mind and memory systems; and (3) *cognitive learning theories* provide a contemporary view of how people learn, think, and acquire knowledge.

Disorders in Psychological Processing

As noted in Chapter 1, a critical element of the federal definition of learning disabilities in IDEA 1997 is that students with learning disabilities have disorders in one or more of the basic psychological processes needed for school learning. Psychological processes are underlying abilities in such areas as perception and motor, linguistic, and memory functions. Disorders in psychological processes are intrinsic limitations that interfere with a student's learning.

The recognition that psychological processing dysfunctions are related to a student's inability to learn provided the foundation for the field of learning disabilities. For educators and other professionals, the notion of **psychological processing disorders** offers a refreshing and hopeful new way to view students who cannot learn and to plan teaching for them. For parents, it offers a logical way to understand their child's inability to learn, without blaming the child for not trying, the teachers for not teaching, or themselves for poor parenting. The theory of psychological processing disorders offers a useful perspective for assessing and teaching students with learning disabilities (Torgesen, 1991; Adelman & Taylor, 1991; Kirk, 1987). (See Chapters 4 and 9.)

Teaching Based on Psychological Processing Concepts   Fundamental to the psychological processing view is the belief that students differ in their underlying abilities to process and use information, factors which affect learning. First, the teacher ascertains a student's psychological processing abilities and disabilities through observations or tests. Then the teacher can select appropriate teaching methods based on this information. Deficits in auditory and visual perception have received the most attention. For example, a student with an auditory processing deficit might encounter difficulty with instructional approaches that are primarily auditory (such as phonics). Similarly, a student with a visual processing deficit might experience obstacles in learning to read by methods that are primarily visual (such as a sight-word method).

Three different teaching plans evolve from the psychological processing view: (1) the training-the-deficit process, (2) teaching through the preferred process, and (3) the combined approach.

- *Training-the-Deficit Process.*   The purpose of this method is to help the student, through practice and training, to build and develop those processing functions that are weak. The teaching plan is to strengthen the deficit process to ameliorate the disability, thereby preparing the student for further learning.

- *Teaching Through the Preferred Process.*   This approach uses the student's psychological processing strength (or learning style) as the basis of teaching. The contention is that instruction should be based on teaching methods and treatment procedures that take advantage of the student's strengths and circumvent the student's processing weaknesses.

- *The Combined Approach.*   The third teaching approach based on the processing concept combines aspects of the two previously mentioned methods. The teacher instructs the student using a method that capitalizes on the processing strengths while concurrently using methods to strengthen the weaknesses.

The theory of disorders in psychological processing has been a contentious issue in the field of learning disabilities. Critics argue that psychological processing tests are not reliable and valid measures, that teaching based on psychological processing information may not help students learn, and that psychological processing deficits may not be the cause of learning failure (Kavale, 1990; Kavale & Forness, 1990; Arter & Jenkins, 1977; Larsen & Hammill, 1975). Yet federal and other definitions of learning disabilities, as well as most state criteria, recognize that students with learning disabilities have psychological processing disorders that are "intrinsic" to the individual and that psychological processing disorders are related to academic failure (Mercer, Jordan, Allsop, & Mercer, 1996). The term *intrinsic* implies that the problem is internal, within the child, rather than due to an external cause, such as the environment.

The debate about psychological process has abated in recent years. We today recognize that more than one psychological process is needed to perform most academic tasks. Reading, for example, requires both visual and auditory skills. Focusing on single deficit areas (such as auditory or visual processing disorders) is overly simplistic because it fails to account for the broad range of learning problems. The concept of psychological processing problems, moreover, continues to have strong intuitive appeal and to contribute valuable procedures for assessment and teaching (Kavale, 1990; Hammill, 1990).

Contemporary cognitive learning theories encompass some of the basic ideas of psychological processing within more complex and elaborate theories of learning and disorders of learning. These ideas are explored later in this chapter in the section on cognitive learning theories.

The Information-Processing Model of Learning

The information-processing model of learning traces the flow of information during the learning process, from the initial reception of information, through a processing function, and then to an action. Figure 6.2 pictures the flows of information in a computer system, within a model that engineers refer to as an *input-output* or *black box* model. With a computer, there are *input* devices (such as a keyboard), *processing* functions (the central processing unit of the computer), and *output* devices (such as the monitor screen).

The analogy to the human learning system is shown in Figure 6.3. Again there are *inputs* (such as auditory stimuli), *processing functions* (cognitive processes such as associations, thinking, memory, and decision making), and *output* (actions and behaviors). Thus, like the computer, the human brain takes in information (input), stores and locates it (memory systems), organizes information and facilitates operations and decisions (central processing system-executive functions), and generates responses to the information (output) (Goetz, Hall, & Fetsco, 1989).

Figure 6.4 is a pictorial diagram of the information-processing system. The model pulls together many of the concepts contributing to cognitive theory and provides a useful way to conceptualize the processes and

Figure 6.2

The Computer System

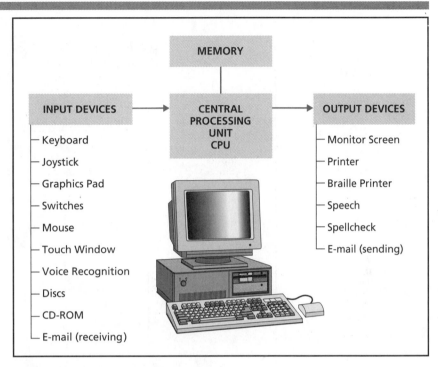

Figure 6.3

The Human Information-Processing System

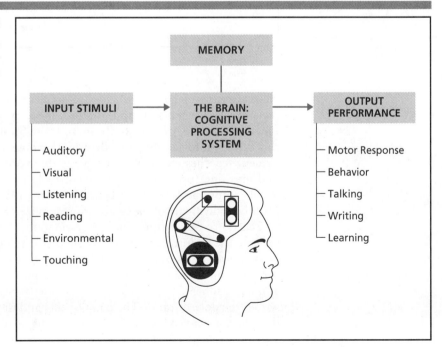

Figure 6.4

An Information-Processing Model of Learning

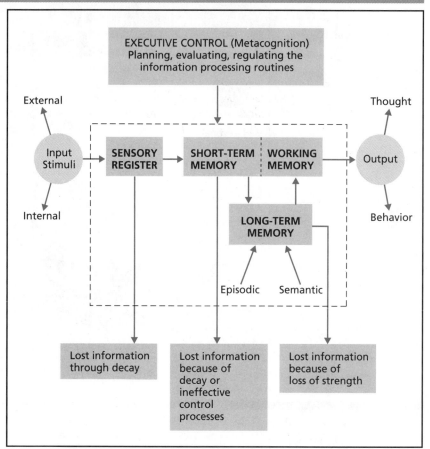

characteristics of human learning. The information-processing model depicts the components of input, output, memory, and an executive control function (Greeno, Collins, & Resnick, 1996; Swanson, 1996). To illustrate this flow of information, a student is shown a word (input stimulus). The student searches memory to recognize the word and determine its sound and meaning (processing and executive function) and, finally, says the word (output performance). If the memory of the word has decayed or is lost, the individual will be unable to recognize or say the word.

Central to the information-processing model is the **multistore memory system.** The multistore memory system conceptualizes a flow of information among three types of memory: (1) sensory register, (2) short-term memory (or working memory), and (3) long-term memory (Atkinson & Shiffrin, 1968; Broadbent, 1958). The three memory types are shown in Figure 6.4 within the dotted frame. The components and the flows of information of the information-processing model of learning are discussed next.

Sensory Register   Information is first received through the senses—vision, hearing, touch, smell, taste, and so on. Stimuli can be from internal or external sources. Most of the stimuli that bombard one's input receptors are unimportant, are not attended to, and do not reach the sensory register. However, once the mind attends to selected input stimuli, that information flows into the first memory system, the **sensory register**. The sensory register system serves as an input buffer, which helps to interpret and maintain the information from the input receptor long enough for it to be perceived and analyzed. **Perception** is important at this stage because it gives meaning to the stimuli. Perception depends upon the individual's past experiences and ability to organize and attach meaning to the stimulus event. To illustrate how past experiences shape perception, a 3-year-old was asked to identify a square shape printed on a page. His personal and unique perception of the shape was clear when he responded, "That's a TV."

Sensation and perception take place when the stimulus is present; they are ongoing activities. Memory pertains to sensations and data *already* received and perceived. Memory (imagery, or "mind's eye") is our ability to store and retrieve previously experienced sensations and perceptions when the stimulus that originally evoked them is no longer present. Examples of sensations and perceptions that occur only in the mind are a musician "listening" to music played at an earlier time; a cook "tasting" the sourness of a lemon to be used; a carpenter "feeling" the roughness of sandpaper used yesterday in a job; and a gardener "smelling" the sweetness of lilacs while looking only at the buds on the tree. A 3-year-old was helped to understand the nature of memory. Her mother asked the youngster to close her eyes and think about a peanut butter and jelly sandwich. Yes, the child said she could "see" the jelly dripping down the sides of the bread; she could "smell" the peanut butter; and she could even "taste" the first bite. The sandwich that had become so vivid existed in her memory.

Significance for Teaching   Information-processing theory suggests that a copy of an experience is stored very briefly, perhaps for a few seconds, in the sensory register. Unless there is an effort to pay attention to it, the information is immediately lost from the sensory register. The significance for teaching is that the student must be attending; the lesson must be planned to initially spark the attention of the student. In computer terms, we must make sure the power is on. Attention-getting techniques that teachers frequently use include flicking lights, ringing a bell, or saying, "This information is important" or even, "This will be on the test."

Short-Term or Working Memory   Short-term memory is also a temporary storage facility. With the first system, the sensory register, the individual is not consciously aware of information. In short-term memory, however, the individual becomes very consciously aware of information. **Short-term memory** is considered **working memory**. The pertinent information or current problem is receiving the person's conscious attention, and the individual can act on it. When a person thinks of a new problem, the new information replaces the old information in working or short-term memory. The old information either decays and is lost or is placed into long-term storage (Swanson, 1987, 1996)). Short-term memory is similar to the material you work with on the computer screen. To return to the computer analogy, the information is temporary, and it will be lost when the power is turned off unless the information has been saved.

Significance for Teaching   In terms of teaching, we should recognize that information remains in short-term memory for a short period of time. Unless it is acted on in some way, information in short-term memory will be lost. A common characteristic of students with learning disabilities is having problems remembering verbal information (Mastropieri & Scruggs, 1998). Some of the strategies or actions that can extend the time that information stays in short-term memory include:

1. *Rehearsal*, or *repeating the information.*   Rehearsal slows the forgetting process and helps in transferring the information to long-term memory. For example, when you look up a telephone number, repeating the number may help you to remember it long enough to dial it.

2. *Chunking*, or *grouping the information.*   It is easier to remember grouped information than isolated bits of information. For example, a social security number can be chunked into three groups: a chunk of three numbers, a chunk of two, and a group of four: 123-44-1830.

3. *Organizing the information.*   This makes the information less complicated and relates the parts to each other. (Food can be organized in four basic food groups—dairy, cereals, fruits and vegetables, and meats.)

4. *Key Words.*   This is mnemonic technique, in which a word is linked to another word that is familiar (Mastropieri & Scruggs, 1998). The linkage is that part of the word (the initial sound or rhyming element) that is similar to the key word. The key-word method is useful when pairs of items, such as foreign language words, technical words, or names, have to be learned. For example, when you are introduced to someone, you will more easily recall the person's name if you link the name with a characteristic, such as "tall Tony" or "blue-eyed Bonnie."

Long-Term Memory and Retrieval   **Long-term memory** is the permanent memory storage. To learn and retain information for long periods of time, information must be transferred from short-term to long-term memory. It is thought that information placed into long-term memory remains there permanently. It is evident from neurological research and clinical experiences that memories remain in long-term storage for a very long time (Semb & Ellis, 1994).

The problem people face in long-term memory is not storage but **retrieval,** that is, how to recall (or remember) information stored in long-term memory. As shown in Figure 6.4, information from short-term memory is lost unless it is saved in long-term memory. Before one can think about a problem, the stored information must be retrieved from long-term memory and placed into short-term or working memory (or consciousness). In the computer analogy, when one wishes to work on a saved file, the file from long-term storage must be loaded into the desktop (short-term or working memory).

There are two types of long-term memory: *episodic* and *semantic*. *Epi-sodic* memories are images—visual and other sensory images of events in one's life. The episodic memory of one's first carnival, for example, might be triggered by the sound of a merry-go-round. *Semantic* memories consist of the storage of general knowledge, language, concepts, and generalizations.

The retrieval of odd bits of long-term memory is sometimes triggered by strange events. One such event occurred at a recent national education conference when a participant noted a vaguely familiar woman in the lobby. After observing her for several minutes, he walked up to her and blurted out, "Hilltop 5-4260." Indeed, that had been her telephone number some twenty-five years earlier. Although the conference participant recalled the phone number, he could not remember her name.

Significance for Teaching   The way information is stored in long-term memory helps with the process of retrieval. Through instruction in learning strategies, teachers can help students with the retrieval process (Scruggs & Mastropieri, 1991). (Chapter 9 discusses learning strategies, and Chapter 11 discusses some of the strategies used in reading to improve semantic memory.) The following strategies help with the storage and retrieval of information in long-term memory:

1. *Organizing schemes.*   Many of the recommended study techniques are methods of organizing information to make it easier to recall from long-term memory. For example, in studying a country in social studies, use a word web to link key information about the country: Weather, crops, rivers, etc.

2. *Using prior knowledge.*   New information that is linked to something the student already knows is much easier to retrieve. To know something is not only to have received information but also to have interpreted it and related it to other knowledge. Teachers must recognize that learning depends on what the student already knows and must build links between old and new knowledge.

3. *Making the information meaningful.*   Students can strengthen their long-term memory if they make the information meaningful by linking it to something they already know. Learning depends on what one already knows or on prior knowledge. Teachers can help students by providing background knowledge and linkages to what is already in the long-term memory.

Executive Control   **Executive control** refers to a component of the information-processing model that deals with directing the course and regulation of one's own thinking and mental activity. The term *metacognition* is often used in conjunction with executive control. (Metacognition is discussed in more detail in the section on learning strategies later in this chapter.) Executive control directs the flow of thinking, manages the cognitive processes during learning, and keeps track of what information is being processed. It involves the planning, evaluating, and regulation of the information-processing routines. It determines which mental activities occur and which processing components receive system attention resources, or one's concentration. One's motivation and goals are important factors in directing the priorities and the problems that will receive attention (Swanson, 1996; Flavell, 1987).

To return once more to our computer analogy, the executive function is likened to the operating system of the computer. The operating system intervenes and controls the allocation and interface between the program and the resource. It keeps track of what each program is doing and when the program needs to use some system resources, such as a disk drive or print instructions.

Executive decisions require *metacognitive* skills—skills that involve "thinking about thinking." Metacognitive functions require that students (1) have knowledge of strategies to control their learning, and (2) are able to select the appropriate method for the problem at hand.

Significance for Teaching   It is not enough to memorize information; students must also have the metacognitive skills to decide to use the information. Research with students with learning disabilities shows that they must learn to activate and select the strategies to use the information they have (Deshler et al., 1996; Lenz et al., 1996). Learning strategies instruction for metacognitive skills are discussed later in this chapter.

Cognitive Learning Theories

Contemporary theories of cognitive learning extend and elaborate the earlier psychological processing concepts of learning. To succeed in the general education classroom, students with learning disabilities must learn the complex concepts and fundamental problem-solving skills of the content areas in the gene5al education curriculum. They confront a number of challenges in the content areas, such as organizing information on their own, having limited background knowledge for many academic activities, and needing sufficient feedback and practice to retain abstract information (Gersten, 1998; Greeno, Collins, & Resnick, 1996; Palinscar & Klenk, 1992).

A number of instructional strategies stem from cognitive theories of learning, which help students with learning disabilities grasp the concepts and subject matter of the general education curriculum. Some of these effective and validated instructional approaches are discussed in other sections of this book: *scaffolding* (p. 137), *learning strategies instruction* (p. 322), and *peer tutoring* (p. 163). In this section, we will discuss two additional effective cognitive learning strategies: *anchored instruction* and *graphic organizers*.

Anchored Instruction   Anchored instruction refers to the kind of teaching that occurs in an *apprenticeship*, a setting in which a knowledgeable adult and a learner work jointly on a real-life problem. Learning in such a setting is geared to solving a genuine problem, rather than just reading about it. Anchored instruction is motivating for learners and increases generalization because student apprentices learn through experience how the knowledge they have acquired applies to real world (Gersten, 1998).

Graphic Organizers   **Graphic organizers** are visual representations of concepts, knowledge, or information that incorporate both text and pictures. They make it easier for a person to understand the information by allowing the mind "to see" complex relationships. Research shows that graphic organizers have proven to be very useful for students with learning disabilities (Fisher, Schumaker, & Deshler, 1995). Some types of graphic organizers described in this book are: Venn diagrams (see p. 452), hierarchical (top-down) organizers (see p. 451), word webs (see p. 424), concept maps, and mind mapping. In this section we discuss concept maps and mind mapping.

Concept Map   With a concept map, students or teachers can cluster ideas and words that go together. The activity serves to activate the students' construction of a concept. Figure 6.5 shows a concept map that a thirteen-year-old created on the topic "Chicago sports" to prepare for a writing project.

Figure 6.5

Graphic Organizer: Concept Map on Chicago Sports

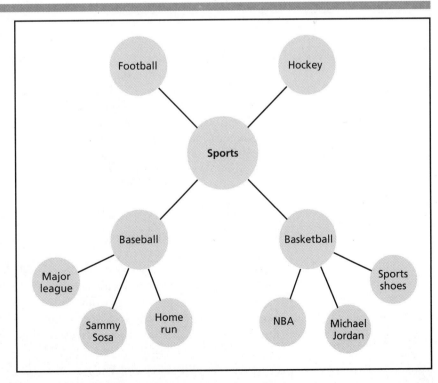

Figure 6.6

Mind Mapping on
Homework

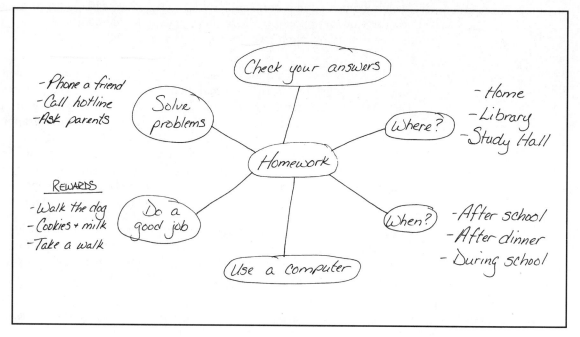

Mind Mapping   **Mind mapping** is a strategy that employs a pictorial method to transfer ideas from the mind(s) of a student or group of students onto a large piece of paper, a transparency, or a large class chart. Ideas are produced randomly, and certain words or ideas will trigger other ideas, which will lead to other suggestions or pictures. It is much easier to mind map than to create an outline because the ideas do not have to be organized or sequenced. Figure 6.6 shows a mind map that a group of students constructed on the topic of "homework."

Implications of Cognitive Psychology for Learning Disabilities

Since cognitive psychology analyzes how people learn, it has many implications for teaching students with learning disabilities. Teaching strategies based on cognitive psychology can help students learn to attend, to remember, to understand, to think, and to enjoy learning. The following guidelines can help teachers apply cognitive strategies as they work with students with learning disabilities:

The social interactions between the teacher and the student, and among students, are critical to the learning process.
(© Elizabeth Crews)

1. ***Help students <u>construct knowledge</u>.*** Knowledge cannot be given directly to students. Instead, each person must construct or build his or her own knowledge. The student's ability to acquire knowledge depends in part on what the student already knows. For example, a child who knows that 2 + 2 = 4 can learn the new number fact 2 + 3 more easily if it is linked to the existing knowledge 2 + 2. Another illustration of how one's scheme of the world drives behavior can be seen in the actions of 3-year-old Cassandra, who geared up for her first day of play school. Her prior knowledge of school consisted of observations of her 6-year-old sister going to school carrying her lunch box and backpack. Based on her prior knowledge of school (her schema), Cassandra insisted that her mother provide her with a lunch box and backpack for her one hour of play school.

2. ***Link new information to prior knowledge.*** Learning is a cumulative process that depends on prior knowledge and past experiences. The more one knows about a subject, the more one can acquire through a learning experience. What students learn depends on the experiences they bring to the learning situation. Since new knowledge is built on what is already known, students must learn to use the experiences, knowledge, and skills they already possess.

Teachers should start with what students already know, and then help them to build and to link new information. In reading, this might mean using the student's existing knowledge of words, books, and stories as the starting point for teaching reading. In arithmetic, the child's arithmetic knowledge of counting could be used as the initial point for teaching mathematics.

3. *Begin instruction at the appropriate level.* It is important for teachers to find the right difficulty level at which to aim the lesson. According to Vygotsky's theory of the zone of proximal development (ZPD), there are several levels of the student's learning. At the lower end, students can learn almost independently; they can easily generalize and make it on their own. At the upper end of the range, the level is beyond the children's capabilities, so that even with very carefully structured instruction, the students will not be able to grasp the skill and transfer it to themselves. The zone of proximal development is the midpoint in this range, the level at which instruction should take place. This level is called the "Goldilocks" level because it is neither too hard nor too easy, and students can successfully learn at this level under adult guidance.

4. *Provide a guiding social environment.* A critical element of learning is the social and reciprocal relationship between the teacher and the student. The teacher serves as a guide for the student, providing the information and support necessary for the student to learn and grow intellectually. This support is referred to as *scaffolding* because the student uses this help while she or he builds a firm understanding that will eventually allow her or him to solve the problem or accomplish the task independently.

5. *Develop automaticity in certain skills.* Certain kinds of knowledge must become automatic, almost subconscious, requiring little processing effort. Successful reading, for example, requires rapid and fluent recognition of words. For efficient responses, many areas of performance must become automatic and habitual. Examples of such **automaticity** include remembering words when speaking, inserting the proper syntactic word form in sentences, and remembering words by sight when reading. Students with reading disabilities cannot quickly recall words, colors, numbers, and pictures. Students with mathematics disabilities cannot rapidly recall arithmetic facts. Students with learning disabilities tend to be slower and more gradual in their acquisition of automatization abilities. They must exert so much effort on tasks that should be automatic that they have less effort remaining to attack other areas of the learning process, such as arithmetic problem solving or reading comprehension. These students need more practice and repetition to develop certain automatic responses.

6. *Use activities that motivate students to want to learn.* Motivation energizes and directs behavior. It is the drive to accomplish goals and the desire to learn. Much of school learning requires hard work for a long period of time and demands that students are active, involved, committed, and interested for a sustained period They must work hard to figure out the meaning of what they read or to solve an arithmetic problem. Because students with learning disabilities find these school challenges so arduous, it is especially important that their teachers demonstrate that they have confidence in them and believe that they will succeed. To maintain motivation,

teachers must make learning enjoyable and display pleasure at their students' achievements.

Activities with the potential to motivate students to learn should:

- make learning enjoyable for the student
- enable the teacher to show pleasure and pride in the student's progress
- involve topics that are of interest to the student
- supply extrinsic incentives that students will want to work for
- allow students to make choices and autonomous decisions about the course of the lesson
- use novelty and variety to keep the student's interest
- project intensity, sincerity and enthusiasm

LEARNING STRATEGIES INSTRUCTION   In this section, we discuss some instructional applications of cognitive theories. We review metacognition, learning strategies, styles of learning, and the social context of learning.

Metacognition

Metacognition refers to the awareness of one's systematic thinking about learning. It is the ability to facilitate learning by taking control and directing one's own thinking processes. People exhibit metacognitive behavior when they do something to help themselves learn and remember, such as preparing shopping lists to remember what to buy, outlining difficult technical chapters to help themselves understand and remember the material, or rehearsing and repeating what has just been learned to help stabilize and strengthen their learning. These behaviors indicate an awareness of one's own limitations and the ability to plan for one's own learning and problem solving (Swanson, 1996). The Case Example entitled "Metacognitive Shopping Behavior" offers other examples.

Efficient learners use metacognitive strategies, but students with learning disabilities tend to lack the skills to direct their own learning. However, once they learn the metacognitive strategies that are used by efficient learners, they can apply them in many situations. Some metacognitive strategies needed for school learning are classification, checking, evaluation, and prediction (Gersten, 1998; Kluwe, 1987).

Classification   This is a strategy for determining the type, status, or mode of a learning activity. Individuals ask themselves, "What am I doing here?" or "Is this activity important to me?"

Checking   This strategy involves taking steps during the process of problem solving to determine progress, success, and results. For example, individuals

---

CASE EXAMPLE

METACOGNITIVE SHOPPING BEHAVIOR

A common example of metacognitive behavior that is familiar to most people is the activity of planning for grocery shopping. Most people must engage in this activity, and they have developed plans that work for them. The following grocery shopping plans are metacognitive behaviors which are based on prior knowledge and experience. They include ways to enhance memory (through writing, visualization, or review) and to organize and prepare for future activities (making meals, eating, and entertaining). When a group of people were asked how they plan for their grocery shopping, their answers differed widely, revealing a correspondingly wide range of metacognitive styles. Some of those answers follow:

- I keep a pad of paper in a convenient spot, and as I discover needs during the week, I jot my needed purchases on the note pad. I take this list with me to the store, and it becomes my guide for shopping.

- I think about what I need and write a list of needs just before going shopping. I take this list with me and then check each item on the list as I take it off the grocery shelves.

- I open my kitchen cabinets just before going shopping, and the visualization of missing items gives me enough information to complete my grocery shopping.

- I walk up and down the aisles, and items that I need just pop up.

- I buy only items that are on sale and stock up on these items.

- I carefully plan my shopping to use the coupons I have acquired.

- I go to the store and buy merchandise that looks as though it would be good to eat when I get home. After I get home, I usually find that I forgot some necessary items and have to go to the store again.

- To avoid impulsive buying, I always eat something before going shopping.

- I plan on how much money I will spend, use a calculator, and stop when that amount is reached.

- I don't do regular shopping. I eat all my meals out.

- I do not plan for grocery shopping. That is my husband's job.

---

may say to themselves, "I remember most of the lesson," "My planning is pretty detailed and careful," "I still have a long way to go before I get there," or "There's something I do not understand here."

Evaluation   Evaluation goes beyond checking and provides information about quality. For example, an individual may think, "My plan is not good enough to rule out any risks," or "I have done a good job."

Prediction   This activity provides information about the possible alternative options for problem solving and possible outcomes. The person may think, "If I decide to work on this problem, the technical details will be hard to accomplish. I will have to get someone to help me with them," or "I should be able to finish the paper in four days."

Learning Strategies

The **learning strategies approach** to instruction focuses on *how* students learn rather than on *what* they learn. Efficient learners can count on a number of learning strategies to help them learn and remember. Students with learning disabilities do not have a repertoire of learning strategies. When teachers help students acquire learning strategies, students *learn how to learn.*

What strategies are used by people who learn in an efficient and well-functioning manner? Successful learners control and direct their thinking processes to facilitate learning. They ask themselves questions, and they organize their thoughts. They connect and integrate the new materials they are trying to learn with prior experience and with knowledge they already possess. They also try to predict what is to come and monitor the relevance of new information. In other words, good learners have learned how to go about the business of learning, and they have at their disposal a repertoire of cognitive strategies that work for them (Deshler, Ellis & Lenz, 1996; Lenz, Ellis & Scanlon, 1996; Ellis et al., 1991).

In contrast, students with learning disabilities usually lack these functional learning strategies. They do not know how to control and direct their thinking to learn, how to gain more knowledge, or how to remember what they learn. In short, they are not aware of the tricks of the trade that proficient learners use to organize their thoughts or to plan an approach to solve complex problems. Students with learning disabilities must first become aware of and acquire learning strategies to facilitate learning and remembering. Fortunately, research shows that once they receive learning strategies instruction, they become privy to the best-kept secrets about how to obtain academic success and do use these strategies in many contexts (Gersten, 1998; Deshler et al., 1996; Lenz et al., 1996; Pressley, 1991).

A widely used model of strategy instruction for students with learning disabilities is the *Strategies Intervention Model* (SIM). The SIM learning strategies were developed over many years at the University of Kansas Center for Research on Learning (Lenz et al., 1996; Deshler et al., 1996). (Because it is geared for adolescents with learning disabilities, the SIM model is discussed in Chapter 9.)

Some examples of learning strategies for students with learning disabilities are described in Table 6.2. Learning strategies can be used in every area of the curriculum—in the teaching of reading, writing, mathematics, social studies, and science. In addition, learning strategies for specific academic areas are woven throughout various chapters of this text, especially in the Teaching Strategies sections; see Reading Comprehension (Chapter 11) and adolescents (Chapter 9).

Styles of Learning

One's style of learning encompasses general behavior, attitude, and temperament when presented with a learning task. The learning styles in an

Table 6.2

Learning Strategies

The following learning strategies were developed at the University of Kansas Institute for Learning. They are designed to help students with learning disabilities meet the challenges of the school curriculum.

Materials that can be purchased without training

Score Skills (Social Strategies)	Cooperative Problem Solving
Teamwork Strategy	Progress Program (Daily Report Cards)
Self-Advocacy Strategy	Surface Counseling

Purchase of these materials requires training
(Contact the Training Coordinator at the Center for Research on Learning.)

Learning Strategies: Acquisition	Learning Strategies: Storage	Learning Strategies: Expression
Word Identification Strategy	First-Letter Mnemonic Strategy	SLANT: A Strategy for Class Participation
Visual Imaging Strategy	Paired Associate Strategy	Sentence Writing Strategy
Self-Questioning Strategy	Vocabulary Strategy	Paragraph Strategy
Paraphrasing Strategy		Error Monitoring Strategy
		Assignment Completion Strategy
		Test-Taking Strategy

Information about these strategies and strategies materials can be obtained from the University of Kansas Center for Research on Learning, 3061 Dole Center, University of Kansas, Lawrence, KS 66045, (785) 864-4780 and Edge Enterprises, Inc., P.O. Box 1304, Lawrence, KS 66044, (785) 749-1473. Training coordination at the Center for Research on Learning. Phone: (785) 864-4780; web site: **http://www.ku-crl.org**.

Source: Strategic Instruction, University of Kansas Center for Research on Learning.

academic situation influence the effectiveness of learning. For example, the learning style of a student may be at odds with the style required to succeed in a traditional education system. Analysis of the student's learning style offers insight into the nature of the learning difficulties (Carbo & Hodges, 1988; Dunn, 1988; Carbo, Dunn, & Dunn, 1986). A student's learning style might also reflect the values of his or her culture. For example, the child's culture might not consider punctuality as important as getting a job completed well (Alverez, 1998).

Behavioral Temperaments   Research shows that even infants have different personalities and behavioral temperaments. Thomas and Chess (1977) verified this common observation of parents. Some babies are alert and responsive; others are irritable or passive. Moreover, the research shows that these temperamental patterns set the stage for the child's later reaction to the world. Temperamental differences are important in understanding children with learning disabilities and their reactions to school learning (Keogh & Bess, 1991).

Reflective Versus Impulsive Learning Styles   Another way of analyzing styles of learning is to determine whether the student's learning behavior is reflective or impulsive. In the *reflective style*, the student proceeds with careful deliberation, considering alternatives before choosing a response to a problem. In the *impulsive style*, the student responds very quickly, without considering possible alternatives.

Individuals with learning disabilities often respond in an impulsive style, a behavior that is detrimental to school performance. Impulsive students speak without first considering their thoughts and race through written assignments without monitoring right and wrong answers. In a task requiring matching objects, they draw lines from one object to another without first carefully inspecting the page. Impulsive students seem to come to decisions too quickly, without sufficient time between the stimulus and the response.

Impulsive behaviors may stem from a basic lack of alternative cognitive strategies. Students who respond impulsively may not have other ways readily at hand for coping with the assignment and should be helped to acquire a number of alternative learning strategies (Torgesen, 1991).

Active Versus Passive Styles   Another way to view students' styles of learning is to consider whether they are *active* or *passive*. Efficient learning requires an *active* and *dynamic* involvement in the learning process. **Active learners** efficiently use many cognitive strategies. They work at structuring the information (organization), asking themselves questions about the material (self-questioning), and comparing the new information to what they already know. They are intensely involved and have a desire to learn, or motivation (Brown & Campione, 1986; Walker, 1985).

Students with learning disabilities, on the other hand, have learned to approach the learning task in a *passive* manner. They probably lack interest in learning because past learning experiences were often dismal exercises in failure and frustration. Not believing that they can learn, these students do not know how to go about the task of learning. As a consequence, they become **passive** and dependent **learners**, a style that has been referred to as **learned helplessness**.

The Social Interactions of Learning

The social environment significantly influences learning itself. The learning process is more than an individualistic, student-centered activity. The social interactions between the teacher and the student and those among students are critical ingredients in the learning process. Theories that emphasize the social context of learning include Vygotsky's (1978) social influences of learning, Feuerstein's (1980) concept of the teacher as mediator, and Palinscar and Brown's (1984) reciprocal teaching. These theories are reviewed in this section.

Vygotsky: Social Influences of Learning The social nature of cognitive development and the role that interpersonal relationships play in this development were first observed some fifty years ago by Lev Vygotsky, a Russian psychologist. (Vygotsky's concept of the *zone of proximal development* was discussed earlier in the section on cognitive psychology.) Vygotsky (1978) observed that social influences are crucial in the learning processes. Learning is an interpersonal, dynamic social event that depends on at least two people, one better informed or more skilled than the other. Human learning occurs as a transfer of responsibility, be it learning to play the violin, doing arithmetic, learning Spanish, reading, writing, or repairing an automobile. All of these learning abilities pass along the interpersonal plane and require the instructor's analysis of the task relative to the student's current ability. Learning and cognitive development are enhanced when the student works collaboratively with an adult or with other students.

Feuerstein: The Teacher as Mediator The work of an Israeli psychologist, Reuven Feuerstein, emphasizes the important social role of the teacher as a mediator in building the student's cognitive potential for learning (Feuerstein, 1980). Feuerstein's innovative method for assessing intellectual potential and remediating cognitive deficits demonstrates that the human organism can be modified at all ages and stages of cognitive development. The method suggests that the cognitive functioning of adolescents can be greatly increased (Feuerstein, Rand, Jensen, Kaniel, & Tzuriel, 1987; Messerer, Hunt, Meyers, & Lerner, 1984).

Two basic components of the Feuerstein approach are assessment and instruction. The assessment instrument is known as the *learning potential assessment device* (LPAD) (Feuerstein, 1979). The teaching method is called *instrumental enrichment* (Feuerstein, 1980). Instrumental enrichment is a set of carefully structured materials. The most critical element of the program, however, is the specially trained teacher, who provides "mediated learning experiences." The teacher first selects what is to be taught—specific events, concepts, ideas, or principles. The teacher then highlights the attributes of these stimuli by interrelating them with the personal experiences of the pupils. Pupils come to understand that what is being discussed has a purpose that is both useful and meaningful, and they will be able to effectively use what they are being taught. The success of the Feuerstein program depends on the specially trained teacher, or mediator. The program instruments themselves provide only opportunities through which mediated learning experiences can occur. It is the teacher-mediator who shapes these opportunities and brings them to the attention of the learner.

Palinscar and Brown: Reciprocal Teaching In the technique called **reciprocal teaching**, cognitive strategies are taught through a social dialogue between the teacher and students. In this form of teaching, teachers and students take turns leading discussions about shared text materials (Palinscar & Brown, 1984; Palinscar, Brown, & Campione, 1991; Palinscar & Klenk, 1992). In their initial study, Palinscar and Brown (1984) trained a group of seventh-grade poor readers in reading comprehension. The seventh graders' reading scores were about 2.5 years below grade level. Through the reciprocal teaching method, they were trained in four learning strategies: *summarizing* the content of a passage, *asking questions* about a central point, *clarifying* the difficult parts of the material, and *predicting* what would happen next.

The reciprocal teaching approach employs the following procedures:

1. First the teacher and the students read the material silently.

2. The teacher then explains and models the strategies of summarizing, questioning, clarifying, and predicting by saying aloud the thoughts that he or she uses in those learning strategies.

3. Next, the students read another passage, and they are given the responsibility of demonstrating the strategies out loud for the other students in the group. At first, many students may be hesitant, and their demonstrations may be imperfect. The teacher provides guidance and encouragement to help students perfect their demonstrations. (As mentioned earlier, this type of guidance and support is referred to as *scaffolding*.)

4. Finally, each student is expected to demonstrate abilities in the strategies of summarizing, questioning, clarifying, and predicting.

Research with reciprocal teaching suggests that it is an effective teaching approach. Students improved in their reading comprehension and in their ability to summarize, question, clarify, and predict using reading passages (Palinscar & Klenk, 1992; Palinscar, Brown, & Campione, 1991).

Implications of Learning Strategies Instruction for Learning Disabilities

The approaches of learning strategies instruction have practical teaching implications. Students with learning disabilities can develop metacognitive abilities to control their own learning. Once they are taught effective learning strategies, they can use them in learning situations and can become active, involved learners who accept responsibility for their own learning. Effective learning occurs in a social context where the interrelationship between student and teacher is critical.

Chapter Summary

1. Theories about learning and teaching are needed to understand learning disabilities. Theory building implies a progression of ideas that builds upon the contributions of earlier theories.

2. The theories of developmental psychology stress the natural progression of the child's growth and the sequential development of cognitive abilities. A state of readiness is needed for the child to acquire certain

abilities. Forcing a child into trying to learn before that state of readiness has been reached can lead to academic failure.

3. Behavioral psychology provides an approach to learning disabilities that emphasizes explicit teaching and direct instruction. The behavioral unit consists of the antecedent event, the target behavior, and the consequent event. Explicit teaching means that teachers are clear about what needs to be accomplished. Direct instruction focuses on the teaching of academic skills.

4. Through behavior analysis, teachers examine an academic task in terms of the subskills that lead to the achievement of that task.

5. Learners go through stages of learning: *acquisition*, *proficiency*, *maintenance*, and *generalization*.

6. Cognitive psychology deals with the human processes of learning, thinking, and knowing. A progression of theories about learning disabilities stem from cognitive psychology: disorders of psychological processing, the information-processing model, and cognitive learning theories.

7. Theories about disorders of psychological processing focus on the unique learning characteristics of students with learning disabilities and how they affect achievement. Analysis emphasizes the processing deficiencies and inadequacies in prerequisite skills, particularly auditory and visual processing.

8. The information-processing model describes the flow of information within the individual. It is likened to a computer process that includes internal or external input; the processing function, in which the individual uses an executive function; and, finally, outputs in the form of performance.

9. The multistore model of three types of memory is the core of the information-processing model. The three memory systems are the sensory register, the short-term or working memory, and the long-term memory. Executive control is another important component of the model.

10. Cognitive learning theories emphasize the learner's own elaborations of knowledge and ways to help students grow in their capacity to monitor and guide their own thinking. Cognitive psychology emphasizes that students construct their own knowledge and that learning depends upon prior knowledge.

11. Learning strategies instruction applies cognitive learning theories to teaching. The topics of this section include metacognition, learning strategies, styles of learning, and the social interactions involved in learning.

12. The learning strategies approach focuses on *how* students learn rather than on *what* they learn. Students learn to use strategies that enable them to control their own learning.

13. Learning occurs in a social environment, and the relationship between teacher and student is a critical element.

Questions for
Discussion and
Reflection

1. Discuss developmental psychology as it applies to learning disabilities. How can developmental delays lead to learning disabilities?

2. What are the approaches to instruction that are based on theories of behavioral psychology? How do the principles of behavioral psychology apply to teaching students with learning disabilities?

3. What is meant by the term *disorders of psychological processing*? Discuss the implications of this concept for instruction in the field of learning disabilities.

4. What are the three memory systems of the information-processing model? How are these systems related? How can the information-processing model of learning be applied to teaching students with learning disabilities?

5. What are the basic concepts of cognitive psychology? How can these concepts be translated into teaching students with learning disabilities? Compare cognitive and behavioral psychology in terms of curriculum.

6. What is meant by the term *metacognition*? Discuss the problems of students with learning disabilities with regard to metacognitive strategies.

Key Terms

active learners *(p. 215)*

antecedent event *(p. 193)*

automaticity *(p. 210)*

behavior analysis *(p. 194)*

behavioral unit *(p. 193)*

cognitive abilities *(p. 198)*

concrete operations stage *(p. 189)*

consequent event *(p. 193)*

developmental delays *(p. 187)*

direct instruction *(p. 194)*

executive control *(p. 205)*

explicit teaching *(p. 194)*

formal operations stage *(p. 189)*

graphic organizers *(p. 207)*

information-processing model
   (p. 200)

learned helplessness *(p. 215)*

learning strategies approach
   (p. 213)

long-term memory *(p. 204)*

metacognition *(p. 211)*

mind mapping *(p. 208)*

multistore memory system
   (p. 202)

passive learners *(p. 215)*

perception *(p. 203)*

preoperational stage *(p. 189)*

psychological processing disorders
   (p. 199)

readiness *(p. 191)*

reciprocal teaching *(p. 216)*

retrieval *(p. 204)*

sensorimotor period *(p. 189)*

sensory register *(p. 203)*

short-term (working) memory
   (p. 203)

stage of learning *(p. 195)*

target behavior *(p. 193)*

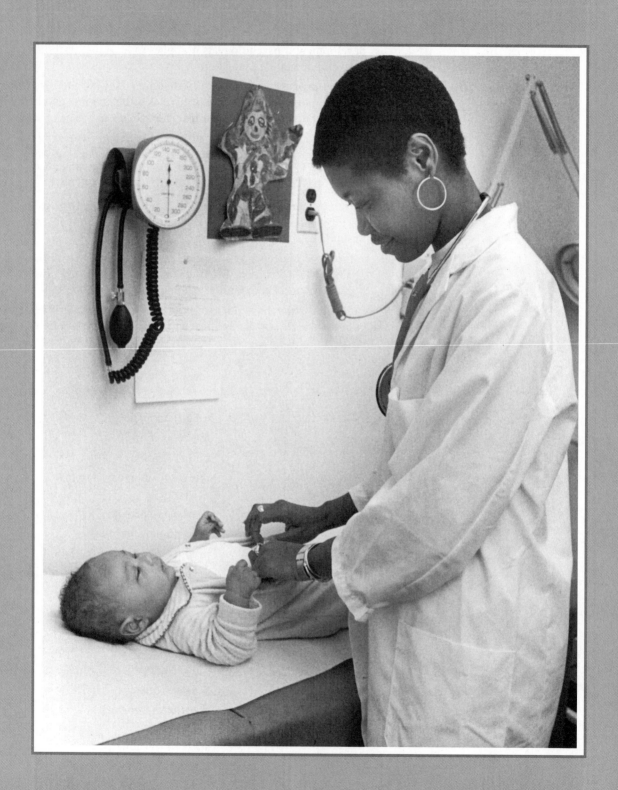

7 Medical Aspects of Learning Disabilities

This chapter discusses medical aspects of learning disabilities. We will examine the value of medical information for teachers, the physiology of the brain, recent brain research, the neurological examination, attention deficit disorder, various medical treatments, and the involvement of several medical specialties.

The medical profession has long been an indispensable participant in the field of learning disabilities. As noted in Chapter 2, medical scientists conducted basic brain research that became central to the early development of the field. Current neuroscience research continues to uncover new information about the brain and new ways to diagnose and treat learning disabilities.

Medical specialists who deal with children with learning disabilities include pediatricians, family practice physicians, pediatric neurologists, child and adolescent psychiatrists, ophthalmologists, and otologists. Physicians are often the first professionals to come in contact with a child with learning disabilities; they also become involved with assessment, diagnosis, and treatment, and may become key members of a student's IEP team. Often they continue to monitor these children over a long period of time.

THE VALUE OF MEDICAL INFORMATION FOR EDUCATORS

No one discipline can remain productive in isolation. Training programs for pediatricians today recognize the multidisciplinary nature of child health and include relevant educational concepts and procedures about learning disabilities. There is a corresponding need for teachers to learn about relevant medical aspects of the field for the following reasons:

- *Learning occurs in the brain.* Teachers need basic information about the central nervous system and its relationship to learning and to learning disabilities. All learning involves the neurological process that occurs within the brain, a major part of the **central nervous system.** A dysfunction in that system can seriously impair the processes of learning. We cannot artificially separate behavior and learning from what happens in our bodies.

- *Physicians are actively involved in treating children with learning disabilities.* Medical specialists often participate in the assessment and treatment of students with learning disabilities. Teachers must therefore understand the vocabulary and concepts of medical sciences to interpret medical reports about their students and to discuss the findings with physicians and parents. When medications are prescribed, teachers should be asked to provide feedback to parents and physicians about the medications' effectiveness.

- *Advances in medical technology affect children with learning disabilities.* Medical procedures now save the lives of many children who probably would not have survived only a few years ago, but sometimes these children have learning disabilities in later life. For example, the treatment for childhood leukemia may lead to problems in attention and concentration, memory, sequencing, and comprehension on school tasks. Advances in neonatology may lead to increases in the survival rates of babies with very low birth weights, but some of these infants encounter learning disabilities later in life.

■ *Awareness of current brain research.*   Informed educators need up-to-date information about the brain and learning. Scientific investigations that attempt to unravel the mysteries of the human brain and learning are fascinating in themselves. Knowledge about the brain is increasing rapidly and promises to further our understanding of the enigma of learning disabilities.

NEUROSCIENCES AND THE STUDY OF THE BRAIN

The **neurosciences** are the cluster of disciplines that investigate the structure and function of the brain and the central nervous system. In this section, we briefly examine several facets of the neurosciences: the structure and functions of the brain, recent brain research, and neuropsychology.

The Brain: Its Structure and Functions

All human behavior is mediated by the brain and the central nervous system. The behavior of learning is one of the most important activities of the brain. From a neurological perspective, learning disabilities represent a subtle malfunction in this most complex organ of the human body. See Figure 7.1.

The Cerebral Hemispheres   The human brain is composed of two halves, the right hemisphere and the left hemisphere, which appear on casual inspection to be almost identical in construction and metabolism. Each **cerebral hemisphere** contains a frontal lobe, a temporal lobe, an occipital lobe, a parietal lobe, and a motor area (see Figure 7.1). The motor area of each hemisphere controls the muscular activities of the opposite side of the body. Thus, the movements of the right hand and foot originate in the motor area of the left hemisphere. Both eyes and both ears are represented in each hemisphere (Gaddes, 1985).

Right Brain, Left Brain: Differences in Function   Although the two halves of the brain appear almost identical in structure, they differ in function, and these differences appear very early in life.

The left hemisphere reacts to and controls language-related activities. For more than 90 percent of adults, language function originates in the left hemisphere, regardless of whether the individual is left-handed, right-handed, or a combination of the two. Language is located in the left hemisphere in 98 percent of right-handed people and in about 71 percent of left-handed people (Hiscock & Kinsbourne, 1987).

Figure 7.1

The Brain

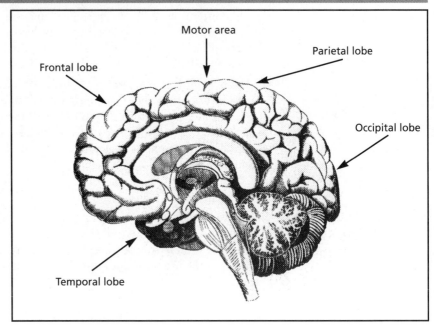

The right hemisphere deals with nonverbal stimuli. Spatial perception, mathematics, music, directional orientation, time sequences, and body awareness are located in the right brain.

Thus, even though visual and auditory nerve impulses are carried to both cerebral hemispheres simultaneously, it is the left hemisphere that reacts to linguistic stimuli, such as words, symbols, and verbal thought. Consequently, adult stroke patients with brain injury in the left hemisphere often suffer language loss in addition to an impairment in the motor function of the right half of the body.

This duality of the brain has led to speculation that some people tend to approach the environment in a "left-brained" fashion whereas others use a "right-brained approach." Left-brained individuals are strong in language and verbal skills while "right-brained" individuals have strengths in spatial, artistic, and mechanical skills. These differences in brain function warrant further discussion because the concept may provide some insight into differences in learning styles.

Cerebral Dominance   Samuel Orton, a physician and early investigator of reading and language difficulties, theorized that the reversal of letters and words (which he called *strephosymbolia,* or twisted symbols) was symptomatic of a failure to establish **cerebral dominance** in the left hemisphere, the location of the language area (Orton, 1937). According to Orton's theory, the left hemisphere should be the dominant or controlling hemisphere, and the interference of the right hemisphere during language activities causes language confusion. Current findings usually show that the left hemisphere does specialize in the language function and the right hemisphere controls nonverbal functions. However, the two hemispheres of the brain do not work altogether independently; there are many interrelating elements and functions. The learning process depends on both hemispheres and their interrelating functions. Inefficient functioning of either hemisphere reduces the total effectiveness of individuals and affects their acquisition and use of language (Cotman & Lynch, 1988; Hiscock & Kinsbourne, 1987; Duane, 1986; Gaddes, 1985).

Lateral Preference   The issue of **lateral preference** is the subject of a related controversial theory, which proposes a relationship between learning disorders and a tendency to use either the right or left side of the body or a preference for the right or left hand, foot, eye, or ear. The term *consistent laterality* refers to the tendency to perform all functions with one side of the body. *Mixed laterality* is a tendency to mix the right and left preference in the use of hands, feet, eyes, and ears. A student's laterality may be tested through observation of simple behaviors—such as throwing a ball, kicking a stick, seeing with a tube, and listening to a watch—or through more sophisticated means used in neuropsychology. There are mixed research findings about the relationship between reading ability and lateral preferences (Biegler, 1987; Obrzut & Bolick, 1991).

Recent Brain Research

Research on the brain and its relationship to behavior and learning has accumulated slowly, in part because the technologies for studying the structure and function of the brain have only recently become available. Today neuroscientists can vastly extend their studies of the structure and functions of the brain because of technological advancements which have created opportunities for a better understanding of the relationship of the brain and learning disabilities.

Dyslexia   Many of the brain investigations involve studies of individuals with **dyslexia**, a puzzling type of learning disability that interferes with learning to read. A definition of dyslexia from the International Dyslexia Association is shown in the box entitled "What is Dyslexia?"

Reading is an extremely complex human task that requires an intact and well-functioning brain and central nervous system. The case example entitled "Recollections of Individuals with Dyslexia" illustrates the serious consequences of having dyslexia.

For almost a century, scientists conjectured that there was a neurological basis for dyslexia and that the difficulty in acquiring reading skills stemmed from abnormal brain function. With growing knowledge about the brain

WHAT IS DYSLEXIA?

The word dyslexia is derived from the Greek "dys" (meaning poor or inadequate) and "lexis" (words or language). Dyslexia is a learning disability characterized by problems in expressive or receptive, oral or written language. Problems may emerge in reading, spelling, writing, speaking, or listening. Dyslexia is not a disease; it has no cure. Dyslexia describes a different kind of mind, often gifted and productive, that learns differently. Dyslexia is not the result of low intelligence. Intelligence is not the problem. An unexpected gap exists between learning aptitude and achievement in school. The problem is not behavioral, psychological, motivational, or social. It is not a problem of vision; people with dyslexia do not "see backward." Dyslexia results from differences in the structure and function of the brain. People with dyslexia are unique, each having individual strengths and weaknesses. Many dyslexics are creative and have unusual talent in areas such as art, athletics, architecture, graphics, electronics, mechanics, drama, music, or engineering. Dyslexics often show special talent in areas that require visual, spatial, and motor integration. Their problems in language processing distinguish them as a group. This means that the dyslexic has problems translating language into thought (as in listening or reading) or thought into language (as in writing or speaking).

Source: International Dyslexia Association. (1998). **http://www.interdys.org.**

and its relationship to reading, there is now convincing evidence that the brains of people with dyslexia do indeed differ in structure and function from the brains of normal persons.

The brain studies that investigate dyslexia include (1) brain-imaging studies, (2) postmortem anatomical studies, and (3) genetic studies. Another recent study shows that children with language delays have brains that process sounds slowly (Tallal, Jenkins, & Merzenich, 1997) (see Chapter 10).

Studies Using Brain-Imaging Techniques   Several new technological innovations allow brain scientists to study the active, living brain through imaging techniques.

Magnetic resonance imaging (MRI) is an advanced neuroimaging device that converts signals into a sharp image on a video screen. The MRI generates images of multiple sections of the brain, indicating the shape and location of various brain structures. Research with MRI scans shows that the

CASE EXAMPLE

RECOLLECTIONS OF INDIVIDUALS WITH DYSLEXIA

The following statements by individuals with this severe reading problem reveal the frustration they face in school and the strengths they develop as they meet the challenges of life.

- Charles Schwab, the founder of the successful and innovative stock brokerage firm, observed that his struggle with dyslexia led him to develop other abilities. In 1994, he told *Business Week,* "I've always felt that I have more of an ability to envision, to be able to anticipate where things are going, to conceive a solution to a business problem than people who are more sequential thinkers."

Source: From "Slow Words, Quick Images—Dyslexia as an Advantage in Tomorrow's Workplace," by T. West in *Learning Disabilities and Employment,* by P. Gerber & D. Brown (eds.), 1997, p. 349.

- Marilyn Bartlett earned a Ph.D. and graduated from law school despite having dyslexia, however she failed the New York State Bar Examination five times because her disability involved a very slow reading rate. When Marilyn asked for more time to take the law test, the New York State Board of Law Examiners denied her request. Marilyn then sued the board under the Americans with Disabilities Act. The court ruled that Marilyn's disability limited a major life activity—reading—and that she was entitled to the accommodation of extended time to take the examination.

Source: Bartlett v. *New York State Board of Law Examiners* 93 Civ. 4986 (SS) (S.D.N.Y., 1997.) From "The ADA and LD/ADD in the Workplace: Myths and Realities," by P. H. Latham & P. S. Latham, 1998, *Their World,* 1998/1999, p. 64.

- I am told that before I went to school, I was a spirited little girl who said she was "on her own" at the age of 5. This little girl was the life of a party, very conversational, and very happy. Then I entered kindergarten, and my spirit deflated like a falling hot air balloon. I remember trying to spell my last name and not being able to accomplish this simple task.... The hurt and frustration did not stop after school. It continued when my best friend from preschool told me she could not be my friend anymore because she thought I was stupid.

Source: From "Stephanie's Story," by S. Burlington, 1994, *Perspectives: The Orton Dyslexia Society, 20* (1), p. 38. Reprinted by permission.

- My name is Amy.... Throughout my early years, I was very much like many other children, loving to play and run around with friends. I could play like the other kids my age, but when it came to academics, I was different. At the age of 5 when I could not write the alphabet, I was told that I was severely dyslexic. I learned that by playing sports, I could rechannel some of the frustration I experienced from school work in a positive way. I found that when I figure-skated I would leave the learning problems aside for a while and skate freely on the ice. I skated competitively from the ages 7 to 10.

Source: From "Amy's Story," by A. Elsman, 1993, *Perspectives: The Orton Dyslexia Society, 19* (3), p. 24. Reprinted by permission.

- The burden of being dyslexic is a unique one. Every case is different and every affected person deals with it in his or her own way. I feel fortunate to have met adversity at the young age of 6. Dyslexia is something that will never go away; you can only train yourself to counterbalance it. The lessons that being dyslexic have taught me outweigh the struggle to overcome my impediment.

Source: From "Frederick's Story," by F. C. McMahon, 1992, *Perspectives: The Orton Dyslexia Society, 18* (4), p. 10. Reprinted by permission.

frontal region of the brains of children with dyslexia and learning disabilities is symmetrical and smaller than this region is in normal children (Lyon & Rumsey, 1996; Hynd, 1992; Hynd & Semrud-Clickman, 1989).

Functional magnetic resonance imaging (fMRI) is a new, noninvasive MRI method for studying the human brain as it is working. Shaywitz and Shaywitz (1998) used the fMRI to image the brains of 32 nondyslexic and 29 dyslexic adults while they attempted to perform a progressively complex series of reading tasks, including letter recognition, rhyming letters and words, and categorizing words. Figure 7.2 maps the location within the brain for phonological processing, word meaning, and letter identification. The study found measurable differences in brain activity between dyslexic and nondyslexic subjects. During reading, subjects with dyslexia showed a pattern of underactivation in a larger posterior brain region, an area which connects the visual areas with the language areas.

Brain electrical activity mapping (BEAM) is a procedure to monitor brain wave activity. BEAM technology is a major advancement from the older electroencephalogram (EEG) procedures. The BEAM procedures use computers to convert and map electrical brain waves that subjects produce in response to sounds, sights, and words. The research of Duffy and McAnulty (1985) and Duffy (1988) found that the electrical activity produced by the brains of individuals with dyslexia differed in major ways from the activity of normal brains. Differences were found in the left hemisphere, the medial frontal lobe, and the occipital lobe, which is the brain's visual center.

Figure 7.2

An fMRI brain image illustrating the mapping of reading activities within the brain

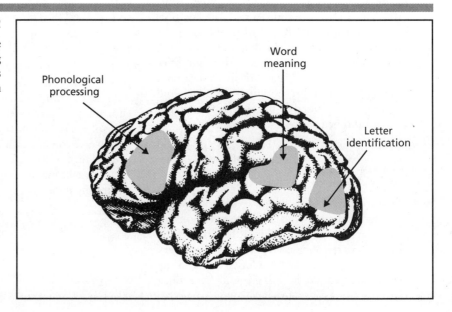

Positron emission tomography (PET) is a device that permits the measurement of metabolism within the brain. Zametkin et al. (1990) used the PET technique to study adults with attention deficit hyperactivity disorder (ADHD). This study demonstrated that cerebral glucose metabolism in the brains of subjects with ADHD differed significantly from that of control subjects. The subjects with ADHD had less metabolic activity and had less glucose in the brain.

Postmortem Anatomical Studies   Strong evidence that the brain structure of dyslexic individuals is different from that of normal readers has been gained from postmortem anatomical studies. These are autopsy studies of the brain tissues of deceased individuals who had dyslexia. Many of these individuals were young men who died suddenly in circumstances such as motorcycle accidents. At the time of death, the brains of these people were donated for study to an ongoing dyslexia research center at Harvard Medical School's Department of Neurology at Beth Israel Hospital in Boston. Thus far, the brain tissues of eight such people—six males and two females—have been studied. A remarkable and consistent finding is that all the cases have the same abnormality in the area of the brain known as the *planum temporale*, an auditory area that lies on the superior surface of the temporal lobe. The planum temporale is located in both the left and right hemispheres. In the left hemisphere this area is the center of language control. In most people, the planum temporale is asymmetrical; that is, the area is larger in the left hemisphere than in the right hemisphere. However, in the postmortem studies of the subjects with dyslexia, the planum temporale was symmetrical; that is, the areas were similar in size in the right and left hemispheres. The postmortem studies also revealed that for the subjects with dyslexia, this language area in the left hemisphere of the brain was smaller and had fewer brain cells, whereas the area in the right hemisphere was larger and contained more cells than are found in normal individuals (Filipek, 1995; Duane, 1989; Galaburda, 1990). These postmortem studies correlate with evidence gathered through the use of new imaging techniques.

Genetics of Learning Disabilities   Knowledge of genetics and inheritability of learning disabilities and dyslexia increased significantly in the last decade (Pennington, 1995). Two types of genetic studies are the family studies and the twin studies.

The *family studies* began with a study conducted in Scandinavia showing that dyslexia aggregates in families (Hallgren, 1950). Since then, more extensive family studies continue to show strong evidence that the tendency for severe reading disabilities is inherited and appears to have a genetic basis (Pennington, 1995; Pennington, Smith, Kimberling, Green, & Haith, 1987).

The *twin study* research provides further evidence that genetics play a significant role in dyslexia (Pennington, 1995; DeFries, Fulker, & LaBuda,

1987; DeFries, Stevenson, Gillis, & Wadsworth, 1991; Olson et al., 1991). Twins have similar characteristics in terms of reading disabilities, even when they are reared apart.

Neuropsychology

Neuropsychology is a branch of psychology that combines psychology and neurology. The neuropsychologist assesses the development and integrity of the individual's central nervous system and the relationship between brain function and behavior (Fennel, 1995). Most of the research in neuropsychology has been applied to the behavior of adults with brain injury. However, recent work in this specialized field has been directed toward research and applications in the area of learning disabilities (Fennel, 1995; Swanson, 1996; Hynd, 1992; Lyon et al., 1991).

A neuropsychological examination is specifically designed to identify subtle or overt neurobehavioral problems that contribute to the child's difficulty in making normal academic progress. Several broad domains in functioning are addressed in the neuropsychological examination: intellectual, attentional, memory, learning, language, sensorimotor, frontal executive, and social-emotional (Fennel, 1995). Neuropsychological evaluations also analyze hemispheric differences, that is, differences in functions between the left and right hemispheres of the brain (Hiscock & Kinsbourne, 1987).

Neuropsychological test batteries that assess brain functions in children include the *Halstead-Reitan Neuropsychological Test Battery for Children* (ages 9 to 14) and the *Reitan-Indiana Neuropsychological Battery for Children* (ages 5 to 8). Use of these tests requires training in neuropsychology and in administering tests. A test of information processing functions is the *Swanson Cognitive-Processing Test* (Appendix C).

THE NEUROLOGICAL EXAMINATION

Neurological examinations can be conducted by any of several medical specialists—the family practice physician, the pediatrician, the developmental pediatrician, the pediatric neurologist, or the child psychiatrist. (These specialists are discussed in more detail later in the chapter.) The neurological examination of a child or adolescent suspected of having learning disabilities has two distinct components: the conventional neurological assessment and the examination for **soft neurological signs,** minimal or subtle neurological deviations such as coordination difficulties in visual-motor, fine motor, or gross motor activities.

A carefully performed and judiciously interpreted neurological examination can contribute to the understanding of the functional status of a child with learning disabilities. Levine (1994) warns, however, that parents and schools should not have unrealistic expectations about the results of neurological examinations. A conventional neurological examination will not reveal many soft signs and will probably fail to find any abnormalities in patients whose primary complaint is the inability to learn (Rapkin, 1995; Levine, 1987, 1994). There are also a number of difficulties in interpreting neurological findings:

1. A wide range of soft signs of minimal neurological dysfunction occurs among students who *are* learning satisfactorily.

2. Because the student's neurological system is not yet mature and is continually changing, it is often very difficult to differentiate between a developmental lag and a dysfunction of the central nervous system.

3. Many of the tests for soft signs are psychological or behavioral rather than neurological.

The ultimate test of healthy neurological function is efficient learning. The unique human ability to learn is attributable to the highly complex organization of the brain and nervous system. This section gives a brief overview of the conventional neurological assessments and the neurological examinations for soft signs.

Conventional Neurological Assessment

In the conventional neurological examination, the physician first obtains a careful, detailed medical history. The information includes a family history (for clues of a genetic nature); details of the mother's pregnancy, the birth process, and the neonatal development; and the child's developmental history. The physician obtains information about all illnesses, injuries, and infections that the child has had. The developmental history includes information about motor behavior (the age at which the child crawled, stood, and walked) and language skills. Additional information about the student's hearing, vision, feeding, sleeping, toilet-training, and social and school experiences is collected (Levine, 1987; Rapkin, 1995).

An examination of the *cranial nerves* gives information relating to vision, hearing, taste, and vestibular function (the sense of balance), as well as such characteristics as facial expression, chewing, swallowing, and the ability to speak. The function of the various cranial nerves is evaluated by noting the child's responses to certain stimuli, the condition of various organs, and the child's ability to perform certain tasks.

The conventional neurological examination also assesses the control of *motor function*. The child's reflexes are tested and sensory nerves are assessed through tests of perception or tactile stimulation.

Other special medical procedures that might be requested include an EEG to measure the electrical activity of the brain, x-rays of the skull and

Obtaining a thorough medical history of the child and family is an important first step in the neurological examination. *(© F. Pedrick/ The Image Works)*

the blood vessels of the brain, biochemical studies, endocrinologic studies, or genetic examinations.

Examination for Soft Neurological Signs

Soft neurological signs can be detected through a neurological examination that goes beyond the conventional examination. As noted earlier, the neurological anomalies most often seen in people with learning disabilities are not gross deviations but rather fine, subtle, and minor symptoms. These soft signs include mild coordination difficulties, minimal tremors, motor awkwardness, visual-motor disturbances, deficiencies or abnormal delay in language development, and difficulties in reading and arithmetic skills. Another soft sign is hyperactivity, which is also recognized as a characteristic of attention deficit disorder.

Neurologists use a number of tests to detect soft signs of central nervous system dysfunction (Levine, 1987). Some of these tests could also be used by teachers as informal motor tests. Many of the tests used to detect soft

Figure 7.3

Geometric Forms

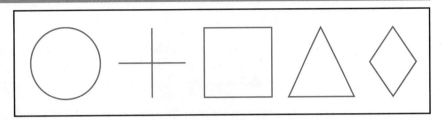

neurological signs have been borrowed or adapted from psychological assessment procedures. We will look at visual-motor, gross-motor, and fine-motor tests.

Visual-Motor Tests   A number of visual-motor tests are used to evaluate a patient's ability to copy various geometric forms. Children can copy the forms in Figure 7.3 at the following ages:

Figure	Age
Circle	3
Cross	4
Square	5
Triangle	6–7
Diamond	7

Other commonly used visual-motor tests are the *Bender-Gestalt Test,* in which the patient is asked to copy nine geometric forms, and the *Goodenough-Harris Drawing Test,* which requires the patient to draw a picture of a human figure. The scoring of the Goodenough-Harris test depends on the body detail represented.

Gross-Motor Tests   Gross-motor tests assess postural skills, movement, and balance. The child's walking gait is also observed. Children can normally perform the following tasks at the ages indicated:

Task	Age
Hopping on either foot: The child is asked to hop on the right foot, then on the left.	5
Standing on one foot: The child is asked to stand on one foot (first the right, then the left) and to maintain balance.	6
Tandem walking (heel-to-toe): The child is asked to walk by placing the heel of one foot directly in front of the toe of the other.	9

Two tests of crossing the midline in the execution of movements are also given:

Touching nose and left ear and then nose and right ear. Observers note the rapidity with which the automatic takeover of motor movements is introduced.

Finger-nose test. The patient is asked to touch a finger to his or her nose and to the examiner's finger repeatedly. Facility in alternating movement is observed.

Fine-Motor Tests   The *finger-agnosia* test assesses the patient's ability to use tactile sensation to recognize, often with eyes closed, which finger is being touched by the examiner. The tasks and the normal age at which each task can be performed follow:

Task	Age
Recognition of thumb	4
Recognition of index finger	5–6

Other tests of tactile perception are recognition of objects by touch, recognition of two simultaneous contacts as the examiner touches two parts of the child's body (such as face and hand), recognition of letters or numbers by touch, recognition of letters or numbers drawn in the palm of the hand, and facility in moving the tongue (vertically and horizontally).

The *finger dexterity* test requires the child to touch each finger in turn to the thumb. Each hand is tested separately.

ATTENTION DEFICIT DISORDER

Attention deficit disorder (ADD) constitutes a neurological condition characterized by developmentally inappropriate attention skills, impulsivity, and, in some cases, hyperactivity. This condition is thought to be caused by a brain-based neurological dysfunction. ADD is the most commonly diagnosed disorder of childhood, accounting for one-half of all child referrals to outpatient mental health clinics (Barkley, 1998; Goldman, Ganel, Bezman, & Sianez, 1996; Lerner & Lowenthal, 1999; Lerner, Lowenthal, & Lerner, 1995).

Although the terms used to describe this condition—minimal brain damage (MBD), hyperactive child syndrome, attention deficit disorder (ADD), and **attention deficit hyperactivity disorder (ADHD)**—have changed during the past 50 years, the major symptoms associated with the disorder have remained constant (U.S. Department of Education, 1997). The term *ADHD (attention deficit hyperactivity disorder)* is used by the American Psychiatric Association (1994) and is generally used by physicians and psychologists. The term *ADD (attention deficit disorder)* is used by the Department of Education (1991, 1999) and by many educators. We will refer to the condition as attention deficit disorder in this discussion.

The major characteristics of attention deficit disorder are inattention, impulsivity, and sometimes hyperactivity. *Inattention* is the inability to concentrate on a task. *Impulsivity* is the tendency to respond quickly without thinking through the consequences of an action. *Hyperactivity* refers to behavior that has a constant, driving motor activity in which the child races from one endeavor or interest to another. According to the American Psychiatric Association (1994), symptoms of ADD/ADHD must meet several criteria:

1. Severity.   The symptoms must be more frequently and severe than is typical of other children at similar developmental levels.

2. Early onset.   At least some of the symptoms must have appeared before the child is 7 years of age.

3. Duration.   The child's symptoms must have persisted for at least 6 months prior to the diagnosis.

For treatment of ADD/ADHD, most experts recommend a multimodal approach or a combination of treatment methods. These methods include medication, special education services, accommodations, regular classes, behavioral management, family counseling and parent training (Barkley, 1998; Lerner, Lowenthal, & Lerner, 1995; Silver, 1998; National Institutes of Health, 1998; Lerner & Lowenthal, 1999). Teachers need special training to deal with students with ADD/ADHD.

Symptoms of Attention Deficit Disorder at Different Stages of Life

Symptoms of attention deficit disorder change with age. Young children with **hyperactivity** exhibit excessive gross motor activity, such as running or climbing. They are described as being "on the go," "running like a motor," and having difficulty sitting still. They may be unable to sit still for more than a few minutes at a time before beginning to wriggle excessively. It is the *quality* of the motor behavior that distinguishes this disorder from ordinary overactivity, for hyperactivity tends to be haphazard and poorly organized.

Older hyperactive children may be extremely restless and fidgety. They are likely to talk too much in class and may constantly fight with friends, siblings, and classmates. However, by adolescence, hyperactivity may no longer present itself. Although the hyperactivity may diminish, other symptoms may appear, such as behavior problems, low self-esteem, inattentiveness, or even depression.

ADD/ADHD affects children in all areas, disrupting the child's home life, education, behavior, and social life. At home, children with this condition have difficulty accommodating to home routines and parent expectations. They may resist going to bed, refuse to eat, or break toys during play. At school, they have trouble completing their class work, often missing valuable information because of their problems paying attention. They speak aloud out of turn and find themselves in trouble for their behavior. Their social interactions may be undermined by their impulsivity, hyperactivity, and inattention, hampering their ability to make and keep friends. In terms of gender, more boys than girls are diagnosed with ADD/ADHD. Research suggests that the prevalence rate is equal for boys and girls, but boys are more likely to be identified (Shaywitz, Fletcher, & Shaywitz, 1995).

Assessment of Attention Deficit Disorder

Assessment of attention deficit disorder is a necessary step before decisions can be made about treatment and eligibility for services. The diagnosis of attention deficit disorder is usually based on the observation of behaviors. The criteria for these behaviors are described in the *Diagnostic and Statistical Manual of Mental Disorders,* fourth edition (American Psychiatric Association, 1994).

Diagnostic and Statistical Manual of Mental Disorders, Fourth Edition (DSM-IV) The American Psychiatric Association publishes a reference manual entitled the *Diagnostic and Statistical Manual of Mental Disorders* that provides criteria for the diagnosis of all mental disorders and is used by medical specialists and psychologists. The fourth edition of this publication revised the criteria for assessing attention deficit disorder. As already mentioned, the term used in DSM-IV is *attention deficit hyperactivity disorder (ADHD),* and three types of ADHD are specified. Each type requires that the individual display at least six of nine specified symptoms shown in Table 7.1.

1. ADHD-IA. *Primarily Inattentive.* The ADHD-IA subtype refers to children who have primary problems with attention.

2. ADHD-HI. *Primarily Hyperactive and Impulsive.* The ADHD-HI subtype refers to individuals who display behaviors of hyperactivity and impulsivity, but who do not manifest problems with attention.

3. ADHD-C. *Combination of ADHD-IA and ADHD-HI.* The ADHD-C subtype refers to individuals who both have attention problems and display symptoms of hyperactivity and impulsivity.

Identifying Attention Deficit Disorder Using Rating Scales A variety of behavioral assessment methods are used to identify attention deficit disorder. Methods for assessment include teacher rating scales, parent rating scales, and direct observation (Atkins & Pelham, 1991). Rating scales that are frequently used are shown in Table 7.2. A version of the *Conners Rating Scales* is included in the *Study Guide with Case Studies* that accompanies this text.

Rating scales are assessment measures based on reports of behavior observed by teachers and parents. A concern about assessment of ADD/ADHD is the lack of consistent physical evidence to diagnose the condition.

Table 7.1 Criteria for Subtypes of Attention Deficit Hyperactivity Disorder in DSM-IV		
ADHD-IA Subtype: symptoms of inattention	Fails to give close attention to details, makes careless mistakes Has difficulty sustaining attention Does not seem to listen Does not follow through or finish tasks Has difficulty organizing tasks and activities Avoids or dislikes tasks requiring sustained effort Loses things needed for tasks Is easily distracted by extraneous stimuli Is often forgetful in daily activities	
ADHD-HI Subtype: symptoms of hyper-activity and impulsivity	**Hyperactivity** Fidgets with hands or feet, squirms in seat Leaves seat in classroom or in other situations Runs about or climbs excessively Has difficulty playing or engaging in leisure activities quietly Talks excessively Acts as if "driven by motor" and cannot sit still **Impulsivity** Blurts out answers before questions are completed Has difficulty waiting in line or awaiting turn in games or activities Interrupts or intrudes on others	
ADHD-C: Combined subtype	Symptoms of both IA and HI	

Source: American Psychiatric Association, *Diagnostic and Statistical Manual of Mental Disorders,* Fourth Edition. Washington, D.C.: American Psychiatric Association, 1994. Reprinted with permission. Copyright © 1994 American Psychiatric Association.

Many children with ADD/ADHD will be missed or their conditions over-diagnosed. A recent promising neuroscientific study used a brain scan with a functional magnetic resonance imaging (MRI) device to identify a biological "signature" within the brains of children with attention deficit disorder (Vaidya et al., 1998). The study used the fMRI to scan the brains of 16 boys between the ages of 8 and 13 while they were playing a simple game. The researchers were able to detect which parts of the brain responded to specific actions and medications. The researchers were also able to distinguish

Table 7.2 Rating Scales for Assessing Attention Deficit Disorder		
	Rating Scale	**Reference**
	Behavior Assessment System for Children (BASC)	Reynolds and Kemphaus, 1992
	Child Behavior Checklist for Ages 4–16	Achenbach, 1981
	Child Behavior Checklist for Ages 2–3	Achenbach & Edelbrock, 1986
	Conners Rating Scales	Conners, 1989a; 1989b

children with ADD/ADHD from normal children by using the fMRI. This type of research is in its earliest stages, so scientists caution that the findings must be broadened and replicated by other researchers.

Attention Deficit Disorder

Frequently children with ADD/ADHD have a **co-occurring condition** that must also be considered in the assessment, instruction, and treatment. It is estimated that 25–40 percent of children with learning disabilities display symptoms of ADD/ADHD (Silver, 1998; Shaywitz, Fletcher, & Shaywitz, 1995). It is estimated that about 40–60 percent have co-occurring behavioral disorders (Tankersley & Landrum, 1997). Also, many children with ADD/ADHD also have social disorders, and many are gifted and talented.

Eligibility of Children with Attention Deficit Disorder for Services

In 1991, The U.S. Department of Education issued a Clarification Memorandum on ADD/ADHD to establish the eligibility of children with attention deficit disorder for special education and related services. In 1999, the Regulations for the 1997 Individuals with Disabilities Act (IDEA) added ADD/ADHD to the list of conditions that could render a child eligible for services under the category of *other health impaired* (OHI). (See Appendix F.) Thus, a child with ADD/ADHD may qualify for special education and related services under the category *other health impaired*. In addition, the regulations state that the term *limited strength, vitality, or alertness* in the definition of *other health impaired*, when applied to children with ADD/ADHD, includes a child's heightened alertness to environmental stimuli that results in limited alertness with respect to the educational environment. (See Appendix F.) Children with ADD/ADHD may be eligible for services under other categories of IDEA if they meet the applicable criteria for those disabilities. Thus, children with ADD/ADHD may be eligible for services under one of three categories of disability: (1) other health impaired, (2) learning disabilities, or (3) emotional disturbances.

The Department of Education further indicates that a child with ADD/ADHD may be eligible for services in the general education classroom under **Section 504 of the Rehabilitation Act of 1973,** even if that child does not qualify for special education and related services. If the child is found to have "a physical or mental impairment which substantially limits a major life activity" (e.g., learning), then the school must make an "individualized determination of the child's education needs for regular or special education or related aids and services." Under Section 504, reasonable accommodations must be provided within the general education classroom (IDEA, 1997).

MEDICAL TREATMENTS FOR ATTENTION DEFICIT DISORDER AND LEARNING DISABILITIES

Many different kinds of treatments are prescribed for individuals with attention deficit disorder and learning disabilities, including medication and various forms of diet control. Medical treatments for these conditions are among the most controversial issues in the field. Some treatments lack sufficient empirical research; additional scientific evidence must be gathered before they can be widely accepted (Silver, 1998).

Medication

Many students with attention deficit disorder and learning disabilities receive medication to improve their attention and to control their hyperactive behavior. A recent survey showed that medication was prescribed in 96.4% of all cases (National Institutes of Health, 1998). The ideal medication should control hyperactivity, increase attention span, and reduce impulsive and aggressive behavior without inducing insomnia, loss of appetite, drowsiness, or other serious toxic effects (Goldman et al., 1996; National Institutes of Health, 1998). Finding ideal medications is not an easy task. It requires close cooperation among medical professionals, school personnel, and family members. The use of psychostimulant medications has been studied extensively and in general shows that there are short-term improvements in symptoms and in academic performance when they are prescribed (Goldman, Ganel, Bezman, & Sianez, 1996; National Institutes of Health, 1998).

The following groups of drugs are prescribed for children: *psychostimulants* (Ritalin, Dexedrine, Cylert, Adderall); *antidepressants* (Tofranil and Norpramin); and *antihypertensive* medication (Clonidine). The psychostimulants are the most commonly prescribed type of medication (Table 7.3).

Psychostimulant Medications   Psychostimulants are the most widely used type of medication for treating attentional and hyperactivity disorders, and are estimated to be used by 3 percent of elementary students in the United States. The usefulness of psychostimulants in reducing hyperactivity was first reported more than fifty years ago, when children taking the psychostimulant benzedrine showed longer attention spans and an improved ability to concentrate, with a corresponding decrease in hyperactivity and oppositional behavior (Bradley, 1937).

Current research on ADD/ADHD suggests that the psychostimulant medication affects the brain in these individuals by increasing the arousal or alertness of the central nervous system (DuPaul, Barkley, & McMurray, 1991). It is thought that these individuals do not produce sufficient **neurotransmitters—**

Table 7.3

Psychostimulant
Medications Used for
Treatment of Attention
Deficit Disorder

Brand name	Generic name	Onset of action	Duration of action
Ritalin	Methylphenidate	30 minutes	3–5 hours
Dexedrine	Dextroamphetamine	30 minutes	3–5 hours
Cylert	Pemoline	2–4 weeks	long-lasting
Adderall	Combination of Dextroamphetamine and Amphetamine	30 minutes	8 hours

chemicals within the brain that transmit messages from one cell to another across a gap, or synapse—and that the psychostimulants work by stimulating the production of the chemical neurotransmitters needed to send information from the brain stem to the parts of the brain that deal with attention (Busch, 1993; Goldstein & Goldstein, 1990). The psychostimulant medications appear to lengthen the children's attention spans, control impulsivity, decrease distractibility and motor activity, and improve visual-motor integration (Barkley, 1998).

The psychostimulant medications most frequently prescribed for attention deficit disorder are Ritalin, Dexedrine, Cylert, and Adderall. Ritalin and Dexedrine become effective in less than 30 minutes; Cylert, however, takes up to four weeks.

The duration of effect for Ritalin and Dexedrine is three to five hours. Consequently, unless a second dose is taken during the school day, the effects of a morning dose of either of these two medications will wear off during the course of the day. The psychostimulants Cylert and Adderall are taken in one daily dosage, and their effects are long-lasting.

The side effects of stimulant medications include insomnia and loss of appetite, but these effects are usually transient and diminish as tolerance develops (Barkley, 1998). For a few children, a more serious side effect of Ritalin is that it can trigger tics or Tourette's syndrome. If one of these situations occurs, the medication must be changed.

A "rebound effect" sometimes occurs with children on psychostimulants. The child's behavior can significantly deteriorate in the late afternoon or evening after a daytime dose of the stimulant. This wearing off of the medication can cause the child to temporarily exhibit more impulsivity, distractibility, and hyperactivity than was previously observed (Parker, 1992). If this occurs, an additional low dose may be needed in the late afternoon.

Other Medications   About 75–85 percent of children with ADD/ADHD show general improvement with psychostimulant medication. For those who do not improve, other medications can be tried. Other medications used for ADD/ADHD are antidepressant medications (Norpramin, Tofranil, Elavil, and Prozac) and antihypertensive medications (clonidine) (Barkley, 1998).

School Responsibility in Monitoring Medication   Teachers play an important role in improving the effectiveness of medical treatment. Teachers should be aware of the student's medication so that they will be able to provide feedback to doctors and parents about the medication's effect on the student in school. The physician needs this feedback to gauge the effectiveness of the medication and to make appropriate modifications.

One problem related to the use of prescribed medication for students with learning disabilities is defining the responsibilities of the school. Schools should have written policies to regulate the storage and administration of prescribed medication.

Nutrition

Research in nutritional biochemistry suggests that there is a significant relationship between diet and brain function. Excesses and/or deficiencies in certain dietary components contribute to the functioning of the central nervous system and therefore have direct effects on behavior (Fishbein & Meduski, 1987).

It is known that protein and calorie deficiency in early life can result in permanent anatomical and biochemical changes in the brain. Intelligence in undernourished children is diminished, and there is increasing evidence that learning disorders result from undernutrition. Early malnutrition impairs growth of both the body in general and the central nervous system in particular. The severity of the deficit is related to the age at which malnutrition occurs, its degree, and its duration. The first six months of life are a critical nutrient period because at this time maximal postnatal brain-cell division occurs in the human infant. Damage incurred during the first six months of life is probably permanent.

Diet Control

There are several diet-related theories concerning the cause or treatment of hyperactivity and learning disorders. Among them are theories of food additives, hypoglycemia, and allergies.

Removal of Food Additives   One of the most controversial and widely discussed treatment theories is that of Feingold (1975), who proposed that **food additives** in a child's diet induce hyperactivity. Feingold noted that artificial flavors, preservatives, and colors have increased in the American diet and that youngsters today consume a large variety of food additives. Therapy consists of the **Feingold diet**, which controls the child's diet and removes food additives.

Although numerous studies have been conducted on the Feingold diet, most have found that the method is not effective in controlling hyperactivity (Silver, 1998). Nevertheless, the Feingold diet continues to enjoy popularity and has many supporters among parents of hyperactive children.

Control of Blood-Sugar Level   Another diet-related theory of the cause of learning disorders suggests that many children with learning disabilities have hypoglycemia, a deficiency in the level of blood sugar (Silver, 1987; Runion, 1980). Therapy consists of controlling the child's eating pattern. Without diet control, according to the theory, the blood-sugar level decreases about an hour after eating, and the child's energy for learning is drained. Several research studies show that sugar in the diet does not increase hyperactivity (Barkley, 1995).

Treatment for Allergies   According to some researchers, many children develop both diet- and environment-related *allergies* that adversely affect learning. The treatment in this approach is removal of the element causing the allergy. Crook (1983) and Rapp (1986) reported success with this treatment. Among the food ingredients thought to impair learning and induce hyperactivity are sugar, milk, corn, eggs, wheat, chocolate, and citrus (Lowenthal & Lowenthal, 1995; Crook & Stevens, 1986). According to Silver (1998), the current research does not clarify the relationship between allergies and learning disabilities.

MEDICAL SPECIALTIES INVOLVED WITH LEARNING DISABILITIES

Pediatrics and Family-Practice Medicine

The pediatrician and the family-practice physician are the medical specialists who are usually responsible for the care of children and adolescents. The role of the child-care physician today extends beyond the care of physical ailments; responsibilities today include understanding the problems of learning and behavior. Pediatricians should be able to recognize disabilities, developmental delays, atypical language, and motor and behavior growth. They are also expected to know about special education services offered by the schools and to be familiar with the rights that children with disabilities have under state and federal law (Levine, 1987).

When parents become concerned about a child's behavior at home or poor performance in school, they often turn to the pediatrician for help. The parents might report that the child overreacts to everything, is constantly in motion, is silly at inappropriate times, does not see the consequences of his or her actions, cannot control his or her behavior, or is overly affectionate, indiscriminate, or gullible. The child may have poor relations with peers, a low tolerance of frustration, and frequent temper tantrums. In school the child may have a short attention span, be easily distracted, be disorganized in working, and vary in mood from day to day or even from hour to hour. The child may have problems in reading or may not seem to understand numbers and arithmetic concepts.

Many pediatricians see their role as central in the total management of the child in terms of both physical and mental health, including language development, school adjustment, and academic learning. Therefore, pediatricians are increasingly aware of learning disabilities.

Developmental pediatrics is an emerging subspecialty within pediatrics. This subspecialty combines expertise in child development with medical knowledge, especially in genetics, neurology, and psychiatry. These specialists should be familiar with the contributions of nonmedical professionals who deal with children and should be able to work as members of interdisciplinary teams.

Neurology

If neurological involvement is suspected, a child or adolescent with learning disabilities may be referred to a neurologist, a physician specializing in the development and functioning of the central nervous system. Overt disturbances of motor function (such as cerebral palsy, epilepsy, and cortical blindness or deafness) and overt neurological abnormalities (such as the absence of certain reflexes or asymmetry of reflex responses) can be readily detected by the neurologist. However, children with learning disabilities do not have obvious impairments; they are more likely to display soft neurological signs—minimal, subtle, refined deviations.

The subspecialty within the field of **neurology** that deals with learning disabilities is *pediatric neurology*. Specialists in this field have the experience, training, and professional perspective to diagnose and treat children and youth with learning disabilities.

Ophthalmology

When a child has difficulty in school, parents often contact an eye specialist, particularly if the problem is poor reading. Two specialties that deal with eye care are ophthalmology and optometry. An **ophthalmologist** is a medical specialist who is concerned with the organic health of the eye as well as with refractive errors (American Academy of Ophthalmology, 1987). The ophthalmologist considers the physiology of the eye and its organic aspects, diseases, and structure. An *optometrist* is the nonmedical specialist concerned with vision and its measurement and correction. The optometrist is more likely to stress the uses of the eye. *Developmental optometrists* are interested in developmental vision, visual perception, and visual training as well as refractive errors (American Optometric Association, 1985).

Many pediatricians see their role as central in the total management of the child in terms of both physical and mental health, including language development, school adjustment, and academic learning. (© Billy E. Barnes/ Stock Boston)

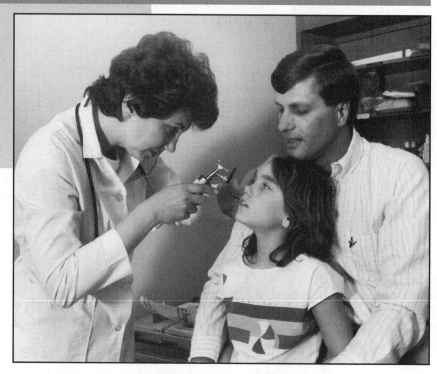

Visual Findings as Factors in Reading Problems   Because visual deficiency may be a factor in certain cases of reading disability, students with reading problems should have a visual examination as part of their diagnosis. Teachers should be alert to such symptoms as facial contortions, forward tilting or thrusting of the head, tension during close work or when looking at a distant object, poor sitting posture, frequent rubbing of eyes, excessive head movements, avoidance of close work, and frequent loss of place during reading. The eye specialist will examine the child for visual acuity, refractive errors, and binocular difficulties.

Visual acuity refers to the ability to see forms or letters clearly from a certain distance. The Snellen chart, a visual screening test used in many schools, tests visual acuity at twenty feet from the chart, that is, *far-point visual acuity*. A score of 20/20 means that the subject sees at twenty feet what the normal eye sees at twenty feet. A score of 20/40 indicates that the subject sees at twenty feet what the normal eye sees at forty feet. Other instruments are needed to assess *near-point visual acuity* at sixteen inches, the distance used in reading. Persons who pass a far-point visual acuity test may fail the near-point test.

Refractive errors are due to a defect of the lens and are of three types: *myopia* (nearsightedness), *hyperopia* (farsightedness), and *astigmatism* (blurring of vision resulting from an uneven curvature of the front of the eye).

Some research studies suggest that problems of binocular vision have more implications for reading than refractive errors do. *Binocular difficulties* occur because the two eyes are not functioning together. Three binocular conditions are *strabismus* (lack of binocular coordination), *inadequate fusion* (poor accommodation of focus of the eye lens to fuse the two images), and *aniseikonia* (unequal size or shape of ocular images in the two eyes).

Learning and reading are probably more dependent on the processes of visual discrimination and visual perception than on either visual acuity or refractive conditions. Visual discrimination and visual perception allow us to interpret visual sensory stimulation. Disturbances in visual perception, however, are not due to organic ocular abnormalities but rather to perceptual processing dysfunctions (see Chapter 8).

Scotopic Sensitivity Syndrome (Tinted Lenses) **Scotopic sensitivity syndrome** is described as a difficulty in processing full-spectrum light efficiently, which causes a reading disorder (Irlen, 1991). It is one of the most controversial explanations of certain types of reading disabilities. Treatment consists of using tinted lenses and colored overlays to eliminate the light sensitivity. Some researchers have reported the method to be beneficial (Robinson & Conway, 1990; O'Connor, Sofo, Kendall, & Olsen, 1990). Others, including both ophthalmologists and optometrists, are doubtful about the value of tinted lenses for treating reading problems (American Academy of Pediatrics, 1998). This method of treatment is not intended for most people with reading problems, but some individuals who have problems with light sensitivity have reported improvement (Silver, 1998).

Otology

Our ability to hear sounds and language in the environment is a crucial factor in the learning of language. The medical specialist responsible for the diagnosis and treatment of auditory disorders is the **otologist.** An audiologist is a nonmedical specialist who specializes in hearing impairment. **Audiology** spans a number of functions, including the testing and measurement of hearing, the diagnosis and rehabilitation of those who are deaf and hard-of-hearing, and the scientific study of the physical process of hearing.

Hearing is most frequently measured by means of a pure-tone audiometer. This electronic device produces pure tones near the outer ear, and the subject states whether he or she hears a sound. A second method of assessing hearing is through a bone conduction test. This method measures certain types of hearing loss by conducting sound waves directly to the inner ear by way of the bones of the ear. In tests for auditory disorders, two dimensions of hearing are considered—intensity and frequency.

Intensity refers to the relative loudness of the sound and is measured in decibels (dB). The louder the sound, the higher the decibel measure. Ordinary conversation measures in the 56- to 60-decibel range. A hearing threshold of 30 decibels is set as the minimum level at which children begin to encounter problems in school. *Frequency* refers to the pitch, or vibrations, of a given sound wave and is measured in cycles per second. A person may have a hearing loss at one frequency but be able to hear well at another. In speech, such consonant sounds as *s, sh,* and *z* are high-frequency sounds; vowels, such as *o* and *u,* are low-frequency sounds.

Hearing level is the intensity level in decibels at which a person begins to detect sounds in various frequency levels. When children are screened for hearing loss, the audiometer may be set at an intensity of 15 to 20 decibels. In a comprehensive sweep check test, the child is tested at frequencies of 250, 500, 1,000, 2,000 and 8,000 cycles per second.

About 0.14 percent of students have hearing impairments. This number includes students who are deaf and those who have hearing disabilities. In addition, many children suffer temporary hearing loss as a result of infected adenoids or tonsils, wax in their ears, or other correctable abnormalities. When such a temporary impairment occurs during certain developmental stages in early childhood, it may have a detrimental effect on learning, particularly on language learning.

The common ear condition in children known as **otitis media** has a detrimental effect on learning. Otitis media is the inflammation of the middle ear accompanied by fluid medial to the ear drum. The cause may be an infection, allergies, or inflamed adenoids or tonsils. Otitis media may cause a mild and fluctuating hearing loss that interferes with language development and with the acquisition of good auditory perception, and it can lead to learning disabilities. The case histories of students with learning disabilities show a markedly higher occurrence of otitis media (Reichman & Healey, 1983).

A sensory hearing loss, then, is an important consideration in diagnosing and treating a student with learning disabilities. Problems in auditory perception are not caused by organic hearing abnormalities. The subject of auditory perception is discussed in greater detail in Chapter 8.

Psychiatry

Many children with learning disabilities are referred to child psychiatrists, who play an important role in their treatment. Many referrals to psychiatric facilities are made because of academic difficulties. With increasing recognition of the emotional factors that accompany learning disabilities, child psychiatrists have assumed important roles as members of diagnostic and treatment teams.

A psychiatric approach to learning disabilities takes into account the complex relationship between organic factors and emotional elements. Psychiatrists often work with parents and other family members as well as with the student. In addition, they should communicate and coordinate their efforts with the school and with the educational treatment. The child psychiatrist certainly is a very visible medical professional at conferences, in the literature, in research, and on learning disabilities teams (Silver, 1998).

Other Medical Specialties

The discussion in this chapter does not exhaust the medical specialties concerned with or contributing to the field of learning disabilities. Practitioners and researchers in the fields of endocrinology, biochemistry, and genetics are very much involved with the problems of students who cannot learn in a normal fashion. They treat such youngsters, function as members of diagnostic teams, and contribute important findings to the literature. The future may hold important breakthroughs from these disciplines.

Chapter Summary

1. Medical information about learning disabilities has value for teachers. Learning occurs within the brain, and what happens in the body and the central nervous system affects a student's learning. Physicians often participate in the assessment and treatment of a student with learning disabilities. Teachers should understand the vocabulary and concepts of the various medical subspecialties. Advances in medical technology may have an effect on the prevalence of learning disabilities.

2. The neurosciences consist of various specialties that study the structure and function of the brain.

3. The brain has two hemispheres—the right and the left. Each hemisphere controls different kinds of learning, although the learning process depends on both hemispheres and their interrelationships. Theories about cerebral dominance, lateral preference, and hemispheric differences are applied to learning disabilities. Recent brain research provides strong evidence that dyslexia has a neurological basis. Familial and twin studies suggest that a tendency for severe reading disabilities is genetic.

4. Neuropsychology combines neurology and psychology and studies the relationship between brain function and behavior. Neuropsychologists are beginning to apply their research to the field of learning disabilities.

5. The neurological examination for learning disabilities is conducted by a family-practice physician, pediatrician, neurologist, or psychiatrist. It consists of two parts: the standard neurological assessment and the examination for soft signs—minimal neurological deviations.

6. Attention deficit disorder (ADD/ADHD) is recognized as a disability under special education law, and eligibility for services is available under one of three existing categories: other health impaired, learning

disabilities, or severe emotional disturbance. Some children with ADD/ADHD are served through Section 504 of the Rehabilitation Act. Teachers must provide services for students with attention deficit disorder.

7. A number of medical treatments are used for individuals with learning disabilities. Some treatments lack sufficient empirical research support. Treatments include medication therapy and various forms of diet control, including removal of food additives and allergy therapy.

8. The most commonly given medications are psychostimulant medications: Ritalin, Dexedrine, Cylert, and Adderall. Studies show that they help reduce hyperactivity and improve attention.

9. The Feingold diet is a diet-control treatment approach. It eliminates food additives, such as artificial flavors, preservatives, and colors. Most of the research on this method has not shown it to be effective. Other diet-control treatments include therapy for hypoglycemia and treatments for allergies. Most physicians feel that more research is needed before these treatments can be generally prescribed.

10. The medical professionals who typically serve students with learning disabilities include the pediatrician, the family-practice physician, developmental pediatrician, pediatric neurologists, and child psychiatrists.

Questions for Discussion and Reflection

1. Why (or why not) is it important for teachers to have information about the function and dysfunction of the brain? What relevance, if any, does such information have for teaching students with learning disabilities?

2. What are the neurosciences finding out about the brain in relation to dyslexia? What are some of the possible implications of this research for teaching?

3. Many children today are diagnosed with ADD/ADHD. Describe the characteristics of children with attention deficit disorder.. What are some of the possibilities for serving children with ADD/ADHD under IDEA and also under Section 504 of the Rehabilitation Act?

4. Many children with learning disabilities and with attention deficit disorder receive medication as part of their treatment. Discuss the kinds of medications these children receive. What responsibilities are placed upon the school when children take medication?

5. In addition to medication, what other kinds of medical treatment are used for children with learning disabilities? Why are these treatments considered controversial?

6. Different medical specialties contribute to the field of learning disabilities. Describe the contributions of three medical specialties.

Key Terms

attention deficit disorder (ADD) *(p. 234)*

attention deficit hyperactivity disorder (ADHD) *(p. 234)*

audiology *(p. 245)*

brain electrical activity mapping (BEAM) *(p. 228)*

central nervous system *(p. 222)*

cerebral dominance *(p. 224)*

cerebral hemisphere *(p. 223)*

co-occurring conditions *(p. 238)*

developmental pediatrics *(p. 243)*

dyslexia *(p. 225)*

Feingold diet *(p. 242)*

food additives *(p. 241)*

functional magnetic resonance imaging (fMRI) *(p. 228)*

hyperactivity *(p. 235)*

lateral preference *(p. 225)*

magnetic resonance imaging (MRI) *(p. 226)*

neurology *(p. 243)*

neuropsychology *(p. 230)*

neurosciences *(p. 223)*

neurotransmitter *(p. 239)*

ophthalmologist *(p. 243)*

otitis media *(p. 246)*

otologist *(p. 245)*

positron emission tomography (PET) *(p. 229)*

scotopic sensitivity syndrome *(p. 245)*

Section 504 of the Rehabilitation Act of 1973 *(p. 238)*

soft neurological signs *(p. 230)*

8

Young Children with Learning Disabilities

CHAPTER OUTLINE

Young children with learning disabilities and children who are at risk for learning disabilities need to be identified early and provided with appropriate intervention. Because national and state policies now support the provision of early services for young children with disabilities, schools and agencies are expanding their services for young children. In this chapter, we will review the developing field of early childhood special education, with an emphasis on young children with learning disabilities. The topics will cover the importance of the preschool years, precursors of learning disabilities in young children, early childhood programs and placement options, early childhood curriculum, early intervention strategies, and using computer technology.

THE IMPORTANCE OF THE EARLY YEARS

The early childhood years are crucial for all children, but for the child who deviates from the norm in terms of mental, physical, behavioral, developmental, or learning characteristics, these years are especially critical. Research from several disciplines confirms what early childhood educators have long observed—that the early years of life are crucial for establishing a lifelong foundation for learning. If the opportunity for children to develop intellectually and emotionally during these critical years is missed, precious learning time is lost forever.

Children do not *begin* to learn when they enter formal schooling at age 6. During the first 6 years of their lives, young children learn at a rapid pace. They need continuous and intense learning from the moment of birth. By the time they reach school age, they should have mastered many kinds of learning. Parents and others involved with young children need to be actively engaged in promoting learning during the preschool years. Otherwise, their child's intellectual abilities will not grow optimally during these vital years. Children who start school being already behind may never be able to catch up, to keep up, or to take advantage of all the efforts schools make to help them.

Benefits of Early Intervention

Perhaps the most promising success stories in education today are the reports of special programs for young children who have disabilities or who are at risk. The underlying premise of early childhood special education is that early intervention makes a significant difference in child growth and development. When a child's problems are recognized early, school failure can to a large extent be prevented or reduced. Early childhood special education programs first *identify* young children, ages birth through 5, who have have special needs and are likely to encounter difficulty in academic learning, and

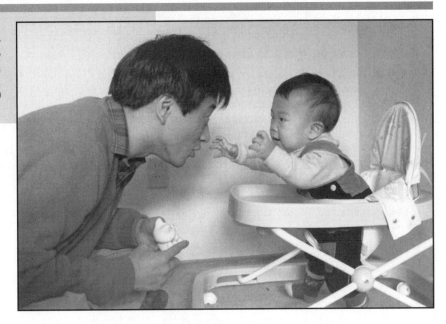

Children at risk dramatically improve when early intervention and work with families are provided. *(© Elizabeth Crews)*

then provide an immediate early intervention program. The case example entitled "A Preschooler with a Disability" illustrates such a situation.

Research demonstrates that early comprehensive and intensive intervention is beneficial for children with disabilities, for their families, and for society.

- *Early intervention helps children with disabilities.* It accelerates cognitive and social development and reduces behavioral problems. Many conditions can be alleviated, other disorders can be overcome to a large extent, and some problems can be managed so that the child can live a better life. Early intervention can avert the occurrence of secondary problems that compound the original difficulty (Lerner, Lowenthal, & Egan, 1998; Fletcher & Foorman, 1994; Bailey & Wolery, 1992).

- *Early intervention benefits the families of young children with special needs.* In the family-centered intervention approach, the child is viewed as part of a family system. When the parents are empowered to be an integral part of the intervention process, the family becomes an essential element in the process of teaching the child and improving child-adult interactions (Dunst, Trivette, & Deal, 1994; Wolery, Werts, & Holcombe, 1994; McGonigel, Kaufmann, & Johnson, 1991; Harbin, Gallagher, & Terry, 1991).

- *Early intervention benefits society.* Early intervention programs offer a substantial financial savings for the community by reducing the number

A PRESCHOOLER WITH A DISABILITY

Lorinda was identified during the local school district's preschool screening program as a high-risk child who needed further assessment and intervention. She performed poorly on tests requiring expressive language skills and on social measures. Lorinda's age was 3 years, 9 months at the time of her testing.

During the interview with Lorinda's mother, the school obtained additional information. Born six weeks prematurely, Lorinda weighed a little more than four pounds at birth and had trouble breathing. She frequently suffered from colds during her first two years, and between the ages of 2 and 3 she had at least eight serious ear infections. Motor development seemed to be normal; she sat up, walked, and crawled at the same ages that her siblings had performed these activities. Her language development, however, was slower than theirs. Although she seemed to understand language when spoken to, she could not use it to make her wants known. She did not use any words until she was 2 years old and even now uses only very short sentences, such as "Me want pizza" or "Him break cup." She often uses the wrong word or simply points to what she wants. She still has temper tantrums, which seem to be triggered by her inability to communicate her needs.

Her mother described her as an "overactive" child compared with the other children. She would "tear the house apart," break the crib, and take all her toys apart. She never sat down, except to watch television, and that activity usually lasted for only a few minutes. When Lorinda turned 3, her mother tried to enroll her in a small play school, but after a few days the director said she could not stay because of her extreme hyperactivity. Without provocation, she grabbed toys from other children and hit or scratched her classmates.

Lorinda's mother had suspected that Lorinda was different, but everyone had told her not to worry—that Lorinda would outgrow her disruptive behavior. The mother expressed relief at having her daughter in the special preschool program. At last, someone else recognized Lorinda's problem and would be working to help her. The hours Lorinda would be in school would offer her mother the first break since Lorinda was born, and she was looking forward to receiving help from the school on home behavior management.

of children needing later special education services (Schweinhart, Barnes, & Weikart, 1993; U.S. Department of Education, 1994).

In summary, early intervention accomplishes the following (Lerner, Lowenthal, & Egan, 1998; Smith & Strain, 1988):

1. Enhances intelligence in some children

2. Promotes substantial gains in all developmental areas (physical, cognitive, language and speech, psychosocial, and self-help)

3. Inhibits or prevents secondary disabilities

4. Reduces family stress

5. Reduces dependency and institutionalization

6. Reduces the need for special education services at school age
7. Saves the nation and society substantial health-care and education costs

Percentage of Young Children Receiving Services

It is difficult to know how many 3- through 5-year-old children who receive special education services have learning disabilities because young children are no longer counted by category of disability (such as learning disabilities or mental retardation). The U.S. Department of Education now categorizes all preschoolers with disabilities as a general group. On the basis of classification data of older students, it is reasonable to estimate that at least 50 percent of the preschool children receiving special education services have learning disabilities.

About 4.6 percent of all preschool children ages 3 through 5 currently receive special education services through the schools. The percentages vary across states, ranging from a low of 1.5 percent to a high of 9.6 percent. Of all preschool children receiving services, 21 percent are 3 years old, 34 percent are 4 years old, and 55 percent are 5 years old. About 1.5 percent of all infants and toddlers (birth through age 2) and their families in the general population receive special education services (U.S. Department of Education, 1998).

PRECURSORS OF LEARNING DISABILITIES IN YOUNG CHILDREN

Precursors of learning disabilities are early symptoms of difficulty in learning in preschool children. Signs of learning disabilities can be observed in the child's motor development, auditory processing, visual processing, speech and language development, or attentional abilities. Often the child will excel in some areas of development while displaying significant difficulty in others. Precursors of learning disabilities are predictive of later difficulty in academic achievement, but early intervention can help children reduce or overcome these potential problems (Lerner, Lowenthal, & Egan, 1998). Young children

Table 8.1

Percentage of Young Children Receiving Special Education Services

Age Group	Percentage of General Population
Birth Through age 2	1.6%
Ages 3 Through 5	4.6%

Data gathered from the U.S. Department of Education (1998). *To assure the free appropriate public education of all children with disabilities. Twentieth annual report to Congress on the implementation of the Individuals with Disabilities Act.* Washington, DC: Government Printing Office.

who lack precursor skills have developmental learning disabilities. In the later school years, they have *academic learning disabilities,* such as problems in reading, writing, and arithmetic (Kirk and Chalfant, 1984).

One reason that learning disabilities may not be identified in young children is that the definition of learning disabilities in the federal law (the Individuals with Disabilities Education Act [IDEA], 1997) emphasizes academic failure in reading, writing, spelling, and mathematics. In the federal definition of learning disabilities, a discrepancy between the child's ability and academic achievement is required. This approach is called the "wait and fail" method because the child must fail before he or she is eligible for identification and services. For this reason preschoolers are not identified as having learning disabilities because they have not yet been exposed to formal academic learning. Waiting for a child to fail in order to become eligible for services is a costly procedure. A more appropriate approach for identifying young children with learning disabilities is to look for precursors of learning disabilities (Lerner, Lowenthal, & Egan, 1998).

Accumulating research shows the importance of early identification of young children who show signs of learning difficulty and the value of providing early intervention. About 74 percent of children who are unsuccessful readers in the third grade are still unsuccessful readers in the ninth grade (Adams, Treiman, & Pressley, 1997; Foorman, et al., 1998; Lyon, Alexander, & Yaffee, 1997; Fletcher & Foorman, 1994). Many studies show that children who are likely to have difficulty in learning to read can be identified during the preschool years, and they can be helped through appropriate and timely instruction. Moreover, the majority of reading problems faced by today's adolescents and adults could have been avoided or resolved in the early years of childhood (Lyon, Alexander, & Yafee, 1997; Adams, 1997; Torgesen, 1997; National Research Council, 1998).

Unfortunately, young children with learning disabilities are not being identified or being given appropriate instruction. In fact, data from the U.S. Department of Education (1998) show that most children with learning disabilities are not identified until ages 9–14. (See Figure 1.2 in Chapter 1). Very few 6-year-old children and relatively few 7- and 8-year-old youngsters receive special learning disabilities services. It is only when children actually fail at ages 9 or 10 that they are finally identified and thus eligible to receive special instruction.

Some precursors of learning disabilities are briefly described next:

■ *Gross-Motor Skills.*   A common precursor for some children with learning disabilities is an awkwardness in gross-motor skills, which require children to use large muscles when moving their arms, legs, torso, hands, and feet. Young children with gross-motor problems appear clumsy in walking, jumping, hopping, running, skipping, throwing, and catching skills. Gross-motor development is discussed later in this chapter.

■ *Fine-Motor Skills.*   Fine-motor activities involve the small muscles used to move fingers and wrists as well as eye-hand coordination and coor-

Human learning begins with motor learning. As children move and play, they learn.
(© Elizabeth Crews)

dination of the two hands. Children with fine-motor skills problems tend to be slow in learning to dress themselves, in learning eating skills, in using buttons and zippers, and in using pencils and crayons. Problems in fine-motor development are evident when children have difficulty doing puzzles, playing building games, accomplishing art projects, and using scissors in cutting activities. In the later elementary years, fine motor difficulties are evident in slow and laborious handwriting. Fine-motor skills are discussed later in this chapter.

■ *Auditory Processing.*   An important precursor of learning disabilities involves auditory processing. The ability to interpret what is heard provides an important pathway for learning. Children who have difficulty learning to read show early signs of difficulties with auditory processing abilities. These children can hear, but their difficulty lies in several dimensions of auditory processing, including phonological awareness, auditory discrimination, auditory memory, and auditory sequencing and blending. Auditory processing precursors are discussed later in this chapter.

■ *Visual Processing.*   Visual processing abilities play a significant role in school learning, particularly in reading. Children with visual processing difficulties can see, but they encounter problems in visual discrimination of letters and words, visual memory, or visual closure. Visual processing and orthographic problems in young children are early signs of learning disabilities, and these precursors are predictive of later reading difficulties. Visual processing precursors are discussed later in this chapter.

■ *Communication and Language Skills.*   Difficulty in acquiring speech and understanding and using language are among the most common precursors of learning disabilities. The ability to use language to communicate one's thoughts is central to learning. Children with communication or language disorders have difficulty understanding the language of others (listening), responding to instructions, initiating communications, explaining, engaging in conversations, and communicating with others. Delays in speech and language acquisition are discussed in Chapter 10.

■ *Problems with Attention.*   Some young children with learning disabilities display behaviors related to attention deficit disorder. Attention deficit disorder includes behaviors of hyperactivity, inattention, and impulsivity. These children cannot regulate or manage their activity levels to meet the demands of the moment. They act as if they were driven by a motor, running and climbing about excessively, being in constant motion, fidgeting and squirming when sitting, and making loud noises. Young children with inattention problems have difficulty concentrating on a task, are easily distracted, shift from one activity to another, and do not finish what they start. Parents and teachers complain that these children do not listen and often lose things. Impulsive young children have problems inhibiting their responses to immediate events and do not think reflectively before acting. They act before considering the consequences of their behavior. They tend to blurt out answers before their teachers have finished the question. These youngsters also find it difficult to share and take turns with their classmates. Attention deficit disorder is addressed in Chapter 7.

MOTOR DEVELOPMENT AND LEARNING

Parents, teachers, physicians, and other professionals often describe a child with learning disabilities as awkward or as lacking manual dexterity. Parents frequently report that their child was slow in acquiring motor skills, such as using eating utensils, putting on clothes, buttoning a coat, catching a ball, or riding a bicycle. Many children with learning disabilities exhibit no motor problems, actually excelling in motor skills. Other children present severe motor incoordination problems and significant delays in motor development. The case example entitled "Motor Coordination Problems" shows a child's difficulties with motor coordination.

The federal Individuals with Disabilities Education Act (IDEA) recognizes the need for physical education for all exceptional children. The child's IEP (individualized education program) can specify adapted physical education, occupational therapy (OT), or physical therapy (PT) as a needed related service. Occupational therapists and physical therapists are medically trained professionals who provide therapy for a variety of motor and physical disorders. Motor activities are typically part of the curriculum in early childhood special education programs. Sometimes the adapted physical education instructor teaches motor activities for young children at the elementary level. More often, the special education or classroom teacher has the responsibility of teaching motor activities.

The Value of Motor Skills and Physical Fitness

Throughout history, philosophers and educators have written about the close relationship between motor development and learning. Plato placed gymnastics at the first level of education in the training of the philosopher-king. Aristotle wrote that a person's soul is characterized by both body and mind. Spinoza advised, "Teach the body to do many things; this will help you to perfect the mind and to come to the intellectual level of thought." Piaget (1936/1952) emphasized that early sensorimotor learning establishes the foundation for later, more complex perceptual and cognitive development. Indeed, a recurring theme throughout the history of special education is the concern for motor development (Sequin, 1866/1970; Itard, 1801/1962; Montessori, 1912).

The current edition of the *Diagnostic and Statistical Manual of Mental Disorders* (DSM) identifies motor skills disorders as developmental coordination disorder (DCD) (American Psychiatric Association, 1994). The criteria for developmental coordination disorder include delays in developmental milestones, dropping things, clumsiness, poor performance in sports, or poor handwriting (Fox, 1998).

Early childhood educators view motor skill growth as a cornerstone in the study of child development (Lerner, Lowenthal, & Egan, 1998). Motor development is typically included in the regular curriculum for preschool children. For preschoolers with learning disabilities who have deficits in motor coordination, balance, rhythm, or body image, the intervention strategies include methods for building motor skills, spatial awareness, and motor planning (Cook, Tessier, & Klein, 1996).

The pioneering theories of learning disabilities focused on sensorimotor and perceptual-motor learning. Today, however, there is much less attention placed on the role of motor development. It is ironic that while learning disabilities programs have deemphasized motor development, the rest of the world seems to be embracing the concept that physical fitness, exercise, and motor activities are essential elements for achieving general well-being and improving life and work for all individuals. The critical role of exercise in fostering general well-being is widely acknowledged today. Indeed, intervening with motor activities can bring about many unanticipated and probably unmeasurable improvements. It can help a child become happier, more confident, and more available for learning, and can also foster social interactions. When the motor curriculum requires the child to go *through, under, over, between,* and *around* obstacles, the child is also learning important cognitive and language skills by learning the instructions.

MOTOR COORDINATION PROBLEMS

Jim is an example of a student with academic learning problems who also shows signs of immature motor development, laterality confusion, and poor awareness of his own body. Jim was brought to a learning disabilities clinic at age 12 for an evaluation because he was doing poorly in school, particularly in reading and arithmetic. An individual intelligence test indicated that Jim's intelligence was above average, and a screening test for auditory and visual acuity showed no abnormalities. His oral language skills seemed good for his age. At first, Jim's posture gave the impression of being unusually straight, almost military in bearing. During the motor testing, however, it was evident that this seemingly straight posture was actually rigidity. When a change in balance occurred because of a required movement, Jim was unable to make the correction within his body position and his relationship to gravity. He lost his balance and fell when he tried to walk in a straight line on the floor. When a ball was thrown to him, he was unable to catch it and lost his balance. Jim's attempts at catching the ball were similar to those of a child of 4 or 5. He was noted to work at times with his left hand, at other times with his right hand; he had not yet established hand preference. Although he had been given swimming lessons several times, he was still unable to swim. All the neighborhood children played baseball after school and on weekends, but Jim could not participate in this sport with youngsters his own age. Consequently, he had no friends, and his teacher identified him as a loner. Evidence of poor motor skills appeared in many academic activities. For example, his handwriting was almost illegible, reflecting his perceptual-motor dysfunction. Jim's father, who had excelled in athletics and had won several sports championships in high school and college, had little patience for working or playing with a son who did not catch on quickly. In fact, because of Jim's abysmal failure in sports, his father was convinced his son was mentally retarded and not "a real boy." For Jim, then, reading was only one part of the difficulty he had in relating to the world. A comprehensive assessment should take into account his poorly developed motor skills, and an individualized instructional plan should help Jim acquire motor experiences to establish a motor awareness of the world.

Concepts of Motor Development

Movement and motor experiences are crucial to human development. Theories of human development generally recognize the significance of motor experiences for child growth. For many children with learning disabilities, difficulties with motor coordination pose a serious problem. Some exhibit motor behaviors that are typical of much younger children. Examples of such motor behaviors are overflow movements (when the child performs a movement with the right arm, the left arm involuntarily performs a shadow movement), poor coordination in gross motor activities, difficulty in fine-motor coordination, poor body image, and lack of directionality. These children are so poor in the physical education activities for their age that they are easily spotted in gym class. They frequently disturb others in the classroom by bumping into objects, falling off chairs, dropping pencils and books, and appearing generally clumsy.

Perceptual-motor behavior refers to the integration of perceptual input and motor output. Human beings have six perceptual systems for receiving raw data about the world: the visual (sight), auditory (sound), tactile (touch), kinesthetic (muscle feeling), olfactory (smell), and gustatory (taste) systems. In education, we emphasize the visual, auditory, kinesthetic, and tactile systems as the most practical approaches for instruction. In the motor learning process, several input channels of sensation or perception are integrated with each other and correlated with motor activity, which in turn provides feedback information to correct the perceptions. Thus, in performing a motor activity such as a somersault, the individual feels the surface of the floor; has a body awareness of space, changing body position, and balance; sees the floor and other objects in relation to changing positions; bears the body thump on the floor; and moves in a certain fashion.

Theories about the relationship of motor development and learning are based on the belief that motor learning lays the foundation for other kinds of learning. Three underlying concepts about motor learning are the following:

1. *Human learning begins with motor learning.*   As children move, they learn. An understanding of the dynamics of learning necessarily involves an understanding of movement and motor development.

2. *There is a natural sequence of developmental motor stages.*   The acquisition of motor skills at each stage of the sequence provides the foundation for learning at the next stage.

3. *Many areas of academic and cognitive performance are based on successful motor experiences.*   Some children need more experiences with gross- and fine-motor coordination activities.

Gross- and Fine-Motor Development   Gross-motor skills involve the large muscles of the neck, trunk, arms, and legs. Gross-motor development involves postural control, walking, running, catching, and jumping. To provide stimulation for gross-motor development, children need safe environments that are free from obstacles, and they need much encouragement from parents and teachers.

Fine-motor skills involve the small muscles. Fine-motor coordination includes coordination of the hands and fingers and dexterity with the tongue and speech muscles. Children develop fine-motor skills as they learn to pick up small objects such as beads or chunks of food, cut with a scissors, grasp and use crayons and pencils, and use a fork and spoon. They need ample opportunities for building with blocks, manipulating small toys, stringing beads, buttoning, and rolling and pounding (Cook, Tessier, & Klein, 1996).

Motor Learning Through Play   Through the normal activities of play, children have many opportunities for motor activity. On the playground, the child's muscles move as they reach, grasp, run, stoop, or stretch. In the normal play environment, the child develops motor skills by playing with toys, using clay, or painting. Playing games can also help build self-concept,

Source: PEANUTS reprinted by permission of UFS, Inc.

social relationships, and acceptance by peers. Motor activities—such as riding bicycles, playing games, and dancing—signal the emergence of various developmental levels. Inability to accomplish these activities with reasonable proficiency may precipitate a chain of failure (Bricker & Cripe, 1992).

Sometimes children with learning disabilities receive instruction in motor skills through **adapted physical education programs.** This is a special physical education program that has been modified to meet the needs of children with disabilities. Helping children with disabilities take advantage of the same physical, emotional, and social benefits of exercise, recreation, and leisure activities that other children enjoy is important in **inclusive environments** (Eastman & Safran, 1986).

Movement games can help children with learning disabilities adjust to general classroom learning. For example, the child's attention span can be lengthened through games and physical activities that require increasing ability to pay attention. The learning of letters can become a physical activity if large letters made of rope are placed on a playground, and games are devised in which the student runs or walks over the shapes of letters. Activities that involve the total body may also serve to focus the attention of the hyperactive child (Cratty, 1988).

Perceptual-Motor Theory

The **perceptual-motor theory** of learning disabilities was formulated by one of the pioneers of learning disabilities, Newell Kephart (1963, 1967, 1971). The perceptual-motor theory suggests that children who have normal perceptual-motor development establish a solid and reliable concept of the world, a stable *perceptual-motor world,* by the time they encounter academic tasks at age 6.

In contrast, some children with learning disabilities have atypical motor development. They must contend with a perceptual-motor world that is still unstable and unreliable. In order to deal with symbolic materials, children must learn to make some rather precise observations about space and time and relate these observations to objects and events. Children with learning disabilities may encounter problems when confronted with symbolic materials because they have an inadequate orientation to what Kephart calls the basic realities of the universe that surrounds them—specifically, the dimensions of space and time. These children lack the necessary motor experiences to internalize a comprehensive and consistent scheme of the world. They cannot adequately organize their information-processing systems, and they are disorganized physically, perceptually, and cognitively.

Sensory-Integration Theory

Another theory of motor development and learning disabilities is the **sensory integration theory,** which comes from the field of occupational therapy (OT) (Goldey, 1998; Fisher, Murray, & Bundy, 1991; Ayres, 1978, 1981). **Occupational therapists** are trained in brain physiology and function. They prescribe specific physical therapies and exercises designed to modify the motor and sensory integration function of patients.

Sensory integration is a theory of the relation between the neurological process and motor behavior (Fisher et al., 1991). Occupational therapists who use sensory integration intervention believe that some children with learning disabilities have disorders in several sensory integration functions, which interfere with the awareness of their body and body movements. In these cases, sensory integration therapy is used to help children with learning disabilities. Usually these methods are used in early childhood special education programs.

Three systems are involved in sensory integration: the tactile system, the vestibular system, and the proprioceptive system (Fisher, et al., 1991; Silver, 1992; Clark, Mailloux, & Parham, 1989).

Tactile System   This system involves the sense of touch and stimulation of skin surfaces. Some children have problems in *tactile defensiveness*; they experience discomfort when touched by another person. Infants with tactile defensiveness do not like to be held or touched. Older children may complain about being bothered by a tag on the back of a shirt, by a seam on a sock, or by clothes that are uncomfortable. These children may lash out and fight when they are brushed against while they are lining up. Children who suffer from touch deprivation need more body contact.

Methods of sensory motor therapy used by occupational therapists for tactile defensiveness include touching and rubbing skin surfaces, using lotions, and brushing skin surfaces.

Vestibular System   This system involves the inner ear and enables individuals to detect motion. The vestibular system allows the individual to tell where the head is in space and how to handle gravity. Children with vestibular disorders fall easily and do not know how to adjust their bodies for the position of their head or for other body movements.

Therapy for vestibular disorders used by occupational therapists consists of exercises in body planning and balance. It includes activities such as spinning in chairs, swinging, and rolling on a large ball to stimulate the vestibular system.

Proprioceptive System   This system involves stimulation from the muscles or within the body itself. Disorders in this system may involve *apraxia*, difficulty in intentional performance of certain body movements. Children with an apraxia problem cannot plan how to move their bodies without bumping into walls, and they cannot direct movements such as buttoning, tying, skipping, or writing.

Therapy for proprioceptive stimulation used by occupational therapists includes having the child use scooter boards and engage in other planned motor behaviors.

Tests of Motor Development

Tests for assessing motor development are listed in Test Inventory 8.1. Additional information on these tests appears in Appendix C.

Young children learn many motor skills through the normal activities of play. *(© Elizabeth Crews)*

PERCEPTUAL PROCESSING

Learning does not suddenly begin when a child reaches age 5 or 6 and enters school. During the preschool years, children are earnestly and actively engaged in learning. During these early years, they master many preacademic skills and acquire a vast amount of knowledge, information, and abilities that are needed later for learning academic subjects (Kirk, 1987). In the preschool years children acquire skills in visual and auditory perception, extend their facility to attend, expand memory and thinking skills, and learn to understand and use language.

Perception is the process of recognizing and interpreting sensory information. It is the intellect's ability to give meaning to sensory stimulation. For example, a "square" must be perceived as a whole configuration, not as four separate lines. Because perception is a learned skill, the teaching process can have a direct impact on the child's perceptual facility.

The concept of perception was one of the productive ideas of Gestalt psychology, a body of study that was influential in the early 1900s in Western Europe, particularly in Germany. (The word *Gestalt* refers to the ability to grasp the wholeness of an experience.) A tenet of Gestalt psychology is that people have an innate inclination to organize information taken from the environment and to make sense of the world by bringing structure and organization to what they perceive.

Ideas from Gestalt psychology influenced the early development of the field of learning disabilities because many of the field's first scholars, such as Alfred Strauss, were trained in Gestalt theory. They recognized that

Test Inventory 8.1

Motor Tests

Bruininks-Oseretsky Test of Motor Proficiency

Peabody Developmental Motor Scales

Purdue Perceptual-Motor Survey

Southern California Test Battery for Assessment of Dysfunction (This battery consists of five tests: *Southern California Kinesthesia and Tactile Perception Tests, Southern California Figure-Ground Visual Perception Test, Southern California Motor Accuracy Test, Southern California Perceptual-Motor Tests,* and *Ayres Space Test.*)

Test of Gross Motor Development

perceptual disorders were a common characteristic of the children they examined and taught (Strauss & Lehtinen, 1947). The strong influence of the concept of perceptual disorders is evident in the federal definition of learning disabilities (the Individuals with Disabilities Education Act) within the phrase *disorder in one of the basic psychological processes.*

Several dimensions of perception have implications for understanding learning disabilities: the perceptual modality concept, overloading of perceptual systems, auditory perception, visual perception, and tactile and kinesthetic perception.

Perceptual Modality Concept

The **perceptional modality concept** is based on the premise that children learn in different ways. Some learn best by listening (auditory), some by looking (visual), some by touching (tactile), and some by performing an action (kinesthetic). Adults, too, have individual learning styles. Some learn best by listening to an explanation; others know that to learn something they must read about it or watch it being done. Still others learn best by writing something down or by going through the action themselves. Some students with learning disabilities appear to have a much greater facility in using one perceptual or learning style over another (see the case example entitled "Perceptual Problems").

To implement the perceptual modality concept in teaching, instructors first assess the child's underlying abilities in terms of perception, assessing the child's strengths and weaknesses in learning through visual, auditory, or tactile styles. On the basis of this information, three alternative methods of instruction are available: (1) strengthening the deficit learning mode, (2) teaching through the preferred learning mode, and (3) combining both methods. (This method is discussed in Chapter 6.)

The concept of underlying perceptual abilities has been controversial because perception occurs within the mind and is not easy to observe, test, and measure (Kavale & Forness, 1987a; Hammill & Larsen, 1978). (See Chapter 6.) Recent research on brain function using the new brain imaging

CASE EXAMPLE

PERCEPTUAL PROBLEMS

Auditory Perception Problems

Eight-year-old Sandra failed many tasks that involved auditory learning. She could not learn nursery rhymes, was unable to take messages correctly over the telephone, forgot spoken instructions, and could not discriminate between pairs of spoken words with minimal contrast or a single phoneme difference (*cat-cap*). She could not tap out the number of sounds in words and found phonics instruction baffling. Sandra was failing in reading, yet she had passed the reading readiness test with ease because it tested performance skills requiring visual learning. At first, Sandra could not remember the arithmetic facts, but there was a sudden spurt in her arithmetic achievement during the second half of first grade. She explained that she solved her arithmetic problems by putting the classroom clock in her head. By "looking" at the minute marks on the clock to perform arithmetic tasks, Sandra did well with visual tasks but poorly in auditory processing, particularly in recognizing sounds in words.

Visual Perception Problems

In contrast, John, at age 8, performed several years above his age level on tasks requiring auditory processing. He had easily learned to say the alphabet in sequence. He also learned poems and nursery rhymes; remembered series of digits, phone numbers, and verbal instructions; and quickly learned to detect phonemes or sounds in words. Visual tasks, however, were difficult. John had much trouble putting puzzles together, seeing and remembering forms in designs, doing block arrangements, remembering the sequence and order of things he saw, and recalling what words looked like in print.

technologies show that different perceptual systems do exist in different areas within the brain.

Sensitive teachers use information about a child's style of learning and perceptual strengths and weaknesses in teaching academic skills. For example, the child who has great difficulty with the auditory perception of the sounds in words (or a deficit in awareness of phonemes) is likely to have difficulty learning phonics. Of course, the child will have to learn to decode words to acquire reading fluency. However, recognizing the pupil's auditory difficulties alerts the teacher to the child's area of difficulty and helps in teaching the child. The child may need additional practice in recognizing sounds in words.

Teachers must consider the child's perceptual difficulties, but they also must move as quickly as possible into the academic area they are trying to improve. For example, a teacher can teach visual discrimination of letters and words in reading instead of discrimination of abstract geometric symbols.

Another important variable to consider is the student's culture and language background. Learning styles differ in various cultures, and the behavior of children will reflect these differences. Children whose first language is not English may have difficulty in auditory perception and phoneme awareness (Mallory & New, 1994).

Overloading of Perceptual Systems

For a few children, the reception of information from one input system interferes with information coming from another. These children have a lower tolerance for receiving and integrating information from several input systems at the same time. An analogy might be made to an overloaded fuse that blows out when it cannot handle any more electrical energy. Unable to accept and process an excess of data, the perceptual system becomes overloaded. Symptoms include confusion, poor recall, retrogression, refusal of the task, poor attention, temper tantrums, or even seizures (Johnson & Myklebust, 1967) or "catastrophic responses" (Strauss & Lehtinen, 1947).

If a child presents such symptoms, teachers should be cautious about using multisensory techniques and should change the method of instruction. One teacher reported that a second-grade girl with learning disabilities was not making progress when taught through simultaneous auditory and visual instruction. The teacher reduced the auditory input by not talking and instead taught reading and arithmetic through visual pictures and examples. The girl now could understand and made great strides in both reading and arithmetic.

Sometimes children learn by themselves to adapt their own behavior to avoid overloading. One boy avoided looking at an individual's face when he engaged in conversation. When asked about this behavior, the boy explained that he found he could not understand what was being said if he watched the speaker's face while listening. The visual stimuli in effect interfered with the boy's ability to comprehend auditory information.

Auditory Perception

Auditory perception—the ability to recognize or interpret what is heard—provides an important pathway for learning. Accumulating research shows that many poor readers have auditory, linguistic, and phonological difficulties (Lyon, 1998; Stahl & Murray, 1994; Ball & Blachman, 1991; Williams, 1991). These children do not have a problem in hearing or in auditory acuity. Rather, they have a disability in auditory perception—the ability to recognize or interpret what is heard. Because abilities in auditory perception normally develop during the early years, many academic teachers mistakenly presume that all students have acquired these skills. Auditory perception skills include phonological awareness, auditory discrimination, auditory memory, auditory sequencing, and auditory blending.

Phonological Awareness   A necessary ability for learning to read is the ability to recognize that the words we hear are composed of individual sounds within the word. This skill is called **phonological awareness.** For example, when an individual hears the word *cat*, the ear hears it as one pulse of sound. But the individual who has acquired phonological awareness knows that the word *cat* is made up of three sounds (or phonemes): /c/a/t/. The child who lacks phonological awareness does not have the system that understands that *cat* has three separate sounds (Torgesen, 1997, 1998; Blachman, 1997; Ball & Blachman, 1991).

Children who have trouble learning to read are often completely unaware of how language is put together. They are unable to recognize or isolate the sounds of words or the number of sounds in a word. For example, when hearing the word *kite*, they cannot tap out three sounds. These children cannot recognize similarities in words. They have difficulty recognizing words that rhyme (for example, *right*, *fight*, and *night*) and alliteration in words (for example, *cat* and *cap*). As a result, these children cannot understand or use the alphabetic principle needed for learning phonics and decoding words.

Skills in phonological awareness abilities are formed during the preschool years. It is very important to assess these abilities before children are taught to read and to provide training for children who have not acquired phonological abilities. Fortunately, research shows that young children can develop phonological awareness through specific instruction and that such teaching has a positive effect on reading achievement (Stahl & Murray, 1994; Ball & Blachman, 1991; Williams, 1991; Chall, 1991; Lerner, 1990; Liberman & Liberman, 1990; Bradley, 1988). Phonological awareness as it relates to reading is also discussed in Chapters 10 and 11.

An informal test of phonological awareness is shown in Table 8.2. In this test, the child is given a word and then asked to say it again but to leave out an element—such as a syllable or a phoneme. For example, the child is given the word *baseball* and asked to say it without *base*. The test becomes progressively more difficult as first syllables and then phonemes are left out.

Auditory Discrimination   **Auditory discrimination** is the ability to recognize a difference between phoneme sounds and to identify words that are the same and words that are different. In testing for this problem, the student is faced away from the examiner (so there will be no visual cue of watching the speaker's mouth) and then asked whether a pair of words are the same or different. The two words (for example, *mitt-mat* or *big-pig*) have a minimal sound difference or contrast of a single phoneme.

Auditory Memory   Auditory memory is the ability to store and recall what one has heard. For example, the student could be asked to do three activities, such as close the window, open the door, and place the book on the desk. Is the student able to store and retrieve through listening to such directions?

Auditory Sequencing   Auditory sequencing is the ability to remember the order of items in a sequential list. For example, the alphabet, numbers, and the months of the year are learned as auditory sequences.

Table 8.2

Informal Test of Phonological Awareness

Give the child two demonstration items to help him or her understand the task. For example, first say the word *cowboy;* then ask the child to say the word. You then tell the child to say the word again but not to say *boy.*

Do the same with the word *steamboat.* Tell the child, "Say it again, but don't say *steam.* "If the child answers both demonstration items correctly, give the following test.

Item	Question	Correct Response
1. Say *sunshine.*	Now say it again, but don't say *shine.*	sun
2. Say *picnic.*	Now say it again, but don't say *pic.*	nic
3. Say *cucumber.*	Now say it again, but don't say *cu.*	cumber
4. Say *coat.*	Now say it again, but don't say /k/.	oat
5. Say *meat.*	Now say it again, but don't say /m/.	eat
6. Say *take.*	Now say it again, but don't say /t/.	ache
7. Say *game.*	Now say it again, but don't say /m/.	gay
8. Say *wrote.*	Now say it again, but don't say /t/.	row
9. Say *please.*	Now say it again, but don't say /z/.	plea
10. Say *clap.*	Now say it again, but don't say /k/.	lap
11. Say *play.*	Now say it again, but don't say /p/.	lay
12. Say *stale.*	Now say it again, but don't say /t/.	sale
13. Say *smack.*	Now say it again, but don't say /m/.	sack

Scoring: Give one point for each correct answer.

Score	Expected Level
1–3	Kindergarten
4–9	Grade 1
10–11	Grade 2
12–13	Grade 3

Source: From J. Rosner, *Helping Children Overcome Learning Difficulties.* Copyright © 1979 by Jerome Rosner. Reprinted by permission from Walker & Company.

Auditory Blending **Auditory blending** is the ability to blend single phonic elements or phonemes into a complete word. Students with such disabilities have difficulty blending, for example, the phonemes *m-a-n* to form the word *man.*

Tests of Auditory Perception Some formal tests of auditory perception are listed in this chapter in Test Inventory 8.2: Tests of Perception, and they are described in Appendix C.

Visual Perception

Visual perception plays a significant role in school learning, particularly in reading. Students have difficulty in tasks requiring the visual discrimination of letters and words, as well as of numbers, geometric designs, and pictures. Within the broad scope of visual perception, several subareas of skills can be identified.

Visual Discrimination   Visual discrimination refers to the ability to differentiate one object from another. In a preschool readiness test, for example, the child may be asked to find the rabbit with one ear in a row of rabbits with two ears. Or, when asked to distinguish visually between the letters *m* and *n*, the child must perceive the number of humps in each letter. The skill of matching identical letters, words, numbers, pictures, designs, and shapes is another visual discrimination task. Objects may be discriminated by color, shape, pattern, size, position, or brightness. The ability to discriminate letters and words visually becomes essential in learning to read. Children who can recognize letters when they are preschoolers do better in reading.

Figure-Ground Discrimination   *Figure-ground discrimination* refers to the ability to distinguish an object from its surrounding background. The student with a deficit in this area cannot focus on the item in question apart from the visual background. Consequently, the student is distracted by irrelevant stimuli.

Visual Closure   *Visual closure* is a task that requires the individual to recognize or identify an object even though the total stimulus is not presented. For example, a competent reader is able to read a line of print when the top half of the print is covered. There are enough letter clues in the remaining portion for the reader to provide visual closure to read the line.

Spatial Relations   *Spatial relations* refers to the perception of the position of objects in space. The child must recognize the placement of an object or a symbol (letters, words, numbers, or pictures) and the spatial relation of that object to others surrounding it. In reading, for example, words must be perceived as separate entities surrounded by space. For the learning of mathematics, abilities in spatial relationships are especially important.

Object and Letter Recognition   *Object recognition* is the ability to recognize the nature of objects when viewing them. This includes recognition of alphabetic letters, numbers, words, geometric shapes (such as a square), and objects (such as a cat, a face, or a toy). The kindergartner's ability to recognize letters, numbers, and geometric patterns has been found to be a dependable predictor of reading achievement (Richek, Caldwell, Jennings, & Lerner, 1996).

Several examples of visual perception tasks used in tests or lessons are shown in Figure 8.1.

Figure 8.1

Examples of Visual
Perception Tasks

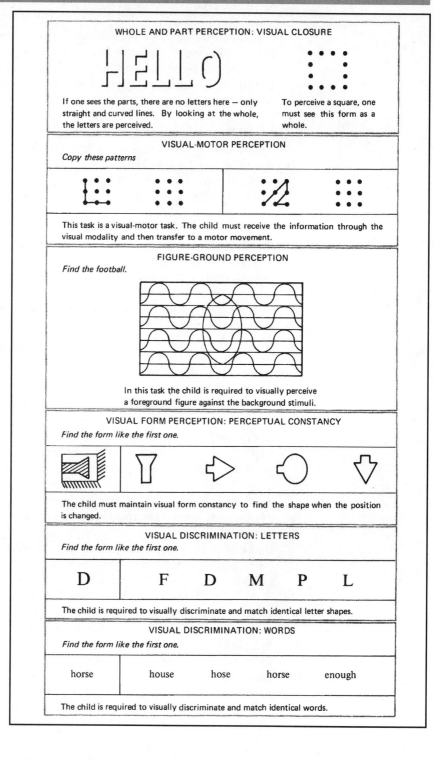

Visual Perception and Reversals   There is an important difference between the perceptual world of *objects* and the perceptual world of *letters* and *words*. During the prereading stage of development, children make a perceptual generalization (sometimes called the "law of object constancy") that an object retains the same name or meaning regardless of the position it happens to be in, the direction it faces, or the modification of slight additions or subtractions. A chair, for example, is a chair regardless of whether it faces left or right, back or front, upside down, or right side up. Whether it is upholstered, has additional cushions, or even has a leg missing, it is still called a *chair*. The child makes similar generalizations about dogs; no matter what its position, size, color, or quantity of hair, a dog is still called a *dog*.

When beginning to deal with letters and words, however, the child finds that this perceptual generalization no longer holds true. The placement of a circle on a stick from left to right or top to bottom changes the name of the letter from *b* to *d* or to *p* or *q*. The addition of a small line changes *c* to *e*. The direction the word is facing changes it from *was* to *saw*, from *no* to *on*, and from *top* to *pot*.

Some students with learning disabilities fail to make the necessary amendments to earlier perceptual generalizations they have formulated. One incident of such confusion happened during a teachers' strike. A boy with this type of difficulty looked at the picket signs and asked why the teachers were picketing if the strike had been called off. The sign was lettered *ON STRIKE*, but the boy read it as *NO STRIKE*. In another such example, a student reversed the letters when making a Christmas card. He printed *LEON* instead of *NOEL*.

Whole and Part Perception   Other differences in visual perceptual processing concern "whole perceivers" and "part perceivers." "Whole perceivers" see an object in its entirety—its gestalt—whereas "part perceivers" tend to focus on minute details, missing the gestalt. Children need to see both the whole and the parts for effective learning. In a task such as reading, learners must be able to move flexibly from the whole to parts. At times they must see the word in its entirety, and at other times they must see a small detail that differentiates it from another word. For example, to differentiate *house* and *horse*, the reader must be able to note details in the words. The word *elephant*, however, is likely to be recognized as a whole or as a sight word. Children who rely on only one of these perceptual styles appear to have difficulty in learning to read.

Children with learning disabilities often exhibit this problem in their coloring of pictures. One sleeve may be colored red, the body of the shirt blue, and the other sleeve yellow. One girl colored each side of the crease in a trouser leg a different color; she saw the parts but not the whole. Jerry, another "part perceiver," identified a tiny difference that the artist had made in two illustrations of an automobile that accompanied a story. Jerry was so concerned with the suspicion that it was a different automobile that he could no longer concentrate on the story. Another child, Paul, was eventually found to have severe learning and perception problems. Paul's atypical styles of perception had been misinterpreted by his kindergarten teacher, who remarked, "Paul has a good deal of ability. He shows originality and has a knack for describing in detail."

Tactile and Kinesthetic Perception

The tactile and kinesthetic systems are two perceptual systems for receiving information. The term *haptic* is sometimes used to refer to both systems.

Tactile perception is obtained through the sense of touch via the fingers and skin surfaces. The ability to recognize an object by touching it, to identify a numeral that is drawn on one's back or arm, to discriminate between smooth and rough surfaces, and to identify which finger is being touched are all examples of tactile perception.

Kinesthetic perception is obtained through body movements and muscle feeling. The awareness of positions taken by different parts of the body and bodily feelings of muscular contraction, tension, and relaxation are examples of kinesthetic perception. The earlier discussion of body image and motor information in the motor development section of this chapter provides a broader view of the kinesthetic system.

The tactile and kinesthetic systems are important sources of information about object qualities, body movement, and their interrelationships. Most school tasks, as well as most acts in everyday life, require both touch and body movement. Tactile and kinesthetic perception play important roles in learning.

Tests of Perception

Tests of perception are listed in Test Inventory 8.2. Additional information on these tests appears in Appendix C.

THE LAW AND YOUNG CHILDREN WITH DISABILITIES

The 1997 Individuals with Disabilities Education Act (IDEA) continues the early childhood special education policies and practices and incorporates the previous early childhood laws (PL 99–457 and PL 102–119). There are two age groups of young children with disabilities identified in the legislation: (1) preschoolers, ages 3 through 5; and (2) infants and toddlers, ages birth to 2. The provisions in the law are different for each of these two groups.

Preschool Children: Ages 3 Through 5

Preschoolers with disabilities, ages 3 through 5, receive the same full rights under the law as older children do. These provisions are specified in **Part B**

Test Inventory 8.2

Tests of Perception

Auditory Perception

Detroit Tests of Learning Aptitude—Primary 2

Detroit Tests of Learning Aptitude—3 (reversed letters, word sequences)

Goldman-Fristoe-Woodcock Auditory Skills Test Battery

Goldman-Fristoe-Woodcock Test of Auditory Discrimination

Illinois Test of Psycholinguistic Abilities (ITPA) (auditory sequential memory, sound blending, and auditory closure)

Test of Auditory Skills Analysis (Rosner, 1979)

Wepman Test of Auditory Discrimination

Visual Perception

Bender-Gestalt Test

Detroit Tests of Learning Aptitude—Primary 2

Detroit Tests of Learning Aptitude—3 (design sequences, design reproduction, picture fragments)

Developmental Test of Visual-Motor Integration

Developmental Test of Visual Perception

Frostig Developmental Test of Visual Perception

Illinois Test of Psycholinguistic Abilities (ITPA) (visual reception, visual association, visual closure, and visual sequential memory)

Motor-Free Test of Visual Perception

Test of Visual-Motor Integration

Visual Retention Test—Revised

Tactile and Kinesthetic Perception

Southern California Kinesthesia and Tactile Perception Tests

(of IDEA 1997). Preschoolers may have a developmental delay in one or more of the following areas:

1. Physical development
2. Cognitive development
3. Communication development
4. Social or emotional development
5. Adaptive development

The following is a summary of the provisions in the law for preschoolers with disabilities:

- Each state must provide a free, appropriate, public education, along with related services, to all eligible children with disabilities ages 3 through 5.

- States may identify preschool children either noncategorically (such as by "developmental delay") or by the category of disability (such as "learning disabilities"). A state that adopts the term "developmental delay" determines whether it applies to children ages 3 through 9 or to ages 3 through 5. (see Appendix F).

- The child study team may use either the IEP (individual education program) or the IFSP (individual family service plan) for children ages 3 through 5. The plan must ensure due process, confidentiality, and the child's placement in the least restrictive environment.

- The state education agency is the lead agency. The law gives the individual state education agencies the responsibility of implementing Part B for preschool children by working through local education agencies or other contracted service agencies.

Infants and Toddlers: Birth Through Age 2

The policies for infants and toddlers with disabilities, birth through age 2, are contained in **Part C (of IDEA 1997)**. Services for infants and toddlers with disabilities are not mandated, but Part C authorizes financial assistance to the states through state grants. Financial assistance is offered to develop and implement a statewide, comprehensive, coordinated, multidisciplinary, interagency program of early intervention services for infants and toddlers, ages birth through 2, with disabilities and for their families. The family system is recognized as critical in the child's development. The teams must use an **individualized family service plan (IFSP),** which includes plans for the family as well as for the child.

The number of infants and toddlers with disabilities is increasing. Recent advances in medical technology have allowed neonates with very low birth weights and substantial health problems to survive. Newborns may have other kinds of problems. For example, there are 375,000 drug-exposed babies and 2,000 HIV-infected babies born each year (National Training Center for Professional AIDS Education Opens, 1992). These fragile infants usually need highly specialized medical attention, and they and their families also require services that medical professionals cannot provide. Infant specialists and infant/toddler service coordinators (or case managers) are key members of the interdisciplinary team in neonatal intensive care units and in child-care centers.

The provisions of the early education law for children ages 3 through 5 years (Part B) and birth through 2 years (Part C) are compared in Table 8.3.

Table 8.3

Comparison of
Legislation for
Preschoolers and for
Infants and Toddlers

	Preschoolers	Infants and toddlers
Age	Ages 3 through 5	Birth through age 2
Eligibility	Category of disability or developmental delay	Developmental delay
Plan	IFSP or IEP	IFSP
Law	Part B/Mandatory	Part C/Permissive
Lead agency	State education agency	Agency appointed by governor
Transition	To regular class or special education class	To program for preschool special education
Primary orientation	Developmental learning	Family-infant interaction
Personnel	Early childhood special education teacher	Service coordinator

Children at Risk

Another concern of the law is for providing assessment and intervention for young children who are at risk. These children may not presently be eligible under the law for services but are at high risk for becoming children with disabilities and for having substantial developmental delays if early intervention services are not provided. The states may choose to serve children who are at risk but are not *required* to serve them.

There is growing evidence that **children at risk** can dramatically improve when early intervention and work with families are provided. For example, low-birth-weight infants significantly gain in cognitive and behavioral function when they receive comprehensive early intervention consisting of home visits, parent training, parent group meetings, attendance at a child development center, pediatric surveillance, and community referral services (Richmond, 1990).

Research also shows the critical effect of the infant's environment on the early development of the brain (Huttenlocher, 1991). During the early months and first years of life, the synapses, or interconnecting links between the neurons in the brain, grow at a phenomenal rate. The brain increases rapidly in size and becomes more effective. The environmental influences and the child's experiences during the earliest years of life play a major role in brain development and affect intelligence and the ability to learn.

Accumulating research on brain development shows that, to maximize intellectual growth, efforts must begin during the first three years of life. The child's environment and experiences in the earliest years influence the development of brain cells and the connections between the cells. Good schooling, skilled teachers, and better living conditions can help older children, but the opportunity to build a better brain exists only in the first few years of life. A happy, nurturing, and stimulating atmosphere can actually help a child become more intelligent for his or her entire life. Early brain development research shows the following (Carnegie Corporation, 1994):

- Environment affects the number of brain cells, the connections among them, and the way the connections are wired. Brain development is much more vulnerable to environmental influences than was previously suspected.

- Brain development before age 1 is more rapid and extensive than previously realized.

- The influence of early environment on brain development is long lasting.

- Early stress has a negative impact on brain function.

Three *categories of risk* are generally recognized: established risk, biological risk, and environmental risk (Shonkoff & Meisels, 1991; Campbell, 1991; Tjossem, 1976):

Established Risk   The *established risk* category includes children with an established diagnosis of developmental delay that invariably results in disability or developmental delay. These conditions are identified through a medical diagnosis early in life. Examples of such conditions include Down syndrome or fragile-X syndrome. Although an evaluation of both child and family is necessary for the purpose of developing an individualized family service plan, no further evaluation is required for the purpose of establishing eligibility.

Biological Risk   The *biological risk* category refers to children who have a diagnosed physical or mental condition that has a high probability of resulting in a developmental delay, such as a very low birth weight. These children require a comprehensive child and family evaluation to determine their eligibility on a case-by-case basis.

Environmental Risk   The *environmental risk* category includes children who are biologically sound but whose early life experiences have been so limiting that they impart a high probability for delayed development. Such experiences include parental substance abuse; significant family social disorganization; extreme poverty; parental intellectual impairment; disturbed parent-child interaction; low parental education; family isolation and lack of support; and a history of inadequate prenatal care, child abuse, or neglect. Children in these environments frequently lack cognitive stimulation for normal development. Such children require a comprehensive child and family evaluation to determine service eligibility (Meisels & Fenichel, 1996).

ASSESSING YOUNG
CHILDREN

A major emphasis in assessment practices today is to use informal, functional assessment measures instead of relying solely on formal standardized tests and testing procedures. There is more authentic assessment and observation of the child in a natural environment (Lerner, Lowenthal, & Egan, 1998).

Phases of Early Identification and Assessment

As Figure 8.2 shows, there are four separate but related phases of identification and assessment of preschoolers with disabilities: (1) **child-find**, (2) screening, (3) diagnosing, and (4) evaluating (Lerner, Lowenthal, & Egan, 1998). Many different tests and assessment procedures can be used during each of these phases.

Child-Find   This first phase refers to ways of finding young children with disabilities in the community. Emphasis is on making initial contact and increasing the public's awareness of services. Preschool children are not usually in the public school system, and communities must therefore make a concerted effort to seek them out. Communities develop methods (such as radio announcements, posters, signs in day-care centers and libraries, and local newspaper articles) to alert families of young children.

Screening   This second phase attempts to identify children who need further study. Emphasis is on ways of quickly surveying many children to identify those who *may* need special services. School districts often encourage families to bring *all* 3- through 5-year-old children in for free evaluation services, even if the family does not suspect a disability. The **screening** is a short, low-cost assessment of children's vision and hearing, speech and language, motor skills, self-help skills, social-emotional maturity, and cognitive development.

Many school systems use screening interviews or questionnaires with the parents of all incoming kindergarten children. Questions are designed to detect those children who are likely to have learning difficulty. The hope is that early detection of high-risk cases will permit plans to be made to help prevent the development of learning disabilities. Table 3.3 (Chapter 3) provides some questions that might be used in such a screening interview.

Diagnosing   The third phase consists of determining the extent of **developmental delay** and devising an intervention program. The emphasis is on methods of comprehensively examining a child through formal and authentic measures to determine if the child's problems warrant special education services. A multidisciplinary team determines the nature of the problem, its severity, and the intervention and placement that the child needs.

Evaluating   The fourth phase concentrates on measuring progress; judging whether a child should remain in a special education program; and

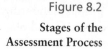

Figure 8.2

Stages of the Assessment Process

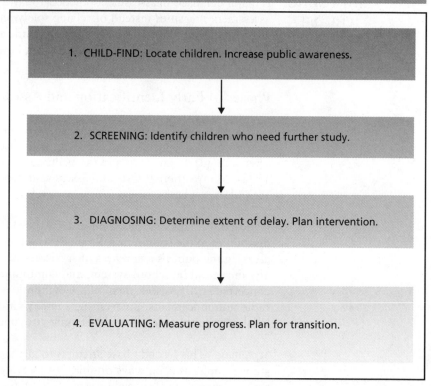

1. CHILD-FIND: Locate children. Increase public awareness.

2. SCREENING: Identify children who need further study.

3. DIAGNOSING: Determine extent of delay. Plan intervention.

4. EVALUATING: Measure progress. Plan for transition.

planning for transition. This stage of the assessment helps determine whether the child still needs special education services, what skills the child has learned and still lacks, and what new placement will be needed.

Areas of Assessment

To evaluate a child's developmental delay, the assessment typically includes an evaluation of cognitive, physical, communication, social-emotional, and adaptive development (Lerner, Lowenthal, & Egan, 1998; Bagnoto, Neisworth, & Munson, 1997).

Cognitive Development   This evaluation includes the assessment of the child's abilities in thinking, planning, and concept development. Examples of cognitive tasks are identifying colors; naming parts of the body; rote counting (up to 10 or so); showing an understanding of one-to-one correspondence ("Show me three blocks"); demonstrating place concepts (on, under, corner, between, middle); identifying given concepts (round, bigger); naming letters; or sorting chips by color, size, and shape.

Physical Development   This category includes fine-motor and gross-motor assessment. This includes the child's overall physical development, gross-motor skills, and fine-motor development. Examples of tasks the child is asked to perform include catching a ball or bean bag, jumping, hopping, skipping, building a four-block design, touching fingers (copying the tester's demonstration by consecutively touching each finger on one hand to the thumb of the same hand, and then repeating the task on the other hand), cutting various patterns with scissors, matching and copying shapes and letter formations, and writing one's own name. The child's visual and auditory acuity are also often assessed.

Communication Development   This evaluation includes speech and language skills and the abilities to understand and use language. Testers might assess articulation by having children say certain words. They can be asked to repeat numbers and sentences spoken by the tester, to describe pictures, to answer problem-solving questions, or to state their first and last names, gender, age, address, and phone numbers. An auditory test—for example, having children copy a series of clapping patterns—may also be included.

Social and Emotional Development   The child's social and affective interactions are recorded through observational notes made by the testers. Typical observations include how well the child relates to adults and to other children.

Adaptive Development   This category refers to the child's self-help skills. It includes such areas as independent toileting skills, dressing skills, eating skills, and the ability to separate from parents.

Problems Related to Early Identification and Assessment

Despite the benefits of early intervention, there are potential dangers in the early identification of preschoolers. First, children do not mature at the same rate, and readiness may simply be a matter of timing. Some children have developmental lags that may disappear by the time they are ready for formal schooling. By labeling a child at 3 or 4 years of age, educators may actually create certain problems. Second, the teacher's low expectations of identified young children may create problems. The term *self-fulfilling prophecy* describes the effects of teacher expectancy on pupil performance (Rosenthal & Jacobson, 1968). There is substantial research showing that teachers act differently toward children for whom they have low expectations. Over time, the child's behavior and achievement conform to the teacher's expectations (Brophy & Good, 1986). Thus early identification might impose limits on what a teacher expects from a pupil, which could in turn reinforce the child's learning and behavior problems.

Finally, the assessment process for young children has some flaws. Many instruments used in early intervention programs fail to demonstrate adequate reliability or test validity, and many have not undergone the evaluation procedures required to be psychometrically sound (Meisels, 1991; McLean, Bailey, & Wolery, 1996). In a screening program, when many children are being tested, errors in judgment are often made, as are errors in the testing procedures and in scoring. Children can be either falsely identified or be missed, as illustrated in the case example entitled "Errors in Testing and Identification."

EARLY CHILDHOOD PROGRAMS

Several different types of programs serve young children with disabilities and children who are at risk for developing disabilities. In this section, we will discuss (1) the Early Education Program for Children with Disabilities (EEPCD), (2) Head Start, and (3) compensatory early childhood programs.

The Early Education Program for Children with Disabilities (EEPCD)

Many of the current services for young children with disabilities are based on demonstration models developed through a program known as EEPCD (the Early Education Program for Children with Disabilities). This Department of Education–sponsored program has been in operation for over twenty-eight years. The model EEPCD projects demonstrated a wide variety of curriculum approaches for many different types of disabilities in a variety of rural and urban settings.

Head Start

Project Head Start, first launched in 1964 under the administration of President Lyndon Johnson, was intended to provide preschool education to the nation's disadvantaged children ages 4 and 5. Its purpose was to offer early educational experiences to preschoolers from homes of poverty who might otherwise come to school unprepared and unmotivated to learn. **Head Start** has become one of the most influential and massive federal social experiments in the history of early childhood education. In 1972, Head Start legislation was amended to include children with disabilities, reserving 10 percent of the total enrollment in Head Start for such children.

Head Start created a fortuitous opportunity to investigate the impact of early intervention. Several heartening longitudinal studies followed up children in these Head Start programs in later life, and the research shows impressive long-term effects of early intervention for environmentally at-risk children. Individuals who had participated in Head Start were evaluated some fifteen years later through a major follow-up study (Lazar & Darling-

CASE EXAMPLE

ERRORS IN TESTING AND IDENTIFICATION

The following example illustrates how test errors can occur and how faulty diagnoses and judgments are made. The parents of a 4-year-old boy were called to a staffing, where a school representative told them that their child performed significantly below the norm on all measures during the district's preschool screening. The parents were informed that mental retardation was suspected, and placement in a special school was recommended. A friend, who was a teacher, accompanied the parents to the staffing and asked to see the test. Upon "eyeballing" the front page of the test, the teacher noted that the child performed either at or above age level on all areas of the test, suggesting that the diagnosis of mental retardation was questionable. Further, the test indicated that the child did not recognize letters and could not count, whereas the child was actually able to do both quite well. When questioned about the scoring and interpretation of the test results, the school representative conducting the staffing explained that she was unfamiliar with the test and that her responsibility was to report to the parents and make placements. As this example illustrates, errors in evaluation and diagnosis do occur, and data should be carefully checked and monitored before any conclusions are drawn.

ton, 1982). The study followed up on 820 Head Start participants, contrasting them with a comparison group that did not have the Head Start experience. The results demonstrated that the Head Start program was very successful. Head Start participants were less likely to be placed in special education classes, were less likely to be retained and required to repeat a grade, consistently scored higher on intelligence tests, and were more likely to finish high school by the age of 18. These encouraging findings led the researchers to conclude that a sensible program of early intervention prevents school failure and reduces the need for remedial programs (Head Start Bureau, 1993).

This study and others demonstrating the benefits of early intervention proved to be politically influential. They indicated to legislators that, in terms of cost-benefit analysis, society got its money back with interest. As a result of the early education experiences of Head Start, there is less need for special education services for children at risk and a decrease in the retention rate, thereby reducing the time these children have to spend in public school. Further, on completion of schooling, the students are more likely to be gainfully employed—to be taxpayers rather than tax receivers—and to be citizens who contribute to society.

Compensatory Early Childhood Programs

There are other notable early education compensatory programs for young children who are at risk for developmental delay or underachievement.

These programs are designed to compensate for the lack of stimulation and education in their home environment. One effective program for environmentally at-risk children is the High/Scope Perry Preschool Program (Schweinhart, Barnes, & Weikart, 1993). The High/Scope program has a Piagetian-based cognitive emphasis curriculum designed to provide young children with the experiences and activities to build thinking skills. The High/Scope research also demonstrates the remarkable benefits of early intervention for at-risk children through extensive follow-up research on individuals who were in the High/Scope program as preschoolers. When the High/Scope participants were tested at ages 15 and 19, they were more committed to school and were doing better than peers who had not shared the preschool experiences. The High/Scope participants had less deviant and delinquent behavior, they had fewer referrals for special education services, and their parents reported that they received greater satisfaction from their children. The follow-up data convincingly demonstrate that individuals with early intervention experiences perform significantly better than comparison groups in cognitive skills, behavior attitudes toward school, and academic achievement (Schweinhart et al., 1993).

EDUCATIONAL PLACEMENTS FOR YOUNG CHILDREN WITH DISABILITIES

Placement Options

Educational placements refer to the site of primary service delivery for young children. Data collected by the U.S. Department of Education (1998) show that children with disabilities (ages 3 through 5) were served in these placements:

Placement for Preschool Children with Disabilities	Percentage
Regular classes	52%
Separate classes	31%
Resource Room	9%
Other (Separate school, Residential, Home/hospital)	8%

In the past, most young children with disabilities were served through special classes. Today, more children are placed in inclusive environments, or regular classes. The goal is to integrate children with disabilities with their peers and to eliminate the stigmatizing effects of segregated programs.

Inclusive Environments

The movement toward inclusive environments to serve young children with disabilities is growing. Over 50 percent of preschool children with disabilities (ages 3 through 5) are currently placed in regular classrooms (U.S. Department of Education, 1998). The *least restrictive environment* (LRE) feature of the federal law (IDEA) requires that the IEP or IFSP team consider a placement that provides the child with disabilities experiences with children who do not have disabilities.

An immediate challenge in providing inclusive environments for preschoolers with disabilities is that most public schools do not offer programs for 3- and 4-year-olds, although they do have kindergartens for 5-year-olds. Children with disabilities are placed in a variety of environments that serve as integrated settings: nursery schools, Head Start classes, day-care centers, other kinds of public early childhood programs, and *reverse mainstreaming* (a program in which typical children are placed in special education classes).

Home-Based, Center-Based, and Combination Services

Home-Based Services   In **home-based programs,** parents become the child's primary teacher. This type of program demands much of the parent(s) in terms of time, dedication, and motivation. In some cases, the professional will solicit the assistance of older siblings, grandparents, and even neighbors to help the parent(s) work with the special needs child.

In the home-based service, a professional child-care provider goes to the child's home, typically one to three times each week. The major responsibility of the child-care provider is to train the parent(s) in their home to work with the child. First, within the home setting, the child's present skills are assessed. Then the professional determines which skills the child has already mastered and which the youngster should be helped to acquire. Next, the professional works with the parent(s) to plan the needed training activities. Finally, the professional demonstrates to the parent(s) how to help the child acquire the skills and how to monitor the child's progress.

Two distinct advantages of the home-based program are that it promotes teaching the child in a natural setting and it fully involves parent(s) in the child's learning. Home-based programs are a particularly viable option with infants and toddlers, in rural or isolated communities, and where transportation problems prevent the child from getting to a center-based program.

Center-Based Services   In center-based programs, the parent (or school-arranged transportation) brings the child to a central facility. The services at the facility can be comprehensive; staff members may represent expertise in many of the related disciplines and services. They may include learning disabilities teachers, early childhood teachers, speech and language pathologists, medical personnel, psychologists, adapted physical education experts, physical therapists, occupational therapists, and social workers. The center also may provide parent training and may offer organized parent support group meetings. Parents are encouraged to carry through the training at home.

Children usually attend a center for three to five hours each day, two to five times each week. A comprehensive curriculum is developed according to the needs and developmental stages of the child. Center-based programs have facilities, equipment, instructional materials, and toys that most parents would not have in the home. In addition, at a center, children can develop social skills by playing with others. Center-based services are particularly useful for 3- to 6-year-old children. In some cases, transporting the child to the center is a problem. Some parents cannot get their child to a center on a regular basis, but buses are expensive, and the trip may be very long for the child. Center-based programs are usually in urban areas, although some do exist in rural settings.

Combination Services   Some flexible programs combine services for young children in the home and in a center. For example, the child may come to the center several times a week, and a professional may visit the child at home every other week. The kinds of services provided in the home and the center will depend on such factors as the needs of the child and parent(s), the age of the child, and the nature of the disability. The major advantage of combination services is their flexibility, for they can be designed to meet each child's unique needs.

Transition to New Placements

Transition means moving the child from one type of organized program to another. Going to a new placement can be a traumatic experience for a young child, and the transition should be carefully planned, coordinated, and monitored. It is important to take steps to ensure a smooth transition. Receiving teachers should observe the child, talk with the parents, attend the annual review, and be familiar with the child's individual education program (IEP) or the individualized family services plan (IFSP).

Transition for Preschool Children   At the completion of the preschool special education program as the child nears age 6, decisions about the next placement must be made. The child is moving from a small instructional group to a larger, less structured environment. The following options for 3- through 5-year-old children are possible (Lerner, Lowenthal, & Egan, 1998):

1. *Regular class.*   Some children will be integrated in a regular kindergarten or first-grade class.
2. *Transition class.*   In this setting, the child receives additional observation and special education intervention for a period of time.
3. *Resource room.*   In this option, the child attends both the general education classroom and a small special education setting for portions of the day.
4. *Separate class.*   This class could be in either the local school or the larger special education district, which would permit a more intensive special education curriculum.

5. *Residential facility.* This setting is used for certain severe cases or when the home is unable to provide the needed care.

Transition for Infants and Toddlers   For infants and toddlers and their families, the transition is particularly difficult. These children will be moving from a personal, small, or one-to-one program to a larger grouping of children. Some will transfer to an early intervention program for preschoolers with disabilities. Some may transfer to a regular preschool program. Transition plans must be made carefully, and the family must understand the plans (Fowler, Haines, & Rosenkoetter, 1990).

EARLY CHILDHOOD CURRICULUM MODELS   The curriculum models for young children with disabilities incorporate elements of both early childhood education and special education. Many early childhood educators today endorse a curriculum model known as **developmentally appropriate practice (DAP).** Other early childhood curriculum models are the enrichment curriculum, direct teaching curriculum, cognitive emphasis curriculum, and combination curriculum. Each of these curriculum models is described in this section.

Developmentally Appropriate Practice (DAP)

The National Association for the Education of Young Children (NAEYC) recommends a set of guidelines for a curriculum for typical young children called developmentally appropriate practice (DAP). The DAP guidelines are based on a contructivist and cognitive philosophy of teaching and learning for young children, emphasizing child-initiated learning, exploratory play, and the child's interests. The guidelines are as follows: (a) activities should be integrated across developmental domains; (b) children's interests and progress should be identified through teacher observation; (c) teachers should prepare the environment to facilitate children's active exploration and interaction; (d) learning activities and materials should be concrete, real, and relevant to the lives of children; (e) a wide range of interesting activities should be provided; and (f) the complexity and challenge of activities should increase as children understand the skills involved (Bredenkamp, 1987; Bredenkamp & Copple, 1997).

Special educators who work with young children with disabilities are concerned that the DAP guidelines do not sufficiently consider the needs of children who have disabilities. The guidelines do not ensure learning outcomes for children with disabilities, who need a curriculum that provides early direct intervention, highly structured learning experiences, and extrinsic motivation (e.g., high rates of praise, tokens, or stickers). Young children with learning disabilities in inclusion placements in regular early childhood programs will need adaptations and modifications of the DAP guidelines (Lerner, Lowenthal, & Egan, 1998; Wolery et al., 1994; Carta, 1995; Bredenkamp, 1993).

Learning activities and materials should be concrete, real, and relevant to the lives of young children. (© Elizabeth Crews/ Stock Boston)

Enrichment Curriculum

The **enrichment curriculum** is based on the "whole child" theory of early childhood education, which encompasses all aspects of child growth—physical, emotional, language, social, and cognitive development. Based on this comprehensive philosophy of the young child's education, the enrichment curriculum offers the child a variety of experiences and many opportunities. The curriculum of the standard nursery school is frequently guided by the enrichment philosophy.

The theories of developmental psychology are the foundation of the enrichment curriculum and reflect a maturational view of child development. The key to this concept of education is the natural growth sequence of the young child. The premise is that under favorable, open circumstances, a child's own inner drive and need to learn will naturally emerge and develop. The role of the teacher is to enhance this natural growth process by providing learning opportunities within an environment that is enriching, encouraging, and nurturing.

The enrichment curriculum classroom typically contains special activities areas—for example, an area for play with large blocks, a place for dress-ups and playhouse materials, a quiet play section, and a creative arts area. Enrichment programs typically have periods of the day assigned for both outdoor and indoor play. A priority for the enrichment class is to stimulate child exploration. Language activities are encouraged through storytelling and conversations. Field trips to the outer world are designed to broaden children's experience levels. Such trips may include visits to museums, the post office, stores, and parks. Although the teacher arranges a general but flexible schedule for the day, activities are often selected by the child. The teacher capitalizes on opportunities for incidental and informal learning.

Direct Teaching Curriculum

Based on principles of behavioral psychology, the **direct teaching curriculum** concentrates on straightforward and structured teaching of specific learning skills, which are selected by the teacher or the program director. The term *early intervention* implies that children will receive explicit teaching. The child's teacher first determines the skills and behaviors that the child needs and then teaches those skills as early as possible.

A substantial body of literature documents that a delay in acquiring early skills may have serious, negative consequences for the child. Children can develop secondary disabilities, have difficulty acquiring more complex skills, and lose out on future educational and occupational opportunities (Carta, 1995). In direct teaching, the teacher's role is to plan and structure learning experiences carefully. Materials and activities are carefully designed to develop these selected skills.

Cognitive Emphasis Curriculum

The cognitive emphasis curriculum is based on the ideas and theories of cognitive psychology, especially the work of Jean Piaget (1970). Of major concern is the way children develop cognitive or thinking abilities, including memory, discrimination, problem solving, concept formation, verbal learning, and comprehension skills. One of Piaget's ground-breaking insights is that children do not think as adults think; rather, they pass through distinct stages of development that are characterized by particular types of thinking. The cognitive emphasis curriculum encourages experiences and actions that help build thinking skills. One program designed for at-risk preschool children is the already mentioned High/Scope Perry Preschool Project (Schweinhart et al., 1993).

Combination Early Childhood Curriculum Models

Programs for young children usually do not follow a single curriculum model; instead, they use elements from several models. They provide some open experiences that are child selected, offer some direct teaching of specific skills, and encourage the development of cognitive skills. In recent years, combination programs have grown out of the research findings in early childhood special education.

Motor Development

The balance of this chapter describes representative activities for teaching young children with learning disabilities. We describe activities for motor development, auditory processing and phonological awareness, visual processing, and tactile and kinesthetic processing. Motor activities are a particularly useful part of the early childhood curriculum. The teaching strategies in this section are subdivided into three target areas: gross-motor skills, fine-motor skills, and body awareness activities.

Gross-Motor Activities

Gross-motor activities involve the ability to move various parts of the body. The purpose of these activities is to develop smoother, more effective body movements and to increase the child's sense of spatial orientation and body consciousness. Gross-motor activities are grouped as walking activities, throwing and catching activities, and other gross-motor activities.

Walking Activities

1. Forward, backward, and sideways walk.   Children walk to a target goal on a straight or curved path marked on the floor. The path may be wide or narrow, but the narrower the path, the more difficult the task. A single line requiring tandem walking (heel-to-toe) is more difficult than a widely spaced walk. A slow pace is more difficult than a running pace. Walking without shoes and socks is more difficult than walking with shoes. Students walk through the same course backward and sideways. In variations, children walk with arms in different positions, carrying objects, dropping objects such as balls into containers along the way, or focusing eyes on various parts of the room.

2. Steppingstones.   Put objects on the floor for steppingstones, identifying placements for right foot and left foot by colors or by the letters *R* and *L*. The student is to follow the course by placing the correct foot on each steppingstone.

3. Box game.   The student has two boxes (the size of shoe boxes), one behind and one in front. The student steps into the front box with both feet, moves the rear box to the front, and then steps into that. The student can use either hand to move the boxes and can use alternating feet. The student should be moving toward a finish line.

4. Line walks.   Draw lines in colors on the floor. Lines can be curved, angular, or spiral. Place a rope on the floor and have the students walk along the side of the rope. A variation is to place a ladder flat on the ground. Students walk between the rungs, forward and backward, and then hop through the rungs.

Throwing and Catching Activities

1. Throwing. Balloons, wet sponges, beanbags, yarn balls, and rubber balls of various sizes can be used to throw objects at targets, to the teacher, or to each other.

2. Catching. Catching is a more difficult skill than throwing. Students can practice catching the previously-mentioned objects thrown by the teacher or by other students.

3. Ball games. Various types of ball games help develop motor coordination. Examples include balloon volleyball or rolling-ball games, bouncing balls on the ground, and throwing balls against the wall.

4. Tire-tube games. Old tire tubes can be used for games of rolling and catching.

5. Rag ball. If students find that throwing and catching a rubber ball is too difficult, a rag ball can be used. Rag balls are made by covering rags or discarded nylon hosiery with cloth.

Other Gross-Motor Activities

1. Balance beam activities. The balance beam is commonly used in the early childhood curriculum. It can be a flat board, either purchased or made from a two-by-four. It can be of various widths; the narrower the width, the more difficult the activities. An eight- to twelve-foot section of two-by-four can be used. Each end of the board is fitted into a bracket that serves as a brace and prevents the board from tipping over. The board can be set flat with the wide surface up or set on its edge with the narrow surface up.

2. Skateboard. The student rides a skateboard lying on the stomach, kneeling, or standing; the surface can be flat or can slope downhill.

3. Jumping jacks. Children jump, putting feet wide apart, while clapping the hands above the head. To vary this activity, the children can make quarter turns, half turns, and full turns, or jump to the left, right, north, or south.

4. Hopping. Children hop on one foot at a time and alternate feet while hopping. Use rhythmical patterns: left, left, right, right; or left, left, right; or right, right, left.

5. Bouncing. Children bounce on a trampoline, bedspring, mattress, or large truck tire tube.

6. Skipping. A difficult activity for children with poor motor coordination, skipping combines rhythm, balance, body movement, and coordination. Many children need help to learn to skip.

7. Hoop games. Hoops of various sizes, from the hula hoop down, can be used to develop motor skills. Have the child twist them around the arms, legs, and waist; bounce balls in them; toss beanbags in them; or step in and out of them.

8. Rope skills. A length of rope can be used in a variety of exercises. Have the child put the rope around designated parts of the body (such as knees, ankles, and hips) to teach body image. Have the child follow directions to put the rope around chairs, under a table, or through a lampshade; to jump back and forth or sideways over the rope; or to make shapes, letters, or numbers with the rope.

Fine-Motor Activities

The following activities give young children experiences with fine-motor activities.

1. Tracing. Students trace lines, pictures, designs, letters, or numbers on tracing paper, plastic, or stencils. Use directional arrows, color cues, and numbers to help children trace the figures.

2. Water control. Children carry and pour water into measured buckets from pitchers to specified levels. Smaller amounts and finer measurements make the task more difficult. Coloring the water makes the activity more interesting.

3. Cutting with scissors. Choose cutting activities that are appropriate for the child's development level. The easiest activity is cutting straight lines marked near the edge of the paper. A more difficult activity is cutting a straight line across the center of the paper. A piece of cardboard attached to the paper helps guide the scissors. Children can cut out marked geometric shapes, such as squares, rectangles, and triangles. By drawing lines in different colors, the teacher can indicate changes of direction in cutting. Children can cut out curving lines and circles, then pictures, and finally patterns made with dots and faint lines.

4. Stencils or templates. Children draw outlines of geometric shapes. Templates can be made from cardboard, wood, plastic, or foam containers. Two styles of templates are (1) a solid shape and (2) frames with the shape cut out.

5. Lacing. A piece of cardboard punched with holes or a pegboard can be used for this activity. A design or picture is made on the board, and then the student follows the pattern by weaving or sewing through the holes with a heavy shoelace, yarn, or cord.

6. Paper-and-pencil activities. Coloring books, readiness books, dot-to-dot books, and kindergarten books frequently provide good paper-and-pencil activities to practice fine-motor and eye-hand development.

7. Clipping clothespins. Clothespins can be clipped to a line or to a box. The child can be timed in this activity by counting the number of clothespins clipped in a specified time.

8. Copying designs. The child looks at a geometric design and copies it on paper.

Body Awareness Activities

The purpose of these activities is to help children develop accurate images of the location and function of the parts of the body.

1. Pointing to body parts. Children point to the various parts of the body: nose, right elbow, left ankle, and so forth. This activity is more difficult with the eyes closed. The child can also lie on the floor and be asked to touch various parts of the body. This activity is more difficult if performed to a rhythmic pattern—using a metronome, for example. As a variation, make a robot from cardboard that is held together at the joints with fasteners and can be moved into various positions. The child can move the limbs of the robot on command and match the positions with his or her own body movements.

2. "Simon Says." This game can be played with the eyes open or closed.

3. Puzzles. Puzzles of people, animals, objects, and so forth can be cut to show functional portions of the body.

4. What is missing? Use pictures with missing body parts. Children either tell or draw what is missing.

5. Life-size drawing. Children lie on a large sheet of paper, and the teacher traces an outline around them. Next, the children fill in and color the clothes and the details of the face and body.

6. Awareness of the body parts through touch. Touch various parts of the student's body while the eyes are closed and ask which part was touched.

7. Games. Games such as "Lobby Loo," "Hokey-Pokey," and "Did You Ever See a Lassie?" help develop concepts of left, right, and body image.

8. Pantomime. Students pantomime actions that are characteristic of a particular occupation, such as those of a bus driver driving a bus, a police officer directing traffic, a mail carrier delivering a letter, or a chef cooking.

9. Following instructions. Instruct the child to put the left hand on the right ear and the right hand on the left shoulder. Other instructions might be to put the right hand in front of the left hand or to turn right, walk two steps, and turn left.

10. Twister. Make rows of colored circles on the floor, an oilcloth, or a plastic sheet, or use the commercial game. Make cards instructing the student to put the left foot on the green circle, the right foot on the red circle, and so on.

11. Water activities.   Gross-motor movements in a pool or lake allow some freedom from the force of gravity. Some activities are easier to learn in the water because it affords greater control, and activities can be done at a slower pace. Swimming is also an excellent activity to strengthen general motor functioning.

Auditory Processing

Many children with learning disabilities need specific instruction to acquire auditory processing skills. Considered in this section are phonological awareness, listening to sounds, auditory discrimination, and auditory memory.

Phonological Awareness   For success at the beginning stages of reading, the child must hear the individual sounds (phonemes) in words and in language. The child must be aware of the fact that the words we hear are comprised of individual sounds (or phonemes) within the words.

Young children should have abundant early literacy experiences with nursery rhymes and word games in which they hear rhymes and similar beginning sounds. Specific suggestions for building phonological awareness are included in Chapter 10 under "Teaching Strategies for Phonological Awareness."

Additional activities for the development of the phonological perception of letter sounds and words are presented in Chapter 10.

Listening to Sounds

1. Listening for sounds.   Children close their eyes and listen to environmental sounds: for example, sounds of cars, airplanes, animals, and other outside sounds; and sounds in the next room. Recorded sounds of planes, trains, animals, and bells can be played back to the students who are then asked to identify them.

2. Sounds made by the teacher.   Children close their eyes and identify sounds that the teacher makes. Examples of such sounds include dropping a pencil, tearing a piece of paper, using a stapler, bouncing a ball, sharpening a pencil, tapping on a glass, opening a window, snapping the lights, leafing through a book, cutting with scissors, opening a drawer, jingling money, or writing on a blackboard.

3. Food sounds.   Ask the children to listen for the kind of food that is being eaten, cut, or sliced, such as celery, apples, or carrots.

4. Shaking sounds.   Place small, hard items, such as stones, beans, chalk, salt, sand, or rice, into containers with covers. Have the children identify the contents by shaking and listening.

5. Listening for sound patterns.   Have the children close their eyes or sit facing away from the teacher. Clap hands, play a drum, or bounce a ball. Rhythmic patterns can be made—for example, slow, fast, fast. Ask students how many counts there were, or ask them to repeat the patterns. As a variation on the previous suggestion, use a cup and a book, for example, to tap out sound patterns.

Auditory Discrimination

1. Near or far.   With eyes closed, the students judge from what part of the room a sound is coming and whether it is near or far.

2. Loud or soft.   Help the students to judge and discriminate between loud and soft sounds that the teacher produces.

3. High and low.   Students learn to judge and to discriminate between high and low sounds that the teacher produces.

4. Find the sound.   One student hides a music box or ticking clock, and the others try to find it by locating the sound.

5. Follow the sound.   The teacher or a student blows a whistle while walking around the room. Through listening, the other students should try to follow the route taken.

6. Blindman's Bluff.   One student in the group says something or makes an animal sound. The blindfolded student tries to guess who it is.

Auditory Memory

1. Do this.   Place five or six objects in front of the student and give him or her a series of directions to follow. For example: "Put the green block in Jean's lap, place the yellow flower under John's chair, and put the orange ball into Joe's desk." The list can be increased as the student improves in auditory memory.

2. Following directions.   Give the student several simple tasks to perform. For example: "Draw a big red square on your paper, put a small green circle underneath the square, and draw a black line from the middle of the circle to the upper right-hand corner of the square." Such activities can be taped for use with earphones at a listening center.

3. Lists of numbers or words.   Help the student hold in mind a list of numbers or single words. Start with two and ask for repetition. Gradually, add to the list as the student performs the tasks. At first, a visual reminder in the form of a picture clue may be helpful.

4. Nursery rhymes.   Have children memorize nursery rhymes and poems and play finger games.

5. Number series.   Give a series of numbers and ask questions about the series. For example, "Write the fourth one: *3, 8, 1, 9, 4.*" Other directions could include having them write the largest, the smallest, the closest to 5, the last, the one nearest their age, and so on.

6. Television programs.   Ask students to watch a television program and remember certain things. For example: "Watch *The Wizard of Oz* tonight and tomorrow tell me all the different lands that Dorothy visited."

7. Going to the moon.   Update the game of "Grandmother's Trunk" or "Going to New York." Say, "I took a trip to the moon and took my space-suit." The student repeats the statement but adds one item, for example, "helmet." Pictures may be used to help with auditory memory.

8. Repetition of sentences.   Say a sentence aloud and ask the student to repeat it. Start with short, simple sentences; then add compound sentences and sentences with complex clauses.

9. Serial order of letters and numbers.   Say several letters in alphabetical order, omitting some. Ask the child to supply omitted letters or numbers: *d, e, f* (pause or tap), *h; 3, 4* (pause or tap), *6, 7.*

10. Ordering events.   Read a selection that relates a short series of events. Have the students retell the story, mentioning each event in order.

Visual Processing

Abilities in visual perception are necessary for academic learning. Good skills in visual discrimination are a strong predictor of first-grade reading achievement. Children who can read letters and numbers, copy geometric patterns, and match printed words tend to do well in first-grade reading.

Visual Perception

1. Pegboard designs.   Using colored pegs, students reproduce colored visual geometric patterns on a pegboard from a visual model made by the teacher or shown on a printed page.

2. Blocks.   Children reproduce models using parquetry blocks. Have children use wood or plastic blocks that are all one color or have faces of different colors to match geometric shapes and have them build copies of models.

3. Finding shapes in pictures.   Students are asked to find all the round objects or designs in a picture, then all the square objects, and so forth.

4. Puzzles.   Students assemble puzzles that are made by the teacher or commercially. Subjects such as people, animals, forms, numbers, or letters can be cut into pieces to show functional parts.

5. Classification.   Students group or classify objects by shapes, sizes, and colors. The objects can be placed in a box or bowl. They can be chips, coins, buttons, beans, and so on.

6. Matching geometric shapes.   Place shapes on cards and have the students play games requiring the matching of these shapes. Collect jars of different sizes with lids, mix the lids, and have students match the lids with the jars.

7. Dominoes.   Make a domino-type game by making sets of cards decorated with sandpaper, felt, self-adhesive covering, or painted dots; have students match the cards with each other.

8. Playing cards.   A deck of playing cards provides excellent teaching material to match suits, pictures, numbers, and sets.

9. Letters and numbers.   Visual perception and discrimination of letters are important reading readiness skills. Games that provide opportunities to match, sort, or name shapes can be adapted to letters and numbers. Bingo cards can be made with letters. As letters are called, the student recognizes and covers up the letters.

10. Visual perception of words.   The ability to perceive words is, of course, highly related to reading. Use games of matching, sorting, grouping, and tracing words.

Visual Memory

1. Identifying missing objects.   Expose a collection of objects. Cover and remove one of the objects. Show the collection again, asking the student to identify the missing object.

2. Ordering from memory.   Expose a short series of shapes, designs, or objects. Have the student place another set of these designs in the identical order from memory. Playing cards, colored blocks, blocks with designs, or mahjongg tiles are among the materials that might be used for such an activity. Show a toy, number, letter, or word for a brief time and then have the child recall it.

3. Stories from pictures.   On a flannel board, place pictures of activities that tell a story. Remove the pictures and have the pupil tell the story by depending on visual memory of the pictures.

4. Repeating patterns.   Make a pattern of wooden beads, buttons, or blocks. Have the child look for a few seconds; then have the child reproduce the pattern.

Tactile and Kinesthetic Processing

For children who do not learn easily through the visual or auditory systems, tactile and kinesthetic perception provides a way to strengthen learning. The following activities stimulate tactile and kinesthetic perception.

1. Feeling various textures.   Children feel various textures, such as smooth wood, metal, sandpaper, felt, flocking, sponge, wet surfaces, and foods. Attach different materials to small pieces of wood. The student touches the boards without looking and learns to discriminate and match the various surfaces.

2. Feeling shapes.   Place various textures cut into geometric patterns or letters on boards. Children can touch them and discriminate, match, and identify these shapes. These shapes can also be made of plastic, wood, cardboard, clay, or the like.

3. Feeling temperatures.   Fill small jars with water to touch as a way of teaching warm, hot, and cold.

4. Feeling weights.   Fill small cardboard spice containers to different levels with beans, rice, and so on. Have the child match weights through shaking and sensing the weights.

5. Smelling.   Put materials of distinctive scents in bottles (cloves, cinnamon, vinegar, and so forth). Have the student identify or match the smells.

6. Recognizing by touch.   Trace designs, numbers, or letters on the child's palms. Ask children to reproduce or to identify the shapes as they feel.

7. Grab bag.   Put various objects in a bag or box. Have the child recognize the object through the sense of touch. The child can also match pairs of objects by feeling their shapes and textures. Use a variety of textures pasted on pieces of wood, Masonite, or plastic.

USING COMPUTER TECHNOLOGY

For young children with learning disabilities, the computer offers many opportunities to explore, play, and learn. The experiences become an integral part of their overall development. The computer bestows a unique magic on children who have special needs by empowering them with a sense of independence and control. The value of the computer may be greater for exceptional youngsters than for others in the population. It is widely acknowledged that computers enable ordinary people to do extraordinary things. But for the child who has special needs, the computer does even more. It enables extraordinary people to do ordinary things.

Computers can help young children develop independence, self-help skills, motor control, visual and auditory concepts, language skills, cognitive skills, and other precursor skills. with the computer young children with disabilities are able to control their environment and to make decisions. Even social skills can be encouraged through cooperative computer activities. Computer activities can help families and teachers meet IEP and IFSP goals (Raskin et al., 1998).

The computer can creatively present colors, distinguish differences such as *larger* and *smaller*, illustrate concepts such as *above* and *below*, and help with shape and letter recognition, counting, matching, and sequencing.

Adaptive peripherals are particularly useful with young children. Speech synthesizers allow the computer to "talk" to the child. Switches can be plugged into the computer, allowing the child to use the computer without

CASE EXAMPLE

USING A COMPUTER WITH A PRESCHOOL CHILD

Twenty-month-old Julia was delighted when she found that the computer allowed her to control her environment by letting her make and implement decisions and practice some newly acquired computer words: *more, all gone, orange,* and *broke.*

By age 3, Julia was playing with the alphabet games on the *Muppet Learning Keys* and with the *Sticky Bear Shapes* program. During lunch one day, she displayed her generalizations computer learning. Holding up her diagonally cut half of a peanut butter-and-jelly sandwich, she said, "Triangle." Then she took two bites from the sandwich from the diagonal side, looked at it, and announced, "Walrus" (the picture identification for *W* on the software program).

the keyboard. Alternative keyboards such as the *Muppet Learning Keys,* and *Power Pad,* and *Intellikeys* are especially useful with young children. With the *Touch Window,* the child can directly touch the screen to control the computer. Most important, young children with disabilities like using the computer. It is an enjoyable, motivating way of learning.

Table 8.4 offers some recommended software for preschool children with learning disabilities (Forgan, 1996). The software programs are divided into the categories of (1) early learning, (2) exploration, (3) communication, (4) beginning users, (5) emergent literacy, and (6) keyboarding skills.

Computers offer many opportunities for young children to explore, play, and learn. These activities empower them with a sense of independence and a sense of control. *(© Elizabeth Crews)*

Table 8.4

Computer Software for Young Children with Learning Disabilities

Program Name	Publisher
Early Learning	
Putt-Putt Joints the Parade	Humongous
Putt-Putt Goes to the Moon	Humongous
The Tree House	Broderbund
Millie's Math House	Edmark
Trudy's Time and Play House	Edmark
Berenstain Bears Get in a Fight	Broderbund
Face Maker Golden Edition	Queue
Exploration	
Just Grandma and Me	Living Books
The Playroom	Broderbund
Little Monster at School	Broderbund
Sammy's Science House	Edmark
Thinking Things Collections I	Edmark
In Grandma's Attic	Soft Key
Communication	
Exploring First Words	Laureate
Exploring First Words II	Laureate
Let's Go to the Moon	Laureate
Beginning Users	
Adventures of Quinn	Edmark
Cause/Effects	Judy Lynn Software
Children's Switch Progressions	J. J. Cooper
Clowns	Colorado Easter Seal Society
Creative Chorus	Laureate
Dino-Maze	Academic Skillbuilders
Early and Advanced Switch Games	R. J. Cooper
Early Concepts Skillbuilders	Edmark
Fundamental Concepts	Judy Lynn Software
Katie's Farm	Lawrence Productions
McGee	Lawrence Productions
Mickey's Colors and Shapes	Disney Software
New Cause and Effects	Colorado Easter Seal Society
Noises	Colorado Easter Seal Society
Old MacDonald II	UCLA Intervention Program

Table 8.4
(continued)

Program Name	Publisher
Beginning Users *(continued)*	
Peek-a-Book on Fundamental Concepts	Judy Lynn Software
This is the Way We Wash Our Face	UCLA Intervention Software
Where's Puff?	UCLA Intervention Software
Emergent Literacy	
New Kid on the Block	Living Books
Harry and the Haunted House	Living Books
Dr. Seuss's ABC CD	Broderbund
Sesame Street Letters	EA*Kids
Kid Works 2	Davidson
Bailey's Book House	Edmark
K.C. & Clyde	Don Johnston
Keyboarding Skills	
Kids Keys	Davidson
Kids on Keys	Queue
Stickybear Typing	Optimum Resources
Mavis Beacon Teaches Typing	Mindspace
Dinosoft Typing Tutor	Maverick

Chapter Summary

1. The early preschool years are critical to a child's development. Early identification and intervention for young children with disabilities are successful means of averting or reducing later failure.

2. Precursors of learning disabilities are early signs of delayed development that are evident during the preschool years.

3. Many young children with learning disabilities are clumsy in their motor skills. Motor learning is a developmental skill and is considered a key curriculum activity for young children.

4. Perceptual processing development is an important domain for young children with learning disabilities. Considerations should be given to the perceptual modality concept, auditory processing, and visual processing.

5. The 1997 Individuals with Disabilities Education Act (IDEA) incorporates provisions for preschool children with disabilities (ages 3 through 5) and also for infants and toddlers with disabilities (ages birth through 2).

6. Assessment for young children with learning disabilities includes several stages: (1) Child-Find, to locate young children with disabilities in the community; (2) screening, to select children who may need more comprehensive testing; (3) diagnosing, to give a comprehensive evaluation with authentic measures and with formal tests; and (4) evaluating, to monitor the child's progress.

7. Programs for young children with disabilities include the Early Education Program for Children with Disabilities (EEPCD), Head Start, and compensatory early education programs.

8. There are several possible education placements for young children with disabilities: regular class, special class, resource room, and others. The inclusive environment is growing as a placement option. Transition to new placements must be considered carefully in the early education programs.

9. Early childhood curriculum models include developmentally appropriate practice (DAP), enrichment curriculum, direct teaching curriculum, and cognitive emphasis curriculum.

10. The chapter suggests the usefulness of early intervention strategies in motor development, auditory processing, visual processing, and tactile/kinesthetic processing.

11. Ways of using the computer with young children with learning disabilities are being explored.

Questions for Discussion and Reflection

1. Why are the early years so important? What are some of the benefits of early intervention?

2. Why are young children with learning disabilities often not identified? How do the diagnostic criteria for learning disabilities sometimes overlook learning disabilities in young children?

3. What are the precursors for learning disabilities found in young children? How can early intervention practices help young children with learning disabilities?

4. Describe the two early childhood age groups covered in the reauthorized Individuals with Disabilities Education Act (IDEA). Compare and contrast the effect of the law for these two age groups.

5. Discuss the importance of transition decisions during the preschool years for children ages birth through 2 and for children ages 3 through 5.

6. Describe three curriculum models for early childhood special education.

7. How has the inclusion movement affected young children with learning disabilities in terms of placement?

Key Terms

adapted physical education programs *(p. 262)*

auditory blending *(p. 270)*

auditory discrimination *(p. 269)*

child-find *(p. 279)*

children at risk *(p. 277)*

developmental delay *(p. 279)*

developmentally appropriate practice (DAP) *(p. 287)*

direct teaching curriculum *(p. 289)*

enrichment curriculum *(p. 288)*

home-based program *(p. 285)*

Head Start *(p. 282)*

inclusive environment *(p. 263)*

individualized family service plan (IFSP) *(p. 276)*

kinesthetic perception *(p. 274)*

occupational therapist *(p. 263)*

Part B (of IDEA 1997) *(p. 274)*

Part C (of IDEA 1997) *(p. 276)*

perception *(p. 265)*

perceptual modality concept *(p. 266)*

perceptual-motor theory *(p. 263)*

phonological awareness *(p. 268)*

precursors of learning disabilities *(p. 255)*

screening *(p. 279)*

sensory-integration theory *(p. 263)*

tactile perception *(p. 274)*

transition *(p. 286)*

visual perception *(p. 271)*

Adolescents and Adults with Learning Disabilities

CHAPTER OUTLINE

For many individuals, learning disabilities are lifelong problems that continue into the adolescent and adult years. Secondary school programs are increasing to serve adolescents with learning disabilities. In this chapter, we will discuss the characteristics of adolescents with learning disabilities, special challenges that arise at the secondary level, transition planning, the types of instruction and programs in the secondary schools, procedures for teaching learning strategies, postsecondary and college programs, and adults with learning disabilities.

ADOLESCENTS WITH LEARNING DISABILITIES

The period of adolescence is well documented as a stage of turmoil and difficult adjustment. The physical, mental, and emotional adjustments that characterize adolescence affect learning. Teenagers with learning disabilities have difficulty in school and social life not only because of their learning disabilities, but also because they must cope with the normal challenges and adjustments presented by adolescence. Since many characteristics of learning disabilities and adolescence overlap, it is hard to know if a particular behavior stems from the learning disability or from normal adolescent development. In many cases, the difficulties stem from both, thus complicating the learning, social, and behavior problems.

Characteristics of Adolescence

The period of adolescence is marked by conflicting feelings about security and independence, rapid physical changes, developing sexuality, peer pressure, and self-consciousness. Many of the characteristics of adolescence can affect the processes of learning (Biehler & Snowman, 2000).

Freedom and Independence Versus Security and Dependence Adolescents want to become independent and separate themselves from their families, but at the same time they also need to keep these ties. According to Erikson's (1968) psychosocial model of development, adolescents must resolve a conflict between their desire for freedom and independence and their desire for security and dependence.

Rapid Physical Changes Adolescence is a period of rapid changes in physical growth and in appearance, including dramatic changes in facial and body structure. Adolescents must develop a new self-image and learn to cope with a different physical appearance as well as new psychological and biological drives.

Developing Sexuality The adolescent period is also one of developing sexuality—another change to which the adolescent must learn to adjust. The sexual dimension of adolescence may be very demanding in terms of time, energy, and worry.

Peer Pressure   Adolescents are greatly influenced by peer pressure and peer values. When the values of friends differ from those of parents, family confrontation and conflict may result.

Self-consciousness   Teenagers tend to be very conscious of themselves—of how they look and of how they compare with group norms. This self-consciousness can lead to feelings of inferiority and withdrawal.

Characteristics of Adolescents with Learning Disabilities

For youth with learning disabilities, the problems of adolescence are compounded by their learning disabilities. The typical characteristics of adolescence present challenges that may negatively affect learning. As illustrated in the case example entitled "Tim, an Adolescent with Learning Disabilities," the adolescent can find it devastating to cope with the symptoms of learning disabilities in addition to those created by normal adolescent development. When one considers the combination of academic difficulties, the characteristics of adolescence, and learning disabilities, it is small wonder that these years are often trying. The following are characteristics of adolescents with learning disabilities (Deshler, Ellis, & Lenz, 1996; Levine & Swartz, 1995):

Passive Learning   Adolescents with learning disabilities have been characterized as **passive learners.** In response to failure-producing experiences, they develop an attitude of **learned helplessness.** They learn to be passive instead of active learners. Instead of trying to solve a problem, they tend to wait passively until the teacher directs them and tells them what to do. In an academic task, they fail to associate new information with what they already know, and they do not elaborate in their thinking (Deshler, Ellis, & Lenz, 1996; Levine & Swartz, 1995; Torgesen, 1991).

Poor Self-concept   Poor self-concept and low self-esteem result from years of failure and frustration. Adolescents with learning disabilities have little confidence in their ability to learn and achieve. Often, too, emotional problems develop from their lack of experiences of success. Adolescents with learning disabilities too often lack self-esteem and self-confidence (Silver, 1998; Deshler et al., 1996).

Social and Behavior Problems   During these critical adolescent years, when friendships and peer approval are so important, problems with social skills create another impediment for adolescents with learning disabilities.

TIM, AN ADOLESCENT WITH LEARNING DISABILITIES

Tim, a 14-year-old freshman at Washington High School, has learning disabilities. His first-semester grades confirmed what he had feared: He failed three subjects—English, algebra, and history. He made only a *D* in general science and received a *C* in physical education and mechanical drawing.

Tim finds that he cannot cope with the assignments, work load, and demands of his courses. Even worse, he cannot read the textbooks, and he does not understand all that goes on in his classes. He also does poorly on the written exams. He feels as though he is drowning, and he knows he needs help.

When Tim was in elementary school, he received intermittent help from the learning disabilities resource teacher. Last year, in eighth grade, Tim was placed in all regular content-area classes and had no resource help or direct special education services. The learning disabilities teacher, his eighth-grade homeroom teacher, and his other subject-area teachers informally discussed Tim's academic progress and planned his program. Tim himself was very involved in these planning sessions. In general, he had a successful year in eighth grade, passing all his subjects with above-average grades, although he had to work hard to do it.

Over the summer, Tim grew so much that he had to buy a complete set of new clothes. His voice has changed, and he finds that he must shave the dark hair sprouting over his upper lip about once a week. Tim has made new friends at the high school and has kept many of his old friends from eighth grade. However, he has not told any of them about his grades. In fact, he is so embarrassed about his grades that he has stopped seeing his friends.

At this point, Tim does not know where to turn. In a conference that the school counselor held with Tim and his parents, they were told that the tests show he has the ability and that he should try harder. His parents are disappointed and angry. Tim is discouraged and depressed. Since the grades were mailed to his parents, he has cut a number of classes. Clearly, without help, there is danger that Tim will become another dropout statistic.

Because adolescents with learning disabilities frequently display social ineptitude, they often have difficulty making and keeping friends. The social and behavior problems become even more evident than the academic problems. The years of failure, low self-esteem, poor motivation, inadequate peer acceptance, and disruptive and maladaptive behavior take their toll (Bryan, 1997; Cole & McLeskey, 1997; Dohrn & Bryan, 1998; Haager & Vaughn, 1997; Scanlon, 1996); see also Chapter 14.

When social malfunctions are extremely disabling and include problems in social interactions and nonverbal communication, they may be diagnosed as nonverbal learning disorders or Asperger's syndrome (Roman, 1998; Thompson, 1997); see also Chapter 14. Web sites for these two social conditions are located at **http://www.nldline.com** (for nonverbal learning disorders) and **http://www.asperger.org** (for Asperger's syndrome).

Attention Deficits Many adolescents with learning disabilities lack the attentional capacity to meet the demands of secondary school. High school

For youths with learning disabilities, the problems of adolescence are compounded.
(© Elizabeth Crews/ Stock Boston)

heightens the demand for students to sustain cognitive effort and to concentrate for extended periods. The requirements of the secondary curriculum can place a strain on the adolescent's capacity to attend to the varied sources of input from teachers, instructional materials, and peers. Given the long periods of concentration needed for studying and listening in class, deficits in attention can seriously impede progress (Barkley, 1998; Goldman, Ganel, Bezman, & Sianez, 1996; Lerner, Lowenthal, & Lerner, 1995).

Levine (1988) relates how a 14-year-old described his attention problem: "I'll tell you just what my head is like. It's like a television set. Only one thing: it's got no channel selector. You see, all the programs keep coming over my screen at the same time" (p. 15).

Lack of Motivation   By the time students with learning disabilities reach secondary school, they have experienced many years of failure. They begin to doubt their intellectual abilities, lack resiliency, and come to believe that their efforts to achieve are futile (Luther, 1993). These feelings in turn lead to a low persistence level; they give up quickly as soon as something appears to be difficult. Even when these adolescents do experience success, they do not believe that they were responsible for the achievement. Instead, they attribute their success to some outside force, such as luck, something the teacher did, or an easy task (Yasutake & Bryan, 1995; Licht & Kistner, 1986). Therefore, even success does not bring much satisfaction or raise their confidence level. Motivating such students to exert the effort needed to learn is very difficult. Yet the best-made decisions about what to teach and the most skillful applications of how to teach will be successful only if students are motivated to learn and can attribute success to their own efforts (Zigmond, 1997; Scanlon, Deshler, & Schumaker, 1996). (See Chapter 14 for a further discussion of attribution theory and motivation.)

Placements of Adolescents with Learning Disabilities and Inclusion at the Secondary Level

The inclusion movement is growing at the secondary level as more adolescents with learning disabilities are placed in regular content-area classes for instruction. Table 9.1 shows the placement or educational environment for students with learning disabilities, ages 12–18. The percentage of adolescents placed in full-time, regular content-area classes increased to 41 percent (from 19 percent, as reported 5 years ago). The placement of adolescents in resource rooms decreased to 40 percent (from 58 percent, as reported 5 years ago). Thus, about 81 percent of secondary students are in regular content-area class for at least a portion of the day. About 18 percent of the secondary students with learning disabilities are in special classes, and about 1 percent are in other settings.

Although 81 percent of the adolescents with learning disabilities are in regular content-area classes for at least a portion of the day, the secondary schools have been slower to develop policies for inclusion than the elementary schools (Cole & McLeskey, 1997). Secondary schools face several obstacles in providing inclusion programs, including (1) the complex curricular material, (2) the larger gap between student skill levels and classroom demands, (3) the broader range of curricular content, (4) secondary school teachers who are content specialists and not trained in meeting the needs of students with disabilities, and (5) outside agencies that exert pressure on secondary schools to meet performance standards.

Table 9.1

Percentages of Adolescents with Learning Disabilities, Ages 12–18, Served in Different Educational Environments

Educational Environment	Percentage of Adolescents with Learning Disabilities
Regular class	41
Resource room	40
Separate class	18
Other placements	1

Source: From *To assure the free appropriate public education of all children with disabilities. Twentieth annual report to Congress on the implementation of the Individuals with Disabilities Education Act,* by the U.S. Department of Education, 1998. Washington, DC: U.S. Government Printing Office, A106.

Effective Inclusion Practices

To make inclusion work at the secondary level, it is necessary to establish partnerships between the **content-area teachers** and the learning disabilities teachers. Partnerships consist of two or more professionals working together in planning and delivering instruction in regular classes that include adolescents with learning disabilities. Several models for having professionals work together have been suggested (Knackendoffel, 1996; Cole & McLeskey, 1997):

Collaborative Teaming   **Collaborative teaming** is an on-going process in which educators with different areas of expertise work together voluntarily to develop creative solutions to problems that are impeding a student's progress. By working as a team, the teachers find a variety of strategies to improve services to students whose needs are not being met satisfactorily in noninclusive settings in which the teacher acts alone. Team members develop supportive and mutually beneficial relationships and share their resources (Knackendoffel, 1996).

Coteaching   **Coteaching** is an approach in which the content-area teacher and the special education teacher instruct students jointly in an educationally integrated setting. Both teachers instruct and provide supportive services. This model capitalizes on the specific and unique skills each professional brings to the classroom (Friend & Cook, 1996).

Collaborative Consultation   **Collaborative consultation** is used when the content-area class has only a few students with learning disabilities. The special education teacher engages in cooperative planning with the content-area teacher but does not directly teach in the classroom. The general education content-area teacher maintains primary responsibility for the instruction (Idol, Paolucci-Whitcomb, & Nevin, 1986).

Thus, inclusion can be promoted at the secondary level through partnerships between the subject teacher and the learning disabilities teacher. The ingredients for developing successful partnerships include (Cole & McLeskey, 1997):

- *Examining current practice.* Subject specialists and learning disabilities teachers examine what they are currently doing and their philosophies of teaching.

- *Determining teacher strengths.* The coteachers discuss their teaching strengths and shortcomings and how their skills are complementary. They should also understand the risks involved in a partnership of coteaching. What will each lose?

- *Developing trust and respect.* The coteachers have to learn to trust each other and to respect the skills and reviews of the partner.

- *Voluntary participation.* Coteaching works best if it is voluntary, not forced.

- *Administrative support.* Teachers need to know that their administrators support the coteaching program.

- *Communication and time.* The coteachers must be willing to provide and to accept interpersonal feedback. Time must be built into the day for planning, communication, and evaluation.

The following are among the benefits of partnerships at the secondary school level to promote inclusion: administrative duties are shared, teachers give more attention to problem behaviors and get to know students better, the feedback from colleagues allow teachers to fine-tune lessons, opportunities are provided for teachers to engage in problem-solving, teachers can model collaboration for students, and teachers can use their strengths to address student needs (Cole & McLeskey, 1997).

SPECIAL ISSUES AT THE SECONDARY LEVEL

The number of adolescents with learning disabilities now outnumbers elementary students. Fifty-four percent of all students served under the category of learning disabilities are ages 12 to 18; about 5 percent are ages 18 through 21 (U.S. Department of Education, 1998).

The data on students with learning disabilities in secondary schools paint a bleak picture. A five-year investigation of secondary school students with learning disabilities conducted by the National Longitudinal Transition Study revealed the extreme difficulties that students with learning disabilities encounter during their secondary school years. Many lack the necessary skills to succeed in general education settings, and many drop out of school (Blackorby & Wagner, 1997; Wagner & Blackorby, 1996).

Challenges for Adolescents with Learning Disabilities

The demands of the secondary school differ significantly from those of the elementary school. Students with learning disabilities move from a pupil-oriented elementary school environment to a content-driven secondary school setting. Often the secondary students lack the requisite skills needed to meet high school academic expectations. If secondary classroom teaching methods are not suited to the student's particular learning strengths and interests, graduating with a high school diploma becomes increasingly problematic (Levine & Swartz, 1995).

What Happens to Students with Learning Disabilities in Secondary School?

About 33 percent of students over the age of seventeen who have learning disabilities complete high school. They may either receive a standard diploma identical to the one awarded to students without disabilities, or they may receive a modified diploma, certification of completion, or other credential documenting their graduation (U.S. Department of Education, 1998). In 1998, a Department of Education report showed that students over fourteen who have learning disabilities exited special education for the following reasons: 13 percent returned to regular education, 32 percent graduated with a high school diploma, 4 percent graduated with a certificate of completion, 33 percent moved, 18 percent dropped out of school, and less than 1 percent reached the maximum age of 22 or died (U.S. Department of Education, 1998).

The high dropout rate of students who are in learning disabilities programs suggests that we are failing to serve these students appropriately. Studies show that there is a significant differential in terms of employment patterns and postschool adjustments between dropouts with learning disabilities and graduates with learning disabilities. Those who stay in school and graduate fare much better than those who leave school. Unfortunately, many students with learning disabilities who drop out of school face an uncertain and grim future in the streets (Zigmond, 1996).

Problems of Adolescents with Learning Disabilities   Adolescents with learning disabilities experience many problems. They can range from mild to severe, and they interfere with mastering many of the subjects of the secondary curriculum. In addition to academic problems, these students have difficulties with cognitive skills, social behaviors, and emotional stability. Many adolescents who have received learning disabilities services at the elementary level continue to need help when they reach junior and senior high school. Some adolescents' problems are not identified until the students enter the secondary school because of the subtle nature of their problems and the increased demands of the secondary curriculum.

Many adolescents with learning disabilities fail regular secondary courses. Almost one out of three youths with learning disabilities fails regular high school courses, and most experience failure before reaching high school (Blackorby & Wagner, 1997; Wagner, 1990). The problems faced by adolescents with learning disabilities are summarized in Table 9.2 (Rieth & Polsgrove, 1994).

Educational Reform and Performance Standards

The educational reform efforts are an influential force in our schools today, with directives coming from national, state, and local sources. The reform movement has led to the establishment of **performance standards** in the content areas such as (English, mathematics, and science), standards that all students are expected to meet. Most states now have written performance standards and have developed assessment tests which are administered to students to measure their mastery of expected performance standards. The results of these assessment tests measure not only the students' skills but

Table 9.2

Problems Faced by
Adolescents with
Learning Disabilities

- Severe deficits in basic academic skills such as reading, spelling, and math
- Generalized failures and below-average performance in content-area courses such as science, social studies, and health
- Deficient work-related skills, such as listening well in class, taking notes, studying, and taking tests
- Passive academic involvement and a pervasive lack of motivation
- Inadequate interpersonal skills

also the effectiveness of schools and districts, holding them accountable for student performance. Some states or school districts reward or sanction individual schools on the basis of whether their student test scores are improving or declining (U. S. Department of Education, 1997; Goertz & Friedman, 1996; McLaughlin, Shepard, & O'Day, 1995).

State or school performance standards also apply to students with learning disabilities, who are also expected to meet these standards. The 1997 IDEA outlines several new requirements concerning the participation of students with disabilities in statewide or districtwide assessments. Each student's IEP must include a plan for how the student will be assessed and what **accommodations** the student needs for the assessment (U. S. Department of Education, 1997, 1999; Shriner, Ysseldyke, & Thurlow, 1994; Rhim & McLaughlin 1997).

In addition to having to meet these performance standards, problems for adolescents with learning disabilities are magnified by the complex set of curriculum demands in high school. When adolescents with learning disabilities are in regular content-area classes for four periods a day, they are usually expected to meet the same requirements that all other students meet. There are often heavy expectations of reading proficiency that many adolescents with learning disabilities cannot meet. In spite of their learning disabilities, they are expected to learn, integrate, manage, and express large amounts of information (Deshler et al., 1996; Zigmond & Baker, 1994; Ellis et al., 1991). The demand for more requirements and for uniform standards creates several problems for students with learning disabilities:

1. As more students fail to meet the higher academic requirements, there is an inordinate increase in the number of students identified with learning disabilities.

2. Because school personnel are judged on their students' abilities to meet uniform standards, schools are less likely to develop a variety of curricular options and instructional strategies.

3. As a larger percentage of students with learning disabilities are unable to meet higher academic standards, they are at risk for dropping out of school.

4. As schools adopt rigid standards, more students with learning disabilities who do remain in school cannot complete the requirements for postsecondary programs and thus have fewer opportunities as adults.

Secondary School Teachers

Many content-area secondary school teachers are not prepared to work with students with learning disabilities. Their training was in their content specialization, be it mathematics, French, physics, or English literature. Many high school educators have not been prepared to provide the needed support for students with specific learning deficits. Therefore, an important collaborative role of the learning disabilities teacher in the high school is to help content-area teachers develop a sensitivity to the needs of students with learning disabilities and to provide them with alternatives for making necessary adjustments in their teaching.

The learning disabilities teacher at the secondary school level has the responsibility of bridging the gap between content-area teaching and special education. In addition to being thoroughly familiar with the field of learning disabilities, the high school special educator must be grounded in the problems of the adolescent and in the curriculum of the high school. Their responsibilities may include assisting students with algebra, with a creative writing assignment, with a mechanical drawing lesson, or with a science experiment. Students want their instruction to have immediacy and relevancy, and they want help that is directly related to their academic assignments. Instruction must be closely tied to what is happening in the subject classroom.

Collaboration involves helping the high school content-area teacher understand the nature of a specific student's problem and how to make the needed accommodations for that student. For example, if the student has a severe reading disability, that student may be helped by taping the lesson. Recordings for the Blind and Dyslexics are books on audiotapes that are accessible to students with learning disabilities. In fact, about 75 percent of those who use Recordings for the Blind and Dyslexics are individuals with learning disabilities. (For further information, see p. 329 in this chapter and contact Recordings for the Blind and Dyslexics; see Appendix D.) During examinations, the student with a severe writing problem might be allowed to give answers orally, to tape answers, or to dictate answers to someone else. Students who work very slowly might be allowed additional time.

"Selling" the learning disabilities concept so that high school teachers are willing to make needed modifications and accommodations is an essential element of the job, and one that requires skill in interpersonal relationships. The role of the high school learning disabilities teacher as a coteacher and collaboration team member is discussed later in this chapter and also in Chapter 5.

TRANSITION
FROM SCHOOL
TO ADULT LIFE

The transition from school to adult life is full of complexities for all adolescents. To successfully negotiate this transition, all adolescents require varying degrees of assistance from friends, family, and school personnel. Adolescents with learning disabilities need extra support and assistance to successfully make this challenging transition.

Transition refers to a change in status from behaving primarily as a student to assuming emerging adult roles. These new roles include employment, becoming a student in postsecondary school, maintaining a home, and experiencing satisfactory personal and social relationships (Halpern, 1994). The research shows that adolescents with learning disabilities receive inadequate **transition planning** that does not help them in seeking employment. They are most likely to find a job on their own, with little support from schools or adult agencies. Relatively few go to college. Only 30 percent actually enroll in any postsecondary school (four-year college, two-year college, or vocational school) (Wagner & Blackorby, 1996).

Transition Legislation

IDEA 1997 has several new requirements that address transition (PL 105–17). The law requires that

1. beginning when the student is age 14 and then updated annually, a statement of transition service needs that focuses on the student's existing program or courses must be written;

2. beginning at age 16, a plan for specific transition services, including interagency responsibilities, must be created;

3. beginning at least one year before the student reaches the age of majority, he or she must be informed of his or her rights.

The law views transition as a set of activities that are based on the needs of the individual student and that are designed to prepare the student for the years beyond secondary school. To ensure that the student completes secondary school prepared for employment or postsecondary education, as well as for independent living, IDEA 1997 requires that an individualized transition plan be written for students with disabilities beginning at age 14 as part of the IEP (Individual Education Plan). Many school districts use an attachment to the student's IEP to indicate transition goals and activities designed to meet those goals. Other schools develop a separate individual-ized transition plan (ITP).

Content of the Transition Plan   The transition plan (IEP/ITP) should in-clude the following (Blalock & Patton, 1996; Stewart & Lillie, 1995; Mar-tin, 1995; Chadsey-Rusch & Heal, 1995):

1. *Current levels of performance.* The transition plan should document the student's current levels of achievement so that the transition team knows where to begin.

2. *Interests and aptitude.* The plan should take into account the student's interests, aptitudes, potential, and vision for the future.

3. *Postschool goals.* The plan should define and project desired postschool goals as identified by the student, parents, and transition teams for community living, employment, postsecondary education and/or training.

4. *Transition activities.* The plan should include specific transition activi-ties in areas such as vocational and career education, work experience, and community-based instruction.

5. *Designate responsible persons.* The plan should designate a person or agency that is responsible for the continuation of the transition after the student's high school years.

6. *Review.* The transition plan should be reviewed and revised as necessary.

Developing Transition Plans

The goals for transition planning for adolescents with learning disabilities follow several different pathways (Dunn, 1996).

Competitive Employment   Most students with learning disabilities go di-rectly into competitive employment from high school. Vocational educators need to be an integral part of the transition team to help these students ex-plore occupations and to gain at least basic knowledge within the various fields. Parents and educators must work together to help students identify areas of interest and potential fields of employment, and also to determine how they can meet the entry-level requirements of those fields. Students will benefit from job experience by participating in a "co-op" project (Ger-ber & Brown, 1997).

Vocational Training   Some students with learning disabilities prepare for a trade after high school by going to a vocational training school or by enter-ing an apprenticeship program.

College Attendance The number of students with learning disabilities who go to college or to a postsecondary school is still quite low, although that number is increasing. Many students with learning disabilities do not consider postsecondary education options because they are not encouraged, assisted, or prepared to do so. However, if transition plans are designed and implemented effectively, many more students could pursue postsecondary education options (Vogel & Reder, 1998; National Joint Committee on Learning Disabilities, 1994; Stewart & Lillie, 1995).

Supported Employment Some transition programs offer a bridge from school to work through supported employment. In this type of program, transition educators seek potential employers to hire special education students. In some cases a job coach works at the employment site, supervising and helping the students over the inevitable rough spots. Job coaches work both for the business that employs the student and for the school or agency (Rusch & Phelps, 1987).

Table 9.3 shows the results of a national survey of the transition goals of students with learning disabilities (Wagner et al., 1993).

Transition Guidelines

Table 9.4 provides guidelines for developing transition plans for students with learning disabilities in high school (Martin, 1995; Stewart & Lillie, 1995).

Table 9.3 **Transition Goals for Students with Learning Disabilities**		

Transition Goal	Description	Percentage
Competitive employment	Seeking job in competitive sector or going into military service	59%
Vocational training	Enrolling in a vocational training program	32%
College attendance	Furthering their education at a four-year college or two-year or community college	28%
Supported employment	Seeking noncompetitive employment in agencies, with job coaches, and with other types of support	4%

Source: From Wagner et al. (1993), *The Secondary School Programs of Students with Disabilities: A Report from the National Longitudinal Transition Study of Special Education Students.* Used by permission.

Table 9.4

Guidelines for Developing Transition Plans for Secondary Students with Learning Disabilities

- *Form an individual transition team for each student to develop the Individual Transition Plan.* Identify resources that are available to meet the goals of the plan.
- *Work with business and industry representatives.* Build relationships for students to meet the goals of the transition plan.
- *Develop a transition curriculum.* Include communication skills, self-esteem development, decision-making skills, career exploration, community living skills, and time management to help students during the transition.
- *Teach self-advocacy skills.* Help students understand the legislative mandates that support requests for accommodations both in the classroom and on the job. Adolescents can use this information in making decisions about their futures. Teach students to advocate for themselves. Many of their interactions require a constructive request for accommodations and services. Students must interact with teachers in high school and in postsecondary school, and with employers. They may need to get services from other agencies. By learning to speak for themselves and to bear the consequences of their actions or inactions, students learn the skills necessary for adulthood.
- *Build competencies in academic skills.* Make sure that students have competencies in reading, writing, mathematics, and computer usage.
- *Teach study skills.* Adolescents need help in test preparation, test taking, and learning strategies.
- *Teach students to use accommodations and modifications appropriately and effectively.*
- *Teach social skills and interpersonal communication skills.*

APPROACHES TO TEACHING ADOLESCENTS WITH LEARNING DISABILITIES IN SECONDARY SCHOOL

Several different instructional approaches and curriculum models are being used with students with learning disabilities in junior and senior high school (Cole & McLeskey, 1997; Sitlington, 1996; Rieth & Polsgrove, 1994; Zigmond & Baker, 1994).

Components of Effective Secondary Programs

Essential components of effective secondary programs for students with learning disabilities include the following elements (Zigmond, 1997, 1990):

Intensive Instruction in Reading and Mathematics   Many students with learning disabilities receive failing grades in mainstream courses because of their poor skills in reading, writing, and math. These students still require basic instruction in reading, writing, vocabulary development, and mathematics (Manheimer & Fleischner, 1995; Lane & Brownell, 1995).

Explicit Instruction in Survival Skills   Zigmond (1990) identifies several **functional or survival skills** that are needed for successful functioning in a high school:

- *Behavior control.* This refers to strategies that help students learn how to stay out of trouble in school and alternative ways of responding to situations that arise in the everyday course of school.

- *Teacher-pleasing behavior.* These consist of skills to help students acquire behavior patterns that will make teachers consider them in a positive light. Examples of such patterns include looking interested, volunteering responses, and looking busy—in short, looking like a good student.

- *Study skills and test-taking skills.* These are essential strategies for high school survival, such as organizing time, approaching a textbook, taking notes from a lecture or text, organizing information, studying for tests, and taking tests.

Curriculum Models for Serving Adolescents with Learning Disabilities at the Secondary Level

Several instructional approaches and curriculum models are used with adolescents with learning disabilities in junior and senior high schools (Cole & McLeskey, 1997; Sitlington, 1996; Deshler, Ellis, & Lenz, 1996). These include basic skills instruction, tutorial instruction, functional skills instruction, work-study programs, and collaboration programs. Learning strategies instruction, an important approach, is discussed in the next major section.

Basic Academic Skills Instruction   The objective of teaching basic skills is to remediate the student's academic deficits. **Basic academic skills instruction** usually focuses on improving the student's abilities in reading and mathematics. Students receive instruction at a level that approximates their achievement or instructional level. For example, if a 16-year-old student is reading at fifth-grade level, reading instruction for that student would be geared to the fifth-grade level.

Tutorial Programs   The objective of **tutorial instruction** is to help students in their specific academic-content subjects. For example, if Alex experiences failure or difficulty in his American history class, his instruction will focus on the specific history material he is studying. The goal is to help Alex succeed in the regular curriculum. The learning disabilities resource teacher must know the requirements of all academic subjects in which students may have difficulty.

Functional or Survival Skills Instruction   The objective of the functional skills instruction model is to equip students to function in society. Students are taught what are often called "survival skills"—that is, skills that will enable them to get along in the world outside of school. The curriculum in-

A high school curriculum can incorporate work-study or vocational programs to teach job skills. *(© Bob Daemmrich/The Image Works)*

cludes such subjects as consumer information, completion of application forms (such as job applications), banking and money skills (such as understanding interest rates and installment purchases), life-care skills (such as grooming), and computer literacy. Academic content is geared to the students' careers and life needs. For example, reading is directed toward relevant areas such as directions, want ads, or a driver's instruction manual. Guidance and counseling for self-identity and career planning are also often part of the curriculum.

Work-Study Programs   The objective of **work-study programs** is to provide adolescents with job- and career-related skills as well as actual on-the-job experience. Students in work-study programs typically spend half the day on the job and the remainder in school. While in school, they may study materials that are compatible with their jobs. Sometimes these students take regular courses and also work with a learning disabilities teacher. The work-study approach is particularly successful for students who are not motivated by the high school environment. The learning disabilities teacher serves as a coordinator who integrates education with desired job skills and supervises students in the work site.

Learning strategies instruction offers a viable and promising approach for helping adolescents with learning disabilities learn to take control of their own learning. The objective of this instruction is to teach students *how* to learn rather than *what* is contained in a specific curriculum. Effective strategy instruction involves helping students use procedures that will empower them to accomplish important academic tasks, to solve problems, and to complete work independently. With proficiency in learning strategies, students can overcome or lessen the effects of learning disabilities. Learning strategies are tools that students can use to approach tasks in content classes or other learning situations. In effect, the teacher helps students learn how to learn (Deshler, Ellis, & Lenz, 1996; Lenz, Ellis, & Scanlon, 1996; Oas, Schumaker, & Deshler, 1995; Harris & Pressley, 1991; Ellis et al., 1991).

A *learning strategy* is defined by Lenz et al. (1996, p. 1) as

an individual's approach to a task when it includes how a person thinks and acts when planning, executing, and evaluating performance on a task and its outcome. It includes both *cognitive* (thinking processes) and *behavioral* (overt actions) elements that guide student planning and performance and evaluation of strategy engagement.

Learning strategies research shows that adolescents with learning disabilities are "inefficient learners." It is not that they lack the ability to learn but rather that they go about learning in an inefficient manner. For example, Maria's memory may be adequate for remembering the facts in a history lesson, but she has to put the right kind of learning effort into remembering those facts. Or for Sam, who is having difficulty in science, learning strategies instruction would teach some techniques for organizing his materials for learning, rather than teach him the content of the subject. Thus, the emphasis is on teaching students how to adapt and cope with the changing world, how to "learn how to learn." (See the case example entitled "The Power of Learning Strategies: A Parable" and also Chapter 6.) Instruction in learning strategies has been found to be particularly effective with adolescents with learning disabilities who are above third-grade reading level, are able to deal with symbolic as well as concrete learning tasks, and have an average intellectual ability (Deshler et al., 1996; Lenz et al., 1996). Learning strategies can be applied to all academic areas of the secondary curriculum, as well as to social and behavioral learning.

Guidelines for Teaching Learning Strategies

The intense interest in learning strategies instruction has generated a significant amount of research (Deshler et al., 1996; Slavin, 1991; Palinscar & Brown, 1984; Brown & Campione, 1986; Kulhavy, Schwartz, & Peterson, 1986). The following are some practical guidelines for putting learning strategies instruction into practice:

THE POWER OF LEARNING STRATEGIES: A PARABLE

If you give a starving man a fish, you feed him for a day. But if you teach the man to fish, you feed him for a lifetime.

If you teach an adolescent with learning disabilities a fact, you help him or her for the moment. But if you teach this adolescent how to think about learning, you help him or her for a lifetime.

- Students get more from instruction when their background knowledge is activated or when the teacher elicits, builds, and focuses on appropriate background knowledge. Background knowledge is the strongest predictor of a student's ability to learn new material. The more students know about a topic, the better they comprehend and learn about the topic from the text.

- Successful learners monitor their own progress. They have an idea of how they are doing. In reading, for example, they use their knowledge of text features and appropriate strategies to monitor their own learning.

- Students who are actively involved in their learning are more successful than students who play a more passive role. Effective learners generate questions, make summaries, and help determine the direction of the lesson.

- There is a strong correlation between successful learning and the student's self-concept and positive attitude. Students with high levels of achievement tend to have high self-concepts, and low achievers have poor self-concepts. Success in learning enhances self-concept.

- Successful learners use effective memory strategies. Memory is related to background; those who know more are able to remember more. Short-term memory is limited in capacity. Most of what is learned is forgotten quickly if it is not acted upon or linked with previous learning.

- The opportunity for students to interact with other students is important. Cooperative learning and peer tutoring increase achievement and motivation as well as improve interpersonal relationships. When one student teaches another student, the achievement of both students can improve.

- Questioning helps comprehension. Students learn more effectively when they generate their own questions. Students exposed to higher-order questions understand more than students exposed only to lower-order questions. They tend to give more thoughtful, reflective responses to questions when teachers allow more time for responses and encourage follow-up.

Strategies Intervention Model (SIM)

One widely used model of strategy instruction, the **strategies intervention model (SIM),** was developed and validated through many years of programmatic research with adolescents with learning disabilities by Deshler, Schumaker, and their colleagues at the Kansas Center for Research on Learning. SIM is a recognized, fully developed procedure for teaching learning strategies to adolescents with learning disabilities (Deshler et al., 1996; Lenz et al., 1996; Oas et al., 1995; Ellis et al., 1991). This model is practical and useful. The approach has two phases for helping students cope with the demands of the high school curriculum: (1) teachers must identify the curriculum demands of their students, and (2) teachers must match these school demands with specific learning strategies (Schumaker, Deshler, & Ellis, 1986).

Steps in Teaching Learning Strategies

Central to the SIM model is a series of eight instructional stages (Deshler et al., 1996; Lenz et al., 1996; Ellis et al., 1991). The integrated series of overt acts and cognitive behaviors enables students to solve a problem or to complete a task. The steps for teaching a learning strategy are summarized in Table 9.5 and illustrated in the following steps.

Step 1: Elena Martinez (the teacher) **pretests** *Andrew Fleming (the student) to determine his current learning habits, and she obtains a commitment from him to learn.* Andrew is asked to perform a task that requires the target learning strategy. For example, for the strategy of self-questioning, Martinez asks Andrew to read a passage and answer comprehension questions. She discusses with Andrew the results of his performance and establishes his need for acquiring the learning strategy and a commitment from Andrew to learn this strategy.

Step 2: Ms. Martinez **describes** *the new learning strategy.* Next, Martinez explains to Andrew the steps and behaviors involved in performing the learning strategy. "First, Andrew, you will read a paragraph. Then you will stop reading and ask yourself some questions. As you think of a question, you will either answer it yourself or go back to the paragraph to find the answer. After you have answered all the questions you can think of, you will read the next paragraph."

Step 3: Ms. Martinez **models** *the new learning strategy.* She demonstrates all the steps described in Step 2. While doing so, Martinez "thinks aloud" so that Andrew can witness the entire process.

Step 4: Andrew **verbally rehearses** *the learning strategy.* Andrew rehearses the steps by talking aloud until he reaches the goal of 100 percent correct without prompting from Martinez. Andrew becomes familiar with the steps through a self-instruction procedure.

Table 9.5

Steps for Teaching a Learning Strategy

Stage 1. Teacher Pretests Students and Obtains a Commitment
Phase 1. Orientation and pretest
Phase 2. Awareness and commitment

Stage 2. Teacher Describes the Learning Strategy
Phase 1. Orientation and overview
Phase 2. Presentation of strategy and remembering system

Stage 3. Teacher Models the Strategy
Phase 1. Orientation
Phase 2. Presentation
Phase 3. Student enlistment

Stage 4. Students Verbally Practice the Strategy
Phase 1. Verbal elaboration
Phase 2. Verbal rehearsal

Stage 5. Students Have Controlled Practice and Feedback
Phase 1. Orientation and overview
Phase 2. Guided practice
Phase 3. Independent practice

Stage 6. Students Have Advanced Practice and Feedback
Phase 1. Orientation and overview
Phase 2. Guided practice
Phase 3. Independent practice

Stage 7. Teacher Posttests Students and Obtains a Commitment
Phase 1. Confirmation and celebration
Phase 2. Forecast and commitment to generalize

Stage 8. Students Generalize the Learning Strategy
Phase 1. Orientation
Phase 2. Activation
Phase 3. Adaptation
Phase 4. Maintenance

Source: Adapted from E. Ellis, D. Deshler, B. Lenz, J. Schumaker and F. Clark (1991), An Instructional Model for Teaching Learning Strategies. *Focus on Exceptional Children, 23* (6), p. 11. Reprinted by permission of Love Publishing Company, Denver.

Step 5: Andrew **practices with controlled materials** *and obtains feedback.* Martinez provides materials for Andrew to practice the new learning strategy. By carefully selecting practice materials, she keeps other intervening problems to a minimum. For example, to practice the strategy of self-questioning in reading material, she selects material that is easy enough for Andrew to practice the target strategy without getting bogged down in very difficult vocabulary.

Step 6: Andrew **practices with classroom materials** *and obtains feedback.* Once Andrew has gained proficiency in the strategy with controlled materials, Martinez applies the strategy to materials used in his regular classroom. This step is a stage in developing an application and generalization of the learning strategy. After using the strategy successfully in the resource room, Andrew must learn to generalize the technique to broader learning situations.

Step 7: Ms. Martinez posttests *to determine Andrew's progress and obtains his permission to generalize.*   Instruction is successful if Andrew has progressed sufficiently to cope with curricular demands in the target area.

Step 8: Andrew generalizes *the learning strategy.* The real measure of effective strategy instruction is the degree to which students generalize the acquired strategy to the real world and maintain its use in new settings and situations.

In summary, the goal of the learning strategies approach is to teach adolescents with learning disabilities to become involved, active, and independent learners. After identifying the demands of the curriculum that the student cannot meet, the teacher provides instruction to meet those demands. The cognitive aspects of learning rather than specific subject matter content are emphasized. Research suggests that this is an effective teaching approach because students learn how to learn.

(Note: For additional information about the Strategies Intervention Model, contact the Center for Research on Learning, University of Kansas, 3061 Dole Human Development Center, Lawrence, KS 66045. Phone: (785)864-4780. Web site: **http://www.ku_crl.org.**)

INTO THE ADULT YEARS

For many individuals, a learning disability is a lifelong problem. In this section, we consider post–high school and college programs and adults with learning disabilities.

Postsecondary and College Programs

Postsecondary education includes community colleges, vocational-technical training, and four-year colleges. Adults with learning disabilities are too frequently excluded from postsecondary education because they do not meet the institution's entrance requirements. If they are accepted by a postsecondary school or college, the assistance and modifications they need may not be available at the institution.

Only a few years ago, college was out of the question for most adults with learning disabilities. Today, however, their prospects for a postsecondary education have brightened considerably, and there are many opportunities for such young adults to acquire a college-level education. Many individuals with learning disabilities can look forward to experiencing college and to a better preparation for their futures (Vogel & Reder, 1998; Vogel, 1997; Vogel & Adelman, 1993). The community colleges are often a good choice for young adults with learning disabilities. They bridge the gap between high school and college, and they may offer special programs for individuals with learning disabilities. The case example entitled "Darlene, A College Student with Learning Disabilities" illustrates such a situation.

Section 504 of the Rehabilitation Act   A major factor triggering the growth of postsecondary and college programs is federal legislation. **Section 504 of the Rehabilitation Act** of 1973 (PL 93–112) states that

> no otherwise qualified handicapped individual . . . shall, solely by reason of his/her handicap, be excluded from participation in, be denied the benefits of, or be subject to discrimination under any program or activity receiving federal financial assistance.

Further clarification and interpretation of Section 504 with regard to the requirements of schools and educational institutions are provided by case law and by the Rehabilitation Act Amendments (1976). Since most colleges receive some federal financial assistance, they are subject to the Section 504 regulations (Rothstein, 1998).

According to Section 504, educational institutions are required to make **reasonable accommodations** for students who are identified as having a disability (Rothstein, 1998). Further, learning disabilities are recognized as a category of disability under the Section 504 regulations. As Section 504 is increasingly implemented at educational institutions, adults with learning disabilities are able to enroll in colleges and postsecondary schools in steadily increasing numbers and to receive a variety of services.

Accommodations   Compliance with the regulations of Section 504 requires that colleges allow for modifications and make reasonable accommodations. Some of these accommodations are listed next (Vogel, 1998, Bursuck, Rose, Cowen, & Yahaya, 1989):

- Extending the time allowed to complete a program
- Adapting the method of instruction
- Substituting an alternative course for a required course
- Modifying or substituting courses for the foreign language requirements
- Allowing for part-time rather than full-time study
- Modifying examination procedures to measure achievement without contamination from areas of deficit
- Providing audiotapes of student textbooks
- Providing note takers to help students with lectures
- Offering counseling services to the students
- Developing individualized education programs for students
- Providing basic skills instruction in areas of reading, mathematics, and language

College Entrance Testing for Individuals with Learning Disabilities   Special accommodations are also available for students with learning disabilities who are taking college entrance examinations. Information on accommodations for the Scholastic Aptitude Test (SAT), the GRE, and the GMAT can be obtained from the Educational Testing Service (ETS),

CASE EXAMPLE

DARLENE, A COLLEGE STUDENT WITH LEARNING DISABILITIES

Darlene was the youngest of three children. Her older sister and brother were model students, receiving good grades in school with little effort. For Darlene, however, school was difficult. At first her parents would say, "Why can't you get A's like your brother and sister?" Finally, in sixth grade, her parents realized that Darlene had learning disabilities. She received help during her middle school years, and her grades improved. During her high school years, Darlene, her parents, and the transition team developed a transition plan for college. She wanted to major in art, an area in which she excelled. She worked with her high school counselor and selected a college with a good arts curriculum and a supportive learning disabilities program. Darlene requested special accommodations for the college entrance examinations, and she was admitted to the college of her choice. At the college, she worked with the learning disabilities staff in planning her courses. When she needed any special accommodations in her courses, she knew her rights under the law and was able to advocate for herself. She decided to take three courses per semester instead of four so that she would graduate in five years instead of four. Darlene is now a college senior and looks forward to her graduation. With careful planning and preparation, her college education has been a difficult but happy experience.

Rosedale Road, Princeton, NJ, 08541. Phone: (609)921-9000. Fax: (609)734-5410. Web site: **http://www.etc.org**. Information on special accommodations on the American College Test (ACT) is described in *ACT Assessment Special Testing Guide* (available from ACT Universal Testing Special Testing: 61, PO Box 4028, Iowa City, IA, 52243-4028. Phone: (319)337-1332, Fax: (319)337-1285, web site: **http://www.act.org**.

Special Problems at the College Level   College poses many problems that are not encountered during the high school years. There is less student-teacher contact, and college has long-range assignments and evaluation rather than the day-to-day monitoring that occurs in high school. The student does not have the support network of family and friends that was available during high school. Students also have more unstructured time they must manage, and they must learn to advocate for themselves. In addition, the physical environment is very different, with classes in different buildings, adjustments to roommates, and acclimation to the eating and sleeping patterns of the dormitories. To meet these new demands, students may need a period of transition activities before the college year begins. Some colleges offer an intensive transition program to prepare such students for college challenges. The University of Wisconsin–Whitewater transition program, which occurs over a five-week summer period, is described by Dalke (1993). A resource of college transition programs is in the *K & W Guide for the Learning Disabled* (Kravetz & Wax, 1997).

Another problem many students encounter in college is the foreign language requirement. For many students with learning disabilities, the foreign language requirement becomes a major stumbling block and may even prevent them from completing their college work. Colleges need to develop policies for students with learning disabilities who are unable to complete the foreign language requirement. Such policies could include a method for students to petition for a substitution, a procedure for waiving the foreign language requirement, or a provision of accommodations in foreign language classes (Ganschow, Sparks, & Javorsky, 1998).

One of the greatest challenges faced by college students with learning disabilities is gaining and maintaining the acceptance and cooperation of the academic faculty. Research shows that faculty members often support the concept of providing accommodations for students with learning disabilities. In-service training is needed to help faculty understand the needs of these students and become familiar with the accommodations that can be made (Rose, 1993). Table 9.6 lists ways college faculty members can help college students with learning disabilities (Vogel, 1997).

Table 9.6

Guidelines for Helping College Students with Learning Disabilities

1. Make the syllabus available four to six weeks before the beginning of the class and, when possible, be available to discuss the syllabus with students with learning disabilities who are considering taking the course.

2. Begin lectures and discussions with reviews and overviews of the topics to be covered.

3. Use a chalkboard or overhead projector to outline lecture material, reading what is written or what is on previously prepared transparencies.

4. Use a chalkboard or overhead projector to highlight key concepts, unusual terminology, or foreign words (being mindful of legibility and of the necessity to read what is written).

5. Emphasize important points, main ideas, and key concepts orally in lecture.

6. Give assignments in writing as well as orally and be available for further clarification.

7. Provide opportunities for student participation, question periods, and/or discussion.

8. Provide time for individual discussion of assignments and questions about lectures and readings.

9. Provide study guides for the text, study questions, and review sessions to aid in mastering material and preparing for exams.

10. Allow oral presentations or tape-recorded assignments instead of a written format.

11. Modify evaluation procedures. For example, permit untimed tests and oral, taped, or typed exams instead of written exams. Allow alternative methods to demonstrate course mastery, and provide adequate scratch and lined paper for students with overly large or poor handwriting. Offer alternatives to computer-scored answer sheets.

12. Assist students in obtaining taped textbooks. Contact RFB & D (Recordings for the Blind and Dyslexic)—Phone: (800) 221-4792, web site: **http://www.rfbd.org** (see Appendix D).

Many colleges establish an office of handicapped student services to meet the needs of all students with disabilities on the campus. The office staff is involved with student admission, assessment, counseling, program planning, and communication with faculty.

Finding Colleges for Students with Learning Disabilities   It is difficult to list college programs for students with learning disabilities because these programs are continually being started and changed. However, several available guidebooks that can help prospective students, their families, and counselors are listed in Table 9.7. Many of these guides can be located in libraries.

Adults with Learning Disabilities

The problems created by learning disabilities may not disappear when an individual leaves school. For many, they continue throughout their lives. Through public awareness programs about learning disabilities seen on television and in newspapers and magazine articles, many adults recognize that their problems are related to learning disabilities. For example, an arti-

---

Table 9.7

College Guides and Resources for Learning Disabilities

Dispelling the Myths: College Students with Learning Disabilities, by Katherine Garnett and Sandra La Porta (1990). A monograph for students and educators that explains what learning disabilities are and what faculty members can do to help such students succeed in college. Call NCLD at (888) 575-7373.

Assisting College Students with Learning Disabilities: A Tutor's Manual, by Pamela Adelamna and Debbie Olufs. Call AHEAD at (614) 488-4972.

College Students with Learning Disabilities: A Handbook, by Susal Vogel (1997). A handbook about college-related issues, including Section 504. For students with learning disabilities and college personnel. Contact LDA by phone at (414) 341-1515 or at **http://www.ldanatl.org**.

K & W Guide to Colleges with Programs for Students with Learning Disabilities. A state-by-state guide by Marybeth Kravets and Imy Wax (New York: Random House, 1997). Call NCLD at (212) 545-7510.

Peterson's Guide to Colleges with Programs for Students with Learning Disabilities. A state-by-state guide, 4th ed. (Princeton, NJ: Peterson's Guides, 1997). Call NCLD at (888) 575-7373.

School/Search Guide to Colleges with Programs for Students with Learning Disabilities. A state-by-state guide by Midge Lipkin (Belmont, MA: SchoolSearch Press, 1994). Call (617) 489-5785.

Unlocking Potential: College and Other Choices for Learning Disabled People: A Step-by-Step Guide, by Barbara Scheiber (1992). A book that assists the reader through the postsecondary school selection process. Call Woodbine House at (800) 843-7323.

Source: "College Guides and Resources for Learning Disabilities" from *Their World,* NCLD, 1999. Reprinted with the permission of the National Center for Learning Disabilities, 381 Park Avenue South, New York, NY 10016. **http://www.ncld.org**.

CASE EXAMPLE

FRANK, AN ADULT WITH A LEARNING DISABILITY

Frank is one example of an adult with a learning disability. A 36-year-old man of average intelligence whose specific difficulty was reading, Frank sought help at a university learning disabilities clinic. Employed as a journeyman painter and supporting his wife and two children, he had learned to cope with many daily situations that required reading skills. Although he was unable to read the color labels on paint cans, could not decipher street and road signs, and could not find streets or addresses or use a city map to find the locations of his house-painting jobs, Frank had learned to manage by compensating for his inability to read. He visually memorized the color codes on paint cans to determine their color. He tried to limit his work to a specific area of the city because he could not read street signs. When he was sent into an unfamiliar area, he would ask a fellow worker who could provide directions to accompany him, or he would request help from residents of the area to reach his destination. He watched television to keep abreast of current affairs, and his wife read and answered his correspondence. However, the day inevitably came when advancement was no longer possible unless Frank learned to read. Moreover, his children were rapidly acquiring the reading skills that he did not possess. His disability was a continual threat to him and finally led him to search for help. It is remarkable that after so many years of failure and frustration, Frank recognized that his problem is a learning disability and that he had the fortitude and motivation to attempt once again the formidable task of learning to read.

cle in *Newsweek* brought information about learning disabilities to the general public (Wingert & Kantrowitz, 1997).

What is the life of an adult with learning disabilities like? These adults sometimes have great difficulty finding their niche in the world. They have trouble finding and keeping a job, developing a satisfying social life, and even coping with individual daily living. Many adults with learning disabilities have developed amazing strategies for avoiding, hiding, and dealing with their problems. Such a situation is described in the case example entitled "Frank, an Adult with a Learning Disability."

Surveys of adults with learning disabilities indicate that their major needs are in the following areas: social relationships and skills, career counseling, developing self-esteem and confidence, overcoming dependence, survival skills, vocational training, job procurement and retention, reading, spelling, management of personal finances, and organizational skills. When these adults lose a job, they are uncertain about what has gone wrong (Gerber & Brown, 1997, Brown, 1997).

What is unique about adults with learning disabilities? They are usually self-identified and self-referred. To succeed, they must be intimately involved in both the diagnosis and the remediation process. They are likely to be highly motivated to learn the skills they know they need in life. They want to know what test results mean and what the goals and purpose of the remediation program are. It is their commitment to the remediation program that enables them to succeed.

Since adults are no longer in school, they usually must find other agencies for services. Most clinics are not geared to serving adults with learning disabilities. Thus learning disabilities specialists must enlarge their scope to provide service to adults—a very neglected population. Adults with learning disabilities should learn about their rights under the law (Latham & Latham, 1997).

Some organizations for adults with learning disabilities are

- LDA, Committee for Adults with Learning Disabilities. LDA, 4156 Library Road, Pittsburgh, PA 15234. Web site: **http://www.ldanatl.org.**
- National Association for Adults with Special Learning Needs. P.O. Box 716, Bryn Mawr, PA 19010. Phone: (610) 446-6126 or (800) 869-8336.
- LDPride. Web site: **http://www.ldpride.net/ldpride.htm.**

Literacy Organizations for Teaching Adults to Read   Often adults are motivated to seek instruction in learning to read. The problem is that after individuals with learning disabilities leave school, there are fewer educational options open to them. Some literacy programs designed for adults include

- *Literacy Volunteers of America.*   LVA is a national nonprofit organization that has a network of volunteer tutors to teach reading, writing, and English-speaking skills to adults. LVA can be contacted at 635 James St., Syracuse, NY 13203. LVA can also be reached by phone at (800) 582-8812 or at **http://literacy.kent.edu/LVA.**
- *The Laubach Program.*   The objective of this private organization is to teach literacy to people around the world. Write to Laubach Literacy Action, P.O. Box 131, 1320 Jamesville Ave., Syracuse, NY 13210. It can also be reached by phone at (315) 422-6369 or at **http://www.laubach.org.**
- *ABE (Adult Basic Education) and GED (General Education Degree).* These government-sponsored programs offer education for adults. A person passing the GED examination is awarded a high school equivalency degree.

COMPUTER TECHNOLOGY FOR ADOLESCENTS AND ADULTS

It is essential that all students, especially adolescents and adults, learn to use computers, as they are either making the transition to the working world or are already immersed in it. The *National Educational Technology Standards for Students* are currently used by educators to determine how best to integrate technology into their classrooms. The *NETS* booklet provides technology learning standards for grades pre-K through 12 and offers profiles for ensuring technology literacy in each of the respective grade ranges. Since the standards are intended for all students, both special and general educators should make every effort to involve their students with technology by using these national standards as a guide.

Facility with a computer can go a long way toward bringing people with learning disabilities into the mainstream. Experience with computers helps people develop the unique technological skills needed for many types of jobs. Many individuals with learning disabilities who have great difficulty with reading, spelling, and writing often excel at using computers. Web authoring tools such as Digital Chisel and graphic organizers such as Inspiration make it possible for students to produce web pages and visuals that have practical applications in the working world (Smith & Levine, in press; Raskind, 1998). Students' use of computers has also been shown to contribute to the development and maturation of cognitive abilities. Application of computer activities is discussed in pertinent chapters of this book: reading (Chapter 11), writing and spelling (Chapter 12), and mathematics (Chapter 13). In this section, we will discuss several software programs that are particularly suited to secondary-level students.

HyperStudio is a computer-based multimedia application that is excellent for use with students at the secondary level. With this application, students can use text, graphics, sounds, and music when developing stories and reports. They can use storyboarding techniques to develop a story before entering it into the computer. Students can work individually, in pairs, or in small groups. Smith & Levine (in press) report that with HyperStudio, students with learning disabilities successfully used material from the curriculum subject areas (such as science, history, or social studies) to create exciting projects (Raskind, 1998).

Two other multimedia software programs that have been used successfully with secondary students are Opening Night (Mecc) and Hollywood High (Theatrix Interactive). Students can create plays that demonstrate the use of plot, problem/resolution, setting, and number of characters. Students can also program each character to move (Archibald, 1998).

The Internet is an up-to-date, innovative facet of technology that offers many resources and activities for students with leaning disabilities. In one study, adolescents with learning disabilities went to a cybercamp where they learned to use the Internet. Students who had always seemed reluctant to speak within a group initiated lively discussions with their peers about their "finds" on the Internet. Part of the camp curriculum involved having students keep a journal of interesting places that they found on the Internet and reporting their discoveries to others (Goldstein, 1998). New web sites are continually being developed, and much of the fun of using the web involves finding and exploring them.

Wissick & Gardner (1998) suggest the following web sites for learning how to use the Web:

- Miami Science Museum at **http://www.miamisci.org**
- Modular Web Teaching Pyramid—Wolfgram Memorial Library, Widener University at **http://www2.widener.edu/Wolfgram-Memorial-Library/pyramid.htm** or at **http://www.science.widener.edu/~withers/webeavl.htm**
- NetLearn: Internet Learning Resources Directory at **http://rgu.ac.uk/~sim/research/netlearn/web.htm**
- BCK25KOL lessons at **http://web.csd.sc/edu/bck2skol/fall/**

As a general note, a useful resource for using technology with students with learning disabilities is *Technology for Students with Disabilities: A Decision Maker's Resource Guide* (1997), published by the NSBA and the U.S. Department of Education's Office of Special Education Programs ($25). This book can help educators find assistive technology for students with learning disabilities. For ordering information about this and additional technology publications, contact the ITTE (Institute for the Transfer of Technology to Education at **http://www.nsba.org/itte**.

Chapter Summary

1. Many individuals continue to be affected by their learning disabilities into adolescence and their adult years. Secondary programs are increasing to serve adolescents with learning disabilities.

2. Adolescents with learning disabilities must cope with the dramatic changes in their lives caused by puberty as well as with problems related to their disabilities. Special characteristics of adolescents with learning disabilities include passive learning styles, poor self-concept, inept social skills, attentional disorders, and lack of motivation.

3. More adolescents with learning disabilities are being placed in regular education classes. Several special problems occur at the high school level. The education reform movement and performance standards create pressure for high school graduation. Another difficulty is that content-area teachers are usually not oriented to the problems of students with learning disabilities. Coteaching is used in many inclusive settings.

4. The transition from school to adult life is full of complexities for all adolescents. Adolescents with learning disabilities need extra support and assistance to successfully make this challenging transition. Transition refers to a change in status from behaving primarily as a student to assuming emergent adult roles in the community. Adult roles include employment, postsecondary education, maintaining a home, involvement in the community, and establishing satisfactory personal and social relationships. Transition planning involves the student, school transition personnel, adult agency services, and community supports.

   IDEA 1997 requires that adolescents with identified learning disabilities have written transition plans beginning when they reach age 14. The goals in the plan can be competitive employment, vocational training, going to college, or supported employment.

5. Important components for success in high school include intensive instruction in reading and mathematics, explicit instruction in survival skills, and completion of all required high school courses for graduation. The types of instructional and curriculum programs for learning disabilities in the secondary schools include basic skills instruction,

tutorial instruction, functional skills instruction, and work-study programs.

6. Learning strategies instruction helps adolescents with learning disabilities learn how to learn and become active, efficient learners. The learning strategies approach teaches students *how* to learn rather than *what* to learn. Students can then apply the learning strategies to all areas of the secondary curriculum. The strategies intervention model (SIM) is a method for teaching learning strategies to adolescents with learning disabilities.

7. Postsecondary and college programs for young adults with learning disabilities are growing, and an increasing number of colleges have developed special services for college students with learning disabilities. Section 504 of the Rehabilitation Act provides protection for college students with learning disabilities.

8. For many individuals, learning disabilities do not end with high school graduation. Rather, they continue as a lifelong problem. Adults with learning disabilities are receiving an increasing amount of attention.

9. Mastery of computer skills is becoming increasingly important for all students, especially adolescents and adults. HyperStudio, Opening Night, and Hollywood High are a few of many programs that have been used successfully with secondary students. Research shows that use of the Internet helps motivate students to learn and interact with others.

Questions for Discussion and Reflection

1. Describe three characteristics of adolescents with learning disabilities, and discuss how these characteristics affect high school achievement.

2. Why do special problems that occur at the secondary level affect adolescents with learning disabilities? How do these problems differ for elementary-age students?

3. More secondary students with learning disabilities are being educated in regular classes. How can regular and special education teachers work together?

4. What is a transition plan for secondary students with learning disabilities? What are some of the possible goals for such a transition plan? At what age does the law require the transition plan to be written? Do you think this age is too early or too late?

5. Several different approaches are used for teaching adolescents with learning disabilities. Describe three of these approaches.

6. What is the purpose of using learning strategies instruction for adolescents with learning disabilities? Describe each of the eight steps in learning strategies instruction.

7. How does Section 504 of the Rehabilitation Act affect the education of college students with learning disabilities? Describe three accommodations in college for students with learning disabilities.

8. What kinds of problems do people with learning disabilities encounter in their adult lives? What would you advise for adults with learning disabilities in the world of work?

9. How can computer technology be effectively integrated into the secondary school curriculum? Name a few skills that students with learning disabilities can acquire and build upon through using the computer and Internet.

Key Terms

accommodations *(p. 314)*

basic academic skills instruction *(p. 320)*

collaborative teaming *(p. 311)*

content-area teachers *(p. 311)*

coteaching *(p. 311)*

functional or survival skills *(p. 319)*

learned helplessness *(p. 307)*

learning strategies instruction *(p. 322)*

passive learners *(p. 307)*

performance standards *(p. 313)*

reasonable accommodations *(p. 327)*

Section 504 of the Rehabilitation Act *(p. 327)*

strategies intervention model (SIM) *(p. 324)*

transition planning *(p. 316)*

tutorial instruction *(p. 320)*

work-study program *(p. 321)*

From Theories to Teaching Strategies

10 Oral Language: Listening and Speaking

CHAPTER OUTLINE

art IV considers the major areas of learning that affect children and youth with learning disabilities: oral language (Chapter 10), reading (Chapter 11), written language (Chapter 12), mathematics (Chapter 13), and social/emotional behavior (Chapter 14). In each of these chapters, there are two major sections: *Theories,* the concepts underlying that area of learning, and *Teaching Strategies,* methods for improving skills in that area of learning.

The three chapters on language (Chapters 10–12) constitute an integrated unit. Each chapter focuses on a different form of language: oral language (Chapter 10), reading (Chapter 11), and writing (Chapter 12). Their organic unity comes from the underlying integrated language system.

This chapter highlights oral language, which includes listening and speaking. In the Theories section, we review theories of oral language: the underlying language system, the interrelationships of the forms of language, and the use of language as a communication process. The chapter also discusses theories of language acquisition, linguistic structures, types of language problems exhibited by individuals with learning disabilities, early literacy, and the assessment of oral language. The Teaching Strategies section provides instructional methods for listening (including phonological awareness) and speaking.

THEORIES

Language is a wondrous thing. It is recognized as one of the greatest of human achievements—more important than all the physical tools invented in the last two thousand years. The acquisition of language is unique to human beings. Although other animals have communication systems, only humans have attained the most highly developed system of communication—speech. Language fulfills several very human functions: It provides a means of communicating and socializing with other human beings, it enables the culture to be transmitted from generation to generation, and it is a vehicle of thought.

An untreated language deficit, then, may diminish an individual's capacity to function as a whole person. Many individuals with learning disabilities manifest some aspect of language inadequacy. Unlike physical disabilities, a language disorder cannot be seen. Yet its effects are often more pervasive and insidious than are the effects of acute physical impairments.

We know that language is essential for development, thinking, and human relationships, yet many aspects of language remain mysterious. How is language acquired by the child? What is the connection between symbolic language and the thinking process? What are the links between language and cognitive and social learning? How does a language impairment affect learning? Such questions are still under investigation.

ORAL LANGUAGE, READING, AND WRITING: AN INTEGRATED SYSTEM

Language appears in several forms: *oral language* (listening and speaking), *reading,* and *writing;* all are linked through an integrated language system. Concepts about teaching oral language, reading, and writing have undergone tremendous change. The interrelationships of oral language, reading, and writing serve to build the core of the language system. As children gain competence and intimacy with language in one form, they also build knowledge and experience with the underlying language core, which are then carried into learning language in another form. What the child learns about the language system through oral language provides a knowledge base for reading and writing, and what the child learns about language through writing improves reading and oral language. These interrelationships also affect language difficulties. When a child exhibits language difficulty in one form, the underlying language deficit often reappears in other forms. For example, a child who has a language delay at age 5 may have a reading disorder at age 8 and a writing disorder at age 14 (Adams, Foorman, Lundberg, & Beeler, 1998; Torgesen, 1998; Liberman, 1997; Lyon, 1995b, 1996).

Early experiences in listening, talking, and learning about the world provide the foundation for learning written language. Early language experiences in turn become the foundation for reading. Through experience with oral language, children learn about the linguistic structures of language, expand their vocabularies, and become familiar with different types of sentences. They are building vocabulary (or semantic knowledge) and an awareness of sentence structure (syntactic knowledge) that they will use in reading and writing. Examples of oral language experiences that help children develop such knowledge include learning words; hearing stories, songs, and rhymes; and recognizing repeated refrains in books (Adams et al., 1998; Richek, Caldwell, Jennings, & Lerner, 1996). Functional knowledge about sentence sequences or the formation of plurals in one form of language carries over to other forms.

By becoming familiar with the sounds of language, children develop a language base for reading. Poor readers who lack an awareness of phonological sounds need specific practice with language sounds. Phonological experiences promote familiarity with language sounds, establishing the basis for word-recognition skills in reading (Torgesen, 1998; Moats, 1998; Adams et al., 1998; Ball & Blachman, 1991; Lyon, 1995b; Lindamood, 1994).

In summary, language is an integrated system, and many areas of learning depend upon mastery of language and facility with verbal symbols. As the child matures, language plays an increasingly important part in the development of the thinking processes and the ability to grasp abstract concepts. Words become symbols for objects, classes of objects, and ideas. Language permits human beings to speak of things unseen, of the past, and of the future.

Forms of the Language System

The language system encompasses the language forms of listening, speaking, reading, and writing. The acquisition of these language skills follows a general sequence of development: (1) listening, (2) speaking, (3) reading, and (4) writing. As shown in Figure 10.1, the different language forms have an underlying language core that integrates the four forms of language. Moreover, experiences with each language form strengthen the underlying language core, which in turn improves the individual's facility in other language forms.

Historically, as civilization evolved, oral language systems for listening and speaking developed hundreds of thousands of years before the creation of written systems for reading and writing. In fact, in historical terms the written form of language is relatively recent; even today, many societies in the world have only a spoken language and no written language.

People usually develop the oral skills of listening and speaking first, and these are considered the **primary language system.** Reading and writing are considered the **secondary language system** because we are dealing with a symbol of a symbol. Whereas the spoken word is a symbol of an idea or a concrete experience, the written word is a symbol of the spoken word. Hellen Keller's primary language system was finger spelling because she learned it first, and Braille was her secondary system. The case example entitled "Language and Learning" illustrates Helen Keller's first experiences in language learning.

Figure 10.1

Language Forms and the Integrated Language Core

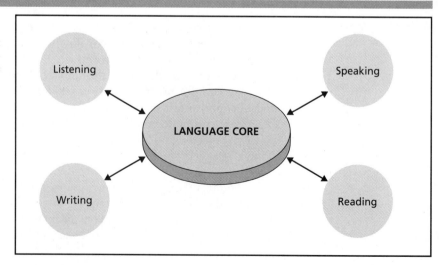

CASE EXAMPLE

LANGUAGE AND LEARNING

HELEN KELLER

One of the most dramatic illustrations of the dependency of thought on language is the experience of Helen Keller as she became aware that things have symbolic names that represent them. The impact of this discovery, made at age 7, changed her behavior from that of an intractable, undisciplined, animal-like child to that of a thinking, language-oriented human being. Her teacher, Anne Sullivan, described the events (Keller, 1961):

> I made Helen hold her mug under the spout while I pumped. As the cold water gushed forth, filling the mug, I spelled "w-a-t-e-r" in Helen's free hand. The word coming so close upon the sensation of cold water rushing over her hand seemed to startle her. She dropped the mug and stood as one transfixed. A new light came into her face. She spelled "water" several times. Then she dropped to the ground and asked for its name and pointed to the pump and the trellis and suddenly turning around she asked for my name . . . All the way back to the house she was highly excited, and learned the name of every object she touched, so

that in a few hours she had added thirty new words to her vocabulary. (pp. 273–274)

Helen Keller also described the transformation caused by her own awareness of language:

> As the cool water gushed over one hand she spelled into the other the word *water,* first slowly, then rapidly. I stood still, my whole attention fixed upon the motion of her fingers.
>
> Suddenly I felt a misty consciousness as of something forgotten—a thrill of returning thought; and somehow the mystery of language was revealed to me. I knew then that "w-a-t-e-r" meant the wonderful, cool something that was flowing over my hand. That living word awakened my soul, gave it light, hope, joy, set it free. . . . I left the wellhouse eager to learn. Everything had a name, and each name gave birth to a new thought. (p. 34)

Helen Keller had learned that a word can be used to signify objects and to order the events, ideas, and meaning of the world about her. Language had become a tool for her to use.

Two of the four forms of the language system can be categorized as input or *receptive language modes*, and the other two are output or *expressive language modes*. Listening and reading are input or *receptive* skills, feeding information into the central nervous system. Speaking and writing are output or *expressive* skills in which ideas originate in the brain and are sent outward.

One implication for teaching is that abundant quantities of input experience and information are needed before output skills can be effectively executed. This principle has been concisely stated as "*intake* before *outgo*." Students should not be assigned to produce output, such as a written theme, before they have been exposed to adequate input experiences, such as discussions, graphic organizers, field trips, or reading. These experiences will enhance the productivity of the output, the written composition. The integrating mechanism between the input and the output is the brain or central nervous system. The relationship between input and output skills is diagrammed in Figure 10.2.

Figure 10.2

Relationship of the Four
Forms of Language

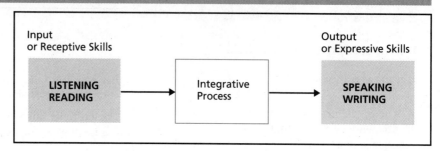

Figure 10.2

Relationship of the Four
Forms of Language

Language as a Communication Process

Language provides a way for people to communicate with each other. There are other methods of communication, such as gesturing, using body language, and using sign language. The communication process between two people consists of sending a message (expressive language) and receiving a message (receptive language). As Figure 10.3 illustrates, *Person A,* who is transmitting an idea to *Person B,* must convert her idea into language symbols. She codes the message into either sound symbols (speaking)

Figure 10.3

**A Model of the
Communication Process**

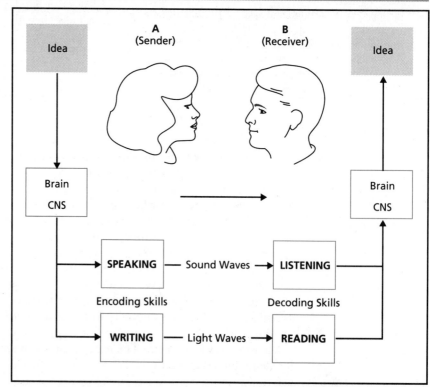

or visual graphic symbols (writing). *Person B,* who receives the message, must then convert the symbols back into an idea. He decodes either the sound symbols (listening) or the visual graphic symbols (reading).

A breakdown can occur anywhere in this process. For example, in the expressive portion of the communication process, the impairment could be in formulating the idea, in coding it into spoken and written language symbols, or in remembering the sequences of previous speaking or writing. In the receptive portion of the communication process, the impairment could be in the reception and perception of the symbols through the eye or ear, in the integration of these stimuli in the brain, or in the recall or memory as it affects the ability to translate the sensory images into an idea. Understanding the communication process helps teachers deal with the communication problems of students with learning disabilities.

THEORIES OF HOW CHILDREN ACQUIRE LANGUAGE

Several factors contribute to the acquisition of language, factors based on behavioral, cognitive, and social theories of language learning. Each perspective augments our understanding of language learning and contributes intervention strategies.

Behavioral Theories

Behavioral theories exaplain that language is learned through environmental influences and that behavioral principles shape language learning. An early behavioral perspective of language learning was proposed by Skinner (1957), who said that language is learned through imitation and reinforcement. The child gradually acquires language through imitation of language sounds in the environment and through the reinforcement of those attempts.

For example, 22-month-old Peter, who was not yet saying words, was sitting in a high chair at a family gathering of about twenty-five people. When Peter gestured that he wanted to get up, his mother said the word "up," and Peter imitated the word. When Peter uttered the sound, all twenty-five people stood up and said "up." Peter looked around and was delighted with the response he had generated. He uttered the sound of "up" again and again, each time eliciting the same response from the group. By the end of the meal, Peter had learned his first word.

The current behavioral view of language learning has expanded with learning principles of behavioral teaching strategies, such as prompting, modeling, positive reinforcements, and scaffolding. In *prompting,* the adult provides a natural verbal cue, such as "What do you want?" when the child points. In *modeling,* the parent or teacher engages in language while the child observes. In providing a *positive reinforcement,* the adult rewards the child for a language attempt with attention and praise. In *scaffolding,* the adult provides graduated cues to assist the child in acquiring more advanced language (for example, if the child says, "Da," the adult could respond with

"Daddy"). In all of these interventions, the adult in the child's environment plays an essential mediating role in shaping language learning opportunities and in bringing them to the child's attention (Lerner, Lowenthal, & Egan, 1998; Cook, Tessier, & Klein, 1996; Fey, Windsor, & Warren, 1995).

Innatist Theories

The innatist theories offer an alternative explanation of language development. This view is based on the concept that language learning is biological (Lenneberg, 1967) and on the psycholinguistic concepts of language learning (Pinker, 1995; Chomsky, 1965). This explanation emphasizes that children are biologically predisposed to learn and use language and that human beings have an innate capacity for dealing with the linguistic universals common to all languages. What the child learns is not a string of words but rather a set of transformational rules. These rules enable the child, as speaker, to generate an infinite variety of novel sentences and, as listener, to understand an infinite variety of sentences (McCormick & Schiefelbusch, 1990; Wiig & Semel, 1984; Chomsky, 1965).

There are two key questions from this perspective:

- What is it about language that enables a child to learn it, internalize it, and use it?
- What is it about a child that permits him or her to learn the language?

In the process of learning a language, the child has a limited number of primary linguistic experiences. At a rather young age, the child hears speech and begins to understand and to repeat certain words and sentences. From these limited experiences, the child soon is able to understand and to produce new sentences. To add to this mystery, children in all cultures have the ability to perform this feat in their native language at about the same chronological and developmental stage. When it is time to enter school, children who are developing along a normal linguistic pattern use language nearly as well as the adults in their immediate environment, using and understanding almost all the common sentence patterns.

The child learning a language does not merely learn a set of sentences but rather internalizes the total language system which is needed for understanding and making new sentences. The transition in language learning from the simple stages of comprehension and expression to the stage at which the child uses a complex mechanism of language is so rapid that accurate notation of the child's language acquisition and development by observation alone is very difficult. In that brief period of transition, the child suddenly learns to use the mechanisms of grammar. The innatist view is that the task of learning human language is so complex that some important aspects of language cannot be learned but are innate within the brain.

In terms of intervention, the innatist theory sees language as a natural human phemonenon, that is, the child's language will develop and flourish

Early literacy refers to the child's first entrance into the world of words, language, books, poetry, and stories. *(© Bob Daemmrich/ The Image Works)*

if the child is given a stimulating language environment. Language learning is compared to learning to walk; rather than being completely acquired, some aspects of spoken language "unfold" or "flower" under appropriate developmental and environmental circumstances. Most children internalize the language system before they reach school age; they understand and respond to the language of others in a meaningful way (Owens, 1995; Fey, Windsor, & Warren, 1995; Lahey, 1988). However, it is estimated that up to 8 percent of children exhibit deviations and delays in language development and require additional time and teaching to internalize the language system. (Tallal et al., 1997).

Cognitive Theories

Cognitive theories provide another view of language learning that highlights the linkages among language, thinking, and experiences (Fey, Windsor, & Warren, 1995; Lahey, 1988; Wiig & Semel, 1984). Vygotsky (1962) proposed that a child (even an infant) begins with some prelinguistic thoughts or existing knowledge base and that the development of language and thinking are independent. Another important factor is that language development requires interpersonal and social experiences (Fey, Catts, & Larrivee, 1995).

Piaget (1970) theorized that language is acquired as the child takes in (assimilates) the language in the environment and then modifies (accommodates) it with his or her own thoughts and knowledge. The child's thoughts and language interact as the thinking processes direct which parts of the language will be assimilated and how they will be accommodated. The controlling factor is the child's existing knowledge base, or *schema*. For example, the infant has some existing thoughts and knowledge about milk. When the word *milk* is used by the parent, the child takes in this new word and modifies the knowledge base by integrating the existing concept of milk with the word *milk*. As children mature, their language becomes more sophisticated because they understand more complex language and modify it with more complex thoughts. Through language experiences, children strengthen, add to, or change their existing knowledge schema, or cognitive structure.

When a child accommodates new information with an existing knowledge schema, the process is often obvious. For example, 4-year-old Aaron had gone fishing several times with his grandfather. He had had the experience of catching the fish, cooking it, and eating it. When Aaron came to his grandparents' house for Thanksgiving and looked at the turkey on the table, he tried to accommodate the new information with his existing fishing schema. His thoughts led to his question, "Did you catch it with your fishing pole, Grandpa?"

In terms of language instruction, the cognitive perspective suggests that the fundamental elements are the interactions of the child, the language, and the environment (Owens, 1995; Windsor, & Warren, 1995; Lahey, 1988). Parents and teachers must ascertain what the child already knows and provide active experiences to build meaning and thinking. As children use their experiences to expand their existing knowledge and language bases, their language and meaning gradually develop.

Social Theories

Social theories of language acquisition stress the interpersonal contributions to language learning, the reciprocal relationship between the child and the parent or others. Language learning is promoted in a naturalistic environment where human relationships help the child become an active processor of language (Lerner, Lowenthal, & Egan, 1998; Vygotsky, 1962).

In terms of intervention, the child and adult have a reciprocal relationship because they influence each other in the communication process. The adult plays a mediating role, shaping learning opportunities to bring them to the attention of the young child. For example, 18-month-old Sarah knew the word *plane* and the phrase *all gone*. While Sarah was sitting at the kitchen table with her mother, an airplane flew over the house. Her mother, initiating a conversation, pointed up questioningly as the plane flew overhead, and Sarah said, "plane." When the noise disappeared, her mother continued the conversation, asking, "What happened?" Sarah replied, "Plane all gone," along with a gesture of extended hands to show "all gone." With her mother's guidance, Sarah produced her first sentence.

LINGUISTICS AND LANGUAGE LEARNING

Linguistics is the systematic study of language and its nature, development, function, and use. Linguistics concepts have implications for every form of language: listening, speaking, reading, writing, spelling, grammar, and usage. Linguistics also offers a useful framework for analyzing any language and the language deviations of students with learning disabilities.

Attitudes Toward Language

Teachers of students with learning disabilities must understand that language is a dynamic, living, changing tool, responsive to the needs and circumstances of the people using it. Language is not a static, unchanging, or prescribed set of rules. Linguists encourage a respect for the various dialects of English and for the diverse languages used in our schools. A student's own language is one of his or her most important links with the outside world. The significance of this can be appreciated when we realize that language provides one of the starting points in the educative process.

Linguistic Systems

A few basic linguistic concepts and terms are needed to discuss linguistic systems: *phonology, morphology, syntax, semantics,* and *pragmatics.*

Phonology   **Phonology** is the system of speech sounds in a language. The smallest unit of sound is a **phoneme**. Different languages and dialects use different phonemes. For example, the word *cat* contains three phonemes: *k-a-t*. Phoneme recognition is important in learning to read as well as in oral language. **Phonics** is the recognition, analysis, and synthesis of phoneme elements in written words. Learning phonics is difficult for some children.

Morphology   **Morphology** is the system of meaning units in a language. The smallest unit of meaning is a **morpheme**. Different languages indicate meaning changes through different morphological forms. In standard English, for example, the word *boy* is one morpheme or meaning unit; and the word *boys* contains two morphemes or meaning units (*boy* plus plurality). A child who has not internalized the morphemic structure of standard English might say, "There are three boy."

Children who are unaware of exceptions to morphemic rules may overgeneralize. For example, they might formulate the past tense of *fight* and *go* as *fighted* and *goed*. Typical preschool and first-grade children have well-established rules of morphology. Children can apply their morphological rules to nonsense words. For example, Berko (1958) showed each child a drawing of a birdlike creature and said, "This is a *wug*." Next, she pointed to a drawing with two of these creatures and asked each child to complete the sentence, "There are two _____." By applying the morpho-logical rule for plurals, children gave the answer of *wugs* by adding the phoneme /z/.

Syntax **Syntax** refers to the grammar system of language—the way the words are strung together to form sentences. Different languages have dif-ferent syntactic or grammatical systems. In the English language (unlike some other languages), word order is extremely important to convey mean-ing. Thus, "John pushes a car" differs in meaning from "A car pushes John." A child with a syntactic language disorder may not have learned how to order words in a sentence. Further, in English we can transform the order of the words—still keeping the same subject—to generate a new meaning. The sentence "Mother is working" can be transformed to gener-ate "Is Mother working?" A child with a syntactic language disorder may be unable to generate such sentence transformations. For example, when children with language disorders are asked to repeat the question form of "Is the boy running?" many simply repeat the simple declarative form "The boy is running."

The active form of a sentence—"Mother bakes cookies"—is easier to comprehend than the passive form: "The cookies are baked by Mother." Children with language disabilities may not understand a passive sentence. To illustrate, when first graders are shown two pictures, one of a cat chasing a dog and the other of a dog chasing a cat, and asked to point to the picture called "The cat is chased by the dog," many children choose the incorrect picture because they do not understand the passive form of the sentence.

Semantics **Semantics** refers to word meaning in language. Pupils who have meager vocabulary understanding or usage and those who have diffi-culty relating a string of words to a meaningful association may have a se-mantic language disorder. The development of vocabulary (the semantic system) continues throughout life. In contrast, the morphology, phonology, and syntax systems normally become firmly established during the preschool years.

A student with a semantic disorder may understand a concept but not possess the appropriate word to express it. For example, referring to twins, one child with learning disabilities talked about the "two girls with the same face." She did not know the word *twin* to communicate her idea.

Pragmatics **Pragmatics** refers to the social side of language, how the speaker uses language in his or her environment. Pragmatics takes into account the relationship between speaker and listener; the speaker's assess-ment of the listener's degree of knowledge; behaviors such as taking turns in conversations, staying on topic, and asking pertinent questions; and other factors, such as general appearance, involvement in the conversation, and eye contact. Some students with learning disabilities have poor skills in interpreting, inferring, comparing, and responding to the language of others, problems which may cause many social difficulties (Owens, 1995; Bryan, 1991b; Lahey, 1988). These individuals have more difficulty in the social use of language, are less effective in their communication attempts, and do poorly in the listening role of a conversation. They interrupt the speaker more frequently in order to insert their own ideas in the conversation (Bryan, 1991b).

Another element of the language system is *intonation,* or the sound patterns of spoken language, including *pitch* (melody), *stress* (accent), and *juncture* (pauses). The intonation system of each language is different. An example of intonational differences is the contrast between the sound of *White House cat* (a certain cat that lives in the residence of the president of the United States) and *white house cat* (a domesticated cat with white fur). Students who have been unable to capture the intonation system of English may speak in a monotone and without expression.

When listening to the intonation pattern of infants, one cannot distinguish the babbling of a 3-month-old Chinese child from that of a Dutch or an American baby of the same age. By the age of 6 months, however, the intonation of the babbling is similar to the intonation of the language in the infant's immediate environment; the babbling is in Chinese, Dutch, or English. The "native language" of a 6-month-old baby can be identified through tape recordings of the baby's babbling. The baby's babble consists of the intonation patterns and the phonemes of the native language.

LANGUAGE PROBLEMS OF STUDENTS WITH LEARNING DISABILITIES

As noted earlier, language problems of one form or another are the underlying basis for many learning disabilities. At least 8 percent of children fail to develop speech and language at or near the expected age (Tallal, Miller, Jenkins, & Merzenich, 1997). Oral language disorders include poor phonological awareness, delayed speech, disorders of grammar or syntax, deficiencies in learning vocabulary, and poor understanding of oral language. Many students with learning disabilities do not do well in situations requiring extensive language interactions and conversations, and they are also less skillful in maintaining a conversation. (Bryan, 1991b). Adolescents and adults with learning disabilities often continue to have poor oral language and communications skills (Vogel & Adelman, 1993; Johnson & Blalock, 1987).

Language disorders also appear in written language performance, affecting reading, writing, or spelling. Students with reading problems often have underlying disabilities in oral language. Young children who exhibit oral language delays as preschoolers usually do acquire oral language skills, but their basic language disorder often reappears several years later as a reading disability (Torgesen, 1998; Tallal, Allard, Miller, & Curtiss, 1997).

In the following section, we discuss several areas related to oral language learning: phonological awareness, temporal acoustical processing, rapid automatized naming (RAN) or word finding, language disorders, nonstandard English, and limited English proficiency.

Phonological Awareness

Phonological awareness (and phonemic awareness) refer to the child's recognition that words are made up of sound elements or phonemes, the sounds of speech. Phonemes are abstract units of language, more abstract than either words or syllables. Learning to reflect about the phoneme sounds of language is more difficult than learning to understand and use language. Many children who have difficulty in learning to read are not sensitive to the phoneme sounds of language and words. Deficits in phonemic processing underlie many of the difficulties encountered by poor readers and spellers (Adams, Foorman, Lundberg, & Beeler, 1998b; Torgesen, 1998; Lyon, 1995b, 1996; Liberman & Liberman, 1990; Ball & Blachman, 1991; Lerner, 1990).

Successful beginning readers must know more than the difference between such words as *cat* and *hat* and must be able to do more than hold these words in memory. They must also have an awareness of phoneme sounds within these words to appreciate that the words *cat* and *hat* differ in a single phoneme sound. Students with poor phonological abilities are unable to tap out the number of sounds within a word such as *cat*. If a child is unable to reflect about the sound elements of language and to perceive the sounds within words, the alphabetic system will remain a mystery (Torgesen, 1998).

Phonological awareness appears to be developmental in children. When children were asked to count the phonemes in familiar monosyllabic words, they showed the following developmental patterns. At age 4, none of the children could count the phonemes, but one-half of them could count the syllables. By age 5, 20 percent could count the phonemes in words, and one-half succeeded in counting the syllables. By the end of first grade, 70 percent of the 6-year-olds could count the phonemes, and 90 percent could count the syllables. However, many children with learning disabilities who have reading problems had not attained these phonological abilities (Mann, 1991).

When children are aware of the phonological system, they can gain entry into the alphabetic system. Written English is an alphabetic system, with written letters of the alphabet representing speech sounds. (Some written languages, such as Chinese, are pictorial.) Research showing a linkage between a lack of phonological awareness and poor reading has been conducted in many alphabetical languages: American English, British English, Swedish, Spanish, French, and Italian (Mann, 1991; Liberman & Liberman, 1990). The implications of phonological awareness for teaching children with learning disabilities are

1. *The skills of phonological awareness can be taught to children.* When children receive training in phonological awareness, they become more successful in reading and spelling than children in control groups who receive other kinds of training (Rosner, 1999; Troia, Roth, Graham, 1998; Torgesen, 1998; Adams et al., 1998b; Bradley & Bryant, 1985).

2. *As early as possible, teachers should help children to become aware of the sounds of speech.* Nursery rhymes, word play, and word games help children understand segmental structure—first in words, then in syllables, and finally in phonemes.

3. *Children should learn the letters of the alphabet as well as the letter names and their sounds.* The sounds of the words can be taught by helping children learn to segment (or break) syllables into phonemes and words into syllables.

The Teaching Strategies section of this chapter presents strategies for building phonological awareness (see p. 364). Tests of phonological awareness are listed in Table 10.1 of this chapter and described in Appendix C.

Temporal Acoustical Processing

One explanation for why children do not develop speech and language at or near the expected ages is that some children have trouble processing sounds quickly enough to distinguish rapid acoustical change in speech. During the course of normal language, the speech sounds come in too fast for these children to recognize and decipher. A series of studies conducted by Paula Tallal and her colleagues over many years suggests that children who have delays in speech and language development may have difficulty with rapid temporal integration of acoustically varying signals and serial memory. These deficits impact central auditory processing in the millisecond time range (Tallal, Allard, Miller, & Curtiss, 1997; Tallal, Miller, Jenkins, & Merzenich, 1997).

The research on **temporal acoustical processing** difficulties in children with language delays led to the development of a computer program called *FastForWord*. This program alters the acoustics of speech, drawing out sounds and then speeding them up—stretching out certain speech sounds and emphasizing rapidly changing speech components by making them slower and louder. The purpose of this program is to help children understand and recognize the acoustically altered speech. Children engage in specifically designed computer games in which they follow spoken commands produced by the computer. The instructions for these computer games require children to distinguish various sound cues. As each child's performance improves, these sound cues gradually become shorter in duration and spaced more closely. The researchers report that the children made great improvements in oral language skills. After four weeks of intensive instruction, their oral language skills improved to the point that they approached or exceeded normal limits for their ages in both speech discrimination and language comprehension. The program encourages the children with rewards and closely monitors their progress. The FastForWord program is used with children ages 5–12 (Tallal, Allard, Miller, & Curtiss, 1997; Tallal, Miller, Jenkins, & Merzenich, 1997; Merzenich, Jenkins, & Tallal, 1996; Tallal, Miller, & Merzenich,

1996; *Time*, 1996; Scientific Learning, 1995). The web site is **http://www. scientificlearning.com.**

Rapid Automatized Naming (RAN): Difficulty with Word Finding

Some children with language delays have difficulty with **rapid automatized naming (RAN)**. That is, they cannot quickly and automatically name objects and are slow with word finding. For example, when given the task of naming pictures as they are shown, these children cannot rapidly produce the names of the pictures. A slowness in word finding and naming is an accurate predictor of later reading and learning disabilities. Slowness in naming is probably due to memory retrieval problems, which make it difficult to access verbal and phonological information (German, 1994; Moats, 1994b; Catts, 1993; Wolf, 1991).

Problems with naming and slow word retrieval affect adolescents and adults with learning disabilities as well as children. Word-finding problems can be lifelong sources of difficulty in reading, learning, and using expressive language (Mann, 1991). One useful program for word-finding problems is the *Word Finding Intervention Program* (Meyer, Wood, Hart, & Felton, 1998; German, 1993, 1994).

Tests for assessing word-finding abilities are listed in Table 10.1 of this chapter and are described in Appendix C.

Language Disorders

Language disorders differ from speech disorders. **Speech disorders** are abnormalities of speech, such as articulation difficulties (for example, the child cannot pronounce the *r* sound), voice disorders (for example, a very hoarse voice), or fluency difficulties (stuttering). Language disorders are much broader, encompassing disorders of the entire spectrum of communication and verbal behavior, including such problems as delayed speech; disorders of vocabulary, word meanings, or concept formations; the misapplication of grammatical rules and syntax; and poor language comprehension.

Many students with learning disabilities have an underlying language disorder. Some children have a **language delay.** They may not talk at all or may use very little language at an age when language normally develops. A child who is not speaking at age 4 has a language delay. The case example entitled "Language Delay" describes Noah's experience with this condition.

As noted in Chapter 7, the relatively common childhood condition known as *otitis media* can seriously impair language learning in children (Hutton, 1984; Reichman & Healey, 1983). *Otitis media* involves an infection of the

CASE EXAMPLE

LANGUAGE DELAY

Noah G., age 5 years and 6 months, was in kindergarten when his parents were contacted about problems he was having in school. The kindergarten teacher said that Noah did not seem to get along with the other children in class. He had no friends, would often "strike" out and hit his classmates, and was especially disruptive during the "conversation time" and story periods. He refused to participate in class activities such as the puppet show that was being prepared for presentation to the parents. The kindergarten teacher said that when she did not know what Noah wanted, this situation often provoked a tantrum.

Mrs. G. said that Noah does not want to go to school and that it is sometimes difficult to get him to go to his class. In describing his developmental history, Mrs. G. said that Noah was born six weeks prematurely, weighing four pounds and five ounces, and that he had been placed in an incubator for a short period. He was a colicky baby and had difficulty nursing. His motor development was average; he crawled at 8 months and walked alone at 12 months. Language development was slow. He spoke his first word at 24 months and did not begin speaking in sentences until age 3. Since he could not communicate with others, he often resorted to pointing and grunting to make his desires known and frequently had temper tantrums when others did not understand what he wanted. Noah does not get along well with his two older sisters. Both sisters are very verbal and do not give Noah much chance to say anything. When Noah is asked a question, his sisters answer before he can respond. Mrs. G. said that the doctor suspected a hearing loss when Noah was younger. He had many colds as a toddler and had a condition the doctor called *otitis media,* with fluid behind the eardrums. The doctor put tubes in Noah's ears when he was 4, and his hearing tested normal after this procedure.

The speech teacher observed Noah during class and reported that he played alone most of the time. During the storytelling period and show-and-tell time, he wandered about the room. Often, when another child was playing with a toy, Noah would grab it. If the other child did not give the toy up readily, Noah would hit his classmate until he got it. He listened very little and did not talk to other children in the class. He seemed to tire of one activity very quickly, moving on to another.

During the multidisciplinary evaluation, the speech teacher checked Noah's hearing with an audiometer, and his auditory acuity was normal. The school psychologist tested Noah with an IQ test, the *Wechsler Preschool and Primary Scale of Intelligence—Revised*. His full-scale IQ score was in the normal range (FSIQ 101), with his performance IQ score (PIQ 119) substantially higher than his verbal IQ score (VIQ 84).

The case conference team recommended that Noah be placed in a developmental kindergarten and receive language therapy from the speech-language pathologist in the school, who would also work with Noah's parents and kindergarten teacher to develop language activities for the home and the inclusion kindergarten.

middle ear that can cause hearing loss. Even if the hearing loss is temporary and mild, it can lead to a language delay if it occurs at stages that are critical for language learning in young children.

Some children use speech but have strange syntactical patterns or confused word order, or they use inappropriate words. The child with this type of language deficit may at age 5 still say, "Why not don't he eats?" Such language disorders may occur even if these children have encountered a rich language environment and have had ample opportunity to hear and participate in Standard English.

Studies show that students who have had various kinds of oral language disorders as preschoolers often have later problems with other forms of language, such as reading and writing. Severe reading problems are associated with language difficulties in both elementary-age children and adolescents. Compared with normal readers, poor readers have less verbal fluency, smaller speaking vocabularies, poorer organizational and integrative skills, and inferior syntactic ability. They exhibit deficits in semantics, syntax, and phonology (Richek, Caldwell, Jennings, & Lerner, 1996; Blachman, 1997).

Language disorders are sometimes referred to as childhood aphasia or developmental aphasia. *Acquired aphasia* is a medical term used to identify adults who lose the ability to speak because of brain damage due to a stroke, disease, or accident. The term **developmental aphasia** is used to describe the child who has severe difficulty in acquiring oral language, and it implies that the disorder is related to a central nervous system dysfunction (Wiig & Semel, 1984).

There are several forms of language disorder. Some children have problems in listening (or receiving symbolic auditory information); others have difficulty in talking (using auditory verbal symbols); and still others have difficulty reading or writing language. The 3-year-old who does not appear to understand simple directions, the 4-year-old who has not yet learned to speak, or the 10-year-old who cannot read or write may have a language disorder.

Receptive and Expressive Language Disorders   Oral language disorders are frequently classified as **receptive language disorders** (problems understanding oral language) or **expressive language disorders** (problems using oral language or talking). Some children have global language disorders, problems with both receptive and expressive language that affect both understanding and the use of language.

Receptive Language Disorders   The process of understanding verbal symbols is called **oral receptive language;** a disorder of this process is called receptive aphasia. Receptive language is a prerequisite for the development of expressive language.

Some children cannot understand the meaning of even a single word. Others have difficulty with more complex units of speech, such as sentences or longer speech units. A child with receptive language problems may be able to understand single words such as *sit, chair, eat,* and *candy* but may have difficulty understanding a sentence using those words, such as "Sit on the chair after you eat the candy." Some children understand a word in one context but are unable to relate it to another context. The word *run* may be understood as a method of locomotion, but the child may not get the meaning when the word is used in reference to baseball, a faucet, a woman's stocking, or a river. *Echolalia,* the behavior of repeating words or sentences in parrotlike fashion without understanding the meaning, is another form of a receptive language disorder.

Some children are unable to discriminate between the pitch levels of two tones (tone discrimination), and others cannot discriminate or blend isolated single-letter sounds. Another receptive language problem is the inability to recognize small word parts within a sentence (morphemic discrimination)—such as the *z* sound difference between "the cows ate grass" and "the cow ate grass."

Expressive Language Disorders   The process of producing spoken language is called **oral expressive language,** and a disorder in this process is called **expressive aphasia** (Owens, 1995; Fey, Windsor, & Warren, 1995; Wiig & Semel, 1984). Children with this disorder depend on pointing and gesturing to make their wants known. Children with oral expressive language disorders can understand speech and language produced by others, they do not have a muscular paralysis that prevents them from talking, and they do well on nonverbal tasks. Yet these children have difficulty in producing speech or in talking (Owens, 1995; Fey, Windsor, & Warren, 1995; Wiig & Semel, 1984).

Language pathologists identify several clinical conditions related to expressive language. **Dysnomia** is a word-finding problem or a deficiency in remembering and expressing words. Children with dysnomia may substitute a word like *thing* for every object they cannot remember, or they may attempt to use other expressions to talk around the subject. For example, when asked to list the foods she ate for lunch, one 10-year-old girl used circumlocution in describing a "round red thing that rhymed with potato," but she was unable to remember the word *tomato.* Another condition is **apraxia,** in which children remember the sound of the word, but they cannot at will move or manipulate their speech musculature to make the appropriate sounds, even though they do not have a paralysis. In yet another type of oral expressive language disorder, a child is able to speak single words or short phrases but has difficulty formulating complete sentences.

Nonstandard English

A **language difference,** in contrast to a language disorder, can also affect school learning. For example, the student's language may be a dialect of **standard English,** such as an Appalachian dialect or Black English. The student's language is similar to that of others in the student's immediate environment, is appropriate for the surroundings, and causes no difficulty in communicating with others within this environment. These students do not have a language disorder, but their language difference can interfere with understanding and using Standard English and with school learning.

There can be a mismatch between the student's language system and the language system of the school. Abstract concepts, scientific analysis, logical thinking, and the communication of subtle ideas require a mastery of a complex, sophisticated language system. Students who use an English dialect and have not learned Standard English may find schoolwork conducted in Standard English to be difficult.

Limited English Proficiency

In today's pluralistic society, an increasing number of students come from homes in which a language other than English is spoken. Currently, more than 15 percent of the students in the United States are identified as Hispanic, and it is expected that by the year 2020, 25 percent of children within the United States will be of Hispanic decent (Gersten, Brengelman, & Jimenez, 1994). Spanish speakers represent 76 percent of the non-English-language population, but there are more than 100 distinct language groups served in the schools of the United States (Ortiz, 1997). Children with limited English proficiency (LEP) have many difficulties in classes taught entirely in English. The number of LEP students is expected to increase to as high as 3.4 million by the year 2000 (Ortiz, 1997).

Children who are truly bilingual understand and use two languages well, their native language and the second language—English. In fact, the research shows that true bilingual abilities are associated with higher levels of cognitive attainment (Hakuta, 1990; Cummins, 1989). Bilingual acquisition involves a process that builds on an underlying base for both languages. The duality of languages does not hamper overall language proficiency or cognitive development for bilingual children.

However, the problem for many linguistically diverse students is that they have **limited English proficiency (LEP)**, difficulty understanding and using English. Some of these students speak only in their native language; others use both English and their native language but still have considerable difficulty with English. A child's native language provides the foundation upon which English language skills are built. Students who use their native language effectively are likely to acquire and use English appropriately, but students who have problems in their native language also experience problems in English as a second language (Ortiz, 1997; Krashen, 1992). Additionally, research shows that a student may acquire conversational English in six months but not have the language proficiency to support the complex demands of academic development in English. Reaching that level may take up to two or more years (Ortiz, 1997; Carrasquillo & Baecher, 1990; Cummins, 1989).

In addition to their limitations in English, some linguistically diverse children also have learning disabilities. They must cope not only with learning English but also with their underlying language disorders and learning disabilities. If a child has a language disorder in his or her primary language, the language problem will also be reflected in the second language (Ortiz, 1997; Garcia & Malkin, 1993).

Methods for learning a second language include *ESL*, *bilingual*, *sheltered English*, and *immersion* methods.

- **ESL** stands for "English as a second language." In this method, students learn through carefully controlled oral repetitions of selected second-language patterns. If students come from many different language backgrounds, this approach might be advisable.

- In the **bilingual method,** students use their native language for part of the school day and use the second language (English) for the other portion of the school day. The objective of the bilingual program is to strengthen school learning through the native language and gradually to add the secondary language. The underlying philosophy is that students will recognize and respect the importance of their native culture and language in American society. In the bilingual method, then, schooling is provided in two languages. Academic subjects are usually taught in the native language, and the student receives oral practice in English. For bilingual students with underlying basic language disorders and learning disabilities, however, learning two languages simultaneously may be confusing (Garcia & Malkin, 1993; Baca & Cervantes, 1989).

- **Sheltered English** is a method of teaching children who have some proficiency in English by having students learn English more rapidly through instruction with printed materials that are written in English, typically used for a content-area subject. The rationale for this approach is that spoken language is fleeting and inconsistent over time. In written language, the text is stable and does not pass the learner by. With written text, students can reread and reconsider what is being learned (Gersten et al., 1994). The sheltered English approach has been used with children whose native language is Spanish. The students continue to use Spanish for part of the day, while English is used in teaching certain subjects with written materials, such as reading or social studies. The teaching of English is merged with this instruction. Wide reading of high-interest stories in English has helped develop English-language competence (Gersten et al., 1994).

- In the **immersion method,** students are "immersed" in, or receive extensive exposure to, the second language. In fact, where there is no formal instruction for a person learning a second language, this is essentially what occurs. Individuals simply learn through this type of repeated exposure as they live daily in the mainstream of the dominant-language society. Immersion is the instructional method for schoolchildren in Canada, where it is used to teach French to English-speaking children by enrolling them in French-speaking immersion schools (Genesee, 1985).

The research on the best methods for teaching students who have learning disabilities and whose native language is not English is still inconclusive. Teachers must be particularly sensitive to the needs of these students and recognize that proficiency in English requires time. These teachers need competencies in both learning disabilities and in teaching students with limited English proficiency. Some suggestions for LEP students who have learning disabilities are given in the box entitled "Effective Practices for LEP Students with Learning Disabilities" (Ortiz, 1997; Gersten et al., 1994).

EARLY LITERACY

The importance of providing young children with a literary environment is recognized as essential to the world of language. **Early literacy** refers to the child's early entrance into the comprehensive world of words, language, books, poetry, and stories. It includes helping children become aware of print, words, and the sounds of language. The early literacy philosophy encourages young children to enjoy experiences with stories and books and encourages early writing (National Research Council, 1998).

It is especially important that children with learning disabilities be given an abundant and rich literature environment. From an early age they should hear stories, tell stories, and even write journals and stories. Story reading helps build oral language experiences. Predictable books should be used that have a pattern or refrain, and one should encourage children to repeat the predictable elements. One should also read and reread favorite stories and have the children listen to them on tapes while following along in their books.

Methods that foster early literacy are described in the box entitled "Activities to Promote Early Literacy" (National Research Council, 1998; Richek et al., 1996):

ASSESSING ORAL LANGUAGE

The purpose of assessing oral language is to determine what language abilities the child has acquired, what language problems (if any) the child exhibits, and how well the child uses language functionally. This information helps in planning the teaching. Assessment should consider the two sides of oral language: listening and speaking. Language assessment measures include informal measures and formal tests.

Informal Measures

Often the most valuable information is obtained by observing as the child uses language functionally in a real environment, such as a class or recreational setting. When rating scales are used in assessment, an informant (usually a parent) provides information about the child's language development and usage. Informal assessments offer valuable information about

ACTIVITIES TO PROMOTE EARLY LITERACY

- *Engage children in oral language activities.* Provide children with many opportunities to talk and to use oral language.
- *Surround young children with a literacy environment.* Supply and read many books, stories, and poems and then discuss them.
- *Introduce concepts about print.* Point out that print carries meaning and can be read from left to right and from top to bottom. Show that words are separated by spaces.
- *Use word and sound games.* Play games to help children become aware that spoken words are constructed from sounds. Teach rhyming games, nursery rhymes, and poetry.
- *Build alphabet knowledge.* Help children recognize alphabet letters and encourage them to write these letters.
- *Make children aware of letter-sound correspondence.* Help children begin to see the relationship between sounds and letters.
- *Encourage early writing.* Have materials for writing available. Children may scribble or just write letters or draw pictures.
- *Help children build a beginning reading vocabulary.* Plan activities to alert children to their first sight words. For example, compile a collection of their favorite words or logos.

the child's language ability, but informal assessment techniques are not standardized.

An informal measure of listening can be obtained by assessing the child's ability to comprehend a story that is read aloud. This listening test is often used as part of an informal reading inventory (IRI). See Chapter 11. The procedure requires the teacher to read aloud stories that are graded for difficulty level. Then the student is asked comprehension questions to determine how well he or she understood this material. In an informal reading inventory, the child's listening level is often compared to the child's reading level (Richek et al., 1996).

Formal Tests

Formal tests are standardized instruments for gathering information about oral language development; a number of examples are listed in Table 10.1. (These and other tests are described more fully in Appendix C.)

EFFECTIVE PRACTICES FOR SUPPORTING LEP STUDENTS WITH LEARNING DISABILITIES

- Be responsive to cultural and individual diversity.
- Teach English-language reading to develop English-language competence.
- Be familiar with assessment tools, recommended practices, and acceptable accommodations for LEP students.
- Help students transfer what is learned in one language to the other language.
- Provide opportunities to move from learning and producing limited word translation and fragmented concepts to using longer sentences and expressing more complex ideas and feelings.
- Encourage home-school collaboration.
- Encourage communication among general and special education staff members.

Table 10.1

Oral Language Tests (These tests are described in Appendix C.)

Test	Age or Grade Tested
Auditory Discrimination Tests	
Wepman Test of Auditory Discrimination	Ages 4–9
Goldman-Fristoe-Woodstock Test of Auditory Discrimination	Ages 2–16+
Auditory Discrimination in Depth (Lindamood)	All ages
General Oral Language Tests	
Boehm Test of Basic Concepts—Revised	Grades K–2
Carrow Elicited Language Inventory	Ages 3–8
Clinical Evaluation of Language Fundamentals—Revised (CELF-R)	K–12
Comprehensive Receptive and Expressive Test	Ages 4–17
Detroit Tests of Learning Aptitude—3 (DTLA-3)	Ages 6–17
Developmental Sentence Scoring Test	Ages 2½–6

Table 10.1 (continued)

Test	Age or Grade Tested
General Oral Language Tests (continued)	
Expressive One-Word Picture Vocabulary Test—Revised	Ages 2–12
Expressive One-Word Picture Vocabulary Test— Upper Extension	Ages 12–15
Fullerton Language Test for Adolescents	Ages 11–adult
Houston Test for Language Development	Ages 6 months– 6 years
Illinois Test of Psycholinguistic Abilities (ITPA)	Ages 2½–10
Let's Talk: Inventory for Adolescents	Ages 7–adult
Let's Talk: Inventory for Children	Ages 4–8
Merrill Screening Test	Grades K–1
Oral Expression Scales—Oral, Written, and Language Scales (OWLS)	Grades K–2
Test for Auditory Comprehension of Language—Revised	Ages 3–10
Test of Adolescent Language and Adult Language— 3 (TOAL-3)	Ages 12–18
Test of Language Development—2: Intermediate (TOLD-2: Intermediate)	Ages 8½–13
Test of Language Development—2: Primary (TOLD-2: Primary)	Ages 4–9 months– 12 years
The WORD Test (Adolescent)	Ages 12–17
The WORD Test (Elementary)	Ages 7–11
Listening Tests	
Brown-Carlsen Listening Comprehension Test	Grades 9–12
Carrow Test for Auditory Comprehension of Language	Ages 3–11
Listening Comprehension Scales—Oral, Written, and Language Scales (OWLS)	Ages 3–21
Northwestern Syntax Screening Test	Ages 3–7
Peabody Picture Vocabulary Test—Revised	Ages 2–18
Sequential Tests of Educational Progress (STEP): *Listening*	Grades K–12
Test de Vocabulario en Images. Peabody (Spanish version of the *Peabody Picture Vocabulary Test—Revised*)	Ages 2½–18
Speech Articulation Test	
Goldman-Fristoe Test of Articulation	Ages 2–16+

(continued)

Table 10.1 (continued)

Test	Age or Grade Tested
Phonological Awareness Tests	
The Assessment of Phonological Processes	Ages 2–12
Bankson-Bernthal Test of Phonology	Ages 3–21
Comprehensive Test of Phonological Processing	Preschool–primary
Lindamood Auditory Conceptualization Test	Preschool–Adult
Test of Awareness of Language Segmentation	Ages 4½–7
Phonological Awareness Test	Ages 3–12
Test of Phonological Awareness	Preschool–primary
Word-Finding Tests	
Test of Word Finding	Ages 6½–13
Test of Adolescent and Adult Word Finding	Ages 12–80

TEACHING STRATEGIES

The integrated language system consists of the language forms of listening, speaking, reading, and writing. Spelling and handwriting can be considered part of writing. This chapter presents teaching strategies for the oral language skills of listening and speaking. Strategies for teaching reading are presented in Chapter 11, and the strategies for the written language skills of writing and spelling are presented in Chapter 12.

Oral language has two contrasting sides: understanding oral language (listening) and producing oral language (speaking).

LISTENING Listening is an often neglected element of language learning. Students are typically expected to acquire the ability to listen without special instruction. However, many students do not acquire functional skills in listening by themselves. Over half the people referred to medical hearing specialists for suspected deafness have no defect in hearing acuity and no organic pathology that would cause their seeming hearing impairment.

Listening is a basic skill that can be improved through teaching and practice. One explanation for poor listening skills is that students today are so bombarded with constant sound that many have actually learned to "tune out" what they do not wish to hear, and they have become skillful at *not* listening. Students who have learned not to listen should be taught to become auditorily attentive and "tuned in."

For some students, a learning problem stems from an inability to comprehend speech, a receptive language disorder. These students may avoid language activities because listening is so distressing.

Listening differs from hearing, which is a physiological process that does not involve interpretation. One can *hear* a foreign language with good auditory acuity but be unable to *listen* to what is being said. In contrast to hearing, listening demands that one select appropriate meanings and organize ideas according to their relationships. In addition, listening calls for evaluation, acceptance or rejection, internalization, and, at times, appreciation of the ideas expressed. Listening is the foundation of all language growth, and the child with a deficit in listening skills will have a disability in all the communication skills.

There are significant differences between listening and reading. The reader can reread and study the material, but the listener can hear the material only once and then it is gone. (Of course, using a tape recorder modifies this difference.) Readers can regulate their own speed, going slower or faster as their purpose and the difficulty of the material dictate, but the listener's speed of listening is set by the speaker. The listener has additional clues from the speaker's voice, gesture, appearance, and emphasis, but the reader cannot derive such supporting information from the printed page. The listener-speaker combination also offers more opportunity for feedback, questioning, and a two-way discussion than reading offers.

When teachers ask students to *listen,* they do not want them simply to *hear,* or to recognize the words being spoken. Students who are directed to listen are expected to comprehend the communication message being sent.

The following techniques are designed to help students develop listening skills. Listening skills can be categorized into successive levels that require increasingly complex abilities:

- Phonological awareness of language sounds
- Understanding words and concepts and building a listening vocabulary
- Understanding sentences and other linguistic elements of language
- Listening comprehension
- Critical listening
- Listening to stories

Children need many opportunities to practice communication skills, both with listening and with oral language activities. *(© Elizabeth Crews/ Stock Boston)*

Phonological Awareness of Language Sounds

As the discussion on p. 352 indicates, important skills for learning to read are perceiving and recognizing phoneme the sounds of our language. For success during the beginning stages of reading, the child must hear individual phoneme sounds of the language and be aware that the words he or she hears are composed of individual sounds within each word. This ability and awareness help prepare the child for learning phonics.

The following language activities are designed to build phonological awareness.

1. Nonsense. Have children listen to and detect the slight change in the name of a familiar story or poem, such as "Baa, Baa, Purple Sheep" or "Twinkle, Twinkle, Little Car."

2. Clapping names. Ask children to clap out syllables in names and words. For example, clap "Jenn-i-pher" (3 claps) or "Zip-pi-ty-doo-dah" (5 claps).

3. Finding things: initial phonemes. Use real objects or pictures of objects. Say the name of the object and ask children which picture or object begins with the same sound. Children can group those objects in one place, put them in one container, or paste their pictures into a chart. For example, the initial consonant *m* may be presented with *milk, money, moon, man,* and *monkey.*

4. Take away a sound. Have children say their names or a word without the initial sound. For example, say, "———enjamin." Children in the group must identify the whole word.

5. Add a sound. Say a word pair, with the second word adding a sound. For example, say "girl, girls" or "mile, smile."

6. Troll talk: blending games. The troll talks funny, saying the sounds of words separately. The children must guess the word by blending the sounds. For example, the troll utters the phonemes "ch-ee-z," "p-e-n," "f-u-n," or "What is your n-ā-m?" The children blend the sounds and identify the word or answer the questions.

7. Nursery rhymes. Read nursery rhymes to the child. Look at the pictures and emphasize the rhyming elements. Children enjoy the many repetitions of nursery rhymes. Occasionally leave off the word that is the rhyming element and have the child say the word: "Jack and Jill went up the———."

8. Rhyming words. Rhyming can be a very enjoyable game for preschoolers. Songs with rhymes and nursery rhymes are valuable sources of rhyming activities. The singer Raffi (1986) has a series of delightful audiotapes that have great appeal to young children. Children find this question, which is asked in one of the songs, very funny: "Did you ever see a fly kissing a tie?" A follow-up game can be developed to think of other rhyming words as substitutes. One group of preschoolers thought of "Did you ever see a hook

Figure 10.4

A Card for Segmenting Speech Sounds

kissing a book?" and "Did you ever see a grandma kissing a pajama?" What an enjoyable way to gain phonological awareness!

9. Segmenting speech sounds. To help children recognize the speech sounds in words, put a picture representing a short word on a card. Draw a rectangle underneath the picture and divide it into the number of phonemes in the word. Have the child say the word slowly, putting a counter in each square as each sound is articulated (Ball & Blachman, 1991). Figure 10.4 illustrates a card for the word *sun.*

10. Counting sounds. Obtain counters such as Popsicle sticks or tongue depressors. Place a picture with a short word on a card. Use words with the same number of letters as sounds (for example, *cap, run,* and *lamp*). For sound counting, say the word slowly and have the child put down a counter for each sound. One set of cards can have both pictures and words, and another can have only the pictures (Richek et al., 1996).

11. Rhyming riddles. The teacher selects a group of words, one to rhyme with *head* and the other to rhyme with *feet.* Then the teacher asks a riddle so that the answer rhymes with either *head* or *feet.* The children then point to the part of their body that has a name that rhymes with *head* or *feet* to answer the riddle. For example, "When you are hungry, you want to———." The children point to their *feet* because *eat* rhymes with it. Repeat by naming other parts of the body to elicit words that rhyme with *hand* or *knee* or with *arm* or *leg* (Richek et al., 1996).

12. Sound substitutions. This activity is harder than rhyming. Raffi (1986) has a song on one of his audiotapes called "Apples and Bananas" that has great appeal for young children and uses phonemic substitution.

> I like to eat, eat, eat
> Apples and Bananas (Repeat)
>
> I like to ate, ate, ate
> Ai-pples and Ba-nainas (Repeat)
>
> I like to oat, oat, oat
> Oa-ples and Ba-noanos (Repeat)
>
> I like to ight, ight, ight
> Igh-pples and Ba-nighnas (Repeat)

13. Deleting sounds. In this activity, children learn to take a word apart, remove one sound, and pronounce the word without that sound—for example, to remove a syllable: "Say *playground.* Now say it without *play.*" It is more difficult to remove a phoneme: "Say *ball.* Now say it without the *b.*" "Say *stack.* Now say it without the *t.*"

14. Beginning sounds. Giving three words like *astronaut, mountain,* and *bicycle,* have the students tell which word begins like *milk.* Ask the children to think of words that begin like *Tom,* to find pictures of words that begin like *Tom,* or to find pictures of words that begin with the sound *T.* Show them three pictures of different objects (for example, a pear, a table, and a car) and ask the students to select the picture of an object with a name that begins like *Tom.*

15. Consonant blends, digraphs, endings, and vowels.   Similar activities can be devised to help the students learn to perceive auditorily and to discriminate other phonic elements.

16. Beating out names.   Beat the syllables in the rhythm and accent of names of the children in the group. For example, for a name like *Marilyn McPhergeson,* you might beat out the following pattern:

Drumbeat: LOUD-soft-soft   soft-LOUD-soft-soft
           1 2 3   4 1 2 3

17. Sound boxes.   Use a box, approximately the size of a shoe box, for each sound being taught. Put the letter representing the sound on the front of the box, and collect toys, pictures, and other objects for the students to place in the appropriate box.

18. Initial consonants—same or different.   Say three words, two of which have the same initial consonant—for example, *car, dog,* and *cat.* Ask the students to identify the word that begins with a different sound.

19. Consonant-blend bingo.   Make bingo cards with consonant blends and consonant digraphs in the squares. Read words and ask the students to cover the blend that begins each word.

20. Hearing syllables.   Say multisyllabic words and have students listen and determine the number of syllables in each word. Clapping or identifying the vowel sounds they hear helps students determine the number of syllables.

21. Substitutions.   Help the students learn to substitute one initial sound for another to make a new word. For example: "Take the end of the word *book* and put in the beginning of the word *hand,* and get something you hang coats on." (The word would be *hook.*)

22. Hearing vowels.   Many children find that vowels are more difficult to hear than consonants. Begin by having students listen for and identify the short vowels; having students refer to key words is helpful. For the short *a,* for example, use a picture of an apple or an astronaut. After the students recognize the short vowel, you can have students identify the long vowel sound. For example, for the long *a* sound, *ape* or *ache.* Then contrast the sound of the short vowel with that of the long vowel. The techniques used for the initial consonants and consonant blends may be adapted for the vowel sounds.

23. Riddle rhymes.   Make up riddle rhymes and encourage students to make up others. One such example is, "I rhyme with *look.* You read me. What am I?"

24. Awareness of rhyming sounds. Have students listen to a series of three words, such as *ball, sit,* and *wall* or *hit, pie,* and *tie,* and tell which two words rhyme.

25. Same or different. Say pairs of words or nonsense words—such as *tag-tack, big-beg, singing-sinking, shin-chin,* and *lup-lub*—and ask the student to determine if they are the same or different.

Understanding Words and Concepts

Listening requires that students acquire a listening vocabulary. Students must understand the names of objects, actions, qualities, and more abstract concepts. It is easier to teach words that carry primary lexical meaning (such as nouns, verbs, adjectives, and adverbs) than to teach structure or function words (such as prepositions and articles) that indicate relationships within sentences.

1. Names of objects. To help students understand names, use actual objects, such as a ball, pencil, or doll. Sometimes you will have to add exaggeration and gestures to help the student with a severe receptive disorder understand the meaning of the word that symbolizes the object.

2. Verb meanings. It is more difficult to teach the concept of a verb than the name of an object. You can illustrate verbs such as *hop, sit,* and *walk* by performing the activity.

3. Pictures. Pictures are useful in reinforcing and reviewing the vocabulary that has been taught.

4. Concepts of attributes. Words that describe the attributes of objects can be taught by providing contrasting sets of experiences that illustrate the attributes. Examples of such sets are *rough-smooth, pretty-ugly, little-big,* and *hot-cold.* Both concrete objects and pictures are useful in teaching attributes.

5. Development of concepts. If you combine experiences with particular objects, you can help students understand the concept beyond the object itself. For example, in learning about the concept of a chair, you might show the students a kitchen chair, an upholstered chair, a folding chair, a lawn chair, a doll chair, and a rocking chair. Through experiences with many chairs, the students develop the concept of chair.

6. Classes of objects. An even broader classification of objects must be made and labeled with a word. For example, the word *food* refers not to any single type of food but to all foods. The students therefore could be taught objects that "are food" and could be asked to remove from a display any objects that "are not food."

Understanding Sentences

Understanding sentences is more difficult than understanding single words. Some students with learning disabilities need structured practice in understanding sentences.

1. Directions. Give simple directions in sentences to provide the students with needed experiences in understanding sentences. For example, you can say, "Give me the blue truck" or "Put the book on the table."

2. Finding the picture. Line up several pictures. State a sentence describing one of them and ask the students to point to the correct picture. You can make this exercise harder by adding more sentences to your description of the picture.

3. Function words. Function or structure words establish structural relationships between parts of a sentence and grammatical meaning. They include noun determiners, auxiliary verbal forms, subordinators, prepositions, connectors, and question words. These words cannot be taught in isolation; they must be taught within a sentence or phrase. You might, for example, teach words such as *on, over, under, behind, in front of, beneath, inside,* and *in* by placing objects *in* a box or *under* a chair while saying the entire phrase to convey the meaning.

4. Riddles. Have students listen to a sentence and fill in the word that fits. For example, for the word *sled,* you might say, "I am thinking of a word that tells what you use to go down a snowy hill."

Listening Comprehension

This skill is similar to what has been called reading comprehension; however, the information is received by hearing rather than by reading language. Thinking is a key component of listening comprehension.

1. Following directions. Read a set of directions for making something. Have the materials ready and ask students to follow the directions step by step.

2. Understanding a sequence of events. Read a story and ask the students to picture the different events in the order in which they happened. Pictorial series, such as comic strips, can help illustrate the events of the story, and you can mix the pictures and ask the students to place the series in the proper chronological order.

3. Listening for details. Read a story to the students and ask detailed questions about it. Phrase your questions as true-false statements or questions that ask who, what, when, where, and how. In another type of detail exercise, you might read a manual on a subject, such as how to care for a new pet, and then ask students to list all the things that should be done.

4. Getting the main idea. Read a short but unfamiliar story and ask the students to make up a good title for the story. Read a story and ask the students to choose the main idea from three choices.

5. Making inferences and drawing conclusions. Read part of a story that the students do not know. Stop at an exciting point and ask the students to guess what happens next. In another approach, read a story that a student has started and explain that the author did not know how to finish it. Ask the other students to suggest an ending.

Critical Listening

Good listening means not only understanding what is said but also being able to listen critically and to make judgments about and evaluations of what is being said.

1. Recognizing absurdities. Tell a short story with a word or phrase that does not fit the story. Ask the students to discover what is funny or foolish about the story. For example, you could say, "It rained all night in the middle of the day," or "The sun was shining brightly in the middle of the night."

2. Listening to advertisements. Have the students listen to advertisements and determine *how* the advertiser is trying to get the listener to buy the products. Adolescents enjoy detecting propaganda techniques.

3. Correct me. Use flannel board figures while telling a story. Plan obvious errors through discrepancies between what is said and what is placed on the board. Have the students listen for and correct the mistakes.

Listening to Stories

Story reading is a useful strategy for building oral language experiences. Frequently reading stories to small groups of children with language problems helps them to acquire language, figure out grammar, and learn the structure of stories (Richek et al., 1996).

1. Read stories frequently (at least once each day) to small groups of five to seven children.

2. To maximize the children's understanding, use strategies (cuing) to focus on the meaning while you read.

3. Involve all the children in the story by asking questions appropriate to their individual levels of language acquisition.

4. Select predictable books (ones that have a pattern, refrain, or sequence) to read aloud, encouraging the children to repeat the predictable element.

5.   Select well-illustrated books (ones with many illustrations closely tied to the text) to read aloud.

6.   Throughout the story, ask the children thought-provoking questions.

7.   Read and reread favorite stories and let the children listen to them on tapes or records while following along in their books.

8.   Provide related follow-up activities using a variety of formats and manipulative materials.

SPEAKING   Oral language, the child's first language, includes listening and speaking. Yet instructional practices too often neglect oral language and emphasize the written forms of communication—reading and writing. The activities in this section focus on speaking.

Stages of Oral Language Development

A general overview of a child's oral language development provides a perspective for viewing language deviations. A child's first attempt to use vocal mechanisms is the birth cry. In the short span of time from the birth cry to the full acquisition of speech, the child goes through many stages.

Vocalization during the first 9 months of life is called *babbling*. During this stage, children produce many sounds, those in their native language as well as those found in other languages. Infants derive pleasure from hearing the sounds they make, and making such sounds gives them the opportunity to use the tongue, larynx, and other vocal apparatuses and to respond orally to others. Children who are deaf begin the babbling stage but soon stop because they receive no satisfaction from hearing the sounds they produce. Parents of children with language disorders often report that their child does not engage in the activities of babbling, gurgling, or blowing bubbles. These children should be encouraged to engage in such oral play to help them have the normal experiences of language acquisition.

By about 9 months, the babbling softens and becomes *jargon*. Children retain the phoneme sounds that are used in the language they hear. Their vocalizations reflect the rhythm and melody of the oral speaking patterns of others around them. Although their intonational patterns may be similar to those of adults, children do not yet use words at this stage; it is as though they are pretending to talk. The parents of children who are diagnosed as having language disabilities often report that their children missed this stage of development.

Chinese children have been observed to have a mastery of basic Chinese intonation patterns by 20 months of age, a feat that is very difficult for an English-speaking adult to accomplish. Yi was a baby from China who was adopted at 10 months of age. Her adoptive parents became concerned about a language disorder because she displayed no signs of language play and did not engage in jargon. The problem was happily solved when the family had lunch at a Chinese restaurant. As soon as Yi heard people talking in Chinese, she spontaneously began "talking" in jargon, using Chinese sounds and intonational patterns.

Single words, such as *mama* and *dada,* normally develop between 12 and 18 months of age. The ability to *imitate* is evident at this stage, and children may well imitate sounds or words that they hear others say or that they themselves produce. Parents often report that their child with language disabilities did not engage in verbal imitation and repetition activities.

Two- and three-word sentences, such as *Baby eat, Daddy home,* and *Coat off,* mark the next stage and follow the use of single words. Once children begin to use language, their skill in making speech increases at a remarkably rapid pace. Between 18 months, when a toddler first produces a two-word utterance, and age 3, many children learn the essentials of English grammar and can produce all linguistic types of sentences. The child's oral language development at age 3 appears to be almost abrupt; the child has an extensive vocabulary and uses fairly complex sentence structures. During this stage, reports become rather hazy—partly because things develop so rapidly and partly because as observers, we do not understand the underlying mechanism of language acquisition. By the time children enter school at age 6, they are fairly sophisticated users of the grammar of their native language, and their understanding vocabulary is large. Their speaking vocabulary is, of course, smaller.

Most children seem to acquire language in a relatively natural and easy manner, without a need for direct teaching. Many children with learning disabilities, however, do not go through the typical developmental stages of language acquisition and exhibit difficulty in acquiring one or several properties of language. Some have difficulty with the phonology of language—differentiating and producing the appropriate sounds. Others have difficulty remembering words or structuring morphological rules. Some have difficulty with grammar or syntax and in putting words together to formulate sentences. Still others have a semantic difficulty in vocabulary development.

Experiences in listening (the input, or receptive, side of language) precede speaking (the output, or expressive, side of language). Listening alone does not produce the ability to speak, but a looping or feedback process must be created in which the child both listens and speaks. The interrelationship of input and output activities provides immediate reinforcement that shapes speaking behavior. Listening to television does not seem to have an impact on the basic language patterns of the viewer. Although the speech on television may be a model of standard American English, the speech patterns of viewers reflect those of their home and peer group rather than those of television performers.

Natural Language Stimulation Activities

Teachers and parents can take advantage of many opportunities in the daily life of a child in school or at home to provide natural language stimulation (Lerner, Lowenthal, & Egan, 1998):

1. Expansion. This is a technique to enlarge and enhance the child's language. In the conversation that follows, the adult expands a child's limited utterance.

Child: "Cookie."
Teacher or parent: "'Cookie? I want cookie.' Well, here it is!"

2. Parallel talk. In this technique, the adult tries to help language develop by supplying language stimulation even when no speech is heard. As the child plays, the teacher or parent guesses what the child is thinking and supplies short phrases describing the actions, thereby placing words and sentences in the child's mind for future reference. For example, if the child is banging a block on the floor, the teacher might say: "There's a block. If I hit the block on the floor, it makes a noise. A big noise. Bang, bang, bang. Block. My block. Bang the block."

3. Self-talk. In this technique, teachers model language by engaging in activities that do not directly involve the child. As teachers complete their own tasks and work in close proximity to the child, they can capitalize on opportunities to use meaningful language stimulation that the child can hear. For example, while cutting some paper, the teacher might say, "I have to cut the paper. Cut the paper. I need scissors. My scissors. Open, shut the scissors. Open, shut. I can cut, cut, cut."

Activities for Teaching Oral Language

Next are listed a number of activities to improve the oral language skills for talking.

Building a Speaking Vocabulary
Some children with language disorders have an extremely limited vocabulary and a very specific, narrow, and concrete sense of the meaning of words. Throughout their lives, people have a much larger listening vocabulary than speaking vocabulary. Young children are able to understand words long before they are able to produce and use them. Children with a language disorder may be able to recognize words when they hear them but be unable to use those words. Adults with known brain injuries may lose their ability to remember words easily as a result of damage to the language area of the brain. This condition, as noted earlier in the chapter, is *dysnomia,* meaning the inability to remember the names of objects. Children may substitute another referent like *thing, whatsit,* or *that* or a gesture or

pantomime for the word they cannot bring to mind. The following exercises can help children use words and build an accessible speaking vocabulary.

1. Naming. Have the children name common objects in or outside the room (chair, door, table, tree, or stone). Have a collection of objects in a box or bag. As each is removed, have the children name it. Have the children name colors, animals, shapes, and so forth. A collection or a file of good pictures of objects provides excellent teaching material. You can make pictures more durable and washable by backing them with cardboard and covering them with a self-adhesive transparent material.

2. Department store. The game of department store (or hardware store, supermarket, restaurant, shoe store, and so on) gives the children an opportunity to use naming words. One child plays the role of the customer and gives orders to another, who is the clerk. The clerk collects pictures of the ordered items and names the items while giving them to his or her customer.

3. Rapid naming. Give the students a specified length of time (such as one minute) to name all the objects in the room. Keep a record of the number of words named to note improvement. You can also ask the students to rapidly name objects in pictures. Another variation could be related to sports, the outdoors, pets, and so forth.

4. Missing words. Have the students say the word that finishes a riddle. For example: "Who delivers the mail? *(mail carrier)*. I bounce a _____ *(ball)*." Read a story to the children, pausing at certain places to leave out words. Have the children supply the missing word. The use of pictures helps in recalling and naming the object.

5. Word combinations. Some words can best be learned as part of a group. When one member of the group is named, the children may be helped to remember the second. For example: *paper-pencil, boy-girl, hat-coat,* and *cats-dogs.* Series such as days of the week and months of the year may also be learned in this fashion.

6. Troublesome words. Be alert for troublesome words. When you note such a word, you may be able to give an immediate lesson on it and then plan for future exercises using that word.

Producing Speech Sounds
Some children have difficulty initiating the motor movements required to produce speech. Such children may be able to remember the words but unable to activate the appropriate speech musculature, although they have no paralysis. As noted earlier in this chapter, the condition has been described as a type of *speech apraxia.* A speech specialist who works with problems of articulation may be helpful in treating this condition.

1. Exercising speech muscles and organs. The children are encouraged to use the various muscles used in speaking for nonspeech activities, such as smiling, chewing, swallowing, whistling, yawning, blowing, laughing, and making various tongue movements.

2. Feeling vibrations and observing sounds. As the teacher makes sounds, the students feel the vibrations of the sounds by touching the teacher's face or throat and observing the mouth movements and shaping during the production of sounds. The use of a mirror is helpful to enable students to observe themselves producing sounds.

Learning Linguistic Patterns

1. Morphological generalizations. Some children have difficulty learning to internalize and use the morphological structure of the language. We all must make generalizations concerning the systems of forming plurals, showing past tense, and forming possessives. We must also learn the exceptions where generalizations do not hold true. For example, the phoneme /s/ or /z/ is usually added to a word in English to show plurality: *three cats* or *two dogs.* In some cases, the sound of /ez/ is added, as in *two dresses,* or the root word is changed, as in *two men.* In a few cases, the word is not changed, as in *four fish.* Children unable to formulate such generalizations can be helped by games in making plurals. It is interesting to note that the morphemic rules of Standard American English do not always hold in dialectical variations. The morphemic generalization in a nonstandard English dialect (as well as in certain other languages) is to use the appropriate quantitative adjective but not pluralize the noun: "That cost two dollar."

2. Use pictures to build morphological generalizations. Ask children to point to the picture that describes the sentence you say aloud. For example, present two pictures, one that shows an activity in process and another that shows that same activity completed. Then say, "The boy is *painting* a picture," and ask students to choose one of the pictures. Follow that by saying, "The picture is now *painted*" and have them choose the appropriate picture. Similarly, you might pair "The dog is running" and "The dogs are running" to show plural forms.

Formulating Sentences
Some children are able to use single words or short phrases but are unable to generate longer syntactic units or sentences. In acquiring language, children must learn to internalize sentence patterns so that they can "generate" new sentences. Some linguists have said that the child becomes a sentence-producing machine. To achieve this state, the child needs many skills, including the ability to understand language, to remember word sequences, and to formulate complex rules of grammar.

1. Experiences with many kinds of sentences. Start with the basic simple sentence and help the child generate transformations. For example, two basic sentences can be combined in various ways:

Basic sentence: "The children play games."
Basic sentence: "The children are tired."
Combined sentences: "The children who are tired play games."
   "The children who play games are tired."

Sentence pattern variations can also be practiced:

Statements	Questions
Children play games.	Do children play games?
Games are played by children.	Are games played by children?
Children do not play games.	Don't children play games?
Children do play games.	Do children play games?

2. Structure words. As mentioned earlier, words such as *on, in, under,* and *who,* which show the relationship among parts of the sentence, are best taught within the sentence. Close observation reveals that many children have hazy concepts of the meanings of such words. You can help students understand these concepts if you ask them to put blocks *in, on,* or *under* a table or chair and then ask them to explain what they did. Words such as *yet, but, never,* and *which* often need clarification. Give a sentence with only the key or class words and then ask the students to add the structure words, as in this example:

"Jack—went—school—sweater."

3. Substitution to form sentences. Have students form new sentences by substituting a single word in an existing kernel sentence. For example:

"I took my *coat* off. I took my *boots* off."
"The child is *reading.* The child is *running.* The child is *jumping.*"

4. Detective game. To help students learn to formulate questions, hide an object and have students ask questions concerning its location until it is found.

Practicing Oral Language Skills

Reading specialists assert that much practice is needed in using and stabilizing newly learned reading skills; they frequently say, "You learn to read by reading." Students with a deficiency in oral expressive language also need practice and multiple opportunities to use words and to formulate sentences. Plans must be made to enable them to practice their speaking skills.

1. Oral language activities. A number of activities can be used to practice the use of oral language and speaking. These include conversations, discussions; radio or television broadcasts; show-and-tell sessions; puppetry; dramatic play; telephoning; choral speaking; reporting; interviewing; telling stories, riddles, or jokes; giving book reports; and role playing.

2. Discussion of objects. Help the students tell about the attributes of an object—its color, size, shape, composition, and major parts—and to compare it with other objects.

3. **Categories.** Place in a box items that can be grouped to teach categories, such as toys, clothes, animals, vehicles, furniture, and fruit. Ask the students to find the ones that go together and tell what they are. You can vary this activity by naming the category and asking the students to find and name the items or by putting items together and asking which do not belong.

4. **Comprehension.** Ask questions that require students to think and formulate responses. For example:

"What would you be if you dressed funny and were in a circus?"

"Why is it easier to make a dress shorter than it is to make it longer?"

"Why should you put a goldfish in a bowl of water?"

5. **"Tell me how** . . . you brush your teeth, go to school, and so forth. Also, tell me why . . .? Tell me where we do . . .?" Such questions can provide an opportunity for valuable practice.

6. **Finishing stories.** Begin a story and let the students finish it. For example:

"Betty went to visit her aunt in a strange city. When the plane landed, Betty could not see her aunt at the airport . . .. "

7. **Peabody Language Kits.** These kits are boxes containing puppets, pictures, and language lessons, all designed to develop oral language abilities. They are published by American Guidance Services.

Improving the Oral Language of Adolescents

Direct instruction in language also helps improve the oral language and communication skills of adolescents with learning disabilities. Sometimes students at the middle school or high school levels appear, at first, to have adequate oral language skills, so their true needs are often overlooked. In addition, the secondary school curriculum emphasizes performance in written language more than in oral language, so their deficiencies may go undetected. On closer observation, however, we find that the oral language of many secondary students with learning disabilities is meager. Many of the methods described earlier work for adolescents, and the following are also useful.

1. **Learning strategies.** Instruction in learning strategies is particularly useful for adolescents. Adolescents should be involved in setting the goals they are trying to reach and in selecting learning strategies to reach these goals. Self-monitoring, verbal rehearsal, and error analysis are the kinds of strategies that have been helpful in reading, and they can also be used for improving oral language (see Chapter 6).

2. **Vocabulary building through classification.** Adolescents can expand their oral vocabularies if they receive help in classifying and organizing

words. For example, they can build lists or hierarchies of words on a topic. For the topic of space exploration, they might use words that classify space vehicles, space inventions, first events that occurred in space, and so on. There are several approaches to this activity. The teacher can supply the words for classifying, the students can supply the words, or the teacher can provide a partial classification system and the students can complete it.

3. **Listening in stages.** Read the beginning of a selection to your students. After they listen to several paragraphs, stop and ask a question: "By now you should be able to answer . . . "This activity, in turn, provides a setting for the next portion of listening.

4. **Reciprocal questioning.** This is a variation of reciprocal teaching. Instead of the teacher asking the questions, the students ask the questions. The technique encourages the development of questioning skills.

5. **Sentence combining.** Say two short sentences aloud and ask students to think of all the ways in which the sentences can be combined into one sentence.

6. **Review of a group discussion.** Have students hold a short discussion on an assigned topic. After the discussion, ask them to analyze the effectiveness of the discussion. Did they keep on the topic? Did they allow others to talk? Did they direct the conversation to the right people? Did they follow through when a point was made?

7. **Explaining how to play a game.** Many students with learning disabilities have difficulty giving explanations and need practice in this activity. Such practice could consist of having students explain to another person how to play a game, how to make something, or how to do something. The recipient of the explanation can be a peer or a younger child. The students could first engage in verbal rehearsal to practice the explanation and then try to be sensitive to whether the listener understands and is able to respond to questions. Examples of subjects for explanation include the rules of a video game, how to cook and peel a hard-boiled egg, or how to play checkers or bingo. It is helpful to follow this exercise with a self-monitoring session on the effectiveness of the explanation.

COMPUTER TECHNOLOGY FOR ORAL LANGUAGE

Computer technology can be helpful in teaching oral language skills. A few select computer software programs are described in this section. Before using these in the classroom, you may wish to review the *National Educational Technology Standards for Students* to determine how they can best be incorporated into your teaching.

- **Earobics.** This is an educational software program to teach auditory and phonological awareness skills. It uses a CD-ROM and six interactive games that teach oral language skills. Cognitive Concepts, Inc., 1123 Emerson St., Evanston, IL 60201. This company may be reached by phone at (888) 328-8199 or at **http://www.cogcom.com**.

- **FastForWord.** This software program alters the acoustics of speech, slowing down the sounds, then speeding them up to help children recognize words. Scientific Learning Corp., 1995 University Ave. Suite 400, Berkeley, CA 94704. This company may be contacted by phone at (888) 665-9707 or at **http://www.scientificlearning.com.**

- **Laureat Learning Systems.** This is a series of software programs for teaching oral language skills to young children with language disorders and to other individuals with disabilities. It trains students in learning cause-and-effect, turn-taking, early vocabulary, syntax, cognitive concepts, auditory processing, and reading. Laureate Learning Systems, 110 E. Spring St., Winooski, VT 05404. This company may be reached by phone at (802) 655-4710 or at **http://www.laureatelearning.com.**

- **Lexia Software.** This is phonics-based interactive reading software that uses multisensory approaches. Lexia Software may be reached by phone at (800) 435-3940, by FAX at (781) 259-1349, or at **http://www.lexialearning.com.**

Chapter Summary

1. Language is perhaps the most important accomplishment of the human being. It is intimately related to all kinds of learning, and an untreated language disorder may diminish an individual's capacity to function as a whole person.

2. Language plays a vital role in learning. It enhances thinking and permits us to speak of things unseen, of the past, and of the future. It also serves to transmit information and to control the environment.

3. Language encompasses the elements of listening, speaking, reading, and writing, which have an underlying integrated language core and a general sequence of development. Oral language is the primary language and consists of listening and speaking. Written language is the secondary language and includes reading and writing.

4. Language is a communication process. Listening and reading are receptive language forms. Talking and writing are expressive language forms. A breakdown can occur anywhere in the communication process.

5. Theories of language acquisition include behavioral, innatist, cognitive, and social theories. Behavioral theories emphasize the role of reinforcement and imitation. Innatist theories stress that language is an innate characteristic in human beings and that there is a wholeness in language learning. Cognitive theories emphasize the role of one's structure of thinking in language learning. Social threories stress the social interactions needed for language learning.

6. Linguistics is the study of language systems and the nature, development, function, and use of language. Linguists encourage a respect for

the various versions of English and for the diverse languages used in our schools. Important linguistic concepts include phonology, morphology, syntax, semantics, and pragmatics.

7. Language problems found among students with learning disabilities include problems with phonological awareness, temporal acoustical processing, rapid automatized naming (RAN), language disorders, and nonstandard English.

8. Limited English proficiency refers to students whose first language is not English and who are in the process of learning and using English. Some children have both limited English proficiency and a language disability.

9. *Early literacy* refers to the child's early entrance into the world of words, language, stories, and books.

10. The Teaching Strategies section suggests activities for teaching listening and oral language.

Questions for Discussion and Reflection

1. Describe the communication process. Discuss the kinds of problems that a student may encounter in communicating.

2. There are several explanations for language acquisition. Compare and contrast two theories of learning language.

3. What are the major linguistic systems? Give an example of each. What kinds of problems can a student with learning disabilities encounter with each of the linguistic systems?

4. Describe a few of the problems faced by students who have limited English proficiency (LEP). Name a few practices that have been shown to be helpful in supporting these students.

5. What intervention strategies can be used for students with language learning disabilities?

6. What is meant by the term *early literacy?* Name a few methods that foster early literacy.

7. What is phonological awareness? Why is it important that young children develop skills in phonological awareness?

Key Terms

apraxia *(p. 357)*

bilingual method *(p. 359)*

developmental aphasia *(p. 356)*

dysnomia *(p. 357)*

early literacy *(p. 360)*

ESL *(p. 359)*

expressive aphasia *(p. 357)*

expressive language disorders *(p. 356)*

immersion method *(p. 359)*

language delay *(p. 354)*

language difference *(p. 357)*

language disorders *(p. 351)*

limited English proficiency (LEP) *(p. 358)*

linguistics *(p. 349)*

morpheme *(p. 349)*

morphology *(p. 349)*

oral expressive language *(p. 357)*

oral receptive language *(p. 356)*

phoneme *(p. 349)*

phonics *(p. 349)*

phonological awareness *(p. 352)*

phonology *(p. 349)*

pragmatics *(p. 350)*

primary language system *(p. 342)*

rapid automatized naming (RAN) *(p. 354)*

receptive language disorders *(p. 356)*

secondary language system *(p. 342)*

semantics *(p. 350)*

sheltered English *(p. 359)*

speech disorders *(p. 354)*

Standard English *(p. 357)*

syntax *(p. 350)*

temporal acoustical processing *(p. 353)*

11 Reading

CHAPTER OUTLINE

T his chapter on reading is the second of three chapters on the integrated language system. Reading is an integral part in the language system; it is closely linked to oral language and writing.

In the first part of this chapter, Theories, we discuss the serious consequences of reading disabilities, the condition of dyslexia, the stages of reading development, the reading process, two approaches to reading instruction, the major components of word recognition and reading comprehension, and assessment of reading.

In the second part of the chapter, Teaching Strategies, we present methods for teaching reading to students with learning disabilities. The section includes procedures for improving word recognition, building fluency, improving reading comprehension, using special remedial methods, dealing with special reading problems, and using computers in reading instruction.

THEORIES

THE CONSEQUENCES OF READING DISABILITIES

Most students with learning disabilities (at least 80 percent) encounter difficulties in reading (Lyon & Moats, 1997; Lyon, 1995b; Kirk & Elkins, 1975). Their poor reading leads to many other types of problems. Opportunities for gainful employment decrease for students with learning disabilities who are poor in reading and in overall educational achievements. Studies of secondary students with learning disabilities show that one-third drop out of school because of poor school performance (Blackorby & Wagner, 1997; Wagner & Blackorby, 1996). Youths who drop out of high school have twice the unemployment rate, have fewer opportunities for continued training, and do not have the qualifications for postsecondary school or college (Gerber, 1997; Coutinho, 1995).

In today's world, high technology and automation have spurred a demand for highly trained people. Old jobs rapidly become obsolete, making the process of retraining a necessity. It is predicted that workers in every occupation will have to retrain themselves to prepare for new jobs many times during their work careers. The ability to read efficiently is a key tool for retraining and for maintaining employment.

We live in a multimedia world, and we obtain many kinds of information through nonprint media. For many purposes, the global environment of television has replaced the world of print. Some educators have even suggested that a "bookless curriculum" be established in our schools—one that instructs through the use of nonprint media designed to relate information and to create appropriate learning experiences. Despite such signs of the declining value of reading in contemporary life, there is also contrasting evidence that reading is assuming a greater role than in the past. For example, although millions of Americans watch television to view momentous occurrences—such as tragic events of nature, special sports events, and critical political happenings—these television viewers are eager to read the newspapers the next day to make the events they have witnessed more coherent, detailed, and comprehensible. Our newest information system is the computer, which brings with it telecommunication, email, the Internet, and the World Wide Web, all of which require users to read the written electronic information on a monitor screen.

Thus, in spite of the new role that nonprint media play in providing a message, illiteracy is more debilitating than ever. If children in our modern society do not learn to read, they do not make it in life. A few generations ago, people managed to get along quite well in the business and social worlds without the ability to read, but in today's world this is no longer possible. Today, students face minimum competency tests, longer periods of compulsory education, job requirements of diplomas and degrees, and more comprehensive school testing. These hurdles, as well as the necessity of filling out application forms and taking licensing examinations, make life for the nonreader very uncomfortable and full of impassable barriers. It is said that "children must learn to read so that they can later read to learn." Indeed, since reading is the basic tool for all academic subjects, failure in school can be traced to inadequate reading skills.

DYSLEXIA

The condition known as **dyslexia** is an unusual type of severe reading disorder that has puzzled the educational and medical communities for many years. Dyslexia is one type of severe learning disability that affects some children, adolescents, and adults. The case example entitled "Dyslexia" provides statements from people with dyslexia about how this problem has affected their lives.

People with this baffling disorder find it extremely difficult to recognize letters and words and to interpret information that is presented in print form. People with dyslexia are intelligent in other ways. For example, they may have very strong mathematics or spatial skills. Although there are a number of different definitions and explanations of dyslexia (see Chapter 7, page 226), there is general agreement on four points (Hynd, 1992):

1. Dyslexia has a biological basis and is due to a congenital neurological condition.
2. Dyslexic problems persist into adolescence and adulthood.
3. Dyslexia has perceptual, cognitive, and language dimensions.
4. Dyslexia leads to difficulties in many areas of life as the individual matures.

People with dyslexia tend to find ingenious ways to hide their disability and cope with their inability to read. Even their close associates may never suspect the truth. For example, an elderly widowed gentleman, caught in

Dyslexia

Adults who have suffered from dyslexia can long recall the anguish of trying to cope with this mysterious condition in a world that requires people to read.

> *Nelson Rockefeller*
> *TV Guide, October 16, 1976*

I remember vividly the pain and mortification I felt as a boy of 8 when I was assigned to read a short passage of a scripture with a community vesper service during the summer vacation in Maine—and did a thoroughly miserable job of it.

There was something wrong with my brain. What had previously been a shadowy suspicion that hovered on the edge of consciousness became certain knowledge the year I was 9 and entered fourth grade. I seemed to be like other children, but I was not like them: I could not learn to read or spell.

> *Eileen Simpson*
> *Reversals: A Personal Account of*
> *Victory over Dyslexia*
> *Boston: Houghton Mifflin, 1979*

The first time I remember shame was when I used the wrong word or got words in the wrong order. Everyone always laughed at me. Perhaps I could have laughed too if I had been able to see the mistake I had made. But I couldn't. What I had said sounded quite logical to me. I would sit there trying hard to think what I had said, then burst out crying.... My lack of reading and writing ability became noted, not only by the teachers, but by the children, too. There was no help or even understanding. Just impatience on the teacher's part.

I can still remember the terror as the class stood up in turn to read aloud. I would start to read with sweaty hands as the print danced before my eyes. I would stammer and sputter in an effort to start. The teacher would look up, see it was me and say crossly, "Oh, for goodness sake; sit down and shut up." . . . I would do anything rather than go to school; powder my face with talcum to make me look pale; scream; have hysterics; be doubled up with pain, be sick.

> *Sue Loftus-Brigham*
> *Dyslexia Need Not Be a Disaster*
> *London: London Dyslexia*
> *Association, 1983*

I am writing to you about my husband's desperate need for help. I think he has dyslexia. Shortly after our marriage I began to notice he never read a newspaper or a book. He asked me to read labels and directions to him, explaining his eyes were not strong enough to see small print. Yesterday, our 7-year-old daughter was reading a book and asked her father to help her with a word. He grew red in the face, ran out of the room, and I found him crying. He admitted the truth. He can't read. He told me that he just can't recognize letters and words.

> *Letter to a reading problems clinic*

the social dating whirl, routinely handled the problem of dining in restaurants by putting down his menu and saying to his companion, "Why don't you order for both of us, dear? Your selections are always delicious." This man hired professionals to handle all of his personal matters, including his checkbook. His friends attributed his actions to wealth, never suspecting his inability to read.

For many years, scholars strongly suspected that dyslexia has a neurobiological basis, but until recently they have lacked the scientific evidence to support this belief. Current research in the neurosciences now offers strong evidence that dyslexia is caused by an abnormality in brain structure, a difference in brain function, and genetic factors (Shaywitz & Shaywitz, 1998; Sherman, 1995; Hynd, 1992; Galaburda, 1990). The fascinating brain research studies on dyslexia and the new technologies for assessing the linkage between brain function and learning are discussed in Chapter 7. While the neuroscientists continue their search for the causes of dyslexia, however, teachers must provide the instruction to teach these individuals how to read.

There are different methods for identifying children with dyslexia. It is important to differentiate between poor readers who have dyslexia and ordinary poor readers ("garden variety" poor readers) (Badian, 1996). The identification of children with dyslexia depends on the definition and criteria used to assess the condition. For example, if the criterion for dyslexia is a discrepancy between an IQ score and a composite reading achievement score, certain types of children will be identified (Aaron, 1997; Shaywitz, Shaywitz, Fletcher, & Makuch, 1992). If the criterion used in identifying the population is a phonological core deficit, other subjects will be identified (Stanovich & Siegel, 1994). If the criterion is "unexpected reading problems" in the light of cognitive strengths, still other individuals may be identified (Lyon, 1995a, 1996).

STAGES OF READING DEVELOPMENT

In the process of learning to read, individuals go through a series of sequential stages of reading development (Chall, 1983, 1987; Cunningham & Stanovich, 1997). These reading stages begin with the prereading stage of early literacy and end with the last stage of mature expert reading. Of course, individuals vary greatly in the rate of their progression through these stages, and many do not reach all of the stages. However, all readers go through the same sequence of development. Table 11.1 presents a brief picture of the six stages of reading development and shows how reading changes from its beginning stage to the advanced stage of mature adult reading.

The early stages of reading development are extremely critical to an individual's success in reading. Accumulating research shows that children who get off to a poor start in reading rarely catch up; poor first-grade readers are likely to continue to be a poor readers (Torgesen, 1998; Lyon & Moats, 1997). The prereading early literacy stage is discussed in Chapter 10. The next stage, decoding, is the ability to decipher new words. Problems with decoding account for about 80 percent of the variance in first-grade reading comprehension and continue to be a major factor in text comprehension as students progress through the grades. As children acquire reading proficiency, they go from global to analytic processing, from approximate to specific linking of sound and symbol, and from text-driven to print-driven reading. The instructional method used should be compatible with the emerging competence of the readers. The early stages that children pass through when learning to read are (Moats, 1998):

Table 11.1

Stages of Reading Development

Stage and Designation	Reading Grade Level	Essential Learnings
Stage 1 Early literacy or pre-reading	Below grade 1 reading level	Early literacy learnings. Awareness of print. Phonological awareness. Reads common signs and labels. Can write one's name.
Stage 2 Decoding	Reading grade levels 1 and beginning 2	Letter-sound correspondences. Knowledge of the alphabetic principle and skill in its use. Identifies about 1,000 of the most common words in the oral language. Can read very simple texts.
Stage 3 Fluency	Reading grade levels 2–3.	Integrates knowledge and skills acquired in Stages 1 and 2. Relies on context and meaning as well as on decoding (phonics for identifying new words). Reads with greater fluency. By the end of Stage 2, can recognize about 3,000 familiar words and derivatives.
Stage 4 Uses reading for learning	Reading grade levels 4–8	Can use reading as a tool for learning new information, ideas, attitudes, and values. Growth in background knowledge, meaning vocabulary, and cognitive abilities.
Stage 5 Multiple viewpoints	High school reading grade levels 9–12	Ability to read widely a broad range of complex materials, expository and narrative, from a variety of viewpoints and at a variety of levels of comprehension: inferential and critical as well as literal.
Stage 6 Construction and reconstruction	College and beyond	Reading for one's own needs and purposes (professional, personal, civic) to integrate one's knowledge with that of others and to create new knowledge.

Adapted from "Reading Development in Adults" by J. Chall, 1987, p. 244 from *Annals of Dyslexia, 37,* 240–251, with permission of the International Dyslexia Association, Feb. 26, 1999.

1. Logographic reading.   Typically, before mid-kindergarten young children begin to recognize a limited vocabulary of whole words through incidental cues such as a logo, a picture, a color, or a shape. For example, parents who have a child at this stage may find that they cannot substitute a generic brand of cereal if their child wants a brand that he or she recognizes from a logo from television advertising. At this beginning stage, children do not associate sounds with symbols or realize that words are composed of **phonemes** or speech sounds.

2. Early alphabetic reading.   To progress in reading, children must grasp the insight that alphabet letters represent abstract speech segments or phonemes (Moats, 1998). At this stage they use alphabet letters to write words. For example, a child might write *KR* for *car, TRKE* for *turkey,* or *PTZU* for *pizza.* Figure 11.1 shows the writing of a child at the early alphabetic stage. Children who are at this stage need a systematic program with

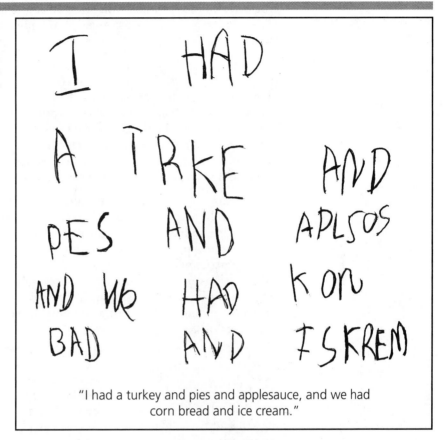

"I had a turkey and pies and applesauce, and we had corn bread and ice cream."

a limited set of sound-symbol correspondences. Teachers can use a limited set of consonants (such as *b, f, j, k, m, p,* and *t*) and one or two vowels (such as *a* or *i*) to teach children how to build words. Children can play word games by changing one sound at a time *(*for example, *hat, bat, hit, bit)*. The instruction should be systematic and explicit as children learn to blend sounds into words and to break words into sounds. After words have been learned, they should be used in sentences.

3. Mature alphabetic reading.   At the next stage of early reading, children know associations for the basic sound-spellings and can use them to decipher simple words. First graders should be able to accomplish this task by the middle of first grade and should also be able to decode predictable syllables. Children begin to recognize word chunks (orthography) such as phonograms *(ell, ack, ame, old)* and word endings *(-ing, -ed -est)* as units (Moats, 1998).

4. Orthographic stages: Recognizing syllables and morphemes.   As whole words, morphemes, and print patterns become increasingly familiar, knowledge of these larger units of print allows children to read more efficiently and to spend less attention on sounding words out letter by letter. At this stage, children use analogy to known words to read new words (for example, *build, guild*).

5. Gaining fluency.   Fluency occurs when children begin to read easily instead of laboring through reading material. Children need many opportunities to read if they are to gain fluency. Knowledge of sound-symbol associations and abundant practice contribute to fluency in word recognition. However, the books read have to be at the right level—not too hard but not too easy. Children like series books; *The Boxcar Children* series; books about horses, animals, and sports figures: and books that hook them into reading independently for themselves.

Unfortunately, because of curriculum demands, less-skilled readers often find themselves reading materials that are too difficult for them to enjoy or to be helpful in building their fluency. As a consequence, poor readers do not have the opportunities to read books and stories at their reading level and to practice newly acquired skills. It is essential that all children be provided with as many reading experiences as possible, regardless of their achievement levels. In fact, frequent reading not only improves reading fluency and reading skills, but it also improves verbal and thinking abilities (Cunningham & Stanovich, 1998).

THE READING PROCESS

Reading is one of the most complex human functions. If teachers understand the nature and complexity of the reading process, they can appreciate why students with learning disabilities have such difficulty acquiring reading skills and becoming fluent readers. Five generalizations about the reading process of effective readers are identified by Anderson, Hiebert, Scott, and Wilkinson (1985):

1. *Reading must be fluent.*   For fluent reading, readers must learn to recognize words easily and quickly. Word identification must be an automatic process, not a conscious, deliberate effort. If readers expend all their concentration on figuring out words, they will be unable to focus on meaning. It is important for readers to "break the code" so they can recognize words quickly and easily.

2. *Reading is a constructive process.*   To bring meaning to the printed text, readers must "construct" the meaning of the written passage by drawing on their existing store of knowledge and experiences. For example, when two boys tried to make cookies, they were puzzled when their cookies stuck to the pan. They had followed the directions in the recipe and greased the bottom of the pan. Their problem was they constructed the meaning of *bottom* to indicate the underside of the pan. The part on which they put the cookies seemed to them to mean the top of the pan. Another instance of faulty construction occurred when a 4-year-old, using her prior experience to bring meaning to her first camping experience, called the tent a "hotel."

As people read and construct their own meaning of a text, they create their own mental version of what they read. For example, in reading a novel, the reader does much more than simply acquire information; the reader actively creates a personal version of the story. The constructed version may differ from the book version: the reader visualizes the characters and the scenery in a story, and probably even supplies details that are not in the book. Thus, if one reader compares his or her mental "image" of a character in the novel with that made by a friend, the two readers will find they have constructed entirely different personal versions of the character in the story. In seeing a movie made from a favorite book, readers find that the actor does not even resemble the image they had constructed.

3. *Reading is strategic.*   Skillful readers use a variety of thinking strategies to construct meaning from the text. They change and direct their reading style, depending on their purpose for reading, the complexity of the material, and their familiarity with the topic. Unlike poor readers, skillful readers monitor their reading comprehension. If something in the text is puzzling, they go back and use "fix-up" strategies, such as rereading or rephrasing to improve their understanding of the reading passage.

4. *Reading requires motivation.*   Learning to read requires sustained attention over a long period of time. Learning to read well takes several years, and teachers must plan to engage the interest of beginning and poor readers to help them become successful readers. Too often poor readers lose motivation. They become inattentive, give up easily, and do not complete their work. Teachers should try to make reading enjoyable and to convey to students the belief that they will learn to read.

5. *Reading is a lifelong pursuit.*   Reading is a continuously developing skill, one that constantly improves with practice. It is not mastered once and for all. From the very beginning and at all stages of reading, learners must have sufficient opportunities to practice and to engage in the process of reading. Teachers must search for strategies that offer many reading opportunities.

TWO APPROACHES TO TEACHING READING

Two philosophies guide the teaching of reading in our schools: (1) whole-language instruction and (2) explicit code-emphasis instruction. Each view embodies important concepts about learning to read. However, there are values in both, and the two approaches can be successfully combined.

Whole-Language Instruction

The far-reaching influence of the reading approach known as **whole-language instruction** is evident in its broad use. Many teachers across the country have responded enthusiastically to the appeal of the whole-language philosophy, so consequently, this approach has shaped the reading curriculum in many of our schools. In fact, research shows that most general education teacher and 80 percent of special education teachers view them-selves as whole-language teachers (Pressley & Rankin, 1994).

The Philosophy of Whole Language   The philosophical view underlying *whole language* is the unity and interrelationships of oral language, read-ing, and writing. The characteristics of the whole-language approach are summarized by Kenneth Goodman (1986, 1989, 1990). Whole-language instruction

- encourages respect for language, for the learner, and for the teacher
- emphasizes the meaning—and not the language itself—in authentic speech and literacy events
- encourages learners to take risks and invites them to use language, in all its varieties, for their own purposes
- advocates that classrooms use all the varied functions and forms of oral and written language

Basic Tenets of Whole-Language Instruction   What are the basic beliefs of whole-language instruction, and what are its implications for students with learning disabilities?

1. *Reading is part of the integrated language system, closely linked to oral and written forms of language.*   Whole-language educators emphasize that active experiences in writing and oral language improve the child's reading. The developing awareness of the interrelatedness of oral and writ-ten language is called **early literacy.** Thus, children begin writing in early childhood whole-language classrooms as early as kindergarten, even before learning to read (Richek et al., 1996). (Figure 11.2 illustrates the writing of a 5-year old in a whole-language kindergarten.)

Learning disabilities educators strongly agree with this tenet. A unifying core underlies speaking, reading, and writing. Teaching methods in the field of learning disabilities emphasize the strong relationships among oral lan-guage, reading, and writing systems. The link between oral language disor-ders and problems in reading is very evident when children who deal poorly with complex syntactic structures and the morphology of spoken language also have difficulty in learning to read (Moats, 1994b; Stanovich, 1994; Wiig & Semel, 1984). Children who have underlying language problems or motor difficulties will probably encounter problems with early writing, and they will need more direct help in writing stories in the early grades than many of their classmates (Juel, 1995). (The case example entitled "Whole-Language Instruction" tells of a kindergartner who learned to write before learning to read.)

2. *Both oral and written language are acquired through natural usage.* Whole-language educators point out that children learn to talk without special exercises and drills. Similarly, it is presumed that children will ac-quire reading skills naturally through exposure to literacy and by being

Figure 11.2

Journal of a First-Grade Student.

"Today I cut my finger with a scissors."

immersed in language and books from infancy (Shanklin & Rhodes, 1989; Toliver, 1990; Goodman, 1986, 1990).

However, learning disabilities educators disagree about this assumption. For students with learning disabilities and many other children, learning to read is not the same as learning to speak. Unlike talking, reading is not innate, natural, or developmental. Written language is a relatively recent invention of civilization. Although all human communities develop an oral communication system, history shows that many civilizations did not develop a written language system. Even today, some communities have no written language system. In addition, we know that some people who are competent speakers never learn to use written language efficiently. Learning to speak is like learning to crawl, walk, or grasp objects. Learning to read, however, is more akin to doing arithmetic or playing checkers. To learn to read, many children need explicit teaching and intensive instruction (Moats, 1998; Pressley & Rankin, 1994).

CASE EXAMPLE

WHOLE-LANGUAGE INSTRUCTION: WRITING BEFORE READING

The following example describes an incident involving a kindergartner who confidently used writing before learning to read. A business call was made to a client's home and the client's 5-year-old answered the phone. The caller's side of the telephone conversation was overheard and went as follows:

"Hello, I want to speak to Mr. John Walsh . . . Oh, he's in the shower? Well, would you please write a message for him? . . . Good. Please write that . . . What? You haven't any paper? . . . Okay, I'll wait until you get a piece of paper . . . You got the paper? Good. Please write that . . . What? You haven't got a pencil? . . . Okay, I'll wait . . . Good. You found a pencil. Please write that Eugene Lerner called. I'll spell that—*E-U-G-E-N-E L-E-R-N-E-R.* My phone number is 708-555-1437. Did you write that down?... Good. Now would you read the message back to me?... What's that? You can write, but you haven't learned to read?"

---

3. *The use of authentic literature provides abundant opportunities for expressive literacy—or for writing.*   Whole-language educators emphasize that beginning from infancy, children should acquire reading skills through exposure to literature and by having many experiences with language, big books, stories, poems, and other books (Shanklin & Rhodes, 1989; Toliver, 1990; Goodman, 1989).

Learning disabilities educators strongly agree. Children with learning disabilities need much exposure to language, books, and stories. They benefit greatly from sharing books and hearing stories. The value of using stories has been part of our culture from Mother Goose to Dr. Seuss (Liberman & Liberman, 1990).

4. *Avoid teaching separate, non-meaningful parts of language or using isolated exercises and drills.*   Whole-language educators maintain that traditional reading methods make learning to read difficult "by breaking whole (natural) language into bite-size, abstract little pieces" (Goodman, 1986). According to Goodman (1986), it was school tradition that "took apart the language into words, syllables, and isolated sounds." The whole-language philosophy maintains that only meaningful reading materials should be used for instruction and that the sound-symbol relationships of the printed language (phonics) will be naturally and incidentally mastered as children learn to read and to write meaningful whole messages. The presumption is that decoding skills do not have to be learned in isolation; instead, these skills will be acquired naturally through reading (Lerner, Cousin, & Richek, 1992).

Learning disabilities educators strongly disagree with this tenet of the whole-language philosophy. Most children with learning disabilities and many other children do not learn the alphabetic principle on their own; they need explicit instruction in the alphabetic code, letters, and their

Children must learn to read so that they can later read to learn. (© Lawrence Migdale/ Stock Boston)

sound equivalents (Moats, 1998; Lyon & Moats, 1997; Adams & Bruck, 1995; Chall, 1991).

Explicit Code-Emphasis Instruction

The second approach to reading instruction emphasizes explicit teaching of decoding skills. Children with learning disabilities usually require systematic, direct instruction in the element of the alphabet code. Research shows that early emphasis on decoding skills leads to higher scores on reading achievement tests (Moats, 1998; Lyon & Moats, 1998; Beck & Juel, 1995; Chall, 1967).

Direct instruction in alphabetic coding (phonics) facilitates early reading instruction. Efficient reading is fluent reading, and to achieve fluency, readers must learn to recognize words easily and quickly. Word identification must be an automatic process, not a conscious, deliberate effort. If readers expend all their concentration on figuring out words, they will be unable to focus on meaning. As stated earlier, it is important for readers to "break the code" so they can recognize words quickly and easily.

In a written alphabetic language such as English, the code involves a system of mapping or seeing the correspondences between letters and sounds. Once a child learns those mappings, the child has "broken the code" and can apply this knowledge to figure out plausible pronunciations of printed words (Moats, 1998; Beck & Juel, 1995; Adams, 1990).

Early attainment of decoding skills is important because this early skill accurately predicts later skill in reading comprehension. Children who get off to a slow start rarely become strong readers. Learning the code leads to wider reading habits both in and out of school. Wide reading in turn provides opportunities to grow in vocabulary concepts and in knowledge of how text is written. Children who do not learn to decode do not have this avenue for growth (Torgesen, 1998; Cunningham & Stanovich, 1998).

Stanovich (1986b) calls the effect of a paucity of reading experiences the "Matthew effect." This is in reference to the Gospel of Matthew, which says that "for unto every one that hath shall be given, and he shall have abundance; but from him that hath not shall be taken away even that which he hath." Stanovich interprets this passage as *the rich get richer.* An analogous effect occurs in reading. Children who get a good start in reading read more and become better readers. In contrast, children who have a poor start in reading do not engage in wide reading and fall further and further behind. They do not enjoy reading, they read less, and go through a negative series of unrewarding reading experiences.

Children with learning and reading disabilities need direct instruction in word recognition, decoding, and phonics to make the relationship between printed letters and sounds explicit. Such **explicit code-emphasis instruction** assists the learning process by providing these children with a basis for remembering the ordered identities of useful letter strings and for deriving the meanings of printed words (Adams & Bruck, 1995).

Integrating Whole-Language and Code-Emphasis Instruction

There is much that is valuable in both whole-language and explicit decoding instruction. Students with learning disabilities need many kinds of instruction, including a balance between whole-language and code-emphasis instruction (Pressley & Rankin, 1994).

We have learned much from the whole-language movement. Students with learning disabilities profit from a literate environment that includes chart stories, in-classroom libraries, and displays of students' work. They gain when teachers model the love of reading, use themes to organize reading and writing instruction, and use rhyming books and pattern books. Teachers should read stories to students, have students read along as they read, develop background knowledge before having students read stories, and encourage students to write stories and keep journals (Pressley & Rankin, 1994).

We also know that students with learning disabilities need explicit instruction in learning the alphabet code, instruction in how sounds and letters are related, and instruction in unlocking unknown words and in systematic phonics. (Moats, 1998).

Fortunately, teachers do not have to choose a single approach to teach reading. Many teachers of students with learning disabilities effectively combine all of these approaches. Written language is like a safe-deposit box: more than one key is needed to unlock it. Students with learning disabilities need all the keys we can give them (Heymsfeld, 1989).

ELEMENTS OF READING: WORD RECOGNITION AND READING COMPREHENSION

The process of teaching reading can be divided into two parts: word recognition and reading comprehension. **Word-recognition skills** enable readers to recognize words and to learn ways to figure out, or unlock, unknown words by decoding printed words, matching letters, and words with sounds. **Reading comprehension** refers to understanding the meaning of what is read. Students must recognize words to comprehend what they read. Just saying the words in a passage without understanding the meaning of the passage is not truly reading (Richek, Caldwell, Jennings, & Lerner, 1996).

Skills in both word recognition and comprehension are needed if the student is to function as a reader. In the traditional reading curriculum, word recognition receives more emphasis in the beginning stages of reading instruction, and comprehension receives more emphasis in the later stages. However, from the initial stages of learning to read, children should have experiences with stories, language, and meaning.

WORD RECOGNITION

Reading requires the ability to recognize words. Once readers develop fluency in word recognition, they can concentrate on the meaning of the text. Without these so-called lower-level reading skills, the higher cognitive skills cannot function (Williams, 1998; Chall, 1991). The readers who must exert effort to recognize words will have little processing capacity remaining for comprehension. Strategies for recognizing words include phonics, sight words, context clues, structural analysis, and combined word-recognition strategies. The Teaching Strategies section of this chapter suggests methods for teaching each of these types of word recognition.

Phonics

Phonics is the word-recognition strategy in which the reader matches a sound to a written letter or letter combination. **Decoding** is another term for the process of making the connection between the sound (phoneme) and the written letter symbol (**grapheme**). At some point the child must acquire the skill of breaking the letter-to-sound code (Stanovich, 1994).

Moats (1998) is critical of many phonics programs because they go from printed letter to sound. She advises, instead, that children should learn by going from sound to letter. Teachers should first teach awareness of the sound system and then should anchor the printed letter (grapheme) to this sound knowledge. The speech-to-print progression is more natural, less confusing, and easier for children to learn.

Phonological Awareness: A Precursor to Learning Phonics   To "break the code" or construct the link between the sounds of speech and the letters of print, the student must realize that speech can be segmented into phonemic units that represent words in print (Adams et al., 1998; Blachman, 1994). Written English is based on the alphabetic principle; that is, letters and letter clusters represent the phonemes (or sounds) of the spoken language

(Henry, 1998). Adults find it simple to understand the idea that the graphic symbols represent the sounds of speech. But many children with learning disabilities have not yet learned this concept and have great difficulty recognizing the relationship between letters and sounds. When they hear the word *man*, for example, they cannot recognize that it contains three sounds. They do not know what the sounds are. They also cannot count the phonemic segments in words. Their lack of **phonological awareness** makes the task of "breaking the code" difficult, thus creating an obstacle for acquiring word-recognition skills.

Children who recognize that speech is made up of sound units and who are proficient at segmenting spoken language into phonemes at an early age learn to read with ease and become better readers (Torgesen, 1998; Torgesen, Wagner, Rashatte, Alexander, & Conway, 1997). The skill of segmenting the sounds in words can be taught, and this training has a positive effect on reading achievement. Methods for developing precursors of reading such as phonological awareness, are described in Chapter 10. Commercial materials for developing phonological awareness include the *Lindemood Phoneme Sequencing Program for Reading, Spelling, and Speech (LiPS), 1998* (Lindamood & Lindamood, 1998) and *Phonological Awareness Training for Reading* (Torgesen & Bryant, 1994). Tests for phonological awareness are listed in Chapter 10 (Table 10.1) and are described in Appendix C.

Instruction in Phonics and Reading Achievement   Studies that compare methods for teaching beginning reading are consistent in one finding: Children who are taught phonics directly and systematically in the early grades receive higher scores on reading achievement tests in the primary years than children who do not receive this training (Lyon & Moats, 1997; Moats, 1998; Chall, 1991). The question is not *whether* children should be taught phonics and word-recognition skills, but *how* these skills can be taught easily and quickly.

Many teachers lack a firm grounding in phonics and phonics generalizations (Moats, 1998; Horne, 1978; Lerner & List, 1970). Some teachers do not remember learning phonics themselves, and many did not receive adequate phonics instruction during their teacher training. (The reader may wish to take the *Foniks Kwiz* in Appendix B. A brief review of phonics generalizations follows the quiz.)

Sight Words

Sight words are the words that are recognized instantly, without hesitation or further analysis. **Fluent reading** requires that most of the words in a selection be sight words. When a selection contains too many difficult (nonsight) words, the reading material is too arduous and frustrating.

Table 11.2 illustrates 220 basic sight words that students should know by the end of third grade. These words are divided into groups according to their difficulty. One of the best and certainly most natural ways to learn

Table 11.2

220 Basic Sight Words

Preprimer	Primer	First	Second	Third
1. the	45. when	89. many	133. know	177. don't
2. of	46. who	90. before	134. while	178. does
3. and	47. will	91. must	135. last	179. got
4. to	48. more	92. through	136. might	180. united
5. a	49. no	93. back	137. us	181. left
6. in	50. if	94. years	138. great	182. number
7. that	51. out	95. where	139. old	183. course
8. is	52. so	96. much	140. year	184. war
9. was	53. said	97. your	141. off	185. until
10. he	54. what	98. may	142. come	186. always
11. for	55. up	99. well	143. since	187. away
12. it	56. its	100. down	144. against	188. something
13. with	57. about	101. should	145. go	189. fact
14. as	58. into	102. because	146. came	190. through
15. his	59. than	103. each	147. right	191. water
16. on	60. them	104. just	148. used	192. less
17. be	61. can	105. those	149. take	193. public
18. at	62. only	106. people	150. three	194. put
19. by	63. other	107. Mr.	151. states	195. thing
20. I	64. new	108. how	152. himself	196. almost
21. this	65. some	109. too	153. few	197. hand
22. had	66. could	110. little	154. house	198. enough
23. not	67. time	111. state	155. use	199. far
24. are	68. these	112. good	156. during	200. took
25. but	69 two	113. very	157. without	201. head
26. from	70. may	114. make	158. again	202. yet
27. or	71. then	115. would	159. place	203. government
28. have	72. do	116. still	160. American	204. system
29. an	73. first	117. own	161. around	205. better
30. they	74. any	118. see	162. however	206. set
31. which	75. my	119. men	163. home	207. told
32. one	76. now	120. work	164. small	208. nothing
33. you	77. such	121. long	165. found	209. night
34. were	78. like	122. get	166. Mrs.	210. end
35. her	79. our	123. here	167. thought	211. why
36. all	80. over	124. between	168. went	212. called
37. she	81. man	125. both	169. say	213. didn't

(continued)

Table 11.2
(continued)

Preprimer	Primer	First	Second	Third
38. there	82. me	126. life	170. part	214. eyes
39. would	83. even	127. being	171. once	215. find
40. their	84. most	128. under	172. general	216. going
41. we	85. made	129. never	173. high	217. look
42. him	86. after	130. day	174. upon	218. asked
43. been	87. also	131. same	175. school	219. later
44. has	88. did	132. another	176. every	220. knew

From Johnson, D. D. (1971, February). The Dolch List reexamined. *The Reading Teacher*, 24(5), 455–456. Reprinted with permission of Dale D. Johnson and the International Reading Association. All rights reserved.

sight words is by actually reading stories. Sight words appear many times in context. Another natural way to expose children to sight words is through language experience stories. Many of the words in these stories are from the sight word list. Students with learning disabilities need other direct approaches to strengthen their sight vocabulary. Some methods for teaching sight vocabulary are presented in the Teaching Strategies section of this chapter.

Unlike some other languages, written English has an inconsistent phoneme-grapheme relationship, or spelling pattern. The relationship between the letter and its sound equivalent is not always predictable. The letter *a*, for example, is given a different sound in each of the following typical first-grade words: *at, Jane, ball, father, was, saw,* and *are.* Another example of this complexity is the phoneme of the long *i,* which has a different spelling pattern in each of the following words: *aisle, aye, I, eye, ice, tie, high, choir, buy, sky, rye, pine,* and *type.* To further complicate the problem of learning to read English, many of the most frequently used sight words in first-grade books have irregular spelling patterns. A few of these words are shown in column A of Table 11.3; column B shows the way they would be spelled with a dependable phoneme-grapheme relationship so that readers could "sound them out." These words thus must be learned as sight words (Richek et al., 1996).

The problems caused by the undependable written form of English can be approached in two ways:

1. *Introduce only a small number of words at a time, selecting words on the basis of frequency of use.* Some beginning reading words are regularly spelled, whereas others have irregular spellings. Words are learned visually through extensive review and through context, meaning, and language. Basal readers, for example, rely on a controlled introduction of a small number of new words.

	Table 11.3	A. English Spelling	B. Phonic Spelling

Table 11.3
Typical First-Grade Sight Words

A. English Spelling	B. Phonic Spelling
of	uv
laugh	laf
was	wuz
is	iz
come	kum
said	sed
what	wut
from	frum
one	wun
night	nite
know	noe
they	thai

2. *Simplify the initial learning phase by selecting only words that have a consistent sound-symbol spelling relationship.*   With this approach, students learn phonics and are exposed to carefully selected words with dependable spellings. Linguistic and phonics methods use this approach and rely on selected words with a dependable spelling pattern.

Eventually, of course, the child must learn about the undependable spelling of many common English words. Through careful selection of the words for reading, students are kept from learning the "awful truth" about spelling until second grade or later. Inevitably, however, the reader must confront the undependable written form of English.

Context Clues

Context clues help a student recognize a word through the meaning or context of a sentence or paragraph in which the word appears. Redundancies in language occur when information from one source repeats or supports information from another source. These language redundancies provide hints about unknown words from the meaning of the surrounding text, helping readers make conjectures and guesses about unfamiliar words.

Instruction in recognizing words through context is best done by actual reading. When students with reading disabilities have consistent practice in reading stories and books, they naturally learn to use context clues. The meaning of the sentence plus the initial sounds in the word may provide enough clues for the reader to recognize the word.

Structural Analysis

Structural analysis refers to the recognition of words through the analysis of meaningful word units, such as prefixes, suffixes, root words, compound words, and syllables. Structural elements include compound words (e.g., *cowboy*), contractions (e.g., *can't*), word endings or inflectional suffixes (e.g., *-s, -ed, -er, est, -ing*), word beginnings or prefixes (e.g., *in-, pre-, un-, re-, ex-*), roots (e.g., *play* in *replaying*), and syllables (i.e., breaking multi-syllabic words into smaller units).

A reader may recognize structural elements of a word (for example, the prefix *re-* and the suffix *-tion* in *repetition*). These clues, combined with the context of the sentence, may be sufficient for recognizing the word.

Combining Word-Recognition Clues

Readers should be encouraged to use all of the word-recognition clues (phonics, sight words, context clues, and structural analysis). However, they will need these strategies only when an unknown word stops the reading process. Readers usually use several clues together until they recognize the unknown word. Students with learning disabilities need practice in each of these word-recognition clues to achieve independence and flexibility and to gain fluency.

READING COMPREHENSION

The purpose of reading is comprehension, that is, to have the ability to gather meaning from the printed page. All reading instruction should provide for the development of reading comprehension abilities.

Although much of the attention and debate in reading focuses on word recognition, the problems related to reading comprehension are far more difficult to solve. The 1997 special education law, the Individuals with Disabilities Education Act (IDEA), indicates that a learning disability can occur in either "basic reading skills" (word recognition) or "reading comprehension." The major problem for many students with learning disabilities is reading comprehension. This ability does not automatically evolve after word-recognition skills are mastered. Most students with learning disabilities eventually learn the basics of word recognition, but many continue to have great difficulty in tasks requiring comprehension of complex passages. They need to learn strategies that will help them become active readers who understand the text (Williams, 1998; Richek et al, 1996).

In this section we examine reading comprehension by looking at strategies to promote reading comprehension, fluency, and understanding narrative and expository materials. The Teaching Strategies section offers some specific strategies for teaching reading comprehension.

Source: PEANUTS reprinted by permission of UFS, Inc.

What Is Reading Comprehension?

As readers try to comprehend the material they read, they must bridge the gap between the information presented in the written text and the knowledge they possess. Reading comprehension thus involves thinking. The reader's background knowledge, interest, and the reading situation affect comprehension of the material. Each person's integration of the new information in the text with what is already known will yield unique information. To understand why an individual is having difficulty with reading comprehension, we must investigate how that person learns and performs in different situations and with different types of reading material.

The following statements about reading comprehension underscore its complexity:

1. *Reading comprehension depends on what the reader brings to the written material.*   Reading comprehension depends on the reader's experience, knowledge of language, and recognition of syntactic structure, as well as on the redundancy of the printed passage (Richek et al., 1996). To appreciate

the importance of the reader's knowledge in reading comprehension, read the following excellent illustration presented by Aulls (1982):

> A newspaper is better than a magazine, and on a seashore is a better place than a street. At first it is better to run than to walk. Also you may have to try several times. It takes some skill but it's easy to learn. Even young children can enjoy it. Once successful, complications are minimal. Birds seldom get too close. One needs lots of room. Rain soaks in very fast. Too many people doing the same thing can also cause problems. If there are no complications, it can be very peaceful. A rock will serve as an anchor. If things break loose from it, however, you will not get a second chance. (Bransford & Johnson, 1972, cited by Aulls, 1982, p. 52)

As a mature reader, you were able to understand every word of this paragraph, yet you probably did not understand the passage and cannot explain what it is about. The reason you had difficulty is that you did not have the appropriate background knowledge to bring to the printed text. Now, we shall expand your background knowledge by telling you that the passage is about *kites*. If you reread the paragraph now, you will find a marked improvement in your reading comprehension. The implication for teaching is that when the reader has limited knowledge to relate to the text content, no amount of rereading will increase comprehension. What students with learning disabilities need in many cases is more background knowledge to improve their comprehension.

2. *Reading comprehension is a language process.*   Reading comprehension is a process for obtaining meaning through language. During the reading process, the reader often cannot complete the thought until the final word or phrase. Consider, for example, two phrases: "the little white pebble" and "the little-understood theory." The word *little* connotes something quite different in each phrase, and the reader cannot know its meaning until the end of the phrase.

Although the eye goes from left to right when reading English text, the mind does not. In many cases the flow of thought in English is not left to right but circular, and certain ideas and words must be held until some part of the sentence permits completion of the thought. For example, "When *Lee* looked at the *note* again, she realized that she should have played *A*-sharp." The meaning of *note* and Lee's gender must be kept in abeyance until the end of the sentence provides the clarification. Sometimes the reader must even delay decisions about pronunciation. In the sentence, "John had *tears* in his shirt," the pronunciation of *tears* cannot be decided until the reader completes the sentence.

The *redundancies* in language offer clues for understanding both oral and written language. Redundancy means sending the same message in other forms. That is, information from one source supports information from another source, reinforcing and enhancing the intended message. Such cues therefore help readers construct the meaning in a written text. The following sentences are examples of redundancies: "Would you reiterate that? Please say it again." (The second sentence explains the first.) "Do you want a piece of cake?" (Both the structure of the sentence and the question mark show that the sentence is an interrogative.) "The girl wore her plaid skirt." (We know the sentence is about a female from the words *girl, her,* and *skirt.*) Students should be taught to look for and to use the redundancies in language.

3. *Reading comprehension is a thinking process.* The relationship between reading and thinking has been noted for a long time. In 1917, Thorndike likened the thinking process used in mathematics to that of reading:

> Understanding a paragraph is like solving a problem in mathematics. It consists of selecting the right elements of the situation and putting them together in the right relations, and also with the right amount of weight or influence or force for each . . . all under the influence of the right mental set or purpose or demands. (p. 329)

Defining reading as thinking, Stauffer (1975) perceived reading as something akin to problem solving. As in problem solving, the reader must employ concepts, develop and test hypotheses, and modify those concepts. In this way, reading comprehension is a mode of inquiry, and methods that employ discovery techniques should be used in the teaching of reading. The key to teaching from this perspective is to guide students to set up their own questions and purposes for reading. Students then read to solve problems that they have devised for themselves. Students can be encouraged first to guess what will happen next in a story, for example, and then to read to determine the accuracy of those predictions. This approach, which is called a **directed reading-thinking activity,** is described in the Teaching Strategies section of this chapter.

4. *Reading comprehension requires active interaction with the text.* Readers must be "active" participants, interacting with the text material. They must actively combine their existing knowledge with the new information of the printed text.

There is evidence that good readers generally do not read every word of a passage; instead, they "sample" certain words to determine the meaning and skip many others. They go back and read every word only when they encounter something unexpected. An excellent example of a reader interacting with the text is provided by Adler (1956):

> When people in love are reading a love letter, they read for all they are worth. They read every word three ways; they read the whole in terms of the parts, and each part in terms of the whole; they grow sensitive to context and ambiguity, to insinuation and implication; they perceive the color of words, the order of phrases, and the weight of sentences. They may even take punctuation into account. Then, if never before or after, they read. (p. 4)

Strategies to Promote Reading Comprehension

Learning to read is not a linear process. Children do not need to master decoding skills before they can learn to comprehend text material. Both skills can be taught at the same time, beginning with the early stage of reading.

Explicit Structured Comprehension Instruction Williams (1998) suggests that students with learning disabilities require a different type of comprehension instruction than typical learners need. Just as students with learning disabilities need explicit structured instruction to learn word-recognition skills, they need explicit, highly structured instruction to learn reading comprehension skills. Incidental, literature-based instruction that is typically used to teach reading comprehension is not sufficient. Williams (1998) taught comprehension to students with learning disabilities through a "Themes Instruction Program" which consists of a series of twelve 40-minute lessons. Each lesson is organized around a single story and is comprised of five parts:

1. Prereading discussion on the purpose of the lesson and the topic of the story that will be read.
2. Reading the story.
3. Discussion of important story information using organized (schema) questions as a guide.
4. Identification of a theme for the story, stating it in general terms so that it is relevant to a variety of stories and situations.
5. Practice in applying the generalized theme to real-life experiences.

Comprehension Activities Before, During, and After Reading Reading comprehension can be taught before reading, during reading, and after reading, as indicated in Table 11.4.

Before reading a story, teachers should motivate and interest children in the reading selection, activate background information, and have them predict what the story will be about. *During reading,* the teacher should direct the students' attention to the difficult or subtle dimensions of the story, anticipate difficult words and ideas, and talk about problems and solutions. *After reading,* comprehension strategies can include having the readers summarize the story, talk about what they liked and that they wished had been different in the story, create graphic organizers, and talk about the characters in the story (Every Child Is Reading, 1998; Richek et al., 1996).

Fluency in Reading

Students must develop fluency to make the bridge from word recognition to reading comprehension (Richek et al., 1996). Reading fluency is the

Table 11.4

Strategies to Promote Reading Comprehension

Before Reading	During Reading	After Reading
Establish a purpose for reading.	Direct attention to difficult or subtle dimensions of the text.	Ask students to retell or summarize the story.
Review vocabulary.	Point out difficult words and ideas.	Create graphic organizers (webs, cause and effect charts, outlines).
Build background knowledge.	Ask students to identify problems and solutions.	Put pictures of story events in order.
Relate background knowledge and information to the story.	Encourage silent reading.	
Encourage children to predict what the story will be about.	Encourage students to monitor their own comprehension while reading.	Generate questions for other children.
Discuss the author, if such knowledge helps to set up the story.		Have students write their own reactions to stories and factual material

ability to recognize words quickly and to read sentences and longer passages in a connected easy manner that indicates understanding of the material. Many poor readers have difficulty reading fluently. Often they do not possess an adequate sight vocabulary and must labor to decode many of the words in the reading passages. With their energies focused on recognizing words, their oral reading is filled with long pauses and many repetitions and is characterized by monotonous expression.

Students need abundant practice in both oral and silent reading to build fluency. Unfortunately, poor readers do not enjoy reading or engage in the wide reading needed to build fluency. Therefore, teachers must use strategies to make reading an enjoyable, positive experience. Methods for building fluency are given in the Teaching Strategies section of this chapter.

Comprehension of Narrative Materials

Two types of reading comprehension materials are narrative materials and expository materials. Narrative materials are stories, usually fiction. Narratives have characters, a plot, and a sequence of events that occur during the story. To read narrative materials effectively, students must be able to identify the following (Richek et al., 1996):

- Important characters
- The setting, time, and place
- The major events in sequence
- The problems that the characters had to solve and how those problems were resolved

Sometimes narratives are inspirational. Readers can leave the limits of their everyday lives and travel to other parts of the world, to space, and to other time periods. Poor readers often respond negatively to narrative materials and have to be strongly encouraged to read stories. It is important to ask for their reactions and to find narrative materials that meet their interests. Different varieties of narrative reading materials are called *genres*. To become good readers, children need to have experiences with a variety of narrative materials; see the box entitled "Narrative Genres."

Comprehension of Expository Materials

Expository materials include informational materials, for example, textbooks used in content areas such as social studies or science. As students move through the grades, the reading tasks that confront them change dramatically. Reading assignments in content-area textbooks take the place of readers and narrative stories. Students are often assigned to read textbooks independently, without supervision or help. They may be required to read a chapter, complete a written assignment on the chapter, prepare for a class activity based on the chapter, and take a test on the content of the chapter. It is not surprising that many students with learning disabilities cannot complete such assignments. A student whose reading has been limited to narrative stories will lack experience with and the ability to do the kind of reading that expository content-area textbooks require.

Instruction at the secondary level places heavy demands on reading proficiency and provides little teacher direction. Major problems in content-area reading for students with learning disabilities include the following:

1. *A heavy emphasis is placed on reading to obtain information.* Content-area instruction is based on presumed proficiency in reading. Students are expected to read, comprehend, and retain large amounts of information—up to fifty pages a week for each mainstreamed class. Further, students may be required to take four content-area classes (for instance, English, science, mathematics, and history). For students with learning disabilities, the reading demand can become overwhelming.

2. *Content textbooks are generally written above the grade level in which they are used.* The textbook could be extremely difficult for the student with learning disabilities to read and understand. If a tenth-grade student is reading, for example, at a fifth-grade level and the social studies textbook is written at an eleventh-grade level, there will be a six-year discrepancy between the student's reading level and the reading level of the textbook.

NARRATIVE GENRES

- Realistic fiction, such as tales about children
- Fantasy, including books with talking animals, science fiction, and horror stories
- Fairy tales, folktales, and tall tales
- Fables
- Mysteries
- Humor, language plays
- Historical fiction set in a period in the past
- Plays
- Narrative poetry, poems that tell stories
- Real-life adventures
- Biographies and autobiographies

3. *Content-area teachers often assume that students have adequate reading ability, and they do not teach reading skills.* At this level, there is little time spent on teaching reading skills, such as organizing or studying an outline. Teachers can help students read content books by making the reading meaningful and connecting it to other material that the students have covered and by encouraging students to review the material to get an orientation to the text as a whole. Teachers can also introduce difficult or technical words before reading the text and alert students to monitor for comprehension as they are reading.

The Teaching Strategies section of this chapter provides some suggestions for helping students read expository materials by using content-area textbooks.

ASSESSING READING There are more methods and tests for assessing reading than for any other area of the curriculum. Reading can be assessed through *informal measures* (such as the informal reading inventory, miscue analysis, and portfolio assessment) or through *formal tests* (such as survey tests, diagnostic tests, and comprehensive batteries).

Informal Measures

One of the simplest methods of assessing reading is to observe informally as the student reads aloud. The teacher can readily detect the student's general reading level, word-recognition abilities, types of errors, and understanding of the material. This method is very practical and can be as informative as elaborate test batteries.

Informal Reading Inventory   The **informal reading inventory (IRI)**, which can be administered quickly and easily, provides a wealth of information concerning the student's reading skills, reading levels, types of errors, techniques of attacking unknown words, and related behavioral characteristics (Johnson, Kress, & Pikulski, 1987).

The informal reading inventory procedure requires the examiner to choose selections of approximately one hundred words in length from a series of graded reading levels. The student reads aloud from several graded levels while the teacher systematically records the errors. If the student makes more than five errors per hundred words, he or she is given progressively easier selections until a level is found at which there are no more than two errors per hundred words. To check comprehension, the teacher asks the student four to ten questions about each selection. By means of the following criteria, an informal reading inventory can determine three reading levels:

1. *Independent reading level.*   The student is able to recognize about 95 percent of the words and to answer about 90 percent of the comprehension questions correctly. (This is the level at which the student is able to read library books or do reading work independently.)

2. *Instructional reading level.*   The student is able to recognize about 90 percent of the words in the selection, with a comprehension score of about 70 percent. (This is the level at which the student will profit from teacher-directed reading instruction.)

3. *Frustration reading level.*   The student is able to recognize fewer than 90 percent of the words, with a comprehension score of less than 70 percent. (If the student does not understand the material, this level is too difficult and should not be used for instruction.)

In addition to informal reading inventories developed by teachers, several standard commercial inventories are available, and they offer a convenient way to administer the reading inventory. They include the *Classroom Reading Inventory,* the *Standard Reading Inventory,* and the *Analytic Reading Inventory* (second edition). They are described in Appendix C. (Also see Appendix C in Richek et al. (1996), which contains a complete *informal* reading inventory that teachers can use.)

Miscue Analysis of Oral Reading   **Miscue analysis** is a psycholinguistic approach to assessing oral reading. Miscues are the deviations from the printed text that the student makes while reading orally. These miscues (sometimes called errors) are viewed as diagnostic opportunities because through them readers reveal their underlying language processes. In effect, the student's own underlying language patterns and structure may give rise to the deviation. The miscue may be a positive effort to preserve comprehension (Goodman & Burke, 1980).

Proficient readers may make oral reading miscues (or errors), but their miscues differ from those of poor readers. The miscues of less proficient readers typically reflect errors of graphic information (for example, *want* for *what*), which make little sense in the context of the passage as a whole. More accomplished readers, however, tend to make miscues that appear quite gross visually (for example, *car* for *automobile*), but they retain the underlying meaning of the passage.

Readers must not only *de*code the words and language of the writer but also *re*code the ideas into their own language pattern to get meaning. The errors are not in decoding the author's language but in recoding it into the reader's linguistic patterns. In the following example, most of the oral errors in reading are not decoding or phonic shortcomings but other kinds of linguistic errors, such as morphological or syntactic errors. The language system of the reader does not correspond to the actual syntactic system of the text.

Text: I am Tiphia, servant *to* Mighty Gwump.
Reader: I am Tiphia, servant *of* Mighty Gwump.

Text: Now he had been *caught.*
Reader: Now he had been *catched.*

Text: Bobby's team *was* the Wildcats.
Reader: Bobby's team *were* the Wildcats.

Text: I *have taken* the book.
Reader: I *has took* the book.

A commercial instrument, the *Reading Miscue Inventory,* contains passages and scoring sheets to help teachers use miscue analysis to analyze a student's oral reading (see Appendix C).

Portfolio Assessment of Reading   Portfolio assessment is an alternative to traditional standardized reading assessment tests. The problem with standardized reading tests is that they do not measure what students are actually doing in the reading classroom and do not closely link the assessment to the reading curriculum. Proponents of portfolio assessment propose that learning is too complex and assessment too imperfect to rely on any single index of achievement (Valencia, 1990a; Wiggins, 1990).

Specifically, **portfolio assessment** consists of keeping samples of the students' reading and writing work. It is relatively easy to collect samples of students' writing during the school year. For reading, the teacher keeps a reflective log, recording the students' reactions to books they read, along with the teacher's own reactions. The log shows the growth of each student in reading comprehension. Samples of language experience stories can be kept in the portfolio. Other assessment methods of this type are observations of students (or "kid watching"), checklists, interviews with students, and collections of student work. By reviewing the students' work over a period of time, teachers, parents, and students themselves are able to evaluate progress (Richek et al., 1996).

Formal Tests

Formal reading tests can be classified as survey tests, diagnostic tests, or comprehensive batteries. *Survey tests* are group tests that give an overall reading achievement level. These tests generally give at least two scores: word recognition and reading comprehension. *Diagnostic tests* are individual tests that provide more in-depth information about the student's strengths and weaknesses in reading. *Comprehensive batteries* are tests with components that measure several academic areas, including reading. Table 11.5 lists some of the widely used formal reading tests in each of these categories. Appendix C provides more information on these tests.

Table 11.5

Commonly Used Formal Reading Tests

Test	Grade or Age Assessed
Survey Tests	
Gates-MacGinitie Reading Tests	Grades 1–12
Metropolitan Achievement Tests	Grades 1–12
SRA Achievement Series	Grades 1–12
Wide-Range Achievement Test 3 (WRAT3)	Ages 5–adult
Diagnostic Tests	
Diagnostic Assessment of Reading with Trial Teaching Strategies (DARTTS)	Grades 1–12, adult
Durrell Analysis of Reading Difficulty	Grades 1–6
Gates-McKillop-Horowitz Reading Diagnostic Tests	Grades 1–6
Stanford Diagnostic Reading Test	Grades 1–12
Woodcock Diagnostic Battery	Grades K–17
Woodcock Reading Mastery Test—Revised	Ages 5–75+
Comprehensive Batteries	
Brigance Diagnostic Inventory of Basic Skills	Grades K–6
Kaufman Test of Educational Achievement	Grades 1–12
Peabody Individual Achievement Test— Revised (PIAT-R)	Ages 5–18
Woodcock-Johnson Tests of Achievement—Revised	Preschool–adult

TEACHING STRATEGIES

This Teaching Strategies section presents approaches, methods, and materials for teaching reading to students with learning disabilities. It is organized as follows: (1) improving word recognition, (2) building fluency, (3) improving reading comprehension, (4) using special remedial methods, (5) dealing with special reading problems, and (6) using computers to teach reading.

Methods and materials intended for students progressing normally in reading can be successfully adapted for students with learning disabilities. Such adaptations include increasing the amount of repetition, allotting more time for the completion of work, providing more examples or activities, offering more review, introducing the work more slowly, expanding the background information, providing more work on vocabulary development, and choosing regular books and materials that are different from those the students have previously used. Sometimes a standard method that failed in one instance seems to work later because it is taught at another time, in another place, or by a different teacher—perhaps one who has the magical clinical touch.

STRATEGIES FOR IMPROVING WORD RECOGNITION

Building Phonological Awareness

A child who is learning to read, as noted earlier, must first become aware of the sounds in words and language. Strategies for teaching phonological awareness such as learning to count the sounds in words to segment the sounds and syllables in words, and to recognize rhyming words, are presented in Chapter 10.

Phonics Methods

Phonics systems and phonics books have been on the market for over 50 years. Many phonics programs today are repackaged as preprinted masters for duplication or as recordings, audiotapes, videotapes, computer software programs, and multimedia packages. There are two phonics approaches—synthetic and analytic. *Synthetic phonics* methods first teach students isolated letters and their sound equivalents. Then they teach students to synthesize or blend these individual phoneme elements into whole words. *Analytic phonics* methods teach students whole words that have a consistent sound-spelling pattern, and they then teach students to analyze the phoneme elements that make up the word.

A typical exercise in phonic materials appears in Figure 11.3. Some of the widely used phonics programs are listed next:

Breaking the Code (Open Court)

Building Reading Skills (McCormick-Mathers)

Figure 11.3

Example of Phonics
Exercises

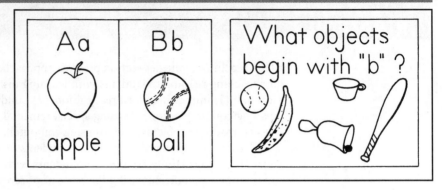

Cove Reading with Phonics (SRA/McGraw-Hill)

Keys to Reading (Economy Company)

New Phonics Skilltexts (Charles E. Merrill)

Phonics We Use (Riverside)

Speech-to-Print Phonics (Harcourt Brace)

Sunform Alphabet (Sundberg Learning Systems)

Wordland Series (Continental Press)

Using Linguistic Readers   Linguistic readers use an analytic phonics approach. Students learn whole words with regular spelling patterns, and they make generalizations about sound elements within the words. Words for the initial reading experience are carefully selected for their consistent and regular spelling pattern, such as words that use a consonant-vowel-consonant (CVC) pattern. Through exposure to words with a minimal contrast of sounds, students are expected to make generalizations about the phoneme-grapheme elements that make up the word. For example, the student is to make a generalization about the short *a* sound by learning words in print such as *can, Nan, van, fan, Dan, pan, man, tan,* and *ran.* These carefully selected, regularly spelled words are then strung together to make sentences, as in the following examples (Bloomfield & Barnhart, 1963, p. 22):

Nan can fan Dan.

Can Dan fan Nan?

Nan, fan Dan.

Dan, fan Nan.

Readers based on this linguistic approach include the following:

Basic Reading Series (Science Research Associates)

Let's Read (Educators' Publishing Service)

Linguistic Readers (Harper and Row)

Merrill Linguistic Readers (Charles E. Merrill)

Phonics Remedial Reading Lessons   These remedial reading lessons consist of words with a consistent phonic pattern that the student reads (Kirk, Kirk, & Minskoff, 1985). The child simply reads words that have been arranged across the page. Part 1 of these drills introduces the most frequent sounds, including short vowels and consonants; Part 2 consists of certain combinations of the previously learned sounds. Part 3 presents less frequently used sounds in whole words, and Part 4 provides supplementary exercises. The drills are based on the principles of minimal change, one response to one symbol, repetition, and social reinforcement. This method is to be used for only a few minutes of an instructional session for students who need practice in decoding skills. See Figure 11.4.

Figure 11.4

Sample Page from
Phonic Remedial
Reading Lessons

Lesson 1-A

a

at	sat	mat	hat	fat
am	ham	Sam	Pam	tam
sad	mad	had	lad	dad
wag	sag	tag	lag	hag

sat	sap	Sam	sad
map	mam	mad	mat
hag	ham	hat	had
cat	cap	cad	cam

sat	am	sad	pat	mad
had	mat	tag	fat	ham
lag	ham	wag	hat	sap
sad	tap	cap	dad	at

map	hag	cat	sat	ham	tap
sap	map	hat	sad	tag	am
Pam	mat	had	tap	hat	dad
fat	mad	at	wag	cap	sag

To the teacher: This lesson introduces many of the consonant sounds. /b/, /r/, /n/, /j/, /x/, and /v/ are introduced in Lesson 1–B. The sounds of /y/, /z/, /k/, and /q/ are not introduced until still later.

From *Phonic Remedial Reading Lessons* by S. A. Kirk, W. Kirk, and E. Minskoff. Copyright © 1985 Academic Therapy Publications. Reprinted by permission.

In addition to recognizing words accurately, readers must read them quickly and fluently. Otherwise, reading is labored and unenjoyable, and the reader loses meaning (Richek et al., 1996; Hasbrouck, 1996).

Repeated Reading

Repeated reading is a strategy for giving the student repeated practice to improve his or her oral reading fluency. It is especially useful with slow, halting readers who accurately identify most words in a passage but have not developed fluency. The method involves the selection of passages that are fifty to two hundred words long and at a difficulty level that enables the reader to recognize most of the words. The student then reads the selection orally three or four times before proceeding to a new passage. Word-accuracy rates and reading speed are usually reported to the student after each reading, and daily practice is recommended (Richek et al., 1996). Some students particularly enjoy repeated reading when the passages are displayed on a computer screen.

Predictable Books

Predictable books contain patterns or refrains that are repeated over and over. Many are based on folktales and fairy tales. For example, in *The Three Billy Goats Gruff,* the question "Who is that trip-trapping over my bridge?" is asked by the troll as each billy goat goes over the bridge. A favorite predictable book is *Brown Bear, Brown Bear.* After the book has been read to young children several times, they are able to predict the wording and begin saying the refrain along with the storyteller. Using predictable books is an excellent way to actively involve children in a story even before they can read. They begin to develop language knowledge and anticipate what will be said. This experience helps develop support for word recognition when they do read the story (Richek et al., 1989).

Neurological Impress Method

Another approach to improving fluency for students with severe reading disabilities is the **neurological impress method** (Langford, Slade, & Barnett, 1974; Heckelman, 1969). It is a system of rapid-unison reading by the student and teacher. The student sits slightly in front of the teacher, and both read together out of one book. The voice of the teacher is directed into the ear of the student at a fairly close range. The student or the teacher places a finger on the word as it is read. At times, the teacher's voice may be louder and faster than the student's, and at other times the teacher may read more softly than the student, who may lag slightly behind. No preliminary preparations are made with the reading material before the student sees it. The goal is simply to cover as many pages as possible within the time available without tiring the student. The theory underlying the method is that the auditory process of feedback from the reader's own voice and from the voice of someone else reading the same material establishes a new learning process.

In the *read-along* method, a similar process occurs. In this method children listen to a tape recording of a story as they read along with the text. In the classroom, headphones may be used so that the tape recording does not disturb other children. There are many commercial stories and tapes available for this purpose.

STRATEGIES FOR IMPROVING READING COMPREHENSION

This section describes strategies to improve reading comprehension. Comprehension is the essence of the reading act. Along with learning to recognize words, children must understand and interact with the text. The section discusses basal readers, activating student background knowledge, building meaning vocabulary and concepts, the reading-writing connection, thinking strategies, and learning strategies for reading.

Using Basal Readers

Basal readers are a sequential and interrelated set of books and supportive materials intended to provide the basic material for the development of fundamental reading skills. A **basal reading series** consists of graded readers that gradually increase in difficulty, typically beginning with very simple readiness and first-grade books and going through the sixth- or eighth-grade level. The books increase in difficulty in vocabulary, story content, and skill development. Auxiliary material, such as teacher's manuals and activity books, often accompany the books. Most basal reading series incorporate an eclectic approach to the teaching of reading, using many procedures to teach readiness, vocabulary, word recognition, comprehension, and the enjoyment of literature.

As the major tool of reading instruction for the past forty years, the basal reader has been the target of continual criticism from diverse groups, including some educators, scholars from other academic disciplines, the popular press, parent groups, political observers, moralists, and, recently, ethnic and women's groups. Critics have scoffed at and satirized the language, phonics presentation, story content, class appeal, pictures, qualities, and environment of the characters of the basal reader. In spite of this highly vocal and severe criticism, basal readers continue to be the major tool for reading instruction in elementary classrooms throughout the country.

Because most basal readers are not committed to any one teaching procedure, publishers are continually modifying them in response to the demands of the times and the consumer market. For example, more phonics and decoding activities are currently being added to basal readers. Other recent basal reader modifications have more literature-based materials and language activities in the early grades. The modifications have also made stories longer and more sophisticated, and added stories that present diverse cultural and ethnic characters.

There are also series of readers produced especially for slow readers. Table 11.6 lists books designed for high interest but easier reading level; the symbol (S) indicates that a book is available in Spanish.

Activating Background Knowledge

The following strategies alert the student to the **background knowledge** needed for reading comprehension and build on student experiences.

The Language Experience Method   The **language experience method** is well-accepted as a method that builds on the student's knowledge and language base, linking the different forms of language—listening, speaking,

Table 11.6

Reading Series for Low Reading Ability and High Interest Level

Series	Reading Level
Challenger (New Readers Press)	1–6
Fastbacks (Fearon)	4–5
Focus: Reading for Success (Spanish version: K–8 *Leer para triunfar*) (Scott, Foresman) (S)	
High Action Reading Series (Modern Curriculum Press)	2–6
High Noon Books (High Noon Publishers)	1–6
Key-Text (Economy Company)	pp–8
New Directions in Reading (Houghton Mifflin)	2–7
The New Open Highways Program (Scott, Foresman)	1–8
Programa de lectura en español (Spanish) (Houghton Mifflin) (S)	K–8
Quest Adventure, Survival (Raintree Publishers)	3–10
Rally (Harcourt Brace Jovanovich)	2–7
The Reading Connection (Open Court)	2–11
Reading for Today (Steck-Vaughn)	1–5
Scott, Foresman Spanish Reading Program (Scott, Foresman) (S)	1–5
Spanish Reading Series (Economy Company) (S)	1–5
Sprint Library (Scholastic)	3–7
Sprint Reading Skills Program (Scholastic)	1–5
Sport Close-ups (Crestwood House)	3–12

reading, and writing. This method uses the student's own experiences and language as the raw material. Students begin by dictating stories to the teacher (or writing stories by themselves). These stories then become the basis of their reading instruction. Through the language experience approach, students conceptualize written material as follows:

What I can think about, I can talk about.

What I can say, I can write (or someone can write for me).

What I can write, I can read.

I can read what others write for me to read.

There is no predetermined, rigid control over vocabulary, syntax, or content. The teacher uses the text or stories that the student composes to develop reading skills. The language experience approach to reading has a vitality and immediacy as well as an element of creativity. The method is effective both in the beginning-to-read stage with young children and in corrective instruction with older pupils. The interest of the student is high because the emphasis is on reading material that grows out of the student's personal experiences and natural language in expressing these experiences. An example of a language experience story is shown in Figure 11.5. (Language experience is also discussed as a writing strategy in Chapter 12.)

The K-W-L Technique   K-W-L is a technique for reading and studying content-area textbooks (Ogle, 1986). The letters represent three questions in three steps of a lesson:

1. K: What I know.   Students think of and state all the knowledge they have on a subject. A group of students can pool their knowledge.

2. W: What I want to find out.   Each student thinks of and writes on a sheet of paper what he or she wants to (or expects to) learn from the reading. Students can then compare their answers to this question.

Figure 11.5

Language Experience Chart

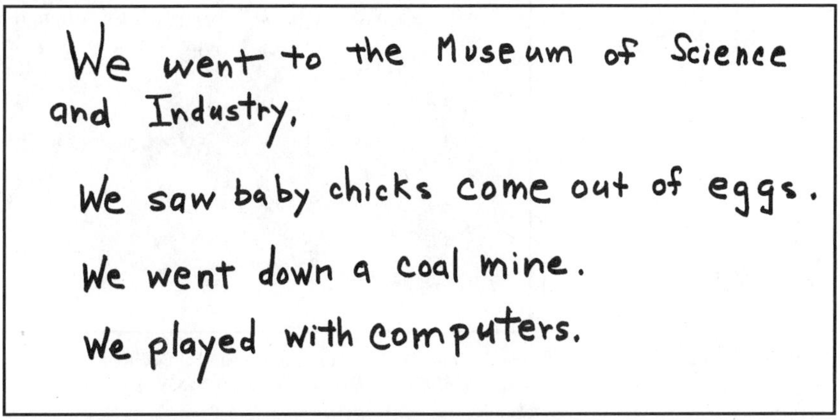

We went to the Museum of Science and Industry.
We saw baby chicks come out of eggs.
We went down a coal mine.
We played with computers.

3. L: What I learned.   Students read the lesson silently and write what they have learned from the reading. Answers to this question can be shared by the group.

Figure 11.6 shows a K-W-L strategy sheet. Groups of students can complete what they already know (K) about a subject, what they want to find out (W), and, after completing the reading, what they have learned (L).

Building Meaning Vocabulary and Concepts

To read effectively, readers need to have knowledge of word meanings and of the concepts underlying the words. The more students read, the more word meanings and language they will acquire. It is important to use strategies that will build the child's vocabulary and understanding of words.

Knowledge of vocabulary and the ability to understand the concepts of words are closely related to reading achievement. Limited vocabulary knowledge can seriously hamper reading comprehension. Further, as words become more abstract, the concepts become more difficult to grasp.

Concepts are commonly explained as ideas, abstractions, or the essence of things. For example, the concept of *chair* refers to an idea, an abstraction, or a symbol of concrete experiences. A person's experiences may have included exposure to a specific rocking chair, an upholstered chair, and a baby's highchair, but the concept *chair* symbolizes a set of attributes about "chairness." The word *chair* allows a person to make an inference about new experiences with chairs, such as a lawn chair, observed for the first time. The word or concept of *chair* by itself does not have an empirical reference point.

Figure 11.6

K-W-L Strategy Sheet

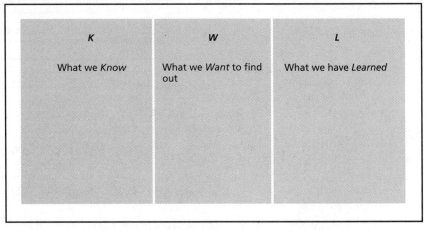

K	*W*	*L*
What we *Know*	What we *Want* to find out	What we have *Learned*

Source: From "K-W-L: Teaching Model That Develops Active Reading of Expository Text," by D. M. Ogle, 1986, *The Reading Teacher, 39,* p. 565.

At a still more abstract level, words become further removed from concrete referents. The concept *chair* is part of a broader concept of *furniture.* Concepts even more removed from the sensory world are ideas such as *democracy, loyalty, fairness,* and *freedom.*

A further confusion in school learning is related to the fact that textbooks present important concepts as technical terms, such as *plateau, continental divide, density of population, pollution, the law of gravity,* or *space exploration.* Problems in reading in the content areas are frequently due not to the difficulty of the words but to the concentration and compactness of the presentation of the concepts.

Since language plays a key role in concept development, language problems are likely to be reflected in faulty conceptual abilities and limited vocabulary development. Students who have meager, imprecise, or inaccurate concepts will have difficulties understanding a reading passage. Illustrations of the consequences of imprecise concept development are given in the case example entitled "Misunderstanding of Concepts."

Expanding Vocabulary   The following activities are designed to expand and build vocabulary:

1. Highlighting multiple word meanings.   Multiple meanings of words often cause confusion in reading. For example, there are many meanings of the word *note.* In music, *note* means the elliptical character in a certain position on the music staff. In arithmetic or business, a *note* might mean a written promise to pay. In English or study hall, a *note* might refer to an informal written communication. In social studies, a *note* might refer to a formal communiqué between the heads of two nations. In science, one might be able to *note* the results of an experiment, meaning to observe them. In English class, the selection of literature might discuss an individual who was a person of great *note,* or importance, in the community. In any lesson, the student could be asked to make *note* of an examination date, meaning to remember it. The teacher could make a *note,* meaning a remark, in the margin of the paper. In material on England, paper money may be called a *bank note.* The student who cannot hold the various concepts of this word in mind will have trouble understanding many areas of the curriculum. By highlighting multiple meanings—through dictionary games, sentence-completion exercises, and class discussion—teachers can offer important help to students who must develop an awareness of one word's different meanings.

2. Providing concrete experiences.   To build vocabulary and develop concepts for reading, students need concrete experiences with words. A first step is to provide students with primary experiences with the word or concept. The next step is to encourage and assist students to draw conclusions from their experiences. As students progress to more advanced stages, teachers can foster skills of classifying, summarizing, and generalizing.

3. Exploring sources of vocabulary.   Since vocabulary is woven into every phase of our lives, new words can be drawn from any aspect of a student's

CASE EXAMPLE

MISUNDERSTANDING OF CONCEPTS

- Some students confuse one attribute of an object with the concept of the object. For example, Paula could not understand the circular concept of the roundness of a plate. When told that the plate was "round" and asked to draw a circle around its edges, Paula said. "That's not round; that's a dish." Students may also confuse the concept of an object with its name. When Paula was asked if the moon could be called by another name, such as *cow,* she responded, "No, because the moon doesn't give milk."

- Misunderstanding a symbol that conveys multiple concepts may have unexpected consequences. Nine-year-old Susie was in tears when she brought home a medical form from the school nurse advising Susie's parents to take their daughter for an eye examination. Susie sobbed that the cause of her anguish was not that she needed eyeglasses, but that the nurse had filled in an *F* in the blank next to the word *sex* on the examination form. That symbol *F* conveyed the concept of a grade, and Susie feared she had failed sex.

- Students often deal with their inability to understand a concept by ignoring it. By failing to read a word they do not know, they may change the entire meaning of a passage. One high school student thought the school was using pornographic material because the people described in the following passage were nude: "The pilgrims did not wear gaudy clothes." Since the boy did not know the meaning of the word *gaudy,* he simply eliminated it from the sentence.

- To make pizza, Lisa and Jaime were told to put it in the microwave oven, heat it, and then bring it to the lunchroom. Thinking they were following the directions, after heating the pizza, they unplugged the microwave oven and carried it (with the pizza inside) to the lunch room.

experience: television, sports, newspapers, advertising, science, and so on. Many students enjoy keeping lists of new words and developing word books.

4. Expanding vocabulary through classification. Another way to learn new words is to attach them to known words. Much vocabulary growth takes place in this manner. Vertical vocabulary expansion involves taking a known word and breaking it down into categories. For example, students take the concept *dog* and break it into many species (*collie, terrier, cocker spaniel*). Horizontal vocabulary growth refers to enrichment and differentiation. Children may first call all animals *dogs*. Then they learn to distinguish cats, horses, and other creatures.

Word Webs   A **word web** is a type of graphic organizer, a strategy for helping build vocabulary and making information easier to understand and learn. Word webs enrich associations with a word and deepen a student's understanding of important concepts. Figure 11.7 is an example of a word web for *ice cream*. A group of students developed the word web by answering three questions: "What is it?" "What is it like?" and "What are some examples?"

Figure 11.7

Word Web

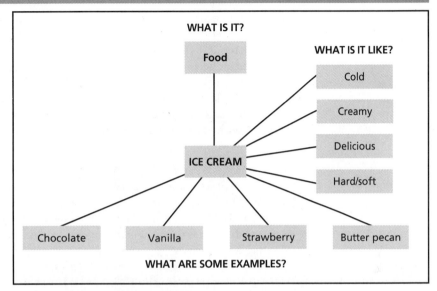

Source: From *Strategic Learning in the Content Areas,* by D. M. Cook (Ed.), 1989, p. 132. Madison: Wisconsin Department of Public Instruction.

Research shows that graphic organizers help students with learning disabilities understand reading material and improve their comprehension (Fisher, Schumaker, & Deshler, 1995). A useful computer program that readily produces many types of graphic organizers is *Inspiration* (Inspiration Software).

Cloze Procedure   The **cloze procedure** is a useful technique for building comprehension and language skills. It is based on the Gestalt idea of closure—the impulse to complete a structure and make it whole by supplying a missing element. When the cloze procedure is applied to the reading process, the following steps are used:

1. Select a passage of reading material.
2. Rewrite the material and delete every *n*th word (for example, every fifth word or every tenth word). Replace the deleted word with a blank line; all lines should be the same length.
3. Ask students to fill in each blank by writing the word they think was deleted.

One advantage of the cloze test over the conventional reading test or other fill-in-the-blank tests is that because words are deleted at random, both *lexical* words and *structural* words are omitted. Lexical words carry primary meaning and are roughly similar to verbs, nouns, adjectives, and adverbs. Relationships are indicated by structural words, such as articles, prepositions, conjunctions, and auxiliary verbs. What the reader supplies provides clues to his or her underlying language processes.

The cloze procedure may be modified and used for a variety of purposes. To teach vocabulary, for example, only the words of the vocabulary lesson can be deleted. In content areas, such as social studies, technical words can be deleted. Or the teacher can delete other selected categories, such as adjectives, adverbs, or prepositions. For students who have difficulty in writing, the cloze words can be printed on cards backed with felt or Velcro, which students place on the appropriate blank space in the written passage.

In the sample cloze exercise that follows, the reading material was retyped with every tenth word deleted and replaced by a standard-size line. Students supply the missing words.

> Fill in the deleted words in the following passage entitled "Farming in Switzerland":
>
> Switzerland is a country of very high, steep mountains _____ narrow valleys. In the valleys are the farms where _____ farmers raise much of the food they need for _____ and their animals. Because the valleys are tiny, the _____ are small. There is no room on them for _____ grassland that is needed for pasturing cows or goats _____ sheep during the summer.*
>
> Answers: *and, the, themselves, farms, the, or*

The Reading-Writing Connection

Dialogue Journals   Dialogue journals are a personal way to integrate reading and writing. To initiate this activity, the teacher gives each student a notebook, and teachers and students write personal messages to each other through the notebook. A variety of topics can be addressed; teachers may ask students how they liked a story or ask them about their pets, birthdays, holidays, or something that happened to them (see Figure 11.8). Some teachers paste a picture, a cartoon, or a Polaroid picture of the student in the journal and ask for student comments. After the student writes something, the teacher responds in the journal. The response may provide some personal information and then ask for more information or may start another topic. Typically, as students get used to the journal, they begin to write more and look forward to a regular interchange through the journal. Figure 11.8 shows a written journal from a bilingual class.

Materials Without Words   To foster reading comprehension, the teacher can use materials that do not have words, such as comic books without captions, silent films, and books of photographs. The students first figure out the story content from the pictures; then they make the transition to printed words. Once the students understand the material, words become meaningful. The students can even write their own dialogue.

Written Conversations   Instead of saying what they wish to communicate to the teacher or to friends, students can write the message and give it to

*From *High Roads*, by P. McKee, M. Harrison, A. McGowen, and E. Lehr, 1962, p. 34. Boston: Houghton Mifflin. Reprinted by permission.

Figure 11.8

Written Journal from a Child in a Bilingual Class

La gente digo que todo parecia
un milagro y eran muy felices.

their teacher or to other students. The teacher's (or classmates') responses should also be written (Richek et al., 1996; Goodman & Burke, 1980). Students in junior high school often surreptitiously send small folded notes to their friends. This activity legitimizes the note exchange ventures.

Thinking Strategies

The Directed Reading-Thinking Activity   The directed reading-thinking activity (DRTA) method promotes the processes of thinking, predicting, and confirming while reading. In this activity, a sentence or a short passage is first read by a group of students. The teacher then encourages the students to predict, by making guesses and establishing hypotheses about what will happen next. Finally, the students read the next short selection to confirm or reject their predictions and also to develop a new prediction for the next part of the story. DRTA promotes group work and social learning. To enhance the group work, teachers can display the stories using big books, overhead transparencies, computer screens, or multimedia computer programs.

With this method, teaching reading becomes a way of teaching thinking, as teachers ask such questions as "What do you think?" "Why do you think so?" and "Can you prove it?" The emphasis is on teaching thinking, and pupils learn to examine, hypothesize, find proof, suspend judgment, and make decisions (Richek et al., 1996).

Advance Organizers   This technique is used to establish a mindset for the reader so that she or he can relate the new material to previously learned information before the material is read. Advance organizers can take several forms: introduction of general concepts, a linkage to previously learned materials, or a study of a complex introductory passage.

Self-Monitoring   In this strategy, students learn to monitor their own mistakes. Specific training is needed for students to learn how to check their own responses and become conscious of errors or answers that do not make sense. Self-monitoring requires active involvement in the learning process rather than passive learning, in which students are not conscious of incongruities. Students are taught how to scan the material before answering a question, and how to stop, listen, look, and think—that is, to consider systematically the alternative approaches and answers before responding to a problem. The aim of self-monitoring is to reduce impulsive, thoughtless answers and to delay responses until a systematic search for the right response has been made.

Questioning Strategies   The types of questions teachers ask stimulate the various types of thinking in which students engage during reading. Many of the questions teachers use demand recall of details. To stimulate comprehension, teachers must also plan questions that provoke conjecture, explanation, evaluation, and judgment. The following examples illustrate the four types of comprehension questions.

Literal comprehension: "What did little brother want to eat?"

Interpretation: "Why was the cookie jar kept on the basement steps?"

Critical reading: "Did Mother do the right thing in leaving the children alone?"

Creative reading: "How would you have solved this problem?"

   With *self-questioning* learning strategies, students develop their own comprehension questions. Students with learning disabilities are taught to use self-questioning strategies while reading. They ask themselves such questions as "What am I reading this passage for? What is the main idea? What is a good question about the main idea?" When students learn to monitor their reading, their comprehension improves significantly (Wong & Jones, 1982).

Learning Strategies for Reading

Learning strategies are discussed in greater detail in Chapters 6 and 9. A major reading comprehension problem for students with learning disabilities is that they tend to be passive and to wait for teacher direction. They do not know how to interact effectively with the text or to merge the information with what they already know. They often read reluctantly, hesitating to ask questions and focusing solely on what they think the teacher wants them to remember. These students may not monitor their reading comprehension. When they are not sure of the meaning of a passage they are reading, they do not take action by going back and trying to understand. Instead, they continue to read and lose even more of the meaning. Often, they are unaware that something is wrong.

Students with disabilities in reading comprehension need instruction that helps them become actively involved in the reading and in trying to reconstruct the author's message. They need to develop metacognitive abilities by learning to recognize their loss of comprehension when it occurs and employing "fix-up" strategies. Learning strategies for improving reading comprehension help students become active, involved learners who are able to direct their own learning (Lane & Brownell, 1995; Lenz, Ellis, & Scanlon, 1996; Deshler, Ellis, & Lenz, 1996). Two learning strategies that focus on reading comprehension are the paraphrasing strategy and the multipass strategy.

Paraphrasing Strategy   In this strategy students learn to put passages into their own words. They use the mnemonic *RAP* to remind themselves to *Read* the paragraph, *Ask themselves* about the main idea and two supportive details, and *Put* the text in their own words (Deshler et al., 1996; Lenz et al., 1996).

Multipass Strategy   In this strategy, students review a text three times to enhance comprehension. In the "survey" pass, they preview the introduction and summary and examine the headings and visual displays of the text. In the "size-up" pass, the student identifies the most important content of the text by reading the chapter questions and surveying the text for the answers. During the "sort-out" pass, the student reads the selection and answers each accompanying question (Lenz et al., 1996; Deshler et al., 1996).

SPECIAL REMEDIAL APPROACHES FOR TEACHING READING

The special methods discussed in this section are designed for students with severe reading problems and are not typically used in the general education classroom. We discuss the following special methods: multisensory methods, the Fernald Method, Reading Recovery, and Direct Instruction Programs.

Multisensory Methods

A collection of programs that are based on the Orton-Gillingham Method comprise the **multisensory methods** for students with severe reading and learning disabilities. They include the Orton-Gillingham program, Project Read, the Wilson Reading Method, Alphabetic Phonics, the Herman Method, and the Spalding Method (Henry, 1998). These multisensory groups have formed an umbrella organization called the International Multisensory Structured Language Council (McIntyre & Pickering, 1995). The multisensory methods have the following similar characteristics (Oakland, Black, Stanford, Nussbaum, & Balise, 1998):

- help anchor verbal information by providing linkages with the visual, auditory, tactile, and kinesthetic pathways for learning
- use highly structured phonics instruction with an emphasis on the alphabetic system
- include abundant drill, practice, and repetition
- have carefully planned sequential lessons
- emphasize explicit instruction in the language rule systems to guide reading and spelling

The multisensory methods use several senses to reinforce learning, as indicated in the acronym **VAKT,** which is formed from the first letter of the words, *visual, auditory, kinesthetic,* and *tactile.* To stimulate all of these senses, children hear the teacher say the word, say the word to themselves, hear themselves say the word, feel the muscle movement as they trace the word, feel the tactile surface under their finger tips, see their hands move as they trace the word, and hear themselves say the word as they trace it. Several of the multisensory methods are described in this section.

The Orton-Gillingham Method   The *Orton-Gillingham method* is an outgrowth of the Orton theory of reading disability (Orton, 1937, 1976). This method focuses on a multisensory, systematic, structured language procedure for reading-decoding and spelling instruction. Initial activities focus on learning individual letter sounds and blending. The student uses a tracing technique to learn single letters and their sound equivalents. These single sounds are later combined into larger groupings and then into short words (Orton, 1976; Gillingham & Stillman, 1970).

Simultaneous spelling tasks are also part of the Orton-Gillingham method. While writing the letters, the students say both the sounds of the letters in sequence and the letter names. The method emphasizes phonics and depends on a formal sequence of learning. Independent reading is delayed until the major part of the phonics program has been covered.

There are a number of extensions and applications of the Orton-Gillingham Method. Project READ, an adaption of the Orton-Gillingham method in the public schools of Minnesota, reported significant gains in reading achievement (Enfield, 1988). A variation of the Orton-Gillingham method was developed by Slingerland (1976), who offered an extensive set of materials. Another adaptation is the *Recipe for Reading* (Traub & Bloom, 1978), which is accompanied by twenty-one supplementary readers.

The Wilson Reading System   The Wilson Reading System (1988) is a multisensory, structured language program based on the Orton-Gillingham philosophy. It provides a step-by-step method for teachers working with students who require direct, multisensory, structured language teaching. The Wilson Reading System targets students who have difficulty decoding independently, reading with fluency, or spelling words, even with the help of a spell-checker or dictionary. The program teaches students the structure of words and language through a carefully sequenced 12-step program that helps them master decoding and improve encoding in English. It directly teaches phonological awareness, phonology, and total word structure, and it takes one to three years to complete. The Wilson program is also used with adults with dyslexia.

The Fernald Method   Grace Fernald (1943, 1988) developed an approach to reading that uses visual, auditory, kinesthetic, and tactile senses, but it differs from the other multisensory programs in that it teaches a whole word (rather than single sounds). The student traces the entire word, thereby strengthening the memory and visualization of the entire word. The Fernald method consists of four stages, but its uniqueness is most evident in Stage 1. The Fernald method is also effective for teaching spelling (see Chapter 12).

Stage 1. It is essential that the student select the word to be learned. The teacher writes the student's word on paper with a crayon. The student then traces the word with his or her fingers, making contact with the paper, thus using both tactile and kinesthetic senses. As the student traces it, the teacher says the word so that the student hears it (using the auditory sense). This process is repeated until the student can write the word correctly without looking at the sample. Once the student learns the word, the sample is placed in a file box. The words accumulate in the box until there are enough words for the student to write a story by using them. The story is then typed so that the student can read his or her own story.

Stage 2. The student is no longer required to trace each word but rather learns each new word by looking at the teacher's written copy of the word and saying it to himself or herself while writing it.

Stage 3. The student learns new words by looking at a printed word and repeating it to himself or herself before writing it. At this point, the student may begin reading from books.

Stage 4. The student is able to recognize new words from their similarity to printed words or to parts of words previously learned. The student now can generalize the knowledge he or she has acquired through the reading skills.

Reading Recovery

Reading Recovery is a reading program designed for first graders who are having difficulty in learning to read. Initially developed for children in New Zealand by Marie Clay (1985, 1993), it is now widely used in the United States. Reading Recovery provides special instruction for children who are at the lowest rank of their first-grade class. All first graders are assessed during the first few weeks of first grade, and those children in the lowest rank are selected for the Reading Recovery Program. Each child in the program then receives one-on-one reading instruction for 30 minutes each day for a period of from 12 to 15 weeks.

The program uses a variety of word-identification and comprehension strategies. The materials include many simple books, particularly predictable and language-pattern books. The program stresses early intervention (in first grade) and the intensive training the teachers receive in Reading Recovery methods (DeFord, 1991; Iverson & Tunmer, 1993).

The research reports on Reading Recovery are mixed. Children initially made greater gains in reading than children in comparable groups. However, some children did not show lasting gains over time. About 30 percent of the children had not been "recovered" one year after they began participating in the program (Pinnell et al., 1994; Center et al. 1995; Shannon & Barr, 1995).

Direct Instruction Programs

Direct instruction has been shown to be highly effective with children who are considered at risk because of poverty (Carnine, Silbert, & Kameenui, 1990). The *Direct Instruction Programs* include a direct instruction reading program (Engelmann & Bruner, 1995). (This reading program is a revision of the former DISTAR reading program.) The Direct Instruction reading programs consist of six levels, roughly corresponding to grades 1 through 6. A sample page from this program is shown in Figure 11.9.

This highly structured reading program consists of lessons based on carefully sequenced skill hierarchies. Based on principles of behavioral psy-

Figure 11.9

Page from a Direct Instruction Program

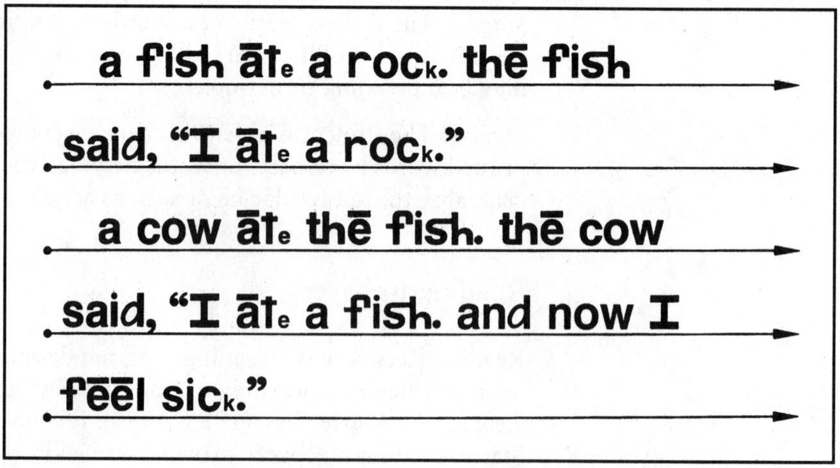

From *Reading Mastery 8 Fast Cycle, Storybook,* 1/e, by S. Engelmann and E. Bruner, copyright © 1995 McGraw-Hill. Reproduced with permission of The McGraw-Hill Companies.

chology, it contains drills and instructional reading, as well as repetition and practice. Students progress in small planned steps, and teacher praise is used as a reinforcement. Teachers are guided in specific procedures and oral instructions through each step of the program. The program uses a synthetic phonics approach, and students are first taught the prerequisite skill of auditory blending to help them combine isolated sounds into words. In addition, the shapes of some alphabet letters are modified to provide clues to the letter sounds. The special alphabet is gradually phased out as children progress.

In these programs, the teacher presents fully scripted lessons; that is, what the teacher says and does is prescribed. The students (individually and in unison as a group) provide the anticipated response. The teacher evaluates the degree of mastery of individuals and of the group on criterion-referenced tasks and tests.

The *Corrective Reading Program* (Engelmann, Becker, Hanner, & Johnson, 1988) is designed for the older student (grades 4 through 12). It consists of two strands: decoding (which follows the regular Direct Instruction format) and comprehension (which uses text materials of interest to the older student). The address for the web site is: **http://www.sra4kids.com.**

METHODS OF DEALING WITH SPECIAL READING PROBLEMS

Students who have great difficulty in acquiring reading skills often encounter special types of problems, such as reversals, finger pointing, lip moving, halting oral reading, and poor silent reading. The following strategies can help students with these special reading problems (Richek et al., 1996).

Reversals

Reversals are the tendency to reverse letters or words that are different only in direction, such as *b* for *d, no* for *on,* or *saw* for *was.* Inversions are another common type of error, such as *u* for *n.* Poor readers with this problem may even write backward, producing "mirror writing."

It is very common for beginning readers to make reversals. At the beginning stages of reading, such errors merely indicate a lack of experience with letters and words. Reversals typically disappear as the student gains experience and proficiency in reading. Therefore, teachers must decide if the reversals are merely developmental (in which case they should be ignored) or if they indicate a disability interfering with reading progress and requiring specific remediation. The following remedial methods are suggested:

1. Concentrate on one letter at a time. For example, start with the letter *b,* make a large chart, and use a memory word, such as *bicycle.*

2. Trace the confusable word or letter on a large card or on the blackboard, or use felt letters so that the student has kinesthetic reinforcement.

3. Underline the first letter of a confusable word, or write the first letter in a color.

4. Use phonics instruction to reinforce the pronunciation of the confusable word.

5. Write the confusable word, and say it while writing.

6. Use memory devices. For example, show that the lowercase *b* goes in the same direction as the capital *B* and that one can be superimposed on the other.

Finger Pointing and Lip Moving

Both finger pointing and lip moving are characteristic normal behaviors in the early stages of reading. Moreover, when material becomes difficult, even mature and efficient readers fall back on these habits because they do help us understand difficult and frustrating material. Some students may need these aids to understand what they are reading.

However, finger pointing and lip moving inhibit fluent reading and should be discouraged when they are no longer needed. Both habits encourage word-by-word reading, vocalization, or subvocalization. Both also inhibit speed and reduce comprehension. The following remedial approaches should be considered:

1. Do not select material that is so difficult that it forces the student to use these behaviors.

2. Extensive finger pointing may be a symptom of visual difficulties. In some cases, the student may need an eye examination.

3. Students should be made aware of their habits and made to understand how they inhibit reading progress.

4. A first stage in eliminating finger pointing can be the use of markers to replace fingers and then the elimination of the marker itself. If the marker is placed *above* the line of print, readers will be able to read as quickly as they can, and the marker will not be a barrier to speed and looking ahead.

5. Students may need to be reminded that they are moving their lips. Increasing the speed of reading also acts to eliminate lip moving.

Disfluent Oral Reading

The repeated reading technique described earlier in this chapter has been found to effectively improve fluency. Poor readers often read in a very hesitant, nonfluent, halting manner. Research shows that teachers tend to interrupt poor readers much more often than they interrupt good readers, thereby discouraging oral reading fluency. To improve oral reading, students need more practice in the skill. Make sure the material is not too difficult, have the students first read the material silently, and tell them you will not interrupt while they are reading.

Inability to Read Silently

Most purposeful reading by adults is silent. Therefore, remedial instruction should include opportunities for students to read silently. To stress the importance of silent reading, it should be done before oral reading. Students need direct motivation to read silently. For example, you might stress the information that the student should find in the text, and follow the silent reading with questions and discussion so that the students will see it as a meaningful activity. Gradually increase the quantity of silent reading that students are expected to do.

Tape-Recorded Textbooks

There are several sources for obtaining the tape-recorded books that are available to students with disabilities. Students who are identified as having learning disabilities are eligible to obtain, at no cost, books recorded for the blind. In addition, new titles can be recorded if needed. For students with severe reading problems, recorded textbooks can be a real boon; using recorded books allows them to keep up with content while continuing to improve their reading skills. For further information, contact Recording for the Blind and Dyslexics, 20 Roszel Road, Princeton, NJ 20542. The organization can also be reached by phone at (800) 221-4792, or at **http://www.bfbd.org**.

COMPUTERS AND READING Computers offer many instructional advantages for students with learning disabilities to practice reading skills. Computer software programs are motivating, they provide time for learning on a private one-to-one basis, they can help develop automaticity, and they offer time to think about passages. Reading software programs are available for the prereading, elementary, secondary, and adult levels.

The dizzying pace of change in computer technology has created a dramatic increase in both the number and quality of software programs to teach reading. Selected reading software programs are listed in Table 11.7, organized by topics in reading. Early reading programs for young children are listed in Chapter 8. The software in Table 11.7 is organized as literacy software, sight words, phonics skills, vocabulary, reading comprehension, reading rate, word webs, and miscellaneous.

New advances in computer technology are available that can help students with disabilities overcome their reading difficulties (Raskind &

Table 11.7

Selected Reading
Software for Students
with Learning
Disabilities

TITLE	PUBLISHER	GRADE LEVEL	TYPE	SYSTEM
Ultimate Word Attack	Davidson	E, S	CD	Mac/Win
Kid Phonics	Davidson	S	CD	Mac/Win
Reader Rabbit	The Learning Co.	E	CD	Mac/Win
Reading Skills Collection	Hartley/Jostens	E, S	CD	Mac/Win
First Phonics	Sunburst	P, E	CD	Mac/Win
Vocabulary Development	Optimum	E, S	CD	Mac/Win
Word Muncher	The Learning Co.	E	CD	Mac/Win
Carmen San Diego WORD Detection	Broderbund	E, S	CD	Mac/Win
Scholastic Smart Book Series	Scholastic	E, S	CD	Mac/Win
Inspiration	Inspiration Software	E, S	CD	Mac/Win
Language Experience Recorder	Teacher Support System	E, S	CD	Mac/Win
Spelling Deluxe	Davidson	E, S	CD	Mac/Win
Hyperstudio	Roger Wagner	E, S	CD	Mac/Win

P=primary   E=elementary   S=secondary

Broderbund Phone: 800-521-6263   Davidson **http://www.davd.com**
Edmark **http://www.edmark.com**   Hartley/Jostens Phone: 800-247-1380
The Learning Co. **http://www.learningco.com**   Sunburst **http://www.sunburst.com**
Optimum Resources Phone: 702-736-2877   Roger Wagner Software **http://www.hyperstudio.com**
Teacher Support System **http://www.edresources.com**

Higgins, 1998; Lewis, 1998; Raskind, 1998). A few activities and software programs you may wish to incorporate into your curriculum include:

- **Computer-based Reading Instruction.**   Reading material on a computer screen that uses hypertext will allow the user to select a word in the text that the computer will pronounce, to click to view a graphic showing the word's meaning, or to click to see a structured analysis of the word (Lewis, 1998).

- **Talking Storybooks.**   These programs present an entire work of children's literature on a CD-ROM disk (Lewis, 1998).

Living Books Series (Broderbund)

Discis Books (Discis Knowledge Research, Inc.)

- **Speech Synthesis.**   These systems will read anything on the screen.

Books on disks. Contact *Recordings for the Blind and Dyslexic* at **http://www.rfbld.org**.

Scanning and reading print with speech synthesizers. These devices use speech synthesizers to read print from a book or on a computer screen.

Students with learning disabilities gain many instructional advantages when using computers to practice reading skills. *(© Bob Daemmrich/ Stock Boston)*

Outspoken. Contact Alva Access Group, Inc., at **http://www.aagi.com/docs/oSM/desc.html.**

Scanning Reader. Contact Arkenstone, Inc., at **http://www.arkenstone.org.arknew.htm.**

Book Wise at **http://www.zerox.com/xis/bookwise/index.html.**

Ultimate Reader. Contact Universal Learning Company at **http://www.universalearn.com/products/index.html.**

Chapter Summary

1. Reading is part of the language system and is closely linked to the other forms of language—oral language and writing.

2. Reading is a major academic difficulty for students with learning disabilities. The detrimental effects of reading disabilities have serious consequences in terms of academic achievement, employment, and success in life.

3. Dyslexia is a learning disability in which the individual encounters extreme difficulty in learning to read. Dyslexia is associated with neurological dysfunction.

4. There are sequential stages of reading acquisition that all individuals learning to read follow.

5. Theories of the reading process emphasize the following ideas: reading must be fluent; it is a constructive process; it must be strategic; reading requires motivation; and reading is a lifelong pursuit.

6. Two views of reading instruction are the whole-language view and explicit instruction of decoding skills (code-emphasis instruction).

7. *Whole language* is a philosophy of teaching reading that emphasizes literacy, the connection between reading and writing, meaning and comprehension, the use of authentic literature, and the avoidance of exercises and drills, such as decoding instructions.

8. Explicit code-emphasis instruction emphasizes direct instruction of phonics and the learning of the alphabetic code.

9. Two major elements of reading are word recognition and reading comprehension. Both are needed for successful reading.

10. Readers need skills in word recognition to develop fluency in reading. Word recognition takes place through phonics, sight words, context clues, and structural analysis. Phonological awareness is the realization that speech can be broken into phonemic units that can be represented by words in print.

11. The purpose of reading is comprehension, or active understanding and involvement with the written material. Fluency is needed for comprehension.

12. Strategies for promoting reading comprehension can be taught before, during, and after reading.

13. Narrative comprehension is the reading of stories.

14. Expository comprehension is the reading of informational material, such as textbooks.

15. There are many ways to assess reading ability. Informal measures include informal reading inventories, miscue analysis, and portfolio assessment. Formal tests include survey tests, diagnostic tests, and comprehensive batteries.

16. The Teaching Strategies section of this chapter presents strategies for teaching reading to students with learning disabilities. Presented are methods for improving word recognition, improving fluency, and improving reading comprehension. This section also presents special remedial methods for readers with severe disabilities and special reading problems, and discusses the use of computers for teaching reading.

Questions for Discussion and Reflection

1. Identify the stages of reading development and tell why they are critical for success in reading.

2. Define the terms *whole-language instruction* and *explicit code-emphasis instruction*. Compare and contrast the philosophies behind each of these methods of instruction.

3. Readers use a variety of methods to recognize words. Describe the different methods of word recognition. What method(s) do you think good readers rely upon?

4. What is reading comprehension? Identify a few strategies used to promote reading comprehension. Describe how students might respond to these strategies.

5. Describe narrative and expository materials. How does the teaching of reading comprehension differ for these two types of materials?

6. Describe two special remedial approaches for teaching reading to students with severe reading disabilities. How might students respond to these approaches?

7. What are the differences between informal and formal methods for assessing reading achievement? Describe a test or an assessment technique for each.

8. Describe a few ways you might successfully incorporate computer technology into a reading curriculum.

Key Terms

background knowledge *(p. 420)*
basal reading series *(p. 419)*
cloze procedure *(p. 425)*
context clues *(p. 403)*
decoding *(p. 399)*
directed reading-thinking activity *(p. 407)*
dyslexia *(p. 387)*
early literacy *(p. 394)*
explicit code-emphasis instruction *(p. 398)*
fluent reading *(p. 400)*
grapheme *(p. 399)*
informal reading inventory (IRI) *(p. 412)*
language experience method *(p. 420)*

miscue analysis *(p. 412)*
multisensory methods *(p. 429)*
neurological impress method *(p. 418)*
phoneme *(p. 390)*
phonics *(p. 399)*
phonological awareness *(p. 400)*
portfolio assessment *(p. 413)*
reading comprehension *(p. 399)*
Reading Recovery *(p. 439)*
sight words *(p. 400)*
structural analysis *(p. 404)*
VAKT *(p. 430)*
whole-language instruction *(p. 393)*
word-recognition skills *(p. 399)*
word web *(p. 424)*

12 Written Language: Written Expression, Spelling, and Handwriting

CHAPTER OUTLINE

Written language is the third form of the integrated language system. Interconnecting linkages bridge written language with oral language and reading. The Theories section of this chapter considers three areas of written language: written expression, spelling, and handwriting. Word processing as a computer skill is also discussed because it is an important dimension of written language and strengthens the connections among the forms of language. The Teaching Strategies section of this chapter presents specific instructional techniques in written expression, computer word processing, spelling, and handwriting to help students with learning disabilities develop their written language skills.

THEORIES

Many people dislike writing. Their disdainful attitude is depicted in the story of the New York City taxicab driver who skillfully guided his cab past a pedestrian. The cabby then explained to his passenger why he was so careful: "I always try to avoid hittin' 'em because every time ya hit one, ya gotta write out a long report about it."

Words are the primary means of communication for human beings. It is the way we tell each other what we want and what we don't want, what we think, and how we feel. When words are spoken, they are a wonderful asset—quick, direct, and easy. But when words must be written, they become burdensome, part of a slow and laborious task. Many students with learning disabilities have significant problems in the acquisition and use of written language, and written language problems often continue to adversely effect their lives as adults (Vogel, 1998; Troia, Graham, & Harris, 1998; Gerber & Reiff, 1994; Adelman & Vogel, 1991).

Writing is the most sophisticated and complex achievement of the language system. In the sequence of language development, it is typically the last to be learned, although the early literacy approach encourages children to write even before they learn to read. Through writing, we integrate previous learnings and experiences in listening, speaking, and reading. Proficiency in written language requires an adequate basis of oral language skills, as well as many other competencies. The writer must be able to keep one idea in mind while formulating it into words and sentences and must be skilled in planning the correct graphic form for each letter and word while manipulating the writing instrument. The writer must also possess sufficient visual and motor memory to integrate complex eye-hand relationships. The instructional concept of "writing across the curriculum" has become a persuasive force in the teaching of writing. This means that writing is encouraged in all subjects of the curriculum, not only those in which written language is the center of instruction.

Three components of writing are addressed in this chapter: written expression, spelling, and handwriting.

WRITTEN EXPRESSION Competent writing requires many related abilities, including facility in spoken language, the ability to read, skills in spelling, legible handwriting or skill with computer keyboarding, knowledge of the rules of written usage, and cognitive strategies for organizing and planning the writing.

Individuals with learning disabilities often lack many of these critical writing-related abilities and may have severe problems communicating through writing. Their writing is replete with errors in spelling, punctuation, capitalization, handwriting, and grammar. Their written products tend to be short, poorly organized, and impoverished in terms of development of ideas. Poor skills in written communication and in sharing thoughts through writing can persist over time and into the adult years (Vogel, 1998; Graham & Harris, 1997; Gerber & Reif, 1994). (See the case example entitled "A Written Language Disability.")

The Writing Connection in the Integrated Language System

The web of linkages among the elements of language connects the language forms with each other and also strengthens the underlying language system. Extensive oral language experiences promote reading. Instruction in reading improves performance in writing. Experiences with writing and composing improves one's knowledge of language and skill in speaking and reading. All strengthen the underlying language system (Richek et al., 1996).

The processes used in spoken language, reading, and writing have many similarities. In both reading and writing, people set and revise goals, refining and reconstructing meaning as they go through the material. They develop expectations about what they will read or write next, form attitudes about the text, and monitor the information they wish to remember or convey. Both use a constructive process. Readers construct meaning as they recode the author's message into their own language; writers construct original ideas in the process of writing the message (Graham & Harris, 1997; Richek et al., 1996; Harris & Graham, 1992).

By its very nature, writing is an active process. The physical aspect of writing literally forces active involvement upon the writers. Writers perform the actions of picking up a pen or pencil (or using a computer keyboard) and recording their thoughts. While people write, they must actively work at producing something that did not exist before by using their own background knowledge and integrating their language skills. The process of revising requires rethinking and reconstruction. Much reading also occurs during the process of writing. When adults write, over half of the "writing" time is actually devoted to reading (Stephens, 1987). As soon as

CASE EXAMPLE

A WRITTEN LANGUAGE DISABILITY

The following news event illustrates the importance of writing skills for successful communication. In an attempted burglary, a would-be robber handed this handwritten note to the bank teller:

I GOT A BUM. I ALSO HAVE A CONTOUR. I'M GOING TO BLOW YOU SKY HEIGHT. I'M NO KILLEN. THIS IS A HELD UP.*

*Possible translation: I got a bomb. I also have a control. I'm going to blow you sky high. I'm no killer. This is a holdup.

Unable to decipher the note, the teller asked the robber for help in reading the message. By the time the robber deciphered the words for the teller, the police had arrived and arrested him. To make the matter worse for the robber, the police were also able to trace him to other bank holdups in which the same spelling and writing errors were made in the burglary note (*Miami Herald*, 1980). Written language skills are required in most occupations today—even to be a successful bank robber.

writers complete a section of writing, they usually reread it. They also reread to see how to connect a previously written section to one they are about to write. When writers complete an entire text, they usually reread it immediately, as well as a few days later. The kind of reading that takes place during writing is intensive, involving much critical analysis (Harris & Graham, 1996).

Early Literacy

The term **early literacy** refers to the child's early entrance into the world of words, language, and stories. The concept of early literacy emphasizes the interrelatedness of the various forms of language in the child's development. Children develop literacy through simultaneous experiences with oral language, reading, and writing.

The early literacy philosophy suggests that writing may be easier than reading and may actually develop earlier than reading (Clay, 1993). Writing is a more self-involving task than reading because the meaning of a writer's message originates from within the writer and is known to the writer in advance. In contrast, reading requires that reader be able to interpret someone else's ideas and use of language, which is a more difficult task for the beginner.

The early literacy view is that writing is beneficial even for primary-age children and should be encouraged (Snow, Burns, & Griffin, 1998; CIERA, 1998; Sulzby & Teale, 1991). When young children write, they directly explore both the functions and the forms of written language. Writing helps children understand that in English print progresses from left to right.

Many young children who have not yet learned this rule of written English reverse this process, writing from right to left (Figure 12.1).

In their early writing experiences, young children should not be required to adhere to criteria of proper form or correct spelling; they should simply be encouraged to explore and to play with writing. Young children are encouraged to use "invented spelling," which means they follow their own spelling rules. Early writing also increases children's awareness of the phonological properties of language. When children attempt to put their ideas into print, they explore and learn about the alphabetic nature of written English. As they begin to realize that words can be segmented into sounds, they acquire important skills for the early stages of reading (Richek et al., 1996). Figure 12.2 is an example of a child's writing in a kindergarten class using an early literacy curriculum.

The Writing Process

Current theories on the teaching of writing call for a major shift in instructional emphasis to the *process* instead of the *product* of writing (Graham & Harris, 1997; Graves, 1994). The traditional product approach emphasized the written assignment (or product) created by the student. The new process approach focuses on the entire process that writers use in developing a written document. In the traditional product approach, teachers' checking and grading of the written product are based on certain expectations of perfection. Students are expected to spell correctly, use adjectives, and compose topic sentences. Their papers are graded on word choice, grammar, organization, and ideas. The papers are then returned to the students with corrections (often in red ink), and students are expected to learn

Figure 12.1

Children Must Learn That Writing in English Goes from Left to Right.

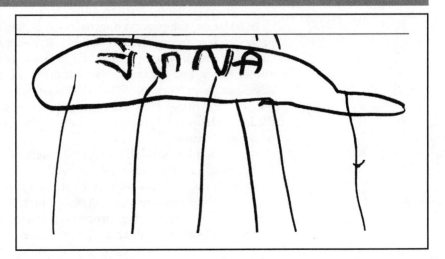

Figure 12.2

Example of a Child's Writing in a Primary Early Literacy Class

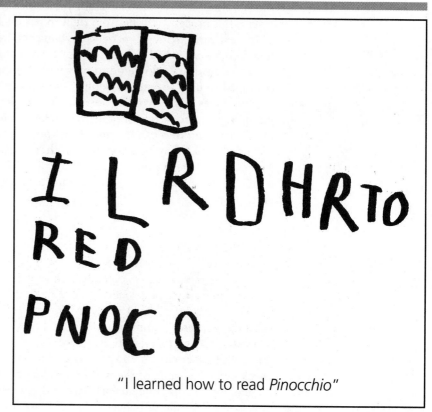

I L R D HR TO
RED
PNOCO

"I learned how to read *Pinocchio*"

and improve their writing skills from these grades and corrections. The more conscientious the teacher, the more conscientiously the corrections fill the students' papers. Too often, the result of the product type of writing instruction is that people learn to dislike writing.

In contrast, the process approach to writing emphasizes the thinking processes that are involved in writing. Teachers are encouraged to understand the complexity of the writing process as they help students think about, select, and organize tasks. Students are encouraged to ask themselves questions, such as "Who is the intended audience? What is the purpose of the writing? How can I get ideas? How can I develop and organize the ideas? How can I translate and revise the ideas so that the reader will understand them?"

Writing is a learned skill that can be taught in a school setting as a thinking-learning activity, with emphasis on the writing process. As a cognitive process, writing requires both backward and forward thinking. Good writers do not simply sit down and produce a text. Rather, they go through several stages of the **writing process**—prewriting, writing (or drafting), revising, and sharing with an audience (Graves, 1983, 1994) (Figure 12.3).

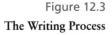

Figure 12.3

The Writing Process

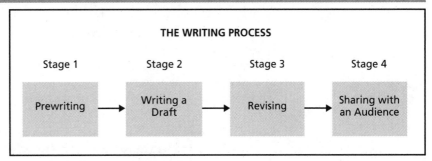

Stage 1: Prewriting During this first stage, the writer gathers ideas and refines them before beginning formal writing. **Prewriting** involves a type of brainstorming, such as talking through some thoughts and ideas, jotting a few notes in a margin, or developing a graphic organizer or list of the main points. During this time, the writer also identifies an intended audience. Students are more willing to write if they choose the topic. They may write about someone they know, a special event, or themselves. Teachers can help by asking the students to make a list of people who are special to them.

Stage 2: Writing a Draft In the second stage of the writing process, the writer records the ideas on paper. Although many people think of this stage as "writing," it actually is only one step in the process. The term **drafting** could be used instead of *writing* to emphasize that this is one version of what eventually will be written, and it will be changed. The first draft of a piece of writing is not for the reader but for the writer. As the writer jots down words, sentences, and paragraphs, these give rise to new ideas or ways to revise ideas already written. At this stage, there may be an overflow of ideas, with little organization or consideration of prose, grammar, and spelling.

Stage 3: Making Revisions Having completed the prewriting and drafting stages, the writer then refines the drafted version of the text by **revising.** Mature writers take the ideas of the first draft and reorganize and polish them. There may be several revisions, with different kinds of changes made in each, such as in content, the way of expressing the ideas, the vocabulary, the sentence structure, and the sequence of ideas. The last revision is editing, which includes checking for grammatical, punctuation, and spelling errors. This stage requires a very critical view of one's own work.

Students with learning disabilities are often reluctant to revise. Just writing the draft has required extensive effort, and making revisions can seem overwhelming. Rewriting of earlier drafts is greatly facilitated by using computers and word processor software programs.

To help writers learn to revise, teachers can model revisions in dictated stories or in their own work. They can have students make suggestions for revising some of the teacher's writing, make the revisions, and share the revised version.

Students can also make suggestions for revising the drafts of their classmates. It is important to make this a positive experience. Be sure to note some good features of a student's work before making suggestions for revision.

Stage 4. Sharing with an Audience   This fourth stage is important because it gives value and worth to the entire writing process. It provides students with the opportunity to receive feedback and to perceive themselves as authors responding to an audience. In this final stage, the writer considers the audience for whom the material is intended and whether the ideas will be well communicated to the intended reader. The amount of rewriting will depend on the intended audience. The audience could be the teacher, other students in the class, or a larger audience that is reached through publication (Graves, 1994).

Sharing with an audience or publishing can occur as a book is bound and shared with a class or placed in a classroom library. Other forms of sharing could be a presentation, a bulletin board display, or even a puppet show.

Principles for Teaching the Writing Process   The following principles apply to planning instruction for the writing process (Richek et al., 1996):

1. *During the prewriting stage, the writing process requires much time, input, and attention.*   Writers need something to write about. They need sufficient prior experiences to create and stimulate ideas for a good written production. Giving a written assignment (such as "write a one-hundred-word theme on spring") without first supplying a prewriting build-up will not produce a rich written product. Teachers can provide input experiences through activities such as trips, stories, discussions, and oral language activities. Sources of inspiration for writing include reading, art, content-area activities, films, television, newspapers, trips and field experiences, and brainstorming. As much time should be spent in prewriting as in writing.

2. *The writing process frees students from undue concentration on the mechanics of writing.*   Students should realize that all writers make errors in spelling and grammar in the first draft. Although such mistakes should *eventually* be corrected, they need not be fixed immediately. Instead, the student should focus on the content during the drafting stage and then later "clean up" the work through editing.

3. *The writing process helps students revise their work.*   Students often think that their writing is finished when they complete their first draft. When they realize that they must go through the revising stage before their

work will be complete, they begin to think of writing as a process instead of a product. A teacher can demonstrate the imperfections of a first draft by exhibiting first drafts of his or her own writing to show the students that all writing needs to be edited. Students can even form small groups to review and edit each other's work.

4. *Avoid excessive corrections of students' written work.* Students can be discouraged from trying if their attempts to express ideas are met only by having their papers returned full of grammatical, spelling, punctuation, and handwriting corrections in red ink, with heavy penalties for mistakes. As one pupil remarked, "An *F* looks so much worse in red ink." By receiving negative reinforcements, students soon learn to beat the game—they will limit their writing vocabulary to words they know how to spell, keep their sentences simple, avoid complex and creative ideas, and keep their compositions short.

Self-regulated Strategy Development (SRSD)

Self-regulated strategy development (SRSD) is suggested as an explicit approach to teaching writing that can be used along with the writing process (Troia, Graham, & Harris, 1998; Harris & Graham, 1996). Students with learning disabilities need structure and direction to acquire writing strategies. The goals of SRSD are (1) to help students develop a knowledge of writing and the skills strategies involved in the writing process, (2) to support students in the ongoing development of the abilities needed to monitor and manage their writing, and (3) to promote students' development of positive attitudes about writing and about themselves as writers.

The six stages of the SRSD model of writing are (Harris & Graham, 1996):

1. **Development of background knowledge.** Working within a group, students think about what is known about the topic and find additional information from a variety of sources.

2. **Discuss it.** The students talk about and discuss what they have learned with each other and with their teacher. They then discuss a specific writing strategy that they plan to use.

3. **Model it.** The students model how to use a writing strategy, thinking out loud as they work.

4. **Memorize it.** Students review and say aloud the parts of the writing strategy.

5. **Support it.** Students begin to write a story by using the writing strategy.

6. **Independent performance.** Students now use the writing strategy independently.

Strategies for Writing

Students with learning disabilities find writing tasks challenging, so teachers must provide adequate structure to help them carry out a writing assignment. A variety of writing strategies can help students find ideas for writing, share their ideas on paper, use interesting and descriptive vocabulary, and make the writing purposeful (Harris & Graham, 1996; Martin & Manno, 1995; Mastropieri & Scruggs, 1994).

Written Conversations   In this strategy, two students, or a student and a teacher, sit beside each other and communicate. The partners cannot speak, and writing is the only communication allowed. If one person's message is unclear, the partner must ask for clarification in writing. Used on a regular basis, this strategy helps students learn to record their thoughts in writing. For example, to "catch up on the news," the teacher can ask the student in writing how things are going. The teacher can also write a greeting and message, and the student can answer (Richek et al., 1996). Or the student can write something, and the teacher can respond in writing. For this exchange each writer can use a different-colored pen or pencil. Figure 12.4 shows an example of a written conversation.

Personal Journals   In a personal journal, students record personal events or experiences in writing. They practice writing by recording day-to-day accounts of events in their lives and their feelings about these experiences, which they can read later on (see Figure 12.5). Each student needs a journal, usually a notebook of lined paper. Students often create titles for their journals and decorate the title page. Time is set aside (usually at least a few periods a week) to record personal thoughts in journals. It is easier for stu-

Figure 12.4

An Example of Written Conversation

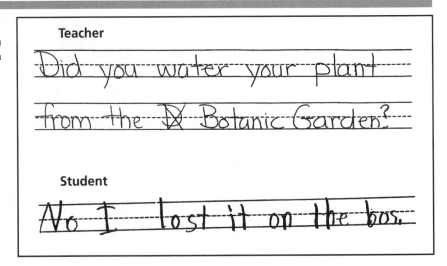

Figure 12.5

A Journal Entry

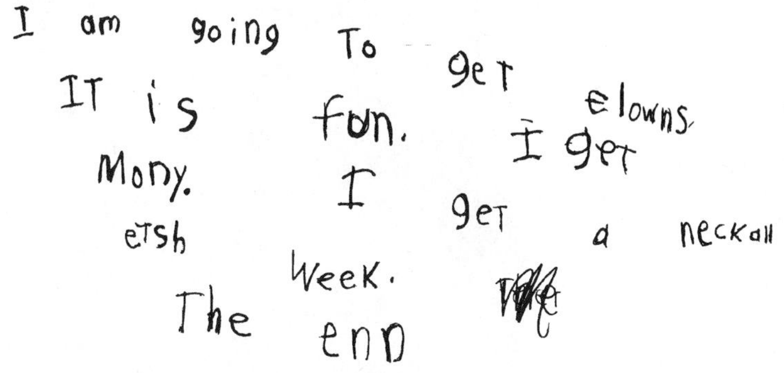

I am going To get

IT is fun. I get elowns

Mony. I get

etsh a neckall

The week.

The enp

I am going to get an allowance. It is fun. I get money.
I get a nickel each week. The end.

dents to read and write if they use only one side of a page (Richek et al., 1996).

Students may choose to share some of their journal entries, but they should have the choice of not doing so. If a student does not want the teacher to read a journal entry, he or she can fold a page in half lengthwise, and the teacher will then not read all folded pages. Teachers should also be careful not to correct grammatical and spelling errors because this practice undermines the student's confidence and may decrease the amount of writing.

Some students with learning disabilities may lack the confidence to maintain a journal. Teachers can help students overcome this problem by modeling journal writing. They can help students who cannot think of journal topics with suggestions, such as favorite places, special people, favorite stories, things I like to do, things I don't like to do, things that make me angry, and things I do well. A list of "Ideas for Writing" could be put on a chart in the room or placed in the student's journal on an "Ideas" page.

Patterned Writing   In this strategy, the students use a favorite predictable book with a patterned writing, and then they write their own version. This method gives students the security of a "frame" to use to write a personalized response. One favorite frame is *Brown Bear, Brown Bear, What Do You See?* (Martin, 1992). Each page of this book contains a refrain, such as "Brown bear, brown bear, what do you see? I see a blue bird looking at me." Students make up their own refrain and illustrate it. The finished writing of several students can be put together into a book and placed on the library table for others to read.

Graphic Organizers   Graphic organizers are visual displays that organize and structure ideas and concepts. In the context of reading, graphic

By its very nature, writing is an active process. When people write, they must actively work at producing something that did not exist before by using their own background knowledge and integrating that with their language skills.
(*Bob Daemmrich*)

organizers help students understand the reading material, and research shows that reading comprehension improves when students use graphic organizers (Fisher, Schumaker, & Deshler, 1995). In the context of writing, graphic organizers can help students generate and organize ideas as they prepare for a writing assignment (Deshler, Ellis, & Lenz, 1996).

The Venn diagram is one graphic organizer in which there are two intersecting circles. This graphic is useful for preparing for a "compare and contrast" writing assignment. For example, in comparing two people in history, one puts the descriptors of one person in one circle, the characteristics of the other person in the second circle, and the common characteristics in the intersecting section. Figure 12.6 shows a Venn diagram comparing oranges and apples.

A writing strategy using a graphic organizer that uses a top-down design is suggested by Korinek and Bulls (1996). Called *SCORE-A*, this strategy includes the following steps: *S* (select a subject), *C* (create categories), *O* (obtain sources), *R* (read and take notes), *E* (evenly organize the information), and *A* (apply the process writing method). Figure 12.7 shows an example of this strategy as the student prepares a writing project for social studies.

Computers and Word Processing

Word processing is one of the most widely used computer applications. It offers an excellent means of teaching writing and integrates the language systems. With this effective tool, writing becomes a less arduous task

Figure 12.6

Venn Diagram
Comparing Oranges
and Apples

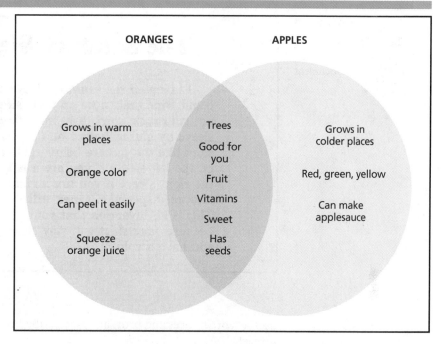

Figure 12.7

Sample Top-Down
Graphic Organizer

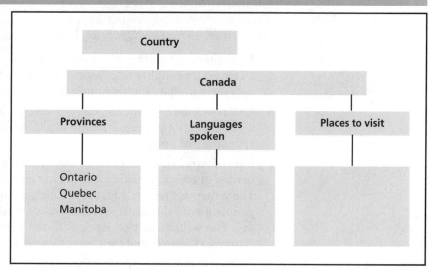

Source: Adapted from "Score A: A Student Research Paper Writing Strategy" by L. Korinek and J. A. Bulls, *Teaching Exceptional Children, 26* (4), 1996, p. 61. Copyright © 1996 by The Council for Exceptional Children. Reprinted with permission.

for many individuals with learning disabilities. With a computer, students can write without worrying about handwriting and can revise without making a mess of the written document. In Figure 12.8, a fourth grader

Figure 12.8

"The Sanitary Sleeve," a Word-Processing Document

The Sanitary Sleeve

I invented the sanitary sleeve so people could wipe their nose on their sleeve and not ruin their shirt. You make a sanitary sleeve by gluing Velcro on the sleeve of your shirt like the picture below (glue the Velcro on the left sleeve if you are a lefty and on the right sleeve if you are a righty). You'll also need special Kleenex with Velcro on it. This is an invention that your Mom will like because your shirt will stay clean even when you have a cold.

uses a word-processing program to describe his "invention" for a science project.

Advantages of Word Processing   As the writing tool of the contemporary classroom, word processing supports writing in the following ways (MacArthur, 1996; Lewis, Ashton, Haapa, Kieley, & Fielden, in press):

- *Motivation.*   Students are motivated to write because word processing increases their ability to produce neat, error-free copies. It also encourages them to share their writing and to publish it in a variety of formats.

- *Collaboration.*   Students learn to collaborate in the writing process with teachers and peers because of the visibility of the screen and the anonymity of printed text.

- *Ease of revision.*   The editing power of the computer eases the physical burden of revising, making it easier to correct, revise, and rewrite a text. The writer can readily add, correct, delete, and revise and can freely experiment until the display screen shows exactly what he or she wants to say. The writer can also work with the printed copy to make further changes, if desired, and then enter those changes into the computer.

- *Help with fine-motor problems.*   Typing is inherently easier and neater than handwriting, especially for students with fine-motor problems. At any point, by clicking "print," the writer can obtain a printed copy. Word processing eliminates the difficult task of recopying or retyping and encourages the student to expend energy on the important part of the writing process—thinking about content, editing, and revising. (To use a computer word-processing program effectively, the writer must learn keyboarding, or typing skills. Keyboarding is discussed in this chapter in the section on handwriting instruction.)

- *Special features.*   Word-processing software such as Clarisworks and Microsoftworks has many special features, such as spell-checkers or thesauruses, grammar-checkers, and speech synthesis programs that make the process of writing easier.

Word processing can assist students with learning disabilities by making it easier for them to write, to correct and revise, and to share their writing with others. However, direct instruction in using word processing for writing, editing, and revising is necessary for this technological tool to have its full impact. Studies indicate that students with learning disabilities prefer using a computer to writing text by hand. When writing text by hand, students make many minor word revisions during the process of recopying. With word processing, they make many minor revisions during the initial composing stage and then tend to add text when they prepare a second draft (Mead, 1995; MacArthur, 1996). The value of computers in writing instruction depends on how adeptly the instructional program takes advantage of the capabilities of the computer to support the writing process.

Research shows that students with learning disabilities made fewer spelling errors when using spell-checkers with word-processing software. In addition, the writing of these students improved in terms of quantity, quality, and accuracy (Lewis et al., 1999).

Word-Prediction Programs   Word-prediction programs can be very helpful for poor writers. Word-prediction programs work together with a word processor to "predict" the word the user wants to enter into the computer. When the user types the first one or two letters of a word, the program offers a list of words beginning with that letter. The user simply selects the desired word. The word-prediction software can also predict the next word in a sentence, even before the letters of the next word are entered. The prediction is based on syntax, spelling rules, word frequency, redundancy, and repetitive factors. The word-prediction software is helpful for students with learning disabilities who have difficulty in writing, keyboarding, spelling, and grammar (Raskind & Higgins, 1998; Lewis, 1998). A popular word-prediction program is Co-writer (see Table 12.1, Computers and Writing).

Speech-Recognition Systems   Speech-recognition systems allow a person to operate a computer by speaking to it. Using it in combination with a word processor, the user dictates to the system through a microphone, and the spoken words are converted to text on the computer screen. The computer "learns" to recognize the speech of the individual using it. The more the system is used, the more accurate it becomes in recognizing the user's spoken language. Speech-recognition systems may be particularly helpful to those individuals who have oral language abilities that are superior to

Table 12.1

Computers and Writing

Type of Computer Program	Name	Company
Word-processing programs	Clarisworks	Claris **http://www.claris.com**
	Microsoftworks	Microsoft **http://www.microsoft.com**
	Bank Street Writer	Broderbund **http://www.broderbund.com**
Word-processing programs that combine text and graphics	Children's Writing and Publishing Center	The Learning Co. **http://www.learningco.com**
	Writing Center	The Learning Co. **http://www.learningco.com**
	Student Writing Center	The Learning Co. **http://www.learningco.com**
Talking word-processing programs	Write: Out Loud Talking Textwriter	Don Johnston **http://www.donjohnston.com**
		Scholastic **http://www.donjohnston.com**
Word-prediction programs	Co-writer	Don Johnston **http://www.donjohnston.com**
Speech recognition systems	Dragon Dictate	Dragon Systems **http://www.dragonsys.com**
	Dragon Naturally Speaking	Dragon Systems **http://www.dragonsys.com**
	Kurzweil L & H	Applied Intelligence, Inc. **http://www.kurzweil.com**
	Voice Express	IBM Special Needs Systems **http://www.ibm.com**
	ViaVoice	IBM Special Needs Systems **http://www.ibm.com**

their written language abilities (Raskind & Higgins, 1998). Some speech-recognition systems are listed in Table 12.1.

Word-Processing Programs   Many excellent word-processing programs are available for students at all levels. Table 12.1 describes some of the programs used in schools.

Writing Email Messages   A widely used and exciting method for encouraging writing and sharing written messages with an audience is through electronic mail (email). Many classes are linking up with other classes through the computer Internet, providing children with the opportunity to write to each other. In addition, there are commercial services specifically designed for telecommunication for children.

Email is a quick and inexpensive way to transmit information. A child can write and send a message, and then the message is stored in a "mailbox" within a host computer system until the receiver logs on and reads his or her mail. A class in California can communicate via email with a class in

Alaska or in Mexico. Children can develop friendships across districts, states, and even nations.

Assessment of Written Expression

The assessment of writing usually focuses on the written product. Although the writing process involves many stages of writing (prewriting, writing, rewriting, and sharing with an audience), methods for assessing these stages are not readily available to the teacher. As with other areas of instruction, both informal and formal measures can be used to assess writing. Some of these measures are listed in Table 12.2; these tests are more fully described in Appendix C.

SPELLING   Spelling has been called "the invention of the devil." Continuing this spiritual analogy, someone has quipped that the ability to spell well is "a gift from God." Spelling is one curriculum area in which neither creativity nor divergent thinking is encouraged. Only one pattern or arrangement of letters can be accepted as correct; no compromise is possible. What makes spelling so difficult is that the written form of the English language has an inconsistent pattern; there is no dependable one-to-one correspondence between the spoken sounds of English and the written form of the language. Therefore, spelling is not an easy task, even for people who do not have learning disabilities.

Spelling a word is much more difficult than reading it. In reading, several clues—context, phonics, structural analysis, and configuration—help the reader to recognize a word in print. Spelling offers no such opportunities to draw on peripheral clues. Many individuals who have trouble spelling words are skilled in recognizing them in reading. However, individuals who are poor in decoding words in reading are almost always poor in spelling as well.

Table 12.2

Tests of Written Expression

Test	Age or Grade Assessed
Oral and Written Language Scales (OWLS)— *Written Expression Scale*	Ages 3–21
Test of Adolescent & Adult Language—3 (TOAL-3)	Ages 12–25
Test of Early Written Language	Ages 2–4
Test of Written Expression (TOWE)	Ages 5–17
Test of Written Language—3 (TOWL-3)	Ages 7–18
Woodcock-Johnson Psychoeducational Battery— Revised, Tests of Achievement	Grades K–17

Figure 12.9

Developing Prephonetic Writing: Making Letters

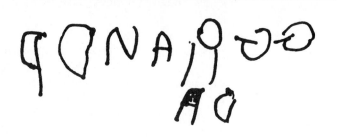

Developmental Stages of Learning to Spell

Children go through several distinct stages of spelling development, following a general progression of spelling knowledge. The rate of progression differs among children with different spelling abilities, but all children pass through the stages in order. Moreover, the spelling errors that children make reflect their current developmental stage (Ferroli & Shanahan, 1987; Henderson, 1985). There are overlaps in the ages at which children pass through each developmental stage of spelling. The stages and their accompanying ages and characteristics follow:

Stage 1: Developing prephonetic writing (ages 1–7). Children scribble, identify pictures, draw, imitate writing, and learn to make letters (Figure 12.9).

Stage 2: Using letter names and beginning phonetic strategies (ages 5–9). Children attempt to use phoneme representations but exhibit limited knowledge. They use invented spelling by letter name (for example, *HIKT* for *hiked*, *LRN* for *learn*, or *TRKE* for *turkey*). Children may be able to spell some sight words correctly (Figure 12.10).

Stage 3: Using written word patterns (ages 6–12). Spelling attempts are readable, pronounceable, and recognizable, and they approximate conventional spelling, even though they are not precise (for example, *offis* for *office* or *alavater* for *elevator*). The child's invented spellings follow rules of short vowels and long vowel markers. Most sight words are spelled correctly (Figure 12.11).

Stage 4: Using syllable junctures and multisyllabic words (ages 8–18). Students display errors in multisyllabic words. Invented spelling errors occur at syllable juncture and *schwa* positions and following deviational rules (for example, *useage* for *usage*). (The term *schwa* refers to unaccented syllables and reflects common spelling errors, such as *cottin* for *cotton.)* Multisyllabic sight words may or may not be transferred to spelling performance.

Figure 12.10

Pictures and Beginning Phonetic Stages

"I'm going apple picking on Sunday"

Figure 12.11

Written Word Patterns

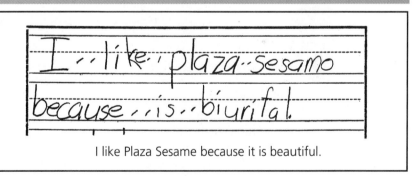

I like Plaza Sesame because it is beautiful.

Stage 5: Developing a mature spelling perspective (ages 10–adult). Invented spellings now are viewed as errors. Many individuals continue to have great difficulty with spelling, even if they follow the rules. Because of the many exceptions in English, individuals should learn to rely on backup sources, such as dictionaries, computer spelling checks, and electronic spellers. (*Franklin Spelling Tutor,* from Franklin Learning Resources, is one example of an electronic speller.)

Problems Related to Spelling

Spelling requires many different abilities. For example, a child who lacks phonological awareness will not recognize that there are phonemes or sounds within spoken words, and have difficulty with the spelling-to-sound linkages that are necessary in spelling (Torgeson, 1998). Some children are initially unable to read a spelling word. Other children do not know how to apply phonics and structural analysis to spell a word. Still others are poor at visualizing the appearance of the word. Some children have such poor motor facility that they cannot write the word.

To spell a word correctly, an individual must not only have stored the word in memory but must also be able to completely retrieve it from memory, without help from visual clues. Poor spellers who cannot remember or visualize the letters and the order of the letters in words benefit from activities to help strengthen and reinforce the visual memory of the spelling words. Fernald (1943, 1988), for example, developed a tracing technique to teach spelling by reinforcing the visual image of the word, drawing on the tactile and kinesthetic senses. (The Fernald method is described in the Teaching Strategies section of this chapter.)

Some poor spellers have difficulty with auditory memory and cannot hold the sounds or syllables in their minds. These students need instruction that will help them recognize the sounds of words and build phonological skills.

Motor memory is also a factor in spelling, for the speller must remember how the word "felt" motorically when it was previously written. Students with motor memory problems need more practice writing the spelling words.

Invented Spelling

Invented spelling is the beginning writer's attempt to write words by attending to their sound units and associating letters with them in a systematic although unconventional way (Richek et al., 1996). Examples of invented spellings used by young children are *nabor* for *neighbor, ez* for *easy, neck all* for *nickel*, and *1000ilnd* for *thousand island*. Examples of writing with invented spelling are shown in Figures 12.12 and 12.13.

Children who are encouraged to use invented spelling and to compose anything they want in whatever way they can are much more willing to write. They learn to take risks in a failure-free environment, and they come to understand that writing is a pleasurable form of communication in which thoughts are translated into symbols that mean something to other people. Figure 12.13 illustrates the writing of a first-grade student who was able to express deep emotional feeling about a ladybug. Research shows that children who were allowed to invent their own spelling at an early age tend to spell as well as or better than children who were not given this instruction (Ehri & Wilce, 1985). It is important that teachers who use in-

Figure 12.12

**Examples of Invented
Spelling**

Swimming Pool. I am going in.

vented spelling as an instructional technique make sure that parents understand the philosophy and purpose of the method. The case example entitled "Learning the Awful Truth About Spelling" tells of a child who was
encouraged to use invented spelling and was later shocked when told that
spelling has rules.

   A critical factor in using invented spelling is the child's phonological
awareness of the sounds of language. One study showed that kindergartners'
insights into the segmental structure of speech underlie their proficiency in

Figure 12.13

Example of Invented
Spelling

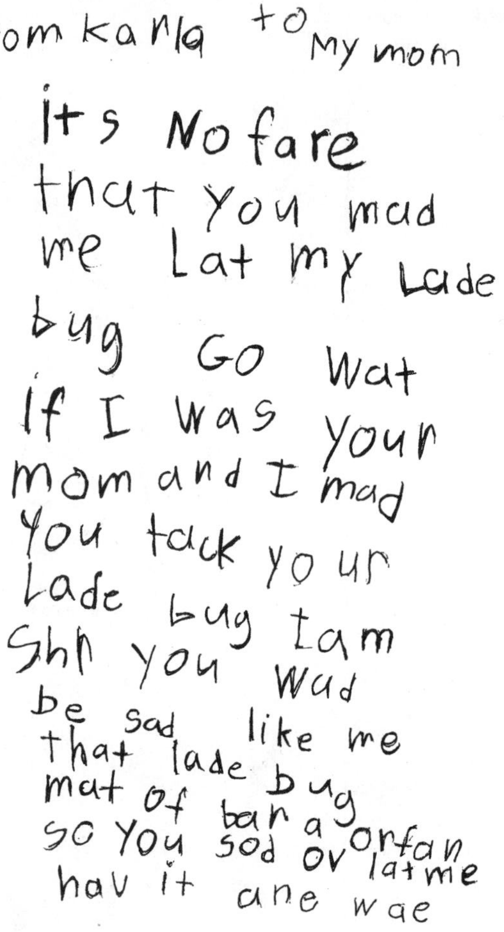

From karla to my mom

It's No fare
that you mad
me Lat my Lade
bug Go Wat
If I was your
mom and I mad
you tack yo ur
Lade bug tam
Shr you Wud
be sad like me
that lade bug
mat of bar a orfan
so You sod ov lat me
hav it ane wae

"From Karla to my mom. It's no fair that you made me let my lady bug go. What if I was your mom and I made you take your lady bug. I am sure you would be sad like me. That lady bug might have been an orphan. So you should have let me have it anyway."

invented spelling and are a crucial factor in early spelling learning (Liberman, Rubin, Duques, & Carlisle, 1985).

Self-Questioning Strategies for Spelling

Cognitive learning strategies involve spelling activities such as self-questioning and self-monitoring. Self-questioning helps students with learning

CASE EXAMPLE

LEARNING THE AWFUL TRUTH ABOUT SPELLING

Some children who use invented spelling are jolted when they realize that there are strict rules about correct spelling. Brian had been in third grade for two weeks in the fall semester when he asked his mother to transfer him to a different third-grade class. Brian explained that the reason for his request was that his current teacher was not a very good teacher. When his mother probed further, Brian confided that his third-grade teacher thought there was only one way to spell a word.

disabilities develop spelling learning strategies. Students are taught to ask themselves the following questions, which are listed on a prompt card:

1. Do I know this word?
2. How many syllables do I hear in this word? (Write down the number.)
3. I will spell out the word.
4. Do I have the right number of syllables?
5a. If the word has the right number of syllables, am I unsure of the spelling of any part of the word? If I am, I will underline that part and try spelling the word again. Now, does it look right to me? If it does, I will leave it alone. If it still does not look right, I will underline the part I am not sure of and try again.
5b. If the word I spelled does not have the right number of syllables, let me hear the word in my head again, and find the missing syllable. Then I will go back to Step 2.
6. When I finish spelling, I tell myself I am a good worker. I have tried hard at spelling.

Multisensory Approaches to Spelling

Using several senses helps to reinforce the learning of spelling words. Multisensory learning involves the senses of visual, auditory, kinesthetic, and tactile learning. Two multisensory spelling approaches are the *multisensory method* and the *Fernald method*, which are described in the strategies for teaching spelling, later in this chapter (page 476).

Two Theories of Word Selection for Teaching Spelling

In selecting words for teaching spelling, there are two alternative approaches: the **linguistic approach** and the **word-frequency approach**.

Linguistic Approach to Spelling   The linguistic approach to spelling is based on the contention that the spelling of American English is sufficiently rule-covered to warrant an instructional method that stresses phonological, morphological, and syntactic rules or word patterns. This might also be called a phonics or word-family approach to spelling since it selects words to teach phonics generalizations, structural analysis, or linguistic patterns.

The linguistic approach to teaching spelling capitalizes on the underlying regularity between the phonological and morphological elements in the oral language and their graphic representations in written language.

In spite of the seemingly numerous exceptions to the rules of spelling, research demonstrates that English spelling has predictable patterns and an underlying system of phonological and morphological regularity. One in-depth analysis examined seventeen thousand words. The correct spelling pattern was predicted for phoneme sounds 90 percent of the time when the main phonological facts of position in syllables, syllable stress, and internal constraints underlying the orthography were taken into consideration (Hanna, Hodges, & Hanna, 1971).

Teachers can help students discover underlying linguistic patterns by selecting words for spelling instruction based on linguistic patterns. For instance, when teaching the spelling pattern of the phoneme *oy*, the teacher should include words such as *boy*, *joy*, *Roy*, and *toy* to help learners form a phonological generalization. The teaching of spelling can be merged with phonics instruction so that phonics and word-analysis skills are practiced during the spelling lesson.

Word-Frequency Approach to Spelling   In the word-frequency approach to spelling instruction, words for spelling instruction are chosen on the basis of frequency of use rather than phonological patterns. The criteria for word selection are frequency of use, permanency, and utility. A core of spelling words that are most frequently used in writing was determined through extensive investigations of the writing of children and adults (Fitzgerald, 1951). In fact, a relatively small number of words do most of the work. The following estimate of needed spelling words is given by Rinsland (1945):

100 words make up more than 60% of elementary students' writing.

500 words make up more than 82% of elementary students' writing.

1,000 words make up more than 89% of elementary students' writing.

2,000 words make up more than 95% of elementary students' writing.

A few words in our language are used over and over. In fact, only 2,650 words and their derivative repetitions make up about 95 percent of the writing of elementary-school children. A basic list of 3,500 words covers the needs of children in elementary school (Fitzgerald, 1955). Sixty percent of our writing consists of the one hundred words shown in Table 12.3.

Table 12.3

The One Hundred Most Common Words in Written Language

a	eat	in	our	there
all	for	is	out	they
am	girl	it	over	this
and	go	just	play	time
are	going	know	pretty	to
at	good	like	put	too
baby	got	little	red	tree
ball	had	look	run	two
be	has	made	said	up
big	have	make	saw	want
boy	he	man	school	was
but	her	me	see	we
can	here	mother	she	went
Christmas	him	my	so	what
come	his	name	some	when
did	home	not	take	will
do	house	now	that	with
dog	how	of	the	would
doll	I	on	them	you
down	I'm	one	then	your

The word-frequency approach to spelling is based on the belief that there are so many exceptions to spelling rules that occur in the most frequently used words that it is difficult to convey patterns and rules to beginning spellers. Examples of the irregular relationship between phonemes (the spoken sounds) and graphemes (the written symbols) are easy to cite. George Bernard Shaw, an advocate of spelling reform, is credited with the suggestion that the word *fish* be spelled *ghoti: gh* as in cough, *o* as in *women, ti* as in *nation*. Following phonic generalizations, the word *natural* could be spelled *pnatchurile*. The many inconsistencies that exist in English spelling are illustrated in the following limericks:

A king, on assuming his reign,
Exclaimed with a feeling of peign:
"Tho I'm legally heir
No one here seems to ceir
That I haven't been born with a breign."

A merchant addressing a debtor,
Remarked in the course of his lebtor

That he chose to suppose
A man knose what he ose
And the sooner he pays it, the bedtor!

A young lady crossing the ocean
Grew ill from the ship's dizzy mocean,
She called with a sigh
And a tear in her eigh,
For the doctor to give her a pocean.

And now our brief lesson is through—
I trust you'll agree it was trough;
For it's chiefly designed
To impress on your minged
What wonders our spelling can dough!*

One teacher found that students' spelling of the word *awful* was varied and included *offul, awfull, offel,* and *offle.* Each is an accurate phonetic transcription of the oral sounds of the word.

Assessment of Spelling

Informal Tests   Informal and teacher-constructed spelling tests are particularly useful. Curriculum-based assessment also offers a way to obtain information on spelling that is directly linked to instruction (Moats, 1994a).

A short informal spelling test, as shown in Table 12.4, was developed by selecting ten words from a frequency-of-use word list (Durrell, 1956). The

Table 12.4

Informal Spelling Test

Grade 1	Grade 2	Grade 3	Grade 4	Grade 5	Grade 6	Grade 7
all	be	after	because	bread	build	although
at	come	before	dinner	don't	hair	amount
for	give	brown	few	floor	music	business
his	house	dog	light	beautiful	eight	excuse
it	long	never	place	money	brought	receive
not	must	in	sent	minute	except	measure
see	ran	gray	table	ready	suit	telephone
up	some	hope	town	snow	whose	station
me	want	live	only	through	yesterday	possible
go	your	mother	farm	bright	instead	straight

*Reprinted by special permission of Dr. Emmett Albert Betts, *Phonetics Spelling Council.*

Table 12.5			
Tests of Spelling	Test	Type	Age or Grade Assessed
	Brigance Diagnostic Inventory of Basic Skills	Battery	Grades K–6
	Peabody Individual Achievement Test—Revised (PIAT-R)	Battery	Grades K–12
	Spellmaster Assessment and Teaching System	Spelling	Grades 2–adult
	Test of Written Spelling—2 (TWS-2)	Spelling	Grades 1–12
	Wide-Range Achievement Test 3 (WRAT3)	Battery	Ages 5–adult

student is asked to spell on paper words from each grade list until three words in a grade list are missed. The student's spelling level can be estimated as that at which only two words are missed.

The *Diagnostic Screening Test for Developmental Dyslexia* is designed to test and classify the types of spelling errors that a student is making (Boder & Jarrico, 1982). Errors are classified in three categories:

1. Dysphonetic dyslexia (spelling errors reflect inaccurate phonic spellings). The spelling errors that fall in this category have some of the correct letters, but the letters are placed in bizarre positions, such as *ronaeg* for *orange, lghit* for *light,* or *heows* for *whose.* This type of error reflects a primary deficit in sound-symbol integration. Students with this problem read and spell primarily through visualization.

2. Dyseidetic dyslexia (spelling errors reflect phonic-equivalent errors). The misspellings in this category include mistakes such as *lisn* for *listen, atenchen* for *attention, pese* for *peace, det* for *debt,* and *sofer* for *chauffeur.* This type of error reflects a primary deficit in the ability to perceive and recall whole words as a gestalt. Students with this problem read and spell primarily through the process of phonic analysis.

3. Dysphonetic-dyseidetic dyslexia (mixed type in which both kinds of errors are reflected). Students with these error patterns make both types of errors, and they are considered the most severe cases.

Formal Tests   Some formal tests of spelling are individual spelling tests, and others are part of a comprehensive academic achievement battery. Table 12.5 shows some commonly used spelling tests. (For further discussion, see Appendix C.)

HANDWRITING

Three different ways to produce writing are currently taught in schools: (1) manuscript writing (a type of printing), (2) cursive writing (sometimes called *script*), and (3) keyboarding (or typing).

Even though the use of computer word processing is becoming more common in our schools, handwriting remains a necessary competency. Handwriting is still the major means by which students convey to teachers what they have learned. In many life situations, adults find handwriting an unavoidable necessity.

Handwriting is the most concrete of the communication skills. It can be directly observed, evaluated, and preserved, providing a permanent record of the output. The process of handwriting is intricate and depends on many different skills and abilities. Writing requires accurate perception of the graphic symbol patterns. The act of writing entails keen visual and motor skills that depend on the visual function of the eye, the coordination of eye movements, smooth motor coordination of eye and hand, and control of arm, hand, and finger muscles. Writing also requires accurate visual and kinesthetic memory of the written letters and words.

Extremely poor handwriting is sometimes called **dysgraphia**, and this condition may reflect other underlying deficits (Deuel, 1995). Poor handwriting may be a manifestation of fine-motor difficulties because the child is unable to execute efficiently the motor movements required to write or to copy written letters or forms. Students may be unable to transfer the input of visual information to the output of fine-motor movement, or they may have difficulty in activities requiring motor and spatial judgments. Some students exhibit dystrophic problems when they cannot go from a far-point visual task of seeing a letter or word on a chalkboard to then copying that form on a piece of paper, a near-point visual task. Other underlying shortcomings that interfere with handwriting performance are poor motor skills, faulty visual perception of letters and words, and difficulty in remembering visual impressions. Poor instruction in handwriting may also contribute to poor writing.

Figure 12.14 illustrates the attempts of two 10-year-old boys with handwriting disabilities to copy some writing materials.

Manuscript Writing

Handwriting instruction usually begins with **manuscript writing** in kindergarten, where children begin to write letters of the alphabet. Manuscript writing usually continues in first, second, and third grade.

Manuscript writing has certain advantages: It is easy to learn because it consists of only circles and straight lines, and the letter forms are closer to the printed form used in reading. Some educators believe it is not essential to transfer to cursive writing at all since the manuscript form is legal, legible, and probably just as rapid. Many children with learning disabilities find manuscript writing easier than cursive writing. The manuscript letters are shown in Figure 12.15.

Figure 12.14

Illustrations of the Handwriting of Two 10-year-old Boys with Handwriting Disabilities (In both cases the boys were asked to copy from a sample.)

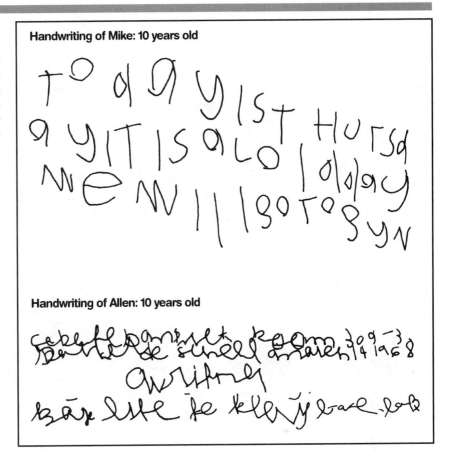

Cursive Writing

In **cursive writing** (sometimes called *script*) the letters are connected. The transfer to cursive writing is typically made somewhere in the third grade, although schools teach cursive writing as late as fifth grade. In an earlier era, writing instruction emphasized the flourishes of cursive writing, but today the goal is to teach functional handwriting. Cursive writing has certain advantages: It minimizes spatial judgment problems for the student, and it has a rhythmic continuity and wholeness that are missing from manuscript writing. In addition, errors of reversals are virtually eliminated with cursive writing. However, many students with learning disabilities find it difficult to make the transfer to cursive writing after they have learned manuscript writing. Samples of cursive letters are shown in Figure 12.15.

Figure 12.15

Sample Manuscript and
Cursive Alphabets

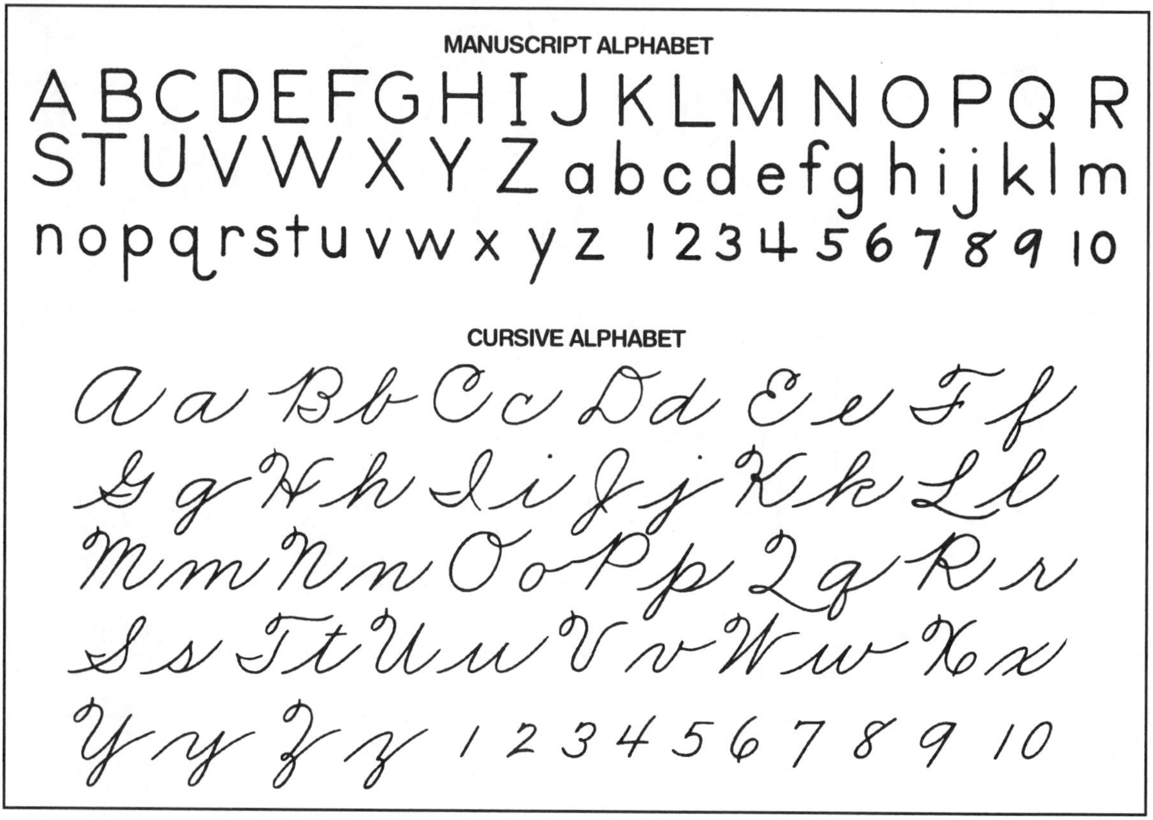

Source: From the *Sample Manuscript Alphabet,* Grade 3, and the *Sample Cursive Alphabet,* Grade 3 (Columbus, OH: Zaner-Bloser, 1958). Used by permission.

Another handwriting form is the *D'Nealian* writing system (Thurber & Jordan, 1981). This system helps students make the transition to cursive writing more easily. The D'Nealian system is a simplified cursive writing style in which manuscript letters have the basic forms of the corresponding cursive letters. Most of the manuscript letters are made with a continuous stroke that produces a kind of connected-manuscript writing, and the student does not have to lift the pencil. Students with handwriting learning disabilities can more easily transfer from manuscript writing to this modified form of cursive writing.

The Left-handed Student

Left-handed people encounter a special handwriting problem because their natural tendency is to write from right to left on the page. In writing from left to right, left-handers have difficulty seeing what they have written. Their hand covers it up and tends to smudge the writing as it moves over the paper. To avoid the smudging, some left-handed students begin "hooking" their hand when they start using ball-point pens.

Left-handedness today is accepted as natural for some people. The student who has not yet stabilized handedness should be encouraged to write with the right hand. However, a student with a strong preference for the left hand should be permitted to write as a "lefty," even though this creates some special problems in writing and requires special instruction. Research shows that left-handers can learn to write just as quickly as right-handers. For manuscript writing, the paper should be placed directly in front of the left-handed student, without a slant. For cursive writing, the top of the paper should be slanted north-northeast, opposite to the slant used by the right-handed student. The pencil should be long, gripped about one inch from the tip, with the eraser pointing to the left shoulder. The position of the hand should be curved, with the weight resting on the outside of the little finger, and "hooking" should be avoided.

Many word-processing programs include adjustments to change the mouse to a left-handed clicking position.

Keyboarding or Typing Skills

The skills needed to use a computer keyboard are referred to as either **keyboarding** or *typing* skills. The ability to type on a keyboard is considered one of the survival skills in today's society. For students who have severe problems in handwriting, learning to use word-processing program offers a very welcome and feasible solution to their handwriting problems. Keyboarding is motorically easier and the output is certainly more legible for the reader. However, simply putting a child in front of a computer is not enough; it is essential to provide explicit and consistent instruction in keyboarding. Teaching students the correct finger positions is much better than allowing them to develop the bad habits of a hunt-and-peck method.

Learning to type is hard work and requires direct and regular instruction over an extended period of time, with ample opportunities for drill and practice. Sufficient time must be provided in the schedule for keyboarding instruction and for the child to practice the skills.

Good keyboarding software programs for children, such as Type to Learn (Sunburst at **http://ww.sunburst.com**) and Mario Teaches Typing (Brain Storm at **http://www.learningco.com**), are based on sound instructional principles. They begin by demonstrating how each new key should be pressed, showing a keyboard on the screen and demonstrating key strokes by highlighting specific keys. As students practice using the new keys, they receive feedback on their accuracy. There are frequent opportunities for practice, and the programs contain drills emphasizing both accuracy and speed. Good programs keep a running record of the students' proficiency level so that students can keep track of how fast they type (in words per minute) and how many errors they make. Children also enjoy computer typing games.

TEACHING STRATEGIES

The balance of this chapter presents specific instructional strategies for teaching written language in the areas of written expression, word processing, spelling, and handwriting.

STRATEGIES FOR TEACHING WRITTEN EXPRESSION

Many students with learning disabilities reach upper elementary or secondary levels with little exposure to and little experience with written expression. Intense instruction to improve poor reading skills often overshadows instruction in writing. Learning to write requires abundant time and opportunities for various kinds of writing.

Principles for Instruction in the Writing Process   The following principles guide the teaching of writing (Bos & Vaughn, 1998):

1. **Provide opportunities for sustained writing.**   Student writers need sufficient time to think, reflect, write, and rewrite. The fact is that many students with learning disabilities spend less than ten minutes per day composing. It is recommended that composing time be extended to 50 minutes each day, four days each week. Break the writing time into several smaller segments for some students.

2. **Establish a writing community.**   The atmosphere of the writing classroom should foster writing activities and encourage cooperative writing work. Teachers can also use individual writing folders containing the students' current writing projects, a list of finished pieces, ideas for future topics, and writing assistance materials such as individual spelling dictionaries. Keep materials and books in one place so students can begin their writing without having to request teacher assistance.

3. **Allow students to choose their own topics.**   Writing projects are most successful when students have a personal interest in the subject. If they need

more information, reading and other source materials should be readily available.

4. Model the writing process and strategic thinking.   The act of writing is encouraged when teachers and peers model the cognitive processes involved in writing. For example, the teacher could model the writing stages by thinking aloud: "I want to plan a mysterious setting for my story. What about a haunted house? Next, I must decide on the characters in this story . . ." (Graham & Harris, 1997).

5. Develop a sense of audience.   In the traditional writing curriculum, students write for the teacher and think they must match the teacher's standards of "rightness." Teachers can expand the students' sense of audience by having them engage in peer collaboration, consulting, group sharing, and publication. Students should have opportunities to discuss the writing progress with peers who are not writing experts. When the writing projects are finished, students can read their material to an audience of peers and discuss their work.

6. Transfer ownership and control of the writing to the students.   A goal of the writing process is to transfer ownership and control to the writer. As the students learn to internalize the strategies that are being taught, they should gradually take more responsibility for their writing and be able to work without teacher direction.

7. Capitalize on current student interests.   Teachers should be aware of students' interests and be on the alert for relevant events that can become the subject for writing. Interests in sports, school, local and national news, trips, family vacations, or holidays offer subjects for writing. One teacher found that trolls (the little dolls with the homely elf-like features and colorful hair) were reemerging as a popular toy. So many students were bringing them to school that the teacher had to limit students to one troll guest a day. Capitalizing on their interest, the teacher had students design their own trolls in drawings and write stories telling why the manufacturer should adopt their troll designs. Although the teacher had asked students to write one troll-design story, they kept writing more during their free time. Some students wrote as many as twenty descriptions (Alexander, 1992).

8. Avoid punitive grading.   Do not allow grading practices to discourage students. Consider grading only ideas, not the technical form, for some assignments, or give two grades—one for ideas and one for technical skills. If a student makes errors in many areas, you might correct only one skill, such as capitalization. When the student masters that skill, you can concentrate on another area.

9. Differentiate between personal and functional writing.   *Personal* and *functional* writing lessons have different goals, and students should understand that different skills are required for each. In personal writing, the goal is to develop ideas and express them in written form, and there is less need for technical perfection. In contrast, a goal of functional writing is to learn the form of the output. The final product, such as a business letter, requires the writer to adhere to certain standards and structure. By separating these two goals, one can develop different kinds of writing skills for each.

10. Provide abundant input. Students need something to write about. Before asking students to write, make sure that they have had enough first-hand experiences, such as trips, creative activities, or watching television shows, movies, or sports events, that can be drawn upon for writing material. Talking about the experiences is also helpful.

11. Schedule frequent writing. Students need frequent writing experiences to develop skills in writing. An assignment to write a certain number of pages per week in a personal journal that will not be corrected (or even read) by the teacher is an excellent technique for providing necessary practice and improving the quality of writing.

12. Use the cloze procedure. The cloze method (discussed in Chapter 12) can also be used to teach written expression. Write a sentence with a word deleted and have the students try to insert as many different words as possible. For example, "John _____ the ball." Sentences can be taken from reading material.

13. Combine sentences. This approach to teaching written expression is especially useful for adolescents and adults. The teacher writes several separate kernel sentences. The students must combine those sentences into a more complex sentence by adding clauses and connectors.

STRATEGIES FOR USING WORD-PROCESSING SOFTWARE

The following are some suggested activities for using computer word processing to teach writing:

1. Expanding vocabulary. Using a word-processing program, write a sentence or short paragraph on the computer. Use the computer thesaurus to find synonyms for several words.

2. Learning story sequence. Place several sentences about a series of events in incorrect order. Have the students use the "cut" and "paste" functions to put them in the proper sequence.

3. Building vocabulary. Have the student use the "find" and "replace" functions to find overused words, such as *very* or *nice*, and substitute other appropriate words. The students may wish to use a thesaurus.

4. Beginning a story. Put the beginning of a story on a disk and have each student continue the narrative. Each child's story can be compared with others. In another variation, begin a story on a disk and then have one student write the next segment, another student write the following segment, and so on.

5. Keeping an electronic diary or journal.   Keeping a journal of daily events has proved to be an effective technique for improving reading and writing skills. Instead of writing on paper, the student can use a computer with word-processing software.

6. Sending email.   Students can use the email to send personal, semipersonal, and class messages. The messages can be sent between students in the class, between the teacher and the students, or between the students and students in other classes throughout the world.

7. Posting electronic bulletin boards.   Students can be responsible for posting news on sports, music events, school programs, club meetings, and the like on computer "bulletin boards."

8. Writing book reports.   To make writing a book report on the computer easier, develop a template with key topics such as title of the book, author, type of book, summary, and the student's name. To write the book report, the student loads the template and fills out the information next to each topic.

9. Writing a class newsletter.   A newsletter can be written with any word-processing program. Several commercial programs allow users to write, illustrate, paste up, and print pages that resemble a newspaper or newsletter. One such software program is the Children's Writing and Publishing Center (The Learning Company at **http://www.learningco.com**).

10. Using graphics.   Graphics can easily be added to many of the previously mentioned activities. Art clips often come with word-processing software programs. They can be purchased separately on disks, graphics can be scanned in with a scanner, or students can create their own art graphics.

11. Expanding the writing process to the Web.   Students who have access to the Internet can find a wealth of information (such as text, pictures, photographs, and charts) about a topic of their interest. Topics such as dinosaurs, baseball, sports figures, or the history of Canada can be investigated through a search engine. Yahooligans is a safe search engine for children. With material gathered from their searches, the students can develop stories and reports or develop web pages to show their reports to others (Smith, Boone, & Higgins, 1998). For more information on building web toolboxes, see the web site at **http://www.ed.sc.edu/caw/toolbox.html**.

STRATEGIES FOR TEACHING SPELLING

The following teaching strategies are for teaching spelling:

1. Auditory perception and memory of letter sounds.   Provide practice in auditory perception of letter sounds, strengthen knowledge of phonics and structural analysis, and develop skills in applying phonic generalizations. (See Chapter 8 for specific techniques.)

2. Visual memory of words.   Help the students strengthen visual memory so that the visual image of a word can be retained. Materials should be clear and concise, and the students should be helped to focus attention on the activity. The students might use a pocket flashlight as an aid in focusing attention. Flash cards and computer spelling software can also be used to develop speed and strengthen memory. (See Chapter 8 for specific methods to develop visual perception and memory.)

3. Multisensory methods in spelling. Students who are told to study spelling lessons are frequently at a loss as to what to do. The following is a multisensory approach that engages the visual, auditory, kinesthetic, and tactile senses:

   a. *Meaning and pronunciation.* Have the students look at the word, pronounce it correctly, and use it in a sentence.
   b. *Imagery.* Ask students to "see" the word and say it. Have them say each syllable of the word, say the word syllable by syllable, spell the word orally, and then use one finger to trace the word, either in the air or by touching the word itself.
   c. *Recall.* Ask students to look at the word and then close their eyes and see it in their mind's eye. Have them spell the word orally. Then ask them to open their eyes and look at the word to see if they were correct. (If they make an error, they should repeat the process.)
   d. *Writing the word.* Ask the students to write the word correctly from memory, check the spelling against the original, and then check the writing to make sure every letter is legible.
   e. *Mastery.* Have the students cover the word and write it. If they are correct, they should cover and write it two more times.

4. The Fernald method. This method (Fernald, 1943/1988) is a multisensory approach, and it is used to teach reading and writing as well as spelling. Very briefly, it consists of the following steps:

   a. The students are told that they are going to learn words in a new way that has proved to be very successful. They are encouraged to select a word that they wish to learn.
   b. The teacher writes that word on a piece of paper, 4 inches by 10 inches, as the students watch and as the teacher says the word.
   c. The students trace the word, saying it several times, and then write it on a separate piece of paper while saying it.
   d. The students write the word from memory without looking at the original copy. If the word is incorrect, students repeat Step c. If the word is correct, it is put in a file box. The words in the file box are used later in writing stories.
   e. At later stages, this painstaking tracing method for learning words is not needed. Students learn a word by *looking* as the teacher writes it, *saying* it, and *writing* it. At a still later stage, the students can learn by only looking at a word in print and writing it. Finally, they learn by merely looking at the word.

5. The "test-study-test" versus the "study-test" methods. There are two common approaches to teaching spelling in the classroom: the "test-study-test" and the "study-test" plans. The test-study-test method uses a pretest, which is usually given at the beginning of the week. The students then study only those words that were missed on the pretest. This method is better for older students who have fairly good spelling abilities because they do not need to study words they already know. The study-test method is better for young students and for those with poor spelling abilities who would miss too many words on a pretest. The study-test method permits them to study a few well-selected words before the test is given.

6. Listening centers and tapes.   Spelling lessons can easily be put on audiotapes. After students have advanced to a level that enables them to work by themselves, they can complete their spelling lessons in a listening laboratory. Earphones allow for individualized instruction and help many students to block out distracting auditory stimuli.

7. Programmed spelling.   Programmed spelling presents the material in small steps, provides immediate reinforcement, and is designed to be self-instructional.

8. Shorthand dictionaries.   Adults with spelling problems find that dictionaries designed for secretaries who use shorthand transcriptions are a useful spelling tool. Unlike most regular dictionaries, these listings contain the word with its various endings, which are so troublesome in spelling (for example, -*ence* and -*ance*).

9. Follet's Vest Pocket Word Divider.   This is another useful spelling aid, containing fifty thousand words.

10. Electronic spellers and computer spell-checkers.   Students should learn how to use these spelling devices as an aid in spelling.

STRATEGIES FOR TEACHING HANDWRITING

The following activities are representative of useful methods for teaching handwriting:

1. Chalkboard activities.   These activities provide practice before writing instruction is begun. Circles, lines, geometric shapes, letters, and numbers can be made with large, free movements using the muscles of the shoulders, arms, hands, and fingers. (For additional suggestions, see Chapter 8.)

2. Other materials for writing-movement practice.   Finger painting or writing in a clay pan or a sand tray gives the students practice in writing movements. Put a layer of sand, cornmeal, salt, or nondrying clay on a cookie sheet. Use commercial or homemade finger paints for the painting practice. Students use one finger or a pointed stick to practice writing shapes, forms, letters, and numbers. A small, wet sponge can be used to draw shapes on a chalkboard.

3. Position.   Have the students prepare for writing by sitting in comfortable chairs at a table which is at the proper height. Be sure the students' feet are flat on the floor and both forearms are on the writing surface. Each student's nonwriting hand should hold the paper at the top. Have children stand and work at a chalkboard for the initial writing activities.

4. Paper.   For manuscript writing, the paper should be placed without a slant, parallel with the lower edge of the desk. For cursive writing, the paper is tilted at an angle—approximately sixty degrees from vertical—to the left for right-handed students and to the right for left-handed students. To help the student remember the correct slant, place a strip of tape parallel to the top of the paper at the top of the desk. It may be necessary to attach the paper to the desk with masking tape to keep it from sliding.

5. Holding the pencil. Many children with writing disorders do not know how or are unable to hold a pencil properly between their thumb and middle finger, with the index finger riding the pencil. They should grasp the pencil above the sharpened point. A piece of tape or a rubber band placed around the pencil can help the student hold it at the right place.

If a student has difficulty grasping the pencil, the pencil can be put through a practice golf ball (the kind with many holes). Have the pupil place the middle finger and thumb around the ball to practice the right grip. Large, primary-size pencils, large crayons, and felt-tip pens are useful for the beginning stages of writing. Clay might also be placed around the pencil to help the student grasp it. Short pencils should be avoided since it is impossible to grip them correctly.

6. Stencils and templates. Make cardboard or plastic stencils of geometric forms, letters, and numbers. Have the students trace the form with one finger, a pencil, or a crayon. (Clip the stencil to the paper to prevent it from moving.) Then remove the stencil and reveal the figure that has been made. The stencil can be cut so that the hole creates the shape or, in reverse, so that the outer edges of the stencil create the shape.

7. Tracing. Make heavy black figures on white paper and clip a sheet of onionskin or transparent paper over the letters. Have the students trace the forms and letters. Start with diagonal lines and circles, then horizontal and vertical lines, geometric shapes, and finally, letters and numbers. The students may also trace a black letter on paper with a crayon or felt-tipped pen or may use a transparent sheet. Another idea is to put letters on transparencies and project the images onto a chalkboard or a large sheet of paper. Students can then trace over the images.

8. Drawing between the lines. Have the students practice making "roads" between double lines in a variety of widths and shapes. Then ask the students to write letters by going between the double lines of outlined letters. Use arrows and numbers to show the direction and sequence of the lines.

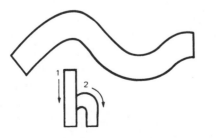

9. Dot-to-dot. Draw a complete figure and then draw an outline of the same figure by using dots. Ask the students to make the figure by connecting the dots.

10. Tracing with reducing cues. Write a complete letter or word and have the students trace it. Then write the first part of the letter or word and have the students trace your part and then complete the letter or word. Finally, reduce the cue to only the upstroke and have the students write the entire letter or word.

11. Lined paper. Begin by having students use unlined paper. Later, have them use paper with wide lines to help them determine the placement of letters. It may be helpful to use specially lined paper that is color-cued to aid in letter placement. Regular lined paper can also be color-cued to help students make letters.

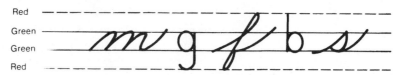

12. Template lines. For students who need additional help in stopping at lines, tape can be placed at bottom and top lines. Windows can be cut out of cardboard to give further guidance for spacing letters. The following is a picture of a piece of cardboard with three windows for one-line, two-line, and three-line letters. One-line letters are those that fit in a single-line space: *a, c, e, i, m, n.* Two-line letters are those with ascenders only: *b, d, b, k, l, t.* Three-line letters are those with descenders: *f, g, j, p, q, z, y.*

13. Letter difficulty. In terms of ease, cursive letters are introduced in the following order: beginning letters—*m, n, t, i, u, w, r, s, l,* and *e;* more difficult letters—*x, z, y, j, p, h, b, k, f, g,* and *q;* and combinations of letters—*me, be, go, it, no,* and so forth.

14. Verbal cues. Students are helped in the motor act of writing by hearing the directions for forming letters—for example, "down-up-and-around." When using this technique, teachers must take care not to distract the students with these verbal instructions.

15. Words and sentences. After the students learn to write single letters, instruction should proceed to writing words and sentences. Spacing, size, and slant are additional factors to consider at this stage.

Chapter Summary

1. This chapter examined theories and teaching strategies for three areas of written language: written expression, spelling, and handwriting.

2. Written expression is considered the most complex and difficult language skill to achieve and the most common communication disability.

3. Writing is one of the elements of the integrated language system.

4. Individuals with learning disabilities often have significant problems in communicating through writing, a difficulty that persists over time.

5. The writing process consists of the stages of prewriting, writing, revising, and sharing with an audience. Emphasis in instruction should be on the process rather than on the product.

6. Strategies for writing include using written conversations, personal journals, patterned writing, and graphic organizers.

7. Word processors offer an excellent means of teaching writing because they integrate all the language systems.

8. Spelling is particularly difficult in English because of the irregularity between the spoken and written forms of the language. Children go through several distinct stages of spelling development. Their rates of progression differ, but they all pass through the stages in order.

9. Invented spelling is the beginning writer's attempt to write words and should be encouraged. These spellings are developmental approximations of the correct spellings.

10. Two theories of word selection to teach spelling are the linguistic approach and the word-frequency approach.

11. Handwriting is a fine-motor skill that causes difficulty for many individuals with learning disabilities. Special consideration must be given to teaching manuscript writing and cursive writing and to instructing the left-handed student. Many students with handwriting problems

are helped by using computers and word processors. It is important to teach students typing or keyboarding skills.

12. Specific teaching strategies are described for writing, word processing, spelling, and handwriting.

Questions for Discussion and Reflection

1. What are the differences between instruction that focuses on the written product and instruction that focuses on the writing process?

2. Describe the stages of the writing process.

3. How can graphic organizers help students with learning disabilities write?

4. Discuss the advantages of computer word processing for writing.

5. What is invented spelling? Do you think it should be encouraged? Why or why not?

6. Identify the two major forms of handwriting taught in the schools. Discuss the advantages and disadvantages of each form of handwriting.

7. Discuss how the characteristics of learning disabilities affect the writing of students with learning disabilities in written expression, spelling, and handwriting.

8. What kind of computer programs and devices are available to help students with writing problems?

Key Terms

cursive writing *(p. 469)*

drafting *(p. 447)*

dysgraphia *(p. 468)*

early literacy *(p. 444)*

graphic organizers *(p. 451)*

invented spelling *(p. 460)*

keyboarding *(p. 471)*

linguistic approach to spelling *(p. 463)*

manuscript writing *(p. 468)*

prewriting *(p. 447)*

revising *(p. 447)*

sharing with an audience *(p. 448)*

word-frequency approach to spelling *(p. 463)*

word processing *(p. 452)*

writing process *(p. 446)*

13 Mathematics

CHAPTER OUTLINE

S ome individuals with learning disabilities do well in language and reading, but their nemesis is mathematics and quantitative learning. Two mathematics problem areas for students with learning disabilities are specified in IDEA 1997 (the Individuals with Disabilities Education Act of 1997): (1) mathematics calculation and (2) mathematics reasoning. Both interfere with achievement in school and success in life.

In the Theories section of this chapter, we examine mathematics disabilities, precursors of mathematic learning in young children, characteristics of mathematics disabilities, mathematics disabilities at the secondary level, changing views of mathematics education, theories of mathematics instruction, and assessing mathematics abilities. In the Teaching Strategies section, we discuss the overall mathematics curriculum; the principles of mathematics instruction; activities for teaching mathematics concepts, skills, and problem solving; and using technology and computers in mathematics instruction.

THEORIES

Mathematics is a symbolic language that enables human beings to think about, record, and communicate ideas concerning the elements and relationships of quantity. It is also a universal language for all cultures and civilizations. In every culture, social class, and ethnic group, children live in a natural environment that is rich in quantitative information and events. In some cultures children count blocks; in others they count stones (Ginsburg, 1997). The scope of mathematics includes the ability to think in quantitative terms, as well as the operations of counting, measurement, arithmetic, calculation, geometry, and algebra.

MATHEMATICS DISABILITIES

Many individuals with learning disabilities encounter major problems in learning mathematics. It is estimated that about 26 percent of students with learning disabilities receive assistance for problems in mathematics (Miller, Butler, & Lee, 1998; Rivera, 1997). Often the mathematics difficulties that emerge in elementary school continue through the secondary school years (Shulev, Manor, Auerbach, & Grodd-Tour, 1998; Miller & Mercer, 1997; Deshler, Ellis, & Lenz, 1996). Not only is a mathematics learning disability a debilitating problem in school, but it also continues to impair adults in their daily lives (Patton, Cronin, Bassett, & Koppel, 1997; Adelman & Vogel, 1991).

The term **dyscalculia** is a medically oriented word that describes a severe disability in learning and using mathematics. Analogous to *dyslexia,* a severe reading disability with medical connotations, dyscalculia is described as a specific disturbance in learning mathematical concepts and computation associated with a central nervous system dysfunction (Rourke & Conway, 1997). Research shows that without direct intervention, dyscalculia persists. Almost one-half of the children who were identified with dyscalculia in the fourth grade are still classified as having dyscalculia three years later (Shalev, Manor, Auerbach, & Grodd-Tour, 1998).

However, not all students with learning disabilities encounter difficulty with number concepts. In fact, some individuals with severe reading disabilities do well in mathematics, and exhibit a strong aptitude in quantitative thinking.

The identification and treatment of mathematics disabilities have received much less attention than problems associated with reading disabilities (Rivera, 1997). One-third of the instructional time in resource rooms is spent on mathematics. However, in most inclusive classrooms, the mathematics curriculum does not pay sufficient attention to learning differences in mathematics among students. For students with learning disabilities, the regular mathematics curriculum does not allot sufficient time for instruction, for guided practice, or for practical applications. Studies of math programs used in inclusive classes show that they have these deficiencies (Cawley, Parmar, Yan, & Miller, 1998; Carnine, 1997; Montague, 1997; Vaughn & Wilson, 1994):

- Insufficient assurance that students have relevant prior knowledge for the lesson
- Too rapid a rate for introducing many of the concepts
- Lack of coherence in the presentation of mathematics strategies
- Poor communication and a lack of conciseness in many instructional activities
- Insufficient guided practice to help students move from the initial teaching stage to working independently
- Not enough review to ensure that students will remember what they have learned

PRECURSORS OF MATHEMATICS LEARNING IN YOUNG CHILDREN

For some children, difficulties with numerical relationships begin at an early age. The ability to count, match, sort, compare, and understand one-to-one correspondence hinges on the child's experiences in manipulating objects. A child with attention problems, unstable perceptual skills, or difficulties in motor development may not have had sufficient or appropriate experiences with the activities of manipulation that pave the way for understanding space, form, order, time, distance, and quantity.

When expected to perform mathematics assignments, some children have not acquired the needed early skills for mathematics learning. Yet these children may be introduced to a mathematics concept or skill before they are ready to learn it. As a result, they do not truly understand and are confused. Learning mathematics is a sequential process, and children must acquire skills at an earlier stage before going on to the next stage. Early math learning includes one-to-one correspondence, classification, and seriation. Teachers who work with students with mathematics disabilities (even with older students) must often gear instruction toward these unlearned early skills.

Spatial Relationships

Typically, young children learn by playing with objects such as pots and pans, boxes that fit into each other, and objects that can be put into containers. These play activities help develop a sense of space, sequence, and order. Parents of children with mathematics disabilities, however, often report that their children did not enjoy or play with blocks, puzzles, models, or construction-type toys as preschoolers. Students with mathematics learning disabilities may have missed these early number-learning experiences.

Many concepts of **spatial relationships** are normally acquired at the preschool age. But often children destined to have mathematics disabilities are baffled by such concepts as *up-down, over-under, top-bottom, high-low, near-far, front-back, beginning-end*, and *across*. A disturbance in spatial relationships can interfere with the understanding of the entire number system. For example, the child may be unable to perceive distances between numbers on number lines or rulers and may not know if the number 3 is closer to 4 or to 6 (Lowenthal, 1998).

Sense of Body Image

Some children with poor number sense have an inaccurate or imprecise **body image.** They may be unable to understand the basic relationship of the body parts. When asked to draw a picture of a human figure, they may draw the body parts as completely unrelated or misplaced, with stick legs coming from the head, or with no body at all.

Visual-Motor and Visual-Perception Abilities

Children with mathematics disabilities may have difficulty with activities requiring visual-motor and visual-perception abilities. Some may be unable to count objects in a series by pointing to each of them and saying, "One, two, three, four, five." Children with this difficulty must first learn to count by physically grasping and manipulating objects. Grasping is an earlier skill in neuromotor and perceptual development than pointing to objects.

Some children are unable to see objects in groups (or sets)—an ability needed to identify the number of objects quickly. Even when adding a group of three with a group of four, some students with mathematics disabilities persist in counting the objects one by one to determine the total number in the two groups at far beyond the age at which this behavior is considered normal (Fox, 1998; Thornton, Langruall, & Jones, 1997; Ginsburg, 1997).

Inability to visually perceive a geometric shape as a complete and integrated entity is a visual-perception problem. A square may not appear as a square shape but as four unrelated lines, as a hexagon, or even as a circle.

Other youngsters have difficulty in learning to perceive number symbols visually. They might confuse the vertical strokes of the number 1 and the number 4, or they may confuse the upper half of the number 2 with portions of the number 3.

Some children with poor mathematics abilities do poorly in visual-motor tasks. Because of their disorders in perceiving shapes, recognizing spatial relationships, and making spatial judgments, they are unable to copy geometric forms, shapes, numbers, or letters. These children are likely to perform poorly in handwriting as well as in arithmetic. When children cannot write numbers easily, they also cannot read and align their own numbers properly. As a result, they make errors in computation. They must learn to copy and line up numbers accurately to calculate problems in addition and subtraction, in place value, and in multiplication and division (Thornton, et al., 1997).

Concepts of Direction and Time

Basic concepts of time are typically acquired during the preschool years. Expressions such as "10 minutes ago," "in a half-hour," and "later" are usually part of the preschooler's understanding and speaking vocabulary. By the end of first grade, students are expected to tell time to the half-hour, and by the middle grades to the nearest minute. Many students with mathematics disabilities have a poor sense of direction and time. They become lost easily and cannot find their way to a friend's house or home from school. They sometimes forget whether it is morning or afternoon and may even go home during the recess period, thinking the school day has ended. They have difficulty estimating the time span of an hour, a minute, several hours, or a week, and they cannot estimate how long a task will take. They may not be able to judge and allocate the time needed to complete an assignment.

Memory Abilities

For success in mathematics, the learning of computational operations is essential and requires reliable memory skills. For efficient math learning, the computational facts of adding, subtracting, multiplying, and dividing must become automatic. Children with severe memory deficits may understand the underlying number system but may be unable to recall number facts quickly. If a child's grasp of basic computation facts is not at a level of automaticity, the child must expend undue time and energy in counting to come up with the answer (Thornton et al., 1997; Montague, 1997; Bley & Thornton, 1989).

CHARACTERISTICS OF MATHEMATICS DISABILITIES

Each student who encounters difficulties in mathematics is unique; not all exhibit the same traits. However, there are a number of characteristics of learning disabilities that affect quantitative learning (Rivera, 1997; Johnson, 1995). In this section we discuss these characteristics of mathematics disabilities in information processing, language and reading, cognitive learning strategies, and math anxiety.

Information-Processing Components

Many of the elements of information processing are linked to mathematics disabilities, such as paying attention, visual-spatial processing, auditory processing, memory and retrieval, and motor skills (Miller & Mercer, 1997). Table 13.1 shows how problems with elements of information processing affect math performance.

Language and Reading Abilities

Early concepts of quantity are evidenced by the child's use of language, such as *all gone, that's all, more, big,* and *little.* Although some children with mathematics disabilities have superior verbal language skills and may even be excellent readers, for many children the mathematics disability is compounded by oral language and reading deficiencies. Their language problems may cause them to confuse mathematics terms such as *plus, take away, minus, carrying, borrowing,* and *place value.* Arithmetic word problems are particularly difficult for students with reading disabilities. If they are unable to read or do not understand the underlying language structure of the mathematics problem, they cannot plan and perform the tasks required to solve the problem (Cawley et al., 1998; Ginsburg, 1997; Thornton, et al., 1997).

Cognitive Learning Strategies

Some mathematics disabilities in adolescents can be be attributed to the student's lack of appropriate strategies for attacking and solving math problems. Students need strategies for visualizing the problem, for knowing what is being asked, and for deciding on methods for solving the problem. Research shows that students with learning disabilities often use no strategies or select an inappropriate strategy. These students may be slow to develop

Table 13.1

Information-Processing Factors and Problems in Math Performance

Information-Processing Factors	How Problems in Information Processing Affect Mathematics Performance
Attention	√ Difficulty maintaining attention to do steps in algorithms or problem solving √ Difficulty in sustaining attention during instruction
Visual-Spatial Processing	√ Loses place on the worksheet √ Difficulty seeing differences between numbers, coins, or operation symbols √ Problems in writing across the paper in a straight line √ Problems with direction: up-down, left-right, aligning numbers √ Difficulty using a number line
Auditory Processing	√ Difficulty doing oral drills √ Problems in "counting on" from within a sequence
Memory and Retrieval	√ Cannot remember math facts √ Forgets steps when doing a problem √ Difficulty telling time √ Forgets multiple-step word problems
Motor Problems	√ Writes numbers illegibly, slowly, and inaccurately √ Difficulty in writing numbers in small spaces

Source: The ideas for this table were suggested by S. Miller & C. Mercer. (1997). Educational Aspects of Mathematics Disabilities. *Journal of Learning Disabilities, 30* (1), p. 50.

and apply strategies for remembering and retrieving information, but if they are provided with instruction, they can acquire and use mathematics learning strategies successfully (Rivera, 1997; Montague, 1997; Deshler et al., 1996; Lenz, Ellis, & Scanlon, 1996; Miller, 1996).

Math Anxiety

Math anxiety, an emotion-based reaction to mathematics, causes individuals to freeze up when they confront math problems or when they take math tests. The anxiety may stem from the fear of school failure and the loss of self-esteem. Anxiety has many repercussions. It can block the school performance of students with learning disabilities by making it difficult for them to initially learn the mathematics, it impedes their ability to use or transfer the mathematics knowledge they do have, and it becomes an obstacle when they try to demonstrate their knowledge on tests (Barkley, 1998; Slavin, 1991).

Many students and adults with learning disabilities report that anxiety is a constant companion. One individual said that she sprinkled anxiety wherever she went, making calm people nervous and nervous people fall apart. She described her feelings: "I couldn't get out the right words. I trembled and my insides writhed" (Smith, 1991). Some guidelines for dealing with math anxiety are given in Table 13.2.

MATHEMATICS DISABILITIES AT THE SECONDARY LEVEL

For students in junior and senior high school, the mathematics learning disabilities differ from those at the elementary level. The secondary mathematics curriculum becomes increasingly more sophisticated and abstract as it is based on the presumption that the basic skills have been learned. The increased mathematics requirements at the high school level and the pressure of more testing are likely to adversely affect students with learning disabilities.

The states are increasing their high school mathematics requirements for graduation. High school graduation is contingent upon passing mathematics courses such as algebra that previously were required only of students in a college preparatory curriculum. Many states and school districts now include algebra as a graduation requirement for all students (Jones, Wilson, & Bhojwani, 1997; Miller & Mercer, 1997).

Table 13.2

Guidelines for Dealing with Math Anxiety

1. **Use competition carefully.** Have students compete with themselves rather than with others in the class or school. In a competitive situation, make sure that students have a good chance of succeeding

2. **Use clear instructions.** Make sure that students understand what they are to do in math assignments. Ask students to work sample problems and be sure that they understand the assignment. When doing a new math procedure, give students plenty of practice and examples or models to show how the work is done.

3. **Avoid unnecessary time pressures.** Give students ample time to complete math assignments in the class period. Give occasional take-home tests. If necessary, reduce the number of problems to be completed.

4. **Try to remove pressure from test-taking situations.** Teach students test-taking strategies. Give practice tests. Make sure that the test format is clear and that students are familiar with the format. For example, a student may be familiar with the problem in the following format:

$$7$$
$$+8$$

The same child may be unfamiliar with a test format that presents the same problem in a different form:

$$7 + 8 =$$

One way to reduce math anxiety is to ask students to do sample problems to make sure they understand the assignment. *(© Jeff Greenberg/ Stock Boston)*

Many secondary students with learning disabilities succeed in advanced mathematics courses, but others shy away from algebra, geometry, statistics, and calculus. In the past students with learning disabilities who faced mathematics disabilities were advised to continue remedial or basic math courses. If algebra is to be required for a high school diploma, we must consider how best to prepare students with learning disabilities to succeed in this subject.

Common mathematics difficulties at the secondary level include division of whole numbers, basic operations (including fractions), decimals and percentages, fraction terminology, multiplication of whole numbers, place value, measurement skills, and the language of mathematics (Jones et al., 1997). Adolescents with learning disabilities continue to have memory deficits that interfere with the automatic learning of computation facts. Adolescents who are having such difficulty appreciate techniques that will help them learn and remember calculation facts. Students with severe problems in mathematics need instruction with emphasis on learning basic skills to help them acquire functional abilities for successful living.

In developing an appropriate math curriculum for secondary students with learning disabilities, three interrelated variables must be considered (Deshler et al., 1996):

1. The characteristics of the learner
2. The demands of the secondary school
3. The anticipated postsecondary demands

Many students with learning disabilities can succeed in advanced mathematics courses. They need these courses because a large number will be going on to postsecondary education and college, and many will enter professions such as engineering or computer science that require competencies in advanced mathematics. Their mathematics curriculum will include fractions, decimals, algebra, geometry, trigonometry, calculus, and probability.

Effective instructional strategies in mathematics for secondary students include the following:

- *Provide many examples.* Students need to have many examples that illustrate the concept being taught. Often teachers provide too few examples (Miller, 1996; Carnine, 1997).

- *Provide practice in discriminating various problem types.* Secondary students with mathematics disabilities have problems with discrimination. They ignore the operation sign and add instead of subtract. Once a skill is learned, the math problem should be placed with different problems so that the student will learn to discriminate and generalize (Carnine, 1997).

- *Provide explicit instruction.* Students with mathematics disabilities need direct instruction that is organized with step-by-step presentations (Miller, 1996; Carnine, 1997).

- *Separate confusing elements.* Since mathematics terminology can be confusing, only one math term should be taught at a time. For example, in teaching fractions, one should teach *denominator* during one lesson and *numerator* during a later lesson (Miller, 1996).

CHANGING VIEWS ABOUT MATHEMATICS EDUCATION

Mathematics education seems to be particularly prone to the vagaries of international events and national political pressures. As a result, we have witnessed wide swings in the philosophy of teaching mathematics over the past forty years.

For example, the modern math curriculum was triggered over forty years ago when U.S. leaders became concerned about the nation's competitive abilities in mathematics because the former Soviet Union had launched *Sputnik*, thereby beating the United States in the space race. Unfortunately, the modern math approach compounded the mathematics problems of individuals with mathematics learning disabilities. Another phase in mathematics education was the **back-to-basics movement,** which swung to an emphasis on mathematics calculation skills with intensive teaching of computation facts. This movement neglected instruction in mathematics concepts, quantitative thinking, and problem solving.

The Educational Reform Movement

Today the competitive edge of the United States is again threatened by the poor mathematics performance of the nation's students. International comparisons on mathematics achievement show that students in the United States have lower math scores than students in other countries (Ginsburg, 1997). The nation's response to low mathematics achievement is the educational reform movement. The recommended solution is to set higher standards for mathematics, require more testing of mathematics competencies, and increase the mathematics courses in the high school curriculum. A consequence of the educational reform movement is that many students with learning disabilities who already have difficulty with mathematics are faced with higher standards and expectations.

Math Curriculum Recommendations of the NCTM

The **National Council of Teachers of Mathematics (NCTM)** (1989, 1991) has identified four basic principles that should underlie math instruction at every level. Students should understand the following:

- Mathematics as problem solving
- Mathematics as reasoning
- Mathematics as communication
- Mathematics as a connection with the real world

The National Council for Supervisors of Mathematics (NCSM) (1988) identified components of essential mathematics, which are shown in Table 13.3. In addition, the NCTM proposed major goals of instruction for grades 9 through 12 (Romberg, 1993):

- Students should be actively involved in constructing and applying mathematical ideas.
- Problem solving should be a means as well as a goal for instruction.
- Teachers should employ effective questioning techniques that promote students' interaction.
- Students should use calculators and computers as tools for learning and doing mathematics.

Table 13.3

Twelve Components of Essential Mathematics

1. Problem solving
2. Communicating mathematical ideas
3. Mathematical reasoning
4. Applying mathematics to everyday situations
5. Alertness to the reasonableness of results
6. Estimation
7. Appropriate computational skills
8. Algebraic thinking
9. Measurement
10. Geometry graphs
11. Statistics
12. Probability

Source: From the National Council of Teachers of Mathematics, 1991. *Professional Standards for Teaching Mathematics.* Reston, VA: Author.

- Teachers should create opportunities for students to communicate mathematical ideas, both orally and in writing.
- Students should understand the interrelatedness of mathematical topics.
- The curriculum should provide systematic review of material that has been mastered by embedding practice in the context of new topics and problem situations.
- Assessment of learning should be an integral part of instruction.

Special educators note that the NCTM goals and principles are for all students. It is important to learn how to implement these goals for students with learning disabilities, especially in inclusive settings (Miller & Mercer, 1997; Cawley & Reines, 1996).

LEARNING THEORIES FOR MATHEMATICS INSTRUCTION

In mathematics, as in other academic areas, different theories of learning lead to different approaches to teaching. We look at several approaches to mathematics instruction for students with mathematics disabilities.

Progression from Concrete to Abstract Learning

The learning of mathematics is a gradual process. It is not a matter of either knowing it or not knowing it. Instead, the learning of mathematics is a continuum that gradually increases in strength. As mathematics learning progresses, knowledge slowly builds from concrete to abstract learning, from incomplete to complete knowledge, and from unsystematic to systematic thinking (Ginsburg, 1997; Baroody & Ginsburg, 1991).

To help students progress from concrete to abstract learning, three sequential levels of mathematics instruction are suggested (Miller & Mercer, 1997; Miller, 1996):

1. *The concrete level.*   At this level children use actual materials, such as objects in the environment, blocks, cubes, poker chips, or place value sticks. Children can physically touch, move, and manipulate these objects as they work out solutions to number problems.

2. *The semiconcrete level.*   Once the students master the skill on the concrete level, instruction progresses to the semiconcrete or representational level. Students use pictures or tallies (marks on the paper) to represent the concrete objects as they do the mathematics problem.

3. *The abstract level.*   At this level, students use only the numbers to solve mathematics problems without the help of semiconcrete pictures or tallies.

Constructive Learning

Constructive learning is based on the view that children construct their own solutions to mathematics problems. Each child must actively build his or her own mental structures of mathematics.

The research on constructive mathematics thinking shows that young children in all cultures develop informal knowledge about numbers. They construct early concepts about numbers as they develop meanings in mathematics. Children naturally invent and rely on their own arithmetic procedures because these methods allow them to cope with their environment in a meaningful manner. For example, children in all cultures initially rely on their own methods of counting to compute sums. When given a task of counting a set of three objects and a set of four objects, four-year-old children will "count all," starting with the number 1. Later, they develop a strategy of "count on," starting with the larger set. In this example, they would begin with 4 and add onto this number (Ginsburg, 1997; Baroody & Ginsburg, 1991; Resnick & Klopfer, 1989).

Constructive learning instruction in mathematics requires that children become actively involved in mathematics. It encourages children to develop and use invented mathematics for solving problems, as illustrated in the case example entitled "Children's Construction of Mathematics Knowledge." Through these experiences children build mathematics mental structures.

Learning mathematics, thus, is viewed as an active process and learning is about doing. Use of hands-on learning materials is encouraged to allow students to explore ideas for themselves through manipulative materials. These materials enable them to construct models with something they can see and touch and to create real world experiences. The constructive view of mathematics learning is epitomized in this Chinese proverb:

I hear and I forget. I see and I remember. I do and I understand.

CASE EXAMPLE

CHILDREN'S CONSTRUCTION OF MATHEMATICS KNOWLEDGE

The following example illustrates how a young child uses estimation skills.

Four-year-old Lee had just had his first experience sleeping overnight in a tent. Lee, his brother, and his grandparents erected a tent, in which they placed four sleeping bags for their overnight campout. When Lee excitedly described the experience to his parents the next day, they asked if they could come along next time. Lee did not answer immediately and spent some time considering the question. After estimating the space, he responded to his parents, "No, you cannot come with us because the tent is not big enough to hold two more sleeping bags."

The following problems show how young children construct solutions to subtraction problems (Lindquist, 1987).

Problem A: Jane had 8 trucks. She gave 3 to Ben. How many trucks does she have left?

Problem B: Jane has 8 trucks. Ben has 6 trucks. How many more trucks does Jane have than Ben?

In problem *A,* a young child counts out eight trucks and gives three away. Then the child counts the trucks that are left. In problem *B,* the child counts out eight trucks for Jane and a set of six trucks for Ben. The child then matches Jane's trucks to Ben's. Finally, the child counts to see how many more trucks Jane has than Ben. The child has constructed meaning and does not ask "Should I add or subtract?"

Direct Instruction

Direct instruction is a method of mathematics teaching that helps students achieve mastery of mathematics skills through instruction that is explicit, carefully structured, and planned. It is a comprehensive system that integrates curriculum design with teaching techniques to produce instructional programs in mathematics (Carnine, 1997). The sequential nature of mathematics makes the direct instruction approach particularly adaptable to the content of mathematics. Direct instruction is compatible with instructional philosophy of mastery learning and effective teaching.

Mathematics programs based on direct instruction are highly organized and carefully sequenced. Instruction follows an ordered plan. Teachers determine the objectives of the teaching, plan the teaching through task analysis, provide explicit instruction, and plan for continuous testing (Carnine, 1997; Tarver, 1992; Carnine, Granzin, & Becker, 1988). Also emphasized are the allocation of sufficient time for learning, enough practice to master the skills, and a focus on essential concepts (Simmons & Kameenui, 1996).

The steps for direct instruction of mathematics are as follows:

1. *Target a specific mathematics objective to be accomplished.* This goal must be measurable and observable. For example, the goal may be

that the student will write the answers to twenty multiplication problems (numerals 1 through 7) in 10 minutes with 90 percent accuracy.

2. *Specify the subskills needed to reach that objective.*

3. *Determine which of these skills the student already knows.* For example, does the student already know the numerals 1 through 5 easily in multiplication? Can the student already do the task accurately but very slowly?

4. *Sequence the steps needed to reach the objective.* If the student already knows the multiplication of 1 through 5, then the steps for teaching multiplication of only 6 and 7 will be needed. If the student already knows 1 through 7 but does the problems very slowly, then the teaching should provide drill and practice to speed up the computations.

A substantial body of research supports the direct instruction approach to teaching mathematics. The research shows that direct instruction is an effective approach to improving mathematics achievement of students with learning disabilities (Carnine, 1997; Elliott & Shapiro, 1990).

Cognitive Learning Strategies

Instruction in cognitive strategies is another instructional approach. The goal is to help students with mathematics disabilities acquire strategies for meeting the challenges of mathematics and taking control of their own mathematics learning. As discussed in Chapter 6, a learning strategy is an individual's approach to a task; it includes how the person thinks and acts when planning, executing, and evaluating his or her performance of a task and its outcomes (Montague, 1997; Deshler et al., 1996; Lenz et al., 1996).

Learning strategies instruction is particularly useful for adolescents with learning disabilities who have not acquired the strategies needed for mathematics learning. These students need specific instruction in developing their own independence and success in learning mathematics and in monitoring their thinking about mathematics (Deshler et al., 1996; Lenz et al., 1996).

With cognitive strategies students are encouraged to talk to themselves and to ask themselves questions about the mathematics problems. Examples of this kind of mathematics thinking and self-questioning are "What is missing?" or "Do I need to add or subtract?" Or students might comment, "Oh, I've had this same kind of problem come out wrong before" or "I need to draw this on paper in order to see what is missing."

One procedure requires students to actively pursue the following eight steps (Montague & Bos, 1986):

1. Read the problem aloud.

2. Paraphrase the problem aloud.

3. Visualize the information.

4. State the problem aloud.

5. Hypothesize and think the problem through aloud.

6. Estimate the answer aloud.

7. Calculate and label the answer.

8. Self-check by using the self-questioning technique to ask if the answer makes sense.

Problem Solving

Mathematics **problem solving** refers to the kind of thinking needed to work out mathematics word problems. Problem solving is identified as the top priority for the math curriculum by the National Council of Teachers of Mathematics (NCTM) and is rapidly assuming a larger part of the curriculums of both regular and special education (Parmar & Cawley, 1997; Rivera, 1997; Resnick, 1989).

Problem solving is the most difficult area of mathematics for many students with learning disabilities. These students need extensive guidance and practice to learn to combine thinking and language with the calculation skills and concepts required to solve mathematics problems.

To solve mathematics problems, students must analyze and interpret information so that they can make selections and decisions. Problem solving requires that students know how to apply mathematics concepts and use computation skills in new or different settings (Montague, Applegate, & Marquard, 1993; Cawley & Miller, 1989).

Research on how students go about solving problems in mathematics shows that first and second graders readily invent their own ways to solve simple word problems. However, by the middle grades, they stop their personal problem-solving attempts and begin to rely on rote procedures they have learned in school. Middle-grade students tend to automatically compute with whatever numbers are in the problems. Strategy instruction for mathematics problem solving has been effective with upper elementary and secondary and postsecondary students (Montague, 1997). For example, four questions students can ask themselves for solving algebra word problems are (Hutchinson, 1993):

1. Have I written an equation?

2. Have I expanded the terms?

3. Have I written out the steps to solve my solution on a worksheet?

4. What should I look for in a new problem to see if it is the same kind of problem?

Middle-grade students should be encouraged to continue to create and use their own ways to solve mathematics problems, as illustrated in the case

CASE EXAMPLE

ENCOURAGING A PROBLEM-SOLVING ATTITUDE

The following example of a word problem illustrates how teachers can encourage an inventive problem-solving attitude (Lindquist, 1987).

Problem: Rebecca wants to sell 30 boxes of Girl Scout cookies. She has sold 25. How many more must she sell? The teacher asks if anyone can draw a picture to show this problem.

One student drew the following figure to solve this problem:

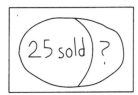

example entitled "Encouraging a Problem-Solving Attitude." To encourage a problem-solving attitude, teachers should help structure the students' responses to problems by talking with them about those responses. Encouraging such a dialogue raises the level of the students' answers. Teachers can help by giving children many word problems to work out and by listening to the students' thinking aloud about the word problems. It is also important to encourage the use of different strategies to solve math problems and to ask students, "How did you get your answer?"

One instructional program to teach arithmetic problem solving to students with learning disabilities used four types of arithmetic work problems: addition, subtraction, two-step problems, and problems with extraneous information (Fleischner, Nuzum, & Marzola, 1987). Students used calculators so that they could concentrate on problem solving rather than computation. In this study, students were taught the processes of solving story problems for 30 minutes twice a week for six weeks. They were given prompt cards to help them focus on the following steps for problem solving:

1. *Read:* What is the question?
2. *Reread:* What is the necessary information?
3. *Think:* a. Putting together = Add
   b. Taking apart = Subtract
   c. Do I need all the information?
   d. Is it a two-step problem?
4. *Solve:* Write the equation.
5. *Check:* Recalculate, label, and compare.

Commercial Programs   Several commercial mathematics programs have been designed to take into account the types of math problems encountered by students with learning disabilities. Table 13.4 lists some of these programs.

ASSESSING MATHEMATICS ABILITY

Information about a student's abilities and proficiency in mathematics can be gathered through both formal tests and informal measures. Formal instruments include standardized survey tests, individually administered achievement tests, and diagnostic math tests. Informal methods include clinical interviews, informal inventories, dynamic assessment procedures, curriculum-based assessment, and analysis of the student errors.

Formal Tests

Formal mathematics tests include standardized survey tests; some are designed for group administration, and some are individually administered achievement tests. There are also diagnostic math tests. It is important to check the validity, reliability, and standardization procedures of tests before using them (Bryant & Rivera, 1997; Salvia & Ysseldyke, 1998).

Standardized Survey Tests   Survey tests provide information on the general level of a student's mathematics performance.

Group Survey Tests   Group survey tests are designed for group administration. Usually data are available on a test's reliability, validity, and standardization procedures. Often there are accompanying manuals with tables

Table 13.4

Commercial Mathematics Programs for Students with Learning Disabilities

Program	Publisher
Computational Arithmetic Program	Pro-Ed
Corrective Mathematics Program	Science Research Associates
Cuisenaire Rods	Cuisenaire
DISTAR Arithmetic Kits	Science Research Associates
Key Math Early Steps Program	American Guidance Services
Key Math Teach and Practice	American Guidance Services
Project Math	Educational Progress
Mastering Math	Steck-Vaughn
Matter of Facts	Creative Publications
Semple Math	Stevenson Learning Skills

Adolescents with mathematics disabilities benefit from specific instruction in learning strategies to develop independence and success in mathematics.
(© Bob Daemmrich/ Stock Boston)

for various kinds of score interpretations, including grade scores, age scores, standard scores, and percentiles. Most of the survey tests in mathematics are part of a general achievement test battery. Some of the most widely used tests are listed in Table 13.5. (Further description appears in Appendix C.)

The standardized achievement tests are useful as screening instruments because they identify those students whose performance scores are below expected levels (Salvia & Ysseldyke, 1998). The major test batteries are well constructed, generally have excellent technical characteristics, and cover most items in the mathematics curriculum. Since they are paper-and-pencil tests that rely on multiple-choice responses, the diagnostic information that can be obtained from them is limited.

The group survey tests can also be given to individuals, and students with learning disabilities are often tested with them.

Individually Administered Achievement Tests   A second type of survey achievement test is commonly used when a student is suspected of having a learning disability. These tests are designed for individual assessment. They often yield more diagnostic information than the group survey tests, providing information on specific areas of mathematics difficulty and more clues for planning instruction. These commonly used norm-referenced measures include the *Wide Range Achievement Test 3* (WRAT3), the *Peabody Individual Achievement Test—Revised* (PIAT-R), and the *Kaufman Test of Educational Achievement* (KTEA). In addition, a number of commonly

Test	Grade or Age
Group Standardized Survey Tests	
California Achievement Tests	Grades K–12
Comprehensive Test of Basic Skills	Grades K–12
Iowa Tests of Basic Skills	Grades K–12
Metropolitan Achievement Tests	Grades K–12
Science Research Associates (SRA) Achievement	Grades K–12
Stanford Achievement Tests	Grades K–12
Individually Administered Achievement Tests	
Brigance Comprehensive Inventory of Basic Skills	Grades K–9
Brigance Diagnostic Inventory of Essential Skills	Grades 6–adult
Peabody Individual Achievement Test—Revised (PIAT-R)	Grades 6–12
Kaufman Test of Educational Achievement (KTEA)	Grades K–12
Wide Range Achievement Test 3 (WRAT3)	Age 5–adult
Woodcock-Johnson Psychoeducational Battery of Achievement	Grades K–12
Diagnostic Math Tests	
Diagnostic Mathematics Inventory/Mathematics System	Grades 1–12
Diagnostic Tests and Self-Helps in Arithmetic	Grades 3–8
Enright Diagnostic Inventory of Basic Arithmetic Skills	Grades 4–Adult
Key Math—Revised	Grades K–6
Sequential Assessment of Mathematics Inventory	Grades K–8
Stanford Diagnostic Mathematics Test (SDMT)	Grades K–12
Test of Early Mathematics Ability	Grades Preschool–3
Test of Mathematical Abilities (TOMA)	Grades 3–12

used criterion-referenced measures are available, such as the *Brigance Diagnostic Inventory of Essential Skills,* which provides extensive information about math achievement patterns. Some of the widely used individual tests are listed in Table 13.5 and are described in Appendix C.

Diagnostic Math Tests   Diagnostic math tests are available for both group and individual administration. Group tests serve two purposes: to provide diagnostic information for student program planning and to assist in program evaluation for administrative purposes. Individual tests generally are used to evaluate patterns of strength and weakness or skills mastered or unmastered in arithmetic (Fleischner, 1994). The diagnostic math tests include the *Stanford Diagnostic Mathematics Test* (SDMT), the *Key Math—Revised*, the *Enright Diagnostic Inventory of Basic Arithmetic Skills*, the *Sequential Assessment of Mathematics Inventories, The Test of Mathematical Abilities* (TOMA), and the *Test of Early Mathematics Ability*. The individually administered diagnostic math tests differ from each other in technical characteristics and in the type of information that they provide about students with learning disabilities (Fleischner, 1994). These tests are listed in Table 13.5 and described in Appendix C.

Informal Measures

Informal measures offer an alternative way to obtain information about a student's performance and abilities in mathematics (Vaughn & Wilson, 1994). Through informal measures, teachers can consider these questions: What previous knowledge did the student bring to this problem? To what extent are the ideas accurate and complete? What strategy did the student employ to solve the problem? What is the child ready to learn now? (Ginsburg, 1997; Baroody & Ginsburg, 1991). Observations of a student's daily behavior in mathematics class and performance on homework assignments and on teacher-made tests or tests that accompany the textbook can provide information for basic assessment decisions.

In this section we look at the following informal measures to assess mathematics: the informal inventory, the clinical interview, analysis of mathematics errors, and curriculum-based assessment.

Informal Inventories   Informal tests can be devised by teachers to assess the student's mathematics skills (Bryant & Rivera, 1997). Once the general area of difficulty is determined, a more extensive diagnostic test of that area can be given. A sample informal arithmetic test appears in Figure 13.1. Teachers can easily construct informal tests to assess the student's achievement in a specific math skill or a sequence of math skills. The informal test can be tailored to an individual student.

Analyzing Mathematics Errors   Teachers should be able to detect the types of errors a student with a mathematics disability is making so that instruction can be directed toward correcting those errors. This information is obtained by examining the students' work or by asking students to explain how they went about solving a problem. When teachers observe the methods used by a student, they can deduce the thought processes the

Figure 13.1

Informal Inventory of
Arithmetic Skills

Addition

3	8	25	20	15	77	5
+5	+0	+71	+49	+ 7	+29	2
						+7

$5 + 7 = \square$ $\qquad$ $3 + \square = 12$ $\qquad$ $\square + 7 = 15$

233	879	648
+ 45	+ 48	745
		+286

Subtraction

7	25	78	72	546	6762
−5	− 9	−23	−49	−222	−4859

$5 - 2 = \square$ $\qquad$ $7 - \square = 4$ $\qquad$ $\square - 3 = 5$

Multiplication

5	6	24	86	59	25
×3	×7	× 2	× 7	×34	×79

$6 \times 3 = \square$ $\qquad$ $7 \times \square = 56$ $\qquad$ $\square \times 5 = 20$

Division

$2\overline{)10}$ $\qquad$ $4\overline{)16}$ $\qquad$ $8\overline{)125}$ $\qquad$ $11\overline{)121}$ $\qquad$ $12\overline{)108}$

$12 \div 4 = \square$ $\qquad$ $24 \div \square = 6$ $\qquad$ $\square \div 9 = 6$

student is using. The four types of mistakes listed next are among the most common errors of calculation.

Place Value **Place value** is the aspect of the number system that assigns specific significance to the position a digit holds in a number. Students who make this error do not understand the concepts of place value, regrouping, carrying, or borrowing. For example:

$$\begin{array}{r} 75 \\ -27 \\ \hline 58 \end{array} \qquad \begin{array}{r} 63 \\ +18 \\ \hline 71 \end{array}$$

These students need concrete practice in the place value of 1s, 10s, 100s, and 1,000s. Effective tools for such practice are an abacus and a place value box or chart with compartments. Students can sort objects such as sticks, straws, or chips into compartments to show place value.

Computation Facts Students who make errors in basic adding, subtracting, multiplying, and dividing need more practice and drill. A handy multiplication chart, like the one in Figure 13.2, might be useful in checking their work. For example:

$$\begin{array}{r} 6 \\ \times 8 \\ \hline 46 \end{array} \qquad \begin{array}{r} 9 \\ \times 7 \\ \hline 62 \end{array}$$

Using the Wrong Process Some students make errors because they use the wrong mathematical process. For example:

$$\begin{array}{r} 6 \\ \times 2 \\ \hline 8 \end{array} \qquad \begin{array}{r} 15 \\ -3 \\ \hline 18 \end{array}$$

These students need work in recognizing symbols and signs.

Working from Right to Left Some students reverse the direction of calculations and work from left to right. For example:

$$\begin{array}{r} 35 \\ +81 \\ \hline 17 \end{array} \qquad \begin{array}{r} 56 \\ +71 \\ \hline 28 \end{array}$$

These students need work in place value.

Figure 13.2
Multiplication Chart

1	**2**	**3**	**4**	**5**	**6**	**7**	**8**	**9**	**10**	**11**	**12**
2	4	6	8	10	12	14	16	18	20	22	24
3	6	9	12	15	18	21	24	27	30	33	36
4	8	12	16	20	24	28	32	36	40	44	48
5	10	15	20	25	30	35	40	45	50	55	60
6	12	18	24	30	36	42	48	54	60	66	72
7	14	21	28	35	42	49	56	63	70	77	84
8	16	24	32	40	48	56	64	72	80	88	96
9	18	27	36	45	54	63	72	81	90	99	108
10	20	30	40	50	60	70	80	90	100	110	120
11	22	33	44	55	66	77	88	99	110	121	132
12	24	36	48	60	72	84	96	108	120	132	144

In addition, *poor writing skills* cause many math errors. When students cannot read their own writing or fail to align their numbers in columns, they may not understand what to do.

Curriculum-Based Assessment   The procedure of curriculum-based assessment (see Chapter 3) provides a useful way to measure mathematics learning and progress. Curriculum-based assessment closely links assessment to the material that is being taught in the mathematics curriculum. The procedure usually involves teacher-constructed tests that measure student progress on curricular objectives relating to a student's individualized education program objectives. In relation to mathematics, curriculum-based assessment consists of four steps (Shinn & Hubbard, 1992; Baroody & Ginsburg, 1991):

1.   Identify target skills. (The skill might be math computation—adding two-digit numbers.)

2.   Determine the objectives to be met. (For example, in a period of four weeks, the student will be able to write correctly the answers to 20 two-digit addition problems in 5 minutes.)

3.   Develop test items to sample each skill. (Assemble a collection of two-digit number problems.)

4.   Develop criteria to measure achievement. (The student will write answers without errors to twenty randomly selected two-digit math problems in a 5-minute period.)

TEACHING STRATEGIES

The rest of this chapter presents teaching strategies for the teaching of mathematics. It includes a discussion of the mathematics curriculum in our schools, some principles of teaching mathematics, and activities for teaching mathematics concepts, skills, and problem solving.

THE MATHEMATICS CURRICULUM

Regular education teachers and special education teachers need to have a general picture of the overall mathematics curriculum. It is important to know what the student has already learned in the mathematics curriculum and what mathematics learnings lie ahead.

The Sequence of Mathematics Through the Grades

Mathematics is a naturally cumulative subject typically taught in a sequence that introduces certain skills at each grade level. For example, learning multiplication depends on knowing addition. The major topics that are covered in the mathematics curriculum from kindergarten through grade 8 include numbers and numeration; whole numbers—addition and subtraction; whole numbers—multiplication and division; decimals; fractions; measurement; geometry; and computer education, a subject that is beginning to show up in many math programs.

Although the sequence may vary somewhat in different programs, the general timetables of instruction are as follows:

Kindergarten.   Basic number meanings, counting, classification, seriation or order, recognition of numerals, writing of numbers

Grade 1.   Addition through 20, subtraction through 20, place value of 1s and 10s, time to the half-hour, money, simple measurement

Grade 2.   Addition through 100, subtraction through 100, ordering of 0 to 100, skip-counting by 2s, place value of 100, regrouping for adding and subtracting

Grade 3.   Multiplication through 9s, odd or even skip-counting, place value of 1,000s, two- and three-place numbers for addition and subtraction, telling time

Grade 4.   Division facts, extended use of multiplication facts and related division facts through 9s, two-place multipliers

Grade 5.   Fractions, addition and subtraction of fractions, mixed numbers, long division, two-place division, decimals

Grade 6.   Percentages, three-place multipliers, two-place division, addition and subtraction of decimals and mixed decimals, multiplication and division of decimals and mixed decimals by whole numbers

Grade 7.   Geometry, rounding, ratios, simple probability

Grade 8.   Scientific notion, using graphs, complex fractions, more complex applications, word problems

The Secondary Mathematics Curriculum

The content areas for grades 9 through 12 identified by the Commission on Standards for School Mathematics of the NCTM (1989) are as follows:

1.   Algebra
2.   Functions
3.   Geometry from a synthetic perspective
4.   Geometry from an algebraic perspective
5.   Trigonometry
6.   Statistics
7.   Probability
8.   Discrete mathematics

9. Conceptual underpinnings of calculus

10. Mathematical structure

Certain general principles of mathematics learning offer a guide for effective mathematics instruction. The principles discussed here include developing prenumber concepts (a readiness skill for mathematics learning), teaching from the concrete to the abstract, providing opportunities and time for practice, generalizing the concepts and skills that have been learned, working with the student's strengths and weaknesses, building a solid foundation of mathematics concepts and skills, providing a balanced mathematics program, and using computers.

Teach Precursors of Mathematics Learning

It is important to check into the previously acquired number learnings to ensure that the student is ready for what needs to be learned. Time and effort invested in building a firm foundation can prevent many later difficulties as the student tries to move on to more advanced and more abstract mathematics processes. The following basic prenumber learnings are essential. If they are lacking, they must be taught:

1. Matching (concept of "same" and grouping of objects)

2. Recognizing groups of objects (recognizing a group of three without counting)

3. Counting (matching numerals to objects)

4. Naming a number that comes after a given number (being able to state, for example, that 8 comes after 7)

5. Writing numerals from 0 to 10 (getting the sequence correct, overcoming reversals and distortions)

6. Measuring and pairing (estimating, fitting objects, one-to-one correspondence)

7. Sequential values (arranging like objects in order by quantitative differences)

8. Relationships of parts to the whole and parts to each other (experimentation with self-correcting materials to discover numerical relationships)

9. Operations (manipulation of the number facts to 10 without reference to concrete objects)

10. The decimal system (learning the system of numeration and notation beyond 10 and base 10)

Progress from the Concrete to the Abstract

Pupils can best understand a math concept when teaching progresses from the concrete to the abstract. A teacher should plan three instructional stages: *concrete, semiconcrete,* and *abstract.* (Miller et al., 1998; Miller, 1996).

In the **concrete instruction** stage, the student manipulates real objects in learning the skill. For example, the student could see, hold, and move two blocks and three blocks to learn that they equal five blocks.

In the **semiconcrete-level instruction** stage, a graphic representation is substituted for actual objects. In the following example, circles represent objects in an illustration from a worksheet:

$$OO + OOO = 5$$

At the **abstract level of instruction,** numerals finally replace the graphic symbols:

$$2 + 3 = 5$$

Provide Opportunity for Practice and Review

Students need many opportunities for review, drill, and practice to over-learn the math concepts since they must be able to use these concepts almost automatically. There are many ways to provide this practice, and teachers should vary the method as often as possible. Such techniques can include worksheets, flash cards, games, behavior management techniques (such as rewards for work completed), and computer practice (special software programs that give immediate feedback).

Teach Students to Generalize to New Situations

Students must learn to generalize a skill to many situations. For example, they can practice computation facts with many story problems that the teacher or students create and then exchange. The goal is to gain skill in recognizing computational operations and applying them to various new situations.

Teach Mathematics Vocabulary

The vocabulary and concepts of mathematics are new and must be learned. The student may know the operation but not know the precise term applied to the operation. Table 13.6 shows the vocabulary for basic mathematics operations.

Table 13.6

Math Terms and
Operations

Operation	Terms		
Addition	3	→	addend
	+5	→	addend
	8	→	sum
Subtraction	9	→	minuend
	−3	→	subtrahend
	6	→	difference
Multiplication	7	→	multiplicand
	×5	→	multiplier
	35	→	product
Division	7	→	quotient
	6⟌42		
			divisor

Consider the Student's Strengths and Weaknesses

Teachers must understand the student's abilities and disabilities in addition to the mathematics attainment levels and the operations that the student can perform. How do the student's areas of disability affect the math learning? What other tasks does the student approach in this manner? How far back is it necessary to go to ensure a firm foundation in number concepts? What techniques, approaches, and materials appear to be most promising? Some specific suggestions follow:

1. Determine whether the student comprehends number structure and arithmetic operations. Does the student understand the meaning of spoken numbers? Can the student read and write numbers? Can the student perform basic arithmetic operations? Given two numbers, can the student tell which is larger and which is smaller?

2. Determine the student's skills in spatial orientation. Has the student established a left-right directionality or shown evidence of spatial disorientation?

3. To what extent does language ability contribute to the student's problems in mathematics? Does the student's ability to understand language (receptive language) and use language (expressive language) affect mathematics learning?

4. Does poor reading ability interfere with mathematics learning? Can the student read numbers? Can the student read the words in directions and story problems? Does the student understand the sentences in the story problems?

5. Are there memory or attention problems that interfere with the student's mathematics learning? Does the student have difficulty remembering math facts?

Build a Solid Foundation of Mathematics Concepts and Skills

Poor teaching can actually make a student's mathematics problems even worse. Mathematics should be taught in a way that solidifies the mathematics concepts so that they are stable and remain available to the student. These guidelines can help students develop a solid foundation of mathematics thinking:

1. Emphasize answering questions rather than merely doing something.
2. Generalize the teaching to many different kinds of applications and experiences with different ways of handling the problem.
3. Provide thorough instruction so that students receive the practice they need.
4. Help students gain confidence in their mathematics ability. Many adults become alarmed and defensive when faced with a mathematical problem because they lost confidence during their early arithmetic instruction.

Provide a Balanced Mathematics Program

Good mathematics instruction must be balanced and should include an appropriate combination of three elements: *quantitative concepts, number skills,* and *problem solving*. All three are essential for mathematics learning (Bley & Thornton, 1989).

Quantitative Concepts   Concepts refer to basic understandings. Students develop a concept when they are able to classify or group objects or when they can associate a label with a class. An example is recognizing that *round* objects form a group and that the name applied to objects in that group is *circle*. Another example of a concept is the formulation of rules or regularities. To illustrate, a concept is developed when the student learns that when a number is multiplied by 10, the product is that number followed by a 0.

Number Skills   Concepts refer to basic understandings; skills refer to something one does. The processes of doing the number facts—the basic operations in addition, subtraction, multiplication, and division—are examples of mathematics skills.

A skill can be performed well or not so well, quickly or slowly, easily or with great difficulty. Skills tend to develop by degrees and can be improved through instructional activities.

Problem Solving Skills   Mathematics concepts and skills are applied to problem solving. Usually, the application involves the selection and use of some combination of concepts or skills in a new or different setting. An example is the problem of measuring a board of lumber. The concepts involved in a rectangle and parallel sides come into play, as well as the skills of measuring, multiplying, and adding. To teach problem solving in mathematics, the teacher must help a student identify analogous situations—that is, think of situations that are similar to the present problem and then use these similarities by applying the same concepts and skills in both situations.

ACTIVITIES FOR TEACHING MATHEMATICS

The instruction activities in this section are grouped into three categories: *quantitative concepts, number skills,* and *problem solving.*

Teaching Mathematics Concepts

Classification and Grouping

1. Sorting games.   Give students objects that differ in only one attribute, such as color or texture, and ask them to sort the objects into two different boxes. For example, if the objects differ by color, have students put red items in one box and blue items in another box. At a more advanced level, increase the complexity of the classification of the attributes, asking students to sort, for example, movable objects from stationary objects. Another variation is to use objects that have several overlapping attributes, such as shape, color, and size. You might present children with cutouts of triangles, circles, and squares in three colors (blue, yellow, and red) and two sizes (small and large). Ask the students to sort them according to shape and then according to color. Then ask them to discover a third way of sorting.

2. Matching and sorting.   A first step in the development of number concepts is the ability to focus on and recognize a single object or shape. Have the student search through a collection of assorted objects to find a particular type of object. For example, the student might look in a box of colored beads or blocks for a red one, search through a collection of various kinds of nuts for all the almonds, choose the forks from a box of silverware, look in a box of buttons for the oval ones, sort a bagful of cardboard shapes to pick out the circles, or look in a container of nuts and bolts for the square pieces.

3. Recognition of groups of objects.   Domino games, playing cards, concrete objects, felt boards, magnetic boards, cards with colored disks, and mathematics workbooks all provide excellent materials for developing concepts of groups.

4. Number stamp. Using a stamp pad and a stamp (the eraser on the end of a pencil will serve very well), the student can make a set of numerals with matching dots. Two students can play the classic card game "War" with one standard deck of cards and one deck made with stamped dots; the first player to recognize and claim matching cards can take them.

Ordering

1. Serial order and relationships. When teaching the concept of ordering, you might ask the student to tell the number that comes after 6 or before 5 or between 2 and 4. Also, ask the student to indicate the first, last, or third of a series of objects. Other measured quantities can be arranged by other dimensions, such as size, weight, intensity, color, volume, and pitch of sound.

2. Number lines. A **number line** is a sequence of numbers forming a straight line that allows the student to manipulate computation directly. Number lines and number blocks for the students to walk on are helpful in understanding the symbols and their relationships to each other.

3. Pattern games. Ask the student to discover patterns by selecting the next object in a series that you have begun. For example, in a pattern of red, white, red, white, the student should choose a red object as the next item in the sequence. Increase the complexity of patterns as the exercise progresses.

4. Relationships between concepts of size and length. Have the student compare and contrast objects of different size, formulating concepts of smaller, bigger, taller, and shorter. Make cardboard objects such as circles, trees, houses, and so forth, or collect objects such as washers, paper clips, and screws. Have the student arrange them by size and then estimate the size of objects by guessing whether certain objects would fit into certain spaces.

One-to-One Correspondence: Pairing

One-to-one correspondence is a relationship in which one element of a set is paired with one and only one element of a second set. Pairing provides a foundation for counting. Activities designed to match or align one object with another are useful. Have the student arrange a row of pegs in a pegboard to match a prearranged row, or set a table and place one cookie on each dish, or plan the allocation of materials to the group so that each person receives one object.

Counting

1. Motor activities for counting. Some students learn to count verbally but do not attain the concept that each number corresponds to one object. Such students are helped by making strong motor and tactile responses along with the counting. Looking at visual stimuli or pointing to the objects may not be enough because such students will count erratically, skipping objects or saying two numbers for one object. Motor activities to help students establish the counting principle include placing a peg in a hole, clipping clothespins on a line, stringing beads onto a pipe cleaner, clapping three times, jumping four times, and tapping on the table two times. Use the auditory modality to reinforce visual counting by having students listen to the counts of a drumbeat with their eyes closed. The students may make a mark for each sound and then count the marks.

2. Counting cups. Take a set of containers, such as cups, and designate each with a numeral. Have the students fill each container with the correct number of items, using objects such as bottle caps, chips, buttons, screws, or washers.

Recognition of Numbers

1. Visual recognition of numbers. Students must learn to recognize both the printed numbers *(7, 8, 3)* and the words expressing these numbers *(seven, eight, three)*. They must also learn to integrate the written forms with the spoken symbols. If students confuse one written number with another, color cues may help them to recognize the symbol. You might, for example, make the top of the 3 green and the bottom red. Another activity is to have the students match the correct number with the correct set of objects; felt, cardboard, or sandpaper symbols or groups of objects can be used.

2. Parking lot poster. Draw a "parking lot" on a poster, numbering parking spaces with dots instead of numerals. Paint numerals on small cars and have the students park the cars in the correct spaces.

Motor Activities

1. Work space. Furnish a large table with equipment that can help in performing number tasks. Counting materials such as an abacus, beans, sticks, play money, rulers, and other measuring instruments are among the items the students might use.

2. Puzzles, pegboards, and form boards. These items help the students focus on shapes and spatial relations. If a student has difficulty finding and fitting the missing piece, orally provide some hints by describing the shape being sought.

3. Measurement. Pouring sand, water, or beans from a container of one shape or size to a different container helps the students develop concepts of measurement. Estimating quantities, using measuring cups, and introducing fractions can be emphasized in such activities. Use actual containers and other devices for measuring pints, quarts, half-gallons, gallons, pounds, and half-pounds to teach measurement and to demonstrate relationships of measurement. Another use of measurement is in cooking; consider making Jell-O, using cake mixes, or preparing macaroni and cheese.

Teaching Mathematics Skills

1. Basic computational skills.   Many problems in arithmetic are due to deficiencies in basic computational skills. The student's problem should be evaluated with reference to underlying deficits in learning processes—verbal, spatial, perceptual, or memory factors. Students should be taught the basic skills of **mathematics computation** that they lack, including addition, subtraction, multiplication, division, fractions, decimals, and percentages.

2. Addition.   Knowledge of addition facts provides the foundation for all other computational skills. Addition is a short method of counting, and pupils should know that they can resort to counting when all else fails. Addition can be thought of as *part plus part equals whole.* Important symbols to learn are: + (plus, or "put together") and = (equals, or "the same as"). As with the other areas, begin by using concrete objects, then use cards with sets that represent numbers, and finally use the number sentence with the numbers alone: $3 + 2 = \Box$. From this the students can also learn that $2 + 3 = \Box; \Box + 2 = 5;$ and $3 + \Box = 5$.

Teaching addition using sums between 10 and 20 is more difficult. There are several approaches. It is easier to start with doubles, such as $8 + 8 = 16$. Then ask what $9 + 8$ equals: One more than 16!

Another way is to "make a 10." For example, in $7 + 5$, the pupil takes 3 of the 5, and adds the 3 to the 7 to make 10. Now the students can see that $10 +$ the remaining $2 = 12$. Use movable disks so that the students can actually experience the process:

$$7 + 5 = 12$$
$$10 + 2 = 12$$

The number line provides another way to teach addition. With a number line, the students can visually perceive the addition process.

3. Subtraction.   After the students have a firm basis in addition, introduce subtraction. An important new symbol is − (minus, or "take away"). A student places a set of objects on the desk and then takes away certain objects. How many are left? $6 - 2 = \Box$. Then use cards with sets on them. Find 6 by using a card with a set of 2 and a card with a set of 4. Tell the students you have a set of 6 when the cards are joined. Take away the set of 2 and ask the students what is left.

Another way of illustrating subtraction is using rods, such as Cuisenaire rods. Start with the rod that represents a total sum. Place on top a type of rod that represents part of the sum. Ask the students to find the rod that fills the empty space.

The number line is also useful in subtraction.

Regrouping is an important concept that is introduced in subtraction, along with the ideas of "1s," "10s," and "100s."

4. Multiplication.   Many students with an arithmetic disability do not know multiplication facts (shown in Figure 13.2, page 505). Those students will be unable to learn division until they master multiplication facts.

Multiplication is a short method of adding. Instead of adding $2 + 2 + 2 + 2$, the students can learn $2 \times 4 = 8$. Subtraction is not a prerequisite of multiplication and a student having difficulty with subtraction may do better with multiplication. The symbol to learn is $\times$ (times).

There are several ways of explaining multiplication. One way is the *multiplication sentence*. How much are 3 sets of 2? Using sets of objects, the students can find the total either by counting objects or by adding equal addends.

The concept of reversals (turn-around) can also be introduced. The sentence $3 \times 5 = \square$ does not change in the form $5 \times 3 = \square$.

In the *equal addend approach*, ask the students to show that:

$$3 \times 5 = 5 + 5 + 5, \text{ or } 15$$

In the *number line approach*, students who can use number lines for addition will probably also do well in using them for multiplication. The student adds a unit of 5 three times on the line, to end up at the 15 on the line.

The *rectangular array approach* contains an equal number of objects in each row. For example, 3×5 is shown as:

```
0 0 0 0 0
0 0 0 0 0
0 0 0 0 0
```

5. Division.   This computational skill is considered the most difficult to learn and to teach. As mentioned earlier, basic division facts come from knowledge of multiplication facts. Long division requires many operations, and students must be able to do all the steps before they can put them together. The new symbol is $\div$ (divide).

There are a number of ways to approach division. Sets can be used: $6 \div 3 = \square$. Draw a set of 6 and enclose three equal sets. The missing factor is seen as 2:

How many subsets are there? How many objects are there in each set?

The number line can also be used. By jumping back a unit of 3, how many jumps are needed?

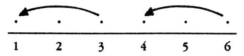

The *missing factors* approach uses known multiplication facts and reverses the process: $3 \times \Box = 12$. Then change to a division sentence: $12 \div 3 = \Box$.

6. Fractions.   Geometric shapes are commonly used to introduce fractional numbers. The new symbol is shown next:

$$\frac{1}{2} \begin{array}{l} \rightarrow \text{number of special parts} \\ \rightarrow \text{total number of equal parts} \end{array}$$

Start with halves, followed by quarters and then eighths. Cut shapes out of flannel or paper plates. Figure 13.3 illustrates common fractions.

7. Learning the computational facts.   Once the concepts behind the facts are known, the students must memorize the facts themselves. Many different learning opportunities are needed. Students can write the facts, say them, play games with facts, take speed tests, and so forth. Also helpful are flash cards, rolling dice, playing cards, or even learning a fact a day. A wide variety of methods should be used.

To learn computational skills, students with an arithmetic disability require much experience with concrete and manipulative materials before moving to the abstract and symbolic level of numbers. Objects and materials that can be physically taken apart and put back together help the students to observe visually the relationship of the fractional parts of the whole.

There are fifty-six basic number facts to be mastered in each mode of arithmetic computation (addition, subtraction, multiplication, and division), if the facts involving the 1s $(3 + 1 = 4)$ and doubles $(3 \times 3 = 9)$ are

Figure 13.3

Some Common Fractions

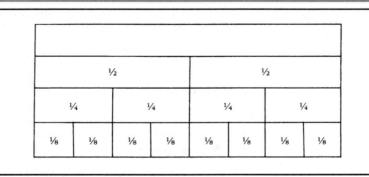

not included. Examples of number facts are 3 + 4 = 7; 9 − 5 = 4; 3 × 7 = 21; 18 ÷ 6 = 3. In the computational skill of addition, for example, there are eighty-one separate facts involved in the span from 1 + 1 = 2 to 9 + 9 = 18. Few students have trouble with the 1s (5 + 1 = 6) or with the doubles (2 + 2 = 4). Therefore, if these facts are omitted, there are fifty-six basic addition facts to be mastered. Similarly, without the 1s and doubles, there are fifty-six facts to be mastered in each of the other computation areas—subtraction, multiplication, and division.

8. The two-weeks facts: 7 + 7.   Students circle two full calendar weeks and count the number of days in each week (see Figure 13.4.) to learn that 7 + 7 = 14 (Thornton, 1984).

9. Subtraction of 9s from teen numbers.   One useful technique to help students learn subtraction of 9s from the teen numbers is the following. Consider the following problem: 16 − 9 = ☐. Adding the 1 and 6 gives the correct answer of 7. This technique works with subtracting 9s from all teen numbers.

10. Tapping out combinations.   Tap out combinations of numbers on a table or have the students tap out the combinations. This reinforces number learning through the kinesthetic and auditory system.

11. Reinforcement of auditory expression.   Some students find it helpful to relate the number sequences and facts aloud.

12. Arrangements.   Give students the numbers 1, 2, 3. Ask them in how many ways they can be arranged: 1-2-3; 1-3-2; 2-1-3; 2-3-1; 3-1-2; 3-2-1 (or 3 × 2 + 1 = 6). Another arrangement puzzle is this one: If four children sit around a square table, in how many ways can they arrange themselves? (4 × 3 × 2 × 1 = 24).

13. Puzzle cards of combinations.   Make cardboard cards on which problems of addition, subtraction, multiplication, and division are worked. Cut each card in two so that the problem is on one part and the answer is on the other. Each card must be cut uniquely, so that when the students try to assemble the puzzle, only the correct answer will fit.

14. Rate of perception of number facts.   The use of computer programs or flash cards is a way to increase the rate of recognition of sets of objects, number symbols, and answers to number facts. A quick exposure device can be made by putting information on transparencies, then cutting the transparencies into strips and inserting them in a filmstrip projector. By covering the lens with a sheet of cardboard and exposing the material for a short period of time, students practice rapid recognition of number facts.

15. Playing cards.   An ordinary deck of cards becomes a versatile tool for teaching number concepts. Some of the activities that can be accomplished with a deck of cards are arranging suits in sequential order by number, matching sets, adding and subtracting the individual cards, and quickly recognizing the number in a set.

Figure 13.4

Calendar for
Learning Facts

Sun	Mon	Tue	Wed	Thur	Fri	Sat
1	2	3	4	5	6	7
8	9	10	11	12	13	14
15	16	17	18	19	20	21
22	23	24	25	26	27	28

Teaching Problem Solving

The eventual goal of mathematics instruction is to apply the concepts and skills in problem solving. The goals set by the National Council for Teachers of Mathematics (1989) call for more emphasis on problem solving at all levels. Effective strategies for teaching problem solving and applications to students with learning disabilities include the following:

1. Word story problems.   Use word story problems that are of interest to the students and within their experience.

2. Posing problems orally.   This strategy is especially important for students with reading problems.

3. Visual reinforcements.   Use concrete objects, drawings, graphs, or other visual reinforcements to clarify the problem, demonstrate solutions, and verify the answers. Have students act out the problem.

4. Simplifying.   Have students substitute smaller and easier numbers for problems with larger or more complex numbers so that they can understand the problems and verify the solutions more readily.

5. Restating.   Have students restate the problems in their own words. This verbalization helps the students structure the problems for themselves and also shows whether they understand the problems.

6. Assessing given information.   Select problems with too little or too much information and have students determine what is still needed or what is superfluous.

7. Supplementary problems.   Supplement textbook problems with your own, which could deal with classroom experiences. Including students' names makes the problem more realistic.

8. Time for thinking.   Allow students enough time to think. Ask for alternative methods for solving the problems. Try to understand how the students thought about the problem and went about solving it.

9. Steps in solving word problems.   Many students with learning disabilities have difficulty with word problems. Although problems in reading may be a factor, the difficulty is often in thinking through the math problems.

Students tend to begin doing computations as soon as they see the numbers in the problems. The following steps are helpful in teaching word problem applications:

a. *Seeing the situation:* Have the students first read the word problem and then relate the setting of the problem. The students do not need paper and pencil for this task. They should simply describe the setting or situation.

b. *Determining the question:* Have the students decide what is to be discovered: What is the problem to be solved?

c. *Gathering data:* The word problem often gives much data—some relevant, some not relevant to the solution. Ask the students to read the problem orally or silently and then list relevant and irrelevant data.

d. *Analyzing relationships:* Help the students analyze the relationships among the data. For example, if the problem states that the down payment on an automobile costing $250 is 25 percent, the students must see the relationship between these two facts. Seeing relationships is a reasoning skill that students with learning disabilities often find difficult.

e. *Deciding on a process:* Students must decide which computational process should be used to solve the problem. Here students should be alert to key words such as *total* or *in all,* which suggest addition, and *is left* or *remains,* which suggest subtraction. They should next put the problem into mathematical sentences.

f. *Estimating answers:* Have the students practice estimating what a reasonable answer might be. If the students understand the reasoning behind the problem, they should be able to estimate answers.

g. *Practice and generalization:* After students have thought through and worked out one type of problem, the teacher can give similar problems with different numbers.

10. Time. Time concepts involve a difficult dimension for many students with learning disabilities to grasp, so they may require specific instructions to learn how to tell time. Real clocks or teacher-made clocks are needed to teach this skill. A teacher-made clock can be created by using a paper fastener to attach cardboard hands to a paper plate. A sequence for teaching time might be the hour (1:00), the half-hour (4:30), the quarter-hour (7:15), 5-minute intervals (2:25), before and after the hour, minute intervals, and seconds. Use television schedules of programs or classroom activities and relate them to clock time.

11. Money. The use of real money and lifelike situations is an effective way to teach number facts to some students. Have them play store, make change, or order a meal from a restaurant menu and then add up the cost and pay for it. All of these situations provide concrete and meaningful practice for learning arithmetic.

USING TECHNOLOGY FOR MATHEMATICS INSTRUCTION

Calculators

The calculator has revolutionized functional arithmetic. Calculators are being used everywhere—in grocery stores, restaurants, real estate firms, used car salesrooms, and college classes. There is undoubtedly an important place for the calculator in our instructional planning. Students must be required to learn the computation facts, but there are times for using the calculator as well. As noted earlier in this chapter, the National Council of Teachers of Mathematics (1989) recommended that students be allowed to use calculators on math tests. How can students in school be taught how to make efficient use of the calculator?

Calculators are suggested for lessons that aim to teach mathematics reasoning, not calculation skills per se. In doing a mathematics reasoning problem, students often become so bogged down in computation that they never get to the reasoning aspects of the lesson. By using calculators, students can put their energies into understanding the mathematical concept rather than on performing the underlying calculation process.

A low-cost pocket calculator is easily accessible and handy. It can be used to compute basic facts as well as more complicated math processes, and it is also useful for self-checking. Because it is more socially acceptable than other counting systems, it is particularly helpful for adults who have not memorized basic computation facts. Students do need instruction in the proper way to use a calculator, so lessons must be designed to teach calculation skills.

Students with learning disabilities might find "talking" calculators useful. The talking calculator is a calculator with a speech synthesizer. When a number, symbol, or operation is pressed, it is vocalized by the speech synthesizer. The user gets auditory feedback and can double-check the answers (Raskind & Higgins, 1998).

Secondary students and adults are likely to need programmable calculators to perform more complex math functions.

Computers

The rapid pace of change in computer applications has made this technology even more useful for teaching mathematics. The revolution in computers has brought the Internet, CD-ROMs, multimedia, and other communication applications, all of which have many uses in teaching mathematics.

Many mathematics software programs, although not specifically designed for students with learning disabilities, may be useful. Computers motivate students, and the mathematics software programs can individualize, provide feedback, and offer repetition (Lewis, 1998; Raskind & Higgins, 1998). These programs should have as little clutter as possible and should offer concise, clear directions, moving from simple and concrete directions to longer and more complex ones. The programs should question the

Table 13.7

Selected Mathematics
Software for Students
with Learning
Disabilities

Title	Publisher	Grade Level	Type	System
Math Blaster	Davidson	E, S	CD	Mac/Win
Math Blaster Algebra	Davidson	S	CD	Mac/Win
Math Rabbit	The Learning Co.	E	CD	Mac/Win
Math Muncher Deluxe	The Learning Co.	E	CD	Mac/Win
Math Keys	MECC/The Learning Co.	E/S	CD	Mac/Win
Sticky Bears Math Splash	Optimum	P, E	CD	Mac/Win
Math Pad	Intellitools	E	CD	Mac/Win
Carmen San Diego Math Detection	Broderbund	E, S	CD	Mac/Win
Mighty Math Cosmic Geometry	Edmark	S	CD	Mac/Win
Mighty Math Astro Algebra	Edmark	S	CD	Mac/Win
Thinking Things	Edmark	E, S	CD	Mac/Win
The Graph Club	Tom Snyder	E	CD	Mac/Win
Factory DeLuxe	Sunburst	E	CD	Mac/Win
Basic Number Facts	Gameco	E	CD	Mac/Win
Computerized Math Pre Test Preparation Series	Chariot	S	CD	Mac/Win
Math Word Problem Series	Optimum Resources	S	CD	Mac/Win
Hot Dog Stand	Sunburst	E, S	CD	Mac/Win

P=primary   E=elementary   S=secondary

Broderbund Phone: (800) 521-6263 Chariot at **http://www.edresources.com** Davidson at **http://www.david.com** Edmark at **http://www.edmark.com** Gameco Chariot at **http://www.edresources.com** The Learning Co. at **http://www.learningco.com** Sunburst at **http://www.sunburst.com** Optimum Resources Phone: (702) 736-2877 Tom Snyder at **http://teachstp.com** Intellitools at **http://www.intellitools.com**

student frequently (asking, for example, "Are you sure? Do you want to change your answer?") They should also provide immediate feedback to the student. Math programs range from drill-and-practice programs to problem-solving programs.

Related to the area of mathematics, other types of computer software are useful for students with learning disabilities. *Databases* allow students to organize information and display it in various ways. *Spreadsheets* (such as Lotus 1-2-3, Excel, and Quattro Pro) allow students to keep track of quantitative information, to model the problem, and to display it through charts. *Graphic organizers* (such as Inspiration) facilitate brainstorming and allow students to organize information (Lewis, 1998). Woodward (1998) suggests that the *World Wide Web* can be used to teach mathematics to students with learning disabilities. Woodward has developed a web strand called Math Concepts, which is located at **http://www.ups.edu/community/tofu/.**

A large-scale examination of how computers affect the learning of mathematics in American classrooms found that, when used selectively by trained teachers in middle schools, they can significantly enhance mathematics performance (Educational Testing Service, 1998).

A good source for mathematics software programs for students with learning disabilities is Closing the Gap's *Resource Directory* (1998). Table 13.7 lists some mathematics software for students with learning disabilities.

Chapter Summary

1. Some students with learning disabilities have severe difficulty in learning mathematics. For others, particularly students with verbal-language disabilities, mathematics seems to be an area of strength. Dyscalculia, a severe disability in learning and using mathematics, is associated with an neurological dysfunction.

2. Precursors of mathematics learning in young children include abilities in spatial relations, visual-motor and visual-perception processing, body image, sense of direction and time, and memory abilities.

3. Characteristics of mathematics disabilities are related to information processing, language an reading, cognitive learning strategies, and math anxiety.

4. Mathematics disabilities are different at the secondary school level because of the advanced mathematics curriculum taught there.

5. Views about teaching mathematics have changed over the years in response to national concerns. We have witnessed a modern math movement and a back-to-basics movement. Now we are concerned with educational reforms and the pressures of testing.

6. There are several learning theories of math instruction for students with learning disabilities. Mathematics should be taught in three stages: concrete, semiconcrete, and abstract. Constructive learning in mathematics encourages children to build their own mathematics solutions to problems. Direct instruction emphasizes the objectives to be taught and the sequential steps needed to reach those objectives. Learning strategies instruction teaches students how to control and direct their own learning in mathematics. Problem-solving approaches emphasize the thinking that students need to find solutions to mathematics problems.

7. Students' mathematics abilities can be assessed through informal and formal measures. Each provides a different kind of information about mathematics performance.

8. The content of the mathematics curriculum is sequential and cumulative. Different elements of mathematics are taught at different grade levels.

9. Principles of instruction in mathematics stress that the students should have prenumber concepts and the readiness for further mathematics learning. Instruction should progress from the concrete to the abstract, and ample opportunity for practice and review should be provided. The students must learn to generalize concepts that have been learned and must possess the vocabulary for basic mathematics operations. Teachers should work with the students' strengths and weaknesses and build a solid foundation of mathematics skills and concepts. A balanced mathematics program should be planned and should teach concepts, skills, and problem solving.

10. Students should learn basic computational facts, but they should be allowed to use calculators for some purposes in the classroom. Calculators should be part of the mathematic curriculum.

11. Teachers need a variety of strategies for teaching mathematics concepts, skills, and problem solving. A balanced program should offer students with learning disabilities adequate instruction with a variety of strategies for each of these three components of mathematics.

12. Computers have many useful applications in teaching mathematics to students with learning disabilities.

Questions for Discussion and Reflection

1. The Individuals with Disabilities Education Act of 1997 (IDEA 1997) recognizes two areas in which students can have mathematics disabilities. Describe these two areas and discuss the implications for services.

2. Characteristics of learning disabilities can affect the learning of mathematics. Select four characteristics of students with mathematics disabilities and describe how these characteristics can affect mathematics learning.

3. How has the teaching of mathematics changed over the years, and what effect have these changes had on students with learning disabilities?

4. Do you think calculators should be used in mathematics instruction? Why or why not? Discuss how they could be used.

5. How can computers be used in the teaching of mathematics?

6. Describe how students can be instructed to go from concrete learning to abstract learning.

Key Terms

abstract-level instruction *(p. 509)*

body image *(p. 486)*

back-to-basics movement *(p. 493)*

concrete instruction *(p. 509)*

constructive learning *(p. 495)*

direct instruction *(p. 496)*

dyscalculia *(p. 484)*

math anxiety *(p. 489)*

mathematics computation *(p. 515)*

number line *(p. 513)*

number skills *(p. 511)*

one-to-one correspondence *(p. 513)*

place value *(p. 504)*

problem solving *(p. 498)*

quantitative concepts *(p. 511)*

semiconcrete-level instruction *(p. 509)*

spatial relationships *(p. 486)*

time concepts *(p. 520)*

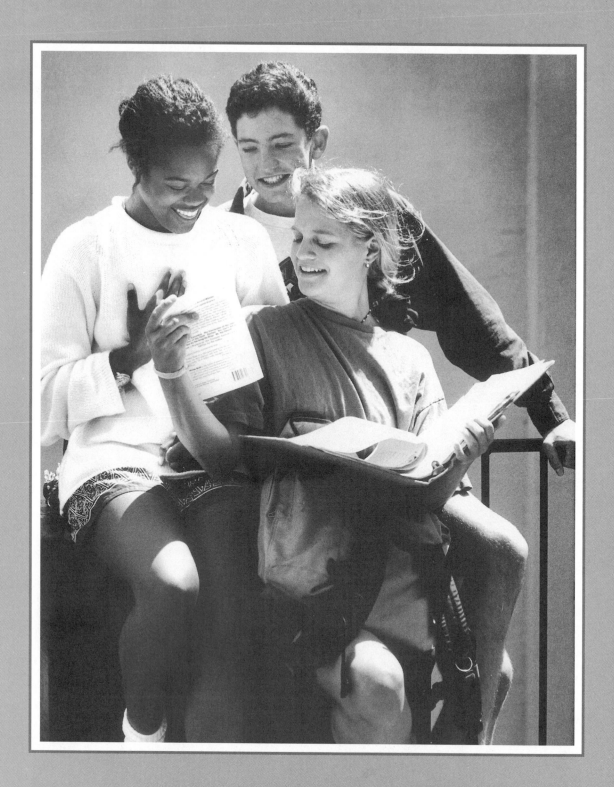

Social and Emotional Behavior

Learning disabilities encompass more than academic difficulties. A comprehensive understanding of the puzzle of learning disabilities requires consideration of the social, emotional, and behavioral spheres of the individual's life. How do these problems impinge upon school learning, and what strategies can help students in these nonacademic domains? The Theories section of this chapter reviews concepts underlying nonverbal, social, emotional, and behavioral dimensions of learning disabilities. The Teaching Strategies section offers various interventions for teachers to use in helping students develop social competence, build self-esteem, and improve their behavior. This section also suggests ways to modify the inclusive classroom to accommodate students with learning disabilities.

THEORIES

In this section we examine nonverbal learning disabilities (NLD), deficits in social skills, and emotional and behavioral problems of individuals with learning disabilities. Several diverse theories underlie each of these problematic areas, and each theory leads to a different approach to intervention.

NONVERBAL LEARNING DISABILITIES (NLD)

The condition of **nonverbal learning disabilities (NLD)** has captured a growing interest among researchers and practitioners. Nonverbal learning disabilities are considered to be a subtype of learning disabilities that differs markedly from academic, linguistic, and cognitive disabilities. NLD are believed to have a neurological basis that involves a dysfunction in the right hemisphere. They are characterized by serious difficulties with social interactions and in interpersonal skills. For example, individuals with NLD have difficulty in understanding those subtle cues inherent in nonverbal communication that play such an important role in social interaction. Children with NLD often have high verbal intelligence, tend to be early talkers, are highly verbal, and do well on reading and decoding in the primary years; therefore, their nonverbal learning problems are often missed. These children often have poor visuospatial and nonverbal problem-solving abilities and low arithmetic skills. Problems with NLD become more evident in the later elementary school years, during adolescence, and in the adult years (Rourke, 1989, 1995; Tsatsanis, Fuerst, & Rourke, 1997; Dimitrovsky, Spector, Levy-Shiff, & Vakil, 1998; Thompson, 1997).

Goleman (1995), in his popular book *Emotional Intelligence,* points out that people who do well in life have the qualities of social deftness, persistence, empathy, self-awareness, impulse control, zeal, and self-motivation.

The inspiring stories of individuals with learning disabilities who become successful adults describe people who have these qualities and also have learned to compensate for their linguistic and reading shortcomings (Mc-Grady & Lerner, in press; Gerber & Brown, 1997). Individuals with nonverbal learning disabilities, however, lack the qualities that Goleman calls "emotional intelligence."

People with nonverbal learning disabilities have difficulty adapting to new or novel situations. Despite their high verbal intelligence and high scores on receptive and expressive language measures, they inaccurately read nonverbal signals and cues, and they lack the social ability to comprehend nonverbal communication cues. If they do not perceive subtle cues in the environment, they do not know when something has gone far enough, do not recognize the idea of personal "space," and cannot interpret the facial expressions of others. These social cues are normally intuitively grasped through observation, but individuals with NLD need to be taught these social skills through direct and explicit instruction (Thompson, 1997; Dimitrovsky, et al., 1998; Tsatsanis et al., 1997).

Adults with nonverbal learning disabilities are likely to have great difficulty in the workplace. Their problems include poor self-concept, mental health problems, difficulty in social relationships, and terse or curt response styles. Transitions are difficult since these individuals like routine and find it difficult to take on new responsibilities and assignments. Unable to reflect on the nature and seriousness of their own problems, they tend to attribute their failures, as well as their successes, to others instead of to themselves. Their coping mechanisms are often misinterpreted as "emotional" or "motivational" problems (Thompson, 1997; Price, 1997; Tsatsanis et al., 1997: Rourke, 1995).

A web site for nonverbal learning disabilities is located at **http://www. nldline.com.**

Deficits in Social Skills

As a subtype of nonverbal disabilities, deficits in **social skills** are probably the most crippling type of problem that a student can have. In terms of total life functioning, a social problem may be far more disabling than an academic dysfunction. (See the case example entitled "Social Skills Disabilities.") A social disability affects almost every aspect of life—in school, at home, and at play.

Severe social learning disabilities include problems in social interactions and nonverbal communication. These students may be identified as having *nonverbal learning disabilities* (NLD) or *Aspergers Syndrome* (Roman, 1998; Thompson, 1997). For further information about NLD, visit **http:// www.nldline.com** and for information about Aspergers Syndrome, see **http://www.aspergers.org.**

CASE EXAMPLE

SOCIAL SKILLS DISABILITIES

The following case examples illustrate social disabilities. These disabilities may not be recognized because they do not prevent students from using verbal language with fluency or from learning to read.

WANDA: IMPULSIVE BEHAVIOR

Nall (1971) described a 12-year-old girl with a social disability, who, she predicted, would not be able to get along in a secondary school because of her poor skills in social perception. The girl read well, performed well in math, and wrote well; she just could not get along with others. She was too impulsive. What she thought, she said. She scratched where it itched. She went where she happened to look. When she finally was academically ready to enter high school, she could not be sent. She would not have lasted there a day.

SAMUEL: DISRUPTIVE SOCIAL BEHAVIOR

Six-year-old Samuel was judged by a psychologist to have an IQ score in the high superior range. He was able to read simple stories by the time he entered first grade. However, Samuel's mother was frequently called in for parent-teacher conferences because of her son's highly disruptive social behavior. The kindergarten teacher reported that Samuel was bossy, turned other children away from him, and had been a "social problem" all year. The first-grade teacher said that Samuel found it difficult to accept "no" for an answer, stamped his feet, cried frequently, pushed others so he could be first in line himself, and alienated the other children by kissing and hugging them to gain affection.

Samuel's mother also described her son's social behavior at home as intolerable. Sitting still for even a few minutes seemed to be impossible,

and he ate so rapidly that he stuffed half his sandwich into his mouth all at once. Samuel would invite a classmate to his house to play and then be so excited that he couldn't do much but run around. The classmate would soon tearfully beg Samuel's mother to go home, and Samuel would also be in tears because of the frustration of trying so hard and not knowing what went wrong. His mother also reported several other incidents typical of children with social perception deficits. Once, for example, when a neighbor girl arrived to play with Samuel, he exclaimed to her, "You sure are a fat one!" The would-be friend left in tears, but Samuel could not understand what he had done wrong. On another occasion, when Samuel was invited to a birthday party, his behavior was so antisocial that the mother of the birthday child phoned Samuel's parents to ask them to take him home.

BECKY: INEPT SOCIAL BEHAVIOR

Becky, a 13-year-old with high average intelligence, constantly said the wrong thing at the wrong time. She seemed unaware of the consequences of her inappropriate remarks. Her parents found they could not have any personal conversations at dinner because she would tell someone about the conversation. Becky had told her Uncle Al, for example, that her parents said he was lazy and irresponsible.

Becky desperately wanted to have friends and to have people like her, but her remarks often offended others and turned them away. For instance, Becky wanted very much to go to a summer camp, but she was rejected by the camp program because she failed the intake interview. When asked by the camp counselor why she would be attending camp, Becky replied that her parents wanted to go to Europe and that was the only way they could get rid of her. With such a response, the interviewer decided that Becky was not a good candidate. Becky did not perceive the inappropriateness of her response or the reaction of the interviewer.

Becky's problems with social perception continued in high school. Her classmates and teachers found her behavior and remarks annoying and disruptive. She did not know how to accept constructive criticism without making an unsuitable rejoinder, and she did not know and use socially acceptable techniques for disagreeing with others. During class, she constantly raised her hand to demand recognition, made challenging remarks, and commented critically in an undertone while the teacher was talking to the class. In Becky's freshman year, her science teacher notified Becky's mother that Becky would receive a grade of B. The science teacher explained that although her average numerical score in the course entitled her to a grade of A, he was lowering Becky's grade because of her behavior. Her poor perception of appropriate social behavior caused her to be an extremely disturbing and disruptive element in the science class.

In school, students need well-developed social and interactive skills in dealing with peers and adults; those who have social perception problems are often at a great disadvantage. (© Jeffrey W. Myers/ FPG International)

Many students with learning disabilities have poor social skills. They lack sensitivity to others, have a poor perception of social situations, and suffer social rejection (Bryan, 1997, Haager & Vaughn, 1997; Rourke, 1995). However, not all students with learning disabilities encounter difficulties with social skills. In fact, for many the social sphere is an area of strength. They are socially competent at making and maintaining friends, and they work at pleasing teachers and parents (Vaughn & Haager, 1994). However, it is estimated that more than one-third of students with learning disabilities have problems with social skills (Bryan, 1997; Voeller, 1994). Some individuals have a social disability but do well in academic domains; others have both social and academic disabilities.

The student's social disability may be a primary and discrete disability, separate from academic and learning problems. It can also reflect a secondary problem if it is the failure to learn that creates secondary emotional and social problems.

Some definitions of learning disabilities (e.g., by the Interagency Committee on Learning Disabilities, 1988) recognize the component of social disabilities. Most definitions, however, such as the federal definition in the Individuals with Disabilities Education Act of 1997 (IDEA 1997), do not mention social disabilities.

Social Competencies

Competencies in social skills are needed for successful daily living. Social skills enable children to successfully interact with peers, teachers, and others; accurately recognize and sensitively respond to emotions expressed by others; or express desires and preferences in socially acceptable ways. Social competencies enable students to identify and solve social problems in a socially acceptable manner (for example, disagreements about who can play with a toy or invitations to sneak out of school with a group of peers) (Friend & Bursuck, 1996).

Social competence means that students establish the following social skills (Rourke, 1995; Vaughn & Haager, 1994; Bos & Vaughn, 1994):

1. **Positive relationships with others.**   Does the student make and maintain positive relationships with peers, parents, and teachers?

2. **Accurate and age-appropriate social cognition.**   How does the student think about self and others, and how well does the child understand and interpret social situations?

3. **The absence of maladaptive behaviors.**   Does the student exhibit behavior problems that interfere with social functioning (disruptive behaviors, anxiety, attention problems, or lack of self-control)?

4. **Effective social behaviors.**   Has the student developed effective social behaviors, such as initiating contact with others, responding cooperatively to requests, and giving and receiving feedback?

Indicators of Social Disabilities

Several behaviors indicate problems in social disabilities.

Poor Social Perception   **Social perception** is the ability to understand social situations, as well as a sensitivity to the feelings of others. Students with problems in social perception perform poorly in the kinds of independent activities expected of students of the same chronological age. They are inept at judging moods and attitudes of the people in their environment, and they are insensitive to the atmosphere of a social situation. They tend to display inappropriate behaviors, to make inappropriate remarks, and to not know how to disagree with others in acceptable ways. (See the case example entitled "A Nonverbal Learning Disability," on page 534.)

Lack of Judgment   Developing social perception is similar in some ways to developing academic skills such as reading or mathematics. In both instances, individuals must learn to anticipate processes, and they must compare the actual result with the expected result. Based on this feedback, individuals must adjust their behavior.

People with social perception problems are likely to have difficulty in each of these steps. They do not anticipate the social processes of others, and they are unable to confirm whether the social behavior of the person matches anticipated behavior. In addition, they cannot adjust their own behavior in light of such comparisons. One consequence is that they appear to lack tact and sensitivity. They may, for example, inappropriately share very personal information with casual acquaintances. At the same time, they may not know how to make appropriate investments in establishing a close relationship with those with whom they wish to be friends (Osman, 1987).

Difficulties in Perceiving How Others Feel   People with social disabilities appear to be less attuned than their peers to the feelings of others. They may use inappropriate behavior or language because they do not know if the person to whom they are reacting is sad or happy, approving or disapproving, accepting or rejecting. In addition, they are insensitive to the general atmosphere of a social situation. Research shows that individuals with social disabilities are poor in detecting or perceiving the subtle social cues given by others, an insensitivity that is a source of difficulty in interacting with peers and parents (Thompson, 1997; Rourke, 1995; Silver, 1998). For example, most children can "sense" a parent's emotional status by body language and know whether to approach or avoid a parent when he or she comes home from work. Children with social perception deficits, however, do not pick up on the subtle messages usually conveyed by facial expression, body language, or tone of voice, and they miss the "Not now" signal that these cues send (Silver, 1998).

A NONVERBAL LEARNING DISABILITY

Jimmy, 9 and a half years old, is an example of a student with a nonverbal learning disability. On the *WISC 3 (Wechsler Intelligence Scale for Children,* third edition), Jimmy received an IQ score of 127, putting him in a high intelligence classification. He did particularly well on the sections that required verbal and language responses. Yet on the *Goodenough-Harris Drawing Test,* his drawing of a man ranked at the sixth percentile for his age.

Jimmy had many problems in the area of social perception. Although he performed satisfactorily in many academic subjects, his teachers consistently reported that his social behavior in school was both strange and disturbing. The speech teacher dismissed him because of his abnormal delight and hilarity when others in the class made mistakes. Another teacher reported that he seemed unconscious of wrongdoing, that he made odd statements totally out of context, and that he was not well accepted by other children. Another report commented that Jimmy had not developed skills in social situations. Although he wanted to be accepted by others and have friends, he did not seem to know the appropriate manner of gaining friends and instead tended to antagonize other students. As seems to be true of some other students with nonverbal learning disabilities, Jimmy also did poorly in perceptual-motor tasks and seemed to have a poor understanding of spatial relationships. The psychologist reported poor performance in perceptual-motor and coordination activities on the *Bender-Gestalt Test.*

Problems in Socializing and Making Friends   Parents of children with social disabilities report that their children have considerable difficulty making friends. During times when there are no planned activities, such as after-school hours, weekends, or holidays, their loneliness becomes especially acute (Tur-Kaspa, Weisel, & Segrev, 1998).

Research shows that the social life of youngsters with social disabilities differs from that of other students. When they attempt to initiate social interactions, they are often ignored. Even strangers can detect these youngsters after viewing them on a videotape for only a few minutes (Bryan, 1991a, 1991b). In conversing with others, students with social disabilities tend to make more nasty and competitive statements. When working with a partner, they tend to resist the initiatives of the partner for cooperative work. These youngsters are often viewed as hostile and are at risk for social neglect and rejection (Vaughn & Haager, 1994).

Problems in Establishing Family Relationships   The family is the core of a child's life. Children desperately need the satisfaction and assurance of relations in the primary family. Even with the intimate family, however, the numerous problems in social skills, behavior, language, and temperament make it hard for a child with social disabilities to establish a healthy family relationship. As a consequence, the youngster may not receive satisfaction from the family sphere and may even be rejected by parents as well as by peers and teachers (Silver, 1998).

Social Disabilities in the School Setting   Successful adjustment in school, especially in inclusive settings, requires competencies in social skills. Essential social competencies in school include such skills as refraining from interrupting when others are talking, communicating needs in a socially acceptable manner, sharing with others, awaiting one's turn, and being able to follow directions.

In the school environment, students with social disabilities do not deal well with others, they are the last ones chosen, and they are not well accepted by classmates or teachers. When these children attempt to initiate a social interaction with a teacher, the teacher often ignores them. In inclusive classroom settings, they behave differently—they are more "off-task" and distractible, initiate more interactions with the teacher, and engage in more nonproductive activity (Bryan, 1997; Voeller, 1994; Vaughn & Haager, 1994).

Social Disabilities in Adolescents and Adults   Many adolescents with learning disabilities have no social problems and do well in social situations (Hazel & Schumaker, 1988). However, for those who do have social disabilities along with their learning disabilities, adolescence is a very trying stage of life. Their social problems affect friendships, employment, and family relationships, and keep them from full and successful participation in school, work, social circles, and family (Scanlon, 1996). These students engage in fewer activities related to extracurricular events and go out with friends less frequently than their classmates do (Price, 1997).

During the stage of adolescence, being different is not tolerated. Instead, being just like everyone else in the peer group is a criterion that must be met before a sense of difference and a pride in individual differences can emerge. The emerging sense of identity as a person is an important step in growing up. However, adolescents with learning disabilities are already different. Social acceptance may elude them because they are inept at sports, dancing, engaging in other activities with peers, making small talk, or listening to others. Some adolescents withdraw into the house, content with watching television, listening to the stereo, or reading. Others become so desperate for social acceptance that they are overly vulnerable to peer pressure, and their inappropriate acts lead to trouble (Silver, 1998).

For adults with learning disabilities, social disabilities often continue to impact many aspects of life. Feelings of inadequacy and poor self-concept continue. Studies show that difficulties in getting and keeping a job are among the major complaints of adults with learning disabilities. Problems that continue into adulthood include the failure to make friends, to establish relationships, and to find a satisfying social life. Social disabilities also interfere with employment (Price, 1997; Gerber & Brown, 1997; Scanlon, 1996; Johnson & Blalock, 1987).

Teaching Nonverbal and Social Skills

Teaching nonverbal and social skills is even more challenging than teaching academic skills. Some students need direct instruction in social behavior, many planned opportunities for social interaction, and recognition of social improvement through positive reinforcers. Among the methods for teaching social skills are direct instruction, individual teaching, group teaching, role playing, game-playing skills, and strategies instruction (Thompson, 1997; Deshler et al., 1996; Rourke, 1995; Moore, Cartledge, & Heckaman, 1995; Farmer & Farmer, 1996). Social skills instruction typically involves social modeling, behavioral rehearsal, and behavior transfer or generalization. Strategies for developing social competence are presented in the Teaching Strategies section at the end of this chapter. Several programs for teaching social skills are presented in Table 14.3 on page 550.

EMOTIONAL PROBLEMS The emotional scars of repeated failure and the inability to achieve and develop a sense of competence and self-worth are often indelible. Psychodynamic development and personality structure have important implications for understanding the emotional consequences of learning disabilities (Weinberg, Harper, Emslie, & Brumback, 1995; Silver, 1998). In considering the emotional issue, the critical question is, How does the student with learning disabilities *feel*?

Causes and Effects of Emotional Problems

Let us compare the emotional and personality development of achieving students to the emotional development of individuals with learning disabilities. Successful achievers have a multitude of gratifying experiences for developing important basic feelings of self-worth and hundreds of opportunities for self-satisfaction as well as the enjoyment of pleasing others. For achieving youngsters, the parent-child relationship is mutually satisfying because normal accomplishments stimulate parental responses of approval and encouragement. As a result of their own feelings of accomplishment and their awareness of the approval of those around them, these children develop a sense of self-worth and prideful identity. They establish healthy identifications with their mothers, fathers, and other key figures in their lives. They build feelings of self-worth, tolerance for frustration, and consideration for others (Rock, Fessler, & Church, 1997; Silver, 1989).

In contrast, the emotional and personality development of students with learning disabilities follows a very different pattern. If the central nervous system is not intact and not maturing in a normal manner, disturbances in motor and perceptual development lead to dissatisfaction with one's self. Failed attempts at mastering tasks induce feelings of frustration rather than feelings of accomplishment. Instead of building self-esteem, the thwarted attempts produce an attitude of self-derision and, at the same time, fail to stimulate the parents' normal responses of pride. Parents become anxious and disheartened, reactions which can result in either rejection or overprotection.

With such a developmental scenario, it is not surprising that many students with learning disabilities develop emotional problems. These reactions can take many forms, including conscious refusal to learn, overt hostility, resistance to pressure, clinging to dependency, quick discouragement, fear of success, and withdrawal into a private world. If the problems are so severe that they interfere with further learning, the student may be referred for psychological or psychiatric counseling (Silver, 1992, 1995b).

Low Self-Concept

Research shows that students with learning disabilities often have very negative views of themselves. The feelings within themselves and the response from outside mold a concept of a threatening world in which they feel insecure and a view of themselves as inept. They do not receive the normal satisfactions of recognition, achievement, or affection. Their unsuccessful academic and/or social experiences lead to disappointment, frustration, feelings of incompetence, lack of self-worth, and a poor self-concept (Rock et al., 1997; Silver, 1992, 1995b).

The battering of the developing personality continues and increases in school. Donald, a 9-year-old who was failing in school and had virtually no opportunities for success, was losing his self-concept and the belief that he was indeed a person with an individual identity. In response to a class assignment to write an autobiographical sketch, all he wrote was "My name is Donald Turner. I am average."

School is often a place that makes no allowances for the shortcomings of these students, a place where teachers are unable to comprehend their difficulties. Ironically, the characteristic inconsistency and unpredictability of learning disabilities may account for an occasional academic breakthrough during which these students perform well, and such random moments of achievement may serve to make matters worse. The teacher may be convinced that the student could do it "if she just tried harder." Failure now may be viewed purely in terms of bad behavior, poor attitude, or lack of motivation. Increased impatience and blame from the teacher intensify the student's anxiety, frustration, and confusion.

The Quality of Resiliency

Although a person's feeling of self-worth is threatened by continual failure, not all individuals with learning disabilities develop low self-esteem. Some have remarkable resiliency and are able to preserve self-confidence and self-worth (Freiberg, 1993; Luther, 1993; Werner, 1990).

What are the factors that enable individuals to keep on trying, and how can the school help? Self-worth is gained through mastery of a skill or task, through perceived respect from peers, and through one's feelings of competence. Students who believe that they have competencies in areas other than academic work are less likely to be devastated by school failure. To maintain their sense of self-worth, students need a support system from sources such as teachers, parents, and peers who will acknowledge that these students possess other competencies. The support system preserves their self-worth by keeping failure to a minimum, increasing the visibility of their nonacademic talents, skills, and competencies, and emphasizing *learning* goals over *performance* goals. For example, the student can be given credit for going about the task in the correct manner (a learning goal) even though the final answer may not be accurate (the performance goal).

It is fascinating to observe individuals who have achieved greatness and maintained a sense of belief in their self-worth and in what they were doing, despite having faced years of rejection and ridicule. Gertrude Stein, the famous poet, submitted poems to editors for about twenty years before one was finally accepted for publication. Van Gogh sold only one painting during his lifetime. Frank Lloyd Wright was rejected as an architect during much of his life. So, too, many individuals with learning disabilities have overcome failure and rejection because they strongly believed in themselves. The stories of adults with learning disabilities who have succeeded against the odds are inspiring, and their resilience is evident in their success (Gerber & Brown, 1997; Smith, S. L., 1991; Gerber & Reiff, 1991).

Mastery of tasks brings
respect from peers.
(© James Carroll)

Strengthening Self-Esteem

Successful experiences build **self-esteem**—the feelings of self-worth, self-confidence, and self-respect. It is often of little value to try to determine if the learning failure or the emotional problem is the primary precipitating factor. A more constructive approach is to help the students accomplish an educational task so that their feelings of self-worth are oriented in a positive direction. Their accomplishments can increase their ability to learn and strengthen their emotional outlook. The beginning of this mutual reinforcement cycle is also the beginning of effective treatment (Silver & Hagin, 1990).

Parents and teachers can help build self-esteem by providing a strong support system to promote students' feelings of control and power over their destiny. Students should be helped to develop skills in decision making and be provided with opportunities to make decisions. They should learn to recognize the causes of success and failure so that they stop blaming themselves and begin instead to feel that their efforts will influence the outcome. Those who work with these students must help them develop coping mechanisms and strategies that will allow them to respond constructively to failure.

Teaching strategies to build self-esteem and to enhance a healthy mental attitude are presented in the Teaching Strategies section of this chapter and in Chapter 4.

Students with learning disabilities sometimes exhibit co-occurring behavioral problems. The behavior problems must be considered in the planning of instruction (Hardwerk & Marshall, 1998).

Attention Deficit Hyperactivity Disorder (ADHD)

Attention deficit disorder is characterized by persistent difficulties in attention span, by poor impulse control, and sometimes by **hyperactivity.** (Legislative and medical aspects of attention deficit disorder are discussed in Chapters 2 and 7.) In school, these students are impulsive, have a loud presence in the classroom, and constantly ask questions and make comments and demands. They tend to become unpopular members of the classroom group. Teachers should understand that although the behaviors of these students are at times annoying, their behavior is not intentional or part of a ploy to defy educational authority. The activity level of students with attention deficit disorder is not always under their voluntary control (Lerner, Lowenthal, & Lerner, 1995).

Children who have attention problems but no overt behavioral problems are often overlooked because they do not cause behavioral disturbances in the classroom. However, even though they may not come to the attention of teachers, they may be at risk for academic failure.

Behavior problems often lead to school failure and rejection by peers, which in turn can lead to low self-esteem and frustration. Table 14.1 suggests some accommodations that teachers can make in the classroom for students with attention, behavior, and hyperactivity problems.

Motivation

Motivation is the force that energizes and directs one's drive to accomplish goals. Theories of motivation focus on such questions as how students become interested enough to initiate learning, what causes them to move toward a particular goal, and what causes an individual to sustain that interest over an extended period of time to reach that goal. Students need a strong desire to learn in school because much of academic learning requires persistent and hard work over a long period of time.

Students with learning disabilities may appear to be unmotivated, but their lack of motivation may actually result from chronic academic failure. The process of losing motivation begins when they first doubt their intellectual abilities. They then start to view their achievement efforts as futile,

Table 14.1

Tips for Teachers: Accommodating for Students with Problems in Behavior, Attention, or Hyperactivity

The following suggestions can help students with attention deficit disorder function in the classroom.

1. **Placement in the classroom.** Seat the student in an area with minimal extraneous distractions and where you can readily ascertain whether the student is attending. This may be at the front of the room, but should be away from doors and windows. Try not to place the youngster near the air conditioner, heater, or high traffic areas.

2. **Plan varied activities so students can move.** Modify classroom routine to enable the student to get up and move around the classroom periodically. For example, have the student pass out papers or put books away. Such activities break up the time that the student must sit in one spot, and the physical involvement helps to focus the student's attention.

3. **Provide as much structure and routine as possible.** Establish a routine and keep it the same from one day to another. On days when something unusual will occur, prepare the student by explaining what event will happen and when it will occur.

4. **Require a daily assignment notebook.** This activity helps the student to organize his or her time, to know what is to be done, and to designate when it has been accomplished. Make sure the student writes down the correct assignments each day.

5. **Make sure you have the student's attention before you teach.** An attention signal, such as a hand sign, a light touch, or eye contact, is sometimes helpful. It is important to gain the student's attention before speaking.

6. **Make directions clear and concise.** Directions should be consistent with daily instructions. Simplify complex directions and avoid multiple commands.

7. **Break assignments into workable chunks.** Students with attention deficit disorder should not be expected to work independently for a long period of time. If workbook or assignment sheets are cluttered and confusing, adapt them by breaking them into chunks. Less material will be on the page, and the material will be better organized.

8. **Give extra time as needed.** Students with attention deficit disorder may work at a slower pace. Give them extra time and do not penalize them if they cannot complete their work within a limited time frame.

9. **Provide feedback on completed work as soon as possible.** Students should know how they are doing and should have opportunities to make their own corrections. When possible, let them check their own work.

10. **Encourage parents to set up appropriate study space at home.** Show parents how to establish routines, with a set time for studying. Ask parents to review and check completed homework. Request that they also check the organization of the student's backpack or book bag.

11. **Make use of learning aids.** Many students with attention deficit disorder enjoy using computers, calculators, tape recorders, and other learning aids. These tools help structure learning and maintain interest.

12. **Find something that the student does well and encourage that interest.** Every child has strengths or special interests in certain activities. Find those areas and foster growth in that activity.

13. **Provide ample praise and rewards.** Be sure to acknowledge good or improved behavior. Inform the student through praise and rewards.

14. **Modify the testing situation.** If necessary, provide additional time or practice, or decrease the work required on the test.

eventually asking themselves, "Why try if you know you are going to fail?" After encountering repeated failure in the classroom, they develop negative and defeatist attitudes about school learning. As a consequence, they have fewer opportunities to experience personal control over learning outcomes and eventually begin to doubt that they are in control of their academic destinies (Schmid & Evans, 1998 Groteluschen, Borkowski, & Hale, 1990).

in Control

Attribution Theory   Attribution theory provides one way to look at motivation. The term **attribution** refers to the way people explain to themselves the causes of their successes. Research shows that students with learning disabilities differ from their peers. They tend to attribute their successes to factors outside of their control, such as random luck or the teacher, and they blame their failures on their lack of ability, the difficulty of the task, the teacher, or other random factors (Stipek, 1993; Kistner, Osborn, & LaVerrier, 1988; Chapman, 1988).

In contrast, youngsters who are successful achievers have a different attribution style. They attribute failure to their own lack of effort and also attribute success to their own effort. Feeling in control of the situation, good learners persevere on difficult tasks, delay gratification, and are actively involved in the learning situation (Stipek, 1993; Deci et al., 1992).

 Students with learning disabilities should be guided to change their attribution styles to become more persistent and independent learners.

Behavior Management

Behavior management is an application of behavioral psychology for managing student behavior. In using behavior management methods, an arrangement of environmental events is systematically planned and structured to modify observable student behavior. Behavior management methods are used both to strengthen desired behaviors and to decrease or eliminate undesired behaviors. Strategies for changing the student's behavior are described in the Teaching Strategies section of this chapter.

The Behavioral Unit—ABC   The core of the theory of behavior management is the ABC behavioral unit (antecedent, behavior, consequence). *A* is the *antecedent* event (or stimulus); *B* is the target *behavior* (or child's response); and *C* is the *consequent* event or (reinforcement) (Alberto & Troutman, 1995; Haring & Kennedy, 1992). (See Figure 6.1, page 193.) We may think of target behavior as an event sandwiched between two sets of environmental influences, those that precede the behavior (the antecedent event or stimulus) and those that follow the behavior (consequent events or reinforcements). Changing a behavior requires an analysis of these three components, as illustrated next.

A. Antecedent Event or Stimulus.   Careful and systematic observation and tabulation should be made of the specific events that precede the behavior of interest. The two following examples specify a stimulus event. The *noise* (antecedent event or stimulus) in the next room is so distracting that Noreen cannot do her work. When *the teacher asks Charlie to read* (antecedent event or stimulus), he begins to disturb others in the classroom by hitting them.

B. Target Behavior or Response.   This is the behavior to be changed or accomplished by the student. For example, the goal might be to have the student complete five arithmetic problems in 2 minutes. The evidence of learning should be observable. For example, the goal of "teaching a student to be sociable" is too broad and too difficult to observe; however, the behavior of saying "thank you" when offered food is specific and observable.

C. Consequent Event or Reinforcement.   This refers to the event that follows the target behavior. It is important to observe the effects of various reinforcements or rewards on the behavior of a particular student and to analyze the patterns of response to rewards. This information allows one to construct a reward system that will promote the desired behavior. Positive and immediate reinforcements are most effective in fostering the desired behavior. Examples include stars and stickers, raisins, tokens, points, praise, flashing lights, or simply the satisfaction of knowing that the answer is correct. The following are examples of consequent events. After Annette reads five pages, she receives *two tokens that are exchangeable for toys*. In teaching reading to Serena, the desired behavior is having her say the sound equivalent of the letter *a* every time a stimulus card with the letter *a* is shown. For each correct response, Serena immediately receives a positive reinforcement, such as *a piece of low-sugar cereal, stars, points, money, praise,* or *attention*.

Reinforcement Theory   Reinforcement theory is a major concept in behavioral management, which is based on the principle that people do what they are reinforced for doing. The use of reinforcement and behavior management methods are strategies of major significance for teaching students with learning disabilities. In applying reinforcement theory to modifying the behavior of students with learning disabilities, the teacher must do the following (Lovitt, 1991):

1. Identify potential reinforcers that will motivate the student and accelerate performance on a specific task.
2. Identify the student responses or behavior that should trigger the reinforcer.

3. Arrange the environment so that the student is reinforced for the desired behavior. If a student responds in a certain way, then a certain reinforcer should occur.

4. When the student's performance is accurate, increase the reinforcer, and when the student makes an error, decrease the reinforcer.

5. Eventually, have the student make independent instructional decisions, such as corrections and establishment of reinforcement values.

A strongly critical view of reinforcement theory and behavior modification is expressed by Kohn (1993) in his book with the provocative title *Punished by Rewards: The Trouble with Gold Stars, Incentive Plans, A's, Praise, and Other Bribes*. Kohn argues that this method of "Do this and you will get that" and dangling goodies (ranging from candy bars to sales commissions) in front of people in the same way that we train the family pet is a short-run solution that is ineffective in the long run.

Cognitive Behavior Modification

Cognitive behavior modification is a self-instructional approach to learning. Developed by Meichenbaum (1977), cognitive behavior modification requires individuals to talk to themselves out loud, give themselves instruction on what they should be doing, and reward themselves verbally for accomplishments. Individuals learn to motivate themselves through self-talk, self-reinforcement, and self-monitoring.

The self-instructional cognitive behavior modification program involves the following steps:

1. The teacher models or performs a task while talking to himself or herself out loud as students observe.

2. Students then perform the same task while talking to themselves, under the teacher's guidance.

3. Students quietly whisper the instructions to themselves while going through the task.

4. Students use inner or private speech while performing the task.

5. Students self-monitor their performance by telling themselves how they did. For example, "I did well" or "Next time I should slow down."

Cognitive behavior modification has often been used with adults in such settings as weight-loss programs. Students with learning disabilities can use the procedure for all kinds of learning, schoolwork, and homework. The goal of cognitive behavior modification is not only to change the person's behavior but also to increase the person's awareness of the behavior and the thinking associated with it. Many of the ideas inherent in cognitive behavior modification are incorporated into learning strategies instruction.

ASSESSING SOCIAL AND EMOTIONAL BEHAVIORS

Assessing a student's social skills and emotional status is difficult. Observational techniques are the most direct way of judging a student's social and emotional behaviors. In fact, teachers who have daily contact with students in the classroom are excellent judges of the students' social and emotional reactions. Other assessment methods include inventories, checklists, and rating scales. Several of these instruments are listed in Table 14.2 and are described more fully in Appendix C.

Interview instruments are actually questionnaires that help a teacher interview the parent, the student, another teacher, or someone else who has contact with the student. *Student inventories* are given to the student to complete.

Sociometric techniques provide information about the child's popularity and acceptance by classmates. They are designed to identify the students who are the most and least liked in their classes. One sociometric technique is to ask students to nominate the three (or another number of) classmates they like most.

Table 14.2

Instruments to
Assess Social and
Emotional Behaviors

Instrument	Age or Grade Assessed
Interview Instruments	
AAMD Adaptive Behavior Scale	Ages 3–16
Scales of Independent Behavior	Ages infant–adolescent
Vineland Adaptive Behavior Scale	Ages birth–adult
Rating Scales	
Burks' Behavior Rating Scales	Grades 1–9
Child Behavior Checklist (Achenbach)	Ages 2–16
Devereux Adolescent Behavior Rating Scale	Ages 13–18
Devereux Child Behavior Rating Scale	Ages 8–12
Devereux Elementary School Behavior Rating Scale	Grades K–6
Pupil Rating Scale (Revised): Screening for Learning Disabilities	Grades K–6
Weller-Strawser Scales of Adaptive Behavior	Ages 6–18
Student Inventories	
Coppersmith Self-Esteem Inventories	Elementary age
Piers-Harris Children's Self-Concept Scale	Grades 4–12

TEACHING STRATEGIES

This section presents teaching strategies for developing social competencies, building self-esteem, applying behavior management techniques, and making accommodations in inclusive classrooms.

DEVELOPING SOCIAL COMPETENCIES

Students who are socially competent learn social skills effortlessly through daily living and observation. Students with social deficits need conscious effort and specific teaching to learn about the social world, its nuances, and its silent language. Just as we teach students to perform schoolwork—to read, write, spell, do arithmetic, and pass tests—we can teach students with social disabilities how to live with and relate to other people. And just as we must use different methods to teach different academic skills, so must we use a variety of methods to teach students how to get along with others.

The activities in this section are designed to develop social skills. They are divided into the following categories: self-perception, sensitivity to other people, social maturity, social skills and learning strategies, and social skills training.

Self-Perception

1. Awareness of body parts. Have students locate the parts of the body on a doll, on a classmate, or on themselves. Make a cardboard person with movable limbs. Put the "person" in various positions—for example, with the left leg and right arm out—and have the students duplicate the positions.

2. Puzzles. Make a puzzle from a picture of a person and have the students assemble the pieces. Cut the puzzle so that each major part is easily identifiable.

3. Completing pictures. Have the students complete a partially drawn figure or tell what is missing in an incomplete picture.

4. Scrapbooks. Help students put together scrapbooks about themselves. Include pictures of them at different stages of growth, pictures of their families and pets, a list of their likes and dislikes, anecdotes about their past, accounts of trips, awards they have won, and so on.

Sensitivity to Other People

The spoken language is only one means of communication; there is also a "silent language" with which people communicate without the use of words, relying instead on gestures, stance, facial expressions, and tone of voice. Students with social deficits need help in learning how to decode the communication messages conveyed by this "silent language." For example, such students often fail to understand the meaning implied in facial expressions and gestures.

1. Pictures of faces.   Draw pictures of faces or collect pictures of faces and have the students ascertain whether the faces convey the emotion of happiness or sadness. Other emotions to be shown include anger, surprise, pain, and love (Dimitrovsky et al., 1998).

2. Gestures.   Discuss the meanings of various gestures, such as waving good-by, shaking a finger, shrugging a shoulder, turning away, tapping a finger or foot, and stretching out arms.

3. Videos and story situations.   Find pictures, short videos, or story situations in which the social implications of gesture, space, and time are presented.

4. What the voice tells.   Help the students learn to recognize implications in the human voice beyond the words themselves. Have the students listen to a voice on a tape recorder to determine the mood of the speaker and to decipher the communication beyond the words.

Social Maturity

Social development involves growing from immaturity to maturity, from dependence to independence. Among all species of animal life, the human infant is perhaps the most dependent on others for sheer survival at birth. The road from complete dependence to relative independence is the long and gradual growth toward social maturity. Social maturity involves recognizing the rights and responsibilities of self and others, making friends, cooperating with a group, following procedures agreed on by others, making moral and ethical judgments, and gaining independence in going places.

1. Anticipating consequences of social acts.   Role playing, creative play, stories, and discussions can help students see what happens if the rules of a game or the rules of manners are broken.

2. Establishing independence.   Encourage the students to go places alone. Make simple maps with directions to follow and talk about the various steps to take in getting to the desired location. Use a walking map, if necessary. Plan activities so that the students make simple purchases alone. Plan activities that provide opportunities for them to talk to other people, ask directions, interview others, and so on.

3. Making ethical judgments.   Help the students learn cultural mores and learn to make value judgments. For example, students can discuss and analyze age-appropriate dilemmas and situations involving acts such as telling lies, stealing, and protecting a friend.

4. Planning and implementing.   Have the students make plans for a trip, activity, party, picnic, or meeting. Then help the students successfully implement the plans to gain a sense of independence and maturity.

5. Solving the "weekend problem."   A consequence of a social disability is that students often have difficulty making friends. Parents frequently complain of a "weekend problem," when their child appears to have nothing to do. Without companions and friends, summers and vacations often are difficult periods for such youngsters. This situation requires the initiative and cooperation of parent groups and community organizations to develop appropriate solutions to the weekend problem.

Learning Strategies for Social Skills

Learning strategies are useful for helping students acquire academic skills, and they are also effective in teaching social skills (Deshler, Ellis, & Lenz, 1996; Lenz, Ellis, & Scanlon, 1996). Social strategies instruction changes students' typical patterns of responses to social situations. Students learn to develop new cognitive responses to social problems and to think about their social actions.

Learning strategies techniques include teaching students to stop and think before responding, to verbalize and rehearse social responses, to visualize and imagine the effect of their behavior, and to preplan social actions.

The response of many students with learning disabilities in social situations is impulsive—they act without considering what is required and without thinking through possible solutions or the consequences of various courses of action. Through instruction in the strategies of self-verbalization and self-monitoring, students can be taught self-control to keep from giving immediate, nonreflective responses. The students are trained to verbalize and ask themselves questions such as "What am I supposed to be doing?" In other words, they are taught to stop and think before responding. Teachers can model social learning strategies by talking out such thoughts as "Does this problem have similarities to other problems I have encountered?" or "What are three possible solutions?" The students then practice these skills of self-verbalization, or thinking out loud. The self-monitoring method has been found to reduce inappropriate social responses (Deshler & Schumaker, 1986).

Social skills strategies include direct instruction, prompting, modeling, rehearsal, and reinforcement (Carter & Sugai, 1988). Several social skills strategies are presented next.

1. The FAST strategy.   This social skills strategy is a four-part mnemonic device to aid in interpersonal problem solving. It helps students with learning disabilities develop questioning and monitoring skills, generate a range of solutions, select a long-range plan to solve the problem, and implement the plan (McIntosh, Vaughn, & Bennerson, 1995). The steps for the FAST strategy are as follows:

F	Freeze and think.	What is the problem? Can I state the problem in behavioral terms?
A	Alternatives	What could I do to solve the problem? List the possible alternatives.
S	Solution	Which alternatives will solve the problem? Which are safe and fair? Select the best long-run solution.
T	Try it.	How can I implement the solution? If this particular solution fails to solve the problem, return to the second step and pick another alternative solution that might solve the problem.

2. Judging behavior in stories.   Read or tell an incomplete story that involves social judgment. Have the students anticipate the ending or complete the story. A short video of a social situation provides an opportunity to discuss critically the activities of the people in the video. For example, discuss the consequences of a student's rudeness when an acquaintance tries to begin a conversation, of a student's making a face when asked by her mother's friend if she likes her new dress, or of hitting someone at a party.

3. Grasping social situations through pictures.   A series of pictures can be arranged to tell a story involving a social situation. Have the students arrange the pictures and explain the story. Comics, readiness books, beginning readers, and magazine advertising all provide good source materials for such activities. These series can also be pictures on transparencies.

4. Learning to generalize newly acquired social behaviors.   After students learn socially appropriate behaviors, they must learn to generalize these behaviors to many settings, such as an inclusive classroom, the home environment, playgrounds, and other social situations. Students need many opportunities to practice and maintain newly acquired skills. Collaboration between special and regular teachers is needed to make plans for generalizing in inclusive classrooms (Deshler, Ellis, & Lenz, 1996).

5. Learning conversation skills.   Students must learn how to converse with others: They must learn how to extend greetings, introduce themselves, find a topic to talk about, listen actively, ask and answer questions, and say good-bye.

6. Friendship skills.   Students must learn how to make friends, give a compliment, join group activities, and accept thanks.

7. Game-playing skills.   Social skills can be taught to students through the activity of playing games with others. The instruction involves social modeling, behavioral rehearsal, and behavior transfer while playing games (Moore, Cartledge, & Heckaman, 1995).

Table 14.3

Social Skills Programs

ASSET: A Social Skills Program for Adolescents with Learning Disabilities (Research Press). A social skills program based on instruction in learning strategies.

DUSO (Developing Understanding of Self and Others) (American Guidance Services). Activities and kits to stimulate social and emotional development in children in grades K–4.

LCEE: Life-Centered Career Education (Council for Exceptional Children). Functional activities that are work related.

Learning to Get Along (Research Press). Teaching students skills for being in group activities.

The SCORE Skills: Social Skills of Cooperative Groups (Edge Enterprises). Learning strategies for working in a cooperative learning curriculum.

Skillstreaming the Adolescent: A Structured Learning Approach to Teaching Prosocial Skills (Research Press). Activities for developing social skills in adolescents.

Skillstreaming the Elementary School Child: A Guide for Teaching Prosocial Skills (Research Press). Activities for developing social skills in elementary school children.

Social Skills Instruction for Daily Living (American Guidance Services). Activities for adolescents with learning disabilities.

Social Skills Intervention (American Guidance Services). A social skills program for students with learning disabilities.

The Social Skills Curriculum (American Guidance Services). A curriculum for teaching social skills.

Social Skills on the Job (American Guidance Services). Work-related social skills activities.

TAD (Toward Affective Development) (American Guidance Services). Group activities, lessons, and materials to stimulate psychological and affective development for students in grades 3 through 6.

The Walker Social Skills Curriculum: The Accepts Program (Pro-Ed). Activities for developing social skills within the school curriculum.

Social Skills Programs

A number of commercial programs are designed to help students develop social skills. Several are listed in Table 14.3.

SELF-ESTEEM STRATEGIES The student whose failure to learn is accompanied by emotional problems may be the victim of a continuous cycle of failure to learn and emotional reaction to the failure. In this cycle, the failure to learn leads to adverse emotional responses—feelings of self-derision and anxiety, which augment the failure-to-learn syndrome. Teachers must find a way to reverse this cycle—to build feelings of self-worth, to increase self-confidence and self-concept, and to provide an experience of success. Teaching should be designed to reverse this cycle of failure.

1. Psychiatric and psychological services. The most severely affected students may need psychiatric or psychological treatment before or during educational treatment. If so, appropriate referrals should be made.

2. Building a therapeutic relationship. For most students with learning disabilities, the teacher can provide a type of therapy through skilled and sensitive clinical teaching. (Specific techniques for building such a relationship are discussed in Chapter 4, pages 128–132.)

3. Bibliotherapy. This is an approach for helping students understand themselves and their problems through books in which the characters learn to cope with problems similar to those faced by the students. By identifying with a character and working out the problem with the character, students are helped with their own problems. Books designed to explain the learning problem to the students are also useful.

4. Magic circle. Participants are seated in a circle. They are encouraged to share their feelings, to learn to listen, and to observe others. The program seeks to promote active listening, to focus on feelings, to give recognition to each individual, and to promote greater understanding. Sample circle topics include:

It made me feel good when I . . .

I made someone feel bad when I . . .

Something I do very well is . . .

What can I do for you . . . ?

5. Use of creative media. Teachers can use art, dance, and music as therapy techniques for promoting the emotional involvement of students with learning disabilities.

6. Counseling. Students' reactions to failure and to success depend in part on their attitudes, emotional status, beliefs, and expectations. Healthier emotional attitudes can be developed through counseling, both individually and in groups.

BEHAVIOR MANAGEMENT STRATEGIES

Behavior management techniques are useful for students with learning disabilities. Many teachers intuitively use many of these procedures, but precise application of behavior management requires that the procedures are systematic and that the behaviors to be changed are observable and measureable.

Reinforcement

A reinforcement is a consequent event that occurs after a person makes a behavior response. The reinforcement has the effect of increasing or strengthening the target behavior.

A **positive reinforcement** involves responding to the child's behavior with a reinforcement, which increases the likelihood that the person will make a similar response in similar situations in the future. For example, if Matthew is rewarded for bringing in his homework, he is more likely to do it again. If 4-year-old Trudy, who has delayed speech, is given a piece of low-sugar cereal after she says a word, she is likely to try saying a word again.

A **negative reinforcement** is an adverse consequence, and the individual behaves to avoid the adverse stimulus. For example, the driver of an automobile will buckle a seatbelt in the car to avoid the annoying buzz of the seatbelt warning system.

Sometimes teachers or parents inadvertently reinforce inappropriate behavior. For example, if Jim, who usually shouts out answers, is recognized by the teacher as soon as he raises his hand, he will tend to raise his hand in the future. If Willie clowns around and the teacher pays attention to him, the teacher's negative attention to his actions can reinforce an undesirable behavior. The box entitled "Finding Reinforcers" describes some items that can be used as positive reinforcers.

Response Cost   **Response cost** involves the loss of positive reinforcers when the child exhibits inappropriate behavior. Lost reinforcers can include a wide range of privileges and activities. For example, if points are given as reinforcers for good behavior, response cost strategies subtract points for aggressive behavior (Fiore, Becker, & Nero, 1993).

Ignoring   Ignoring is the contingent withdrawal of teacher attention when misbehavior occurs. Teachers who give students attention in the form of reprimands or reminders may unknowingly be reinforcing inappropriate classroom behaviors. For example, every time Sam talks out in class, he becomes the center of attention because the teacher tells him how disturbing his actions are. If Sam's behavior is ignored instead of reinforced by verbal comments, it will lessen and eventually cease (Barkley, 1995).

Shaping Behavior

This term refers to the concept of breaking the desired goal into a sequence of ordered steps or tasks, then reinforcing a behavior that the student already shows and gradually increasing the requirement for reinforcement. **Shaping behavior** is sometimes referred to as **successive approximations.** For example, the eventual behavioral goal is to have Patty sit at her desk for 20 minutes. Patty's behavior is shaped by reinforcing the following steps or successive approximations: First, she is reinforced for standing near her desk for a few seconds, then for touching her desk, then for kneeling on her desk, then for sitting at her desk for a few seconds, then for sitting for 2 minutes, and so on.

FINDING REINFORCERS

The success of behavior management depends on finding the appropriate reinforcer to stimulate the target behavior. What is viewed as desirable by one student may hold little interest for another. Ways to find a successful reinforcer include observing the students to see what they choose to do in their free time and requesting information from them and their parents. Reinforcers can be *extrinsic*—something external, such as food or toys—or *intrinsic*—something internal, such as the joy of mastering a task. The reinforcement can be social, such as praise or approval from a teacher or parent. It can be a token to be exchanged for a later reinforcement, or it can take the form of a privilege. A good reinforcement for each individual is simply the one that works. Several suggested reinforcements are noted next:

- *Foods:* nuts, edible seeds, low-sugar cereal, peanuts, popcorn, raisins, fruit
- *Play materials:* baseball cards, toy animals, toy cars, marbles, jump ropes, gliders, crayons, coloring books, clay, dolls, kits, balls, puzzles, comic books, balloons, games, yo-yos, trolls
- *Tokens:* marks on the blackboard or on the student's paper, gold or silver stars, marbles in a jar, plastic chips on a ring, poker chips, tickets, washers on a string
- *Activities or privileges*: having computer time presenting at "show and tell," going first, running errands, having free time, helping with cleanup, taking the class pet home for the weekend, leading the songs, seeing a video, listening to music, doing artwork

Contingency Contracting

The idea that something desirable can be used to reinforce something the student does not wish to do is the essence of contingency contracting. This is the premise of the **Premack principle:** Preferred activities can be used to reinforce less-preferred activities (Premack, 1959). This method is also referred to as "grandma's rule" because grandmothers are alleged to promise, "If you finish your plate, you can have dessert." For example, if Willie prefers constructing models to reading, his opportunity to work on a model would be contingent upon his completing a certain reading assignment. Or Dave, who likes to play ball, can play after he finishes his spelling work.

Contingency contracting is a behavioral management strategy that entails a written agreement between the student and the teacher. The student agrees to do something the teacher desires, and the teacher agrees to provide something the student wants in return. For example, Karen and her teacher have a written agreement that after Karen completes twenty arithmetic problems, she will be given an extra free period.

A contingency contract must be signed by both parties. The written contract should specify the task to be completed, a time limit for the task, a re-

CONTRACT

This contract is an agreement between _____

(student)

and _____ .

(teacher)

_____ will _____

(student)

_____

by _____ .

(date of completion)

If the work described above is completed on time,

_____ will _____

(teacher)

_____

_____

_____

by _____ .

(date of reward)

_____   _____

Signature of student   date

_____   _____

Signature of teacher   date

ward for completing the task, and the individuals who have entered into the agreement. An example of a contract is shown in Figure 14.1.

Token Reinforcements

Token reinforcements are reinforcers that are accumulated to be exchanged later for a more meaningful "backup" reinforcer. The token reinforcer could, for example, be poker chips or plastic objects, which the student saves and exchanges for objects the student desires, such as toys, gum, comic books, games, baseball cards, and so forth. Time must be scheduled for exchanges, and information about exchange rates must be made available. In some programs, a total *token economy* is built into the project— that is, all the activities are built on earning the tokens.

Time-Out

Time-out is a procedure in which a disruptive student is removed from the instructional activities and placed in a designated isolated area for a short period of time. Time-out can be a powerful technique for managing disruptive behaviors with children, but it should be used cautiously. If implemented properly, time-out offers an effective means of managing behavior. Several conditions will increase the likelihood of success with this method (Alberto & Troutman, 1995):

- Time-out should be brief, from 1 to 10 minutes, with young children requiring the least amount of time. A common rule of thumb is no more than 1 minute for every year of the child's age.
- Warn the child only once by stating clearly the broken rule.
- During a time-out the teacher and the other children should ignore the student.
- Actively assist the student's return from time-out by directly engaging the child in ongoing activities.

Home-School Coordination

Programs of **home-school coordination** are intended to improve the behavior of students by combining school and home efforts. Behavioral goals are established for the student, and each day the teacher indicates the goals the student has met. These behavior-management sheets are sent home, signed by the parents to acknowledge the teacher's comments, and then returned to the school. The student is reinforced at home for the positive behaviors displayed at school. A sample home-school behavior-management sheet is shown in Figure 14.2.

Figure 14.2

Home-School Behavior-
Management Sheet

Student: _____ Teacher: _____

Week beginning: _____

Use (S) for satisfactory performance.
Use (U) for unsatisfactory performance.
Use (N) for items that do not apply.

	Mon	Tues	Wed	Thurs	Fri
1. Homework turned in					
2. Began work within 3 minutes of assignment					
3. Followed directions					
4. Followed class and school rules					
5. Paid attention to teacher					
6. Raised hand to speak					
7. Other					

If 80% of applicable boxes are checked, the student will receive 20 minutes of computer time.

Teacher's initials: _____

COMMENTS AND SIGNATURE

	Teacher	Parent
Monday	_____	_____
Tuesday	_____	_____
Wednesday	_____	_____
Thursday	_____	_____
Friday	_____	_____

- Parent signs chart daily.
- Child takes chart home daily.
- Child returns chart to school daily.
- Child receives daily reward.

ACCOMMODATIONS FOR INCLUSIVE CLASSROOMS

Teachers must make **modifications** in the classroom to adjust for the behaviors of students with learning disabilities. Table 14.4 lists some of the target behaviors, along with accommodations that can be made to achieve them.

Table 14.4.

Accommodations for Inclusive Classrooms

Target Behavior	Accommodations
Limiting distractions	■ Seat student near the teacher. ■ Seat student away from noisy places. ■ Seat student with well-behaved students and away from students with problem behaviors. ■ Keep routines simple and direct.
Increasing attention	■ Shorten the task—break it into smaller parts. ■ Shorten homework assignments. ■ Use distributed practice (many shorter sessions). ■ Make tasks more interesting (work with partners, interest centers, groups). ■ Increase the novelty of the task.
Improving organization	■ Provide clear classroom rules and teacher expectations. ■ Establish routines for placing objects in the room. ■ Provide a list of materials for each task. ■ Check that student has homework before leaving school; use assignment books. ■ Use folders to organize materials. ■ Use a different-colored folder for each subject.
Improving listening skills	■ Keep instructions simple and short. ■ Have students repeat instructions aloud, then to themselves. ■ Alert students by using key phrases: "This is important," "Listen carefully." ■ Use visual aids, charts, pictures, graphics, transparencies; write key points on chalkboard.
Managing time	■ Set up a specific routine and adhere to it. ■ Make lists to help students organize tasks. ■ Use behavior contracts that specify the time allotted for activities.
Opportunities for moving	■ Permit students to move in class, sharpen pencils, and get papers and materials. ■ Alternate activities—standing, sitting, moving. ■ Allow students to leave their seats to make a wall chart after they finish a page. ■ Allow students to work while standing or leaning on their desks. ■ Have work centers in the classroom. ■ Use computers; allow children to go to computers during work time.

Chapter Summary

1. A comprehensive understanding of the problems of students with learning disabilities is impossible unless the effects of social, behavioral, and emotional facets of the condition are considered.

2. Nonverbal learning disabilities involve problems in social learning. Children with NLD may initially do well in academic learning, but as they advance through the grades, and social skills become more important for ensuring their success, these students tend to fall behind.

3. The characteristics of social disabilities include poor social perception, a lack of judgment, difficulty in perceiving the feelings of others, problems in socializing and making friends, and problems in family relationships and in school. Social problems continue into the adolescent and adult years.

4. Emotional problems are often associated with learning disabilities. These problems may be the consequences of continual failure. Students with learning disabilities may grow up with little self-confidence, a poor self-concept, and few opportunities to develop feelings of self-worth. The emotional status of students with learning disabilities may further affect their ability to learn. Teachers can help students preserve their self-esteem by emphasizing their strengths.

5. Some students with learning disabilities display behavioral problems, especially if they have a coexisting attention deficit hyperactivity disorder (ADHD). Teachers can modify instruction and the classroom environment to reduce behavior problems.

6. Students with learning disabilities appear to lack motivation, but this lack may be a consequence of chronic academic failure.

7. *Attribution* refers to a person's ideas concerning the causes of events. Students with learning disabilities tend to blame their academic failure on teachers or on the difficulty of the task, not on their own effort. They do not think they control their learning. Motivation can be fostered through attribution training.

8. The theory of behavior management is based on the ABC behavioral unit: A—the antecedent event or stimulus; B—the target behavior or response, and C—the consequent event or reinforcement.

9. Reinforcement theory emphasizes that people do what they are reinforced for doing.

10. Cognitive behavior modification is a procedure of self-instruction for achieving specific goals.

11. Assessment instruments for social-emotional factors include interviews, inventories, checklists, rating scales, and sociometric techniques.

12. Teaching strategies include developing social skills, building self-esteem, behavior-management strategies, and classroom modifications.

13. Students typically learn social-perception skills without direct instruction. However, students with social disabilities often need direct instruction in how to act and respond in social situations.

14. Students with learning disabilities often need strategies for building self-esteem so that they can learn.

15. Behavior-management strategies are effective in changing the behavior of students with learning disabilities. They include reinforcement, response cost, punishment, ignoring, shaping behavior, contingency contracting, token reinforcements, time-out, and home-school coordination.

16. Teachers can make classroom modifications to meet the student's behavioral needs.

Questions for Discussion and Reflection

1. What are nonverbal learning disabilities? What are some specific problems associated with NLD?

2. Why do you think deficits in social skills are identified as "the most crippling type of problem that a student can have"? What are common indicators of social disabilities?

3. What are some causes and effects of emotional problems?

4. What is the ABC behavioral unit? Give an example of each component of the behavioral unit.

5. Describe three behavior-management strategies and give examples of how they could be applied to a student with learning disabilities.

6. Describe three ways that a teacher could make accommodations in an inclusive classroom to meet the behavior needs of a student with learning disabilities.

Key Terms

attention deficit hyperactivity disorder *(p. 540)*

attribution *(p. 542)*

contingency contracting *(p. 553)*

home-school coordination *(p. 555)*

modifications *(p. 557)*

negative reinforcement *(p. 552)*

nonverbal learning disabilities (NLD) *(p. 528)*

positive reinforcement *(p. 552)*

Premack principle *(p. 553)*

response cost *(p. 552)*

self-esteem *(p. 539)*

shaping behavior *(p. 552)*

social perception *(p. 533)*

social skills *(p. 529)*

successive approximations
(p. 552)

token reinforcers *(p. 555)*

APPENDIX

A

Case Study

Case studies are useful because they provide an opportunity to apply knowledge to the assessment-teaching process in an actual situation. The case of Adam Z., a freshman high school student, follows the format outlined in Chapter 3. As noted earlier, any case presentation is necessarily influenced by the theoretical orientation of the case investigators, and professionals often differ in their views of such matters as the selection of assessment instruments, the analysis of that assessment information, and the recommended intervention procedures. The case of Adam Z. is followed through six stages of the assessment-teaching process:

Stage 1. Prereferral activities

Stage 2. Referral and initial planning

Stage 3. Multidisciplinary evaluation

Stage 4. The case conference meeting: Writing the individualized education program

Stage 5. Implementing the teaching plan

Stage 6. Monitoring the student's progress

Identifying Information: Adam Z.

Name of Student: Adam Z.

Age: 14 years, 6 months

Current Placement: High school freshman, grade 9.4

STAGE 1. PREREFERRAL ACTIVITIES

Shortly after the semester started in September, Adam Z.'s high school departmental English teacher, Ms. Sloan, requested a prereferral staffing to discuss Adam, who was doing poorly in her general English class. The informal prereferral staffing included Adam's departmental teachers: his English teacher (Ms. Sloan), his general science teacher, his American history teacher, and his Spanish teacher. Ms. Sloan reported that Adam's problem in English was that he could not read his literature assignments and therefore had little knowledge of the content of this material. After discussing Adam's problem, the members of the prereferral team recommended that a classmate in the English class tape-record the assigned literature readings for Adam so that he could listen to the material. Specifically, they recommended that Adam's classmate Peter be given this assignment because Peter was particularly interested in speech and drama and read well orally.

Ms. Sloan discussed this proposal with Adam and Peter, and they both agreed to give the plan a trial. Peter recorded two of the literature assignments to help Adam study his English homework. However, about one week into this plan, Peter won the lead role in the school play, and frequent rehearsals kept him from making further recordings for Adam. As Peter's interest in the plan waned, so did Adam's, and he began to fall even further behind in English. At the next report period at the end of October, Adam received a failing grade in English. At this point, Ms. Sloan decided to refer Adam for a special education evaluation.

STAGE 2. REFERRAL AND INITIAL PLANNING

Ms. Sloan met with Adam's mother, Mrs. Z., to discuss Adam's failing work in English class. Mrs. Z. related that Adam had always had difficulty in school, beginning in the primary grades. During the elementary years— grades 1 through 8—Adam had attended several schools, but he had not received any special education services. As Mrs. Z. signed the consent form to have the evaluation, she remarked that she hoped Adam would finally receive some help now that he was in high school.

Ms. Sloan subsequently submitted the referral to the special education coordinator in the high school. The initial planning for Adam's multidisciplinary evaluation included the following kinds of assessment information: (1) classroom observation, (2) review of health information and tests of auditory and visual acuity, (3) conference with Adam, (4) developmental and educational history, (5) psychological report and measures of learning aptitude, and (6) measures of present levels of academic achievement.

STAGE 3. MULTIDISCIPLINARY EVALUATION

The multidisciplinary evaluation team consisted of the school psychologist, the learning disabilities teacher, the high school guidance counselor, and the school nurse. Each member of the team was responsible for obtaining certain kinds of evaluation information. A summary of this information follows.

Classroom Observation

The learning disabilities teacher observed Adam during a reading lesson in an American history class. The students in the class were assigned to read a passage concerning the U.S. Constitution and to answer ten multiple-choice questions on the text. Adam exhibited behavior suggesting that he was completing the assignment: He appeared to be reading the selection, then he appeared to be answering the questions, exhibiting such behaviors as scratching his head and looking up at the ceiling, as if thinking, before marking each answer. Upon examination of his test paper and in discussion with him, however, it became evident that the assignment was completely beyond his current achievement level. He had learned to act appropriately and to fake the behavior of looking as though he were doing the same work that the other students were doing.

Review of Health Information and Tests of Auditory and Visual Acuity

The school nurse reviewed the health records, which showed that Adam had been absent often during the primary and elementary years because of frequent colds. Also, his mother had reported that during his early school years he had suffered from otitis media, an inflammatory condition of the middle ear resulting in fluctuating and temporary hearing loss. The school nurse tested Adam's hearing with an audiometer and found that his auditory acuity fell within normal limits. The school nurse gave Adam a visual screening test, and no problems were noted. The other health history indicated no unusual health problems.

Conference with Adam

The guidance counselor met with Adam to discuss the evaluation. Adam clearly recognized that he had a learning problem. He told the counselor that he did not understand why he was so different from the other kids and why he always had so much difficulty learning to read. He thought he had gotten along at his previous school because the teachers had left him alone and had never called on him. Adam also mentioned that he was worried that his parents did not like him because he caused them so much more trouble than his sister did. He confided that he had once convinced a friend to rush into his house shouting, "Help, help! Adam's been run over!" so he could watch his mother's reaction through the window. He quite expected her to say, "Thank goodness for that." When she stood up in a panic, Adam rushed in, telling her it was only a joke. His mother was very angry about his joke, but Adam thought it was worth playing the trick to find out that she really cared.

Developmental and Educational History

The guidance counselor interviewed Mr. and Mrs. Z. and also reviewed Adam's educational history through his cumulative records.

Adam is the younger of two children. His sister is two years older and is an excellent student. Adam, born two months prematurely, weighed four pounds, eight ounces, at birth. He was a colicky baby and was put on a supplemental formula because his weight gain had been slow. He was allergic to the formula and several changes had to be made. Motor developmental milestones were accomplished within the normal range: He crawled at 8 months and walked at 12 months. His language development, however, was slow. Unlike his sister, he did not engage in such activities as cooing, verbalizing, or babbling during his infancy. By age 2, he had not learned to say any words to express himself but only pointed and gestured. His pediatrician referred him to the University Language Disorders Clinic, where he received language therapy for one hour each week until he was 3 years old. At that time, the family moved to a country in Asia, where Mr. Z. was assigned for three years as part of his military service. During this period, Adam did not attend school or receive any language help. The family had a child-care helper who did not speak English. Mrs. Z. said that it wasn't until Adam was 4 years old that she was able to decipher and understand his verbalizations.

Mrs. Z. said that Adam was an extremely active child, getting into everything, and that when he was young, the family could not take him to restaurants or to the homes of friends because of his extremely hyperactive behavior. He seemed to be driven, in constant motion and touching everything. His poor communication skills and hyperactivity interfered with his making friends as a young child. Adam is no longer hyperactive, but he still is not very talkative. He does well in sports activities and is on the football team.

Adam was placed in first grade when the family returned to the United States from their overseas assignment. At the end of the school year, the school suggested that Adam repeat first grade. However, his father would not hear of it, and Adam was enrolled in the second grade of a private school. The family moved three times during Adam's elementary years because of his father's military assignments. He never did repeat a grade during elementary school.

Although Adam does not enjoy school, he does not complain, and he tries hard to succeed. Just before the conference ended, Adam's father commented that as a child he had also had difficulty learning to read in school but has nevertheless done well as an officer in the military service. Mr. and Mrs. Z. said they hoped Adam could be helped through the special services of the school.

Psychological Report and Measures of Learning Aptitude

The school psychologist administered the *Wechsler Intelligence Scale for Children—Third Edition* (WISC-3) to assess Adam's intellectual potential and the *Wide Range Achievement Test—3* (WRAT-3) to screen his academic achievement. The psychologist found that Adam was in the above-average range of intelligence but that his abilities in performance areas were substantially higher than his abilities in language areas. Adam did especially poorly in tasks requiring auditory memory abilities. The WRAT-3 indicated severe problems in reading and spelling, with less severe problems in mathematics. Adam was cooperative during the testing, was aware of his problem, and appeared to be eager to succeed in school. He was well adjusted, considering the many years of failure he had encountered. His scores on these tests follow: WISC-3 Full-Scale IQ, 104; Performance IQ, 120; Verbal IQ, 91.

Verbal subtests	Scaled score	Performance subtests	Scaled score
Information	7	Picture arrangement	13
Comprehension	6	Picture completion	14
Arithmetic	9	Block design	15
Vocabulary	7	Object assembly	14
Similarities	8	Coding	8
Digit span	6		

Wide Range Achievement Test—3 (WRAT-3)

Reading (word recognition)	3.3
Arithmetic	6.0
Spelling	3.0

Measures of Present Levels of Academic Achievement

The learning disabilities teacher administered the following academic tests in their entirety or as partial tests: *Brigance Inventory of Essential Skills; Woodcock-Johnson Psychoeducational Battery, Revised—Tests of Achievement; Key Math—Revised; Clinical Evaluation of Language Fundamentals—Revised* (CELF-R); *Gray Oral Reading Test III; Test of Adolescent and Adult Language* (TOAL-3); and *Test of Written Language—3* (TOWL-3). A brief summary of Adam's test results in several academic areas follows.

Oral Language Abilities: Receptive   Adam scored at or above average on tests of comprehension of oral language sentences and words. When visual input was included, he seemed to do better in receiving and remembering the language.

Oral Language Abilities: Expressive   Problems were evident in Adam's use of oral language, in word finding (retrieval of a precise word), and in syntax. He had difficulty repeating sentences with complex syntactical structures and words with difficult articulation patterns, and his word fluency was poor in terms of quantity, quality, and speed.

Reading   According to the oral reading inventory, Adam's instructional reading level was at the middle third grade. Although he knew basic word-recognition skills, vowels, consonants, and simple word prefixes and suffixes, his efforts to apply this information were slow and laborious. His sight vocabulary was at the third-grade level, but his recognition was somewhat slow. Adam's comprehension of the oral reading passages was surprisingly strong. Considering his difficulty with word-recognition skills, he seemed to make good use of context clues to help understand the story.

Silent reading scores ranged from grade 3.5 to 5.0, generally below the fifth percentile for his age and grade. Observation of Adam during silent reading showed that he spent more time studying the questions than reading the text. He seemed to be looking for words he knew.

Mathematics   Mathematics was an area of significant strength for Adam. He did particularly well in computation and in mental mathematics. However, when he had to read a mathematics word-story problem, the task became more difficult.

Written Language   Written language was an area of great difficulty for Adam. He did poorly in usage, mechanics, and spelling. Both quantity and quality of output were very meager. His handwriting, however, was legible.

STAGE 4. THE CASE CONFERENCE MEETING: WRITING THE INDIVIDUALIZED EDUCATION PROGRAM

The case conference team met and included the following participants: the English teacher, the learning disabilities teacher, the school psychologist, the special education coordinator, Mr. and Mrs. Z., and Adam.

The case conference team agreed that Adam has learning disabilities and requires special education services. He exhibits a severe discrepancy between his potential and his achievement in reading, oral language, and written language.

Adam possesses a number of strengths: intellectual aptitude in the above-average range, with strong abilities in performance areas, mathematics concepts and computational skills, receptive oral language, and physical and motor performance. He does not exhibit behavior problems in school and appears to have a high desire to learn.

Areas of weakness that should be considered include poor reading skills (although he has a knowledge of basic word-attack skills), inadequate skills in oral expressive language, poor written language and spelling skills, and inefficient strategies for coping with the demands of the high school curriculum.

The case conference team felt that Adam's academic problem was severe. Because he had not received any help in the past, he now needs a rather intensive special education program. The team recommended that Adam receive instruction from a learning disabilities resource teacher and that this teacher collaborate with the content-area teachers. The case conference team recommended that Adam be placed in the inclusive regular subject classes for mathematics, physical education, and a career education class, to begin planning for career and work. Adam's learning disabilities teacher will collaborate with the teachers of these classes. Mr. and Mrs. Z. agreed to the plan, and an individualized education program (IEP) was written and signed by all members of the case conference team.

STAGE 5. IMPLEMENTING THE TEACHING PLAN

The learning disabilities teacher developed more specific plans to meet the objectives written into Adam's IEP. The plans included methods for solidifying and practicing reading word-recognition skills, building reading comprehension skills through reading of content-area books, placing Adam into a career education class, teaching learning strategies to improve his ability to help himself learn, and providing direct instruction in oral expression and in writing. The learning disabilities teacher will collaborate by planning and working with the general education and content-area teachers.

STAGE 6. MONITORING THE STUDENT'S PROGRESS

Adam's progress will be reviewed informally on a weekly basis by the learning disabilities teacher. Progress will be monitored in all classes and conferences will be held with each of the departmental teachers (mathematics and career education). The school has special classes for students with learning disabilities in English, social studies, and science. Adam will be placed in these classes and will also receive assistance from the learning disabilities resource teacher. A review of Adam's progress and a reevaluation of his program will be held in six months.

B Phonics

This appendix has two sections. The first part is a short phonics quiz to assess the teacher's knowledge of this subject area. The second part is a brief review of some phonic generalizations.

The purpose of the phonics quiz is to give teachers the opportunity to evaluate their knowledge of phonics. Fluent, accurate decoding and phonics skills are central to skilled reading. Many teachers and prospective teachers lack sufficient knowledge about phonics and structural analysis (Moats, 1998; Horne, 1978; Lerner & List, 1970).

To check your knowledge of phonics, select the correct answer for each of the following fifty questions. Compare your choices with the correct answers printed at the end of the phonics quiz. Score two points for each correct answer. Check the lists that follow the answers for your rating and classification.

Choose the Correct Answer

Consonants

1. Which of the following words ends with a consonant sound?
   (a) piano   (b) baby   (c) relay   (d) pencil   (e) below

2. A combination of two or three consonants pronounced so that each letter keeps its own identity is called a
   (a) silent consonant   (b) consonant digraph   (c) diphthong
   (d) schwa   (e) consonant blend

3. A word with a consonant digraph is
    (a) stop   (b) blue   (c) bend   (d) stripe   (e) none of the above

4. A word with a consonant blend is
    (a) chair   (b) ties   (c) thing   (d) strict   (e) where

5. A soft *c* is in the word
    (a) city   (b) cat   (c) chair   (d) Chicago   (e) none of the above

6. A soft *g* is in the word
    (a) great   (b) go   (c) ghost   (d) rig   (e) none of the above

7. A hard *c* is sounded in pronouncing which of the following nonsense
    words?
    (a) cadur   (b) ceiter   (c) cymling   (d) ciblent   (e) chodly

8. A hard *g* would be likely to be found in which of the following non-
    sense words?
    (a) gyfing   (b) gesturn   (c) gailing   (d) gimber   (e) geit

9. A *voiced* consonant digraph is in the word
    (a) think   (b) ship   (c) whip   (d) the   (e) photo

10. An *unvoiced* consonant digraph is in the word
    (a) those   (b) thirteen   (c) that   (d) bridge   (e) these

Vowels

11. Which of the following words contains a long vowel sound?
    (a) paste   (b) stem   (c) urge   (d) ball   (e) off

12. Which of the following words contains a short vowel sound?
    (a) treat   (b) start   (c) slip   (d) paw   (e) father

13. If *tife* were a word, the letter *i* would probably sound like the *i* in
    (a) if   (b) beautiful   (c) find   (d) ceiling   (e) sing
    Why?

14. If *aik* were a word, the letter *a* would probably sound like the *a* in
    (a) pack   (b) ball   (c) about   (d) boat   (e) cake
    Why?

15. If *ne* were a word, the letter *e* would probably sound like the *e* in
    (a) fed   (b) seat   (c) batter   (d) friend   (e) weight
    Why?

16. A vowel sound represented by the alphabet letter name of that vowel
    is a
    (a) short vowel   (b) long vowel   (c) diphthong   (d) digraph
    (e) schwa

17. An example of the schwa sound is found in
    (a) cotton   (b) phoneme   (c) stopping   (d) preview   (e) grouping

18. A diphthong is in the word
    (a) coat   (b) boy   (c) battle   (d) retarded   (e) slow

19. Which of the following words contains a vowel digraph?
    (a) fill (b) amazing (c) happy (d) cape (e) coat

Syllables

Indicate the correct way to divide the following nonsense words into syllables:

20. lidber
    (a) li-dber (b) lidb-er (c) lid-ber (d) none of these
    Why?

21. sefum
    (a) se-fum (b) sef-um (c) s-efum (d) sefu-m (e) none of these
    Why?

22. skeble
    (a) skeb-le (b) ske-ble (c) sk-eble (d) none of these
    Why?

23. gophul
    (a) gop-hul (b) go-phul (c) goph-ul (d) none of these
    Why?

24. repainly
    (a) rep-ain-ly (b) re-pai-nly (c) re-pain-ly (d) none of these
    Why?

25. How many syllables are in the word *barked?*
    (a) one (b) two (c) three (d) four (e) five

26. How many syllables are in the word *generalizations?*
    (a) four (b) five (c) six (d) seven (e) eight

27. A word with an open syllable is
    (a) pike (b) go (c) bend (d) butter (e) if

28. A word with a closed syllable is
    (a) throw (b) see (c) why (d) cow (e) win

Accent

29. If *trigler* were a word, which syllable would probably be accented?
    (a) trig (b) ler (c) neither (d) both
    Why?

30. If *tronition* were a word, which syllable would probably be accented?
    (a) tro (b) ni (c) tion (d) none of these
    Why?

31. If *pretaineringly* were a word, which syllable would probably be accented?
    (a) pre (b) tain (c) er (d) ing (e) ly
    Why?

Sound of Letter y

32. If *gly* were a word, the letter *y* would probably sound like the
    (a) *e* in *eel* (b) *e* in *pet* (c) *i* in *isle* (d) *i* in *if* (e) *y* in *happy*
    Why?

33. If *agby* were a word, the letter *y* would probably sound like
    (a) *e* in *eel*   (b) *e* in *egg*   (c) *i* in *ice*   (d) *i* in *if*   (e) *y* in *cry*
    Why?

Silent Letters

34. *No* silent letters are found in which of the following nonsense words?
    (a) knip   (b) gine   (c) camb   (d) wron   (e) shan

35. *No* silent letters are in
    (a) nade   (b) fruting   (c) kettin   (d) foat   (e) pnam

Terminology

36. A printed symbol made up of two letters representing one single phoneme or speech sound is a
    (a) schwa   (b) consonant blend   (c) phonetic   (d) digraph
    (e) diphthong

37. The smallest sound-bearing unit or a basic sound of speech is a
    (a) phoneme   (b) morpheme   (c) grapheme   (d) silent consonant
    (e) schwa

38. A study of all the speech sounds in language and how these sounds are produced is
    (a) phonics   (b) semantics   (c) orthography   (d) etymology
    (e) phonetics

39. The application of speech sounds to the teaching of reading letters or groups of letters is called
    (a) phonics   (b) phonemics   (c) orthography   (d) etymology
    (e) phonetics

40. The study of the nature and function of human language using the methodology and objectivity of the scientist is
    (a) phonetics   (b) phonology   (c) linguistics   (d) morphology
    (e) semantics

41. The approach to beginning reading that selects words that have a consistent sound-symbol relationship (CVC) is the
    (a) basal reader approach   (b) phonics approach
    (c) linguistics approach   (d) language-experience approach
    (e) initial teaching alphabet approach

42. The approach to beginning reading that uses a simpler, more reliable alphabet to make the decoding of English phonemes less complex is the
    (a) basal reader approach   (b) phonics approach
    (c) linguistics approach   (d) language-experience approach
    (e) initial teaching alphabet approach

43. A *phonic element* is similar to which word in linguistic terminology?
    (a) syntax   (b) phoneme   (c) morpheme   (d) grapheme
    (e) intonation

44. The study of structural analysis is similar to what element of linguistics?
    (a) syntax   (b) phonology   (c) morphology   (d) graphology
    (e) intonation

The Utility of Phonic Generalizations

In examining both the words that are exceptions to the rules and the words that conform to the rules, researchers have found a varying percentage of utility in the generalizations in Items 45–48. How frequently does each hold true?

45. When there are two vowels side by side, the long sound of the first one is heard and the second is usually silent.
    (a) 25%   (b) 45%   (c) 75%   (d) 90%   (e) 100%

46. When there are two vowels, one of which is a final *e*, the first vowel is long and the *e* is silent.
    (a) 30%   (b) 60%   (c) 75%   (d) 90%   (e) 100%

47. When a vowel is in the middle of a one-syllable word, the vowel is short.
    (a) 30%   (b) 50%   (c) 75%   (d) 90%   (e) 100%

48. When a word begins with *kn*, the *k* is silent.
    (a) 30%   (b) 50%   (c) 70%   (d) 90%   (e) 100%

49. The first American educator to advocate the teaching of phonics as an aid to word recognition and pronunciation was
    a. Noah Webster in *The American Blueback Spelling Book*, 1790.
    b. William McGuffey in *McGuffey's Readers*, 1879.
    c. Leonard Bloomfield, *Language*, 1933.
    d. Rudolph Flesch in *Why Johnny Can't Read*, 1955.
    e. Charles Fries, *Linguistics and Reading*, 1963.

50. Most reading authorities agree that
    a. the sight-word method is the best way to teach reading.
    b. the phonics method is the best way to teach reading.
    c. structural or morphemic analysis is the best way to teach reading.
    d. there is no one best way to teach reading.

Nonsense Words Quiz

Read the following nonsense words, applying phonic generalizations to determine their appropriate pronunciations.

bongtrike	gingabution
plignel	recentively
abcealter	fudder
conborvement	gentropher
crangle	craipthrusher
magsletting	wonaprint
phister	knidderflicing
flabinstate	

Answers to Phonics Quiz

1. d
2. e
3. e
4. d
5. a
6. e
7. a
8. c
9. d
10. b
11. a
12. c
13. c: Long vowel with silent *e*.
14. e: With two vowels, first is long, second is silent
15. b: One-syllable ending in vowel is long.
16. b
17. a
18. b
19. e
20. c: Divide between two consonants.
21. a: Vowel, consonant, vowel.
22. b: In words ending in -*le*, the consonant precedes the *le*.
23. b: Consonant digraphs are not divided.
24. c: Prefix and suffix are separate syllables.
25. a
26. c
27. b
28. e
29. a: Accent first of two syllables.
30. b: Accent syllables before -*tion* ending.
31. b: Accent syllable with two adjacent vowels.
32. c. *y* at end of one-syllable word has a long *i* sound.
33. a: *y* at end of multisyllable word has a long *e* sound.
34. e
35. b
36. d
37. a
38. e
39. a
40. c
41. c
42. e
43. b
44. c
45. b
46. b
47. c
48. e
49. a
50. d

Rating Scale

Score	Rating
92–100	EXCELLENT Congratulations! You do know your phonics.
84–91	GOOD A brief refresher will help, though.
75–83	FAIR Study with your favorite third grader.
68–74	POOR You need to learn about our written language system before teaching a student to read.

A REVIEW OF COMMON PHONIC GENERALIZATIONS

Consonants

Consonants are the letters that are not vowels. Consonant speech sounds are formed by modifying, altering, or obstructing the stream of vocal sound with the organs of speech. These obstructions may be stops, fricatives, or resonants. Consonant sounds are relatively consistent and have a regular grapheme-phoneme relationship. They include *b, d, f, h, j, k, l, m, n, p, r, s, t, v, w, y* (initial position).

Consonants c *and* g

Hard *c* pronounced like *k* when followed by *a, o, u (cup, cat)*.

Soft *c* pronounced like *s* when followed by *i, e, y (city, cent)*.

Hard *g* when followed by *a, o, u (go, gay)*.

Soft *g* when followed by *i, e, y;* sounds like *j (gentle, gyp)*.

Consonant Blends

A consonant blend is a combination of two or three consonant letters blended in such a way that each letter in the blend keeps its own identity: *bl, sl, cl, fl, gl, pl, br, cr, dr, fr, gr, pr, tr, sc, sk, sl, sw, sn, sp, sm, spl, spr, str, ng, nk, tw, dw*.

Consonant Digraphs

A consonant digraph is a combination of two consonant letters representing one phoneme or speech sound that is not a blend of the two letters: *sh, ch, wh, ck, ph, gh, th*.

Silent Consonants

Silent consonants are the consonants that, when combined with specific other letters, are not pronounced. In the examples that follow, the silent consonants are the ones in parentheses, and the letters shown with them are the specific letters that cause them to be silent in combination. (There are exceptions, however.)

i(gh)	sight, bright
m(b)	comb, lamb
(w)r	wren, wrong
(l)k	talk, walk
(k)n	knew, knife
s(t)	listen, hasten
f(t)	often, soften

Vowels

The vowels are the letters *a, e, i, o, u,* and sometimes *y*. The vowel speech sounds are produced in the resonance chamber formed by the stream of air passing through in the oral cavity.

Short vowels: a, e, i, o, u (**sometimes** *y*).   A single vowel in a medial position usually has the short vowel sound: consonant, vowel, consonant (CVC). A diacritical mark called a breve ˘ may indicate the short vowel: păt, săd, lĕd, sĭt, pŏt, cŭp, gўp.

Long vowels: a, e, i, o, u, (sometimes y).   The long vowel sounds the same as the alphabet letter name of the vowel. It is indicated with the diacritical mark $\bar{e}$, called a macron: $g\bar{o}$, $c\bar{a}ke$, $\bar{e}el$, $\bar{\imath}ce$, $n\bar{o}$, $\bar{u}niform$, $cr\bar{y}$.

Double Vowels: Vowel Digraph

Frequently, when two vowels are adjacent, the first vowel has the long sound, whereas the second is silent. Some research has shown this generalization to hold true about 45 percent of the time: *tie, coat, rain, eat, pay*.

Final e

In words with a vowel-consonant-*e* pattern (VC*e*), the vowel frequently has the long sound and the *e* is silent. Research has shown this generalization to hold true about 60 percent of the time: *make, Pete, slide, hope, cube*.

Vowels Modified by r

Vowels followed by the letter *r* are neither long nor short, but the sound is modified by the letter *r*. This generalization holds true about 85 percent of the time: *star, her, stir, horn, fur*.

Diphthong

A diphthong consists of two adjacent printed symbols representing two vowels, each of which contributes to a blended speech sound: *joy, toil, cow, house, few*.

Schwa Sound

This is the vowel sound in an unaccented syllable and is indicated with the symbol ə: b*a*lloon, eat*e*n, beaut*i*fy, butt*o*n, circ*u*s.

Syllabication

Number of Syllables

There are as many syllables in a word as there are vowel sounds heard: *bruise* (one syllable), *beautiful* (three syllables).

Two Consonants (VC-CV)

If the initial vowel is followed by two consonants, divide the word between the two consonants. This rule holds true about 80 percent of the time: *con-tact, let-ter, mar-ket.*

Single Consonant (V-CV)

If the initial vowel is followed by one consonant, the consonant usually begins the second syllable. Although there are many exceptions to this rule, the generalization holds true about 50 percent of the time: *mo-tor, na-tion, stu-dent.*

Consonant -le (C-le) Endings

If a word ends in *-le*, the consonant preceding the *-le* begins the last syllable. This generalization holds true about 95 percent of the time: *ta-ble, pur-ple, han-dle.*

Consonant Blends and Consonant Digraphs

Consonant blends and digraphs are not divided when separating a word into syllables. This holds true 100 percent of the time: teach-er, graph-ic, de-scribe.

Prefixes and Suffixes

Prefixes and suffixes usually form a separate syllable: *re-plac-ing, dis-cour-age-ment.*

Suffix -ed

If the suffix *-ed* is preceded by *d* or *t*, it forms a separate syllable and is pronounced *-ed*. If the suffix *-ed* is not preceded by a *d* or *t*, it does not form a separate syllable. It is pronounced like *t* when it follows an unvoiced consonant, and it is pronounced like *d* when it follows a voiced consonant: *sanded (ed), patted (ed), asked (t), pushed (t), tamed (d), crazed (d).*

Open and Closed Syllables

Syllables that end with a consonant are closed syllables, and the vowel is short: *can-*vass. Syllables that end with a vowel are open syllables, and the vowel is long: *ba-*by.

The y Sound in One-Syllable Words and Multisyllable Words

When the *y* is the final sound in a one-syllable word, it usually has the sound of a long *i*: *cry, my, ply.*

When the *y* is the final sound of a multisyllable word, it usually has the long *e* sound: *funny, lady.*

Accent

When there is no other clue in a two-syllable word, the accent frequently falls on the first syllable. This generalization is true about 80 percent of the time: *pen′ cil, sau′ cer.*

In inflected or derived forms of words, the primary accent usually falls on or within the root word: *fix′ es, un touched′.*

Two vowels together in the last syllable of a word give a clue to an accented final syllable: *re main′, re peal′.*

If two identical consonants are in a word, the syllable before the double consonant is usually accented: *big′ ger, win′ ner.*

The primary accent usually falls on the syllable preceding these suffixes: *-ion, -ity, -ic, -ical, -ian, -ial, -ious.* For example, *at ten′ tion, hys ter′ ical, bar bar′ ian, bil′ ious.*

C Tests

This appendix provides an alphabetical listing of a number of tests that are useful in assessing students with learning disabilities. The list includes tests that were mentioned in this text as well as some tests that were not discussed. The descriptive material about each test is brief and not designed to be evaluative. Since tests are frequently revised and new forms of manuals are issued, it is desirable to obtain a current catalog from the publisher before placing an order. The publisher appears after the test name; publishers' addresses are provided in Appendix D.

In selecting tests, the user should consider the technical qualities of the test: its purpose, reliability, validity, standardization procedures, types of scores that are provided, ease of administration and scoring, and time and training needed to administer the test. The **Standards for Educational and Psychological Tests** (American Educational Research Association, 1985) is a comprehensive guide for test users and developers; it sets the standard for the kinds of information that should be in test manuals, for the kinds of information that should be provided on the technical adequacy of tests, and for test use.

AAMR Adaptive Behavior Scale. American Association of Mental Retardation. There are two editions of the AAMR Adaptive Behavior Scale: the School Edition (ages 3–21) and the Residential and Community Edition (ages 18–79). Assesses the total life-functioning abilities of individuals through an interview with an informant. 20 minutes.

Adaptive Behavior Inventory. Pro-Ed. Tests self-care, communication, and social, academic, and occupational skills. Ages 6–19.

Ammons Full-Range Picture Vocabulary Test (Forms A and B). Psychological Test Specialists. An individually administered test of receptive language vocabulary. Preschool to adult.

Analytic Reading Inventory. Charles E. Merrill. Criterion-referenced informal reading inventory that yields independent, instructional, and frustration reading levels and listening, miscues, and comprehension analysis. Grades 1–6.

Attention Deficit Disorder Evaluation Scale. Hawthorne Educational Services. Two versions: Home Version and School Version. Rating Scales. School Version, ages 4–5 to 21 years. Three subscales—inattentive, impulsive, hyperactive. Home Version, ages 4–20.

Auditory Discrimination in Depth (Lindamood). Riverside. Auditory perception skills of sounds, letters, and words. All ages.

Auditory Discrimination Test (Wepman). Western Psychological Services. An individual test of a child's ability to distinguish whether two spoken words are the same or different. Ages 5–8.

BASC—Behavior Assessment System For Children. AGS. A coordinated system of instructions that evaluate the behavior, thoughts, and emotions of children and adolescents. Ages 4–18. 20 minutes.

Basic Achieving Skills Individual Screener (BASIC). Psychological Corporation. Individual test of reading, mathematics, spelling, and writing. Grades 1–12.

Basic Schools Skills Inventory. Pro-Ed. Identifies areas of difficulty in school performance. Ages 4–7.

Bender-Gestalt Test. Western Psychological Services. An individually administered test of a person's performance in copying designs. The Koppitz Scoring (E. Koppitz, **The Bender-Gestalt Test for Young Children,** New York: Grune & Stratton, 1963) provides a developmental scoring system for young children. Ages 5–10.

Boder Test of Reading-Spelling Patterns. Grune & Stratton. A diagnostic screening test of subtypes of reading disability. Differentiates two characteristics of reading and spelling disability: visual gestalt (ability to develop sight vocabulary) and auditory analysis (ability to develop phonic word analysis skills). All ages.

Boehm Test of Basic Concepts—Revised. Psychological Corporation. Diagnostic group test of understanding of concepts. Grades K–2.

Brigance Assessment of Basic Skills. Curriculum Associates. Tests of reading, language arts, and arithmetic. Grades K–6.

Brigance Assessment of Basic Skills—Spanish Edition. Curriculum Associates. For students with limited English proficiency. Grades K–8.

Brigance Comprehensive Inventory of Basic Skills. Curriculum Associates. Criterion-referenced tests of readiness, reading, language arts, and mathematics. Grades K–9. 15–90 minutes.

Brigance Inventory of Early Development—Revised. Curriculum Associates. Assesses functional skills of preschool children. Ages 1–7.

Brigance Inventory of Essential Skills. Curriculum Associates. Measures minimal academic and vocational competencies. Designed for secondary students. Grades 6–adult.

Bruinicks-Oseretsky Test of Motor Proficiency. AGS. Individually administered test of gross- and fine-motor development. Ages 4–16.

Burk's Behavior Rating Scales. Western Psychological Services. Measures eighteen categories of behavior, including self-blame, anxiety, withdrawal, dependency, attention, impulse control, sense of identity, and social conformity. Grades 1–9.

California Achievement Tests: Reading and Mathematics. California Testing Bureau. A battery of group tests to assess several areas of academic achievement. Grades 3–8.

Carrow Elicited Language Inventory. Riverside. Assessment of language proficiency in spoken language. Ages 3–8.

Child Behavior Checklist (T. Achenbach & C. Edelbrock, Burlington, VT: University of Vermont, Department of Psychiatry). Checklists for teachers and parents. Measures behavior and hyperactivity. Parent checklists for ages 2–3 and for ages 4–18. Teacher's Report Form, ages 5–18. 20 minutes.

Classroom Reading Inventory. William C. Brown. A reading inventory that can be administered to individuals or groups. Grades Preprimary–8.

Clinical Evaluation of Language Fundamentals—Revised (CELF-R). Psychological Corporation. Individual screening test and diagnostic battery to measure oral language abilities. Grades K–12.

Comprehensive Receptive and Expressive Vocabulary Test. Riverside. Individual vocabulary test with two subtests—expressive vocabulary and receptive vocabulary. Ages 4–17. 45 minutes.

Conners Rating Scales. Multi-Health Systems. Conners Teacher Rating Scale, ages 3–17. Conners Parent Rating Scale, ages 3–17. Rating scales for hyperactivity. Parents and teachers provide information to determine the child's level of hyperactivity. 10–15 minutes.

Coopersmith Self-Esteem Inventories. Publishers Test Services. Self-report questionnaires that consist of short statements such as "I can usually take care of myself." The subject answers with either "like me" or "unlike me." Measures attitude toward the self in social, academic, and personal contexts. Elementary age.

Denver Developmental Screening Test—Revised. Denver Developmental Materials. Identifies delays in young children in the areas of fine-motor, adaptive, gross-motor, personal-social, and language development. Ages 1 month–6 years. 20 minutes.

Detroit Tests of Learning Aptitude—4 (DTLA-4). Pro-Ed. An individual test of mental functions that has subtests measuring various areas of mental processing. In addition to an overall score, the tests yield nine composite scores. Ages 6–17. 30–60 minutes.

Developmental Sentence Scoring Test. Northwestern University Press. A speech sample from fifty complete utterances (sentences) is obtained from the child and then scored and analyzed. Ages 2–6.

Developmental Test of Visual-Motor Integration. Western Psychological Services. A visual-motor test of the subject's abilities in copying designs. Ages 5–15.

Devereux Adolescent Behavior Rating Scale. Devereux Foundation. A scale for teacher rating of behavior of adolescents. Ages 13–18.

Devereux Child Behavior Rating Scale. Devereux Foundation. A rating scale for use by parent or teacher. Ages 8–12.

Devereux Elementary School Behavior Rating Scale. Devereux Foundation. A rating scale that identifies eleven school-related behaviors, such as disturbance, impatience, attention, withdrawal, inability to change, slowness, and quitting before completing a task. Grades K–6.

Diagnostic Assessment of Reading with Trial Teaching Strategies (DARTTS). Riverside. Identifies strengths and weaknesses in reading through six areas: word recognition, word analysis, oral reading, silent reading comprehension, spelling, and word meaning. Identifies student reading levels. 20–30 minutes.

The Trial Teaching Strategies provide a series of teaching sessions to identify the most effective methods and materials for individual students. Provides three reading levels: potential, instructional, and independent. 30 minutes.

Diagnostic Mathematics Inventory Mathematics System. CTB/ McGraw-Hill. Individual inventory of student achievement in mathematics. Grades 1–12.

Diagnostic Reading Inventory. Kendall/Hunt. Individual informal reading inventory with graded word lists and graded oral and silent reading passages. Grades 1–8.

Diagnostic Screening Test for Developmental Dyslexia. Grune & Stratton. A diagnostic analysis and classification of spelling errors. All ages.

Diagnostic Tests and Self-Helps in Arithmetic. California Testing Bureau. Test designed to diagnose arithmetic difficulties. Grades 3–8.

DIAL-R. AGS Edition. Developmental Indicators for the Assessment of Learning—Revised (DIAL-R). AGS. A prekindergarten screening test for identifying children with learning problems. Preschool age.

Durrell Analysis of Reading Difficulty. Psychological Corporation. A battery of diagnostic tests designed to help in the analysis and evaluation of specific reading difficulties. Grades 1–6. 30–60 minutes.

Ekwall Reading Inventory. Allyn & Bacon. Informal reading inventory of oral and silent reading. Grades Preprimary–9; 20–30 minutes.

Enright Diagnostic Inventory of Basic Arithmetic Skills. Curriculum Associates. Determines the student's performance levels in addition, subtraction, multiplication, and division of whole numbers, fractions, and decimals. Grade 4–adult.

Gates-MacGinitie Reading Tests. Teachers College Press. A general test of silent reading designed for group administration. Five forms. Grades 1–12.

Gates-McKillop-Horowitz Reading Diagnostic Tests. Teachers College Press. Battery of tests for individual administration, designed to give diagnostic information about a student's reading skills. Grades 1–6. 60–90 minutes.

Gilmore Oral Reading Test. Psychological Corporation. An individually administered oral reading test that gives information about word accuracy, rate, and comprehension. Grades 1–8. 15–20 minutes.

Goldman-Fristoe Test of Articulation. American Guidance Services. Tests the articulation of words and sentences. Ages 2–16+. 30 minutes.

Goldman Fristoe-Woodcock Test of Auditory Discrimination. American Guidance Services. Tests auditory discrimination of phonemes against a quiet background and against a noisy background. Ages 2–16+.

Goodenough-Harris Drawing Test. Psychological Corporation. Provides a score of nonverbal intelligence obtained through an objective scoring of a student's drawings of a human figure. Ages 3–15. 13–15 minutes.

Gray Oral Reading Tests (3rd ed.). Pro-Ed. Two forms. An individually administered oral reading test. Thirteen passages for oral reading and comprehension questions. Grades Preprimary–12.

Halstead-Reitan Neuropsychological Test Battery for Children. Reitan Neuropsychology Laboratory. Designed to test brain behavior functions in children. Ages 9–14.

Houston Test for Language Development. Houston Test Company. A checklist to be completed by an observer who has ready access to the child. Ages 6 months–6 years.

Illinois Test of Psycholinguistic Abilities (ITPA). University of Illinois Press. Individually administered test containing twelve subtests of dimensions of mental processes. Scores obtained on subtests can be used for diagnostic purposes. Ages 2–10. 60 minutes.

Informal Reading Inventory (Appendix D in M. Richek, J. Caldwell, J. Jennings, & J. Lerner, *Reading Problems: Assessment and Reading Strategies*, Allyn & Bacon, 1996. An informal reading inventory of oral and silent reading, including word-recognition and reading-comprehension passages and questions. Grades Preprimary–8.

Iowa Tests of Basic Skills. Houghton Mifflin. Group test of several academic areas: reading, arithmetic, language, and work-study skills. Ages 3–9.

Kaufman Assessment Battery for Children (K-ABC). AGS. Individual test of intelligence and achievement. Yields four major scores: sequential processing, simultaneous processing, mental processing composite, and achievement. Ages 2–12. 1 hour.

Kaufman Brief Intelligence Tests. AGS. Verbal and nonverbal subtests. Provides IQ score. Ages 4–90. 15–30 minutes.

Kaufman Test of Educational Achievement (K-TEA). AGS. Individually administered tests of reading, mathematics, and spelling. Grades 1–12. Brief form: 20–30 minutes; comprehensive form: 50–75 minutes.

Key Math–Revised. American Guidance Services. Measures fourteen arithmetic subskills. Individually administered. Four levels of evaluation. Grades K–6.

Keystone Visual Survey Service for Schools. Keystone View. Individually administered visual screening device to determine the need for further referral for a visual examination. Ages 2–18.

The Learning Disabilities Diagnostic Inventory (LDDI). An individual rating scale to help identify intrinsic processing disorders and learning disabilities. Ages 8.0–17.11. 1–20 minutes.

Learning Styles Inventory. Price Systems. Uses responses to 100 true-false items to identify students' preferred learning conditions. Grades 3–12.

Leiter International Performance Scale. Stoelting. Nonverbal test of mental abilities. Ages 2–18. 1.5 hours.

Lincoln-Oseretsky Motor Development Scale. Stoelting. Individual tests of a variety of motor skills. Ages 6–14.

Lindamood Auditory Conceptualization Test. Riverside. Measures speech sound discrimination and perception of number, order, sameness, or difference of speech sounds. Preschool to adult. 10 minutes.

McCarthy Scales of Children's Abilities. Psychological Corporation. General intellectual levels and strengths and weaknesses in several ability areas. Ages 2.5–8.5. 45–60 minutes.

Metropolitan Achievement Tests. Psychological Corporation. Group-administered battery of tests that measures several areas of academic achievement: reading, spelling, and arithmetic. Grades K–12.

Monroe Diagnostic Reading Tests. Nevins. Individually administered diagnostic reading test of oral reading and word recognition. Grades 1–4. Untimed.

Monroe Reading Aptitude Tests. Riverside. Group-administered test to measure readiness for reading. Nonreading test that assesses several areas of mental functioning. Ages 6–9.

Motor-free Test of Visual Perception. Academic Therapy Publications. Test of visual perception that does not require a motor component. Ages 4–8. 10 minutes.

Nebraska Test of Learning Aptitude. Hiskey Publications. An individual test of intellectual potential used widely with the deaf or hard-of-hearing. Ages 7–17. 40–60 minutes.

Nelson-Denny Reading Test. Riverside. Group or individual general reading assessment. Grades 9–adult.

Nelson Reading Skills Test. Riverside. Diagnostic reading battery. Grades 3–9.

Northwestern Syntax Screening Test. Northwestern University Press. Individually administered test of receptive and expressive language. Ages 3–7.

Oral and Written Language Scales (OWLS). AGS. Listening Comprehension and Oral Expression; individual test assesses listening and oral expression skills. Ages 3–21. 1–25 minutes. Written Expression Scale; test assesses written language. Ages 5–21. 15–25 minutes.

Ortho-rater. Bausch & Lomb. Individual visual screening test. Grades 1–12.

Otis-Lennon School Ability Test. Psychological Corporation. Group test of general mental ability and scholastic aptitude. Grades K–12. 45–80 minutes.

Peabody Development Motor Scales. Riverside. Early childhood development program provides both in-depth assessment and an instructional program in gross-motor and fine-motor skills, eye-hand coordination, finger dexterity, reflexes, balance, and locomotion. Ages birth–83 months. 10–20 minutes.

Peabody Individual Achievement Test—Revised (PIAT-R). AGS. Individually administered test of five subjects: mathematics, reading recognition, reading comprehension, spelling, and general information. Grades K–12.

Peabody Picture Vocabulary Test—III. AGS. An individually administered test of receptive language vocabulary. Ages 2–18.

Piers-Harris Children Self-Concept Scale. Western Psychological Services. Students respond "yes" or "no" to statements such as "I am a happy person." Statements can be read by the teacher or the students. Measures six factors: behavior, intellectual status, physical appearance, anxiety, popularity, and happiness. Grades 4–12. 20 minutes.

Prescriptive Reading Inventory. CTB/McGraw-Hill. Criterion-referenced reading test; five levels. Grades K–9.

Purdue Perceptual-Motor Survey. Charles E. Merrill. A series of tests for assessing motor development and motor skills. Ages 4–10. 10–15 minutes.

Reading Miscue Inventory: Alternative Procedures. Richard C. Owen. Analyzes strategies used for oral reading miscues. Grades 1–8.

Reitan-Indiana Neuropsychological Battery for Children. Reitan Neuropsychology Laboratory. Designed to test brain behavior functions in children. Ages 5–8.

Rosner Informal Test of Auditory Perception Skills. In J. Rosner, *Helping Children Overcome Learning Difficulties*, New York: Walker & Co., 1975, pp. 47–79.

Scales of Independent Behavior. Riverside. Noncognitive measures of adjustment in the social, behavioral, and adaptive areas. Measures functional independence and adaptive behavior in motor skills, social and communication skills, personal living skills, and community living skills.

Sequential Assessment of Mathematics Inventory. Psychological Corporation. Individual assessment battery. Classroom survey. Gives information about student's strengths and weaknesses in math. Grades K–8.

Sequential Tests of Educational Progress (STEP). CTB/McGraw-Hill. A battery of achievement tests, including tests of reading and listening vocabulary and comprehension. Grades K–12.

Slingerland Screening Tests for Identifying Children with Specific Language Disability. Educator's Publishing Service. Three sets of group-administered screening tests with informal scoring. Grades 1–4.

Slosson Intelligence Test—Revised. Slosson Educational Publications. A short, individual screening test of intelligence for use by teachers and other professionals for a quick estimate of mental ability. Ages birth–adult; 10–20 minutes.

Slosson Oral Reading Test. Slosson Educational Publications. Brief test of word recognition. Primary grades–high school. 3–5 minutes.

Snellen Chart. American Optical Co. Wall chart with rows of letters gradually decreasing in size. Tests far-point vision at 20 feet. 2–3 minutes.

Social Skills Rating System. AGS. Rating scales to assess social skills, problem behaviors, and academic competence. Preschool–adult.

Southern California Test Battery for Assessment of Dysfunction. Western Psychological Services. A battery containing the following separate tests: **Southern California Kinesthesia and Tactile Perception Tests; Southern California Figure-Ground Visual Perception Test; Southern California Motor Accuracy Test; Southern California Perceptual-Motor Tests;** and **Ayres Space Test.** Ages 3–10.

SRA Achievement Series: Reading. Science Research Associates. Group tests of several areas of academic achievement, including reading. Grades 1–12.

Standard Reading Inventory. Klamath Printing Co. Informal reading inventory. Grades Preprimary–7.

Stanford Achievement Test: Reading. Psychological Corporation. Group test of academic achievement, including reading. Grades 1–10.

Stanford Diagnostic Mathematics Test (3rd ed.). Psychological Corporation. Group test to diagnose the nature of arithmetic difficulties. Grades K–12.

Stanford Diagnostic Reading Test. Psychological Corporation. Group test to diagnose the nature of reading difficulties; measures comprehension, vocabulary, syllabication, auditory skills, phonetic analysis, and reading rate. Grades 1–12.

Stanford-Binet Intelligence Scale (4th ed.). Riverside. Individual test of general intelligence, yielding MA and IQ scores; to be administered by trained examiners. Ages 2–adult. 60–90 minutes.

Swanson Cognitive Processing Test. Pro-Ed. Individually administered test battery: 11 subtests that measure different aspects of intellectual abilities and information processing potential.

Templin-Darley Test of Articulation. Bureau of Educational Research, University of Iowa City. Test of ability to pronounce sounds of English. Individual. 15 minutes.

Test of Adolescent/Adult Word Finding. Riverside. 40-item test. Ages 12–80. 20–30 minutes.

Test of Adolescent Language (TOAL-2). Pro-Ed. Assesses the language ability of adolescent students. Ages 12–19.

Test for Auditory Comprehension of Language—Revised. Carrow. Riverside. Individual test of language and understanding. Forms in Spanish and English. Ages 3–11. 10–15 minutes.

Test of Early Mathematics Ability—2. Pro-Ed. Test of early math functioning. Useful with older students who have mathematics problems. Preschool–Grade 3.

Test of Language Development—3: Intermediate (TOLD-3: Intermediate). Pro-Ed. Individually administered diagnostic test of spoken language, including articulation, word discrimination, oral vocabulary, picture vocabulary, sentence initiation, and grammar. Identifies receptive and expressive language deficits of intermediate-level children. Ages 8.5–12.11. 40 minutes.

Test of Language Development—3: Primary (TOLD-3: Primary). Pro-Ed. Identifies specific receptive and expressive language skills of primary-age children. Ages 4.0–8.11. 40 minutes.

Test of Mathematical Abilities—2. Pro-Ed. Assesses abilities in arithmetic story problems and computation. Tests attitude toward mathematics and understanding of mathematics vocabulary. Grades 3–12.

Test of Non-verbal Intelligence (TONI—3). Pro-Ed. Tests nonlanguage cognitive abilities. Ages 6–18. 60 minutes.

Test of Phonological Awareness. Pro-Ed. Tests young children's awareness of individual sounds in words. Grades K–2.

Test of Reading Comprehension (TORC) (3rd ed.). Pro-Ed. Assessment of reading comprehension abilities. Grades 2–12. 30 minutes.

Test de Vocabulario en Imagenes Peabody. AGS. Spanish version of the Peabody Picture Vocabulary Test. Ages 2.5–18.0. 10–15 minutes.

Test of Word Finding. Riverside. Individual test that assesses expressive language problems as a result of word-retrieval difficulties. Subjects name nouns and verbs and complete sentences. Ages 6.6–12.11. 20–30 minutes.

Test of Word Knowledge. Psychological Corporation. Assesses knowledge of words, meanings, and expressive and receptive vocabulary. Level 1, ages 5–8, 25–30 minutes. Level 2, ages 8–17, 40–65 minutes.

Test of Written Language—3 (TOWL-3). Pro-Ed. A test of written expression. Ages 7–18.

Test of Written Spelling—3 (TOWS-3). Pro-Ed. Dictated word test selected from ten basal reader programs. Grades 1–12.

Vineland Adaptive Behavior Scales. American Guidance Services. Individual test that measures communication, daily living skills, specialization, and motor skills. Interview edition, survey form and interview edition, expanded form and classroom edition. Information derived by an interview with an informant, usually a parent. Ages birth–adult. 30 minutes.

Visual Retention Test—Revised. Psychological Corporation. Individually administered test of visual perception and memory of designs. Ages 8–adult.

Wechsler Adult Intelligence Scale—Revised (WAIS-R). Psychological Corporation. An individual intelligence test that yields verbal, performance, and full-scale scores. To be administered by trained examiners. Ages 15–adult. 60 minutes.

Wechsler Individual Achievement Test. AGS. Individual test with eight subtests: basic reading, math reasoning, spelling, reading comprehension, numerical operations, writing, oral expression, written expression. Ages 5–19. 30–75 minutes.

Wechsler Intelligence Scale for Children—Third Edition (WISC-3). Psychological Corporation. Individual intelligence test that yields verbal and performance scores and a full-scale IQ score. To be administered by trained examiners. Ages 6–16. 60 minutes.

Wechsler Preschool and Primary Scale of Intelligence—Revised (WPPSI-R). Psychological Corporation. Individual intelligence test, similar to the WISC-3, that yields verbal, performance, and full-scale IQ scores. To be administered by trained examiners. Ages 4–6. 60 minutes.

Wepman Test of Auditory Discrimination. Language Research Associates. Individual test of auditory discrimination of phoneme sounds. Ages 5–9.

Wide-Range Achievement Test—3 (WRAT-3). Jastak Associates. A brief individual test of word recognition, spelling, and arithmetic computation. Ages 5–adult.

Woodcock Reading Mastery Test—Revised. American Guidance Services. Individual tests of identification of words, word attack, word comprehension, and passage comprehension. Criterion- and norm-referenced scores. Ages 5–adult.

Woodcock-Johnson Psychoeducational Battery—Revised (WJ-R). Riverside. Individual battery of tests in two parts: cognitive tests and achievement tests. Complete test: 2 hours. Grades K–17. **Woodcock-Johnson Achievement Tests** contain academic achievement tests in reading, mathematics, written language, and knowledge. **Woodcock-Johnson Cognitive Tests** measure long-term retrieval, short-term memory, processing speed, auditory processing, visual processing, comprehension knowledge, and fluid reasoning.

Woodcock Reading Diagnostic Battery. Riverside. A diagnostic test of reading achievement and reading abilities. 50–60 minutes. Ages 4–90.

D

Contact Information for Educational Publishers and Organizations

The following directory contains, in alphabetical order, the names and addresses of the publishers of tests, publishers of other materials, and organizations mentioned in this book.

Academic Therapy Publications, 20 Commercial Blvd., Novato, CA 94947. **http://www.atpub@aol.com**

Achenbach, Thomas A., Department of Psychiatry, University of Vermont, Burlington, VT 05401.

A.D.D. Warehouse, 300 NW 70th Ave., Suite 102, Plantation, FL 33317. **http://www.addwarehouse.com**

AGS (American Guidance Services), 4201 Woodland, PO Box 99, Publishers Building, Circle Pines, MN 55014-1796. **http://www.agsnet.com**

Allyn & Bacon, 160 Gould St., Needham Heights, MA 02194. **http://www.abacon.com**

American Association of Mental Retardation, 5201 Connecticut Ave. NW, Washington, DC 20015.

American Psychological Association, 1200 17th St. NW, Washington, DC 20036.

American Speech and Hearing Association, 9030 Old Georgetown Rd., Washington, DC 20014.

Bausch & Lomb Optical Co., Rochester, NY 14602.

Broderbund Software, 500 Redwood Blvd., PO Box 6121, Novato, CA 94948-6121.

Paul H. Brookes, PO Box 10624, Baltimore, MD 21285-0624. **http://www.pbrookes.com**

CHADD (Children and Adults with Attention Deficit Disorder), 8181 Professional Pl., Suite 201, Landover, MD 20785. http://www.CHADD.org

Closing the Gap, PO Box 68, Henderson, MN 56044. http://www.closingthe gap.com

Cognitive Concepts, Inc., 1123 Emerson St., Evanston, IL 60201. http://www.cogcon.com

Consulting Psychologists Press, 577 College Ave., Palo Alto, CA 94306.

Continental Press, 520 E. Bainbridge St., Elizabethtown, PA 17022.

Council for Exceptional Children, 1920 Association Dr., Reston, VA 22091. http://www.cec.sped.org

Crestwood Co., PO Box 04513, Milwaukee, WI 53204.

CTB/Macmillan/McGraw-Hill, 20 Ryan Ranch Rd., Monterey, CA 93940-5703.

Cuisenaire Co. of America, 12 Church St., New Rochelle, NY 10885.

Curriculum Associates, 5 Esquire Rd., PO Box 2001, North Billerica, MA 08162-0901. http://www.curriculumassociates.com

Davidson & Associates, 19840 Pioneer Ave., Torrance, CA 90503. http://www.davd.com

Devereux Foundation Press, 19 S. Waterloo Rd., Devon, PA 19333.

Don Johnston, Inc., 1000 N. Rand Rd., Building 115, PO Box 639, Wauconda, IL 60084-0639.

Dragon Systems, 320 Nevada St., Newton, MA 02160. http://www.dragonsys.com

EA*Kids, 533 Chard Court, Grayslake, IL 60030.

Edmark Corp., PO Box 97021, Redmond, WA 98073-9721. http://www.edmark.com

Educational Service, PO Box 219, Stevensville, MI 49127.

Educational Testing Service, Princeton, NJ 08540.

Educator's Publishing Service, 75 Moulton St., Cambridge, MA 02138-9101.

Franklin Learning Resources, Franklin Plaza, Burlington, NJ 08016-4907. (800) 266-5626.

Hartley, 9920 Pacific Heights Blvd., San Diego, CA 92121-4330.

Hawthorne Educational Services, 800 Gray Oak Dr., Columbia, MO 65201. (800) 542-1673

Marshall Hiskey Publications, 5640 Baldwin, Lincoln, NE 68507.

Houghton Mifflin Co., 222 Berkeley St., Boston, MA 02116-3764. http://www.hmco.com

Houston Press, University of Houston, Houston, TX 77000.

Humongous, 13110 NE 177th Place, Woodenville, WA 98072.

IntelliTools, 55 Leveroni Ct., Suite 9, Novato, CA 94949. (800) 899-6687, http://www.intellitools.com

International Dyslexia Associations (IDA) 8600 LaSalle Rd. Chester Bldg. #382, Baltimore, MD 21206-2044. http://www.interdys.org

International Dyslexia Society, http://www.intdys.org.

International Reading Association, 800 Barksdale Rd., Newark, DE 19711.

Jastak Associates, PO Box 3410, Wilmington, DE 19804-0250.

Keystone View Co., 2212 E. 12th St., Davenport, IA 52803.

Klamath Printing Co., 320 Lowell St., Klamath Falls, OR 97601.

Language Research Associates, PO Box 2085, Palm Springs, CA 92262.

Laureate Learning Systems, 110 E. Spring St., Winooski, VT 05404. http://www.laureatelearning.com

LDONLINE, http://www.ldonline.org

LDResources, 202 Lake Rd., New Preston, CT 06777. http://www.ldresources.com

Learning Disabilities Association of America, 4156 Library Rd., Pittsburgh, PA 15234. http://www.ldanatl.org

Learning Disabilities Association of Canada, 323 Chapel St., Ottawa, Ontario, Canada, KIN 7Z2.

Learning Resources, 380 N. Fairway Dr., Vernon Hills, IL 60061. (800) 222-3909, http://www.learningresources.com

The Learning Co., 6493 Kaiser Dr., Fremont, CA 94555. http://www.learningco.com

Lekotek, 2100 N. Ridge Ave., Evanston, IL 60201. (847) 328-0001, http://www.lekotek.org

Lexia Software. http://www.lexialearning.com

Lindamood-Bell Learning Process, 416 Higeura St., San Luis Obispo, CA 93401.

Living Books, 160 Pacific Ave. Mall, San Francisco, CA 94111.

Love Publishing Co., 6635 E. Villanova Pl., Denver, CO 80222.

Mafex Associates, 90 Cherry St., PO Box 519, Johnstown, PA 16906.

Maverick, 9801 Dupont Center, Bloomington, MN 55431.

McCormick-Mathers Publishing Co., 450 W. 33rd St., New York, NY 10001.

MECC, 6160 Summit Dr. N., St. Paul, MN 55430-4003.

Charles E. Merrill, 1300 Alum Creek Dr., Columbus, OH 43216.

Mindscape Educational Software, 1345 Diversy Pkwy., Chicago, IL 60614.

Modern Curriculum Press, 13900 Prospect Rd., Cleveland, OH 44136.

MultiHealth Systems, 908 Niagara Falls Blvd., North Tonawanda, NY 14120-2060.

National Center for Learning Disabilities, 381 Park Ave. South, Suite 1401, New York, NY 10016. http://www.ncld.org

National Education Association Publications, 1201 16th St. NW, Washington, DC 20036.

Open Court Publishing Co., PO Box 599, La Salle, IL 61301.

Optimum Resources, 59 Hilltech La., Hilton Head Island, SC 29926. http://www.stickybear.com

Price Systems, PO Box 3271, Lawrence, KS 66044.

Pro-Ed, 5341 Industrial Oaks Blvd., Austin, TX 78735. http://www.proedinc.com

The Psychological Corp., 555 Academic Court, San Antonio, TX 78204-2498. http://www.psychcorp.com

Psychological Test Specialists, PO Box 9229, Missoula, MT 59807.

Queue, 338 Commerce Dr., Fairfield, CT 06430.

Reader's Digest Services, Educational Division, Pleasantville, NY 10570.
Recordings for the Blind and Dyslexic, 20 Roszel Rd., Princeton, NJ 08540.
Reitan Neuropsychology Laboratory, 1338 E. Edison St., Tucson, AZ 85719.
Research Press, Box 31773, Champaign, IL 61826.
Riverside Publishing Co., 425 Spring Lake Dr., Itaska, IL 60143. http://www.
    riverpub.com
RJ Cooper & Associates, 1 Athenauem Pl., Cambridge, MA 02142.
Roger Wagner Publishing, 1050 Pioneer Way, Suite P, El Cagon, CA 92020.
    http://www.care@hyperstudio.com

Scholastic Magazine and Book Services, 50 W. 44th St., New York, NY 10036.
Scholastic Software, 730 Broadway, Dept. JS, New York, NY 10003.
Sheffield Publishing Co., PO Box 357, 9009 Antioch Rd., Salem, WI 53168.
Scientific Learning Corp., 1995 University Ave., Suite 400, Berkeley, CA 94770-
    1074. http://www.scientificlearning.com
Skills Bank Corp., Parview Center 1, 7104 Ambassador Rd., Baltimore, MD
    21244. http://www.skillsbank.com
Slosson Educational Publications, PO Box 280, East Aurora, NY 14052.
Soft Key, 1 Athenaeum Pl., Cambridge, MA 02142.
SRA/Macmillan/McGraw-Hill, 220 E. Danieldale Rd., DeSoto, TX 75115-8815.
Steck-Vaughn Co., PO Box 26015, Austin, TX 78755. http://www.
    steck-vaughn.com
Stoelting Co., 1350 S. Kostner St., Chicago, IL 60623.
Sunburst Communications, 1010 Castleton St., Pleasantville, NY 10570. http://
    www.sunburst.com

Teachers College Press, Teachers College, Columbia University, 1234 Amsterdam
    Ave., New York, NY 10027.
Tom Snyder Productions, 80 Coolidge Hill Rd., Watertown, MA 02172-2817.
    http://www.teachsp.com
Train, Inc., Neshamini Plaza II, Suite 101, Bensalem, PA 19020.

UCLS Intervention Program for Children with Disabilities, 1000 Veteran Ave.,
    Room 2310, Los Angeles, CA 90095. email: twebb@pediatrics.medscho.
    ucla.edu
United States Government Printing Office, Superintendent of Documents, Washing-
    ton, DC 20025.

Vineyard Video Productions, Box 780L, West Tisbury, MA 02575. (800) 664-6119

Western Psychological Services, 12031 Wilshire Blvd., Los Angeles, CA 90025-
    1251.
WETA Video, 22-D Hollywood Ave., Ho-Ho-Kus, NJ 07423. (800) 343-5540
    (tel.), (201) 652-1973 (fax)
Wilson Language Training Co., 175 W. Main St., Millbury, MA 05127-4441.
    http://www.wilsonlanguage.com

APPENDIX E

Glossary

abstract-level instruction At this level of mathematics instruction, students manipulate symbols without the help of concrete objects or representational pictures or tallies.

accommodations Refers to adjustments and modifications within a general education program to meet the needs of students with disabilities. Required under Section 504 of the Rehabilitation Act.

achievement The measure of the child's level of academic skills, usually as measured by a test.

active learning Dynamic involvement in the learning process.

adapted physical education Physical education programs that have been modified to meet the needs of students with disabilities.

adaptive behavior scales A rating scale of information provided by an informant who knows the child (such as the parent). It is usually obtained during an interview with the parent and provides information about the student's self-help skills, communication skills, daily living skills, socialization, and motor skills.

affect Refers to children's perception of themselves.

alternative assessment Assessment procedures that, in contrast to traditional assessment, assess the child in the natural setting, use the school curriculum, and draw on what the child does in the classroom. Includes informal assessment measures.

annual goals General estimates of what the student will achieve in one year. These goals should represent the most essential needs of the student. Annual goals are part of the written individualized education program.

antecedent event In behavioral psychology, the situation that precedes the target behavior.

aphasia Impairment of the ability to use or understand oral language, usually associated with an injury or abnormality of the speech centers of the brain. Several classifications are used, including expressive aphasia, receptive aphasia, developmental aphasia, and acquired aphasia.

apraxia   Difficulty in directing one's motor movements.

assessment stage   This is the stage during which tests are given (multidisciplinary evaluation) and decisions are made (the case conference or IEP meeting).

assistive technology   Any technology that enables an individual with a disability to compensate for specific deficits. It includes low-tech or high-tech equipment.

attention deficit disorder (ADD)   Difficulty in concentrating and staying on a task. It may or may not be accompanied by hyperactivity. Used by the U.S. Department of Education.

attention deficit hyperactivity disorder (ADHD)   Difficulty in concentrating and staying on a task, accompanied by hyperactivity. The condition of ADHD is identified and defined by the American Psychiatric Association's *Diagnostic and Statistical Manual of Mental Disorders,* fourth edition.

attribution   A person's ideas concerning the causes of his or her successes and failures.

audiology   A discipline that spans a number of functions, including the testing and measurement of hearing, the diagnosis and rehabilitation of those who are deaf and hard-of-hearing, the scientific study of the physical process of hearing, and the broadening of knowledge and understanding of the hearing process.

auditory blending   The ability to synthesize the phonemes of a word in recognizing the entire word. In an auditory blending test, the individual sounds of a word are pronounced with separations between each phoneme sound. The child must combine the individual sounds to say and recognize the word.

auditory discrimination   The ability to recognize a difference between phoneme sounds; also the ability to identify words that are the same and words that are different when the difference is a single phoneme element (for example, *big-pig*).

auditory perception   The ability to recognize or interpret what is heard.

authentic assessment   Assessment that makes realistic demands on the child, is set in real-life contexts, and is based on the child's curriculum.

automaticity   In cognitive learning theory, the condition in which learning has become almost subconscious and therefore requires little processing effort.

background knowledge   Information and experiences that are gained about the topic of instruction or about a reading selection.

back-to-basics movement   Educational instruction that emphasizes intensive teaching of academic skills. In reading, the emphasis is on word-recognition skills; in mathematics, it is on computation facts.

basal readers   A sequential and interrelated set of books and supportive material intended to provide the basic material for the development of fundamental reading skills.

basic skills instruction   Instruction focusing on direct teaching, especially in reading and mathematics. Students receive instruction at a level that approximates their achievement or instructional level.

behavior analysis   The process of determining the subskills or steps needed to accomplish a task.

behavioral approach   An approach to teaching that concentrates on the sequence of learning skills and on changing a child's behavior through contingencies (such as reward, punishment, and so on).

behavioral unit   In behavioral psychology, the core unit that constitutes an action and its environment. It consists of the antecedent event, the target behavior, and the consequent event.

benchmarks   A term used in the 1997 IDEA, referring to short-term objectives.

bibliotherapy   A technique of using characters in books to help children work through personal problems.

bilingual approach   A teaching method in which students use their native language for part of the instructional day and English for part of the instructional day.

brain electrical activity mapping (BEAM)   A procedure using a machine to monitor brain wave activity.

brain-injured child   A child who before, during, or after birth has received an injury to or suffered an infection of the brain. As a result of such organic impairment, there are disturbances that prevent or impede the normal learning process.

case conference meeting   The Individual Education Program (IEP) meeting at which decisions are made about the child's IEP.

case history   A compilation of the student's background, development, and other information. Case-history information is usually obtained from parents and from the student's school and medical histories. Often this information is obtained by interview.

center-based program   A program offered at a central facility for comprehensive services for young children and delivered by staff members with expertise in disciplines related to intervention and therapy for young children.

central nervous system   The organic system comprising the brain and the spinal cord.

central nervous system dysfunction   A disorder in learning caused by an impairment in brain function.

cerebral dominance   The theory that one hemisphere of the brain controls major functions. In most individuals, the left side of the brain controls language function and, in this theory, is considered the dominant hemisphere.

cerebral hemisphere   One of the two halves (the right hemisphere and the left hemisphere) that constitute the human brain.

Child Service Demonstration Centers (CSDCs)   Federally supported demonstration programs for children with learning disabilities.

Child-Find   Ways of locating young children with disabilities in the community.

children at risk   Children who are at risk for poor development and learning failure. Three categories of at risk are established risk, biological risk, and environmental risk.

Children with Specific Learning Disabilities Act (PL 91–230) A law passed in 1969 that first recognized children with learning disabilities.

clinical teaching   A method of teaching that tailors learning experiences to the unique needs of a particular child.

cloze procedure   A technique that is useful in testing, in teaching reading comprehension, and in determining readability (or difficulty level of the material). The cloze procedure involves deleting words from the text and inserting underlined blank spaces. Measurement is made by counting the number of blanks that students can correctly fill.

cognitive abilities   Clusters of human abilities that enable one to know, be aware, think, conceptualize, reason, criticize, and use abstractions.

cognitive emphasis curriculum   A curriculum that focuses on helping children develop thinking and cognitive abilities. Many of the concepts and curriculum programs of this approach stem directly from the ideas of Jean Piaget.

cognitive processing   The mental processes involved in thinking and learning, such as perception, memory, language, attention, concept formation, and problem solving.

cognitive psychology A branch of psychology that deals with the human processes of thinking, learning, and knowing.

conceptual disorder Difficulty in thinking and organizing thoughts.

concrete instruction A method of teaching in which the child manipulates real objects for learning.

concrete operations stage In Piaget's theory, the stage at which children can systematize and organize thoughts on the basis of past sensual experience.

consequent event In behavioral psychology, the reinforcement that follows the behavior.

constructive learning A theory of learning that is based on the idea that children can build their own mental structures. In mathematics, they create their own number ideas.

content-area teachers High school teachers whose primary orientation and expertise is the subject matter of their specialty. In contrast, elementary teachers tend to have an orientation and more expertise in child development.

context clues Clues that help readers recognize words through the meaning or context of the sentence or paragraph in which the words appear.

contingency contract A behavioral management strategy that entails a written agreement between the student and the teacher stating that the student will be able to do something he or she wants if he or she first completes a specified task.

continuum of alternative placements An array of different placements that should be available in a school system to meet the varied needs of students with disabilities.

co-occurring conditions A term used to describe conditions that exist along with an attention deficit disorder. Also called *comorbidity*.

coteaching The process of two professionals working together to seek a joint solution. Often refers to the joint efforts of the special education teacher and the general education classroom teacher.

criterion-referenced tests Tests that measure the student's abilities in specific skills (rather than tests that compare a student to others in a norm group).

cultural and linguistic diversity Representation by many different cultures and language groups.

current achievement level A student's present stage of performance in an academic area.

curriculum-based assessment Assessment designed to measure student performance on the student's curriculum activities and materials. The student's performance on an academic task is repeatedly measured and charted to assess changes in learning performance.

cursive writing The style of writing sometimes called script. The individual letters are joined in writing a word. Children typically learn cursive writing in third grade.

developmental and educational Refers to a child's achievement in developmental and academic areas.

developmental aphasia The term used to describe a child who has severe difficulty in acquiring oral language. This term implies that the disorder is related to a central nervous system dysfunction.

developmental delay A term designating that a child is slow in a specific aspect of development, such as in cognitive, physical, communication, social/emotional, or adaptive development. It is considered a noncategorical label for identifying a young child for services.

developmental learning disabilities   Deficits in the requisite skills that a child needs to learn academic subjects. They include motor, perceptual, language, and thinking skills.

developmental pediatrics   A medical specialty that combines expertise in child development with medical knowledge. The medical areas of pediatrics, genetics, neurology, and psychiatry are particularly important.

developmentally appropriate practice (DAP)   Guidelines for a curriculum for young children based on a constructivist philosophy emphasizing child-initiated learning, exploratory play, and the child's interests.

diagnostic teaching   Teaching designed for the purpose of gathering further information about a student.

diagnostic tests   Tests that provide specific evaluative information about a child's functioning.

direct instruction   A method associated with behavioral theories of instruction. The focus is directly on the curriculum or task to be taught and the steps needed to learn that task.

direct services   The learning disabilities teacher works directly with a child to provide instructional services.

direct teaching curriculum   A curriculum based on direct instruction of specific preselected learning and academic skills.

directed reading-thinking activity   A guided method of teaching reading comprehension in which readers first read a section of text, then predict what will happen next, and then read to verify the accuracy of the predictions.

discrepancy score   A mathematical calculation for quantifying the discrepancy between the student's current achievement and his or her potential.

distractibility   The tendency to attend to irrelevant external stimuli, a practice which detracts from attending to the task at hand.

drafting   A stage in the writing process in which a preliminary version of the written product is developed.

dynamic assessment   Evaluation of a student by noting how the student performs during instruction in an interactive teaching environment.

dyscalculia   A medical term indicating lack of ability to perform mathematical functions. The condition is associated with neurological dysfunction.

dysgraphia   Extremely poor handwriting or the inability to perform the motor movements required for handwriting. The condition is associated with neurological dysfunction.

dyslexia   A severe reading disorder in which the individual cannot learn to read or does not acquire fluent and efficient reading skills. Research suggests that there is a connection between dyslexia and neurological dysfunction.

dysnomia   A deficiency in remembering and expressing words. Children with dysnomia may substitute a word like thing for many objects when they cannot remember the name of the object. They may attempt to use other expressions to talk around the subject.

early literacy   The child's early entrance into the world of words, language, and stories. Literacy emerges in children through simultaneous experiences with oral language, reading, and writing.

ecological system   The several environments within which an individual lives and grows, including home and school, as well as social and cultural environments.

educational reform movement   A general movement throughout the United States to improve education in schools. As a result of educational reform, curriculum requirements in high schools have become more stringent.

eligibility criteria   Standards for determining whether a student can be classified as having learning disabilities and will be eligible for learning disabilities services.

email   Electronic mail allows a user to send messages to another user's private "mailbox" within the host computer of the electronic network.

enrichment curriculum   A preschool curriculum based on a maturational view of child development. This "traditional" program of nursery schools assumes a natural growth sequence for the young child's abilities within a nurturing environment.

ESL (English as a second language) approach   A method of teaching English to students whose native language is not English.

executive control   A component in the information-processing model that refers to the ability to control and direct one's own learning. It is also referred to as *metacognition.*

explicit code-emphasis instruction   Systematic and direct teaching of decoding and phonics skills.

explicit instruction   Teachers are clear about what should be taught and how it should be done. Students are not left to make inferences from experiences on their own.

explicit teaching   *See* explicit instruction.

expressive language disorder   Difficulty in using language (or speaking).

Feingold diet   A diet that eliminates artificial flavors, artificial preservatives, and artificial colors in an attempt to control hyperactivity in children. (*See* food additives.)

fluent reading   The act of reading quickly and smoothly. Fluency requires the reader to recognize words easily. The word-identification process must be automatic, not a conscious deliberate effort.

food additives   Artificial flavors, artificial preservatives, and artificial colors that are put into food. (*See* Feingold diet.)

formal operations stage   In Piaget's theory, the stage at which children can work with abstractions.

formal standardized tests   Commercially prepared tests that have been used with and standardized on large groups of students. Manuals that accompany the tests provide derived scores on student performance, such as grade scores, age scores, percentiles, and standard scores.

full inclusion   The policy of placing and instructing all children, including all categories of disability and levels of severity, in their neighborhood school and in the general education classroom.

functional magnetic resonance imaging (fMRI)   A new MRI method for studying the live human brain at work.

functional or survival skills instruction   Teaching survival skills to enable students to get along in the outside world.

general education classroom   The regular class, in which most students in school receive instruction.

general tests   Tests that provide overall scores but not diagnostic information.

giftedness   Refers to children and youth who display evidence of high performance capability in areas such as intellectual, creative, artistic, or leadership spheres or in specific academic fields, and who require services or activities not ordinarily provided by the school in order to develop such capabilities.

grapheme The written representation of a phoneme sound.

graphic organizer Visual representation of concepts, knowledge, or information that incorporates both text and pictures to make the material easier to understand.

Head Start A preschool program intended to provide compensatory educational experiences for children from low-income families who might otherwise come to school unprepared and unmotivated to learn. Head Start is sponsored by the Office of Child Development.

home-based program A system of delivering intervention services to very young children in their homes. Parent(s) become the child's primary teacher. A professional child-care provider goes to the child's home, typically one to three times per week, to train the parent(s) to work with the child.

home-school coordination A behavior management strategy for helping a child learn. Progress at school is reinforced at home.

hyperactivity A condition characterized by uncontrollable, haphazard, and poorly organized motor behavior. In young children, excessive gross-motor activity makes them appear to be on the go, and they have difficulty sitting still. Older children may be extremely restless or fidgety, may talk too much in class, or may constantly fight with friends, siblings, and classmates.

IDEA 1997 Acronym for the 1997 Individuals with Disabilities Education Act.

immersion approach An approach in which students receive extensive exposure to a second language.

inclusion The policy of placing children into regular or general education classes for instruction.

inclusive environment Placing children with disabilities in an inclusive or regular classroom with typical children.

indirect services The learning disabilities teacher works with the classroom teacher as a consultant to provide services for a child with a learning disability.

individualized education program (IEP) The written plan for the education of an individual student with learning disabilities. The plan must meet requirements specified in the rules and regulations of IDEA.

Individualized Family Service Plan (IFSP) A plan for young children that includes the family as well as the child.

Individuals with Disabilities Education Act (IDEA) The special education law assuring that students with disabilities have a free, appropriate, public education.

informal assessment measures Ways of evaluating performance that are not formal standardized tests. These can include teacher-made tests, diagnostic teaching, commercial nonstandardized tests, curriculum-based assessment, and so on.

informal reading inventory An informal method of assessing the reading level of a student by having the student orally read successively more difficult passages.

information processing A systems approach to cognitive processing. The information processing model emphasizes the flow of information, the memory system, and the interrelationships among the elements of cognitive processes.

Interagency Committee on Learning Disabilities (ICLD) A committee commissioned by the U.S. Congress and made up of representatives from twelve agencies of the Department of Health and Human Services and the Department of Education to develop a federal definition of learning disabilities.

invented spelling   The beginning writer's attempt to write words. The young writer attends to the sound units and associates letters with them in a systematic, although unconventional, way.

keyboarding   The process of typing on a computer keyboard.

kinesthetic perception   Perception obtained through body movements and muscle feeling, such as the awareness of positions taken by different parts of the body and bodily feelings of muscular contraction, tension, and relaxation.

language delay   Slowness in the acquisition of language. The child with a language delay may not be talking at all or may be using very little language at an age when language normally develops.

language difference   A language problem of students who use nonstandard English and whose native language is not English. A language difference can interfere with school learning.

language disorder   The term that refers to children with a language delay or language disabilities.

language experience method   A method of teaching reading based on the experiences and language of the reader. The method involves the generation of experience-based materials that are dictated by the student, written by the teacher, and then used as the material for teaching reading.

lateral preference   A tendency to use either the right or left side of the body or to favor using the hand, foot, eye, or ear of one side of the body.

lead agency   The agency with primary responsibility for programs for young children with disabilities. The governor of each state appoints the lead agency for infants and toddlers from birth through age 2. The state education agency is the lead agency for preschoolers ages 3 through 5.

learned helplessness   A trait of students with learning disabilities in which they exhibit passiveness and do not take on the responsibility for their own learning.

learning disabilities   A disorder in one or more of the basic processes involved in understanding spoken or written language. It may show up as a problem in listening, thinking, speaking, reading, writing, or spelling or in a person's ability to do math, despite at least average intelligence. The term does not include children who have learning problems which are primarily the result of visual, hearing, or physical handicaps, mental retardation, or emotional disturbance, or of environmental, cultural, or economic disadvantage. Individuals with learning disabilities encounter difficulty in one or more of seven areas: (1) receptive language, (2) expressive language, (3) basic reading skill, (4) reading comprehension, (5) written expression, (6) mathematics calculations, or (7) mathematics reasoning.

learning quotient   A score that reports a discrepancy between what the child is capable of achieving and what he or she has actually achieved.

learning strategies approach (instruction)   A series of methods to help students direct their own learning, focusing on how students learn rather than on what they learn.

learning strategies instruction   *See* learning strategies approach.

least restrictive environment   (LRE) A term in special education law that indicates that children with disabilities should be placed in an environment that has typical or nondisabled children.

life skills   The knowledge and abilities that a student needs to adapt to real-life situations.

limited English proficiency (LEP)   The term used to describe students whose native language is not English and who also have difficulty understanding and using English.

linguistic approach to spelling   A theory of word selection and instruction in spelling. It is based on the belief that the spelling of English is sufficiently rule-covered to warrant a method of selection and instruction that stresses phonological, morphological, and syntactic rules or word patterns.

linguistics   The scientific study of the patterns, nature, development, function, and use of human language.

long-term memory   Permanent memory storage that retains information for an extended period of time.

magnetic resonance imaging (MRI)   An advanced neurology device that converts signals into a shape on a video screen, thereby permitting the study of the living brain.

mainstreaming   Placing children with disabilities within the general education classroom.

manuscript writing   The form of handwriting sometimes called *printing*. This form of writing, closer to the printed form, is easier to learn than cursive writing because it consists of only circles and straight lines.

mastery learning   An approach that is compatible with instructional methods advocated by behavioral psychologists. It is based on sequential steps. Instructional programs using this approach are highly structured and carefully sequenced. They require very directive teaching.

materials approach   An approach to teaching that is based on the materials used for instruction.

math anxiety   Refers to a debilitating emotional reaction to mathematics situations.

mathematics computation   The basic mathematical operations, consisting of addition, subtraction, multiplication, division, fractions, decimals, and percentages.

mathematics problem solving   The kind of thinking needed to solve mathematics problems. The individual must analyze and interpret information as the basis for making selections and decisions.

mediation   A process of resolving disputes between the parent and the school in a nonadversarial fashion.

megavitamins   Massive doses of vitamins, sometimes given as orally administered pills, capsules, or liquids to treat children with learning disabilities.

mental retardation   Significantly subaverage general intellectual functioning existing concurrently with deficits in adaptive behavior and manifest during the developmental period.

metacognition   The ability to facilitate learning by taking control and directing one's own thinking process.

mind mapping   A technique that employs a pictorial method to transfer ideas from a student's mind onto a piece of paper.

minimal brain dysfunction (MBD)   A term that refers to mild or minimal neurological abnormality that causes learning difficulties.

miscue analysis   An evaluation of the errors the student makes in oral reading.

modern math   A widely used math curriculum of the 1970s, designed to teach the concepts underlying mathematics instead of the mechanics of arithmetic.

modification   Reasonable changes to accommodate needs of students with disabilities in general education classrooms.

morpheme   The smallest meaning unit of a language system.

morphology   The linguistic system of meaning units in any particular language; for example, the word *played* contains two meaning units (or morphemes): play + ed (past tense).

multidisciplinary evaluation   The assessment process in which specialists from several disciplines evaluate a child and coordinate their findings.

multiple intelligences   Many different talents or intelligences, such as verbal or linguistic intelligence and visual or spatial intelligence.

multisensory methods   A collection of programs based on the Orton-Gillingham method that use several sensory avenues to teaching reading.

multistore memory system   The central idea in the information-processing model of learning. Information is seen as flowing among three types of memory: the sensory register, short-term memory, and long-term memory.

National Joint Committee on Learning Disabilities (NJCLD)   An organization of representatives from several professional organizations and disciplines involved with learning disabilities.

NCTM   National Council of Teachers of Mathematics.

negative reinforcement   An event following a response that decreases the likelihood that the response will occur again.

neurological impress method   An approach for teaching reading to students with severe reading disabilities that consists of a system of rapid-unison reading by the student and the instructor.

neurology   A medical specialty concerned with the development and functioning of the central nervous system.

neuropsychology   A discipline that combines neurology and psychology and studies the relationship between brain function and behavior.

neurosciences   Disciplines that are involved with the study of the brain and its functions.

neurotransmitter   The chemicals that transmit messages from one cell to another across the synapse (a microscopic space between nerve cells).

nonverbal learning disabilities   Poor skills in nonacademic areas of learning, such as poor social skills.

nonverbal learning disorders   *See* nonverbal learning disabilities.

norm-referenced tests   standardized tests that compare a child's performance to that of other children of the same age.

number line   A sequence of numbers forming a straight line that allows the student to manipulate computation directly. Number lines help students develop an understanding of number symbols and their relationship to each other.

observation   Careful watching of a student's behavior, usually in the classroom setting.

occupational therapist   A therapist who is trained in brain physiology and function and who prescribes exercises to improve motor and sensory integration.

one-to-one correspondence   A relationship in which one element of a set is paired with one and only one element of a second set.

one-to-one instruction   Teaching with one teacher and one student.

ophthalmologist   A medical specialist concerned with the physiology of the eye, its organic aspects, diseases, and structure.

oral expressive language   The skills required to produce spoken language for communication with other individuals. Difficulty in producing spoken language is called *expressive language disorder.*

oral receptive language   Understanding of the language spoken by others. Listening is a receptive oral language skill.

otitis media   Middle-ear infection that may cause temporary hearing loss and may impede language development.

otologist   The medical specialist responsible for the diagnosis and treatment of auditory disorders.

parent support groups   Small groups of parents who meet to obtain information about their children with disabilities and to discuss common problems.

parents' rights   Used in the 1997 IDEA for procedural safeguards to protect the rights of parents.

Part B   The part of the law (IDEA) that refers to regulations for children with disabilities. In reference to early childhood, Part B covers preschoolers with disabilities ages 3 through 5.

Part C   The part of the law (IDEA) that covers infants and toddlers from birth through age 2.

passive learning style   A characteristic of students with learning disabilities who tend to wait until the teacher directs them and tells them what to do. A lack of interest in learning. (*See* learned helplessness.)

pedagogy   The art of teaching.

peer tutoring   A method of instruction in which the student is taught by a peer or classmate.

perception   The process of recognizing and interpreting information received through the senses.

perceptual disorder   A disturbance in the ability to perceive objects, relations, or qualities; difficulty in the interpretation of sensory stimulation.

perceptual modality concept   The notion that children have preferred channels for learning (for example, auditory or visual). Information on the child's perceptual strengths and weaknesses is used in planning instruction.

perceptual-motor behavior   Behavior that integrates perceptual input and motor output.

perceptual-motor match   Kephart's term for the process of comparing and collating the two kinds of input information. Perceptual data become meaningful when correlated with previously learned motor information.

perceptual-motor skill   A behavior that requires the efficient interaction of visual perception with motor actions.

perceptual-motor theory   The theory that a stable concept of the world depends on being able to correlate perceptions and motor development.

performance assessment   A method of assessing students by observing and assessing what they actually do in the classroom.

performance tests   Standards in the content areas that all students are expected to meet.

perseveration   The behavior of being locked into continually performing an action.

personal writing   Writing about personal ideas. There are fewer requirements in terms of form than for functional writing.

phoneme   The smallest sound unit of a language system.

phonics   An application of phonetics to the teaching of reading in which the sound (or phoneme) of a language is related to the equivalent written symbol (or grapheme).

phonological awareness   A child's recognition of the sounds of language. The child must understand that speech can be segmented into syllables and phonemic units.

phonology   The linguistic system of speech sounds in a particular language. The word *cat,* for example, has three sounds (or phonemes).

place value   The aspect of the number system that assigns specific significance to the position a digit holds in a numeral.

placement   The selection of the appropriate setting for teaching a child.

portfolio assessment   A method of evaluating student progress by analyzing samples of the student's classroom work.

positron emission tomography (PET)   A procedure that permits one to measure metabolism within the brain.

positive reinforcement   An event following a response that increases the likeli-hood that the person will make a similar response in similar situations in the future.

potential for learning   A term that refers to intellectual ability, whether measured by an intelligence test, a test of cognitive abilities, clinical judgment, or other means.

pragmatics   The social side of language; the social context and social customs surrounding language.

precursor skills   Skills that are necessary for academic learning, such as motor and perceptual skills and language skills.

precursors   Early signs of learning problems in young children.

Premack principle   A behavioral method using preferred activities to reinforce less preferred activities. This concept is also referred to as "Grandma's Rule": for example, "If you finish your vegetables, you can have dessert."

preoperational stage   One of Piaget's developmental stages of learning. During this stage children make intuitive judgments about relationships and also begin to think with symbols.

prereferral activities   Preventive procedures taken prior to referral for special education evaluation and intended to help regular teachers work more successfully with the child in the regular classroom.

present levels of educational performance   The levels at which the student is currently achieving in various developmental and academic areas. The written individualized education program must include a statement of the child's present levels of educational performance.

prewriting   The first step of the writing process, in which writers evoke and gather ideas for writing.

primary language   The child's first language, usually oral language. In relation to bilingual students it can refer to the student's native language.

problem solving   The kind of thinking needed to work out mathematics word problems.

procedural safeguards   Regulations in federal law that are designed to protect the rights of students with learning disabilities and their parents.

psychological processing disorders   A phrase in the federal definition of learning disabilities that refers to disabilities in visual or auditory perception, memory, or language.

psychotherapeutic approach   An approach to teaching that concentrates on the student's feelings and relationship with the teacher.

Public Law 94–142   Public Law 94–142 is the Education for All Handicapped Children Act. It was passed by Congress in 1975. The law guarantees a free and appropriate public education to children with disabilities. This law was reauthorized in 1990 and is in the reauthorization of the Individuals with Disabilities Education Act (IDEA) that was implemented in 1997.

Public Law 99–457   A law that targets young children with disabilities. The provisions are incorporated in IDEA 1997.

Public Law 101–476   This is the Individuals with Disabilities Education Act (IDEA) passed by Congress in 1990. It updated PL 94–142, the education of Handicapped Children Act.

Public Law 105–17   The 1997 Individuals with Disabilities Education Act that was passed by Congress in 1997.

rapid automatized naming (RAN)   The ability to quickly and automatically name objects and pictures of objects.

rapport   A close relationship between teacher and child that is based on total acceptance of the child as a human being worthy of respect.

rating scales   A ranking of student behavior as judged by a parent, teacher, or other informant.

readiness   The state of maturational development that is necessary before a skill can be learned.

reading comprehension   Understanding of the meaning of printed text.

Reading Recovery   A reading program first used in New Zealand in which first graders who rank very low in reading are selected for a period of intensive reading instruction.

reasonable accommodations   The phrase used in Section 504 of the Rehabilitation Act to describe what can fairly easily be done in a setting to make adjustments for an individual with a disability.

reauthorized Individuals with Disabilities Education Act   PL 105–17, passed in 1997. A special education law that reauthorized and updated the 1990 IDEA.

receptive language disorder   Difficulty in understanding oral language or listening.

reciprocal teaching   A method of teaching through a social interactive dialogue between teacher and student which emphasizes the development of thinking processes.

referral   The initial request to consider a student for a special education evaluation.

referral stages   The initial stages of the IEP process. They include the prereferral activities and the referral activities.

regular education classroom   *See* general education classroom.

regular education initiative   A proposal advanced by the Office of Special Education and Rehabilitative Services (OSERS) that students with many types of learning problems and low achievers can be served effectively through the regular education classroom.

regulations   The Department of Education rules to implement the 1997 Individuals with Disabilities Education Act.

representational-level instruction   Mathematics instruction that is between the concrete and abstract levels. It is semiconcrete in that students use pictures or tallies to represent objects as they do mathematics problems.

residential school   An educational institution in which students live away from home and receive their education. A residential school may be sponsored by a government agency or may be privately managed.

resource room   A special instructional setting, usually a room within a school. In this room, small groups of children meet with a special education teacher for special instruction for a portion of the day. Children spend the remainder of the day in the general education classrooms.

response cost   A punishment for a behavior, or response, in which positive reinforcers are withdrawn.

revising   A stage of the writing process in which the writer reworks a draft of a written product.

scaffolded instruction   Teacher supports for the student, particularly at the initial stage of learning a task.

scotopic sensitivity syndrome   A difficulty in processing full-spectrum light efficiently, which causes a reading disorder.

screening   A type of assessment using ways to survey many children quickly to identify those who may need special services.

secondary language system   The student's second language, usually written language. In the case of bilingual students, it may refer to their second language (English).

Section 504 of the Rehabilitation Act   Federal law that covers all agencies and institutions receiving financial assistance and that requires that no otherwise qualified handicapped individual shall be excluded from participation.

self-esteem   Feelings of self-worth, self-confidence, and self-concept that provide an experience of success.

semantics   A linguistic term referring to the vocabulary system of language.

sensorimotor period   One of Piaget's developmental stages of learning. During this stage children learn through senses and movements and by interacting with the physical environment.

sensory integration theory   A theory stemming from the field of occupational therapy that physical exercises can modify the brain.

sensory register   The first memory system in the information-processing model that interprets and maintains memory information long enough for it to be perceived and analyzed.

separate class   A special class for children with disabilities taught by a teacher with special training. Children in a separate class usually spend most of the day in this setting.

separate school   A school for students with learning disabilities that students attend during the day. They return home after school.

service coordinator   The professional who serves as a case manager for children ages birth through 2 years and their families.

severe discrepancy   A significant difference between a child's current achievement and intellectual potential.

shaping behavior   *See* successive approximations.

sharing with an audience   A stage of the writing process in which the final written product is read by others.

sheltered English   A method of teaching children who have some proficiency in English to learn English more rapidly by having them use materials written in English.

short-term instructional objectives   Specific steps to be accomplished to reach the annual goal written in the individualized education program.

short-term (working) memory   A second memory storage within the information-processing model. It is a temporary storage facility serving as working memory as a problem receives one's conscious attention.

sight words   Words that a student recognizes instantly, without hesitation or further analysis.

skills sequence   The sequence of steps involved in learning a skill.

social perception   The ability to understand social situations, as well as sensitivity to the feelings of others.

social skills   Skills necessary for meeting the basic social demands of everyday life.

soft neurological signs   Minimal or subtle neurological deviations that some neurologists use as indicators of mild neurological dysfunction.

sound counting   Activities to help students count the number of sounds in a word. Counters (such as Popsicle sticks or tongue depressors) are often used.

spatial relationship   Concepts such as up-down, over-under, top-bottom, high-low, near-far, beginning-end, and across. A disturbance in spatial relationship can interfere with the visualization of the entire number system.

speech disorder   A disorder of articulation, fluency, or voice.

stages of acceptance   The different emotions parents go through when they learn they have a child with disabilities.

stages of child development approach   An approach to teaching that is based on a model of child development.

stages of learning   The stages a person goes through in mastering material, such as acquisition, proficiency, maintenance, and generalization.

Standard English   The linguistic system of English recognized by the literate culture and used in school.

strategies intervention model (SIM)   An instructional method for teaching learning strategies to adolescents with learning disabilities.

structural analysis   The recognition of words through the analysis of meaningful word units, such as prefixes, suffixes, root words, compound words, and syllables.

successive approximations   A behavioral method that is also referred to as *shaping behavior*. Desired goals are broken down into a sequence of ordered steps or tasks, behavior that the child already emits is reinforced, and then requirements are gradually increased with appropriate reinforcement until the child reaches the desired goal.

syntax   The grammar system of a language; the linguistic rules of word order; the function of words in a sentence.

tactile perception   Perception obtained through the sense of touch via the fingers and skin surfaces.

task analysis   A teaching approach that analyzes an activity by breaking it down into a sequence of steps.

Technology Act   Technology-Related Assistance for Individuals with Disabilities Act of 1994 (PL 103–218).

temporal acoustical processing   The ability to process sounds of language rapidly enough to distinguish speech sounds and words.

time concepts   The sense of time, which is not easily comprehended by some students with learning disabilities, who may be poor at estimating the span of an hour, a minute, several hours, or a weekend and may have difficulty estimating how long a task will take. Trouble with time concepts characterizes students with mathematics disabilities.

token reinforcers   Reinforcements that are accumulated to be exchanged at a later time for a more meaningful "back-up" reinforcer.

traditional assessment   An evaluation procedure that measures students with standard norm-referenced tests.

transition   The process of moving from one type of program to another. In early childhood programs it can be from the birth-through-2 program to the ages 3-through-5 program, or from the ages 3-through-5 program to another educational placement. For adolescents transition refers to the passage from school to the adult world.

transition planning   Planning for making the change from being a student to being an adult. Students with learning disabilities need help with this process.

tutorial instruction   Teaching designed to help students meet requirements in their specific academic-content subjects and to achieve success in the regular curriculum. This teaching is usually accomplished through one-to-one instruction or in small groups.

VAKT   The abbreviation for *visual, auditory, kinesthetic,* and *tactile* learning, a multisensory approach for teaching reading that stimulates all avenues of sensory input simultaneously.

visual discrimination   The ability to note visual differences or similarities between objects, including letters and words.

visual perception   The identification, organization, and interpretation of sensory data received by the individual through the eye.

whole language   Whole language is a philosophy about reading that embraces the wholeness of the integrated language forms—oral language, reading, and writing. It makes extensive use of literary materials.

whole-language instruction   Teaching that uses the whole-language philosophy by integrating oral language, reading, and writing. It uses a wide variety of books and literary materials.

word-frequency approach to spelling   A method of word selection and instruction for spelling. Words are selected for spelling instruction on the basis of how frequently they are used in writing.

word processing   Writing with a computer (as contrasted with writing by hand or on a conventional typewriter).

word-recognition skills   Strategies for recognizing words, including phonics, sight words, context clues, structural analysis, and combinations of these strategies.

word retrieval   The ability to recall words.

work-study program   A high school program in which students work on a job for a portion of the day and go to school for a portion of the day.

World Wide Web (WWW)   Interconnected pages or sites with textual and graphic information on the Internet.

writing process   The process whereby writers go through a series of stages during writing. The four stages of the writing process are (1) prewriting, (2) writing or drafting, (3) revising, and (4) sharing with an audience.

zone of proximal development (ZPD)   A term, used by Vygotsky, envisioning a range of levels of difficulty for a student. The lower end is very easy, the upper end beyond the student's capacity. The ZPD is the midpoint and is an appropriate level for learning.

Final Regulations for the 1997 Individuals with Disabilities Education Act (IDEA 1997)

The final regulations accompanying the Individuals with Disabilities Education Act (IDEA) amendments of 1997 appear in the March 12, 1999, Federal Register. Some of the major issues addressed in this package of regulations are provided in this appendix.

INDIVIDUALIZED EDUCATION PROGRAMS AND GENERAL CURRICULUM

Prior to 1997, the law did not specifically address general curriculum involvement of disabled students. The 1997 amendments shifted the focus of the IDEA to one of improving teaching and learning, with a specific focus on the individualized education program (IEP) as the primary tool for enhancing the child's involvement and progress in the general curriculum.

The final regulations reflect the new statutory language which requires that the IEP for each child with a disability include

- a statement of the child's present levels of educational performance including how the child's disability affects the child's involvement and progress in the general curriculum;
- a statement of measurable annual goals related to meeting the child's disability-related needs in order to enable the child to be involved and progress in the general curriculum;
- a statement of the special education and related services, and supplementary aids and services; and
- a statement of the program modifications or supports for school personnel that will be provided for the child to advance appropriately toward attaining the annual goals, be involved and progress in the general

curriculum, and participate in extra-curricular and other nonacademic activities and to be educated and participate with other children with disabilities and nondisabled children.

GENERAL STATE AND DISTRICT-WIDE ASSESSMENTS

The 1997 amendments specifically require that, as a condition of state eligibility for funding under Part B of IDEA, children with disabilities are included in general state and district-wide assessment programs. The amendments also address timelines and reporting requirements.

The *final regulations* essentially incorporate these statutory provisions on general state and district-wide assessments verbatim. These provisions require that states and local education agencies (LEAs) must

- provide for the participation of children with disabilities in general state and district-wide assessments, with appropriate accommodations and modifications in administration, if necessary;
- provide for the conduct of alternate assessments not later than July 1, 2000, for children who cannot participate in the general assessment programs; and
- make available and report to the public the assessment results of disabled children with the same frequency and in the same detail as the assessment results of non-disabled children.

REGULAR EDUCATION TEACHER INVOLVEMENT

Prior to 1997, the law did not include a regular education teacher as a required member of the IEP team. Under the 1997 IDEA amendments, the IEP team for each child with a disability now must include at least one of the child's regular education teachers if the child is, or may be, participating in the regular education environment. The new law also indicates that the regular education teacher—to the extent appropriate—participates in the development, review, and revision of the IEP of the child.

The final regulations package clarifies that

- if a child has more than one regular education teacher, the LEA may designate which teacher (or teachers) will be on the IEP team;
- depending upon the child's needs and the purpose of the specific IEP meeting, the regular education teacher need not be required to participate in all decisions made as part of the meeting, be present throughout the entire meeting, or attend every meeting;
- the extent to which it would be appropriate for the regular education teacher member of the IEP team to participate in IEP meetings must be decided on a case-by-case basis; and
- each of the child's teachers, including the regular education teacher(s) and provider(s) must be informed of his or her responsibilities related

to implementing the child's IEP and the specific accommodations, modifications, and supports that must be provided for the child.

GRADUATION WITH A REGULAR DIPLOMA

Neither the old nor the revised IDEA speaks directly to the issue of students with disabilities graduating with a regular high school diploma. However, the 1997 amendments placed greater emphasis on involvement of disabled students in the general curriculum and in state and district-wide assessment programs.

The final regulations incorporate the Department of Education's long-standing policy clarifying that

- graduation from high school with a regular diploma is considered a change in placement requiring prior written notice;
- a student's right to free and appropriate public education (FAPE) is terminated upon graduation with a regular high school diploma. (The statutory requirement for reevaluation before a change in a student's eligibility does not apply.); and
- a student's right to FAPE is not terminated by any other kind of graduation certificate or diploma.

DISCIPLINE

Prior to 1997, the IDEA only specifically addressed the issue of discipline in a provision that allowed personnel to move a child to an interim alternative educational placement for up to forty-five days if the child brought a gun to school or to a school function. The IDEA 1997 incorporated prior court decisions and Department of Education policy that allow school personnel to remove a child for up to ten school days at a time for any violation of school rules as long as there is not a pattern. Additionally, a child with disabilities cannot be long-term suspended or expelled from school for behavior that is a manifestation of his or her disability, and services must continue for children with disabilities who are suspended or expelled from school. The IDEA 1997 also expanded the authority of school personnel to move a student to an interim alternative educational placement for up to forty-five days if the student is in knowing possession of any dangerous weapon or illegal drug or selling or soliciting the sale of controlled substances. The IDEA 1997 also added a new ability of schools to request a hearing officer to remove a child for up to forty-five days if keeping the child in his or her current placement is substantially likely to result in injury to the child or others. The amendments added provisions requiring schools to assess children's troubling behavior and to develop positive behavioral interventions to address that behavior. The provisions also defined how to determine whether behavior is a manifestation of a child's disability.

The final regulations incorporate these statutory provisions and provide additional specificity on a number of key issues.

Services During Periods of Disciplinary Removal

- Schools do not need to provide services during the first ten school days in a school year that a child is removed.

- During any subsequent removal that is for less than ten school days, schools provide services to the extent determined necessary to enable the child to appropriately progress in the general curriculum and appropriately advance toward achieving the goals of his or her IEP. In cases involving removals for ten school days or less, school personnel, in consultation with the child's special education teacher, make the service determination.

- During any long-term removal for behavior that is not a manifestation of disability, schools provide services to the extent determined necessary to enable the child to appropriately progress in the general curriculum and appropriately advance toward achieving the goals of his or her IEP. In cases involving removals for behavior that is not a manifestation of the child's disability, the child's IEP team makes the service determination.

Conducting Behavioral Assessments and Developing Behavioral Interventions

- Meetings of the IEP team to develop behavioral assessment plans or, if the child has one, to review the behavioral intervention plan are only required when the child has first been removed from his or her current placement for more than ten school days in a school year and when commencing a removal that constitutes a change in placement. If other subsequent removals occur, the IEP team members review the child's behavioral intervention plan and its implementation to determine if modifications are necessary and only meet if one or more team members believe that modifications are necessary.

Manifestation Determinations

Manifestation determinations are only required if a school is implementing a removal that constitutes a change of placement.

Change of Placement

The final regulations clarify that a change of placement occurs if a child is removed for more than ten consecutive school days or is subjected to a series of removals that constitute a pattern because they cumulate to more than ten school days in a school year, and because of factors such as the length of each removal, the total amount of time the child is removed, and the proximity of the removals to one another.

Removals of up to Ten School Days at a Time

The final regulations clarify that school personnel may remove a child with a disability for up to ten school days and for additional removals of up to ten school days for separate acts of misconduct as long as the removals do not constitute a pattern.

ATTENTION DEFICIT DISORDER AND ATTENTION DEFICIT HYPERACTIVITY DISORDER

Neither the old nor the revised IDEA included attention deficit disorder or attention deficit hyperactivity disorder as a separate disability category.

Relying on the Department of Education's long-standing policy, the final regulations clarify that

- ADD and ADHD have been listed as conditions that could render a child eligible under the "other health impaired" (OHI) category of Part B of IDEA and

- the term "limited strength, vitality, or alertness" in the definition of "OHI," when applied to children with ADD and ADHD, includes a child's heightened alertness to environmental stimuli that results in limited alertness with respect to the educational environment.

DEVELOPMENTAL DELAY

Prior to the 1997 IDEA amendments, states could define and require LEAs to use the developmental delay category for children ages three through five. The 1997 IDEA amendments allowed states to define developmental delay for children ages three through nine and authorized LEAs to choose to use the category and, if they do, they are required to use the state's definition.

The final regulations make the following clarifications:

- A state that adopts the term *developmental delay* determines whether it applies to children ages three through nine, or to a subset of that age range (e.g., ages three through five).

- If an LEA uses the term *developmental delay,* the LEA must conform to both the state's definition of that term and to the age range that has been adopted by the state.

- If the state does not adopt the term *developmental delay,* an LEA may not independently use that term as a basis for establishing a child's eligibility under Part B of IDEA.

- Any state or LEA that elects to use the term *developmental delay* for children ages three through nine may also use one or more of the disability categories for any child within that age range if it is determined, through the evaluation under Part B of the IDEA, that the child has an impairment under Part B of the IDEA and because of that impairment needs special education and related services.

DEFINITION OF DAY AND SCHOOL DAY

Prior to 1997, the law included only the term *day* that was interpreted by the Department of Education to mean *calendar day.* Now, the law uses the terms *day, business day,* and *school day.*

The final regulations clarify that

- *day* means a calendar day, unless otherwise indicated as business day or school day;

- *business day* means Monday through Friday, except for federal and state holidays, unless holidays are specifically included in the designation of business day;
- *school day* means any day (including a partial day) that children are in attendance at school for instructional purposes; and
- *school day* has the same meaning for all children with and without disabilities.

CHARTER SCHOOLS

The IDEA Amendments of 1997 contain two specific provisions on public charter schools:

1. In situations in which charter schools are public schools of the LEA, the LEA must serve children with disabilities in those schools in the same manner that it serves children with disabilities in its other schools. The LEA must also provide Part B funds to those schools in the same manner as it provides Part B funds to its other schools.

2. A state education agency (SEA) may not require a charter school that is an LEA to jointly establish its eligibility with another LEA unless it is explicitly permitted to do so under the state's charter school statute.

The final regulations clarify that

- Part B final regulations apply to all public agencies, including public charter schools that are not included as LEAs or Education Service Agencies (ESAs) and are not a school of an LEA or ESA;
- the term *local education agency* includes public charter schools that are established as an LEA under state law;
- the term *public agency* includes among the list of examples of a public agency, public charter schools that are not otherwise included as LEAs or ESAs and are not a school of an LEA or ESA;
- children with disabilities who attend public charter schools and their parents retain all rights under Part B of the IDEA; and
- compliance with Part B of the IDEA is required regardless of whether a public charter school receives Part B funds.

PARENTALLY PLACED CHILDREN WITH DISABILITIES IN PRIVATE SCHOOLS

Prior to 1997, the law did not extensively address the education of children with disabilities placed in private schools by their parents. These children were served based on the limited provisions of the statutes and on the Education Department's General Administrative Regulations (EDGAR) and the department's long-standing policy interpretation. The 1997 amendments included some of the old language and incorporated the Education Department's long-standing policy interpretation. Specifically, the final regulations clarify that

- the term "service plan" has been adopted for use in lieu of "IEP" for parentally placed children in private schools;

- Part B services must be provided in accordance with a "service plan" that, to the extent appropriate, meets specified IEP requirements;

- child-find activities for private school children with disabilities must be comparable to that in the public schools;

- public agencies must consult with representatives of parentally placed private school children with disabilities on how to conduct child-find activities for those children in a manner that is comparable to that for public school children;

- each LEA must consult with representatives of private school children with disabilities to decide how to conduct the annual count of the number of those children;

- the costs of child-find activities for private school children with disabilities may not be considered in determining whether the LEA met the minimum expenditure requirements; and

- the due process procedures under Part B apply to child-find activites for private school children with disabilities, including evaluations, but do not apply to the other provisions regarding children with disabilities enrolled by their parents in private schools.

*   *   *

For further information about the IDEA 1997 statute and implementing regulations, contact the Department of Education at (202)205-5465 or **http://www.ed.gov/offices/OSERS/IDEA.**

Source: IDEA Partnership Projects. Council for Exceptional Children. ASPIIRE and ILIAD. http://www.ideapractices.org.

Resources

Internet Resources

ADD Warehouse, 300 NW 70th Ave., Suite 102, Plantation, FL 33317. (954) 792-8100, (954) 792-8944, **http://www.addwarehouse.com**

Alva Access Group (Braille displays, "outspoken" software), 5801 Christie Ave., Suite 475, Emeryville, CA 94608. (510) 923-6280, **www.aagi.com/docs/oS-Mdesc.html**

Arkenstone, (a provider of reading systems for people with visual and reading disabilities, "scanning reader" software). **www.arkenstone.org.arknew.html**

Association on Higher Education and Disability (AHEAD), PO Box 21192, Columbus, OH 43221. (614) 488-4972, **http://www.ahead.org**

(C.H.A.D.D.) Children and Adults with ADHD, 8181 Professional Pl., Suite 201, Landover, MD 20785. (800) 233-4050, **http://www.CHADD.org**

Council for Exceptional Children, 1920 Association Dr., Reston, VA 20191-1589. (888) 232-7733, **http://www.cec.sped.org/bk/tec-jour.htm**

Cuisenaire Dale Seymour Publications (K–12 Math, Manipulatives, Science, Arts, Teacher Resources), 10 Bank St. White Plains, NY 10016-5026. (800) 237-3142, **http://www.cuisenaire.com**

Earobics Cognitive Concepts, 1123 Emerson St., Suite 202, Evanston, IL 60201. (888) 328-8199, **http://www.cogcon.com**

FastForWord, Scientific Learning Corp., 1995 University Ave., Suite 400, Berkeley, CA 94704-1074. (888) 665-9707, **http://www.scientificlearning.com**

615

International Dyslexia Association, Chester Building, 8600 La Salle Rd., Suite 382, Baltimore, MD 21286-2044. (410) 296-0232, http://www.interdys.org

The Laubach Program, Laubach Literacy Action, PO Box 131, Syracuse, NY 13210. (315) 422-6369, http://www.laubach.org

Laureat Learning Systems, 110 E. Spring St., Winooski, VT 05404. (802) 655-4710, http://www.laureatelearning.com

LD Online The Coordinated Campaign for Learning Disabilities (CCLD), http://www.ldonline.org

Lexia Software (phonics-based interactive reading software), 11A Lewis St., PO Box 466, Lincoln, MA 01773. (800) 435-3942, http://www.lexialearning.com

Literacy Volunteers of America, 635 James St., Syracuse, NY 13203. (800) 582-8812, http://www.205.185.23.173/home/body.html

Miami Science Museum. (305) 854-4242, http://www.miamisci.org

National Center for Learning Disabilities, 381 Park Ave. South, Suite 1401, New York, NY 10016. (888) 575-7373, (212) 545-7510, http://www.ncld.org

National School Boards Association, Institute for the Transfer of Technology to Education (ITTE). http://www.nsba.org/itte/index.html

NetLearn:Internet Learning Resources Directory. http://www.rgu.ac.uk/~sim/research/netlearn/web.html

Recordings for the Blind and Dyslexic, 20 Roszel Rd., Princeton, NJ 08540. (800) 221-4792, http://www.rfbd.org

Tools for Understanding (math concepts, online lessons for learning), John Woodward, Professor, School of Education, University of Puget Sound, 1500 N. Warner, Tacoma, WA 98416. http://www.ups.edu/community/tofu/

Universal Learning Co., ("ultimate reader" software), 39 Cross St., Peabody, MA 01960. http://www.universalearn.com/products/index.html

Video Resources

A child's first words. [Videotape]. This is a videotape on how speech and language development in children under age 4 can affect their ability to learn. It alerts parents to the milestones of good speech and language acquisition in children under age 4 and tells them how to get help if they need it. 18 minutes. $21. Learning Disabilities Association of America.

A leader's guide for youth with learning disabilities. [Videotape]. This video tape shows how leaders of groups can integrate individuals with learning disabilities into regular programs similar to scouts. This film, which includes comments by Dr. Larry Silver throughout, uses as an example the Boy Scouts. 10 minutes. $24.50. Learning Disabilities Association.

Activity-based intervention. [Videotape]. This practical videotape illustrates how activity-based intervention can be used to turn everyday events and natural interactions into opportunities to promote learning in young children who are considered at risk for developmental delays or who have mild to significant disabilities. 14 minutes. $39.00. Paul H. Brookes, P.O. Box 1-624, Baltimore, MD 21285-0624. Phone (800) 638-3775. **www.http://pbrookes .com**

ADHD: Inclusive instruction and collaborative practices. [Videotape]. This videotape is a presentation by Sandra Rief that shows ways that general education teachers can serve children with diverse needs in the regular classroom. 38 minutes. $99. National Professional Resources. 25 S. Regent St., Port Chester, NY 10573. Phone: (800) 453-7461, Fax: (914) 937-9327.

ADHD in the classroom: Strategies for teachers. [Videotape]. Russell Barkley presents a videotape designed to inform teachers of practical ways that will help them provide a better learning atmosphere for all of their students. ADD Warehouse, 300 Northwest 70th Avenue, Suite 102, Plantation, FL 33317. Contact by phone at (954) 792-8944 or at **http://www.addwarehouse.com**

ADHD: What do we know? [Videotape]. This videotape is narrated by a well-known ADHD expert, Russell A. Barkley. It discusses what is known about the condition of Attention Deficit Hyperactivity Disorder and assessment methods. 35 minutes. $75. Guilford Publications, Dept. 8A1, 72 Spring St., New York, NY 10012 (800) 365-7006.

All children learn differently. [Narrated by Steve Allen]. [Videotape]. Pittsburgh, PA: LDA. This video interviews 12 specialists in medicine perception, language, and education. It takes a nutritional-educational approach to the remediation of learning disabilities, calling for the "right professional team" for each person. 30 min. $42.

Emotional intelligence. [Videotape]. Daniel Goleman explains what emotional intelligence is, why (and how) it can be learned, and how it affects the work of educators and school professionals. 40 minutes. $89.95. Paul H. Brookes, P.O. Box 10624. Baltimore, MD 21285-0624. Phone (800) 638-3775. **http://www.pbrookes.com**

The employment interview and disclosure: Tips for job seekers with learning disabilities. [Videotape]. Very few of us have a natural talent for job interviewing. But it is a skill that all of us can learn. The first thing to realize is that verbal communication is only part of the interaction. This videotape covers all aspects of an interview, including résumé and cover letter, promptness, appearance, body language, and attitude. 25 minutes. $22.95. Learning Disabilities Association of America.

Enhancing strategies for instruction: Critical teaching behaviors. [Videotape]. This videotape demonstrates each of the teaching behaviors that are critical for teachers. Research on Learning at the University of Kansas. 30 minutes. $50. Edge Enterprise, P.O. Box 104, Lawrence, KS 66044. Phone: (785) 749-1473.

Every child is learning. [Videotape]. This is a videotape to help parents, teachers, and early-care providers recognize early warning signs for language and learning disabilities. 45 minutes. $89.95. National Center for Learning Disabilities, 381 Park Avenue, South Suite 1401, New York, NY 10016. Phone: (888) 575-7373.

Helping students master social skills. [Videotape]. This videotape describes ways to teach social skills from the learning strategies. It was developed at the Center for Research on Learning at the University of Kansas. 30 minutes. $50. Edge Enterprise, P.O. Box 104, Lawrence, KS 66044. Phone: (785) 749-1473.

Homework and learning disabilities. [Videotape]. This videotape offers practical techniques for solving homework problems. It clarifies responsibilities of teachers, students, and parents. 34 minutes. $99. The Menninger Clinic and Center for Learning Disabilities, P.O. Box 829, Topeka, KS 66601-0820. Phone: (800) 345-6036.

How are kids smart? Multiple Intelligences in the classroom. [Videotape]. Howard Gardner describes multiple intelligences and shows teachers and administrators how to use these strengths to enhance children's growth. 31 minutes. $69. Paul H. Brookes, P.O. Box 10624, Baltimore, MD 21285-0624. Phone (800) 638-3775. **http://www.pbrookes.com.**

How difficult can this be?—A learning disabilities workshop. [Videotape]. Ho-Ho-Kus, NJ: WETA Video. This unique video allow viewers to experience the same frustration, anxiety, and tension that children with learning disabilities face in their daily lives. Teachers, social workers, psychologists, parents, and friends who have participated in Richard Lavoie's workshop reflect upon their experience and the way it changed their approach to LD children. 45 min. $39.95. Contact WETA for orders.

How to help your child succeed in school: Strategies and guidance for parents of children with ADHD and/or learning disabilities. [Videotape]. Sandra Rief presents the most essential information needed for every parent of children with ADHD and /or learning disabilities to help their child succeed in school. This videotape includes developmental reading, writing, and math skills, building organization and study skills, surviving the daily homework assignments, and coping with learning difficulties. 56 minutes. $46. ADD Warehouse, 300 Northwest 70th Avenue, Suite 102, Plantation, FL 33317. (954) 792-8944.

How to help your child succeed in school. [Videotape]. This videotape presents strategies and guidance for parents of children with ADHD and/or learning disabilities in reading, writing, and math skills: organization and study skills; and ability to do daily homework assignments. Presented by Sandra Rief. 56 minutes. $49.95. Paul H. Brookes. P.O. Box 10624, Baltimore, MD 21285-0624. Phone (800) 638-3775. **http://www.pbrookes .com**

I'm not stupid. [Videotape]. Depicts the constant battle of the child with learning disabilities in school. It points our how the child is often misdiagnosed as slow, retarded, emotionally disturbed, or lazy. Recommended for parents, teachers, administrators, or students. $22. Learning Disabilities Association. (LDA).

Keys to success in learning strategies instruction. [Videotape]. This videotape explains the theory and procedures of learning strategies instruction developed at the Center for Research on Learning at the University of Kansas. 30 minutes. $75. Edge Enterprise, Inc., P.O. Box 104, Lawrence, KS 66044. Phone: (785) 749-1473.

Keys to success in social skills instruction. [Videotape]. This videotape describes the teaching of social skills from the learning strategies perspective. It was developed at the Center for Research on Learning at the University of Kansas. 30 minutes. $75. Edge Enterprises, Inc., P.O. Box 104, Lawrence, KS 66044. Phone: (785) 749-1473.

Last one picked, first one picked on. [Videotape]. Rick Lavoi addresses the social problems children with learning disabilities face and offers some practical solutions for teachers and parents. 60 minutes. $49.05. WETA.

Learning disabilities and self-esteem with Robert Brooks. Look what you've done! Stories of hope and resilience. [Videotape]. Whether they've failed a spelling test or dropped an easy pop fly, kids with learning disabilities hear those words far too often. It's no wonder they often give up hope. And it's no wonder we sometimes overlook what Dr. Robert Brooks calls the "every-day courage" of our children. Dr. Brooks, a nationally known expert on learning disabilities, says we need to find each child's "islands of competence" and then build on those strengths. He offers practical strategies for helping children develop the confidence and resilience they will need to succeed. 65 minutes. $49.95. WETA Video, 22-D Hollywood, Ave., Ho-Ho-Kus, NJ 07423. Phone: (800) 343-5540. Fax: (201) 652-1973.

Learning disabilities/learning abilities. Tape 3: Reading is not a natural skill: Teaching children the code to unlock language. [Videotape]. This videotape shows how children can master reading through explicit, multisensory, systematic teaching. 45 minutes. $79.95. Vineyard Productions.

Learning disabilities/learning abilities. Tape 5: ADD/ADHD/LD: Understanding the connection. [Videotape]. This videotape gives views from medical professionals, parents, teachers, and children on ADD/ADHD and tells how they create learning problems. 30 minutes. $79.95. Vineyard Productions.

Learning disabilities/learning abilities. Tape 6: Teaching math: A systematic approach for children with learning disabilities. [Videotape]. This videotape explains the connection between math learning problems, dyslexia, and attention disorders; shows teaching techniques; and more. 51 minutes. $79.95. Vineyard Productions.

Learning disabilities. Tape 1: Understanding learning disabilities through demonstration and description. [Videotape]. West Tisbury, MA: Vineyard Video

Productions. This video defines the spectrum of learning disabilities, dyslexia, and ADD, as well as the importance of phonological awareness and its effect on reading. 45 min. $79.95.

Learning disabilities. Tape 2: The teaching: What LD students need. [Videotape]. This videotape offers a full explanation of teaching methods, phonemic awareness, and more. 55 minutes. $79.95. Vineyard Video Productions.

Learning disabilities Tape 4: Children and parents and schools and strengths. [Videotape]. This videotape gives an overview of parent-school communication, parent advocacy, assessment, and the importance of stressing the ability of children with learning disabilities. 45 minutes. $79.95. Vineyard Video Productions.

Learning disability: A family crisis. [Videotape]. When a child's learning disability is discovered, the family may experience an emotional crisis. This videotape dramatizes what happens in the family of an 8-year-old boy when his learning disability is diagnosed by the school staff. The multifaceted process of identification and treatment is complicated by the emotional reaction of the parents, who must struggle to come to terms with the child's disability. Parental support is a key factor in the successful treatment of learning disabilities. 45 minutes. $165. Menninger Clinic and Center for Learning Disabilities. (800) 345-6036.

Mathematics: With manipulatives. [Videotape]. A series of six videotapes with Dr. Marilyn Burns demonstrating, using manipulatives to teaching mathematics for grades K–6. The videotape covers base ten blocks, pattern blocks, Cuisenaire rods, color tiles, geoboards, and six models. Cuisenaire, 10 Bank St., White Plains, NY 1006-5026. Contact by phone at (800) 237-3142. or at http://www.cuisenaire.com. 20 minutes. $89 each.

1-2-3-Magic: Training your preschooler and preteens to do what you want. [Videotape]. 2 hours. $40. Child Management Press, Glen Ellyn, IL. This videotape is also available from ADD Warehouse.

Reach for the stars. [Videotape]. This videotape presents an inspiring story for people with learning disabilities. Each year the Lab School of Washington, DC, presents awards to selected entertainers, athletes, scholars, and business people who have accomplished great success in their fields despite their learning disabilities. 22 minutes. $22. Learning Disabilities Association of America.

Study strategies made easy video: A practical plan for school success. Grades 6–12. [Videotape]. Shows students, parents, educators, and health professionals how to help secondary school students develop study strategies. 44 minutes. $47. ADD Warehouse, 300 Northwest 70th Avenue, Suite 102, Plantation, FL 33317. (954) 792-8944.

The 3 Rs for special education: Rights, resources, results. [Videotape]. This videotape helps parents learn how to navigate the steps of the special education system and work toward securing the best education and services for their children. Special education professionals and parents offer advice on planning for the future. the videotape also features reviews of the laws. 50 minutes. $49.95. Paul H. Brookes. P.O. Box 10624, Baltimore, MD 21285-0624. Phone (800) 638-3775. http://www.pbrookes.com

We can learning: Understanding and helping children with learning disabilities. [Videotape]. A five-part videotape series about children with learning disabilities. Produced by the National Center for Learning Disabilities (NCLD), along with WNBC. $39.95. NCLD, 381 Park Avenue South, Suite 1401, New York, NY 10016. Phone (212) 545-7510.

When the chips are down. . .Learning disabilities and discipline strategies for improving children's behavior. [Videotape]. Rick Lavoie offers practical advice on dealing with behavioral problems quickly and effectively. He show how preventive discipline can anticipate many problems before they start. 62 minutes. $56. Learning Disabilities Association of America, 4156 Library Road, Pittsburgh, PA 15234. (414) 341-1515.

When the chips are down . . . Strategies for improving children's behavior: Learning disabilities and discipline with Richard Lavoi. [Videotape]. Host Richard Lavoi, a nationally known expert on learning disabilities, offers practical advice on dealing with behavioral problems quickly and effectively. He show how preventive discipline can anticipate many problems before they start. He explains how teachers and parents can create a stable, environment in which children with learning disabilities can flourish. 62 minutes. $49.95. WETA Video, 22-D Hollywood Ave., Ho-Ho-Kus, NJ 07423. Phone: (800) 343-5540, Fax: (201) 652-1973.

PRINT RESOURCES FOR LEARNING DISABILITIES AND EDUCATION

Adams, A., Foorman, B., Lundberg, I., & Beeler, T. (1998a). The elusive phoneme. *American Educator, 22* (1 & 2), 18–31.

Bagnoto, S. J., Neisworth, J., & Munson, S. (1997). *Linking assessment and early intervention.* Baltimore: Paul H. Brookes.

Bailey, D., & Wolery, M. (1992). *Teaching infants and preschoolers with disabilities.* New York: Macmillan.

Barkley, R. (1998). *Attention deficit hyperactivity disorder.* New York: Guilford.

Blachman, B. (Ed.). (1997). *Foundations of reading acquisition and dyslexia: Implications for early instruction.* Mahwah, NJ: Lawrence Erlbaum.

Blackorby, J., & Wagner, M. (1997). The employment outcomes of youth with learning disabilities: A review of findings from the NLTS. In P. Gerber & D. Brown (Eds.), *Learning disabilities and employment* (pp. 57–76). Austin, TX: Pro-Ed.

Bredenkamp, S., & Copple, C. (Eds.), (1997). *Developmentally appropriate practices in early childhood programs.* (Rev. Ed.). Washington, DC: National Association for the Education of Young Children.

Bricker, D., & Cripe, J. (1992). *An activity-based approach to early intervention.* Baltimore: Paul H. Brookes.

Brooks, R. B. (1997). Resilience, courage, and hope: A precious gift for our children. *Attention!* (Spring, 1997), 36–41.

Bryan, R. (1997). Assessing the personal and social status of students with learning disabilities. *Learning Disabilities: Research and Practice, 13* (1), 63–76.

Carnine, D. (1997). Instructional design in mathematics for students with learning disabilities. *Journal of Learning Disabilities, 30,* (2), 134–141.

Cawley, J., Parmar, R., Yan, W., & Miller, J. (1998). Arithmetic computation performance of students with learning disabilities: Implications for curriculum. *Learning Disabilities Research and Practice, 13,* 68–74.

Chall, J. (1983). *Stages of reading development.* New York: McGraw-Hill.

Chall, J. (1987). Reading development in adults. *Annals of Dyslexia, 37,* 240–251.

Clay, M. (1993). *Reading Recovery: A guidebook for teachers in training.* Portsmouth, NH: Heinemann.

Cole, C., & McLeskey, J. (1997). Secondary inclusion program for students with mild disabilities. *Focus on Exceptional Children, 29* (6), 1–15

Cook, R. E., Tessler, A., & Klein, M. (1996). *Adapting early childhood curricula for children in inclusive settings.* Englewood Cliffs, NJ: Macmillan.

Cummins, J. (1996). *Negotiating identities: Education for empowerment in a diverse society.* Los Angeles: California Association for Bilingual Education.

Cunningham, A., & Stanovich, K. (1997). Early reading acquisition and its relation to reading experience and ability ten years later. *Developmental Psychology, 33* (6), 934–945.

Cunningham, A., & Stanovich, K. (1998). What reading does for the mind. *American Educator, 22* (1 & 2), 8–17.

Department of Education. (1997). *To assure the free appropriate public education of all children with disabilities.* Nineteenth Annual Report to Congress on the Implementation of the Individuals with Disabilities Education Act. Washington, DC: U.S. Government Printing Office.

Dimitras, H., & Donahue, M. (1997). Conversational and social problem-solving skills in adolescents with learning disabilities. *Learning Disabilities: Research and Practice, 23* (4), 213–220.

Dimitrovsky, L., Spector, H., Levy-Shiff, R., & Vakil, E. (1998). Interpretation of facial expressions of affect in children with learning disabilities with verbal or nonverbal deficits. *Journal of Learning Disabilities, 31,* (3), 286–292, 312.

Dunst, C. J., Trivette, D. M., & Deal, A. G. (1994). *Supporting and strengthening families.* Cambridge, MA: Brookline Books.

Erickson, R., Ysseldyke, J., Thurlow. M., & Elliot, J. (1998). Inclusive assessments and accountability systems: Tools of the trade in educational reform. *Teaching Exceptional Children, 31* (2), 24–29.

Every child is reading. (1998). An action plan of the learning first alliance. *American Educator, 22* (1 & 2), 52–63.

Fey, M., Windsor, J., & Warren, S. (Eds.). (1995). *Language intervention: Preschool through the elementary years.* Baltimore: Paul H. Brookes.

Fisher, J., Schumaker, J., and Deshler, D. (1995). Searching for validated inclusion practices: A review of the literature *Focus on Exceptional Children, 28* (4), 1–20.

Fletcher, J. (1998). IQ discrepancy: An inadequate and iatrogenic conceptual model of learning disabilities. *Perspectives: The International Dyslexia Association, 24* (4), 495–500.

Gardner, H. (1993). *Multiple intelligences: The theory in practice.* New York: Wiley.

Gerber, P. (1997). Life after school: Challenges in the workplace. In P. Gerber & D. Brown (Eds.), *Learning disabilities and employment* (pp. 3–18). Austin, TX: Pro-Ed.

Gerber, P., & Brown, D. (Eds.). (1997). *Learning disabilities and employment* Austin, TX: Pro-Ed.

Gersten, R. (1998). Recent advances in instructional research for students with learning disabilities: An overview. *Learning Disabilities: Research and Practice, 13* (3), 162–170.

Ginsburg, H. (1997). Mathematics learning disabilities: A view from developmental psychology. *Journal of Learning Disabilities, 30,* (1), 20–33.

Goldman, L., Ganel, M., Bezman, R., & Sianez, P. (1996). Diagnosis and treatment of attention deficit/hyperactivity disorder in children and adults. *JAMA (Journal of the American Medical Association), 279* 1100–1106.

Goldstein, S, & Mather, N. (1998). *Overcoming underachievement: An action guide to helping your child succeed in school.* New York: Wiley.

Goleman, D. (1995). *Emotional intelligence.* New York: Bantam Books.

Graham, S., & Harris, K. (1997). Whole language and process writing: Does one size fit all? In J. Lloyd, E. Kameenui, & D. Chard (Eds.), *Issues in educating students with disabilities* (pp. 239–261). Mahwah NJ: Lawrence Erlbaum.

Greeno, J., Collins, A., & Resnick, L. (1996). Cognition and learning. In B. Berliner & R. Calfee (Eds.), *Handbook of educational psychology* (pp. 15–46). NY: Macmillan.

Haager, D., & Vaughn, S. (1997). Assessment of social competence. In J. Lloyd, E. Kameenui, & D. Chard (Eds.), *Issues in educating students with disabilities* (pp. 129–152). Mahwah, NJ: Lawrence Erlbaum.

Handwerk, M., & Marshall, R. (1998). Behavioral and emotional problems of students with learning disabilities, serious emotional disturbances, or both conditions. *Journal of Learning Disabilities, 31,* (4), 327–338.

Harris, K., & Graham, S. (1996). *Making the writing process work: Strategies for composition and self-regulation.* Cambridge, MA: Brookline Books.

Henry, M. (1998). Structured, sequential, multisensory teaching: The Orton legacy. *Annals of Dyslexia, 48,* 3–26.

IDEA 1997. Individuals with Disabilities Education Act (IDEA): PL 105–17. (1997). Note to the regulations for eligibility for children with attention deficit disorder.

Katz, M. (1997). *On playing a poor hand well.* New York: W.W. Norton

Kauffman, J., & Hallahan, D. (1997). The diversity of restrictive environments: Placement as a problem of social ecology. In J. Lloyd, E. Kameenui, & D. Chard (Eds.), *Issues in educating students with disabilities* (pp. 325–342). Mahwah, NJ: Lawrence Erlbaum.

Knachendoffel, E. A. (1996). Collaborative teaming in the secondary school. In D. Deshler, E. Ellis, & B. Lenz (Eds.), *Teaching adolescents with learning disabilities* (pp. 517–616). Denver: Love.

Kohn, A. (1995). *Punished by rewards: The trouble with gold stars, incentive plans, a's, praise, and other bribes.* Boston: Houghton Mifflin.

Langone, J. (1998). Managing inclusive instruction settings: Technology, cooperative planning, and team-based organization. *Focus on Exceptional Children, 30* (8), 1–15.

Latham, P., & Latham, P. (1996). *Documentation and the law: For professionals concerned with ADD/LD.* Pittsburgh, PA: Learning Disabilities Association.

Latham, P., & Latham., P. (1997). Legal rights of adults with learning disabilities in employment. In P. Gerber & D. Brown (Eds.), *Learning disabilities and employment* (pp. 39–58). Austin, TX: Pro-Ed.

Lerner, J., Lowenthal, B., & Egan, R. (1998). *Preschool children with special needs: Children at risk and children with disabilities.* Needham Heights, MA: Allyn & Bacon.

Lerner, J. W., Lowenthal, B., & Lerner, S. (1995). *Attention deficit disorders: Assessment and Treatment.* Pacific Grove CA: Brooks/Cole.

Lewis, R. (1998). Assistive technology and learning disabilities Today's realities and tomorrow's promises. *Journal of Learning Disabilities, 31* (1), 16–26.

Lewis, R., Ashton, T., Haapa, B, Kieley, C., & Fielden, C. (in press). Improving the writing skills of students with learning disabilities: Are word processors with spelling and grammar checkers useful? *Learning Disabilities: A Multidisciplinary Journal.*

Liberman, A. M. (1997). How theories of speech affect research in reading and writing. In Blachman, B. (Ed.), *Foundations of reading acquisition and dyslexia: Implications for early intervention.* Mahwah, NJ: Lawrence Erlbaum.

Lloyd, J., Kameenui, E., & Chard, D. (Eds.). (1997). *Issues in educating students with disabilities.* Mahwah, NJ: Lawrence Erlbaum.

Lyon, G. R. (1996). Learning disabilities. *The Future of Children, 6* (1), 54–76.

Lyon, G. R. (1997). Progress and promise in research in learning disabilities. *Learning Disabilities: A Multidisciplinary Journal, 8* (1), entire issue.

Lyon, G. R., Alexander, D., & Yaffee, S. (1997). Programs, promise, and research in learning disabilities. *Learning Disabilities: A Multidisciplinary Journal, 8,* 1–6.

MacArthur, C. (1996). Using technology to enhance the writing process of students with learning disabilities. *Journal of Learning Disabilities, 29,* 344–354.

Mastropieri, M., & Scruggs, T. (1998). Construction of more meaningful relationships in the classroom: Mnemonic research into practice. *Learning Disabilities: Research & Practice, 13* (3), 138–145.

McGrady, H., and Lerner, J. (in press). The Education Lives of Young Adults with Learning Disabilities. In P. Rods, A. Garrod, and M. Boscardin (Eds.), *Learning Disabilities and Life Stories.* New York: Teachers College Press.

McLean, M., Bailey, D., & Wolery, M. (Eds.). (1996). *Assessing infants and preschoolers with special needs.* Englewood Cliffs, NJ: Prentice-Hall.

McLesky, J., & Waldron, N. (1995). Inclusive elementary programs: Must they cure students with learning disabilities to be effective? *Phi Delta Kappan, 77* (5). 542–546.

Miller, S., Butler, F., & Lee, K. (1998). Validated practices for teaching mathematics to students with learning disabilities: A review of the literature. *Focus on Exceptional Children, 31* (1), 1–24.

Miller, S., & Mercer, C., (1997). Education aspects of mathematics disabilities. *Journal of Learning Disabilities, 30,* (1), 47–56.

Moats, L. (1998). Teaching decoding. *American Educator, 22* (1 & 2), 42–65.

Montague, M. (1997). Cognitive strategy instruction in mathematics for students with learning disabilities. *Journal of Learning Disabilities, 30,* (2), 164–177.

National educational technology standards for students (1998, June). International Society for Technology in Education (ISTE), NETS Project. Contact ISTE at 1787 Agate Street, Eugene, OR 97403-1923 or at **http://www. ISTE.org.**

National Institutes of Health. (1998). Diagnosis and treatment of attention deficit hyperactivity disorder. NIH Consensus Statement.

National Joint Committee on Learning Disabilities. (1997). Operationalizing the NJCLD Definition of Learning Disabilities for Ongoing Assessment in Schools. *Perspectives: The International Dyslexia Association, 23,* (4) 29–33.

National Research Council. (1998). *Preventing reading difficulties in young children.* Washington, DC: National Academy of Sciences.

Ortiz, A. (1997). Learning disabilities occurring concomitantly with linguistic differences. *Journal of Learning Disabilities, 30,* 331–332.

Owens, R. E. (1995). *Language disorders: A functional approach to assessment and intervention.* New York: Merrill/Macmillan.

Patton, J., Cronin, M., Bassett, D., & Koppel, A. (1997). A life skills approach to mathematics instruction: Preparing students with learning disabilities for real-life math demands of adulthood. *Journal of Learning Disabilities, 30,* (2), 178–187.

Price, L. Psychosocial issues of workplace adjustment. In P. Gerber & D. Brown (Eds.), *Learning disabilities and employment* (pp. 275–306). Austin, TX: Pro-Ed.

Raskind, M. & Higgins, E. (1998). Assistive technology for postsecondary students with learning disabilities: An overview. *Journal of Learning Disabilities, 31,* (1), 27–40.

Raskind, M. H. (1998). Literacy for adults with learning disabilities through assistive technology. In S. Vogel and S. Reder (Eds.), *Learning disabilities, literacy, and adult education* (pp. 253–274). Baltimore: Paul H. Brookes.

Rivera, D. (1997). Mathematics education and students with learning disabilities: Introduction to special series. *Journal of Learning Disabilities, 30,* (1), 2–19.

Rosenshine, B. (1997). Advances in research on instruction. In J. Lloyd, E. Kameenui, & D. Chard (Eds.), *Issues in educating students with disabilities.* (pp. 197–220). Mahwah, NJ: Lawrence Erlbaum.

Rothstein, L. (1998). Americans with Disabilities Act, Section 504, and adults with learning disabilities in adult education and transition to employment. In S. Vogel & S. Reder (Eds.), *Learning disabilities, literacy, and adult education* (pp. 29–43). Baltimore: Paul H. Brookes.

Rourke, B., & Conway, J. (1997). Disabilities of arithmetic and mathematical reasoning: Perspectives from neurology and neuropsychology. *Journal of Learning Disabilities, 30,* (1), 34–46.

Rourke, B., & Fuerst, D. R. (1995). *Learning disabilities syndrome of nonverbal learning disabilities: Neurodevelopmental manifestations.* New York: Guilford.

Salend, S. (1998). Using portfolios to assess student performance. *Teaching Exceptional Children, 31* (2), 26–43

Salvia, J., & Ysseldyke, J. (1998). *Assessment.* Boston: Houghton Mifflin.

Shaywitz, B., & Shaywitz, S. (1998). Functional disruption in the organization of the brain for reading in dyslexia. *Proceedings of the National Academy of Sciences, 95* (5), 2636–2641.

Silver, L. (1992). *The misunderstood child.* New York: Times Books.

Silver, L. (1998). *The misunderstood child.* New York: Times Books.

Smith, C., & Strick, L.(1997). *Learning Disabilities: A to Z: A Parent's Complete Guide to Learning Disabilities from Preschool to Adulthood.* New York: The Free Press.

Smith, S. (1991). *Succeeding against the odds.* Los Angeles: Jeremy P. Tarcher.

Smith, S., Boone, R., & Higgins, K. (1998). Expanding the writing process to the web. *Teaching Exceptional Children, 30* (5), 22–33.

Tallal, P., Allard, L., Miller, S., & Curtiss, S. (1997). Academic outcomes of language impaired children. In C. Hulme and M. Snowling (Eds.). *Dyslexia: Biology, cognition, and intervention* (pp. 167–179). London: Whurt, British Dyslexia Association.

Thompson, S. (1997). *The source for nonverbal learning disorders.* East Moline, IL: LinguiSystems.

Thornton, C., Langruall, C., & Jones, G. (1997). Mathematics instruction for elementary students with learning disabilities. *Journal of Learning Disabilities, 30,* (2), 142–150.

Torgesen, J. (1998). Catch them before they fall. *American Educator, 22* (1 & 2), 32–41.

Troia, G., Graham, S., & Harris, H. (1998). Teaching students with learning disabilities to mindfully plan when writing. *Exceptional Children, 65* (2), 235–252.

Tsatsanis, K., Fuerst, D., & Rourke, B. (1997). Psychosocial dimensions of learning disabilities: External validation and relationship with age and academic functioning. *Journal of Learning Disabilities, 30,* (5), 490–502.

Turnbull, A., & Turnbull, H. (1996). *Families, professionals, and exceptionality.* Upper Saddle River, NJ: Merrill.

Umansky, W., & Hooper, S. (1998). *Young children with special needs.* Columbus, OH: Prentice-Hall.

Utley, C., Mortweet, S., & Greenwood, C. (1997). Peer-mediated instruction and interventions. *Focus on Exceptional Children, 29* (5), 1–23.

Vaughn, S., Schumm, J., & Arguelles, M. (1997). The ABCDEs of Co-Teaching. *Teaching Exceptional Children, 30* (2), 26–29.

Vogel, S. A. (1997). *College students with learning disabilities: A handbook.* Pittsburgh, PA: Learning Disabilities Association of America.

Vogel, S. A., & Reder, S. (1998). *Learning disabilities, literacy, and adult education* Baltimore: Paul H. Brookes.

Wasik, B. (1998). Using volunteers as reading tutors: Guidelines for successful practices. *Reading Teacher, 51* (7), 262–270.

William, J. P. (1998). Improving comprehension of disabled readers. *Annals of Dyslexia, 48,* 213–238.

Wilson, B. A. (1988). *Wilson reading system.* Millbury, MA: Wilson Language Training.

Wingert, P., & Kantrovitz, B. (1997, October 27). Why Andy couldn't read. *Newsweek, 56–64.*

Wissick, C., & Gardner, J. E. (1998). A learner's permit to the World Wide Web. *Teaching Exceptional Children, 30* (5), 8–15.

Yell, M., & Shriner, J. (1997). The IDEA Amendments of 1997: Implications for special and general education teachers, administrators, and teacher trainers. *Focus on Exceptional Children, 30* (1), 1–19.

Zigmond, N. (1997). Educating students with disabilities: The future of special education. In J. Lloyd, E. Kameenui, & D. Chard (Eds.), *Issues in educating students with disabilities* (pp. 377–390). Mahwah, NJ: Lawrence Erlbaum.

References

A Fable for Teachers. (1974). *Reading Today International, 3* (2), 1.

Aaron, P. G. (1997). The impending demise of the discrepancy formula. *Journal of Review of Educational Research, 67* (4), 461–502.

Achenbach, T. M. (1981). *Child behavior checklist for ages 4–16.* Burlington, VT: University of Vermont Department of Psychiatry.

Achenbach, T. M., & Edelbrock, C. (1986). *Child behavior checklist for ages 2–3.* Burlington, VT: University of Vermont Department of Psychiatry.

Adams, A., Foorman, B., Lundberg, I., & Beeler, T. (1998a). The elusive phoneme. *American Educator, 22* (1 & 2), 18–31.

Adams, A., Foorman, B., Lundberg, I., & Beeler, T. (1998b). *Phonemic awareness in young children.* Baltimore: Paul H. Brookes.

Adams, M., Treisman, R., & Pressley, M. (1997). Reading, writing, and literacy. In I. E. Siegel & K. A. Renninger (eds.). *Handbook of Child Psychology* (5th ed.). Volume 4. *Child Psychology in Practice* (pp. 275–355). New York: Wiley.

Adams, M. J. (1990). *Beginning to Read.* Cambridge, MA: MIT Press.

Adams, M. J., & Bruck, M. (1995). Resolving the "Great Debate." *American Educator, 19* (2), 7, 1–20.

Adelman, H., & Taylor, L. (1991). Issues and problems related to the assessment of learning disabilities. In H. L. Swanson (Ed.), *Handbook on the assessment of learning disabilities: Theory, research, and practice* (pp. 21–44). Austin, TX: Pro-Ed.

Adelman, P., & Vogel, S. (1991). The learning disabled adult. In B. Wong (Ed.), *Learning about learning disabilities* (pp. 564–594). San Diego: Academic Press.

Adler, M. (1956). *How to read a book.* New York: Simon & Schuster.

Alberto, P., & Troutman, A. (1995). *Applied behavior analysis for teachers.* (4th ed.). Englewood Cliffs, NJ: Prentice-Hall.

Alberto, P., & Troutman, A. (1998). *Applied behavior analysis for teachers.* (5th ed.). Englewood Cliffs, NJ: Prentice-Hall.

Algozzine, B. (1991). Curriculum-based assessment. In B. Wong (Ed.), *Learning about learning disabilities* (pp. 40–59). San Diego: Academic Press.

Alverez, L. (1998). A short course in sensitivity training: Working with Hispanic families of children with disabilities. *Focus on Exceptional Children, 31* (1), 73–78.

American Educational Research Association, American Psychological Association, & National Council on Measurement in Education (1985). *Standards for educational and psychological testing.* Washington, DC. American Psychological Association.

American Psychiatric Association. (1994). *Diagnostic and statistical manual of mental disorders.* (4th ed.) (DSM IV). Washington, DC: American Psychiatric Association.

Anderson, R., Hiebert, E., Scott, J., & Wilkinson, I. (1985). *Becoming a nation of readers: The report of the Commission on Reading.* Washington, DC: National Institute of Education.

Archibald, D. J. (1998, December). I have this great software: Now what do I do? Paper presented at the Cove Conference, Northbrook, IL.

Arter, J., & Jenkins, J. (1977). Differential diagnosis: Prescriptive teaching—A critical appraisal. *Review of Educational Research, 49,* 517–555.

Artiles, A., & Trent, S. (1997). Forging a research program on multicultural preservice teacher education in special education: A proposed analytic scheme. In J. Lloyd, E. Kameenui, & D. Chard (Eds.), *Issues in educating students with disabilities* (pp. 275–304). Mahwah, NJ: Lawrence Erlbaum.

Artiles, A., Trent, S., & Kuan, L. (1997). Learning disabilities empirical research on ethnic minority students: An analysis of twenty-two years of studies published in selected reference journals. *Learning Disabilities: Research & Practice, 12* (2), 82–91.

Atkins, M., & Pelham, W. (1991). School-based assessments of attention-deficit hyperactivity disorder. *Journal of Learning Disabilities, 24,* 197–204.

Atkinson, R., & Shiffrin, R. (1968). Human memory: A proposed system and its control processes. In K. Spence & J. Spence (Eds.), *The psychology of learning and motivation: Advances in theory and research* (Vol. 2). New York: Academic Press.

Aulls, M. (1982). *Developing readers in today's elementary schools.* Boston: Allyn & Bacon.

Ayres, A. (1981). *Sensory integration and the child.* Los Angeles: Western Psychological Services.

Baca, L., & Cervantes, H. (1989). *The bilingual special education interface.* St. Louis, MO: Times Mirror/Mosby.

Badian, N. A. (1996). Dyslexia: A validation of the concept at two age levels. *Journal of Learning Disabilities, 29* (1), 102–112.

Bagnoto, S. J., Neisworth, J., & Munson, S. (1997). *Linking assessment and early intervention.* Baltimore: Paul H. Brookes.

Bailey, D., & Wolery, M. (1992). *Teaching infants and preschoolers with disabilities.* New York: Macmillan.

Ball, E. W., & Blachman, B. A. (1991). Does phoneme awareness training in kindergarten make a difference in early word recognition and spelling? *Reading Research Quarterly, 26* (1), 49–66.

Barkley, R. (1990). *Attention deficit hyperactivity disorder: A handbook for diagnosis and treatment.* New York: Guilford Press.

Barkley, R. (1995). *Taking charge of ADHD: The complete authoritative guide for parents.* New York: Guilford Press.

Barkley, R. (1998). *ADHD and the nature of self control.* New York: Guilford.

Barkley, R. (1998). *Attention deficit hyperactivity disorder.* New York: Guilford.

Baroody, A., & Ginsburg, H. (1991). A cognitive approach to assessing the mathematical difficulties of children labeled "learning disabled." In H. L. Swanson (Ed.), *Handbook on the assessment of learning disabilities* (pp. 117–228). Austin: Pro-Ed.

Bateman, B. (1992). Learning disabilities: The changing landscape. *Journal of Learning Disabilities, 25,* 29–36.

Bateman, B. D. (1994). Toward a better identification of learning disabilities. *Learning Disabilities: A Multidisciplinary Journal, 5* (2), 95–99.

Beck, I. L., & Juel, C. (1995). The role of decoding in learning to read. *American Educator, 19* (2), 8, 21–25, 39–42.

Bender, L. (1957). Specific reading disability as maturational lag. *Bulletin of the Orton Society, 7,* 9–18.

Berko, J. (1958). The child's learning of English morphology. *Word, 14,* 15–17.

Biehler, R., & Snowman, J. (1997). *Psychology applied to teaching.* Boston: Houghton Mifflin.

Blachman, B. (1994). What have we learned from longitudinal studies of phonological processing and reading? Some unanswered questions: A response to Torgesen, Wagner, & Rashott. *Journal of Learning Disabilities, 27,* 287–291.

Blachman, B. (Ed.). (1997). *Foundations of reading acquisition and dyslexia: Implications for early instruction.* Mahwah, NJ: Lawrence Erlbaum.

Blackorby, J., & Wagner, M. (1997). The employment outcomes of youth with learning disabilities: A review of findings from the NLTS. In P. Gerber & D. Brown (Eds.), *Learning disabilities and employment* (pp. 57–76). Austin, TX: Pro-Ed.

Blalock, G., & Patton, J. R. (1996). Transition and students with learning disabilities: Creating sound futures. *Journal of Learning Disabilities, 29* (1), 7–16.

Bley, N., & Thornton, C. (1989). *Teaching mathematics to the learning disabled.* Austin, TX: Pro-Ed.

Bloomfield, L., & Barnhart, C. (1963). *Let's read* (Pt. 1). Bronxville, NY: C. I. Barnhart.

Boder, E., & Jarrico, S. (1982). The Boder test of reading-spelling patterns: A diagnostic screening test for subtypes of reading disability. Orlando, FL: Grune & Stratton.

Bond, G., Tinker, M., Wasson, B., & Wasson, J. (1984). *Reading difficulties: Their diagnosis and correction.* Englewood Cliffs, NJ: Prentice-Hall.

Boone, R., and Higgins, K. (1998). Digital publishing. *Teaching Exceptional Children, 30* (5), 4–5.

Bos, C., & Fletcher, T. (1997). Sociocultural considerations in learning disabilities inclusion research: Knowledge gaps and future directions. *Learning Disabilities: Research & Practice 12* (2), 92–99.

Bos, C. S., & Vaughn, S. (1994). *Strategies for teaching students with learning and behavior problems.* (3d ed.). Needham Heights, MA: Allyn & Bacon.

Bos, C. S., & Vaughn, S. (1998). *Strategies for teaching students with learning and behavior problems.* (4th ed.). Boston: Allyn & Bacon.

Bradley, C. (1937). The behavior of children receiving benzedrine. *American Journal of Psychiatry, 94,* 577–585.

Bradley, L. (1988). Rhyme recognition and reading and spelling in young children. In W. Ellis (Ed.), *Intimacy with language: A forgotten basic in teacher education.* Baltimore, MD: Orton Dyslexia Society.

Bradley, L., & Bryant, R. (1985). *Rhyme and reason in reading and spelling* (International Academy for Research in Learning Disabilities, Monograph Series No. 1). Ann Arbor: University of Michigan Press.

Bredenkamp, S. (Ed.). (1987). *Developmentally appropriate practice in early childhood programs serving children from birth through age 8.* Washington, DC: National Association for the Education of Young Children.

Bredenkamp, S. (1993). The relationship between early childhood education and early childhood special education. *Topics in Early Childhood Special Education, 13,* 258–273.

Bricker, D., & Cripe, J. (1992). *An activity-based approach to early intervention.* Baltimore: Paul H. Brookes.

Broadbent, D. (1958). *Perception and communication.* London: Pergamon Press.

Broca, P. (1879). Anatomie comparée circonvolutions cérébrales. *Review of Anthropology, 1,* 387–498.

Brooks, R. B. (1991). *The self esteem teacher.* Circle Pines, MN: American Guidance Services.

Brophy, J. E., & Good, T. L. (1986). Teacher behavior and student achievement. In M. C. Wittrock (Ed.), *Handbook of research on teaching* (3rd ed., pp. 328–375). New York: Macmillan.

Brown, A., & Campione, J. (1986). Psychological theory and the study of learning disabilities. *American Psychologist, 41,* 14–21.

Bryan, R. (1997). Assessing the personal and social status of students with learning disabilities. *Learning Disabilities : Research and Practice, 13* (1), 63–76.

Bryan, T. (1991a). Assessment of social cognition: Review of research in learning disabilities. In H. Swanson (Ed.), *Handbook on the assessment of learning disabilities* (pp. 285–312). Austin, TX: Pro-Ed.

Bryan, T. (1991b). Social problems and learning disabilities. In B. Wong (Ed.), *Learning about learning disabilities* (pp. 190–231). San Diego: Academic Press.

Bryan, T. (1997). Assessing the personal and social status of students with learning disabilities. *Learning Disabilities: Research and Practice, 12* (1), 63–76.

Bryan, T., Sullivan-Burnstein, K., & Mathur, S. (1998). The influence of affect on social information processing. *Journal of Learning Disabilities, 31,* 418–426.

Bryant, B., & Rivera, D. (1997). Educational assessment of mathematics skills and abilities. *Journal of Learning Disabilities, 30,* 57–68.

Bryant, B., & Seay, P. (1998). The Technology-Related Assistance to the Individuals with Disabilities Act: Relevance to individuals with learning disabilities and their advocates. *Journal of Learning Disabilities, 31* (1), 4–15.

Bursuck, W. D., Rose, E., Cowen, S., & Yahaya, M. (1989). Nationwide survey of postsecondary education services for students with learning disabilities. *Exceptional Children, 56,* 236–254.

Busch, B. (1993). Attention deficits: Current concepts, controversies, management, and approaches to classroom instruction. *Annals of Dyslexia, 43,* 5–25.

Campbell, P. (1991). Evaluation and assessment in early intervention for infants and toddlers. *Journal of Early Intervention, 15,* 36–45.

Carbo, M., Dunn, R., & Dunn, K. (1986). *Teaching students to read through their individual learning styles.* Reston, VA: Reston Publishing Co.

Carbo, M., & Hodges, H. (1988). Learning styles strategies can help students at risk. *Teaching Exceptional Children, 20,* 55–58.

Carnegie Corporation. (1994). *Starting points: Meeting the needs of our youngest children.* New York: Author.

Carnine, D. (1997). Instructional design in mathematics for students with learning disabilities. *Journal of Learning Disabilities, 30* (2), 134–141.

Carnine, D., Granzin, A., & Becker, W. (1988). Direct instruction. In J. Braden, J. Zins & M. Curtis (Eds.), *Alternative educational delivery systems: Enhancing instructional options for all students* (pp. 327–349). Washington, DC: National Association for School Psychologists.

Carnine, D., Jones, E., & Dixon, R. (1995). Mathematics: Educational tools for diverse learners. *School Psychology Review, 23* (3), 406–427.

Carnine, D., Silbert, J., & Kameenui, E. J. (1990). *Direct instruction in reading.* Columbus, OH: Merrill.

Carrasquillo, A. L., & Baecher, R. E. (Eds.) (1990). *Teaching the bilingual special education student.* Norwood, NJ: Ablex.

Carta, J. J. (1995). Developmentally appropriate practice: A critical analysis as applied to young children with disabilities. *Focus on Exceptional Children, 27* (5), 1–15.

Carter, J., & Sugai, G. (1989). Survey on prereferral practices: Responses from state departments of education. *Exceptional Children, 55,* 298–302.

Catts, H. W. (1993). The relationship between speech-language impairments and reading disabilities. *Journal of Speech and Hearing Research, 36* (5), 948–958.

Cawly, J., & Miller, J. H. (1989). Cross-sectional comparisons of the mathematics performances of children with learning disabilities: Are we on the right track toward comprehensive programming? *Journal of Learning Disabilities, 22,* 250–254, 259.

Cawley, J., Parmar, R., Yan, W., & Miller, J. (1998). Arithmetic computation performance of students with learning disabilities: Implications for curriculum. *Learning Disabilities Research and Practice, 13,* 68–74.

Cawley, J. F., & Reines, R. (1996). Mathematics as communication. *Teaching Exceptional Children, 28* (2), 29–34.

Cazden, C. (1992). *Whole language plus: Essays on literacy in the United States and New Zealand.* New York: Teachers College Press.

Center, Y., et al. (1995). An evaluation of reading recovery. *Reading Research Quarterly, 30* (2), 240–263.

Chadsey-Rusch, J., & Heal, L. (1995). Building consensus from transition experts on social integration outcomes and interventions. *Exceptional Children, 62,* 165–186.

Chalfant, J., & Pysh, M. (1989). Teacher assistance teams: Five descriptive studies on 96 teams. *Remedial and Special Education, 10* (6), 49–58.

Chalfant, J., & Pysh, M. (1993). Teacher assistance teams: Implications for the gifted. In C. J. Maker (Ed.), *Critical issues in gifted education: Vol. 888-Gifted students in the regular classroom* (pp. 32–48). Austin, TX: Pro-Ed.

Chalfant, J. C. (1989). Diagnostic criteria for entry and exit from services: A national problem. In L. Silver (Ed.), *The assessment of learning disabilities* (pp. 1–26). Boston: College Hill Press.

Chall, J. (1967, 1983). *Learning to read: The great debate.* New York: McGraw-Hill.

Chall, J. (1983). *Stages of reading development.* New York: McGraw-Hill.

Chall, J. (1987). Reading development in adults. *Annals of Dyslexia, 37,* 240–251.

Chall, J. S. (1991). American reading instruction: Science, art and ideology. In W. Ellis (Ed.), *All language and the creation of literacy* (pp. 20–26). Baltimore, MD: Orton Dyslexia Society.

Chapman, J. (1988). Cognitive-motivational characteristics and academic achievement of learning-disabled children: A longitudinal study. *Journal of Educational Psychology, 80,* 357–365.

Chapman, J. (1992). Learning disabilities in New Zealand: Where kiwis and kids with LD can't fly. *Journal of Learning Disabilities, 26* (6), 363–370.

Chomsky, N. (1965). *Aspects of the theory of syntax.* Cambridge, MA: MIT Press.

CIERA (Center for the Improvement of Early Reading Achievement). (1998). *Improving the reading achievement of America's children: Ten research-based principles.* Washington, DC: Department of Education.

Clark, F., Mailloux, Z., & Parham, D. (1989). Sensory integration and children with learning disabilities. In P. N. Pratt & A. S. Allen (Eds.), *Occupational therapy for children* (pp. 457–507). St. Louis: C. V. Mosby.

Clay, M. (1985). *The early detection of reading difficulties* (3rd ed.). Portsmouth, NH: Heinemann.

Clay, M. (1993). *An observation survey of early literacy achievement.* Portsmouth, NH: Heinemann.

Clay, M. (1993). *Reading recovery: A guidebook for teachers in training.* Portsmouth, NH: Heinemann.

Clements, S. (1966) *Minimal brain dysfunction in children: Terminology and identification* (NINDS Monograph No. 3, Public Health Services Publication No. 1415). Washingon, DC: U.S. Department of Health, Education, and Welfare.

Closing the Gap. (1996). *Resource directory: Hardware, software, products, organizations.* Henderson, MN: Author.

Closing the Gap. (1998). *The 1998 Resource Directory.* Henderson, MN: Closing the Gap.

Coben, S., & Vaughn, S. (1994). Gifted students with learning disabilities: What does the research say? *Learning Disabilities: A Multidisciplinary Journal, 5* (2), 87–94.

Cohen, S. (1971). Dyspedagogia as a cause of reading retardation in learning disorders. In B. Bateman (Ed.), *Learning disorders: Reading* (Vol. 4, pp. 269–293). Seattle: Special Child Publications.

Cole, C., & McLeskey, J. (1997). Secondary inclusion programs for students with mild disabilities. *Focus on Exceptional Children, 29* (6), 1–15.

Conderman, G. (1995). Social status of sixth and seventh grade students. *Learning Disabilities Quarterly, 19,* 13–24.

Cone, T., & Wilson, L. (1981). Quantifying a severe discrepancy: A critical analysis. *Learning Disability Quarterly, 4,* 359–372.

Conners, C. K. (1989). *Conners parent rating scales.* North Tonawanda, NY: Multi-Health Systems.

Cook, R., Tessier, A., & Klein, M. (1996). *Adaptive Early Childhood Curriculum for Children in Inclusive Settings.* New York: Macmillan.

Coordinated Campaign for Learning Disabilities. (1998). *Learning disabilities: Information, strategies, resources.* Washington, DC: Communication Consortium Media Center.

Cordini, B. (1992). *Living with a Learning Disability.* Carbondale, IL: Southern Illinois University Press.

Cotman, C., and Lynch, G. (1988). The neurobiology of learning and memory. In J. Kanvanagh & T. Truss, Jr. (Eds.), *Learning disabilities: Proceedings of the national conference* (pp. 1–69). Parkton, MD: York Press.

Coutinho, M. (1995). The national profile and recent studies regarding characteristics, integration, secondary school experiences, and transitions of youth with specific learning disabilities: Summary and implications. In Learning Disabilities Association (Ed.), *Secondary education and beyond: Providing opportunities for students with learning disabilities* (pp. 13–45). Pittsburgh: Learning Disabilities Association.

Coutinho, M., & Malouf, D. (1993). Performance assessment and children with disabilities: Issues and possibilities. *Teaching Exceptional Children, 25* (4) 62–67.

Cratty, B. J. (1988). *Adapted physical education in the mainstream.* Denver: Love Publishing.

Crook, W. (1983). Let's look at what they eat. *Academic Therapy, 18,* 629–631.

Crook, W. G., & Stevens, L. (1986). *Solving the puzzle of your hard-to-raise child.* New York: Life Sciences Press.

Cruickshank, W., Bentzen, F., Ratzeburgh, F., & Tannhauser, M. (1961). *Teaching methods for brain injured and hyperactive children.* Syracuse, NY: Syracuse University Press.

Cummins, J. (1989). A theoretical framework for bilingual special education. *Exceptional Children, 56,* 111–120.

Cummins, J. (1996). *Negotiating identities: Education for empowerment in a diverse society.* Los Angeles: California Association for Bilingual Education.

Cunningham, A., & Stanovich, K. (1997). Early reading acquisition and its relation to reading experience and ability ten years later. *Developmental Psychology, 33* (6), 934–945.

Cunningham, A., & Stanovich, K. (1998). What reading does for the mind. *American Educator, 22* (1 & 2), 8–17.

da Fonseca, V. (1996). Assessment and treatment of learning disabilities in Portugal. *Journal of Learning Disabilities, 29* (2), 114–117.

Dalke, C. (1993). Making a successful transition from high school to college: A model program. In S. Vogel & P. Adelman (Eds.), *Success for students with learning disabilities* (pp. 57–80). New York: Springer-Verlag.

DeFord, D. (1991). On noble thoughts, or toward a clarification of theory and practice within a whole language framework. In W. Ellis (Ed.), *All language and creation of literacy* (pp. 27–39). Baltimore, MD: Orton Dyslexia Society.

DeFries, J. C., Fulker, D. W., & LaBuda, M. C. (1987). Reading disability in twins: Evidence for a genetic etiology. *Nature, 329,* 537–539.

DeFries, J. C., Stevenson, J., Gillis, J., & Wadsworth, S. J. (1991). Genetic etiology of spelling deficits in the Colorado and London twin studies of reading disability. *Reading Writing, 3,* 271–283.

Deno, E. (1970). Special education as developmental capital. *Exceptional Children, 37,* 229–237.

Deno, S. L. (1985). Curriculum-based measurement: The emerging alternative. *Exceptional Children, 52,* 219–232.

Deshler, D., Ellis, E. S, & Lenz, B. K (1996). *Teaching adolescents with learning disabilities: Strategies and methods.* Denver: Love Publishing.

Deshler, D., & Schumaker, B. (1988). An instructional model for teaching students how to learn. In J. Graden, J. Zins, & M. Curtis, (Eds.), *Alternative educational delivery sys-*

tems: Enhancing instructional options for all students. Washington, DC: National Association of School Psychologists.

Deuel, R. K. (1995). Developmental dysgraphia and motor skills disorders. *Journal of Child Neurology, 10* (Suppl. 1), S6–S7.

Dewey, J. (1946). *The public and its problems.* Chicago: Gateway.

Di Pasquale, G., Moule, A., & Flewelling, R. (1980). The birth date effect. *Journal of Learning Disabilities, 13,* 234–238.

Diamond, G. (1983). The birth date effect: A maturational effect? *Journal of Learning Disabilities, 16,* 161–164.

Dimitras, H., & Donahue, M. (1997). Conversational and social problem-solving skills in adolescents with learning disabilities. *Learning Disabilities Research and Practice, 23* (4), 213–220.

Dimitrovsky, L., Spector, H., Levy-Shiff, R., & Vakil, E. (1998). Interpretation of facial expressions of affect in children with learning disabilities with verbal or nonverbal deficits. *Journal of Learning Disabilities, 31* (3), 286–292, 312.

Dohrn, E., & Bryan, T. (1998). Coaching parents to use causal attributions and task strategies when reading with their children. *Learning Disabilities: A Multidisciplinary Journal, 9* (2), 33–46.

Duane, D. (1986). Neurodiagnostic tools in dyslexic syndromes in children: Pitfalls and proposed comparative study of computer tomography, nuclear magnetic resonance, and brain electrical activity mapping. In G. Pavlidis & D. Fisher (Eds.), *Dyslexia: Its neuropsychology and treatment* (pp. 65–86). New York: John Wiley.

Duane, D. (1989). Neurobiological correlates of learning disorders. *Journal of the American Academy of Child and Adolescent Psychiatry, 28,* 314–318.

Duffy, F. (1988). Neurophysiological studies in dyslexia. In D. Plum (Ed.), *Language, communication and the brain.* New York: Raven Press.

Duffy, F., & McAnulty, G. (1985). Brain electrical activity mapping (BEAM): The search for a physiological signature of dyslexia. In F. Duffy & N. Geschwind (Eds.), *Dyslexia: A neuroscientific approach to clinical evaluation* (pp. 105–122). Boston: Little, Brown.

Dunn, C. (1996). Status report on transition planning for individuals with learning disabilities. *Journal of Learning Disabilities, 29* (1), 17–30.

Dunn, L. (1968). Special education for the mildly retarded: Is much of it justifiable? *Exceptional Children, 35,* 5–22.

Dunn, R. (1988). Teaching students through the perceptual strengths or preferences. *Journal of Reading, 31,* 304–309.

Dunst, C. J., Trivette, D. M., & Deal, A. G. (1994). *Supporting and strengthening families.* Cambridge, MA: Brookline Books.

DuPaul, G., Barkley, R., & McMurray, M. (1991). Therapeutic effects of medication on ADHD: Implications for school psychologists. *School Psychology Review, 20,* 203–219.

Durrell, D. (1956). *Improving reading instruction.* New York: Harcourt, Brace & World.

Eastman, M., & Safran, J. (1986). Activities to develop your students' motor skills. *Teaching Exceptional Children, 19,* 24–27.

Educational Testing Service (1998). *Does it compute?* Princeton, NJ: Author.

Ehri, L. (1994). Development of the ability to read words: Update. In R. Ruddell, M. Ruddell, & H. Singer (Eds.), *Theoretical models and the process of reading* (4th ed., pp. 323–358). Newark, DE: International Reading Association.

Ehri, L., & Wilce, L. (1985). Movement into reading: Is the first stage of printed word reading visual or phonetic? *Reading Research Quarterly, 20,* 163–179.

Elliot, S. (1992). Authentic assessment: An introduction to the neo-behavioral approach to classroom assessment. *School Psychology Quarterly, 6* (4), 62–67.

Elliott, S. (1998). Performance assessment of students' achievement: Research and practice. *Learning Disabilities: Research & Practice, 31* (4), 233–241.

Elliott, S., & Shapiro, E. (1990). Intervention techniques and programs for academic performance problems. In T. Gutkin & C. Reynolds (Eds.), *The handbook of school psychology*. New York: John Wiley.

Ellis, E., Deshler, D., Lenz, K., Schumaker, J., & Clark, F. (1991). An instructional model for teaching learning strategies. *Focus on Exceptional Children, 23*(6), 1–23.

Enfield, M. (1988). The quest for literacy. *Annals of Dyslexia, 38*, 8–21.

Engelmann, S., Becker, W. C., Hanner, S., & Johnson, G. (1988). *Corrective reading program: Series guide*. Chicago: Science Research Associates.

Engelmann, S., & Bruner, E. C. (1995). *Direct instruction-reading*. Worthington, OH: SRA Macmillan/McGraw-Hill.

Erikson, E. H. (1968). *Identity: Youth and crisis*. New York: Norton.

Every child is reading. (1998). An action plan of the Learning First Alliance. *American Educator, 22* (1 & 2), 52–63.

Fabbro, F., & Masutto, C. (1994). An Italian perspective on learning disabilities. *Journal of Learning Disabilities, 27* (3), 139–141.

Farmer, T., & Farmer, M. (1996). Social relationships of students with exceptionalities in mainstream classrooms: social networks and homophily. *Exceptional Children, 62* (5), 431–450.

Farr, R., & Carey, F. (1986). *Reading: What can be measured?* Newark, DE: International Reading Association.

Feingold, B. (1975). *Why your child is hyperactive*. New York: Random House.

Fennel, E. B. (1995). The role of neuropsychological assessment in learning disabilities. *Journal of Child Neurology, 10* (Suppl. 1), S36–S41.

Fernald, G. (1988). *Remedial techniques in basic school subjects*. Austin, TX: Pro-Ed (Original work published 1943).

Ferroli, L., & Shanahan, T. (1987). Kindergarten spelling: Explaining its relation to first-grade reading. In J. E. Readence & R. S. Baldwin (Eds.), *Research in literacy: Merging perspectives* (pp. 93–99). Thirty-sixth Yearbook of the National Reading Conference. Rochester, NY: National Reading Conference.

Feuerstein, R. (1979). *The dynamic assessment of retarded performers: The learning potential assessment device, theory, instruments, and techniques*. Baltimore: University Park Press.

Feuerstein, R. (1980). *Instrumental enrichment: An intervention program for cognitive modifiability*. Baltimore: University Park Press.

Feuerstein, R., Rand, Y., Jensen, M., Kaniel, S., & Tzuriel, D. (1987). Prerequisites for assessment of learning potential: The LAPD model. In C. Lidz (Ed.), *Dynamic assessment: An interactional approach to evaluating learning potential*. New York: Guilford Press.

Fey, M., Catts, H., Larrivee, L. (1995). Preparing preschoolers for the academic and social changes. In M. Fey, J. Windsor, & S. Warren (Eds.), *Language intervention: Preschool through the elementary years*. (pp. 3–38). Baltimore: Paul H. Brookes.

Fey, M., Windsor, J., & Warren, S. (Eds.). (1995). *Language intervention: Preschool through the elementary years*. Baltimore: Paul H. Brookes.

Filipek, P. (1995). Neurobiologic correlates of developmental dyslexia: How do dyslexics' brains differ from those of normal readers? *Journal of Child Neurology, 10* (Suppl. 1), S62–S85.

Fiore, T. A., Becker, E. A., & Nero, R. C. (1993). Educational interventions for students with attention deficit disorder. *Exceptional Children, 60* (2), 163–173.

Fishbein, D., & Meduski, J. (1987). Nutritional biochemistry and behavioral disabilities. *Journal of Learning Disabilities, 20*, 505–512.

Fisher, A., Murray, E., & Bundy, A. (1991). *Sensory integration: Theory and practice*. Philadelphia: F. A. Davis.

Fisher, J., Schumaker, J., and Deshler, D. (1995). Searching for validated inclusion practices: A review of the literature. *Focus on Exceptional Children, 28* (4), 1–20.

Flavell, J. (1987). Speculations about the nature and development of metacognition. In F. Weinert & R. Kluwe (Eds.), *Metacognition, motivation, and understanding* (pp. 21–30). Mahwah, NJ: Lawrence Erlbaum Associates.

Fleischner, J., Nuzum, M., & Marzola, E. (1987). Devising an instructional program to teach arithmetic problem-solving skills to students with learning disabilities. *Journal of Learning Disabilities, 20*(4), 214–217.

Fleischner, J. E. (1994). Diagnosis and assessment of mathematics learning disabilities. In G. R. Reid (Ed.), *Frames of reference for the assessment of learning disabilities* (pp. 441–458). Baltimore: Paul Brookes.

Fletcher, J. (1998). IQ discrepancy: An inadequate and iatrogenic conceptual model of learning disabilities. *Perspectives: The International Dyslexia Association, 24* (4), 10–11.

Fletcher, J., Francis, D., Shaywitz, S., Lyon, G., Foorman, B., Stubbing, K., & Shaywitz, B. (1998). Intelligence testing and the discrepancy model for children with learning disabilities. *Learning Disabilities: Research & Practice, 13* (4), 186–203.

Fletcher, J. M., & Foorman, B. R. (1994). Issues in definition and measurement of learning disabilities: The need for early intervention. In G. R. Lyon (Ed.), *Frames of reference for the assessment of learning disabilities* (pp. 185–200). Baltimore: Paul Brookes.

Fletcher, J. M., Shaywitz, S. E., Shankweiler, D. P., et al. (1994). Cognitive profiles of reading disability: Comparisons of discrepancy and low achievement definitions. *Journal of Educational Psychology, 86,* 6–23.

Fletcher, T. V., & DeLopez, C. (1995). A Mexican perspective on learning disabilities. *Journal of Learning Disabilities, 28* (9), 530–534, 544.

Flynn, J. (1998). School-based assessment of attention deficit disorder, *Attention!, 5* (1) 37–40.

Foorman, B., Francis, D., Fletcher, J., Schat-Schneider, C., & Mehta, P. (1998). The role of instruction in learning to read: Preventing reading failure in at-risk children. *Journal of Educational Psychology, 90,* 1–15.

Forgan, J. (1996). *Developmentally Appropriate Software for Young Children.* Presentation at the Council for Exceptional Children Annual Conference. Orlando, FL.

Forness, S., Sinclair, E., & Guthrie, D. (1983). Learning disability discrepancy formulas: Their use in actual practice. *Learning Disability Quarterly, 6,* 107–114.

Fowler, S. A., Haines, A. H., & Rosenkoetter, S. E. (1990). The transition between early intervention services and preschool services: Administration and policy issues. *Topics in Early Childhood Special Education, 9,* 55–65.

Fox, A. (1998). Clumsiness in children: Developmental coordination disorders. *Learning Disabilities: A Multidisciplinary Journal 9* (2), 57–63.

Frankenberger, W., & Fronzaglio, K. (1991). A review of states' criteria and procedures for identifying children with learning disabilities. *Journal of Learning Disabilities, 24,* 495–500.

Freiberg, H. J. (1993). A school that fosters resiliency in inner-city youth. *Journal of Negro Education, 62,* 364–376.

Friend, M., & Bursuck, W. (1996). *Including students with special needs: A practical guide for classroom teachers.* Needham Heights, MA: Allyn & Bacon.

Friend, M., & Cook, L. (1996). *Interactions: Collaboration skills for school professionals.* White Plains, NY: Longman.

Fuchs, D., & Fuchs, L. (1995). Inclusive schools movement and the radicalization of special education reform. In J. Kauffman & D. Hallahan (Eds.), *The illusion of full inclusion* (pp. 213–242). Austin, TX: Pro-Ed.

Fuchs, D., & Fuchs, L. (1998). Researchers and teachers working together to adapt instruction for diverse learners. *Learning Disabilities: Research & Practice 13* (3), 126–137.

Fuchs, L. S., & Deno, S. L. (1994). Must instructionally useful performance assessment be based in the curriculum? *Exceptional Children, 61* (1), 15–24.

Gaddes, W. H. (1985). *Learning disabilities and brain function: A neuropsychological approach.* New York: Springer-Verlag.

Galaburda, A. (1990). The testosterone hypothesis: Assessment since Geschwind and Behan, 1982. *Annals of Dyslexia, 40,* 18–38.

Galagan, J. (1985). Psychoeducational testing: Turn out the lights, the party's over. *Exceptional Children, 52*(3), 288–299.

Gallagher, N. (1995). The impact of learning disabilities on families. *Journal of Child Neurology, 10* (Suppl. 1), S112–S113.

Ganschow, L., Sparks, R., & Javorksy, J. (1998). Foreign language and learning difficulties: An historical perspective. *Journal of Learning Disabilities, 31* (2), 248–258.

Garcia, S. B., & Malkin, D. H. (1993). Toward defining programs and services for culturally and linguistically diverse students in special education. *Teaching Exceptional Children, 26* (1), 52–58.

Gardner, H. (1983). *Frames of mind.* New York: Basic Books.

Gardner, H. (1993). *Multiple intelligences: The theory in practice.* New York: Wiley.

Gardner, H., and Hatch, T.(1989). Multiple intelligences go to school. *Educational Researcher, 18,* 4–10.

Genesee, F. (1985). Second-language learning through immersion: A review of U.S. programs. *Review of Educational Research, 55*(4), 541–561.

Gerber, P. (1997). Life after school: Challenges in the workplace. In P. Gerber & D. Brown (Eds.), *Learning disabilities and employment* (pp. 3–18). Austin, TX: Pro-Ed.

Gerber, P., & Brown, D. (Eds.). (1997). *Learning disabilities and employment.* Austin, TX: Pro-Ed.

Gerber, P., & Reiff, H. (Eds.) (1994). *Learning disabilities in adulthood: Persisting problems and evolving issues.* Boston: Andover Medical Publishers.

Gerber, P. J., & Reiff, H. B. (1991). *Speaking for themselves: Ethnographic interviews with adults with learning disabilities.* Ann Arbor: University of Michigan Press.

German, D. (1993). *Word Finding Interactive Programs.* Itaska, IL: Riverside Publishing.

German, D. (1994). Word finding difficulties in children and adolescents. In G. P. Wallach & K. G. Butler (Eds.), *Language learning abilities in school-age children and adolescents* (pp. 323–347). Needham Heights, MA: Allyn & Bacon.

Gersons-Wolfenberger, D., & Ruijssenaars, W. (1997). Dyslexia: A report of the committee on dyslexia in the health council of the Netherlands, *Journal of Learning Disabilities, 30,* 209–213.

Gersten, R. (1998). Recent advances in instructional research for students with learning disabilities: An overview. *Learning Disabilities: Research & Practice 13* (3), 162–170.

Gersten, R., Brengelman, S., & Jimenez, R. (1994). Effective instruction for culturally and linguistically diverse students: A reconceptualization. *Focus on Exceptional Children, 27* (1), 1–16.

Giffin, M. (1996). Introduction: The journey toward the national summit on teacher preparation. *Teaching: The Nationals Lifeline.* (pp. 10–11). New York: National Center for Learning Disabilities.

Gillingham, A., & Stillman, B. (1970). *Remedial training for children with specific difficulty in reading, spelling, and penmanship.* Cambridge, MA: Educators Publishing Service.

Ginsburg, H. (1997). Mathematics learning disabilities: A view from developmental psychology. *Journal of Learning Disabilities, 30* (1), 20–33.

Goertz, M., & Friedman, D. (1996). State education reform and students with disabilities: A preliminary analysis. Alexandria, VA: Center for Policy Research on the Impact of General and Special Education Reform, National Association of State Boards of Education.

Goetz, E., Hall, R., & Fetsco, T. (1989). Information processing and cognitive assessment. I: Backgrounds and overview. In J. Hughes & R. Hall (Eds.), *Cognitive behavioral psychology in the schools: A comprehension handbook* (pp. 87–115). New York: Guilford Press.

Goldey, E. (1998). New angles on motor and sensory coordination in learning disabilities: A report on the 1998 LDA medical symposium. *Learning Disabilities: A Multidisciplinary Journal, 9* (2), 65–72.

Goldman, L., Ganel, M., Bezman, R. & Sianez, P. (1996). Diagnosis and treatment of attention deficit/hyperactivity disorder in children and adults. *JAMA (Journal of the American Medical Association), 279* (14), 1100–1106.

Goldstein, C. (1998). Learning at cybercamp. *Teaching Exceptional Children, 30* (5), 16–21.

Goldstein, K. (1939). *The organism.* New York: American Books.

Goldstein, S., & Goldstein, M. (1990). *Managing attention disorders in children: A guide for practitioners.* New York: Wiley.

Goldstein, S., & Mather, N. (1998). *Overcoming underachievement: An action guide to helping your child succeed in school.* New York: John Wiley.

Goleman, D. (1995). *Emotional intelligence.* New York: Bantam Books.

Goodman, K. (1989). Whole language *is* whole: A response to Heymsfeld. *Educational Leadership, 46,* 69–70.

Goodman, K. S. (1986). *What's whole in whole language?* Portsmouth, NH: Heinemann.

Goodman, K. S. (1990). The past, present, and future of literacy education: Comments from the pen of distinguished educators, Part I. *The Reading Teacher, 43,* 302–311.

Goodman, K. S. (1992). Why whole language is in today's agenda in today's education. *Language Arts, 69,* 353–363.

Goodman, Y., & Burke, C. (1980). *Reading strategies: Focus on comprehension.* New York: Holt, Rinehart & Winston.

Graham, S., & Harris, K. (1997). Whole language and process writing: Does one size fit all? In J. Lloyd, E. Kameenui, & D. Chard (Eds.), *Issues in educating students with disabilities,* (pp. 239–261). Mahwah, NJ: Lawrence Erlbaum.

Graves, D. (1983). *Writing: Teachers and children at work.* Portsmouth, NH: Heinemann.

Graves, D. H. (1994). *A fresh look at writing.* Portsmouth, NH: Heinemann.

Greeno, J., Collins, A., & Resnick, L. (1996). Cognition and learning. In B. Berliner & R. Calfee (Eds.), *Handbook of educational psychology* (pp. 15–46). New York: Macmillan

Greenwood, C. R. (1996). Research on the practices and behavior of effective teachers at the Juniper Gardens Child's Project: Implication for the education of diverse learners. In D. L. Speece & B. Keogh (Eds.), *Research on classroom ecologies: Implications for inclusion of children with learning disabilities* (pp. 39–67). Mahwah, NJ: Lawrence Erlbaum.

Groteluschen, A., Borkowski, J., & Hall, C. (1990). Strategy instruction is often insufficient: Addressing the interdependency of executive and attributional processes. In T. Scruggs and B. Wong (Eds.), *Intervention research in learning disabilities* (pp. 81–101). New York: Springer-Verlag.

Haager, D., & Vaughn, S. (1995). Parent, teacher, peer and self-reports of the social competence of students with learning disabilities. *Journal of Learning Disabilities, 28* (4), 205–215, 231.

Haager, D., & Vaughn, S. (1997). Assessment of social competence in students with learning disabilities. In J. Lloyd, E. Kameenui, & D. Chard (Eds.), *Issues in educating students with disabilities* (pp. 129–152). Mahwah, NJ: Lawrence Erlbaum.

Hakuta, K. (1990). Language and cognition in bilingual children. In A. M. Padilla, H. H. Fairchild, & C. Valadez (Eds.), *Bilingual education: Issues and strategies* (pp. 47–59). Newbury Park, CA: Sage.

Hall, S., & Moats, L. (1999). *Straight talk about reading: How parents can make a difference during the early years.* Chicago: Contemporary Press.

Hallgren, B. (1950). Specific dyslexia (congenital word-blindness): A clinical and genetic study. *Acta Psychiatrica Scandinavica Supplementum, 65,* 1–287.

Halpern, A. S. (1994). The transition of youth with disabilities to adult life: A position statement of the Division on Career Development and Transition, The Council for Exceptional Children. *Career Development for Exceptional Individuals, 17,* 115–124.

Hammill, D. (1990). On defining learning disabilities: An emerging consensus. *Journal of Learning Disabilities, 23,* 74–84.

Handwerk, M., & Marshall, R. (1998). Behavioral and emotional problems of students with learning disabilities, serious emotional disturbances, or both conditions. *Journal of Learning Disabilities, 31* (4), 327–338.

Hanna, R., Hodges, R., & Hanna, J. (1971). *Spelling structure and strategies.* Boston: Houghton Mifflin.

Harbin, G. L., Gallagher, J. J., & Terry, D. V. (1991). Defining the eligible population: Policy issues and challenges. *Journal of Early Intervention, 15,* 13–20.

Haring, T., & Kennedy, C. (1992). Behavior analytic foundations of classroom management. In W. Stainback & S. Stainback (Eds.), *Controversial issues confronting special education* (pp. 201–213). Boston: Allyn & Bacon.

Harris, A. (1964). *How to improve reading ability.* New York: David McKay.

Harris, K., & Pressley, M. (1991). The nature of cognitive strategy instruction: Interactive strategy construction. *Exceptional Children, 57,* 392–404.

Harris, K. R., & Graham, S. (1992). *Helping young writers master the craft: Strategy instruction and self regulation of the writing process.* Cambridge, MA: Brookline.

Harris, K. R., & Graham, S. (1997). *Making the writing process work: Strategies for composition and self-regulation.* Cambridge, MA: Brookline Books.

Hasbrouck, J. (1996, April 12). *Oral reading fluency: A review of literature with implications for use with elementary students who are difficult to teach.* Paper given at the Council for Exceptional Children meeting, Orlando, FL.

Hasselbring, T., & Goin, I. (1993). Integrated technology and media. In E. Polloway & J. Patton (Eds.), *Strategies for teaching learners with special needs* (pp. 145–162). New York: Merrill/Macmillan.

Hazel, J., & Schumaker, J. (1988). Social skills and learning disabilities: Current issues and recommendations for future research. In J. Kavanagh & T. Truss, Jr. (Eds.), *Learning disabilities: Proceedings of the national conference* (pp. 293–344). Parkton, MD: York Press.

Head, H. (1926). *Aphasia and kindred disorders of speech.* London: Cambridge University Press.

Head Start Bureau. (1993). *Head Start performance standards on services for children with disabilities.* Office of Human Development: Administration on Children, Youth, and Families. Washington, DC: U.S. Government Printing Office.

Hearne, D., & Stone, S. (1995). Multiple intelligences and underachievement: Lessons from individuals with learning disabilities. *Journal of Learning Disabilities, 28,* 439–448.

Heckelman, R. (1969). A neurological impress method of reading instruction. *Academic Therapy, 4,* 277–282.

Henderson, E. (1985). *Teaching spelling.* Boston: Houghton Mifflin.

Henry, M. (1998). Structured, sequential, multisensory teaching: The Orton legacy. *Annals of Dyslexia, 48,* 3–26.

Hinshelwood, J. (1917). *Congenital word blindness.* London: H. K. Lewis.

Hiscock, M., & Kinsbourne, M. (1987). Specialization of the cerebral hemispheres: Implications for learning. *Journal of Learning Disabilities, 20*(3), 130–143.

Hofmeister, A., Engelman, S., & Carnine, D. (1989). Developing and validating science education videodisks. *Journal of Research in Science Teaching, 26,* 665–677.

Horne, M. (1978). Do learning disabilities specialists know their phonics? *Journal of Learning Disabilities, 11,* 580–582.

Hoyt, C. (1990). Irlen lenses and reading difficulties. *Journal of Learning Disabilities, 23,* 624–627.

Hsu, Chin-chin. (1988). Correlates of reading success and failure in a logographic writing system. *Thalmus, 6*(1), 33–59.

Hutchinson, N. (1993). Effects of cognitive strategy instruction on algebra problem solving of adolescents with learning disabilities. *Learning Disabilities Quarterly, 16,* 34–63.

Huttenlocher, P. (1991). *Neural plasticity.* Paper presented at the Brain Research Foundation Women's Council. University of Chicago, Chicago, September 26, 1991.

Hutton, J. (1984). Incidence of learning problems among children with middle ear pathology. *Journal of Learning Disabilities, 17,* 41–42.

Hynd, G. (1992). Neurological aspects of dyslexia: Comments on the balance model. *Journal of Learning Disabilities, 25,* 110–113.

Hynd, G., & Semrud-Clickman, M. (1989). Dyslexia and brain morphology. *Psychological Bulletin, 106,* 447–882.

Idal, L. (1997). Key questions related to building cooperative and inclusive schools. *Journal of Learning Disabilities 30* (4), 384–395.

IDEA 1997. Individuals with Disabilities Education Act (IDEA): PL 105–17. (1997). Note to the regulations for eligibility for children with attention deficit disorder.

Idol, L., Paulucci-Whitcomb, P., & Nevin, A. (1986). *Collaborative consultation.* Austin, TX: Pro-Ed.

Individuals with Disabilities Education Act (IDEA) Amendments of 1997, PL 105–17, 105th Cong. 1st Sess. (1997).

Interagency Committee on Learning Disabilities (Ed.), (1988). *Learning disabilities: A report to the U.S. Congress.* Washington, DC: U.S. Government Printing Office.

Itard, J. (1962). *The wild boy of Aveyron* (G. Humphrey & M. Humphrey, Trans.). New York: Appleton-Century-Crofts. (Original work published 1801).

Iverson, S., & Tunmer, W. (1993). Phonological processing skills and the reading recovery program. *Journal of Educational Psychology, 85,* 112–120.

Jackson, J. H. (1874). On the nature of duality of the brain. In J. Taylor (Ed.), (1958), *Selected writing of John Hughlings Jackson.* New York: Basic Books.

Johnson, D. (1967). Educational principles for children with learning disabilities. *Rehabilitation Literature, 18,* 317–322.

Johnson, D., & Johnson, R. (1986). Mainstreaming and cooperative learning strategies. *Exceptional Children, 56,* 426–437.

Johnson, D., & Myklebust, H. (1967). *Learning disabilities.* New York: Grune & Stratton.

Johnson, D. J. (1995). An overview of learning disabilities: Psychoeducational perspectives. *Journal of Child Neurology, 10* (Suppl. 1), 52–55.

Johnson, D. J., & Blalock, J. (1987). *Adults with learning disabilities: Clinical studies.* Orlando, FL: Grune & Stratton.

Johnson, M., Kress, K., & Pikulski, J. (1987). *Informal reading inventories.* Newark, DE: International Reading Association.

Jones, E., Wilson, R., & Bhojwani, S. (1997). Mathematics instruction for secondary students with learning disabilities. *Journal of Learning Disabilities, 30,* 151–163.

Juel, C. (1995). The role of decoding in learning to read. *American Educator, 19,* 8–42.

Kameenui, E. (1991). Toward a scientific pedagogy of learning disabilities: A sameness in the message. *Journal of Learning Disabilities, 24,* 364–372.

Katz, M. (1997). *On playing a poor hand well.* New York: W. W. Norton.

Kauffman, J., & Hallahan, D. (1995). *The illusion of full inclusion.* Austin, TX: Pro-Ed.

Kauffman, J., & Hallahan, D. (1997). A diversity of restrictive environments: Placement as a problem of social ecology. In J. Lloyd, E. Kameenui, and D. Chard (Eds.), *Issues in educating students with disabilities* (pp. 325–342). Mahwah, NJ: Lawrence Erlbaum.

Kavale, K. (1990). Variances and verities in learning disability interventions. In T. Scruggs & B. Wong (Eds.), *Intervention in learning disabilities* (pp. 3–33). New York: Springer-Verlag.

Kavale, K., & Forness, S. (1987 a). The far side of heterogeneity: A critical analysis of empirical subtyping research in learning disabilities. *Journal of Learning Disabilities, 20*(6), 374–382.

Kavale, K., & Forness, S. (1987 b). Substance over style: Assessing the efficacy of modality testing and teaching. *Exceptional Children, 54,* 228–239.

Kavale, K., & Forness, S. (1990). Substance over style: A rejoinder to Dunn's animadversions. *Exceptional Children, 56,* 357–361.

Keller, H. (1961). *The story of my life.* New York: Dell.

Keogh, B., & Bess, C. (1991). Assessing temperament. In H. L. Swanson (Ed.), *Handbook on the assessment of learning disabilities* (pp. 313–330). Austin, TX: Pro-Ed.

Keogh, B. K. (1994). A matrix of decision points in the measurement of learning disabilities. In G. R. Lyon (Ed.), *Frames of reference for the assessment of learning disabilities* (pp. 15–58). Baltimore: Paul Brookes.

Kephart, N. (1963). *The brain-injured child in the classroom.* Chicago: National Society for Crippled Children and Adults.

Kephart, N. (1967). Perceptual-motor aspects of learning disabilities. In E. Frierson & W. Barbe (Eds.), *Educating children with learning disabilities* (pp. 405–413). New York: Appleton-Century-Crofts.

Kephart, N. (1971). *The slow learner in the classroom.* Columbus, OH: Charles E. Merrill.

Kirk, S., & Chalfant, J. (1984). *Developmental and academic learning disabilities.* Denver: Love Publishing.

Kirk, S. A. (1963). Behavioral diagnosis and remediation of learning disabilities. In *Proceedings of the Conference on the Exploration into the Problems of the Perceptually Handicapped Child.* Evanston, IL: Fund for the Perceptually Handicapped Child.

Kirk, S. A. (1987). The learning-disabled preschool child. *Teaching Exceptional Children, 19*(2), 78–80.

Kirk, S. A., & Elkins, J. (1975). Characteristics of children enrolled in Child Service Demonstration Centers. *Journal of Learning Disabilities, 8,* 630–637.

Kirk, S. A., Kirk, W., & Minskoff, E. (1985). *Phonic remedial reading drills.* Novato, CA: Academic Therapy Publications.

Kistner, J., Osborn, M., & LaVerrier, L. (1988). Causal attributions of learning-disabled children: Developmental patterns and relation to academic progress. *Journal of Educational Psychology, 80,* 82–89.

Kluwe, R. (1987). Executive decisions and regulation of problem solving behavior. In F. Weinert & R. Kluwe (Eds.), *Metacognition, motivation and understanding* (pp. 31–64). Hillsdale, NJ: Lawrence Erlbaum.

Knackendoffel, E. A. (1996). Collaborative teaming in the secondary school. In D. Deshler, E. Ellis, & B. Lenz (Eds.), *Teaching adolescents with learning disabilities* (pp. 517–616). Denver: Love.

Knoblauch, B. (1998). Rights and responsibilities of parents of children with disabilities. *ERIC EC Digest #567* (May 1998).

Kohn, A. (1995). *Punished by rewards: The trouble with gold stars, incentive plans, A's, praise, and other bribes.* Boston: Houghton Mifflin.

Koppitz, E. (1973). Special class pupils with learning disabilities: A five-year follow-up study. *Academic Therapy, 8,* 133–140.

Korinek, L., & Bulls, J. A. (1996). SCORE-A: A student research paper writing strategy. *Teaching Exceptional Children, 28* (4), 60–63.

Korkunov, V., Nigayev A., Reynolds, L., & Lerner, J. (1998). Special education in Russia: History, reality, and prospects. *Journal of Learning Disabilities, 31* (2), 186–192.

Krashen, S. D. (1992). *Fundamentals of language education.* Torrance, CA: Laredo.

Kravetz, M., & Wax, I. (1997). *K & W guide for the learning disabled.* New York: The Princeton Review.

Kubler-Ross, E. (1969). *On death and dying.* New York: Macmillan.

Kulhavy, R., Schwartz, N., & Peterson, S. (1986). Working memory: The encoding process. In T. Andre & G. Phye (Eds.), *Cognitive classroom learning: Understanding, thinking, and problem solving* (pp. 115–140). San Diego: Academic Press.

Lahey, M. (1988). *Language disorders and language development.* Columbus, OH: Macmillan.

Lane, H. B., & Brownell, M. T. (1995). Literacy instruction: Meeting the needs of adolescents with learning disabilities. In *Secondary education and beyond: Providing opportunities for students with learning disabilities* (pp. 131–148). Pittsburgh: Learning Disabilities Association of America.

Langford, K., Slade, K., & Barnett, A. (1974). An explanation of impress techniques in remedial reading. *Academic Therapy, 9,* 309–319.

Langone, J. (1998). Managing inclusive instruction settings: Technology, cooperative planning, and team-based organization. *Focus on Exceptional Children, 30* (8), 1–15.

Larsen, S., & Hammill, D. (1975). Relationship of selected visual perceptual abilities to school learning. *Journal of Special Education, 9,* 282–291.

Latham, P., & Latham., P. (1997). Legal rights of adults with learning disabilities in employment. In P. Gerber & D. Brown (Eds.), *Learning disabilities and employment* (pp. 39–58). Austin, TX: Pro-Ed.

Lavoie, R. D. (1995). Life on the waterbed: Mainstreaming on the homefront. *Attention! 2* (1), 25–29.

Lazar, I., & Darlington, R. (Eds.). (1982). Lasting effects of early education: A report from the Consortium for Longitudinal Studies. *Monographs of the Society for Research in Child Development, 27* (2–3, Serial No. 195) (Summary Report, DHEW Publication No. OHDS 80–30/79).

LDA Position Paper. (1990). Eligibility for services for persons with specific learning disabilities. *LDA Newsbriefs, 25*(3), 2a–8a.

Learning Disabilities Association of America. (1995). *Secondary education and beyond: Providing opportunities for students with learning disabilities.* Pittsburgh: Author.

Lenneberg, E. (1967). *Biological foundations of language.* New York: Wiley.

Lenz, B. K., Ellis, E. S., & Scanlon, D. (1996). *Teaching learning strategies to adolescents and adults with learning disabilities.* Austin, TX: Pro-Ed.

Lerner, J. (1990). Phonological awareness: A critical element in learning to read. *Learning Disabilities: A Multidisciplinary Journal, 1,* 50–54.

Lerner, J., Cousin, P. T., & Richek, M. (1992). Critical issues in learning disabilities: Whole language learning. *Learning Disabilities Research and Practice, 7,* 226–330.

Lerner, J., Dawson, D., & Horvath, L. (1980). *Cases in learning and behavior problems: A guide to individualized education programs.* Salem, WI: Sheffield Publishing Co.

Lerner, J., Lowenthal, B., & Egan, R. (1998). *Preschool children with special needs: Children at-risk and children with disabilities.* Needham Heights, MA: Allyn & Bacon.

Lerner, J., Lowenthal, B., & Lerner, S. (1995). *Attention deficit disorders: Assessment and teaching.* Pacific Grove, CA: Brooks/Cole.

Lerner, J. W., & Chen, A. (1992). The cross-cultural nature of learning disabilities: A profile in perseverance. *Learning Disabilities: Research and Practice, 8,* 147–149.

Lerner, J. W., & List, L. (1970). The phonics knowledge of prospective teachers, experienced teachers and elementary pupils. *Illinois School Research, 7,* 39–42.

Lerner, J. W., and Lowenthal, B. (1999). Coping with attention deficit disorder. *The world book health and medical annual 1999* (pp. 106–119). Chicago: World Book.

Lerner, J. W., Lowenthal, B., & Egan, R. (1998). *Preschool children with special needs: Children at-risk and children with disabilities.* Needham Heights, MA: Allyn & Bacon.

Levine, M. (1987). *Developmental variation and learning disabilities.* Cambridge, MA: Educators' Publishing Service.

Levine, M. (1988). Learning disability: What is it? *ACLD Newsbriefs, 173,* 1–2.

Levine, M. (1994). *Educational Care: A System for Understanding and Helping Children with Learning Problems at Home and in School.* Cambridge, MA: Educators Publishing Services.

Levine, M., Hooper, S., Montgomery, J., Reed, M., Sandler, A., & Swartz, C. (1993). Learning disabilities: An interactive developmental paradigm. In G. R. Lyon, D. Gray, J. Kavanagh, & N. Krasnegor (Eds.), *Better understanding of learning disabilities* (pp. 199–228). Baltimore: Paul Brookes.

Levine, M. D., & Swartz, C. W. (1995). The unsuccessful adolescent. In Learning Disabilities Association of America (Ed.), *Secondary education and beyond: Providing opportuni-*

ties for students with learning disabilities (pp. 3–12). Pittsburgh: Learning Disabilities Association of America.

Lewis, R. (1998). Assistive technology and learning disabilities: Today's realities and tomorrow's promises. *Journal of Learning Disabilities, 31* (1), 16–26.

Lewis, R., Ashton, T., Haapa, B., Kieley, C., & Fielden, C. (in press). Improving the writing skills of students with learning disabilities: Are word processors with spelling and grammar checkers useful? *Learning Disabilities: A Multidisciplinary Journal.*

Liberman, A. M. (1997). How theories of speech affect research in reading and writing. In B. Blachman, (Ed.), *Foundations of reading acquisition and dyslexia: Implications for early instruction* (pp. 3–20). Mahwah, NJ: Lawrence Erlbaum.

Liberman, I., & Liberman, A. (1990). Whole language vs. code emphasis: Underlying assumptions and their implications for reading instruction. *Annals of Dyslexia, 40,* 51–78.

Liberman, I. Y., Rubin, H., Duques, S., & Carlisle, J. (1985). Linguistic abilities and spelling proficiency in kindergartners and adult poor spellers. In D. Gray (Ed.), *Behavioral measures of dyslexia.* Parkton, MD: York Press.

Lindamood, P. & Lindamood, P. (1998). *The Lindamood Phoneme Sequencing Program for Reading, Spelling, and Speech (LIPS).* Austin, TX: Pro-Ed.

Lindamood, P. C. (1994). Issues in researching the link between phonological awareness, learning disabilities, and spelling. In G. R. Lyon (Ed.), *Frames of reference for the assessment of learning disabilities* (pp. 351–375). Baltimore: Paul Brookes.

Lindquist, M. (1987). Strategic teaching in mathematics. In B. F. Jones et al. (Eds.), *Strategic teaching and learning: Cognitive instruction in the content areas* (pp. 11–134). Washington, DC: Association for Supervision and Curriculum Development.

Lovitt, T. (1991). Behavioral assessment of learning disabilities. In H. L. Swanson (Ed.), *Handbook on the assessment of learning disabilities* (pp. 95–119). Austin, TX: Pro-Ed.

Lowenthal, B. (1998). Precursors of learning disabilities in the inclusive preschool. *Learning Disabilities: A Multidisciplinary Journal 9* (2), 25–32.

Lowenthal, B., & Lowenthal, M. (1995). The effects of asthma on school performance. *Learning Disabilities: A Multidisciplinary Journal, 6* (20), 41–46.

Luther, S. S. (1993). Methodological and conceptual issues in research in childhood resilience. *Journal of Child Psychology and Psychiatry and Allied Disciplines, 34,* 441–453.

Lyon, G. R. (1994). Critical issues in learning disabilities. In *Frames of reference for learning disabilities* (pp. 1–2). Baltimore: Paul Brookes

Lyon, G. R. (1995a). Toward a definition of dyslexia. *Annals of Dyslexia, 45,* 13–30.

Lyon, G. R. (1995b). Research initiatives in learning disabilities: Contributions from scientists supported by the National Institute of Child Health and Human Development. *Journal of Child Neurology, 10* (Suppl. 1), S120–S126.

Lyon, G. R. (1996). Learning disabilities. *The Future of Children, 6* (1), 54–76.

Lyon, G. R. (1997). Progress and promise in research in learning disabilities. *Learning Disabilities: A Multidisciplinary Journal, 8* (1), 1–6.

Lyon, G. R. (1998). Why reading is not a natural process. *Educational Leadership, 55* (6) 14–18.

Lyon, G. R., Alexander, D., & Yaffee, S. (1997). Programs, promise, and research in learning disabilities. *Learning Disabilities: A Multidisciplinary Journal, 8,* 1–6.

Lyon, G. R., Newby, R., Recht, D., & Caldwell, J. (1991). Neuropsychology and learning disabilities. In B. Wong (Ed.), *Learning about learning disabilities* (pp. 375–406). San Diego: Academic Press.

Lyon, R. & Moats, L. C. (1997). Critical conceptual and methodological considerations in reading intervention research. *Journal of Learning Disabilities, 30* (6), 578–588.

MacArthur, C. (1996). Using technology to enhance the writing process of students with learning disabilities. *Journal of Learning Disabilities 29,* 344–354.

Macintosh, R., Vaughn, S., & Bennerson, D. (1995). FAST social skills with a SLAM and a RAP. *Teaching Exceptional Children, 27,* 37–41.

Macmillan, D. L., Semmel, M. I., & Gerber, M. M. (1995). The social context: Then and now. In J. Kauffman & D. Hallahan (Eds.), *The illusion of full inclusion* (pp. 19–38). Austin, TX: Pro-Ed.

Male, M. (1998). *Technology for Inclusion.* Needham Heights, MA: Allyn & Bacon.

Mallory, B., & New, R. (Eds.). (1994). *Diversity and developmentally appropriate practice.* New York: Teachers College Press.

Manheimer, M. A., & Fleischner, J. E. (1995). Helping students with learning disabilities meet the new math standards. *Secondary education and beyond: Providing opportunities for students with learning disabilities* (pp. 149–158). Pittsburgh: Learning Disabilities Association of America.

Mann, L., Cartright, R., Kenowitz, I., Boyer, C., Metz, C., & Wolford, B. (1984). The child service demonstration centers: A summary report. *Exceptional Children, 50*(6), 532–541.

Mann, V. (1991). Language problems: A key to early reading problems. In B. Wong (Ed.), *Learning about learning disabilities* (pp. 130–163). San Diego: Academic Press.

Markowitz, J., Garcia, S., & Eichelberger, J. (1997). *Addressing the disproportionate representation of students from racial and ethnic minority groups in special education: A resource document.* Alexandria, VA: The National Association of State Directors of Special Education.

Martin, B. (1992). *Brown bear, brown bear, what do you see?* New York: Holt, Rinehart, & Winston.

Martin, K. F., & Manno, C. (1995). Use of a check-off system to improve middle school students' story compositions. *Journal of Learning Disabilities, 28,* 139–149.

Martin, R. (1995). Transition services from a legal perspective. In *Secondary education and beyond: Providing opportunities for students with learning disabilities* (pp. 82–89). Pittsburgh: Learning Disabilities Association of America.

Mastropieri, M. (1987). Statistical and psychometric issues surrounding severe discrepancy: A discussion. *Learning Disabilities Research, 3*(1), 29–31.

Mastropieri, M., & Scruggs, T. (1998). Constructing more meaningful relationships in the classroom: Mnemonic research into practice. *Learning Disabilities: Research & Practice, 13* (3), 138–145.

Mastropieri, M. A., & Scruggs, T. E. (1994). *Effective instruction for special education.* Austin, TX: Pro-Ed.

Mather, N. (1998). Relinquishing aptitude-achievement discrepancy: The doctrine of misplaced precision. *Perspectives: The International Dyslexia Association, 24* (4), 4–7.

Mather, N., & Healey, W. C. (1990). Disposing aptitude-achievement discrepancy in the emperial criterion for learning disabilities. *Learning Disabilities: A Multidisciplinary Journal, 1,* 40–48.

Mather, N., & Roberts, R. (1994). Learning disabilities: A field in danger of extinction. *Learning Disabilities: Research and Practice, 9,* 49–58.

McCormick, L., & Schiefelbusch, R. (1990). *Early language intervention.* Columbus, OH: Merrill.

McGonigel, M., Kaufmann, R., & Johnson, B. (1991). A family-centered process for the individualized family service plan. *Journal of Early Intervention, 15,* 55.

McGrady, H., & Lerner, J. (in press). The educational lives of young adults with learning disabilities. In P. Rodis, A. Garrod, & M. Boscardin (eds.). *Learning Disabilities and Life Stories.* New York: Teachers College Press.

McIntyre, C., and Pickering, J. (1995). *Clinical studies of multisensory structured language education for students with dyslexia and related disorders.* Salem, OR: International Multisensory Structured Language Education Council.

McLaughlin, M., Shepard, L., & O'Day, J. (1995). *Improving education through standards-based reform: A report by the National Academy of Education panel on standards-based education reform.* Palo Alto, CA: Stanford University, National Academy of Education.

McLean, M., Bailey, D., & Wolery, M. (Eds.). (1996). *Assessing infants and preschoolers with special needs.* Englewood Cliffs, NJ: Prentice-Hall.

McLeskey, J., & Waldron, N. (1995). Inclusive elementary programs: Must they cure students with learning disabilities to be effective? *Phi Delta Kappan, 77* (5), 542–546.

Mead, M. (1995). Enriching the reading process with software. *Closing the Gap, 13* (5), 1, 11.

Meichenbaum, D. (1977). *Cognitive behavior modification.* New York: Plenum.

Meisels, S., & Fenichel, F. (Eds.). (1996). *New visions for the developmental assessment of infants and young children.* Washington, DC: Zero to Three, National Center for Infants, Toddlers, and Families.

Meisels, S. J. (1991). Dimensions of early identification. *Journal of Early Intervention, 15,* 26–35.

Mercer, C., Jordan, L., Alsop, D., & Mercer, A. (1996). Learning disabilities definitions and criteria used by the state education departments. *Learning Disability Quarterly, 19* (2), 217–232.

Merzenick, M. M., Jenkins, W. M., & Tallal, P. (1996). Temporal processing deficits of language-learning impaired children ameliorated by training. *Science, 271* (5245), 77–80.

Messerer, J. (1997). Adaptive technology: Unleashing the power of the computer for children with disabilities. *Learning and Leading with Technology, 24* (February 1997).

Messerer, J., Hunt, E., Meyers, G., & Lerner, J. (1984). Feuerstein's instrumental enrichment: A new approach for activating intellectual potential in learning disabled youth. *Journal of Learning Disabilities, 17,* 322–325.

Meyer, M., Wood, F., Hart, L., & Felton, R. (1998). Longitudinal course of rapid naming inn disabled and non-disabled readers. *Annals of Dyslexia, 48,* 90–114.

Miller, S., Butler, F., & Lee, K. (1998). Validated practices for teaching mathematics to students with learning disabilities: A review of the literature. *Focus on Exceptional Children, 31* (1), 1–24.

Miller, S., & Mercer, C. (1997). Education aspects of mathematics disabilities. *Journal of Learning Disabilities, 30* (1), 47–56.

Miller, S. P. (1996). Perceptives on mathematics instruction. In D. Deshler, E. Ellis, & B. Lenz. *Teaching adolescents with learning disabilities.* Denver: Love Publishing.

Moats, L. (1998). Teaching decoding. *American Educator, 22* (1 & 2), 42–65.

Moats, L. C. (1994a). Assessment of spelling in learning disabilities research. In G. R. Lyon (Ed.), *Frames of reference for the assessment of learning disabilities* (pp. 333–350). Baltimore: Paul Brookes.

Moats, L. C. (1994b). Honing the concepts of listening and speaking: A prerequisite to the valid measurement of language behavior in children. In G. R. Lyon (Ed.), *Frames of reference for the assessment of learning disabilities* (pp. 229–242). Baltimore: Paul Brookes.

Moats, L. C. (1998). Teaching decoding. *American Educator, 22* (1 & 2), 42–51.

Moll, L. C., & Gonzales, N. (1994). Lessons from research with language minority children. *Journal of Reading Behavior, 26,* 439–456.

Monda-Amayla, L., Dieker, L., and Reed, F. (1998). Preparing students with learning disabilities to participate in inclusive classrooms. *Learning Disabilities: Research & Practice 13* (3), 171–182.

Montague, M. (1997). Cognitive strategy instruction in mathematics for students with learning disabilities. *Journal of Learning Disabilities, 30* (2), 164–177.

Montague, M., Applegate, B., & Marquard, K. (1993). Cognitive strategy instruction and mathematical problem-solving performance of students with learning disabilities. *Learning Disabilities: Research and Practice, 8,* 223–232.

Montague, M., & Bos, C. S. (1986). The effect of cognitive strategy verbal math problem-solving performance of learning-disabled adolescents. *Journal of Learning Disabilities, 19*(1), 26–33.

Montessori, M. (1912). *The Montessori method* (A. E. George, Trans.). New York: Frederick Stokes.

Montessori, M. (1964). *The Montessori method.* New York: Bently.

Moore, R., Cartledge, G., & Heckaman, K. (1995). The effects of social skill instruction and self-monitoring on game-related behaviors of adolescents with emotional or behavioral disorders. *Behavioral Disorders, 20* (4), 253–266.

Morsink, C. et al. (1986). Research on teaching: Opening the door to special education classrooms, *Exceptional Children, 53,* 32–40.

Myklebust, H. (1968). Learning disabilities: Definitions and overview. In H. Myklebust (Ed.), *Progress in learning disabilities* (Vol. 1, pp. 1–15). New York: Grune & Stratton.

Nall, A. (1971). Prescriptive living. In J. Arena (Ed.), *The child with learning disabilities: His right to learn* (pp. 69–77). San Rafael, CA: Academic Therapy Publications.

National Council for Teachers of Mathematics. (1991). *Professional Standards for Teaching Mathematics.* Reston, VA: Author.

National Council of Teachers of Mathematics. (1989). *Curriculum and evaluation standards for school mathematics.* Reston, VA: National Council of Teachers of Mathematics.

National Institutes of Health. (1998). Diagnosis and treatment of attention deficit hyperactivity disorder. NIH Consensus Statement.

National Joint Committee on Learning Disabilities. (1994). *Collective perspectives on issues affecting learning disabilities.* Austin, TX: Pro-Ed.

National Joint Committee on Learning Disabilities. (1997). Operationalizing the NJCLD definition of Learning Disabilities for Ongoing Assessment in Schools. *Perspectives: The International Dyslexia Association, 23* (4), 29–33.

National Research Council. (1998). *Preventing reading difficulties in young children.* Washington, DC: National Academy of Sciences.

National Training Center for Professional AIDS Education Opens. (1992). *DEC Communicator, 18*(3), 5.

NLD web site. **http://www.nldline.com.**

O'Conner, P., Sofo, F., Kendall, L., and Olsen, G. (1990). Reading disabilities and the effects of colored filters. *Journal of Learning Disabilities, 23,* 597–603.

Oakland, T., Black, J., Stanford, G. Nussbaum, N., & Balise, R. (1998). An evaluation of the dyslexia training program: A multisensory method for promoting reading in students with reading disabilities. *Journal of Learning Disabilities, 31,* 14–147.

Oas, B. K., Schumaker, J. B., & Deshler, D. D. (1995). Learning strategies: Tools for learning to learn in middle and high schools. In *Secondary education and beyond: Providing opportunities for students with learning disabilities* (pp. 90–100). Pittsburgh: Learning Disabilities Association of America.

Ogle, D. (1986). K-W-L: A teaching model that develops active reading of expository text. *The Reading Teacher, 39,* 564–570.

Olson, R. K., Gillis, J. J., Rack, J. P., et al. (1991). Confirmatory factor analysis of word recognition and process measures in the Colorado reading project. *Reading Writing, 3,* 235–248.

Opp, G. (1992). A German perspective on learning disabilities. *Journal of Learning Disabilities, 26* (6), 351–360.

Ortiz, A. (1997). Learning disabilities occurring concomitantly with linguistic differences. *Journal of Learning Disabilities, 30* (3), 321–232.

Orton, J. (1976). *A guide to teaching phonics.* Cambridge, MA: Educators Publishing Service.

Orton, S. (1937). *Reading, writing and speech problems in children.* New York: Norton.

Osman, B. (1987). Promoting social acceptance of children with learning disabilities. *Reading, Writing, and Learning Disabilities, 3,* 111–118.

Osman, B. (1997). *Learning disability and ADHD: A family guide to learning and learning together.* New York: John Wiley.

Otto, W., McMenemy, R., & Smith, R. (1973). *Corrective and remedial teaching.* Boston: Houghton Mifflin.

Owens, R. E. (1995). *Language disorders: A functional approach to assessment and intervention.* New York: Merrill/Macmillan.

Palinscar, A., & Brown, A. (1984). Reciprocal teaching of comprehension-fostering and comprehension-monitoring activities. *Cognition and Instruction, 1,* 117–175.

Palinscar, A., Brown, A., & Campione, J. (1991). Dynamic assessment. In H. L. Swanson (Ed.), *Handbook on the assessment of learning disabilities* (pp. 75–94). Austin, TX: Pro-Ed.

Palinscar, H., & Klenk, L. (1992). Fostering literacy learning in supportive contexts. *Journal of Learning Disabilities, 25,* 211–225.

Parker, H. C. (1992). *The ADD hyperactivity handbook for schools.* Plantation, FL: Impact Press.

Parmar, S., & Cawley, J. (1997). Preparing teachers to teach mathematics to students with learning disabilities. *Journal of Learning Disabilities, 30* (2) 188–197.

Patten, B. (1973). Visually mediated thinking: A report of the case of Albert Einstein. *Journal of Learning Disabilities, 6,* 415–420.

Patton, J., Cronin, M., Bassett, D., & Koppel, A. (1997). A life skills approach to mathematics instruction: Preparing students with learning disabilities for real-life math demands of adulthood. *Journal of Learning Disabilities, 30* (2), 178–187.

Pennington, B. (1995). Genetics of learning disabilities. *Journal of Child Neurology, 10* (Suppl. 1), S69–S77.

Pennington, B., Smith, S., Kimberling, W., Green, P., & Haith, M. (1987). Left-handedness and immune disorders in familial dyslexics. *Archives of Neurology, 44,* 634–639.

Piaget, J. (1952). *The origins of intelligence in children* (M. Cook, Trans.). New York: International University Press. (Original work published in 1936.)

Piaget, J. (1970). *The science of education and psychology of the child.* New York: Grossman.

Pinker, S. (1995). *The Language Instinct.* New York: Harper Perennial.

Pinnell, G., et al. (1994). Comparing instructional models for the literacy education of high-risk first graders. *Reading Research Quarterly, 29* (1), 8–39.

PL 103–218. (1994). *Technology-Related Assistance for Individuals with Disabilities Act.* Washington, DC: U.S. Congress.

PL 105–17. (1997). The Individuals with Disabilities Education Act of 1997.

Poteet, J. A., Choate, J. S., & Stewart, S. C. (1993). Performance assessment and special education: Practices and prospects. *Focus on Exceptional Children, 26* (1), 1–20.

Premack, D. (1959). Toward empirical behavior law, I: Positive reinforcement. *Psychological Review, 66,* 219–223.

Pressley, M. (1991). *The cognitive strategy training series.* Cambridge, MA: Brookline Books.

Pressley, M., & Rankin, J. (1994). More about whole language methods of reading instruction for students at risk for early reading failure. *Learning Disabilities: Research and Practice, 9* (3), 157–168.

Price, L., (1997). Psychosocial issues of workplace adjustment. In P. Gerber & D. Brown (Eds.), *Learning disabilities and employment* (pp. 275–306). Austin, TX: Pro-Ed.

Pugach, M. , & Johnson, L. (1988). Peer collaboration. *Teaching Exceptional Children, 20*(3), 75–77.

Raffi. (Singer). (1986). *A children's sampler of singable songs.* Willowdale, Ontario: Shoreline Records, a division of Troubadour Records, Ltd. (cassette).

Rapkin, I. (1995). Physician's testing of children with developmental disabilities. *Journal of Child Neurology, 10* (Suppl. 1), S11–S15.

Rapp, D. J. (1986). *The impossible child in school and at home.* Buffalo, NY: Life Sciences Press.

Raskind, M. & Higgins, E. (1998). Assistive technology for postsecondary students with learning disabilities: An overview. *Journal of Learning Disabilities, 31* (1), 27–40.

Raskind, M. (1998). Assistive technology for individuals with learning disabilities: How far have we come? *Perspectives: The International Dyslexia Association, 24* (2), 20–26.

Raskind, M., & Higgins, E. (1998). Assistive technology for postsecondary students with learning disabilities: An overview. *Journal of Learning Disabilities, 30* (1), 27–40.

Raskind, M., & Higgins, E. (1998). Technology and learning disabilities: What do we know and where should we go? *Perspectives: The International Dyslexia Association, 24* (2), 1.

Raskind, M., Higgins, E., Slaff, M. & Shaw, T. (1998). Assistive technology in the homes of children with learning disabilities: An exploratory study. *Learning Disabilities: A Multidisciplinary Journal, 9* (2), 33–56.

Raskind, M. H. (1998). Literacy for adults with learning disabilities through assistive technology. In S. Vogel and S. Reder (Eds.) *Learning disabilities, literacy, and adult education* (pp. 253–274). Baltimore: Paul H. Brookes.

Regulations for IDEA 1997. (1999). *Federal Register, 64* (48), 12 March 1999. 300. 7 (c) (9) (i).

Reichman, J., & Healey, W. (1983). Learning disabilities in conductive hearing loss involving otitis media. In G. Senf & J. Torgesen (Eds.), *Annual review of learning disabilities: Vol. 1, A Journal of Learning Disabilities reader* (pp. 39–45). Chicago: Professional Press.

Reid, D., Hresko, W., Swanson, H., (Eds.). (1996). *Cognitive approaches to learning disabilities.* Austin, TX: Pro-Ed.

Reid, G. R., & Rumsey, J. (1996). *Neuroimaging: A Window to the Neurological Foundations of Learning and Behavior in Children.* Baltimore: Paul H. Brookes.

Resnick, L. (1989). Developing mathematical knowledge. *American Psychologist, 44,* 162–169.

Resnick, L., & Klopfer, L. (1989). Toward the thinking curriculum: An overview. In L. Resnick & L. Klopfer (Eds.), *Toward the thinking curriculum: Current cognitive research* (pp. 1–18). Alexandria, VA: Association for Supervision and Curriculum Development.

Reynolds, C. (1985). Critical measurement issues in learning disabilities. *Journal of Special Education, 18,* 451–475.

Reynolds, C., & Kamphaus, R. (1992). *Behavior assessment system for children.* Circle Pines, MN: American Guidance Services.

Rhim, L. M., & McLaughlin, M. J. (1997). Building capacity for education reform. *State-level policies and practices: Where are students with disabilities?* Alexandria, VA: Center for Policy Research on the Impact of General and Special Education Reform, National Association of State Boards of Education.

Richek, M., Caldwell, J., Jennings, J., & Lerner, J. (1996). *Reading problems: Assessment and teaching strategies.* Needham Heights, MA: Allyn & Bacon.

Richek, M., List, L., & Lerner, J. (1989). *Reading problems: Assessment and teaching strategies.* Englewood Cliffs, NJ: Prentice-Hall.

Richmond, J. (1990). Low-birth weight infants. *JAMA (Journal of the American Medical Association), 263*(22), 3069–3070.

Rieth, H., & Polsgrove, L. (1994). Curriculum and instructional issues in teaching secondary students with learning disabilities. *Learning Disabilities: Research and Practice, 9* (2), 118–126.

Rivera, D. (1997). Mathematics education and students with learning disabilities: Introduction to special series. *Journal of Learning Disabilities, 30* (1), 2–19, 68.

Roberts, R., & Mather, N. (1995). The return of students with learning disabilities to regular classrooms: A sellout? *Learning Disabilities: Research and Practice, 10* (1), 46–58.

Robinson, G., & Conway, R. (1990). The effects of Irlen colored lenses on students' specific reading skills and their perception of ability: A 12-month validity study. *Journal of Learning Disabilities, 23,* 588–596.

Rock, E., Fessler, M., & Church, R. (1997). The concomitance of learning disabilities and emotional/behavioral disorders: A conceptual model. *Journal of Learning Disabilities, 30* (3), 245–263.

Rockefeller, N. (1976, October 16). *TV Guide,* pp. 12–14.

Roman, M. (1998). The syndrome of nonverbal learning disabilities: clinical description and applied aspects. *Current Issues in Education, 1* (1), (Fall). An electronic journal at **http://cie.ed.asu.edu/index/htm/.**

Romberg, T. A. (1993). NCTM's standards: A rallying flag for mathematics teachers. *Educational Leadership, 50* (5), 36–42.

Rose, E. (1993). Faculty development: Changing attitudes and enhancing knowledge about learning disabilities. In S. Vogel & P. Adelman (Eds.), *Success for students with learning disabilities.* New York: Springer-Verlag, pp. 131–150.

Rosenshine, B. (1986). Synthesis of research on explicit teaching. *Educational Leadership, 43,* 60–69.

Rosenshine, B. (1997). Advances in research on instruction. In J. Lloyd, E., Kameenui, & D. Chard (Eds.), *Issues in educating students with disabilities* (pp. 197–220). Mahwah, NJ: Lawrence Erlbaum.

Rosenshine, B., & Stevens, R. (1986). Teaching functions. In M. Wittock (Ed.), *Handbook of research on teaching* (3rd ed., pp. 376–391). New York: Macmillan.

Rosenthal, R., & Jacobson, L. (1968). *Pygmalion in the classroom.* New York: Holt, Rinehart and Winston.

Rosner, J. (1999). *Helping Children Overcome Learning Difficulties.* New York: Walker & Co.

Roswell, F. G., & Chall, J. S. (1994). DARTTS (Diagnostic Assessments of Reading with Trial Teaching Strategies). Chicago: Riverside.

Rothstein, L. (1998). Americans with Disabilities Act, Section 504, and adults with learning disabilities in adult education and transition to employment. In S. Vogel & S. Reder (Eds.), *Learning disabilities, literacy, and adult education* (pp. 29–43). Baltimore: Paul H. Brookes

Rourke, B., & Conway, J. (1997). Disabilities of arithmetic and mathematical reasoning: Perspectives from neurology and neuropsychology. *Journal of Learning Disabilities, 30* (1), 34–46.

Rourke, B., & Fuerst, D. R. (1995). *Learning disabilities syndrome of nonverbal learning disabilities: Neurodevelopmental manifestations.* New York: Guilford Press.

Rourke, B. P. (1989). *Nonverbal learning disabilities: The syndrome and the model.* New York: Guilford.

Rourke, B. P. (1995). *Syndrome of nonverbal learning disabilities: Neurodevelopmental manifestations.* New York: Guilford.

Runion, H. (1980). Hypoglycemia: Fact or fiction? In W. Cruickshank (Ed.), *Approaches to learning: Vol. 1. The best of ACLD* (pp. 111–122). Syracuse: Syracuse University Press.

Rusch, F., & Phelps, L. (1987). Secondary special education and transition from school to work: A national priority. *Exceptional Children, 53,* 487–492.

Salvia, J., & Ysseldyke, J. (1998). *Assessment* (7th ed.), Boston: Houghton Mifflin.

Scanlon, D. (1996). Social skills strategy instruction. In D. Deshler, E. Ellis, & B. Lenz (Eds.), *Teaching adolescents with learning disabilities: Strategies and methods.* Denver: Love Publishing.

Scanlon, D., Deshler, D., & Schumaker, J. (1996). Can a strategy be taught and learned in secondary inclusive classrooms? *Learning Disabilities Research and Practice, 11* (1), 41–57.

Schmid, R., & Evans, W. (1998). *Curriculum and Instruction for Students with Emotional/Behavioral Disorders.* Reston, VA: Council for Children with Behavioral Disorders.

Schumaker, J., Deshler, D., & Ellis, E. (1986). Intervention issues related to the education of LD adolescents. In J. Torgesen & B. Wong (Eds.), *Psychological and educational perspectives on learning disabilities* (pp. 329–366). New York: Academic Press.

Schumaker, J. B., & Deshler, D. D. (1995). Social skills and learning disabilities. *LDA Newsbriefs* (March/April).

Schweinhart, L. J., Barnes, H. V., & Weikart, D. B. (1993). *Significant benefits: The High/Scope Perry Preschool study through age 27.* Monographs of the High/Scope Educational Research Foundation, No. 10. Ypsilanti, MI: High Scope Press.

Scientific Learning. (1995). *FastfForWord.* Berkeley, CA: Author.

Scruggs, T., & Mastropieri, M. (1991). *Teaching students ways to remember: Strategies for learning mnemonically.* Cambridge, MA: Brookline Books.

Semb, G., & Ellis, J. (1994). Knowledge taught in school: What is remembered? *Review of Educational Research, 64* (2), 253–286.

Senate Report on the Individuals with Disabilities Education Act Amendments of 1997. (1997). (Available at **http://wais.access.gpo.gov**).

Sequin, E. (1970). *Idiocy and its treatment by the physiological method.* New York: Columbia University Press. (Original work published 1866).

Shalev, R. Manor, O., Auerbach, J., & Grodd-Tour, V. (1998). Persistence of developmental dyscalculia: What counts: *The Journal of Pediatrics, 133* (3), 358–362.

Shanklin, N., & Rhodes, L. (1989). Transforming literacy instruction. *Educational Leadership, 47,* 59–63.

Shannon, T., & Barr, R. (1995). Reading recovery: An independent evaluation of the effects of an early instruction intervention for at-risk learners. *Reading Research Quarterly, 30* (4), 958–996.

Shaw, S. F., Cullen, J. P., McGuire, J. M., & Brinckerhoff, L. C. (1995). Operationalizing a definition of learning disabilities. *Journal of Learning Disabilities, 28,* 586–597.

Shaywitz, B., Fletcher, J., & Shaywitz, S. (1995). Defining and classifying learning disabilities and attention deficit hyperactivity disorder. *Journal of Child Neurology, 10* (Suppl. 1), S50–S57.

Shaywitz, B., & Shaywitz, S. (1998). Functional disruption in the organization of the brain for reading in dyslexia. *Proceedings of the National Academy of Sciences, 95* (5).

Shaywitz, B., & Shaywitz, S. (1998). Biological basis for reading disability. *Proceedings of the National Academy of Sciences, 95* (5).

Shaywitz, S., & Shaywitz, B. (1988). Attention-deficit disorder: Current Perspectives. In J. Kavanagh & J. Truss (Eds.), *Learning disabilities: Proceedings of the National Conference* (pp. 369–567). Parkton, MD: York Press.

Shaywitz, S., Shaywitz, B., Fletcher, J., & Makuch, R. (1992). Evidence that dyslexia may represent the lower tail of a normal distribution of reading ability. *New England Journal of Medicine, 36,* 145–150.

Shaywitz, S., Shaywitz, B., & Fletcher, J. (1990). Prevalence of reading disability in boys and girls: Results of the Connecticut longitudinal study. *Journal of the American Medical Association, 264,* 998–1002.

Sherman, G. F. (1995). Dyslexia: Is it all in your mind? *Perspectives: The Orton Dyslexia Society, 21* (4), 1–8.

Shinn, M. R., & Hubbard, D. (1992). Curriculum-based measurement and problem-solving assessment: Basic procedures and outcomes. *Focus on Exceptional Children, 24*(5), 1–20.

Shonkoff, J., & Meisels, S. J. (1991). Defining eligibility for services under PL 99–457. *Journal of Early Intervention, 15,* 21–25.

Shriner, J., Ysseldyke, J., & Thurlow, M (1994). Standards for all American students. *Focus on Exceptional Children, 26* (5), 1–19.

Silver, A., & Hagin, R. (1966). Maturation of perceptual functions in children with specific reading disabilities. *The Reading Teacher, 19,* 253–259.

Silver, A., & Hagin, R. (1990). *Disorders of learning in childhood.* New York: Wiley.

Silver, L. (1989). Psychological and family problems associated with learning disabilities: Assessment and interventions. *Journal of the American Academy of Child and Adolescent Psychiatry, 28,* 319–325.

Silver, L. (1992). *The misunderstood child.* Blue Ridge Summit, PA: Tab Books.

Silver, L. (1992). *The misunderstood child: A guide for parents of children with learning disabilities.* New York: Times Books.

Silver, L. (1995a). Controversial therapies. *Journal of Child Neurology, 10* (Suppl. 1), S96–S99.

Silver, L. (1995b). Knowledge of self: The key to self-esteem and self-advocacy. In Learning Disabilities Association of America (Ed.), *Secondary education and beyond: Providing opportunities for students with learning disabilities* (pp. 223–233). Pittsburgh: Learning Disabilities Association of America.

Silver, L. (1998). *The misunderstood child: Understanding and coping with your child's learning disabilities.* New York: Times Books.

Silver, L. B. (1987). The "magic cure": A review of the current controversial approaches to treatment of learning disabilities. *Journal of Learning Disabilities, 20,* 498–504.

Silver, L. B. (1988). A review of the federal government's Interagency Committee on Learning Disabilities: A report to Congress. *Learning Disabilities Focus, 3*(2), 73–81.

Simmons, D. C., & Kameenui, E. J. (1996). A focus on curriculum design: When children fail. *Focus on Exceptional Children, 28* (7), 1–16.

Skinner, B. (1957). *Verbal behavior.* New York: Appleton-Century-Crofts.

Slavin, R. (1991). *Educational psychology.* Englewood Cliffs, NJ: Prentice-Hall.

Slingerland, B. (1976). *A multisensory program for language arts for specific language disability children: A guide for primary teachers.* Cambridge, MA: Educators Publishing Service.

Smith, B. K., & Strain, P. S. (1988). Early childhood special education in the next decade: Implementing and expanding PL 99–457. *Topics in Early Childhood Special Education, 8,* 34–47.

Smith, C. (1991). *Learning disabilities: The interaction of learner, task, and setting.* Boston: Little, Brown.

Smith, S., Boone, R., & Higgins, K. (1998). Expanding the writing process to the Web. *Teaching exceptional children, 30* (5), 22–33.

Smith, S. L. (1991). *Succeeding against the odds: Strategies and insights from the learning disabled.* Los Angeles: Jeremy P. Tarcher.

Smith, S. L., & Levine, S. E. (in press). Technology the lab school way: Multisensory empowering experience for students with severe learning disabilities and ADHD. *Learning Disabilities: A Multidisciplinary Journal.*

Snow, C., Burns, M. & Griffin, P. (Eds.). (1998). *Report of the committee on the prevention of reading difficulties in young children.* Washington, DC: National Research Council, National Academy of Sciences.

Snow, C., Burns, M., & Griffin, R. (Eds). (1998). *Preventing reading difficulties in young children.* Washington, DC: National Academy Press.

Solan, H. (1990). An appraisal of the Irlen technique of correcting reading disorders using tinted overlays and tinted lenses. *Journal of Learning Disabilities, 23,* 621–623.

Stahl, S. A., & Murray, B. A. (1994). Defining phonological awareness and its relationship to early reading. *Journal of Educational Psychology, 86,* 221–234.

Stainback, W., & Stainback, S. (Eds.). (1992). *Controversial issues confronting special education: Divergent perspectives.* Needham Heights, MA: Allyn & Bacon.

Stainback, W., & Stainback, S. (Eds.). (1996). *Inclusion: A guide for educators.* Baltimore: Paul H. Brookes.

Stanovich, K. & Siegel, L. S. (1994). The phenotypic performance profile of reading disabled children: A regression-based text of the phonological-core variable difference model. *Journal of Educational Psychology, 86,* 24–53.

Stanovich, K. (1993). The construct validity of discrepancy definitions of reading disabilities. In G. R. Lyon, D. Gray, J. Kavanagh, & N. Krasnegor (Eds.), *Better understanding learning disabilities* (pp. 273–307). Baltimore: Paul Brookes.

Stanovich, K. (1994). Are discrepancy-based definitions of dyslexia empirically defensible? In K. Vanden Bos, L. Siegl, D. Bakker, & D. Share (Eds.), *Current directions in dyslexia research* (pp. 15–30). Alblasserdam, Holland: Swetz & Zertlinger.

Stanovich, K. E. (1986b). Matthew effects in reading: Some consequences of individual differences in the acquisition of literacy. *Reading Research Quarterly, 21,* 360–406.

Stauffer, R. G. (1975). *Directing the reading-thinking process.* New York: Harper & Row.

Stephens, R. (1987). *Write/read/write some more.* Paper presented at the Fourth Annual Conference on Adult Reading Problems, Chicago State University, September 27.

Stevens, G., & Birch, J. (1957). A proposed clarification of the terminology to describe brain-injured children. *Exceptional Children, 23,* 346–349.

Stewart, A., & Lillie, P. (1995). Transition plan. In *Secondary education and beyond: Providing opportunities for students with learning disabilities* (pp. 58–81). Pittsburgh: Learning Disabilities Association of America.

Stipek, D. (1993). *Motivation to learn: From theory to practice.* Boston: Allyn & Bacon.

Stone, A. (1998). Moving validated instructional practices into the classroom: Learning from examples about the rough road to success. *Learning Disabilities: Research & Practice 13* (3), 121–125.

Stone, C. A. (1998). The metaphor of scaffolding: Its utility for the field of learning disabilities. *Journal of Learning Disabilities, 13* (4), 344–364.

Strauss, A., & Lehtinen, L. (1947). *Psychopathology and education of the brain-injured child.* New York: Grune & Stratton.

Sugai, G., & Tindal, G. (1993). *Effective school consultation: An interactive approach.* Pacific Grove, CA: Brooks/Cole.

Sulzby, E., & Teale, W. (1991). Emergent Literacy. In. R. Barr, M. Kamil, P. Mosenthal, & D. Pearson (Eds.), *Handbook of reading research, Vol. 2* (pp. 727–758). White Plains, NY: Longman.

Swanson, H. (1987). Informational processing theory and learning disabilities: An overview. *Journal of Learning Disabilities, 20,* 3–7.

Swanson, H. (1996). Informational processing: An introduction. In D. Reid, W. Hresko, & H. Swanson (Eds.), *Cognitive approaches to learning disabilities* (pp. 251–286).Austin, TX: Pro-Ed.

Swanson, H. L. (1993). Learning disabilities from the perspective of cognitive psychology. In G. R. Lyon, D. Gray, J. Kavanagh, & N. Krasnegor (Eds.), *Better understanding learning disabilities* (pp. 199–228). Baltimore: Paul Brookes.

Tallal, P., Allard, L., Miller, S., & Curtiss, S. (1997). Academic outcomes of language impaired children. In C. Hulme and M. Snowling (Eds.). *Dyslexia: Biology, cognition, and intervention* (pp. 167–179). London: Whurt, British Dyslexia Association.

Tallal, P., Jenkins, W., & Merzenich, M. (1997). The role of temporal processing in developmental language-based learning disorders. In B. Blachman (Ed.), *Foundations of reading acquisition and dyslexia* (pp. 49–66). Mahwah, NJ: Lawrence Erlbaum.

Tallal, P., Miller, S. L., & Merzenick, M. M. (1996). Language comprehension in language-learning impaired children improved with acoustically modified speech. *Science, 271* (5245), 81–83.

Tallal, P., Miller, S., Jenkins, W., Merzenich, M. (1997). The role of temporal processing in developmental language-based learning disorders: Research and clinical implications. In B. Blachman (Ed). *Foundations of reading acquisition and dyslexia* (pp. 49–66). Mahwah, NJ: Lawrence Erlbaum.

Tankersley, M. & Landrum, T. (1997). Comorbidity of emotional and behavioral disorders. In J. Lloyd, E. Kameenui, & D. Chard (Eds.), *Issues in educating students with disabilities* (pp. 153–176). Mahwah, NJ: Lawrence Erlbaum.

Tarver, S. (1992). Direct instruction. In W. Stainback & S. Stainback (Eds.), *Controversial issues confronting special education* (pp. 141–152). Needham Heights, MA: Allyn & Bacon.

Taylor, R., Partenio, I., & Ziegler, E. (1983). Diagnostic use of WISC-R subtest scatter: A note of caution. *Diagnostique, 9,* 26–31.

Teeter, P. A., & Semrud-Clikeman, M. (1997). *Child neurology: Assessment and interventions for neuropsychological and neurodevelopmental disorders of childhood.* Needham Heights, MA: Allyn & Bacon.

Thomas, A., & Chess, S. (1977). *Temperament and development.* New York: Bruner/Mazel.

Thompson, L. (1971). Language disabilities in men of eminence. *Journal of Learning Disabilities, 4,* 34–15.

Thompson, S. (1997). *The source for nonverbal learning disabilities.* East Moline, IL: LinguiSystems.

Thorndike, E. (1917). Reading as reasoning: A study in paragraph reading. *Journal of Educational Psychology, 8,* 323–332.

Thornton, C. A. (1984). *Matter of facts.* Oaklawn, IL: Creative Publications.

Thornton, C., Langruall, C., & Jones, G. (1997). Mathematics instruction for elementary students with learning disabilities. *Journal of Learning Disabilities, 30* (2), 142–150.

Thousand, J., & Villa, R. (1991). A futuristic view of the REI: A response to Jenkins, Pious, and Jewell. *Exceptional Children, 57,* 556–562.

Thurber, D. N., & Jordon, D. (1981). *D'Nealian handwriting.* Glenview, IL: Scott, Foresman.

Time. (1996, January 29). pp. 62–64.

Tindal, G., & Nolet, V. (1995). Curriculum-based measurement in middle and high schools: Critical thinking skills in content areas. *Focus on Exceptional Children, 17* (7), 1–22.

Tjossem, T. (1976). Early intervention: Issues and approaches. In T. Tjossem (Ed.), *Intervention strategies for high risk infants and young children* (pp. 3–33). Baltimore, MD: University Park Press.

Toliver, M. (1990). Try it, you'll like it: Whole language. *The Reading Teacher, 43,* 348–349.

Tomlan, P. S., & Mather, N. (1996). Back on track: A response to Shaw, Cullen, McGuire, & Brinckerhoff. *Journal of Learning Disabilities, 29* (2), 220–224.

Torgensen, J., & Wagner, R. (1998). Alternative diagnostic approaches to specific developmental reading disabilities. *Learning Disabilities: Research & Practice, 13* (4), 220–232.

Torgesen J. (1998). Catch them before they fall. *American Educator, 22* (1 & 2), 32–41.

Torgesen, J. (1991). Learning disabilities: Historical and conceptual issues. In B. Wong (Ed.), *Learning about learning disabilities* (pp. 3–39). San Diego: Academic Press.

Torgesen, J. (1993). Variations on theory in learning disabilities. In G. R. Lyon, D. Gray, J. Kavanagh, & N. Krasnegor (Eds.), *Better understanding of learning disabilities* (pp. 153–171). Baltimore: Paul Brookes.

Torgesen, J. (1997). The prevention and remediation of reading difficulties: Evaluating what we know from research. *Journal of Academic Language Therapy, 1,* 11–47.

Torgesen, J. (1998). Catch them before they fall. *American Educator, 22* (1 & 2), 32–51.

Torgesen, J., & Bryant, B. (1994). *Phonological awareness training for reading.* Austin, TX: Pro-Ed.

Torgesen, J., Wagner, R., Rashette, C., Alexander, A., & Conway, T. (1997). Preventive and remedial interventions for children with severe reading disabilities. *Learning Disabilities: A Multidisciplinary Journal, 8.* 51–62.

Traub, N., & Bloom, F. (1978). *Recipe for reading.* Cambridge, MA: Educators Publishing Service.

Troia, G., Graham, S., & Harris, H. (1998). Teaching students with learning disabilities to mindfully plan when writing. *Exceptional Children, 65* (2), 235–252.

Troia, G., Roth, F., & Graham, S. (1998). An educator's guide to phonological awareness: Assessment measures and intervention activities for children. *Focus on Exceptional Children, 31* (3), 1–12.

Tsatsanis, K., Fuerst, D., & Rourke, B. (1997). Psychosocial dimensions of learning disabilities: External validation and relationship with age and academic functioning. *Journal of Learning Disabilities, 30* (5), 490–502.

Tur-Kaspa, H., Weisel, A., & Segrev, L. (1998). Attributes for feelings of loneliness of students with learning disabilities. *Learning Disabilities: Research and Practice, 13* (2), 89–94.

Turnbull, A., & Turnbull, H. (1996). *Families, professionals, and exceptionality.* Upper Saddle River, NJ: Merrill.

Umansky, W., & Hooper. S. (1998). *Young children with special needs.* Columbus, OH: Prentice-Hall.

Underhill, R., Uprichard, A., & Heddens, J. (1980). *Diagnosing mathematics difficulties.* Columbus, OH: Charles E. Merrill.

U.S. Department of Education. (1990). *To assure the free appropriate public education of all handicapped children.* Twelfth Annual Report to Congress on the Implementation of the Handicapped Act. Washington, DC: U.S. Government Printing Office.

U.S. Department of Education. (1991a). *To assure the free appropriate public education of all children with disabilities.* Thirteenth Annual Report to Congress on the Implementation of the Individuals with Disabilities Act. Washington, DC: U.S. Government Printing Office.

U.S. Department of Education. (1991b). *Policy memorandum: Clarification of policy to address the needs of children with attention-deficit disorders within general and/or special education.*

U.S. Department of Education. (1994). *To assure the free appropriate public education of all children with disabilities.* Sixteenth Annual Report to Congress on the Implementation of the Individuals with Disabilities Education Act. Washington, DC: U.S. Government Printing Office.

U.S. Department of Education. (1995). *To assure the free appropriate public education of all children with disabilities.* Seventeenth Annual Report to Congress on the Implementation of the Individuals with Disabilities Education Act. Washington, DC: U.S. Government Printing Office.

U.S. Department of Education. (1997). *To assure the free appropriate public education of all children with disabilities.* Nineteenth Annual report to Congress on the Implementation of the Individuals with Disabilities Education Act. Washington, DC: U.S. Government Printing Office.

U.S. Office of Education. (1977). *Assistance to states for education of handicapped children: Procedures for evaluating specific learning disabilities.* (Federal Register, 42:65082–65085).

Utley, C., Mortweet, S., Greenwood, C. (1997). Peer-mediated instruction and interventions. *Focus on Exceptional Children, 29* (5), 1–23.

Vaidya, C., Austin, G., Kirkorian, G., Ridelhuber, H., Desmond, J., Glover, G. & Gabrieli, J. (1998). Selective effects of methylphenidate in attention deficit hyperactivity disorder: A functional magnetic resonance study. *Proceedings of the National Academy of Sciences, 95* (24), pp. 14494–14499.

Vail, P. (1990). Gifts, talents, and the dyslexias: Wellsprings, springboards, and finding Foleys rocks. *Annals of Dyslexia, 40,* 3–17.

Valencia, S. (1990a). Alternative assessment: Separating the wheat from the chaff. *The Reading Teacher, 44,* 60–61.

Vanderwood, M., McGrew, K., & Ysseldyke, J. (1998). Why we can't say much about students with disabilities during educational reform. *Exceptional Children, 64* (3), 359–370.

Vaughn, S. (1991). Social skills enhancement in students with learning disabilities. In B. Wong (Ed.), *Learning about learning disabilities* (pp. 408–440). San Diego: Academic Press.

Vaughn, S., & Haager, D. (1994). The measurement of assessment of social skills. In G. R. Lyon (Ed.), *Frames of reference for the assessment of learning disabilities: New views of measurement issues* (pp. 555–570). Baltimore: Paul Brookes.

Vaughn, S., & Schumm, J. (1995). Responsible inclusion for students with learning disabilities. *Journal of Learning Disabilities, 28,* 264–270, 290.

Vaughn, S., & Wilson, C. (1994). Mathematics assessment for students with learning disabilities. In G. R. Lyon (Ed.), *Frames of reference for the assessment of learning disabilities* (pp. 459–472). Baltimore: Paul Brookes.

Vaughn, S., Schumm, J., Arguelles, M. (1997). The ABCDEs of Co-Teaching. *Focus on Exceptional Children, 30* (2), 26–29.

Vaughn, S., Zaragoza, N., Hogan, Z., & Walker, J. (1993). A four-year longitudinal investigation of the social skills and behavior problems of students with learning disabilities. *Journal of Learning Disabilities, 26* (6), 404–412.

Villa, A., Thousand, J., Meyers, H., & Nevin, A. (1996). Teacher and administrator perceptions of heterogenous education *Focus on Exceptional Children, 63,* 29–36.

Villa, R., & Thousand, J. (1990). Administrative supports to promote inclusive schooling. In W. Stainback & S. Stainback (Eds.), *Support networks for inclusive schooling: Integrated interdependent education* (pp. 201–218). Baltimore: Paul Brookes.

Voeller, K. K. (1994). Techniques for measuring social competence in children. In G. R. Lyon (Ed.), *Frames of reference for the assessment of learning disabilities: New views of measurement issues* (pp. 525–554). Baltimore: Paul Brookes.

Vogel, A. (1998). Adults with learning disabilities. In S. Vogel & S. Reder (Eds.), *Learning disabilities, literacy, and adult education* (pp. 5–8). Baltimore: Paul H. Brookes.

Vogel, S. A. (1990). Gender differences in intelligence, language, visual-motor abilities, and academic achievement in students with learning disabilities: A review of the literature. *Journal of Learning Disabilities, 23,* 44–52.

Vogel, S. A. (1997). *College Students with Learning Disabilities: A Handbook.* Pittsburgh, PA: Learning Disabilities Association of America.

Vogel, S. A., & Adelman, P. B. (1993). *Success for college students with learning disabilities.* New York: Springer-Verlag.

Voltz, D., Elliot, R., & Harris, W. (1995). Promising practices in facilitating collaboration between resource room teachers and general education teachers. *Learning Disabilities: Research and Practice, 102* (2), 129–136.

Vygotsky, L. (1962). *Thought and language.* Cambridge, MA: MIT Press.

Vygotsky, L. S. (1978). In M. Cole, V. John-Steiner, S. Scribner & E. Souberman (Eds.), *Mind in society: The development of higher psychological processes.* Cambridge, MA: Harvard University Press.

Wagner, M. (1990). *The school programs and school performance of secondary students classified as learning disabled: Findings from the National Longitudinal Transition Study of Special Education Students.* Menlo Park, CA: SRI International.

Wagner, M., & Blackorby, J. (1996). Transition from high school to work or college: How special education students fare? *The Future of Children, 6* (1), 103–120.

Wagner, M., Blackorby, J., Cameto, R., Hebbeler, K., & Newman, L. (1993). *The secondary school programs of students with disabilities: A report from the National Longitudinal Transition Study of Special Education Students.* Menlo Park, CA: SRI International.

Waldron, K., & Saphire, D. (1990). An analysis of WISC-R factors for gifted students with learning disabilities. *Journal of Learning Disabilities, 23,* 481–498.

Walker, N. (1985). Impulsivity in learning disabled children: Past research findings and methodological inconsistencies. *Learning Disabilities Quarterly, 8,* 85–94.

Wasik, B. (1998). Using volunteers as reading tutors: Guidelines for successful practices. *Reading Teacher, 51* (7), 262–270.

Weinberg, W. A., Harper, C. R., Emslie, G. L., & Brumback, R. A. (1995). Depression and other affective illnesses as a cause of school failure and maladaption in learning disabled children, adolescents, and adults. In Learning Disabilities Association of America (Ed.), *Secondary education and beyond: Providing opportunities for students with learning disabilities* (pp. 223–233). Pittsburgh: Learning Disabilities Association of America.

Werner, E. (1990). Protective factors and individual resilience. In *Handbook of early childhood intervention.* New York: Cambridge University Press.

Werner, H., & Strauss, A. (1940). Causal factors in low performance. *American Journal of Mental Deficiency, 45,* 213–218.

Wernicke, C. (1908). The symptom complex of aphasia. In A. Church (Ed.), *Diseases of the nervous system* (pp. 265–324). New York: Appleton.

Wiener, J., & Siegel, J. (1992). A Canadian perspective on learning disabilities. *Journal of Learning Disabilities, 26* (6), 350–370.

Wiggins, G. (1990). *The case for authentic assessment.* ERIC Clearinghouse on Tests, Measurement, and Evaluation. Washington, DC: American Institutes for Research.

Wiig, E., & Semel, E. M. (1984). *Language assessment and intervention for the learning disabled.* Columbus, OH: Charles E. Merrill.

Will, M. (1986). Educating children with learning problems: A shared responsibility. *Exceptional Children, 52,* 411–416.

Williams, J. (1991). The meaning of a phonics base for reading instruction. In E. Ellis (Ed.), *All language and the creation of literacy* (pp. 9–19). Baltimore, MD: Orton Dyslexia Society.

Williams, J. P. (1998). Improving comprehension of disabled readers. *Annals of Dyslexia, 48* 213–238.

Willson, V. (1987). Statistical and psychometric issues surrounding severe discrepancy. *Learning Disabilities Research, 3*(1), 24–28.

Wilson, B. A. (1998). *Wilson reading system.* Millbury, MA: Wilson Language Training.

Wingert, P. & Kantrovitz, B. (1997, October 27). Why Andy couldn't read. *Newsweek,* 56–64.

WISC-III Manual (1991). *Wechsler Intelligence Scale for Children* (3rd ed.). San Antonio: Psychological Corp.

Wolery, M., Werts, M. G., & Holcombe, A. (1994). Current practices with young children who have disabilities: Placement, assessment, and instructional issues. *Focus on Exceptional Children, 26* (6), 1–12.

Wolf, M. (1991). Naming speed and reading: The contribution of the cognitive neurosciences. *Reading Research Quarterly, 25,* 123–141.

Wong, B., & Jones, W. (1982). Increasing metacomprehension in learning-disabled and normally achieving students through self-questioning training. *Learning Disability Quarterly, 5*(3), 228–240.

Woodward, J. (1998). New web site provides math lessons for students with math disabilities. *TAM Connection, 11* (3), 1–2.

World Wide Web and Special Education. (1998). *Teaching Exceptional Children, 30* (5) entire issue.

Yamada, J., & Banks, A. (1994). Evidence for and characteristics of dyslexia among Japanese children, *Annuals of Dyslexia, 44,* 105–119.

Yasutake, D., & Bryan, T. (1995). The influence of induced positive affect on middle school children with and without learning disabilities. *Learning Disabilities: Research and Practice, 10* (1), 38–45.

Yasutake, D., & Lerner, J. (1996). Teachers' perceptions of inclusion. *Learning Disabilities: A Multidisciplinary Journal, 7* (2), 1–4.

Yell, M., & Shriner, J. (1997). The IDEA Amendments of 1997: Implications for special and general education teachers, administrators, and teacher trainers. *Focus on Exceptional Children, 30* (1) 1–19.

Zametkin, A., et al. (1990, November 15). Cerebral glucose metabolism of adults with hyperactivity of childhood onset. *New England Journal of Medicine, 323,* 1361–1364.

Zigmond, N. (1990). Rethinking secondary school programs for students with learning disabilities. *Focus on Exceptional Children, 23,* 1–22.

Zigmond, N. (1995). Models for delivery of special education services to students with learning disabilities in public schools. *Journal of Child Neurology, 10* (Suppl. 1), S86–S91.

Zigmond, N. (1997). Educating students with disabilities: The future of special education. In J. Lloyd, E., Kameenui, & D. Chard (Eds.), *Issues in educating students with disabilities* (pp. 275–304, 377–391). Mahwah, NJ: Lawrence Erlbaum.

Zigmond, N., & Baker, J. (1994). Is the mainstream a more appropriate educational setting for Randy? A case study of one student with learning disabilities. *Learning Disabilites: Research and Practice, 9,* 108–117.

Zigmond, N., Jenkins, J., Fuchs, L. S., Deno, S., Fuchs, D. Baker, J., Jenkins, L., & Coutino, M. (1995). Special education in restructured schools: Findings from three multi-year studies. *Phi Delta Kappan, 76,* 531–540.

Author Index

Aaron, P. G., 389
Adams, A., 256, 341, 352, 397, 398, 399
Adams, M. J., 397
Adelman, H., 199
Adelman, P., 326, 351, 442, 484
Adler, M., 407
Alberto, P., 124, 542, 555
Alexander, A., 400
Alexander, D., 188, 256
Algozzine, B., 194
Allard, L., 351, 353
Allington, 434
Allsop, D., 9, 13, 14, 15, 76, 99, 200
Alverez, L., 214
Anderson, R., 120, 392
Applegate, B., 498
Archibald, D. J., 333
Arguelles, M., 154, 163, 164
Arter, J., 200
Artiles, A., 48, 50, 117
Ashton, T., 454, 455
Atkins, M., 236
Atkinson, R., 202
Auerbach, J., 8, 484, 485
Aulls, M., 406
Austin, G., 237
Ayres, A., 263

Baca, L., 359
Badian, N. A., 389
Baecher, R. E., 358
Bagnoto, S. J., 280
Bailey, D., 253, 282
Baker, J., 136, 314, 319
Balise, R., 429
Ball, E. W., 268, 269, 341, 352, 368
Banks, A., 8
Barkley, R., 234, 235, 239, 240, 241, 242,
    309, 490, 552
Barnes, H. V., 254, 284, 289
Barnett, A., 418
Barnhart, C., 416
Baroody, A., 494, 495, 503, 506
Barr, R., 432
Barry, D., 197
Barsch, R., 38
Bassett, D., 484
Bateman, B., 77, 115, 136
Beck, I. L., 397
Becker, W., 433, 496, 552
Beeler, T., 341, 352, 399
Bender, L., 187
Bennerson, D., 548
Bentzen, F., 44, 160
Berko, J., 349

Subject Index